Accounting WITHDRAWN

An Introduction

Visit the *Accounting: An Introduction, fourth edition* Companion Website at **www.pearsoned.co.uk/mclaney** to find valuable student learning material including:

- Multiple choice questions to help test your learning
- Additional exercises and review questions
- Solutions to end of chapter review questions
- Links to relevant sites on the web
- An online glossary to explain key terms

We work with leading authors to develop the strongest educational materials in Accounting, bringing cutting-edge thinking and best learning practice to a global market.

Under a range of well-known imprints, including Financial Times Prentice Hall, we craft high quality print and electronic publications which help readers to understand and apply their content, whether studying or at work.

To find out more about the complete range of our publishing, please visit us on the World Wide Web at: www.pearsoned.co.uk

4th edition

Accounting
An Introduction

**Eddie McLaney
and
Peter Atrill**

FT Prentice Hall
FINANCIAL TIMES

An imprint of **Pearson Education**
Harlow, England • London • New York • Boston • San Francisco • Toronto
Sydney • Tokyo • Singapore • Hong Kong • Seoul • Taipei • New Delhi
Cape Town • Madrid • Mexico City • Amsterdam • Munich • Paris • Milan

Pearson Education Limited

Edinburgh Gate
Harlow
Essex CM20 2JE
England

and Associated Companies throughout the world

Visit us on the World Wide Web at:
www.pearsoned.co.uk

_____

First published 1999 by Prentice Hall Europe
Second edition published 2002
Third edition published 2005
Fourth edition published 2008

ISBN 978-0-273-71136-0

British Library Cataloguing-in-Publication Data
A catalogue record for this book is available from the British Library

10 9 8 7 6 5 4 3 2 1
11 10 09 08 07

Typeset in 9.5/12.5pt Stone Serif by 35
Printed and bound by Mateu Cromo Artes Graficas, Spain

The publisher's policy is to use paper manufactured from sustainable forests.

Brief contents

Preface • How to use this book • Guided tours • Acknowledgements   xxi–xxviii

1   Introduction to accounting and finance   1

Part 1 Financial accounting   35

2   Measuring and reporting financial position   37
3   Measuring and reporting financial performance   71
4   Accounting for limited companies (1)   115
5   Accounting for limited companies (2)   159
6   Measuring and reporting cash flows   192
7   Analysing and interpreting financial statements   221

Part 2 Management accounting   277

8   Relevant costs for decision making   279
9   Cost-volume-profit analysis   297
10 Full costing   332
11 Costing and pricing in a competitive environment   372
12 Budgeting   430
13 Accounting for control   470

Part 3 Financial management   507

14 Making capital investment decisions   509
15 Financing the business   566
16 Managing working capital   614

Part 4 Supplementary information   657

Appendix A Recording financial transactions   659
Appendix B Glossary of key terms   677
Appendix C Solutions to self-assessment questions   693
Appendix D Solutions to review questions   709
Appendix E Solutions to selected exercises   723
Appendix F Present value table   787

Index   789

Detailed contents

Preface   xxi
How to use this book   xxii
Guided tour of the book   xxiv
Guided tour MyAccountingLab   xxvi
Acknowledgements   xxviii

1 Introduction to accounting and finance   1

Introduction   1
Learning outcomes   1
What are accounting and finance?   2
Who are the users of accounting information?   3
The conflicting interests of users   5
How useful is accounting information?   5
    Evidence on the usefulness of accounting   6

Providing a service   7
But . . . is it material?   8
Weighing up the costs and benefits   9
Accounting as an information system   11
Management and financial accounting   13
Scope of this book   15
Has accounting become too interesting?   15
The changing face of accounting   16
Why do I need to know anything about accounting and finance?   17
Accounting for business   18
What is the purpose of a business?   18
What kinds of business ownership exist?   19
    Sole proprietorship   19
    Partnership   20
    Limited company   20

How are businesses organised?   22
How are businesses managed?   24
What is the financial objective of a business?   25
    Balancing risk and return   28

Not-for-profit organisations   28

Summary   30
Key terms   32
References   32
Further reading   32
Review questions   33

Part 1 Financial accounting

2 Measuring and reporting financial position   37

Introduction   37
Learning outcomes   37

The major financial statements – an overview   38
The balance sheet   42
    Assets   42
    Claims   44

The effect of trading operations on the balance sheet   47
The classification of assets   49
    Current assets   50
    Non-current assets   50

The classification of claims   52
Balance sheet layouts   52
The balance sheet and time   55
Accounting conventions and the balance sheet   55
    Business entity convention   55
    Historic cost convention   56
    Prudence convention   56
    Going concern convention   57
    Dual aspect convention   57

Money measurement   58
    Goodwill and brands   59
    Human resources   60
    Monetary stability   60

Valuing assets on the balance sheet   61
    Tangible non-current assets (property, plant and equipment)   61
    Intangible non-current assets   63
    The impairment of non-current assets   63
    Inventories (stock)   64

Interpreting the balance sheet   65

Summary   66
Key terms   67
Further reading   67
Review questions   68
Exercises   68

3 Measuring and reporting financial performance   71

Introduction   71
Learning outcomes   71

The income statement   72
The income statement and the balance sheet   73
Income statement layout   74
Some further issues   75
    Cost of sales   76

Classification of expenses   77
The accounting period   78

Recognising revenue   79
Long-term contracts   80
Services   81

Recognising expenses   82
When the expense for the period is more than the cash paid
during the period   83
When the amount paid during the year is more than the full
expense for the period   85
Profit, cash and accruals accounting   86

Depreciation   87
Tangible non-current assets (property, plant and equipment)   87
Depreciating intangible assets   93
Depreciation and the replacement of non-current assets   94
Depreciation and judgement   95

Costing inventories   97
First in, first out (FIFO)   97
Last in, first out (LIFO)   98
Weighted average cost (AVCO)   98
Inventories – some further issues   100

Dealing with trade receivables' problems   101
Interpreting the income statement   107

Summary   107
Key terms   109
Further reading   109
Review questions   110
Exercises   110

4 Accounting for limited companies (1)   **115**

Introduction   115
Learning outcomes   115

The main features of limited companies   116
Legal nature   116
Perpetual life   116
Limited liability   117
Legal safeguards   119
Public and private companies   119
Taxation   121
Transferring share ownership: the role of the Stock Exchange   122

Managing a company   123
Strengthening the framework of rules   124
The Combined Code   124

Financing limited companies   128
The owners' claim   128
The basic division   129

Share capital	130
Reserves	131
Altering the nominal value of shares	133
Bonus shares	134
Share capital jargon	136
Raising share capital	136
Borrowings	137
Withdrawing equity	139
The main financial statements	142
The income statement	144
The balance sheet	144
Dividends	145
Accounting for groups of companies	145
Summary	150
Key terms	152
Reference	152
Further reading	152
Review questions	153
Exercises	153

5 Accounting for limited companies (2)   159

Introduction	159
Learning outcomes	159
The directors' duty to account	160
The need for accounting rules	161
Sources of accounting rules	161
Presenting the financial statements	164
Income statement	165
Balance sheet	166
Statement of changes in equity	166
Cash flow statement	168
Explanatory notes	168
General points	168
The framework of principles	169
The IASB framework	169
The auditors' role	170
Directors' report	171
Segmental financial reports	171
Segmental reporting rules	172
Segmental disclosure	173
Problems of segmental reporting	174
Narrative reporting	175
The OFR framework	176
The business review and RS 1	179
Summary financial statements	180
Creative accounting	180
Creative accounting methods	180

Checking for creative accounting 184
Creative accounting and economic growth 185

Summary 185
Key terms 187
Further reading 187
Review questions 188
Exercises 188

6 Measuring and reporting cash flows 192

Introduction 192
Learning outcomes 192

The cash flow statement (or statement of cash flows) 193
Why is cash so important? 194
The main features of the cash flow statement 195
   A definition of cash and cash equivalents 195
   The relationship between the primary financial statements 196
   The form of the cash flow statement 197
   The normal direction of cash flows 199

Preparing the cash flow statement 201
   Deducing net cash flows from operating activities 201
   Deducing the other areas of the cash flow statement 204

What does the cash flow statement tell us? 208

Summary 211
Key terms 212
Further reading 212
Review questions 213
Exercises 213

7 Analysing and interpreting financial statements 221

Introduction 221
Learning outcomes 221

Financial ratios 222
Financial ratio classifications 223
The need for comparison 223
   Past periods 224
   Similar businesses 224
   Planned performance 224

Calculating the ratios 225
A brief overview 227
Profitablility 228
   Return on ordinary shareholders' funds (ROSF) 228
   Return on capital employed (ROCE) 229
   Operating profit margin 230
   Gross profit margin 231

Efficiency 233
   Average inventories turnover period 233
   Average settlement period for trade receivables 234

Average settlement period for trade payables 235
Sales revenue to capital employed 236
Sales revenue per employee 237

Relationship between profitablility and efficiency 238
Liquidity 240
Current ratio 240
Acid test ratio 241
Cash generated from operations to maturing obligations 241

Financial gearing 242
Gearing ratio 244
Interest cover ratio 245

Investment ratios 248
Dividend payout ratio 248
Dividend yield ratio 249
Earnings per share 250
Cash generated from operations per share 250
Price/earnings (P/E) ratio 251

Financial ratios and the problem of overtrading 256
Trend analysis 258
Using ratios to predict financial failure 260
Using single ratios 260
Using combinations of ratios 262
Z score models 263

Limitations of ratio analysis 264

Summary 266
Key terms 268
References 268
Further reading 268
Review questions 269
Exercises 269

Part 2 Management accounting

8 Relevant costs for decision making 279

Introduction 279
Learning outcomes 279

What is meant by 'cost'? 280
Relevant costs: opportunity and outlay costs 282
Sunk costs and committed costs 286
Qualitative factors of decisions 287

Summary 289
Key terms 290
Further reading 290
Review questions 291
Exercises 291

9 **Cost-volume-profit analysis** **297**

Introduction 297
Learning outcomes 297

The behaviour of costs 298
Fixed costs 298
Variable costs 300
Semi-fixed (semi-variable) costs 301
    Estimating semi-fixed (semi-variable) costs 302

Finding the break-even point 303
Contribution 307
Margin of safety 308
Operating gearing 311
    Operating gearing and its effect on profit 311

Profit–volume charts 313
The economist's view of the break-even chart 313
Failing to break even 315
Weaknesses of break-even analysis 315
Using contribution to make decisions: marginal analysis 317
    Accepting/rejecting special contracts 318
    The most efficient use of scarce resources 319
    Make-or-buy decisions 322
    Closing or continuation decisions 323

Summary 325
Key terms 326
Further reading 326
Review questions 327
Exercises 327

10 **Full costing** **332**

Introduction 332
Learning outcomes 332

Why do managers want to know the full cost? 333
What is full costing? 334
Single-product businesses 334
Multi-product businesses 335
    Direct and indirect costs 336
    Job costing 337
    Full (absorption) costing and the behaviour of costs 338
    The problem of indirect costs 340

Overheads as service renderers 340
    Job costing: a worked example 340
    Selecting a basis for charging overheads 344
    Segmenting the overheads 347
    Dealing with overheads on a departmental basis 348
    Batch costing 358
    Full (absorption) cost as the break-even price 359
    The forward-looking nature of full (absorption) costing 359

Using full (absorption) cost information 360
Criticisms of full (absorption) costing 362
Full (absorption) costing versus variable costing 362
  Which method is better? 363
Summary 364
Key terms 366
References 366
Further reading 366
Review questions 367
Exercises 367

11 Costing and pricing in a competitive environment 372
Introduction 372
Learning outcomes 372
Costing and the changed business environment 373
  Costing and pricing in the traditional way 373
  Costing and pricing in the new environment 374
Activity-based costing 374
  An alternative approach to full costing 375
  What drives the costs? 376
  Cost pools 376
  ABC and service industries 377
  Criticisms of ABC 381
Other approaches to cost management 385
  Total (or whole) life-cycle costing 385
  Target costing 388
  Costing quality control 389
  Kaizen costing 390
  Value chain analysis 390
  Benchmarking 392
Non-financial measures of performance 393
  The Balanced Scorecard 394
Measuring shareholder value 401
  The quest for shareholder value 401
  How can shareholder value be created? 401
  The need for new measures 402
  Economic value added (EVA®) 403
Pricing 409
  Economic theory 409
  Some practical considerations 416
  Full cost (cost-plus) pricing 417
  Pricing on the basis of relevant/marginal cost 420
  Target pricing 422
  Pricing strategies 422
Summary 423
Key terms 425
References 425

Further reading   425
Review questions   426
Exercises   426

12 Budgeting   **430**

Introduction   430
Learning outcomes   430

How budgets link with strategic plans and objectives   431
    Collecting information on performance and exercising control   432

Time horizon of plans and budgets   432
Limiting factors   434
Budgets and forecasts   434
Periodic and continual budgets   434
How budgets link to one another   435
How budgets help managers   437
The budget-setting process   440
Using budgets in practice   443
Incremental and zero-base budgeting   446
Preparing the cash budget   447
Preparing other budgets   451
Activity-based budgeting   454
Non-financial measures in budgeting   455
Budgets and management behaviour   455
Who needs budgets?   456
Beyond conventional budgeting   457
Long live budgets!   460

Summary   461
Key terms   462
References   462
Further reading   462
Review questions   463
Exercises   463

13 Accounting for control   **470**

Introduction   470
Learning outcomes   470

Budgeting for control   471
Types of control   472
Variances from budget   473
    Flexing the budget   474
    Sales volume variance   474
    Sales price variance   477
    Materials variance   478
    Labour variances   479
    Fixed overhead variance   480

Reasons for adverse variances   484
Non-operating-profit variances   486
Investigating variances   486

Compensating variances   489
Making budgetary control effective   490
Behavioural issues   490
The impact of management style   491
    Reservations about the Hopwood study   492
    Failing to meet the budget   492

Standard quantities and cost   494
Setting standards   494
    What kinds of standards should be used?   494
    Information gathering   495
    The learning-curve effect   496

Other uses for standard costing   497
Some problems . . .   497
The new business environment   498

Summary   499
Key terms   501
References   501
Further reading   501
Review questions   502
Exercises   502

Part 3 Financial management

14 Making capital investment decisions   **509**
Introduction   509
Learning outcomes   509

The nature of investment decisions   510
Investment appraisal methods   511
Accounting rate of return (ARR)   513
    ARR and ROCE   515
    Problems with ARR   515

Payback period (PP)   518
    Problems with PP   520

Net present value (NPV)   522
    Interest lost   523
    Risk   523
    Inflation   524
    What will a logical investor do?   524
    Using discount tables   527
    Why NPV is better   529
    NPV's wider application   530

Internal rate of return (IRR)   530
    Problems with IRR   533

Some practical points   534

Investment appraisal in practice   537
Dealing with risk   541
    Assessing the level of risk   541
    Reacting to the level of risk   551
Managing investment projects   552
    Stage 1: Determine investment funds available   553
    Stage 2: Identify profitable project opportunities   554
    Stage 3: Evaluate the proposed project   554
    Stage 4: Approve the project   555
    Stage 5: Monitor and control the project   555

Summary   557
Key terms   559
References   559
Further reading   559
Review questions   560
Exercises   560

15 Financing the business   **566**

Introduction   566
Learning outcomes   566

Sources of finance   567
Sources of internal finance   567
Long-term sources of internal finance   568
    Retained profits   568
Short-term sources of internal finance   569
    Tighter credit control   569
    Reducing inventories levels   570
    Delaying payment to trade payables   570
Sources of external finance   570
Long-term sources of external finance   570
    Ordinary shares   571
    Preference shares   572
    Loans (borrowings)   573
    Finance leases and sale-and-leaseback arrangements   580
    Hire purchase   582
Gearing and the long-term financing decision   583
Share issues   586
    Rights issue   586
    Offer for sale and public issue   589
    Private placing   590
    Bonus issue   590
The role of the Stock Exchange   590
    Advantages of a listing   592
    Disadvantages of a listing   594
Alternative Investment Market   596
Short-term sources of external finance   597
    Bank overdraft   597

Debt factoring 597
Invoice discounting 598
Long-term versus short-term borrowing 600
Providing long-term finance for the small business 601
Venture capital 601
Business angels 603
Government assistance 603
Summary 605
Key terms 607
Further reading 607
Review questions 608
Exercises 608

16 Managing working capital **614**
Introduction 614
Learning outcomes 614
The nature and purpose of working capital 615
Managing working capital 616
The scale of working capital 616
Managing inventories 618
Budgeting future demand 620
Financial ratios 620
Recording and reordering systems 620
Levels of control 622
Inventories management models 622
Managing receivables 627
Which customers should receive credit and how much should
they be offered? 627
Length of credit period 629
Cash discounts 631
Debt factoring and invoice discounting 632
Collection policies and reducing the risk of non-payment 632
Managing cash 635
Why hold cash? 635
How much cash should be held? 636
Controlling the cash balance 636
Cash budgets and managing cash 638
Operating cash cycle 638
Cash transmission 641
Bank overdrafts 642
Managing trade payables 642
Controlling trade payables 643
Working capital problems of the small business 644
Managing inventories 644
Credit management 644
Managing cash 645
Managing credit suppliers 645

Summary	646
Key terms	648
Reference	648
Further reading	648
Review questions	649
Exercises	649

Part 4 **Supplementary information**

Appendix A Recording financial transactions	659
Introduction	659
Learning outcomes	659
The basics of double-entry bookkeeping	660
Recording trading transactions	662
Balancing acccounts and the trial balance	665
Preparing the financial statements (final accounts)	669
The ledger and its division	672
Summary	673
Key terms	673
Further reading	674
Exercises	675
Appendix B Glossary of key terms	677
Appendix C Solutions to self-assessment questions	693
Appendix D Solutions to review questions	709
Appendix E Solutions to selected exercises	723
Appendix F Present value table	787
Index	789

Supporting resources

Visit **www.pearsoned.co.uk/mclaney** to find valuable online resources

Companion Website for students
- Multiple choice questions to help test your learning
- Additional exercises and review questions
- Solutions to end of chapter review questions
- Links to relevant sites on the web
- An online glossary to explain key terms

For instructors
- Complete, downloadable Instructor's Manual
- PowerPoint slides that can be downloaded and used for presentations
- Case study material with solutions
- Progress tests, consisting of various questions and exercise material with solutions
- Tutorial/seminar questions and solutions
- Solutions to end of chapter review questions

Also: The Companion Website provides the following features:
- Search tool to help locate specific items of content
- E-mail results and profile tools to send results of quizzes to instructors
- Online help and support to assist with website usage and troubleshooting

For more information please contact your local Pearson Education sales representative or visit **www.pearsoned.co.uk/mclaney**

Preface

This text provides a comprehensive introduction to financial accounting, management accounting and core elements of financial management. It is aimed both at students who are not majoring in accounting or finance and at those who are. Those studying introductory level accounting and/or financial management as part of their course in business, economics, hospitality management, tourism, engineering or some other area should find that the book provides complete coverage of the material at the level required. Students who are majoring in either accounting or finance should find the book useful as an introduction to the main principles, which can serve as a foundation for further study. The text does not focus on technical issues, but rather examines basic principles and underlying concepts. The primary concern throughout is the ways in which financial statements and information can be used to improve the quality of decision making. To reinforce this practical emphasis, there are, throughout the text, numerous illustrative extracts with commentary from real life, including company reports, survey data and other sources.

In this fourth edition we have taken the opportunity to make improvements that have been suggested by students and lecturers who used the previous edition. We have also brought up to date and expanded the number of examples from real life. From 2005, most of the larger UK companies have had to adopt a new set of international rules relating to their main financial statements. These new rules form the basis of the section of the book that deals specifically with accounting for limited companies.

The text is written in an 'open-learning' style. This means that there are numerous integrated activities, worked examples and questions throughout the text to help you to understand the subject fully. You are encouraged to interact with the material and to check your progress continually. Irrespective of whether you are using the book as part of a taught course or for personal study, we have found that this approach is more 'user friendly' and makes it easier for you to learn.

We recognise that most readers will not have studied accounting or finance before, and we have therefore tried to write in a concise and accessible style, minimising the use of technical jargon. We have also tried to introduce topics gradually, explaining everything as we go. Where technical terminology is unavoidable we try to provide clear explanations. In addition, you will find all of the key terms highlighted in the text. These are then listed at the end of each chapter with a page reference. They are also listed alphabetically, with a concise definition, in the glossary given in Appendix B towards the end of the book. This should provide a convenient point of reference from which to revise.

A further important consideration in helping you to understand and absorb the topics covered is the design of the text itself. The page layout and colour scheme have been carefully considered to allow for the easy navigation and digestion of material. The layout features a large page format, an open design, and clear signposting of the various features and assessment material.

More detail about the nature and use of these features is given in the 'How to use this book' section; and the main points are also summarised, using example pages from the text, in the guided tour.

We hope that you will find the book readable and helpful.

Eddie McLaney
Peter Atrill

How to use this book

We have organised the chapters to reflect what we consider to be a logical sequence and, for this reason, we suggest that you work through the text in the order in which it is presented. We have tried to ensure that earlier chapters do not refer to concepts or terms that are not explained until a later chapter. If you work through the chapters in the 'wrong' order, you will probably encounter concepts and terms that were explained previously.

Irrespective of whether you are using the book as part of a lecture/tutorial-based course or as the basis for a more independent mode of study, we advocate following broadly the same approach.

Integrated assessment material

Interspersed throughout each chapter are numerous **Activities**. You are strongly advised to attempt all of these questions. They are designed to simulate the sort of quick-fire questions that your lecturer might throw at you during a lecture or tutorial. Activities serve two purposes:

- To give you the opportunity to check that you understand what has been covered so far.
- To encourage you to think about the topic just covered, either to see a link between that topic and others with which you are already familiar, or to link the topic just covered to the next.

The answer to each Activity is provided immediately after the question. This answer should be covered up until you have deduced your solution, which can then be compared with the one given.

Towards the middle/end of each chapter there is a **Self-assessment question**. This is more comprehensive and demanding than any of the Activities, and is designed to give you an opportunity to check and apply your understanding of the core coverage of the chapter. The solution to each of these questions is provided in Appendix C at the end of the book. As with the Activities, it is important that you attempt each question thoroughly before referring to the solution. If you have difficulty with a self-assessment question, you should go over the relevant chapter again.

End-of-chapter assessment material

At the end of each chapter there are four **Review questions**. These are short questions requiring a narrative answer or discussion within a tutorial group. They are intended to help you assess how well you can recall and critically evaluate the core terms and concepts covered in each chapter. Answers to these questions are provided in the student access Companion Website. At the end of each chapter, except for Chapter 1, there are eight **Exercises**. These are mostly computational and are designed to reinforce your knowledge and understanding. Exercises are graded as 'basic' and 'more advanced', according to their level of difficulty. The basic-level questions are fairly straightforward; the more advanced ones can be quite demanding but are capable of being successfully completed if you have worked conscientiously through the chapter and have attempted the basic exercises. Solutions to five of the exercises in each chapter are provided in Appendix D at the end of the book. A coloured exercise number identifies these five questions. Here, too, a thorough attempt should be made to answer each exercise before referring to the solution. Solutions to the other three exercises and to the review questions in each chapter are provided in a separate Instructors' Manual.

To familiarise yourself with the main features and how they will benefit your study from this text, an illustrated Guided tour is provided on pages xxiv–xxv.

Content and structure

The text comprises 16 chapters organised into three core parts: financial accounting, management accounting and financial management. A brief introductory outline of the coverage of each part and its component chapters is given in the opening double-page spread which precedes each part.

The market research for this text revealed a divergence of opinions, given the target market, on whether or not to include material on double-entry bookkeeping techniques. So as to not interrupt the flow and approach of the financial accounting chapters, Appendix A on recording financial transactions (including Activities and three Exercise questions) has been placed in Part 4.

MyAccountingLab

MyAccountingLab supports this book. This banner reminds students to complete the chapter pre-test to create their personal Study Plan. The results of the test determine the Study Plan going forward.

This banner reminds students to complete the chapter post-test in MyAccountingLab to track their progress and mastery of the topics included in each chapter. Their Study plan will adapt according to the results of the test.

 This icon indicates that there is a Key Concept Animation relevant to the topic covered in the text at that point. Animations of all the Key Concepts are accessible through MyAccountingLab.

 This icon indicates that there is an interactive Study Guide covering the topic at hand available in MyAccountingLab. The Study Guide contains diagrams, video clips and short self test quizzes designed to guide and reinforce the student's learning.

Guided tour of the book

Key terms The key concepts and techniques in each chapter are highlighted in colour where they are first introduced, with an adjacent icon in the margin to help you refer back to them.

Examples At frequent intervals throughout most chapters, there are numerical examples that give you step-by-step workings to follow through to the solution.

Introductions A brief introduction, detailing the topics covered in the chapter, and also showing how chapters are linked together.

Learning outcomes Bullet points at the start of each chapter show what you can expect to learn from the chapter, and provide a brief checklist of the core issues.

Activities These short questions, integrated throughout each chapter, allow you to check your understanding as you progress through the text. They comprise either a narrative question requiring you to review or critically consider topics, or a numerical problem requiring you to deduce a solution. A suggested answer is given immediately after each activity.

'Real World' illustrations Integrated throughout the text, these illustrative examples highlight the practical application of accounting concepts and techniques by real businesses, including extracts from company reports and financial statements, survey data and other insights from business.

Self-assessment questions Towards the end of most chapters you will encounter one of these questions, allowing you to attempt a comprehensive question before tackling the end-of-chapter assessment material. To check your understanding and progress, solutions are provided in Appendix C.

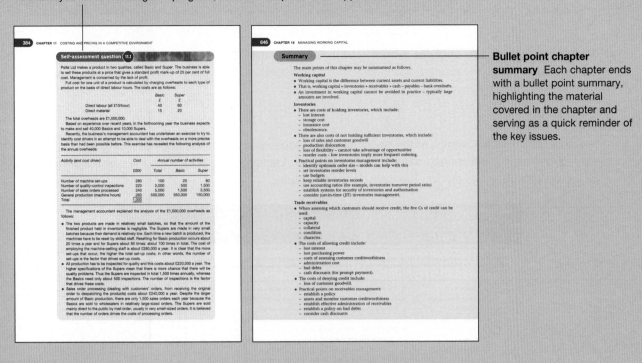

Bullet point chapter summary Each chapter ends with a bullet point summary, highlighting the material covered in the chapter and serving as a quick reminder of the key issues.

Key terms summary At the end of each chapter, there is a list (with page references) of all the key terms introduced in that chapter, allowing you to refer back easily to the essential points.

Review questions These short questions encourage you to review and/or critically discuss your understanding of the main topics covered in each chapter, either individually or in a group. Solutions to these questions can be found in Appendix D.

References Full details of the sources of information referred to in the chapter.

Further reading This section provides a list of relevant chapters in other textbooks that you might wish to refer to in order to pursue a topic in more depth or access an alternative perspective.

Exercises There are eight of these comprehensive questions at the end of most chapters. The more advanced questions are separately identified. Solutions to five questions (those with coloured numbers) are provided in Appendix E, enabling you to assess your progress. Solutions to the remaining questions are available for lecturers only. An additional exercise for each chapter can be found on the Companion Website at **www.pearsoned.co.uk/mclaney**.

Guided tour of MyAccountingLab

MyAccountingLab puts students in control of their own learning through a suite of study and practice tools tied to the online e-book and other media tools. At the core of **MyAccountingLab** are the following features:

Practice tests

Practice tests for each section of the textbook enable students to test their understanding and identify the areas in which they need to do further work. Lecturers can customise the practice tests or leave students to use the two pre-built tests per chapter.

Personalised study plan

Based on a student's performance on a practice test, a personal study plan is generated that shows where further study needs to focus. This study plan consists of a series of additional practice exercises.

Additional practice exercises

Generated by the student's own performance on a practice test, additional practice exercises are keyed to the textbook and provide extensive practice and link students to the e-book and to other tutorial instruction resources.

Tutorial instruction

Launched from the additional practice exercises, tutorial instruction is provided in the form of solutions to problems, detailed differential feedback, step-by-step explanations, and other media-based explanations, including key concept animations.

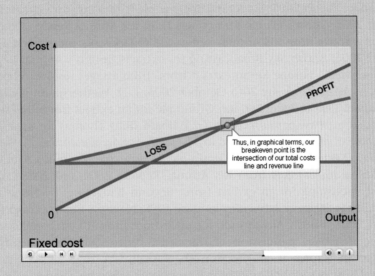

Additional MyAccountingLab tools

1. Interactive study guide
2. Electronic tutorials
3. Glossary – key terms from the textbook
4. Glossary flashcards
5. Links to the most useful accounting data and information sources on the Internet.

Lecturer training and support

We offer lecturers personalised training and support for MyAccountingLab. We have a dedicated team of Technology Specialists whose job it is to support lecturers in their use of our media products, including MyAccountingLab. To make contact with your Technology Specialist please email feedback-cw@pearson.com

For a visual walkthrough of how to make the most of MyAccountingLab, visit www.MyAcountingLab.com

To find details of your local sales representatives go to www.pearsoned.co.uk/replocater

Acknowledgements

We are grateful to the following for permission to reproduce copyright material:

NI Syndication Limited for extracts from 'Dirty Laundry: How companies fudge the numbers' published in *The Times* 22nd September 2002, 'The Thoughts of Warren Buffett' published in *The Times* 26th September 2002 and 'Ryanair alert hits shares' published in *The Times* 4th June 2003; Manchester United Limited for an extract from it's Annual Report 2005; Marks and Spencer plc (company) for extracts from it's Annual Report 2006; Thorntons plc for extracts from it's Annual Report 2006; Alliance Boots plc for extracts from it's Annual Report 2006; Jarvis plc for extracts from it's Annual Report 2006; British Sky Broadcasting for extracts from it's Annual Report 2005; VNU Business Media Europe for an extract from 'JJB massages results to boost profits' published in *Accountancy Age* 20th October 2005; J. D. Wetherspoon plc for extracts from it's Annual Report 2006; Pennon Group plc for an extract from 'Investor Information' published at www.pennon.co.uk; C. William (Bill) Thomas for an extract from 'The Rise and Fall of Enron' published in *The Journal of Accountancy* vol 194 no 3 April 2002; Dr Terry O'Brien CEO LiDICO Group plc for an extract from it's Annual Report 2006; SAB Miller for extracts from it's Annual Reports 2004 and 2005; Harvard Business School Publishing for an extract from 'Beyond Budgeting' by Hope and Fraser published in *Management Accounting* January 1999; Next plc for an extract from it's Annual Report 2006; British Airways plc for an extract from it's Annual Report 2006; Figure 11.5 reprinted by permission of Harvard Business School Press from *The Balanced Scorecard* by Kaplan R. and Norton D., Boston, MA 1996, copyright © 1996 by the Harvard Business School Publishing Corporation, all rights reserved; Figure 14.2 adapted from *Investment appraisal in UK manufacturing: Has it changed since the mid-1990s?* D. Godden, www.cbi.org.

We are grateful to the Financial Times Limited for permission to reprint the following material:

Real World 1.1 Morrison in uphill battle to integrate Safeway, © Ft.com, 26 May 2005; Real World 1.6 Fair Shares?, © Ft.com, 11 June 2005; Real World 1.7 Profit without honour, © Financial Times Weekend, 29/30 June 2002; Real World 1.8 Tsunami: Finding the right figures for disaster, © Ft.com, 7 March 2005; Real World 2.4 Goodwill charges at record levels, © Ft.com, 30 May 2006; Real World 3.8 Household debt adds to rise in bank write-offs, © Financial Times, 28 March 2005; Real World 4.1 Monotub Industries in a spin as founder gets Titan for £1, © Financial Times, 23 January 2003; Real World 4.12 MyTravel set to resume its dividend, © Ft.com, 14 March 2006; Real World 6.1 Eurotunnel takes £1.3bn impairment charge, © Ft.com, 9 February 2004; Real World 6.3 WaterfordWedgwood face some intense questions over its cash flow, © Financial Times, 17 June 2004; Real World 8.2 MFI furniture retail arm bought for £1, © Ft.com, 22 September 2006; Real World 9.4 Ford puts Aston Martin up for auction, © Ft.com, 31 August 2006; Real World 11.14 How to put ideas to work, © Ft.com, 23 May 2006; Real World 14.8 Satellites need space to earn, © Ft.com, 14 July 2003;

Real World 15.3 New appetite develops for Eurobonds, © Financial Times, 18 September 2004; Real World 15.4 Volatility prompts European issuance, © Financial Times, 12 July 2006; Real World 15.5 Gcap attacks note on breaching covenants, © Financial Times, 9 September 2006; Real World 15.13 page 22, © Financial Times, 8 August 2003; Real World 16.2 Poor cash management hits profits, © Financial Times, 29 August 2005; Real World 16.4 Small stores keep up with the big boys, © Financial Times, 5 February 2003.

In some instances we have been unable to trace the owners of copyright material and we would appreciate any information that would enable us to do so.

Introduction to accounting and finance

Introduction

In this opening chapter we begin by considering the roles of accounting and finance. We shall see that both can be valuable tools for decision-making purposes. We shall identify the main users of accounting and financial information and discuss the ways in which this information can improve the quality of decisions that those users make. In subsequent chapters, we develop this decision-making theme by considering in some detail the kinds of financial reports and methods used to aid decision making.

Since this book is concerned with accounting and financial decision making for private-sector businesses, we shall devote some time to examining the business environment. We shall, therefore, consider the purpose of a private-sector business, the main forms of business enterprise and the ways in which a business may be structured. We shall also consider what the key financial objective of a business is likely to be. These factors are important as they all exert an influence on the kind of accounting and financial information produced.

Learning outcomes

When you have completed this chapter, you should be able to:

● Explain the nature and roles of accounting and finance.

● Identify the main users of financial information and discuss their needs.

● Identify and discuss the characteristics that make accounting information useful.

● Explain the purpose of a business and describe how businesses are organised and structured.

MyAccountingLab Remember to create your own personalised Study Plan

What are accounting and finance?

Let us start our study of accounting and finance by trying to understand the purpose of each. **Accounting** is concerned with collecting, analysing and communicating financial information. This information is useful for those who need to make decisions and plans about businesses, including those who need to control those businesses. For example, the managers of businesses may need accounting information to decide whether to:

- develop new products or services (such as a computer manufacturer developing a new range of computers);
- increase or decrease the price or quantity of existing products or services (such as a telecommunications business changing its mobile phone call and text charges);
- borrow money to help finance the business (such as a supermarket wishing to increase the number of stores it owns);
- increase or decrease the operating capacity of the business (such as a beef farming business reviewing the size of its herd); and
- change the methods of purchasing, production or distribution (such as a clothes retailer switching from UK to overseas suppliers).

The information provided should help in identifying and assessing the financial consequences of such decisions.

Though managers working within a business are likely to be significant users of accounting information about that particular business, they are by no means the only users. There are those outside the business (whom we shall identify later) who may need information to decide whether to:

- invest or disinvest in the ownership of the business (for example, buy or sell shares);
- lend money to the business;
- offer credit facilities (for example, a bank to grant an overdraft); and
- enter into contracts for the purchase of products or services.

Sometimes the impression is given that the purpose of accounting is simply to prepare financial reports on a regular basis. While it is true that accountants undertake this kind of work, the preparation of financial reports does not represent an end in itself. The ultimate purpose of the accountant's work is to give people better information on which to base their decisions. This decision-making perspective of accounting dictates the theme of this book and shapes the way in which we deal with each topic.

Finance (or **financial management**), like accounting, exists to help decision makers. It is concerned with the ways in which funds for a business are raised and invested. This lies at the very heart of what a business is about. In essence, a business exists to raise funds from investors (owners and lenders) and then to use those funds to make investments (equipment, premises, inventories and so on) in an attempt to make the business, and its owners, wealthier. It is important that funds are raised in a way that is appropriate to the particular needs of the business and an understanding of finance should help in identifying:

- the main forms of finance available;
- the costs and benefits of each form of finance;
- the risks associated with each form of finance; and
- the role of financial markets in supplying finance.

Once the funds are raised, they must be invested in a way that will provide the business with a worthwhile return. An understanding of finance should help in evaluating:

- the returns from an investment; and
- the risks associated with an investment.

Businesses tend to raise and invest funds in large amounts for long periods of time. The quality of the investment decisions made can, therefore, have a profound impact on the fortunes of the business.

There is little point in trying to make a sharp distinction between accounting and finance. We have already seen that both are concerned with the financial aspects of decision making. There is considerable overlap between the two subjects, for example accounting reports are a major source of information for financing and investment decision making. In this book, we shall not emphasise the distinctions between accounting and finance.

Who are the users of accounting information?

For accounting information to be useful, the accountant must be clear *for whom* the information is being prepared and *for what purpose* the information will be used. There are likely to be various groups of people (known as 'user groups') with an interest in a particular organisation, in the sense of needing to make decisions about it. For the typical private-sector business, the most important of these groups are shown in Figure 1.1. Take a look at this figure and then try Activity 1.1.

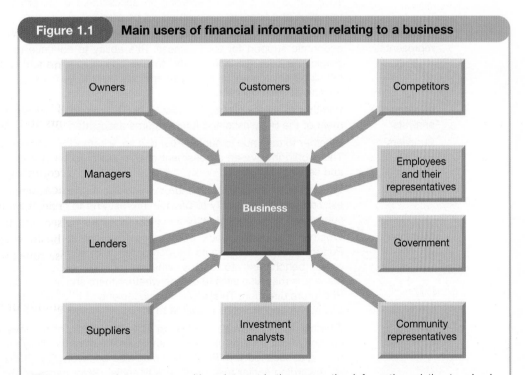

Figure 1.1   **Main users of financial information relating to a business**

There are several user groups with an interest in the accounting information relating to a business. The majority of these are outside the business but, nevertheless, they have a stake in it. This is not meant to be an exhaustive list of potential users; however, the groups identified are normally the most important.

Activity (1.1)

Ptarmigan Insurance plc (PI) is a large motor insurance business. Taking the user groups identified below, suggest, for each group, the sorts of decisions likely to be made about PI and the factors to be taken into account when making these decisions.

Your answer may be as follows:

User group	Decision
Customers	Whether to take further motor policies with PI. This might involve an assessment of PI's ability to continue in business and to meet their needs, particularly in respect of any insurance claims made.
Competitors	How best to compete against PI or, perhaps, whether to leave the market on the grounds that it is not possible to compete profitably with PI. This might involve using PI's performance in various aspects as a 'benchmark' when evaluating their own performance. They might also try to assess PI's financial strength and to identify significant changes that may signal PI's future actions (for example, raising funds as a prelude to market expansion).
Employees	Whether to continue in employment with PI and, if so, whether to demand higher rewards for their labour. The future plans, profits and financial strength of the business are likely to be of particular interest when making these decisions.
Government	Whether PI should pay tax and, if so, how much, whether it complies with agreed pricing policies, whether financial support is needed and so on. In making these decisions an assessment of its profits, sales revenues and financial strength would be made.
Community representatives	Whether to allow PI to expand its premises and/or whether to provide economic support for the business. PI's ability to continue to provide employment for the community, to use community resources and to help fund environmental improvements are likely to be considered when arriving at such decisions.
Investment analysts	Whether to advise clients to invest in PI. This would involve an assessment of the likely risks and future returns associated with PI.
Suppliers	Whether to continue to supply PI and, if so, whether to supply on credit. This would involve an assessment of PI's ability to pay for any goods and services supplied.
Lenders	Whether to lend money to PI and/or whether to require repayment of any existing loans. PI's ability to pay the interest and to repay the principal sum would be important factors in such decisions.
Managers	Whether the performance of the business needs to be improved. Performance to date would be compared with earlier plans or some other 'benchmark' to decide whether action needs to be taken. Managers may also wish to decide whether there should be a change in PI's future direction. This would involve looking at PI's ability to perform and at the opportunities available to it.
Owners	Whether to invest more in PI or to sell all, or part, of the investment currently held. This would involve an assessment of the likely risks and returns associated with PI. Owners may also be involved with decisions on rewarding senior managers. The financial performance of the business would normally be considered when making such a decision.

Although this answer covers many of the key points, you may have identified other decisions and/or other factors to be taken into account by each group.

The conflicting interests of users

We have seen above that each user group looks at a business from a different perspective and has its own particular interests. This means that there is always the risk that the interests of one group will collide with those of another group. Conflict between user groups is most likely to occur over the way in which the wealth of the business is generated and/or distributed. A good example is the conflict that may arise between the managers and the owners of the business. Although managers are appointed to act in the best interests of the owners, there is always a danger that they will not do so. Instead, managers may use the wealth of the business to award themselves large pay rises, to furnish large offices or to buy expensive cars for their own use. Accounting information has an important role to play in reporting the extent to which various groups have benefited from the business. Thus, owners may rely on accounting information to check whether the pay and benefits of managers are in line with agreed policy.

A further example is the potential conflict of interest between lenders and owners. There is a risk that the funds loaned to a business will not be used for purposes that have been agreed. Lenders may, therefore, rely on accounting information to check that the funds have been applied in an appropriate manner and that the terms of the loan agreement are not being broken.

Activity 1.2

Can you think of other examples where accounting information may be used to monitor potential conflicts of interest between the various user groups identified?

Two possible examples that spring to mind are:

- Employees (or their representatives) wishing to check that they are receiving a 'fair share' of the wealth created by the business and that agreed profit-sharing schemes are being adhered to.
- Government wishing to check that the profits made from a contract that it has given to a business are not excessive.

You may have thought of other examples.

How useful is accounting information?

No one would seriously claim that accounting information fully meets all of the needs of each of the various user groups. Accounting is still a developing subject and we still have much to learn about user needs and the ways in which these needs should be met. Nevertheless, the information contained in accounting reports should help users make decisions relating to the business. The information should reduce uncertainty about the financial position and performance of the business. It should help to answer questions concerning the availability of funds to pay owners a return, to repay loans, to reward employees and so on.

Typically, there is no close substitute for the information provided by the financial statements. Thus, if users cannot glean the required information from the financial statements, it is often unavailable to them. Other sources of information concerning the financial health of a business are normally much less useful.

Activity (1.3)

What other sources of information might users use in an attempt to gain an impression of the financial position and performance of a business? What kind of information might be gleaned from these sources?

Other sources of information available include:

● Meetings with managers of the business
● Public announcements made by the business
● Newspaper and magazine articles
● Websites, including the website of the business
● Radio and TV reports
● Information-gathering agencies (for example, agencies that assess businesses' credit-worthiness or credit ratings)
● Industry reports
● Economy-wide reports.

These sources can provide information on various aspects of the business, such as new products or services being offered, management changes, new contracts offered or awarded, the competitive environment within which the business operates, the impact of new technology, changes in legislation, changes in interest rates and future levels of inflation. However, the various sources of information identified are not really substitutes for accounting reports. Rather, they are best used in conjunction with the reports in order to obtain a clearer picture of the financial health of a business.

Evidence on the usefulness of accounting

There are arguments and convincing evidence that accounting information is at least *perceived* as being useful to users. Numerous research surveys have asked users to rank the importance of accounting information, in relation to other sources of information, for decision-making purposes. Generally speaking, these studies have found that users rank accounting information very highly. There is also considerable evidence that businesses choose to produce accounting information that exceeds the minimum requirements imposed by accounting regulations. (For example, businesses often produce a considerable amount of accounting information for managers, which is not required by any regulations.) Presumably, the cost of producing this additional accounting information is justified on the grounds that users find it useful. Such arguments and evidence, however, leave unanswered the question of whether the information produced is actually used for decision-making purposes, that is: does it affect people's behaviour?

It is normally very difficult to assess the impact of accounting on decision making. One situation arises, however, where the impact of accounting information can be observed and measured. This is where the **shares** (portions of ownership of a business) are traded on a stock exchange. The evidence reveals that, when a business makes an announcement concerning its accounting profits, the prices at which shares are traded and the volume of shares traded often change significantly. This suggests that investors are changing their views about the future prospects of the business as a result of this new information becoming available to them and that this, in turn, leads them to make a decision either to buy or to sell shares in the business.

Although there is evidence that accounting reports are perceived as being useful and are used for decision-making purposes, it is impossible to measure just how useful accounting reports are to users. As a result we cannot say with certainty whether the cost of producing those reports represents value for money. Accounting information will usually represent only one input to a particular decision and so the precise weight attached to the accounting information by the decision maker and the benefits which flow as a result cannot be accurately assessed. We shall now go on to see, however, that it is at least possible to identify the kinds of qualities which accounting information must possess in order to be useful. Where these qualities are lacking, the usefulness of the information will be diminished.

Providing a service

One way of viewing accounting is as a form of service. Accountants provide economic information to their 'clients', who are the various users identified in Figure 1.1. The quality of the service provided is determined by the extent to which the needs of the various user groups have been met. In other words, how fit for purpose is the information?

To meet these users' needs, it can be argued that accounting information should possess certain key qualities, or characteristics. These are:

→ ● **Relevance**. Accounting information must have the ability to influence decisions. Unless this characteristic is present, there is really no point in producing the information. The information may be relevant to the prediction of future events (for example, in predicting how much profit is likely to be earned next year) or relevant in helping to confirm past events (for example, in establishing how much profit was earned last year). The role of accounting in confirming past events is important because users often wish to check the accuracy of earlier predictions that they have made. The accuracy (or inaccuracy) of earlier predictions may help users to judge the accuracy of current predictions. To influence a decision, the information must, of course, be available when the decision is being made. Thus, relevant information must be timely.

→ ● **Reliability**. Accounting should be free from significant errors or bias. It should be capable of being relied upon by managers to represent what it is supposed to represent. Though both relevance and reliability are very important, the problem that we often face in accounting is that information that is highly relevant may not be very reliable, and that which is reliable may not be very relevant.

Activity 1.4

To illustrate this last point, let us assume that a manager has to sell a custom-built machine owned by the business and has recently received a bid for it. This machine is very unusual and there is no ready market for it.

What information would be relevant to the manager when deciding whether to accept the bid? How reliable would that information be?

→

Activity 1.4 continued

The manager would probably like to know the current market value of the machine before deciding whether or not to accept the bid. The current market value would be highly relevant to the final decision, but it might not be very reliable because the machine is unique and there is likely to be little information concerning market values.

Where a choice has to be made between providing information that has either more relevance or more reliability, the maximisation of relevance is usually the guiding rule. No matter how reliable the information is, it is useless if it is not relevant. On the other hand, information that is not totally reliable can be useful if it is relevant.

- **Comparability**. This quality will enable users to identify changes in the business over time (for example, the trend in sales revenue over the past five years). It will also help them to evaluate the performance of the business in relation to similar businesses. Comparability is achieved by treating items that are basically the same in the same manner for accounting purposes. Comparability tends also to be enhanced by making clear the policies that have been adopted in measuring and presenting the information.
- **Understandability**. Accounting reports should be expressed as clearly as possible and should be understood by those at whom the information is aimed.

Activity 1.5

Do you think that accounting reports should be understandable to those who have not studied accounting?

It would be useful if anyone could understand accounting reports, but realistically this is not likely to be the case. Complex financial events and transactions cannot always be reported easily. It is probably best that we regard accounting reports in the same way as we regard a report written in a foreign language. To understand either of these, we need to have had some preparation. Generally speaking, accounting reports assume that the user not only has a reasonable knowledge of business and accounting but is also prepared to invest some time in studying the reports.

Despite the answer to Activity 1.5, the onus is clearly on accountants to provide information in a way that makes it as understandable as possible to non-accountants.

But . . . is it material?

The qualities, or characteristics, that have just been described will help us to decide whether accounting information is potentially useful. If a particular piece of information has these qualities then it may be useful. However, this does not automatically mean that it should be reported to users. We also have to consider whether the information is material, or significant. This means that we should ask whether its omission or misrepresentation in the accounting reports would really alter the decisions that users make. Thus, in addition to possessing the characteristics mentioned above, accounting information must also cross the threshold of **materiality**. If the information is not regarded as material, it should not be included within the reports as it will merely clutter them up and, perhaps, interfere with the users' ability to interpret the financial results. The type of information and amounts involved will normally determine whether it is material.

Weighing up the costs and benefits

Having read the previous sections you may feel that, when considering a piece of accounting information, provided the four main qualities identified are present and it is material it should be gathered and made available to users. Unfortunately, there is one more hurdle to jump. Something may still exclude a piece of accounting information from the reports even when it is considered to be useful. Consider Activity 1.6.

Activity 1.6

Suppose an item of information is capable of being provided. It is relevant to a particular decision, it is also reliable, comparable, can be understood by the decision maker concerned and is material.

Can you think of a reason why, in practice, you might choose not to produce the information?

The reason that you may decide not to produce, or discover, the information is that you judge the cost of doing so to be greater than the potential benefit of having the information. This cost–benefit issue will limit the extent to which accounting information is provided.

In theory, a particular item of accounting information should only be produced if the costs of providing it are less than the benefits, or value, to be derived from its use. Figure 1.2 shows the relationship between the costs and value of providing additional accounting information. The figure shows how the value of information received by the decision maker eventually begins to decline. This is, perhaps, because additional information becomes less relevant, or because of the problems that a decision maker may have in processing the sheer quantity of information provided. The costs of providing the information, however, will increase with each additional piece of information. The broken line indicates the point at which the gap between the value of information and the cost of providing that information is at its greatest. This represents the optimal amount of information that can be provided. This theoretical model, however, poses a number of problems in practice. We shall now go on to discuss these.

To illustrate the practical problems of establishing the value of information, suppose that we wish to have a car serviced at a local garage. We know that the nearest garage would charge £250 but believe that other local garages may offer the same service for a lower price. The only ways of finding out the prices at other garages are either to telephone them or to visit them. Telephone calls cost money and involve some of our time. Visiting the garages may not involve the outlay of money, but more of our time will be involved. Is it worth the cost of finding out the price of a car service at the various local garages? The answer, as we have seen, is that if the cost of discovering the price is less than the potential benefit, it is worth having that information.

Figure 1.2 **Relationship between costs and the value of providing additional accounting information**

The benefits of accounting information eventually decline. The cost of providing information, however, will rise with each additional piece of information. The optimal level of information provision is where the gap between the value of the information and the cost of providing it is at its greatest.

To identify the various prices for a car service, there are various points to be considered, including:

- How many garages shall we telephone or visit?
- What is the cost of each telephone call?
- How long will it take to make all the telephone calls or visits?
- How much do we value our time?

The economic benefit of having the information on the price of the service is probably even harder to assess – remember that we have not contacted any garages yet. The following points need to be considered:

- What is the cheapest price that we might be quoted for the car service?
- How likely is it that we shall be quoted a price cheaper than £250?

As we can imagine, the answers to these questions may be far from clear. When assessing the value of accounting information we are confronted with similar problems.

The provision of accounting information can be very costly; however, the costs are often difficult to quantify. The direct, out-of-pocket, costs such as salaries of accounting staff are not really a problem to identify, but these are only part of the total costs involved. There are also less direct costs such as the cost of the user's time spent on analysing and interpreting the information contained in reports.

The economic benefit of having accounting information is even harder to assess. It is possible to apply some 'science' to the problem of weighing the costs and benefits, but a lot of subjective judgement is likely to be involved. Whereas no one would seriously advocate that the typical business should produce no accounting information, at the same time no one would advocate that every item of information that could be seen as possessing one or more of the key characteristics should be produced, irrespective of the cost of producing it.

The characteristics that influence the usefulness of accounting information and which have been discussed in this section and the preceding section are set out in Figure 1.3.

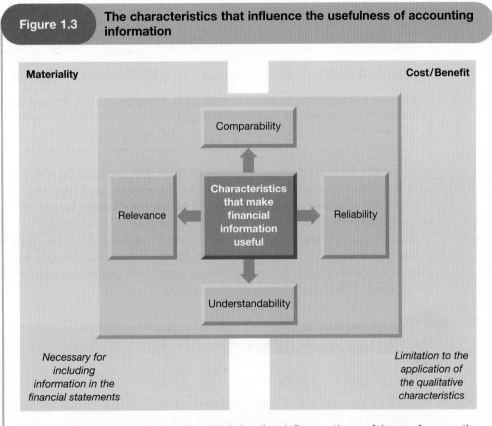

Figure 1.3 | **The characteristics that influence the usefulness of accounting information**

Materiality

Cost/Benefit

Comparability

Characteristics that make financial information useful

Relevance

Reliability

Understandability

Necessary for including information in the financial statements

Limitation to the application of the qualitative characteristics

There are four main qualitative characteristics that influence the usefulness of accounting information. In addition, however, accounting information should be material and the benefits of providing the information should outweigh the costs.

Accounting as an information system

We have already seen that accounting can be seen as the provision of a service to 'clients'. Another way of viewing accounting is as a part of the business's total information system. Users, both inside and outside the business, have to make decisions concerning the allocation of scarce economic resources. To try to ensure that these resources are allocated in an efficient manner, users require economic information on which to base decisions. It is the role of the accounting system to provide that information and this will involve information gathering and communication.

→ The **accounting information system** should have certain features that are common to all valid information systems within a business. These are:

● identifying and capturing relevant information (in this case economic information);
● recording the information collected in a systematic manner;
● analysing and interpreting the information collected;
● reporting the information in a manner that suits the needs of users.

The relationship between these features is set out in Figure 1.4.

Figure 1.4 **The accounting information system**

Information identification → Information recording → Information analysis → Information reporting

There are four sequential stages of an accounting information system. The first two stages are concerned with preparation, whereas the last two stages are concerned with using the information collected.

Given the decision-making emphasis of this book, we shall be concerned primarily with the final two elements of the process: the analysis and reporting of accounting information. We shall consider the way in which information is used by, and is useful to, users rather than the way in which it is identified and recorded.

Efficient accounting systems are an essential ingredient of an efficient business. When the accounting systems fail, the results can be disastrous. **Real World 1.1** provides an example of a systems failure when two businesses combined and then attempted to integrate their respective systems.

Real World 1.1

Blaming the system

FT

When Sir Ken Morrison bought Safeway for £3.35bn in March 2004, he almost doubled the size of his supermarket chain overnight and went from being a regional operator to a national force. His plan was simple enough. He had to sell off some Safeway stores – Morrison has to date sold off 184 stores for an estimated £1.3bn – and convert the remaining 230 Safeway stores into Morrison's. Sir Ken has about another 50 to sell. But, nearly 15 months on, and the integration process is proving harder in practice than it looked on paper. Morrison, once known for its robust performance, has issued four profit warnings in the past 10 months. Each time the retailer has blamed Safeway. Last July, it was because of a faster-than-expected sales decline in Safeway stores. In March – there were two warnings that month – it was the fault of Safeway's accounting systems, which left Morrison with lower supplier incomes. This month's warning was put down to higher-than-expected costs from running parallel store systems. At the time of the first warning last July, Simon Procter, of the stockbrokers Charles Stanley, noted that the news 'has blown all profit forecasts out of the water and visibility is very poor from here on out'. But if it was difficult then to predict where Morrison's profits were heading, it is impossible now. Morrison itself cannot give guidance. 'No one envisaged this,' says Mr Procter. 'When I made that comment about visibility last July, I was thinking on a 12-month time frame, not a two-year one.' Morrison says the complexity of the Safeway deal has put a 'significant strain' on its ability to cope with managing internal accounts. 'This is impacting the ability of the board to forecast likely trends in profitability and the directors are therefore not currently in a position to provide reliable guidance on the level of profitability as a whole,' admits the retailer.

Source: 'Morrison in uphill battle to integrate Safeway', Elizabeth Rigby, FT.com, 26 May 2005.

Management and financial accounting

Accounting is usually seen as having two distinct strands. These are:

- **Management accounting**, which seeks to meet the needs of managers; and
- **Financial accounting**, which seeks to meet the accounting needs of all of the other users identified earlier in the chapter (see Figure 1.1).

The difference in their targeted users has led to each strand of accounting developing along different lines. The main areas of difference are as follows.

- *Nature of the reports produced.* Financial accounting reports tend to be general purpose, that is, they contain financial information that will be useful for a broad range of users and decisions rather than being specifically designed for the needs of a particular group or set of decisions. Management accounting reports, on the other hand, are often specific-purpose reports. They are designed either with a particular decision in mind or for a particular manager.
- *Level of detail.* Financial accounting reports provide users with a broad overview of the performance and position of the business for a period. As a result, information is aggregated and detail is often lost. Management accounting reports, however, often provide managers with considerable detail to help them with a particular operational decision.
- *Regulations.* Financial accounting reports, for many businesses, are subject to accounting regulations that try to ensure they are produced with standard content and in a standard format. The law and accounting rule makers impose these regulations. As management accounting reports are for internal use only, there are no regulations from external sources concerning the form and content of the reports. They can be designed to meet the needs of particular managers.
- *Reporting interval.* For most businesses, financial accounting reports are produced on an annual basis, though large businesses may produce half-yearly reports, and a few produce quarterly ones. Management accounting reports may be produced as frequently as required by managers. In many businesses, managers are provided with certain reports on a daily, weekly or monthly basis, which allows them to check progress frequently. In addition, special-purpose reports will be prepared when required (for example, to evaluate a proposal to purchase a piece of machinery).
- *Time orientation.* Financial accounting reports reflect the performance and position of the business for the past period. In essence, they are backward looking. Management accounting reports, on the other hand, often provide information concerning future performance as well as past performance. It is an oversimplification, however, to suggest that financial accounting reports never incorporate expectations concerning the future. Occasionally, businesses will release projected information to other users in an attempt to raise capital or to fight off unwanted takeover bids. Even preparation of the routine financial accounting reports typically requires making some judgements about the future, as we shall see in Chapter 3.
- *Range and quality of information.* Financial accounting reports concentrate on information that can be quantified in monetary terms. Management accounting also produces such reports, but is also more likely to produce reports that contain information of a non-financial nature, such as physical volume of inventories, number of sales orders received, number of new products launched, physical output per employee and so on. Financial accounting places greater emphasis on the use of objective, verifiable evidence when preparing reports. Management accounting

reports may use information that is less objective and verifiable, but nevertheless provide managers with the information they need.

We can see from this that management accounting is less constrained than financial accounting. It may draw from a variety of sources and use information that has varying degrees of reliability. The only real test to be applied when assessing the value of the information produced for managers is whether or not it improves the quality of the decisions made.

The distinctions between management and financial accounting suggests that there are differences between the information needs of managers and those of other users. While differences undoubtedly exist, there is also a good deal of overlap between these needs.

Activity (1.7)

Can you think of any areas of overlap between the information needs of managers and those of other users?

We thought of two points:

- Managers will, at times, be interested in receiving an historical overview of business operations of the sort provided to other users.
- Other users would be interested in receiving information relating to the future, such as the planned level of profits and non-financial information such as the state of the sales order book and the extent of product innovations.

The distinction between the two areas of accounting reflects, to some extent, the differences in access to financial information. Managers have much more control over the form and content of information they receive. Other users have to rely on what managers are prepared to provide or what the financial reporting regulations require must be provided. Though the scope of financial accounting reports has increased over time, fears concerning loss of competitive advantage and user ignorance concerning the reliability of forecast data have led businesses to resist providing other users with the same detailed and wide-ranging information available to managers.

In the past it has been argued that accounting systems are biased in favour of providing information for external users. Financial accounting requirements have been the main priority and management accounting has suffered as a result. Recent survey evidence suggests, however, that this argument has lost its force. Nowadays, management accounting systems will usually provide for managers information that is relevant to their needs rather than what is determined by external reporting requirements. Financial reporting cycles, however, retain some influence over management accounting and managers are aware of expectations of external users (see reference 1 at the end of the chapter).

Scope of this book

This book covers both financial accounting and management accounting topics. Broadly speaking, the next six chapters (Part 1, Chapters 2 to 7) are concerned with financial accounting topics, and the six thereafter (Part 2, Chapters 8 to 13) with management accounting topics. The final part of the book (Part 3, Chapters 14 to 16) is concerned with the financial management of the business, that is, the chapters examine issues relating to the financing and investing activities of the business. As we have seen, accounting information is usually vitally important for these kinds of decisions.

Has accounting become too interesting?

In recent years, accounting has become front-page news and is a major talking point among those connected with the world of business. Unfortunately, the attention that accounting has attracted has been for all the wrong reasons. We have seen that investors rely on financial reports to help to keep an eye on both their investment and the managers. However, what if the managers provide misleading financial reports to investors? Recent revelations suggest that the managers of some large companies have been doing just this.

Two of the most notorious cases have been those of:

● Enron, an energy-trading business based in Texas, which was accused of entering into complicated financial arrangements in an attempt to obscure losses and to inflate profits; and
● WorldCom, a major long-distance telephone operator in the US, which was accused of reclassifying $3.9 billion of expenses so as to falsely inflate the profit figures that the business reported to its owners (shareholders) and to others.

In the wake of these scandals, there was much closer scrutiny by investment analysts and investors of the financial reports that businesses produce. This led to further businesses, in both the US and Europe, being accused of using dubious accounting practices to bolster profits.

Accounting scandals can have a profound effect on all those connected with the business. The Enron scandal, for example, ultimately led to the collapse of the company, which, in turn, resulted in lost jobs and large financial losses for lenders, suppliers and investors. Confidence in the world of business can be badly shaken by such events and this can pose problems for society as a whole. Not surprisingly, therefore, the relevant authorities tend to be severe on those who perpetrate such scandals. In the US, Bernie Ebbers, the former chief executive of WorldCom, received 25 years in prison for his part in the fraud.

Various reasons have been put forward to explain this spate of scandals. Some may have been caused by the pressures on managers to meet unrealistic expectations of investors for continually rising profits, others by the greed of unscrupulous executives whose pay is linked to financial performance. However, they may all reflect a particular economic environment.

Real World 1.2 gives some comments suggesting that when all appears to be going well with a business, people can be quite gullible and over-trusting.

Real World 1.2

The thoughts of Warren Buffett

Warren Buffett is one of the world's shrewdest and most successful investors. He believes that the accounting scandals mentioned above were perpetrated during the 'new economy boom' of the late 1990s when confidence was high and exaggerated predictions were being made concerning the future. He states that during that period:

> You had an erosion of accounting standards. You had an erosion, to some extent, of executive behaviour. But during a period when everybody 'believes', people who are inclined to take advantage of other people can get away with a lot.

He believes that the worst is now over and that the 'dirty laundry' created during this heady period is being washed away and that the washing machine is now in the 'rinse cycle'.

Source: *The Times*, Business Section, 26 September 2002, p. 25.

Whatever the causes, the result of these accounting scandals has been to undermine the credibility of financial statements and to introduce much stricter regulations concerning the quality of financial information. We shall return to this issue in later chapters when we consider the financial statements.

The changing face of accounting

Over the past twenty-five years, the environment within which businesses operate has become increasingly turbulent and competitive. Various reasons have been identified to explain these changes, including:

● the increasing sophistication of customers;
● the development of a global economy where national frontiers become less important;
● rapid changes in technology;
● the deregulation of domestic markets (for example, electricity, water and gas);
● increasing pressure from owners (shareholders) for competitive economic returns;
● the increasing volatility of financial markets.

This new, more complex, environment has brought new challenges for managers and other users of accounting information. Their needs have changed and both financial accounting and management accounting have had to respond. To meet the changing needs of users there has been a radical review of the kind of information to be reported.

The changing business environment has given added impetus to the search for a clear framework and principles upon which to base financial accounting reports. Various attempts have been made to clarify the purpose of financial accounting reports and to provide a more solid foundation for the development of accounting rules. The frameworks and principles that have been developed try to address fundamental questions such as:

● Who are the users of financial accounting information?
● What kinds of financial accounting reports should be prepared and what should they contain?
● How should items be measured?

In response to criticisms that the financial reports of some businesses are too opaque, accounting rule makers have tried to improve reporting rules to ensure that the accounting policies of businesses are more comparable, more transparent and portray economic reality more faithfully. While this has had a generally beneficial effect, the recent accounting scandals have highlighted the limitations of accounting rules in protecting investors and others.

The internationalisation of businesses has created a need for accounting rules to have an international reach. It can no longer be assumed that users of accounting information relating to a particular business are based in the country in which the business operates or are familiar with the accounting rules of that country. Thus, there has been increasing harmonisation of accounting rules across national frontiers. A more detailed review of the developments mentioned above is included in Chapter 5.

Management accounting has also changed by becoming more outward looking in its focus. In the past, information provided to managers has been largely restricted to that collected within the business. However, the attitude and behaviour of customers and rival businesses have now become the object of much information gathering. Increasingly, successful businesses are those that are able to secure and maintain competitive advantage over their rivals.

To obtain this advantage, businesses have become more 'customer driven' (that is, concerned with satisfying customer needs). This has led to management accounting information that provides details of customers and the market, such as customer evaluation of services provided and market share. In addition, information about the costs and profits of rival businesses, which can be used as 'benchmarks' by which to gauge competitiveness, is gathered and reported.

To compete successfully, businesses must also find ways of managing costs. The cost base of modern businesses is under continual review and this, in turn, has led to the development of more sophisticated methods of measuring and controlling costs. These changes are considered in more detail in Chapter 11.

Why do I need to know anything about accounting and finance?

At this point you may be asking yourself 'Why do I need to study accounting and finance? I don't intend to become an accountant!' Well, from the explanation of what accounting and finance is about, which has broadly been the subject of this chapter so far, it should be clear that the accounting/finance function within a business is a central part of its management information system. On the basis of information provided by the system, managers make decisions concerning the allocation of resources. These decisions may concern whether to:

- continue with certain business operations;
- invest in particular projects; or
- sell particular products.

Such decisions can have a profound effect on all those connected with the business. It is important, therefore, that *all* those who intend to work in a business should have a fairly clear idea of certain important aspects of accounting and finance. These aspects include:

- how financial reports should be read and interpreted;
- how financial plans are made;
- how investment decisions are made;
- how businesses are financed.

Many, perhaps most, students have a career goal of being a manager within a business – perhaps a personnel manager, production manager, marketing manager or IT manager. If you are one of these students, an understanding of accounting and finance is very important. When you become a manager, even a junior one, it is almost certain that you will have to use financial reports to help you to carry out your management tasks. It is equally certain that it is largely on the basis of financial information and reports that your performance as a manager will be judged.

As a manager, it is likely that you will be expected to help in forward planning for the business. This will often involve the preparation of projected financial statements and setting of financial targets. If you do not understand what the financial statements really mean and the extent to which the financial information is reliable, you will find yourself at a distinct disadvantage to others who know their way round the system. As a manager, you will also be expected to help decide how the limited resources available to the business should be allocated between competing options. This will require an ability to evaluate the costs and benefits of the different options available. Once again, an understanding of accounting and finance is important to carrying out this management task.

This is not to say that you cannot be an effective and successful personnel, production, marketing or IT manager unless you are also a qualified accountant. It does mean, however, that you need to acquire a bit of 'street wisdom' in accounting and finance in order to succeed. This accounting and finance book aims to give you just that.

Accounting for business

We have seen that the needs of the various user groups will determine the kind of accounting information to be provided, however, the forms of business ownership and the ways in which a business may be organised and structured will help to shape those needs. Thus, in the sections that follow, we consider the business environment within which accounting information is produced. A discussion of these topics should help our understanding of points that crop up in later chapters.

What is the purpose of a business?

Peter Drucker, an eminent management thinker, has argued that 'The *purpose of business is to create and keep a customer*' (see reference 2 at the end of the chapter). Drucker defined the purpose of a business in this way in 1967, at a time when most businesses did not adopt this strong customer focus. His view therefore represented a radical challenge to the accepted view of what businesses do. Forty years on, however, his approach has become part of the conventional wisdom. It is now widely recognised that, in order to succeed, businesses must focus on satisfying the needs of the customer.

Although the customer has always provided the main source of revenue for a business, this has often been taken for granted. In the past, too many businesses have assumed that the customer would readily accept whatever services or products were on offer. When competition was weak and customers were passive, businesses could operate under this assumption and still make a profit. However, the era of weak competition has passed. Nowadays, customers have much greater choice and are much more assertive concerning their needs. They now demand higher quality services and goods at cheaper prices. They also require that services and goods be delivered faster with an increasing emphasis on the product being tailored to their individual needs. If a business cannot meet these needs, a competitor business often can. Thus the business mantra for the current era is *'the customer is king'*; most businesses now recognise this fact and organise themselves accordingly.

Real World 1.3 provides an illustration of how one business recognises the supremacy of the customer.

Real World 1.3

Customers are top of the apex

Medrad, a US-based leading worldwide provider of medical devices and services recently won a prestigious award for quality, which was presented by President Bush at the White House. The business's chief executive officer (CEO) explaining the business's success said that at Medrad the customer was placed at the top of the business's organisation chart. [An organisation chart is a diagram showing the hierarchy of importance of managers and staff and usually has the CEO at the top.] Why the customer? 'Because the customer can fire (or sack) the whole company at any time,' said the CEO.

Source: 'CEO at bottom of award-winning firm's organisation chart', C. A. Cohen, www.post-gazette.com/businessnews, 13 July 2004.

What kinds of business ownership exist?

The particular form of business ownership has important implications for accounting purposes and so it is useful to be clear about the main forms of ownership that can arise.

There are basically three arrangements:

● sole proprietorship
● partnership
● limited company.

Each of these is considered below.

Sole proprietorship

→ **Sole proprietorship**, as the name suggests, is where an individual is the sole owner of a business. This type of business is often quite small in terms of size (as measured, for example, by sales revenue generated or number of staff employed), however, the number of such businesses is very large indeed. Examples of sole-proprietor businesses can be found in most industrial sectors but particularly within the service sector. Hence, services such as electrical repairs, picture framing, photography, driving instruction, retail shops and hotels have a large proportion of sole-proprietor businesses. The sole-proprietor business is easy to set up. No formal procedures are required and operations can often commence immediately (unless special permission is required because of the nature of the trade or service, such as running licensed premises). The owner can decide the way in which the business is to be conducted and has the flexibility to restructure or dissolve the business whenever it suits. The law does not recognise the sole-proprietor business as being separate from the owner, so the business will cease on the death of the owner.

Although the owner must produce accounting information to satisfy the taxation authorities, there is no legal requirement to produce accounting information relating to the business for other user groups. However, some user groups may demand accounting information about the business and may be in a position to have their demands met (for example, a bank requiring accounting information on a regular basis as a condition of a loan). The sole proprietor will have unlimited liability which means that no distinction will be made between the proprietor's personal wealth and that of the business if there are business debts that must be paid.

Partnership

→ A **partnership** exists where at least two individuals carry on a business together with the intention of making a profit. Partnerships have much in common with sole-proprietor businesses. They are often quite small in size (although some, such as partnerships of accountants and solicitors, can be large). Partnerships are also easy to set up as no formal procedures are required (and it is not even necessary to have a written agreement between the partners). The partners can agree whatever arrangements suit them concerning the financial and management aspects of the business, and the partnership can be restructured or dissolved by agreement between the partners.

Partnerships are not recognised in law as separate entities and so contracts with third parties must be entered into in the name of individual partners. The partners of a business usually have unlimited liability.

Activity 1.8

What are the main advantages and disadvantages that should be considered when deciding between a sole proprietorship and a partnership?

The main advantages of a partnership over a sole-proprietor business are:

- sharing the burden of ownership;
- the opportunity to specialise rather than cover the whole range of services (for example, a solicitors' practice, where each partner tends to specialise in a different aspect of the law);
- the ability to raise capital where this is beyond the capacity of a single individual.

The main disadvantages of a partnership compared with a sole proprietorship are:

- the risks of sharing ownership of a business with unsuitable individuals;
- the limits placed on individual decision making that a partnership will impose.

Limited company

→ **Limited companies** can range in size from quite small to very large. The number of individuals who subscribe capital and become the owners may be unlimited, which provides the opportunity to create a very large scale business. The liability of owners, however, is limited (hence 'limited' company), which means that those individuals subscribing capital to the company are liable only for debts incurred by the company up to the amount that they have agreed to invest. This cap on the liability of the owners is designed to limit risk and to produce greater confidence to invest. Without such limits on owner liability, it is difficult to see how a modern capitalist economy could operate. In many cases, the owners of a limited company are not involved in the day-to-day running of the business and will invest in a business only if there is a clear limit set on the level of investment risk.

The benefit of limited liability, however, imposes certain obligations on such a company. To start up a limited company, documents of incorporation must be prepared that set out, among other things, the objectives of the business. Furthermore, a framework of regulations exists that places obligations on the way in which such a company conducts its affairs. Part of this regulatory framework requires annual financial reports to be made available to owners and lenders and usually an annual general meeting of the owners has to be held to approve the reports. In addition, a copy of the annual financial reports must be lodged with the Registrar of Companies for public inspection. In this way, the financial affairs of a limited company enter the public domain. With the exception of small companies, there is also a requirement for the annual financial reports to be subject to an audit. This involves an independent firm of accountants examining the annual reports and underlying records to see whether the reports provide a true and fair view of the financial health of the company and whether they comply with the relevant accounting rules established by law and by accounting rule makers.

All of the large household-name UK businesses (Marks and Spencer, Tesco, Shell, BSkyB, BA, BT, easyJet and so on) are limited companies.

Limited companies are considered in more detail in Chapters 4 and 5.

Activity 1.9

What are the main advantages and disadvantages that should be considered when deciding between a partnership business and a limited liability company?

The main advantages of a partnership over a limited company are:

- the ease of setting up the business;
- the degree of flexibility concerning the way in which the business is conducted;
- the degree of flexibility concerning restructuring and dissolution of the business;
- freedom from administrative burdens imposed by law (for example, the annual general meeting and the need for an independent audit).

The main disadvantage of a partnership compared with a limited company is:

- the fact that it is not possible to limit the liability of all of the partners.

This book concentrates on the accounting aspects of limited liability companies because this type of business is by far the most important in economic terms. The early chapters will introduce accounting concepts through examples that do not draw a distinction between the different types of business. Once we have dealt with the basic accounting principles, which are the same for all three types of business, we can then go on to see how they are applied to limited companies. It must be emphasised that there are no differences in the way that all three of these forms of business keep their day-to-day accounting records. In preparing their periodic financial statements, there are certain differences that need to be considered. These differences are not ones of principle, however, but of detail.

How are businesses organised?

As we have just seen, nearly all businesses that involve more than a few owners and/or employees are set up as limited companies. This means that the finance will come from the owners (shareholders) both in the form of a direct cash investment to buy shares (in the ownership of the business) and through the owners allowing past profits, which belong to them, to be reinvested in the business. Finance will also come from lenders (banks, for example), who earn interest on their loans, and from suppliers of goods and services being prepared to supply on credit, with payment occurring a month or so after the date of supply, usually on an interest-free basis.

In larger limited companies, the owners (shareholders) are not involved in the daily running of the business; instead they appoint a board of directors to manage the business on their behalf. The board is charged with three major tasks:

- setting the overall direction and strategy for the business;
- monitoring and controlling the activities of the business; and
- communicating with owners and others connected with the business.

Each board has a chairman, elected by the directors, who is responsible for running the board in an efficient manner. In addition, each board has a chief executive officer (CEO), or managing director, who is responsible for running the business on a day-to-day basis. Occasionally, the roles of chairman and CEO are combined, although it is usually considered to be a good idea to separate them in order to prevent a single individual having excessive power.

The board of directors represents the most senior level of management. Below this level, managers are employed, with each manager given responsibility for a particular part of the business's operations.

Activity 1.10

Why are most larger businesses not managed as a single unit by one manager?

Three common reasons are:

- the sheer volume of activity or number of staff employed makes it impossible for one person to manage them;
- certain business operations may require specialised knowledge or expertise;
- geographical remoteness of part of the business operations may make it more practical to manage each location as a separate part, or set of separate parts.

The operations of a business may be divided for management purposes in different ways. For smaller businesses offering a single product or service, separate departments are often created, with each department responsible for a particular function (such as marketing, personnel, finance). The managers of each department will then be accountable to the board of directors. In some cases, individual board members may also be departmental managers.

A typical departmental structure, organised along functional lines, is set out in Figure 1.5.

Figure 1.5 — A departmental structure organised according to business function

This is a typical departmental structure organised along functional lines.

The structure set out in Figure 1.5 may be adapted according to the particular needs of the business. Where, for example, a business has few employees, the personnel function may not form a separate department but may form part of another department. Where business operations are specialised, separate departments may be formed to deal with each specialist area. Example 1.1 illustrates how Figure 1.5 may be modified to meet the needs of a particular business.

Example 1.1

Supercoach Ltd owns a small fleet of coaches that it hires out with drivers for private group travel. The business employs about 50 people. It might be departmentalised as follows:

- *marketing department*, dealing with advertising and with enquiries from potential customers, maintaining good relationships with existing customers and entering into contracts with customers;
- *routing and personnel department*, responsible for the coach drivers' routes, schedules, staff duties and rotas, problems that arise during a particular job or contract;
- *coach maintenance department*, looking after repair and maintenance of the coaches, buying spares, giving advice on the need to replace old or inefficient coaches;
- *finance department*, responsible for managing the cash flows, borrowing, use of spare funds, payment of wages and salaries, billing and collecting charges to customers, processing invoices from suppliers and paying the supplier.

For large businesses which have a diverse geographical spread and/or a wide product range, the simple departmental structure set out in Figure 1.5 will usually have to be adapted. Separate divisions are often created for each geographical area and/or major product group. Each division will be managed separately and will usually enjoy a degree of autonomy. Within each division, however, departments will often be created and organised along functional lines. Some functions providing support across the various divisions, such as personnel, may be undertaken at head office to avoid duplication. The managers of each division will be accountable to the board of directors. In some cases, individual board members may also be divisional managers. A typical divisional organisational structure is set out in Figure 1.6.

Figure 1.6 **A divisional organisational structure**

This is a typical organisational structure for a business that has been divided into separate operating divisions.

Both the divisional structure and departmental structure just described appear to be widely used, although it should be emphasised that other organisational structures may also be found in practice.

How are businesses managed?

We have already seen that the environment in which businesses operate has become increasingly turbulent and competitive. The effect of these environmental changes has been to make the role of managers more complex and demanding. It has meant that managers have had to find new ways to manage their business. This has increasingly led to the introduction of **strategic management**.

Strategic management is designed to provide a business with a clear sense of purpose and to ensure that appropriate action is taken to achieve that purpose. The action taken should link the internal resources of the business to the external environment of competitors, suppliers, customers and so on. This should be done in such a way that any business strengths, such as having a skilled workforce, are exploited and any weaknesses, such as being short of investment finance, are not exposed. To achieve this requires the development of strategies and plans that take account of the business's strengths and weaknesses, as well as the opportunities offered and threats posed by the external environment. Access to a new, expanding market is an example of an opportunity; the decision of a major competitor to reduce prices is an example of a threat. This topic will be considered in more depth in Chapter 12 when we consider business planning and budgeting.

What is the financial objective of a business?

A business is created to enhance the wealth of its owners, and throughout this book we shall assume that this is its main objective. This may come as a surprise, as there are other objectives that a business may pursue that are related to the needs of others associated with the business. For example, a business may seek to provide good working conditions for its employees, or it may seek to conserve the environment for the local community. While a business may pursue these objectives, it is normally set up with a view to increasing the wealth of its owners, and in practice the behaviour of businesses over time appears to be consistent with this objective.

Real World 1.4 provides an example of how many clothes retailers pursue the search for profit.

Real World 1.4

From rags to riches

Progress in the search for profit is reported by the accounting information system. If managers find that the reported profits are inadequate, it can be an important driver for change. This change can, in turn, have a profound effect on the working lives of those both inside and outside the business.

Many clothes retailers have been concerned with profit levels in recent years. This has led them to make radical changes to the ways in which they operate. Low inflation and increased competition in the high street have forced the retailers to keep costs under strict control in order to meet their profit objectives. This has been done in various ways, including:

- moving production to cheaper countries and closing inflexible manufacturing offshoots;
- using fewer manufacturers and working more closely with manufacturers in the design of clothes. This has enabled the retailers to add details, such as embroidery or unusual design features, and to command a higher price for relatively little cost;
- improving communication to suppliers of materials and to manufacturers so that design and sourcing decisions can be made faster and more accurately. This has meant that the time to make garments has been reduced from as much as nine months to just a few weeks;
- predicting more accurately what customers want in order to avoid being left with inventories of unwanted items.

The effect of implementing these changes has been to reduce costs, and thereby improve profits, and to have more flexibility in the cost structure so that the clothes retailers are more able to weather a downturn.

Source: Adapted from 'Margin of success for clothing retailers', *The Times*, 20 November 2002, p. 30.

Within a market economy there are strong competitive forces at work that ensure that failure to enhance owners' wealth will not be tolerated for long. Competition for the funds provided by the owners and competition for managers' jobs will normally mean that the owners' interests will prevail. If the managers do not provide the expected increase in ownership wealth, the owners have the power to replace the existing management team with a new team that is more responsive to owners' needs.

Does this mean that the needs of other groups associated with the business (employees, customers, suppliers, the community and so on) are not really important? The answer to this question is certainly no, if the business wishes to survive and prosper over the longer term. Satisfying the needs of other groups will normally be consistent with increasing the wealth of the owners over the longer term.

We have already discussed the importance of customers to a business. Dissatisfied customers will take their business to another supplier and this will, in turn, lead to a loss of wealth for the owners of the business losing the customers. **Real World 1.5** provides an illustration of the way in which one business acknowledges the link between customer satisfaction and creating wealth for its owners.

Real World 1.5

On a mission

A business will often express its ultimate purpose in the form of a **mission statement**. Mission statements are widely published and frequently adorn the websites and promotional material produced by businesses. The statements are usually concise and try to convey the essence of a business.

J. Sainsbury plc is a leading food retailer which recognises in its mission statement the importance of customers to increasing the wealth of the owners (shareholders), as follows:

What is Sainsbury's mission?

To meet our customers' needs effectively by providing the best quality and choice to meet their everyday shopping needs and thereby provide shareholders with good, sustainable financial returns.

Source: Investor FAQs, www.j-sainsbury.co.uk, August 2006, p. 2.

A dissatisfied workforce may result in low productivity, strikes and so forth, which will in turn have an adverse effect on owners' wealth. Similarly, a business that upsets the local community by unacceptable behaviour, such as polluting the environment, may attract bad publicity, resulting in a loss of customers and heavy fines.

Real World 1.6 provides an example of how two businesses responded to potentially damaging allegations.

Real World 1.6

The price of clothes

FT

US clothing and sportswear manufacturers Gap and Nike have much of their clothes produced in Asia where labour tends to be cheap. However, some of the contractors that produce clothes on behalf of the two companies have been accused of unacceptable practices.

> Campaigners visited the factories and came up with damaging allegations. The factories were employing minors, they said, and managers were harassing female employees.
>
> Nike and Gap reacted by allowing independent inspectors into the factories. They promised to ensure their contractors obeyed minimum standards of employment. Earlier this year, Nike took the extraordinary step of publishing the names and addresses of all its contractors' factories on the internet. The company said it could not be sure all the abuse had stopped. It said that if campaigners visited its contractors' factories and found examples of continued malpractice, it would take action.
>
> Nike and Gap said the approach made business sense. They needed society's approval if they were to prosper. Nike said it was concerned about the reaction of potential US recruits to the campaigners' allegations. They would not want to work for a company that was constantly in the news because of the allegedly cruel treatment of those who made its products.

Source: 'Fair shares?', Michael Skapinker, FT.com, 11 June 2005.

It is important to recognise that generating wealth for the owners is not the same as seeking to maximise the current year's profit. Wealth creation is a longer-term concept, which relates not only to this year's profit but to that of future years as well. In the short term, corners can be cut and risks taken that improve current profit at the expense of future profit. **Real World 1.7** gives some examples of how emphasis on short-term profit can be damaging.

Real World 1.7

Short-term gains, long-term problems

FT

In recent years, many businesses have been criticised for failing to consider the long-term implications of their policies on the wealth of the owners. John Kay argues that some businesses have achieved short-term increases in wealth by sacrificing their longer-term prosperity. He points out that:

> The business of Marks and Spencer, the retailer, was unparalleled in reputation but mature. To achieve earnings growth consistent with a glamour rating the company squeezed suppliers, gave less value for money, spent less on stores. In 1998, it achieved the highest (profit) margin in sales in the history of the business. It had also compromised its position to the point where sales and profits plummeted.
>
> Banks and insurance companies have taken staff out of branches and retrained those that remain as sales people. The pharmaceuticals industry has taken advantage of mergers to consolidate its research and development facilities. Energy companies have cut back on exploration.
>
> We know that these actions increased corporate earnings. We do not know what effect they have on the long-run strength of the business – and this is the key point – do the companies themselves know? Some rationalisations will genuinely lead to more productive businesses. Other companies will suffer the fate of Marks and Spencer.

Source: 'Profit without honour', John Kay, *Financial Times Weekend*, 29/30 June 2002.

Balancing risk and return

All decision making involves the future and business decision making is no exception. There is only one thing certain about the future, which is that we cannot be sure what is going to happen. Risk is therefore an important factor in all financial decision making, and one that must be considered explicitly in all cases. As in other aspects of life, risk and return tend to be related. Evidence shows that returns relate to risk in something like the way shown in Figure 1.7.

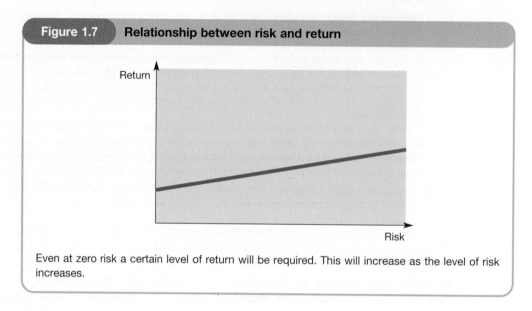

| Figure 1.7 | Relationship between risk and return |

Even at zero risk a certain level of return will be required. This will increase as the level of risk increases.

This relationship between risk and return has important implications for setting financial objectives for a business. The owners will require a minimum return to induce them to invest at all, but will require an additional return to compensate for taking risks; the higher the risk, the higher the required return. Managers must be aware of this and must strike the appropriate balance between risk and return when setting objectives and pursuing particular courses of action.

Not-for-profit organisations

Though the focus of this book is accounting as it relates to private sector businesses, there are many organisations that do not exist mainly for the pursuit of profit. Examples include:

- charities
- clubs and associations
- universities
- local government authorities
- churches
- trade unions.

Such organisations also need to produce accounting information for decision-making purposes. Various user groups need accounting information about these types of organisation to help them to make decisions. These groups are often the same as, or similar to, those identified for private sector businesses. They may have a stake in the future viability of the organisation and may use accounting information to check that the wealth of the organisation is being properly controlled and used in a way that is consistent with its objectives.

Real World 1.8 provides an example of the importance of accounting to relief agencies.

Real World 1.8

FT

When disaster strikes

In the aftermath of the Asian tsunami at the turn of the year, one of the most important issues was ensuring the huge amounts of money raised were providing necessary aid and reconstruction as efficiently and effectively as possible. That does not just mean medical staff and engineers. It also means accountants.

The charity that does this is Mango: Management Accounting for Non-Governmental Organisations (NGOs). It provides accountants in the field and it provides the back-up, such as financial training, and all the other services that should result in really robust financial management in the disaster area.

'In January we had 40 requests for placements,' says Denise Joseph, director of placements at Mango, 'and it was not just for the tsunami. It is an indication of the value that aid agencies place on management accountants. They play a very important role in relief efforts.'

That role will increase. The sheer scale of the money now involved ensures that. Funds for tsunami relief now stand at £365m. In comparison, the funds raised for the Kosovo appeal in 1999 amounted to £53m. 'It is vastly more than previous sums raised,' says Ms Joseph, 'and coupled with this is the pressure to spend money very quickly. So the strain on existing financial controls and management creates extra pressures.'

Mango's work is twofold. It recruits accountants and keeps them on a register to enable a rapid response to the needs of NGOs. And it provides training courses and guidance for them.

For example, Mango has devised a Financial Management Health Check that can be downloaded by NGOs, through which they can gauge the strength of their financial systems. So far, 47,000 copies of the Health Check have been downloaded. 'Aid agencies,' says Ms Joseph, 'achieve different levels of cost effectiveness. We find that if you have someone knowledgeable about financial reporting and that person is separate from the programme manager, it leads to cost savings and efficiencies.'

It is a simple principle. But it is one that can be easily forgotten in the chaos and speed of getting relief to disaster victims. Management accountants can make a huge difference both in making sure the money is spent effectively in the field and that accountability back to the donors is of a high standard.

Source: 'Tsunami: finding the right figures for disaster', Robert Bruce, FT.com, 7 March 2005.

Summary

The main points of this chapter may be summarised as follows.

What are accounting and finance?

- Accounting provides financial information for a range of users to help them make better judgements and decisions concerning a business.
- Finance also helps users to make better decisions and is concerned with the financing and investing activities of the business.

Accounting and user needs

- For accounting to be useful, there must be a clear understanding of *for whom* and *for what purpose* the information will be used.
- There may be conflicts of interest between users over the ways in which the wealth of a business is generated or distributed.
- There is evidence to suggest that accounting is both used and useful for decision-making purposes.

Providing a service

- Accounting can be viewed as a form of service as it involves providing financial information required by the various users.
- To provide a useful service, accounting must possess certain qualities, or characteristics. These are relevance, reliability, comparability and understandability. In addition, accounting information must be material.
- Providing a service to users can be costly and financial information should be produced only if the cost of providing the information is less than the benefits gained.

Accounting information

- Accounting is part of the total information system within a business. It shares the features that are common to all information systems within a business, which are the identification, recording, analysis and reporting of information.

Management and financial accounting

- Accounting has two main strands: management accounting and financial accounting.
- Management accounting seeks to meet the needs of the business's managers and financial accounting seeks to meet the needs of the other user groups.
- These two strands differ in terms of the types of reports produced, the level of reporting detail, the time horizon, the degree of standardisation and the range and quality of information provided.

Is accounting too interesting?

- In recent years, there has been a wave of accounting scandals in the US and Europe.
- This appears to reflect a particular economic environment, although other factors may also play a part.

The changing face of accounting

- Changes in the economic environment have led to changes in the nature and scope of accounting.

- Financial accounting has improved its framework of rules and there has been greater international harmonisation of accounting rules.
- Management accounting has become more outward looking and new methods for managing costs have emerged.

Why study accounting?

- Everyone connected with business should be a little 'streetwise' about accounting and finance. Financial information and decisions exert an enormous influence over the ways in which a business operates.

What is the purpose of a business?

- To create and keep a customer.

What kinds of business ownership exist?

There are three main forms of business unit:

- Sole proprietorship – easy to set up and flexible to operate but the owner has unlimited liability.
- Partnership – easy to set up and spreads the burdens of ownership, but partners usually have unlimited liability and there are ownership risks if the partners are unsuitable.
- Limited company – limited liability for owners but obligations imposed on the way a company conducts its affairs.

How are businesses organised and managed?

- Most businesses of any size are set up as limited companies.
- A board of directors is appointed by owners (shareholders) to oversee the running of the business.
- Businesses are often divided into departments and organised along functional lines, however, larger businesses may be divisionalised along geographical and/or product lines.
- The move to strategic management has been caused by the changing and more competitive nature of business.

What is the financial objective of a business?

- A business may pursue a variety of objectives but the main objective for virtually all businesses is to enhance the wealth of its owners. This does not mean, however, that the needs of other groups connected with the business, such as employees, should be ignored.
- When setting financial objectives the right balance must be struck between risk and return.

MyAccountingLab **Now check your progress in your personal Study Plan**

Key terms

accounting p. 2	accounting information
finance p. 2	system p. 11
financial management p. 2	management accounting p. 13
shares p. 6	financial accounting p. 13
relevance p. 7	sole proprietorship p. 19
reliability p. 7	partnership p. 20
comparability p. 8	limited company p. 20
understandability p. 8	strategic management p. 24
materiality p. 8	mission statement p. 26

References

1 **Contemporary Management Accounting Practices in UK Manufacturing**, *Dugdale D., Jones C. and Green S.*, CIMA Research Publication, vol. 1, no. 13, 2005.

2 **Effective Executive**, *Drucker P.*, Heinemann, 1967.

Further reading

If you would like to explore the topics covered in this chapter in more depth, we recommend the following books:

Accounting Theory, *Riahi-Belkaoui A.*, 5th edn, Thomson Learning, 2004, chapters 1, 2 and 6.

Business Finance: Theory and practice, *McLaney E.*, 7th edn, Prentice Hall, 2006, chapters 1 and 2.

Cost Accounting: A managerial emphasis, *Horngren C., Datar S. and Foster G.*, 12th edn, Prentice Hall, 2005, chapter 1.

Financial Accounting and Reporting, *Elliot B. and Elliot J.*, 11th edn, Financial Times Prentice Hall, 2006, chapter 7.

Managerial Accounting, *Hilton R.*, 6th edn, McGraw-Hill/Irwin, 2005, chapter 1.

Review questions

Answers to these questions can be found at the back of the book on pages 773–4.

1.1 What is the purpose of producing accounting information?

1.2 Identify the main users of accounting information for a university. Do these users differ very much from the users of accounting information for private-sector businesses? Is there a major difference in the ways in which accounting information for a university would be used compared with that of a private-sector business?

1.3 Management accounting has been described as 'the eyes and ears of management'. What do you think this expression means?

1.4 Financial accounting statements tend to reflect past events. In view of this, how can they be of any assistance to a user in making a decision when decisions, by their very nature, can only be made about future actions?

PART 1

Financial accounting

2 Measuring and reporting financial position

3 Measuring and reporting financial performance

4 Accounting for limited companies (1)

5 Accounting for limited companies (2)

6 Measuring and reporting cash flows

7 Analysing and interpreting financial statements

Part 1 of this book deals with the area of accounting and finance usually referred to as 'financial accounting'. Here we shall introduce the three principal financial statements:

- balance sheet
- income statement
- cash flow statement.

In Chapter 2, we provide an overview of these three statements and then go on to consider the first of these, the balance sheet, in some detail. Included in our consideration of the balance sheet will be an introduction to the accounting conventions used when preparing this financial statement. These 'conventions' are generally accepted rules that have evolved to help deal with practical problems experienced by preparers and users.

In Chapter 3 we examine the second of the major financial statements, the income statement. Here we shall be looking at such issues as how profit is measured and the point in time at which it is reported. We shall also consider the accounting conventions used when preparing this financial statement.

The limited company is the most important business form in the UK and in Chapters 4 and 5 we focus on this type of business. As far as accounting is concerned, there is nothing in essence that makes companies different from other types of private-sector business, but there are some points of detail that we need to consider. Chapter 4 examines the nature of limited companies, the way in which they are financed and the accounting issues that specifically relate to this form of business. Chapter 5 considers the duty of directors of a limited company to account to its owners and to others and the regulatory framework imposed on limited companies. Some additional reports prepared by large limited companies are also considered.

Chapter 6 deals with the last of the three principal financial statements, the cash flow statement. This financial statement sets out the sources and uses of cash during an accounting period. We shall see that making profit is not enough. A business must also be able to generate cash to pay its obligations and the cash flow statement helps us to assess its ability to do this.

Reading the three financial statements provides useful information about the business's performance and position for the period concerned. It is possible, however, to gain even more helpful insights about the business by analysing these statements, using financial ratios and other techniques. Combining two figures from the financial statements in a ratio, and comparing this with a similar ratio for, say, another business, can often tell us much more than just reading the figures themselves. In Chapter 7 we consider some of the techniques for analysing financial statements.

Measuring and reporting financial position

Introduction

We saw in the previous chapter that accounting has two distinct strands: financial accounting and management accounting. This chapter, along with Chapters 3 to 7, examines the three major financial statements that form the core of financial accounting. We start by taking an overview of these statements to reveal how each contributes towards an assessment of the overall financial position and performance of a business.

Following this overview, we begin a more detailed examination by turning our attention towards one of these financial statements: the balance sheet. We shall see how it is prepared, and examine the principles underpinning this statement. We shall also consider its value for decision-making purposes.

Learning outcomes

When you have completed this chapter, you should be able to:

- Explain the nature and purpose of the three major financial statements.

- Prepare a simple balance sheet and interpret the information that it contains.

- Discuss the accounting conventions underpinning the balance sheet.

- Discuss the limitations of the balance sheet in portraying the financial position of a business.

 Remember to create your own personalised Study Plan

The major financial statements - an overview

The major financial accounting statements aim to provide a picture of the financial position and performance of a business. To achieve this, a business's accounting system will normally produce three particular statements on a regular, recurring basis. These three are concerned with answering the following questions:

- What cash movements (that is, cash in and cash out) took place over a particular period?
- How much wealth (that is, profit) was generated, or lost, by the business over that period? (Profit (loss) is defined as the increase (decrease) in wealth arising from trading activities.)
- What is the accumulated wealth of the business at the end of that period and what form does the wealth take?

To address each of the above questions, there is a separate financial statement. The financial statements are:

→ - the **cash flow statement**
→ - the **income statement** (also known as the profit and loss account)
→ - the **balance sheet** (also known as the statement of financial position).

When taken together, they provide an overall picture of the financial health of the business.

Perhaps the best way to introduce these financial statements is to look at an example of a very simple business. From this we shall be able to see the sort of information that each of the statements can usefully provide. It is, however, worth pointing out that, while a simple business is our starting point, the principles that we consider apply equally to the largest and most complex businesses. This means that we shall frequently encounter these principles again in later chapters.

Example 2.1

Paul was unemployed and unable to find a job. He therefore decided to embark on a business venture. Christmas was approaching, and so he decided to buy gift wrapping paper from a local supplier and to sell it on the corner of his local high street. He felt that the price of wrapping paper in the high street shops was excessive. This provided him with a useful business opportunity.

He began the venture with £40 in cash. On Monday, Paul's first day of trading, he bought wrapping paper for £40 and sold three-quarters of it for £45 cash.

- **What cash movements took place during Monday?**

  For Monday, a cash flow statement showing the cash movements for the day can be prepared as follows:

Cash flow statement for Monday

	£
Opening balance (cash introduced)	40
Add Cash from sales of wrapping paper	45
	85
Less Cash paid to buy wrapping paper	40
Closing balance of cash	45

- **How much wealth (that is, profit) was generated by the business during Monday?**

    An *income statement (profit and loss account)* can be prepared to show the wealth (profit) generated on Monday. The wealth generated will represent the difference between the value of the sales made and the cost of the goods (that is, wrapping paper) sold:

    ### Income statement (profit and loss account) for Monday

	£
Sales revenue	45
Less Cost of goods sold ($^3/_4$ of £40)	30
Profit	15

    Note that it is only the cost of the wrapping paper *sold* that is matched against the sales revenue in order to find the profit, and not the whole of the cost of wrapping paper acquired. Any unsold inventories (in this case $^1/_4$ of £40 = £10) will be charged against the future sales revenue that it generates.

- **What is the accumulated wealth at Monday evening?**

    To establish the accumulated wealth at the end of Monday's trading, we can draw up a *balance sheet (statement of financial position)*. This will list the resources held at the end of that day:

    ### Balance sheet (statement of financial position) as at Monday evening

	£
Cash (closing balance)	45
Inventories of goods for resale ($^1/_4$ of £40)	10
Total business wealth	55

We can see from the financial statements in Example 2.1 that each statement provides part of a picture portraying the financial performance and position of the business. We begin by showing the cash movements. Cash is a vital resource that is necessary for any business to function effectively. Cash is required to meet debts that may become due and to acquire other resources (such as inventories). Cash has been described as the 'lifeblood' of a business, and movements in cash are usually given close scrutiny by users of financial statements.

However, it is clear that reporting cash movements alone would not be enough to portray the financial health of the business. The changes in cash over time do not tell us how much profit was generated. The income statement provides us with information concerning this aspect of performance. For example, we saw that during Monday the cash balance increased by £5, but the profit generated, as shown in the income statement, was £15. The cash balance did not increase by the amount of the profit made because part of the wealth generated (£10) was held in the form of inventories.

A balance sheet can be drawn up as at the end of Monday's trading, which should provide an insight to the total wealth of the business. Cash is only one form in which wealth can be held. In the case of this business, wealth is also held in the form of inventories (also known as stock). Hence, when drawing up the balance sheet, both forms of wealth held will be listed. In the case of a large business, there may be many other forms in which wealth will be held, such as land and buildings, equipment, motor vehicles and so on.

Let us now continue with our example.

> ## Example 2.1 (continued)
>
> On Tuesday, Paul bought more wrapping paper for £20 cash. He managed to sell all of the new inventories and all of the earlier inventories, for a total of £48.
>
> The cash flow statement for Tuesday will be as follows:
>
> **Cash flow statement for Tuesday**
>
> | | £ |
> |---|---|
> | Opening balance (from Monday evening) | 45 |
> | Add Cash from sales of wrapping paper | 48 |
> | | 93 |
> | Less Cash paid to buy wrapping paper | 20 |
> | Closing balance | 73 |
>
> The income statement for Tuesday will be as follows:
>
> **Income statement for Tuesday**
>
> | | £ |
> |---|---|
> | Sales revenue | 48 |
> | Less Cost of goods sold (£20 + £10) | 30 |
> | Profit | 18 |
>
> The balance sheet as at Tuesday evening will be:
>
> **Balance sheet as at Tuesday evening**
>
> | | £ |
> |---|---|
> | Cash (closing balance) | 73 |
> | Inventories | – |
> | Total business wealth | 73 |

We can see that the total business wealth increased to £73 by the Tuesday evening. This represents an increase of £18 (that is, £73 – £55) over Monday's figure – which, of course, is the amount of profit made during Tuesday as shown on the income statement.

> ## Activity 2.1
>
> On Wednesday, Paul bought more wrapping paper for £46 cash. However, it was raining hard for much of the day and sales were slow. After Paul had sold half of his total inventories for £32, he decided to stop trading until Thursday morning.
>
> Have a go at drawing up the three financial statements for Paul's business for Wednesday.
>
> **Cash flow statement for Wednesday**
>
> | | £ |
> |---|---|
> | Opening balance (from the Tuesday evening) | 73 |
> | Add Cash from sales of wrapping paper | 32 |
> | | 105 |
> | Less Cash paid to buy wrapping paper | 46 |
> | Closing balance | 59 |

Income statement for Wednesday

	£
Sales revenue	32
Less Cost of goods sold (½ of £46)	23
Profit	9

Balance sheet as at Wednesday evening

	£
Cash (closing balance)	59
Inventories (½ of £46)	23
Total business wealth	82

Note that the total business wealth had increased by £9 (that is, the amount of Wednesday's profit) even though the cash balance had declined. This is because the business is holding more of its wealth in the form of inventories rather than cash, compared with the position on Tuesday evening.

We can see that the income statement and cash flow statement are both concerned with measuring flows (of wealth and cash respectively) during a particular period (for example, a particular day, a particular month or a particular year). The balance sheet, however, is concerned with the financial position at a particular moment in time.

Figure 2.1 illustrates this point. The financial statements (income statement, cash flow statement and balance sheet) are often referred to as the **final accounts** of the business.

Figure 2.1   The relationship between the balance sheet, the income statement and the cash flow statement

The income statement and cash flow statement are concerned with measuring flows of wealth and cash (respectively) over time. The balance sheet, however, is concerned with measuring the stock of wealth at a particular moment in time.

For external users (that is virtually all except the managers of the business concerned), these statements are normally backward looking because they are based on information concerning past events and transactions. This can be useful in providing feedback on past performance, and in identifying trends that provide clues to future performance. However, the statements can also be prepared using projected data to help assess likely future profits, cash flows and so on. The financial statements are normally prepared on a projected basis for internal decision-making purposes only, as we shall see in Chapter 12. Managers are usually reluctant to publish these projected statements for external users, as they may reveal valuable information to competitors.

Now that we have an overview of the financial statements, we shall consider each statement in more detail. We shall go straight on to look at the balance sheet. Chapter 3 looks at the income statement, Chapter 6 goes into more detail on the cash flow statement. (Chapters 4 and 5 consider the balance sheets and income statements of limited companies.)

The balance sheet

The purpose of the balance sheet is simply to set out the financial position of a business at a particular moment in time (hence, its alternative name *statement of financial position*). We saw above that the balance sheet will reveal the forms in which the wealth of the business is held and how much wealth is held in each form. We can, however, be more specific about the nature of the balance sheet by saying that it sets out the **assets** of the business on the one hand, and the **claims** against the business on the other. Before looking at the balance sheet in more detail, we need to be clear about what these terms mean.

Assets

An asset is essentially a resource held by the business. For a particular item to be treated as an asset for accounting purposes it should have the following characteristics:

● *A probable future benefit must exist.* This simply means that the item must be expected to have some future monetary value. This value can arise through its use within the business or through its hire or sale. Thus, an obsolete piece of equipment that could be sold for scrap would still be considered an asset, whereas an obsolete piece of equipment that could not be sold for scrap would not be regarded as one.
● *The business must have an exclusive right to control the benefit.* Unless the business has exclusive rights over the resource it cannot be regarded as an asset. Thus, for a business offering holidays on barges, the canal system may be a very valuable resource, but as the business will not be able to control the access of others to the canal system, it cannot be regarded as an asset of the business. (However, the barges owned by the business would be regarded as assets.)
● *The benefit must arise from some past transaction or event.* This means that the transaction (or other event) giving rise to the business's right to the benefit must have already occurred, and will not arise at some future date. Thus an agreement by a business to buy a piece of equipment at some future date would not mean the item is currently an asset of the business.
● *The asset must be capable of measurement in monetary terms.* Unless the item can be measured in monetary terms, with a reasonable degree of reliability, it will not be

regarded as an asset for inclusion on the balance sheet. Thus, the title of a magazine (for example *Hello!* or *Vogue*) that was created by its publisher may be extremely valuable to that publishing business, but this value is usually difficult to quantify. It will not, therefore, be treated as an asset.

Note that all four of these conditions must apply. If one of them is missing, the item will not be treated as an asset, for accounting purposes, and will not appear on the balance sheet.

We can see that these conditions will strictly limit the kind of items that may be referred to as 'assets' in the balance sheet. Certainly not all resources exploited by a business will be assets of the business for accounting purposes. Some, like the canal system or the magazine title *Hello!*, may well be assets in a broader sense, but not for accounting purposes. Once an asset has been acquired by a business, it will continue to be considered an asset until the benefits are exhausted or the business disposes of it in some way.

Activity 2.2

Indicate which of the following items could appear as an asset on the balance sheet of a business. Explain your reasoning in each case.

1 £1,000 owing to the business by a customer who is unable to pay.
2 The purchase of a patent from an inventor that gives the business the right to produce a new product. Production of the new product is expected to increase profits over the period during which the patent is held.
3 The business hiring a new marketing director who is confidently expected to increase profits by over 30 per cent during the next three years.
4 The purchase of a machine that will save the business £10,000 each year. It is currently being used by the business but it has been acquired on credit and is not yet paid for.

Your answer should be along the following lines.

1 Under normal circumstances a business would expect a customer to pay the amount owed. Such an amount is therefore typically shown as an asset under the heading 'trade receivables' (or 'debtors'). However, in this particular case the customer is unable to pay. Hence the item is incapable of providing future benefits, and the £1,000 owing would not be regarded as an asset. Debts that are not paid are referred to as 'bad debts'.
2 The purchase of the patent would meet all of the conditions set out above and would therefore be regarded as an asset.
3 The hiring of a new marketing director would not be considered as the acquisition of an asset. One argument against its classification as an asset is that the business does not have exclusive rights of control over the director. (Nevertheless, it may have an exclusive right to the services that the director provides.) Perhaps a stronger argument is that the value of the director cannot be measured in monetary terms with any degree of reliability.
4 The machine would be considered an asset even though it is not yet paid for. Once the business has agreed to buy the machine, and has accepted it, the machine is legally owned by the business even though payment is still outstanding. (The amount outstanding would be shown as a claim, as we shall see below.)

The sorts of items that often appear as assets in the balance sheet of a business include:

- property
- plant and equipment
- fixtures and fittings
- patents and trademarks
- trade receivables (debtors)
- investments.

Activity 2.3

Can you think of three additional items that might appear as assets in the balance sheet of a business?

You may be able to think of a number of other items. Some that you may have identified are:

- motor vehicles
- inventories (stock)
- computer equipment
- cash at bank.

Note that an asset does not have to be a physical item – it may also be a non-physical right to certain benefits. Assets that have a physical substance and can be touched are referred to as **tangible assets**. Assets that have no physical substance but which, nevertheless, provide expected future benefits (such as patents) are referred to as **intangible assets**.

Claims

A claim is an obligation on the part of the business to provide cash, or some other form of benefit, to an outside party. A claim will normally arise as a result of the outside party providing funds in the form of assets for use by the business. There are essentially two types of claim against a business:

- **Capital**. This represents the claim of the owner(s) against the business. This claim is sometimes referred to as the *owner's equity*. Some find it hard to understand how the owner can have a claim against the business, particularly when we consider the example of a sole-proprietor-type business where the owner *is*, in effect, the business. However, for accounting purposes, a clear distinction is made between the business (whatever its size) and the owner(s). The business is viewed as being quite separate from the owner and this is equally true for a sole proprietor like Paul, the wrapping-paper seller in Example 2.1, or a large company like Marks and Spencer plc. It is seen as a separate entity with its own separate existence and when financial statements are prepared, they relate to the business rather than to the owner(s). This means that the balance sheet should reflect the financial position of the business as a separate entity. Viewed from this perspective, any funds contributed by the owner will be seen as coming from outside the business and will appear as a claim against the business in its balance sheet.

  As we have just seen, the business and the owner are separate for accounting purposes, irrespective of the type of business concerned. It is also true that the operation of the capital section of the balance sheet is broadly the same irrespective of the type of business concerned. As we shall see in Chapter 4, with limited companies the owner's clairm figure must be analysed according to how each part of it first arose. For example, companies must make a distinction between that part of the owner's claim that arose from retained profits and that part that arose from the owners putting in cash to start up the business, usually by buying shares in the company.

→ ● **Liabilities**. Liabilities represent the claims of all other individuals and organisations, apart from the owner(s). Liabilities must have arisen from past transactions or events such as supplying goods or lending money to the business. When a liability is settled it will normally be through an outflow of assets (usually cash).

Once a claim from the owners or outsiders has been incurred by a business, it will remain as an obligation until it is settled.

Now that the meaning of the terms *assets* and *claims* has been established, we can go on and discuss the relationship between the two. This relationship is quite straightforward. If a business wishes to acquire assets, it will have to raise the necessary funds from somewhere. It may raise the funds from the owner(s) or from other outside parties or from both. Example 2.2 illustrates this relationship.

Example 2.2

Jerry and Company start a business by depositing £20,000 in a bank account on 1 March. This amount was raised partly from the owner (£6,000) and partly from borrowing (£14,000). Raising funds in this way will give rise to a claim on the business by both the owner (capital) and the lender (liability). If a balance sheet of Jerry and Company is prepared following the above transactions, it will appear as follows:

Jerry and Company
Balance sheet as at 1 March

	£		£
Assets		**Claims**	
Cash at bank	20,000	Capital (owner's equity)	6,000
		Liability – borrowing	14,000
	20,000		20,000

We can see from the balance sheet that the total claims are the same as the total assets. Thus:

$$\text{Assets} = \text{Capital} + \text{Liabilities}$$

This equation – which is often referred to as the *balance sheet equation* – will always hold true. Whatever changes may occur to the assets of the business or the claims against it, there will be compensating changes elsewhere that will ensure that the balance sheet always 'balances'. By way of illustration, consider the following transactions for Jerry and Company:

2 March	Bought a motor van for £5,000, paying by cheque.
3 March	Bought inventories (that is, goods to be sold) on one month's credit for £3,000. (This means that the inventories will be bought on 3 March, but payment will not be made to the supplier until 3 April.)
4 March	Repaid £2,000 of the amount borrowed to the lender, by cheque.
6 March	Owner introduced another £4,000 into the business bank account.

A balance sheet may be drawn up after each day in which transactions have taken place. In this way, the effect can be seen of each transaction on the assets and claims of the business. The balance sheet as at 2 March will be as follows:

Jerry and Company
Balance sheet as at 2 March

Assets	£	Claims	£
Cash at bank (20,000 – 5,000)	15,000	Capital	6,000
Motor van	5,000	Liabilities – borrowing	14,000
	20,000		20,000

As can be seen, the effect of buying the motor van is to decrease the balance at the bank by £5,000 and to introduce a new asset – a motor van – to the balance sheet. The total assets remain unchanged. It is only the 'mix' of assets that has changed. The claims against the business remain the same because there has been no change in the way in which the business has been funded.

The balance sheet as at 3 March, following the purchase of inventories, will be as follows:

Jerry and Company
Balance sheet as at 3 March

Assets	£	Claims	£
Cash at bank	15,000	Capital	6,000
Motor van	5,000	Liabilities – borrowing	14,000
Inventories (stock)	3,000	Liabilities – trade payable	3,000
	23,000		23,000

The effect of buying inventories has been to introduce another new asset (inventories) to the balance sheet. In addition, the fact that the goods have not yet been paid for means that the claims against the business will be increased by the £3,000 owed to the supplier, who is referred to as a *trade payable* (or trade creditor) on the balance sheet.

Activity (2.4)

Try drawing up a balance sheet for Jerry and Company as at 4 March.

The balance sheet as at 4 March, following the repayment of part of the loan, will be as follows:

Jerry and Company
Balance sheet as at 4 March

Assets	£	Claims	£
Cash at bank (15,000 – 2,000)	13,000	Capital	6,000
Motor van	5,000	Liabilities – borrowing	
		(14,000 – 2,000)	12,000
Inventories (stock)	3,000	Liabilities – trade payable (creditor)	3,000
	21,000		21,000

The repayment of £2,000 of the borrowing will result in a decrease in the balance at the bank of £2,000 and a decrease in the lender's claim against the business by the same amount.

Once assets are revalued, the frequency of revaluation then becomes an important issue as assets recorded at out-of-date values can mislead users. Using out-of-date revaluations on the balance sheet is the worst of both worlds. It lacks the objectivity and verifiability of historic cost; it also lacks the realism of current values. Revaluations should therefore be frequent enough to ensure that the carrying amount of the revalued asset does not differ materially from its fair value at the balance sheet date.

When an item of property, or plant, or equipment is revalued on the basis of fair values, all assets within that particular group must be revalued. Thus, it is not acceptable to revalue some property but not others. Although this provides some degree of consistency within a particular group of assets, it does not, of course, prevent the balance sheet from containing a mixture of valuations.

Intangible non-current assets

For these assets, the 'benchmark treatment' is, once again, that they are measured initially at historic cost. What follows, however, will depend on whether the asset has a finite or an infinite useful life. (Purchased goodwill can provide an example of an asset with an infinitely useful life.) Where the asset has a finite life, any depreciation (or *amortisation* as it is usually termed for intangible non-current assets) following acquisition will be deducted from its cost. Where, however, the asset has an infinite life, it will not be amortised. Instead, it will be tested annually to see whether there has been any fall in value. This point is discussed in more detail in the following section.

Once again, the alternative of revaluing intangible assets using fair values is available. However, this can only be used where an active market exists, which allows fair values to be properly determined. In practice, this is a rare occurrence.

The impairment of non-current assets

There is always a risk that both types of non-current asset (tangible and intangible) may suffer a significant fall in value. This may be due to factors such as changes in market conditions, technological obsolescence and so on. In some cases, this fall in value may lead to the net book value, or carrying amount, of the asset being higher than the amount that could be recovered from the asset through its continued use or through its sale. When this occurs, the asset value is said to be impaired and the general rule is to reduce the asset on the balance sheet to its recoverable amount. Unless this is done, the asset will be overstated on the balance sheet.

Activity (2.15)

With which one of the accounting conventions that we discussed earlier is this accounting treatment consistent?

The answer is the prudence convention, which states that actual or anticipated losses should be recognised in full.

In many situations, a business may use either historic cost, less any depreciation, or a value-based measure when reporting its non-current assets. However, where the former is greater than the latter, the business has no choice; the use of depreciated historic cost is not an option. **Real World 2.4** provides an example of where the application of the 'impairment rule', as it is called, resulted in huge write-downs (that is, reductions in the balance sheet value of the assets) for a well-known mobile phone operator.

Real World 2.4

Talking telephone numbers

FT

The scale of Vodafone's binge on spending on telecom assets at the turn of the century can still be seen six years later after the mobile phone operator on Tuesday announced major write-downs of goodwill for a third successive year.

The £23.5bn write-down in the carrying value of goodwill, flagged earlier this year, is one of the largest corporate write-downs on record.

But it is the £101bn purchase of Germany's Mannesmann in 2000 and the Italian operations it partly inherited from the deal, that has caused the problems.

Broken down, Vodafone ascribed a write-down value of £19.4bn for its assets in Germany, £3.6bn for its Italian operations and £515m for the assets in Sweden. The latter already had an impairment charge of £475m a year ago, and Vodafone has since sold it to Norway's Telenor Mobile.

Vodafone blamed the write-down on the revision of its longer term prospects in the German and Italian markets, which are being hit by tough price competition.

Source: 'Goodwill charges at record levels', FT.com, 30 May 2006.

We saw earlier that intangible, non-current assets with infinite lives must be tested annually to see whether there has been any impairment. Other non-current assets, however, must be also tested where events suggest that impairment has taken place.

Inventories (stock)

It is not only non-current assets that run the risk of a significant fall in value. The inventories of a business could also suffer this fate, which could be caused by factors such as reduced selling prices, obsolescence, deterioration, damage and so on. Where a fall in value means that the amount likely to be recovered from the sale of the inventories will be lower than their cost, this loss must be reflected in the balance sheet. Thus, if the net realisable value (that is, selling price less any selling costs) falls below the historic cost of inventories held, the former should be used as the basis of valuation. This reflects, once again, the influence of the prudence convention on the balance sheet.

Real World 2.5 reveals how one well-known business wrote down the inventories of one of its products following a sharp reduction in selling prices.

Real World 2.5

You're fired!

'You're fired!' is what some investors might like to tell Amstrad, run by *Apprentice* star Sir Alan Sugar. . . . Shares in the company fell nearly 10 per cent as it revealed that sales of its much-vaunted videophone have failed to take off.

Amstrad launched the E3, a phone allowing users to hold video calls with each other, in a blaze of publicity last year. But, after cutting the price from £99 to £49, Amstrad sold just 61,000 E3s in the year to June and has taken a £5.7m stock [inventories] write down.

Source: 'Amstrad (AMT)', *Investors Chronicle*, 7 October 2005.

The published financial statements of large businesses will normally show the basis on which inventories are valued. **Real World 2.6** shows how one well-known business reports this information.

Real World 2.6

Reporting inventories

The 2006 financial statements of Thorntons plc, the chocolate maker, include the following explanation concerning inventories:

> Inventories are recorded at the lower of cost and net realisable value. Cost includes materials, direct labour and an attributable proportion of manufacturing overheads, based on normal operating capacity, according to the stage of production reached. Net realisable value is the estimated value which would be realised after deducting all costs of completion, marketing and selling. Provision is made to reduce the cost to net realisable value having regard to the age and condition of inventory, as well as its saleability.

Source: Thorntons plc Annual Report 2006, p. 25.

Interpreting the balance sheet

We have seen that the conventional balance sheet has a number of limitations. This has led some users of financial information to conclude that the balance sheet has little to offer in the way of useful information. However, this is not really the case. The balance sheet can provide useful insights about the financing and investing activities of a business. We shall consider this in detail in Chapter 7 when we deal with the analysis and interpretation of the financial statements.

Summary

The main points of the chapter may be summarised as follows.

The major financial statements

- There are three major financial statements: the cash flow statement, the income statement (profit and loss account) and the balance sheet (statement of financial position).
- The cash flow statement shows the cash movements over a particular period.
- The income statement shows the wealth (profit) generated over a particular period.
- The balance sheet shows the accumulated wealth at a particular point in time.

The balance sheet

- This sets out the assets of the business, on the one hand, and the claims against those assets, on the other.
- Assets are resources of the business that have certain characteristics, such as the ability to provide future benefits.
- Claims are obligations on the part of the business to provide cash, or some other benefit, to outside parties.
- Claims are of two types: capital and liabilities.
- Capital represents the owner's claim and liabilities represent the claims of others, apart from the owner.

Classification of assets and liabilities

- Assets are normally categorised as being current or non-current.
- Current assets are cash or near cash or are held for sale or consumption in the normal course of business, or for trading, or for the short term.
- Non-current assets are assets that are not current assets. They are normally held for the long-term operations of the business.
- Liabilities are normally categorised as being current or non-current liabilities.
- Current liabilities represent amounts due in the normal course of the business's operating cycle, or are held for trading, or are to be settled within 12 months of, or cannot be deferred for at least 12 months after, the end of the reporting period.
- Non-current liabilities represent amounts due that are not current liabilities.

Balance sheet layouts

- The horizontal layout sets out the assets on one side of the balance sheet and the capital and liabilities on the other side.
- The vertical layout begins with the assets at the top of the balance sheet and places capital and liabilities underneath.

Accounting conventions

- Accounting conventions are the rules of accounting that have evolved to deal with practical problems experienced by those preparing financial statements.
- The main conventions relating to the balance sheet include business entity, historic cost, prudence, going concern and dual aspect.

Money measurement

- Using money as the unit of measurement limits the scope of the balance sheet.

- Certain resources such as goodwill, product brands and human resources are difficult to measure. An 'arm's-length transaction' is normally required before such assets can be reliably measured and reported on the balance sheet.

- Money is not a stable unit of measurement – it changes in value over time.

Asset valuation

- The 'benchmark treatment' is to show property, plant and equipment at historic cost less any amounts written off for depreciation. However, fair values may be used rather than depreciated cost.

- The 'benchmark treatment' for intangible non-current assets is to show the items at historic cost. Only assets with a finite life will be amortised (depreciated) and fair values will rarely be used.

- Where the recoverable amount from tangible non-current assets is below their carrying amount, this lower amount is reflected in the balance sheet.

- Inventories are shown at the lower of cost or net realisable value.

MyAccountingLab **Now check your progress in your personal Study Plan**

 Key terms

cash flow statement p. 38	**non-current (fixed) assets** p. 50
income statement p. 38	**current liabilities** p. 52
balance sheet p. 38	**non-current liabilities** p. 52
final accounts p. 41	**accounting conventions** p. 55
assets p. 42	**business entity convention** p. 55
claims p. 42	**historic cost convention** p. 56
tangible assets p. 44	**prudence convention** p. 56
intangible assets p. 44	**going concern convention** p. 57
capital p. 44	**dual aspect convention** p. 57
liabilities p. 45	**property, plant and equipment** p. 60
current assets p. 50	**fair values** p. 61

Further reading

If you would like to explore the topics covered in this chapter in more depth, we recommend the following books:

Corporate Financial Accounting and Reporting, *Sutton T.*, 2nd edn, Financial Times Prentice Hall, 2004, chapters 2 and 8.

Financial Accounting and Reporting, *Elliott B. and Elliott J.*, 11th edn, Financial Times Prentice Hall, 2006, chapters 16 and 18.

International Financial Reporting Standards (IFRSs), *International Accounting Standards Board*, IAS 16 (revised December 2003), IAS 36 (revised March 2004) and IAS 38 (revised March 2004).

International Financial Reporting Standards in Depth, Vol. 1. Theory and Practice, *Kirk R. J.*, CIMA Publishing, 2005, chapters 2 and 3.

Review questions

Answers to these questions can be found at the back of the book on page 774.

2.1 An accountant prepared a balance sheet for a business. In the balance sheet, the capital of the owner was shown next to the liabilities. This confused the owner, who argued: 'My capital is my major asset and so should be shown as an asset on the balance sheet.' How would you explain this misunderstanding to the owner?

2.2 'The balance sheet shows how much a business is worth.' Do you agree with this statement? Discuss.

2.3 What is meant by the balance sheet equation? How does the form of this equation differ between the horizontal and vertical balance sheet layout?

2.4 In recent years there have been attempts to place a value on the 'human assets' of a business in order to derive a figure that can be included on the balance sheet. Do you think humans should be treated as assets? Would 'human assets' meet the conventional definition of an asset for inclusion on the balance sheet?

Exercises

Exercises 2.5 to 2.8 are more advanced than 2.1 to 2.4. Those exercises with coloured numbers have answers at the back of the book, starting on page 709.

If you wish to try more exercises, visit the students' side of the Companion Website.

2.1 On Thursday, the fourth day of his business venture, Paul, the street trader in wrapping paper (see earlier in the chapter, page 38), bought more inventories (stock) for £53 cash. During the day he sold inventories that had cost £33 for a total of £47.

Required:
Draw up the three financial statements for Paul's business venture for Thursday.

2.2 The 'total business wealth' belongs to Paul because he is the sole owner of the business. Can you explain how the figure for total business wealth by Thursday evening has arisen? You will need to look back at the events of Monday, Tuesday and Wednesday (in this chapter on pages 38 to 41) to do this.

2.3 While on holiday in Bridlington, Helen had her credit cards and purse stolen from the beach while she was swimming. She was left with only £40, which she had kept in her hotel room, but she had three days of her holiday remaining. She was determined to continue her holiday and decided to make some money to enable her to do so. She decided to sell orange juice to holidaymakers using the local beach. On day 1 she bought 80 cartons of orange juice at £0.50 each for cash and sold 70 of these at £0.80 each. On the following day she bought 60 cartons at £0.50 each for cash and sold 65 at £0.80 each. On the third and final day she bought another 60 cartons at £0.50 each for cash. However, it rained and, as a result, business was poor. She managed to sell 20 at £0.80 each but sold off the rest of her inventories at £0.40 each.

Required:
Prepare an income statement and cash flow statement for each day's trading and prepare a balance sheet at the end of each day's trading.

2.4 On 1 March, Joe Conday started a new business. During March he carried out the following transactions:

1 March	Deposited £20,000 in a bank account.
2 March	Bought fixtures and fittings for £6,000 cash, and inventories £8,000 on credit.
3 March	Borrowed £5,000 from a relative and deposited it in the bank.
4 March	Bought a motor car for £7,000 cash and withdrew £200 in cash for his own use.
5 March	A further motor car costing £9,000 was bought. The motor car bought on 4 March was given in part exchange at a value of £6,500. The balance of purchase price for the new car was paid in cash.
6 March	Conday won £2,000 in a lottery and paid the amount into the business bank account. He also repaid £1,000 of the loan.

Required:
Draw up a balance sheet for the business at the end of each day.

2.5 The following is a list of the assets and claims of Crafty Engineering Ltd at 30 June last year:

	£000
Trade payables	86
Motor vehicles	38
Long-term loan from Industrial Finance Co.	260
Equipment and tools	207
Short-term borrowings	116
Inventories	153
Property	320
Trade receivables	185

Required:
(a) Prepare the balance sheet of the business as at 30 June last year from the above information using the vertical layout. (*Hint*: There is a missing item that needs to be deduced and inserted.)
(b) Discuss the significant features revealed by this financial statement.

2.6 The balance sheet of a business at the start of the week is as follows:

Assets	£	Claims	£
Property	145,000	Capital	203,000
Furniture and fittings	63,000	Short-term borrowing (bank overdraft)	43,000
Inventories	28,000	Trade payables	23,000
Trade receivables	33,000		
	269,000		269,000

During the week the following transactions take place:

(a) Inventories sold for £11,000 cash; these inventories had cost £8,000.
(b) Sold inventories for £23,000 on credit; these inventories had cost £17,000.
(c) Received cash from trade receivables totalling £18,000.
(d) The owners of the business introduced £100,000 of their own money, which was placed in the business bank account.
(e) The owners brought a motor van, valued at £10,000, into the business.
(f) Bought inventories on credit for £14,000.
(g) Paid trade payables £13,000.

Required:
Show the balance sheet after all of these transactions have been reflected.

2.7   The following is a list of assets and claims of a manufacturing business at a particular point in time:

	£
Short-term borrowing	22,000
Property	245,000
Inventories of raw materials	18,000
Trade payables	23,000
Plant and equipment	127,000
Loan from Manufacturing Finance Co. (long-term borrowing)	100,000
Inventories of finished goods	28,000
Delivery vans	54,000
Trade receivables	34,000

Required:

Write out a balance sheet in the standard vertical form incorporating these figures. (*Hint:* There is a missing item that needs to be deduced and inserted.)

2.8   You have been talking to someone who had read a few chapters of an accounting text some years ago. During your conversation the person made the following statements:

(a)   The income statement shows how much cash has come into and left the business during the accounting period and the resulting balance at the end of the period.

(b)   In order to be included in the balance sheet as an asset, an item needs to be worth something in the market – that is all.

(c)   The balance sheet equation is:

$$\text{Assets} + \text{Capital} = \text{Liabilities}$$

(d)   Non-current assets are things that cannot be moved.

(e)   Goodwill has an indefinite life and so should not be amortised.

Required:

Comment critically on each of the above statements, going into as much detail as you can.

CHAPTER 3

Measuring and reporting financial performance

Introduction

In this chapter we continue our examination of the major financial statements by looking at the income statement. This statement was briefly considered in Chapter 2 and we shall now examine it in some detail. We shall see how it is prepared and how it links with the balance sheet. We shall also consider some of the key measurement problems to be faced when preparing the income statement.

Learning outcomes

When you have completed this chapter, you should be able to:

- Discuss the nature and purpose of the income statement.

- Prepare an income statement from relevant financial information.

- Discuss the main recognition and measurement issues that must be considered when preparing the income statement.

- Explain the main accounting conventions underpinning the income statement.

 MyAccountingLab Remember to create your own personalised Study Plan

The income statement

In Chapter 2 we examined the nature and purpose of the balance sheet. We saw that this statement is concerned with setting out the financial position of a business at a particular moment in time. However, it is not usually enough for users of the financial statements to have information relating only to the amount of wealth held by a business at one moment in time. Businesses exist for the primary purpose of generating wealth, or profit, and it is the profit generated *during a period* that is the main concern of many users of financial statements. Although the amount of profit generated is of particular interest to the owners of a business, other groups such as managers, employees and suppliers will also have an interest in the profit-generating ability of the business. The purpose of the income statement – or profit and loss account, as it is sometimes called – is to measure and report how much **profit** (wealth) the business has generated over a period. As with the balance sheet that we examined in Chapter 2, the principles of preparation are the same irrespective of whether the income statement is for a sole proprietorship business or for a limited company.

The measurement of profit requires that the total revenue of the business, generated during a particular period, be identified. **Revenue** is simply a measure of the inflow of economic benefits arising from the ordinary activities of a business. These benefits, which accrue to the owners, will result in either an increase in assets (such as cash or amounts owed to the business by its customers) or a decrease in liabilities. Different forms of business enterprise will generate different forms of revenue. Some examples of the different forms that revenue can take are as follows:

- sales of goods (for example, of a manufacturer)
- fees for services (for example, of a solicitor)
- subscriptions (for example, of a club)
- interest received (for example, of an investment fund).

The total expenses relating to each period must also be identified. **Expense** is really the opposite of revenue. It represents the outflow of economic benefits arising from the ordinary activities of a business. This loss of benefits will result in either a decrease in assets (such as cash) or an increase in liabilities (such as amounts owed to suppliers). Expenses are incurred in the process of generating revenue, or attempting to generate it. The nature of the business will again determine the type of expenses that will be incurred. Examples of some of the more common types of expenses are:

- the cost of buying goods that are subsequently sold – known as *cost of sales* or *cost of goods sold*
- salaries and wages
- rent and rates
- motor vehicle running expenses
- insurances
- printing and stationery
- heat and light
- telephone and postage.

The **income statement** simply shows the total revenue generated during a particular period and deducts from this the total expenses incurred in generating that revenue. The difference between the total revenue and total expenses will represent either profit (if revenue exceeds expenses) or loss (if expenses exceed revenue). Thus, we have:

> **Profit (loss) for the period = Total revenue for the period *less* Total expenses incurred in generating the revenue**

The period over which profit or loss is normally measured is usually known as the **accounting period**, but sometimes known as the 'reporting period' or 'financial period'. **Real World 3.1** shows the various forms of revenue generated by a leading football club.

Real World 3.1

Away the lads!

Newcastle United is a well-known football club in the English Premiership. For the year to 31 July 2005, the club generated revenue totalling £87.0m. A breakdown of this amount is provided in Figure 3.1.

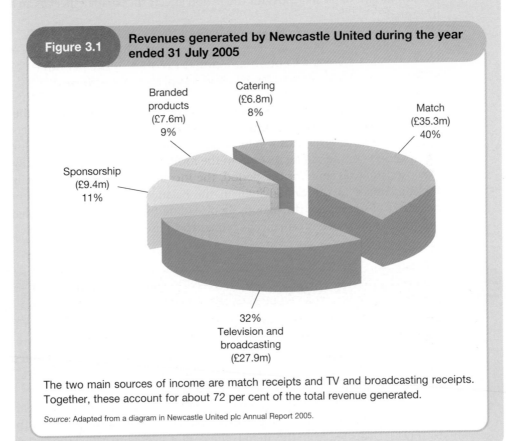

Figure 3.1   Revenues generated by Newcastle United during the year ended 31 July 2005

The two main sources of income are match receipts and TV and broadcasting receipts. Together, these account for about 72 per cent of the total revenue generated.

Source: Adapted from a diagram in Newcastle United plc Annual Report 2005.

The income statement and the balance sheet

The income statement and the balance sheet should not be viewed in any way as substitutes for one another. Rather they should be seen as performing different functions. The balance sheet is, as stated earlier, a statement of the financial position of a business at a single moment in time – a 'snapshot' of the make-up of the wealth held by the business. The income statement, on the other hand, is concerned with the *flow* of wealth over a period of time. The two statements are, however, closely related.

The income statement links the balance sheets at the beginning and the end of an accounting period. Thus, at the start of a new accounting period, the balance sheet shows the opening financial position. After an appropriate period, an income statement is prepared to show the wealth generated over that period. A balance sheet is then also prepared to reveal the new financial position at the end of the period. This balance sheet will incorporate the changes in wealth that have occurred since the previous balance sheet was drawn up.

We saw in Chapter 2 (page 49) that the effect on the balance sheet of making a profit (loss) means that the equation can be extended as follows:

> **Assets = Capital (amount at the start of the period + profit (or – loss) for period) + Liabilities**

The amount of profit or loss for the period affects the balance sheet as an adjustment to capital.

The above equation can be extended to:

> **Assets = Capital (amount at the start of the period) + (sales revenue – expenses) + Liabilities**

In theory, it would be possible to calculate the profit (or loss) for the period by making all adjustments for revenue and expenses through the capital section of the balance sheet. However, this would be rather cumbersome. A better solution is to have an 'appendix' to the capital section, in the form of an income statement. By deducting expenses from revenue for the period, the income statement derives the profit (loss) for adjustment in the capital item in the balance sheet. This figure represents the net effect of trading for the period. By providing this 'appendix', a detailed and more informative view of performance is presented to users.

Income statement layout

The layout of the income statement will vary according to the type of business to which it relates. To illustrate an income statement, let us consider the case of a retail business (that is, a business that buys goods in their completed state and resells them). This type of business usually has straightforward operations and, as a result, the income statement is relatively easy to understand.

Example 3.1 sets out a typical layout for the income statement of a retail business. We can see that trading revenue, which arises from selling the goods, is the first item to appear. Deducted from this item is the cost of sales (also called the cost of the goods sold) during the period. Note that brackets are used to denote when an item is to be deducted. This convention is used by accountants in preference to + or – signs and will be used throughout the text.

Gross profit

→ This first part of the income statement is concerned with calculating the **gross profit** for the period. It is simply the difference between the trading revenue and cost of sales and represents the profit from buying and selling goods without taking into account any other revenues or expenses associated with the business.

Example 3.1

Better-Price Stores
Income statement for the year ended 31 October 2007

	£
Sales revenue	232,000
Cost of sales	(154,000)
Gross profit	78,000
Salaries and wages	(24,500)
Rent and rates	(14,200)
Heat and light	(7,500)
Telephone and postage	(1,200)
Insurance	(1,000)
Motor vehicle running expenses	(3,400)
Depreciation – fixtures and fittings	(1,000)
Depreciation – motor van	(600)
Operating profit	24,600
Interest received from investments	2,000
Loan interest	(1,100)
Profit for the year	25,500

Operating profit

From the gross profit, other expenses (overheads) that have been incurred in operating the business (salaries and wages, rent and rates, and so on) are deducted.

→ The resulting figure is known as the **operating profit** for the accounting period. This represents the wealth generated during the period from the normal activities of the business.

Operating profit does not take account of any income that the business may have from activities that are not included in its normal operations. Better-Price Stores (Example 3.1) is a retailer, so the interest on some spare cash that the business has lent is not part of its operating profit.

Costs of financing the business are also ignored in the calculation of the operating profit.

Profit for the year

Having established the operating profit, we add any non-operating income (such as interest receivable) and deduct any interest payable on borrowings made by the
→ business, to arrive at the **profit for the year** (or net profit). This is the income that is attributable to the owner(s) of the business and which will be added to capital in the balance sheet. As can be seen, profit for the year is a residual: that is, the amount remaining after deducting all expenses incurred in generating the sales revenue for the period and taking account of non-operating income.

Some further issues

Having set out the main principles involved in preparing an income statement, we need to consider some further points.

Cost of sales

 The **cost of sales** (or cost of goods sold) figure for a period can be identified in different ways. In some businesses, the cost of sales is identified at the time a sale has been made. Sales are closely matched with the cost of those sales and so identifying the cost of sales figure for inclusion in the income statement is not a problem. Many large retailers (for example, supermarkets) have point-of-sale (checkout) devices that not only record each sale but also simultaneously pick up the cost of the goods that are the subject of the particular sale. Other businesses that sell a relatively small number of high-value items (for example, an engineering business that produces custom-made equipment) also tend to match sales revenue with the cost of the goods sold at the time of the sale. However, some businesses (for example, small retailers) do not usually find it practical to match each sale to a particular cost of sales figure as the accounting period progresses. They find it easier to identify the cost of sales figure at the end of the accounting period.

Deriving the cost of sales after the end of the accounting period

To understand how this is done, it is important to recognise that the cost of sales figure represents the cost of goods that were *sold* by the business during the period rather than the cost of goods that were *bought* by that business during the period. Part of the goods bought during a particular period may remain in the business, as inventories, and not be sold until a later period. To derive the cost of sales for a period, it is necessary to know the amount of opening and closing inventories (stock) for the period and the cost of goods bought during the period. Example 3.2 illustrates how the cost of sales is derived.

Example 3.2

Better-Price Stores, which we considered in Example 3.1 above, began the accounting year with unsold inventories of £40,000 and during that year bought inventories at a cost of £189,000. At the end of the year, unsold inventories of £75,000 were still held by the business.

The opening inventories at the beginning of the year *plus* the goods bought during the year will represent the total goods available for resale. Thus:

	£
Opening inventories	40,000
Goods bought	189,000
Goods available for resale	229,000

The closing inventories will represent that portion of the total goods available for resale that remains unsold at the end of the period. Thus, the cost of goods actually sold during the period must be the total goods available for resale *less* the inventories remaining at the end of the period. That is:

	£
Goods available for resale	229,000
Closing inventories	(75,000)
Cost of sales (or cost of goods sold)	154,000

These calculations are sometimes shown on the face of the income statement as in Example 3.3.

Example 3.3

	£	£
Sales revenue		232,000
Cost of sales:		
Opening inventories	40,000	
Goods bought	189,000	
	229,000	
Closing inventories	(75,000)	(154,000)
Gross profit		78,000

The above is just an expanded version of the first section of the income statement for Better-Price Stores, as set out in Example 3.1. We have simply included the additional information concerning inventories balances and purchases for the year provided in Example 3.2.

Classification of expenses

The classifications for the revenue and expense items, as with the classifications of various assets and claims in the balance sheet, are often a matter of judgement by those who design the accounting system. Thus, the income statement set out in Example 3.1 could have included the insurance expense with the telephone and postage expense under a single heading – say, general expenses. Such decisions are normally based on how useful a particular classification will be to users. This will usually mean, however, that expense items of material size will be shown separately. For businesses that trade as limited companies, there are rules that dictate the classification of various items appearing in the financial statements for external reporting purposes. These rules will be discussed in Chapter 5.

Activity 3.1

The following information relates to the activities of H & S Retailers for the year ended 30 April 2007:

	£
Motor vehicle running expenses	1,200
Rent received from subletting	2,000
Closing inventories	3,000
Rent and rates payable	5,000
Motor vans cost less depreciation	6,300
Annual depreciation – motor vans	1,500
Heat and light	900
Telephone and postage	450
Sales revenue	97,400
Goods purchased	68,350
Insurance	750
Loan interest payable	620
Balance at bank	4,780
Salaries and wages	10,400
Opening inventories	4,000

→

Activity 3.1 continued

Prepare an income statement for the year ended 30 April 2007. (*Hint*: Not all items shown above should appear on this statement.)

Your answer to this activity should be as follows:

H & S Retailers
Income statement for the year ended 30 April 2007

	£	£
Sales revenue		97,400
Cost of sales:		
Opening inventories	4,000	
Purchases	68,350	
	72,350	
Closing inventories	(3,000)	(69,350)
Gross profit		28,050
Rent receivable		2,000
Salaries and wages		(10,400)
Rent and rates		(5,000)
Heat and light		(900)
Telephone and postage		(450)
Insurance		(750)
Motor vehicle running expenses		(1,200)
Depreciation – motor van		(1,500)
Operating profit		9,850
Loan interest		(620)
Profit for the year		9,230

Note that neither the motor vans, nor the bank balance are included in this statement.

In the case of the balance sheet, we saw that the information could be presented using either a horizontal or a vertical layout. This is also true of the income statement. Where a horizontal layout is used, expenses are listed on the left-hand side and revenues on the right, the difference being either profit or loss. The vertical layout has been used in our examples so far because it is easier to understand and, for this reason, it is now almost always used in practice.

The accounting period

We have seen already that for reporting to those outside the business, a financial reporting cycle of one year is the norm, though some large businesses will produce a half-yearly, or interim, financial statement to provide more frequent feedback on progress. For those who manage a business, however, it is important to have much more frequent feedback on performance. Thus it is quite common for income statements to be prepared on a quarterly, monthly, weekly or even daily basis in order to show how things are progressing.

Recognising revenue

A key issue in the measurement of profit concerns the point at which revenue is recognised. Revenue arising from the sale of goods or provision of a service could be recognised at various points. Where, for example, a motor car dealer receives an order for a new car from one of its business clients, the associated revenue could be recognised by the dealer:

- at the time that the order is placed by the customer;
- at the time that the car is collected by the customer; or
- at the time that the customer pays the dealer.

These three points could well be quite far apart, particularly where the order relates to a specialist car that is sold to the customer on credit.

The point chosen is not simply a matter of academic interest: it can have a profound impact on the total revenues, and therefore total profits, reported for a particular accounting period. If the car transaction straddled the end of an accounting period, the choice made between the three possible times for recognising the revenue could determine whether the revenue is included as revenue of an earlier accounting period or a later one.

When dealing with the sale of goods or the provision of services, the main criteria for recognising revenue are that:

- the amount of revenue can be measured reliably;
- it is probable that the economic benefits will be received.

An additional criterion, however, must be applied where the revenue comes from the sale of goods, which is that:

- ownership and control of the items should pass to the buyer.

Activity 3.2 provides an opportunity to apply these criteria to a practical problem.

Activity (3.2)

A manufacturing business sells goods on credit (that is, the customer pays for the goods some time after they are received). Below are four points in the production/selling cycle at which revenue might be recognised by the business:

1 when the goods are produced;
2 when an order is received from a customer;
3 when the goods are delivered to, and accepted by, the customer;
4 when the cash is received from the customer.

A significant amount of time may elapse between these different points. At what point do you think the business should recognise revenue?

All of the three criteria mentioned above will usually be fulfilled at point 3; when the goods are passed to, and accepted by, the customer. This is because:

- the selling price and the settlement terms will have been agreed and therefore revenue can be reliably measured;
- delivery and acceptance of the goods leads to ownership and control passing to the buyer;
- transferring ownership gives the seller legally enforceable rights that makes it probable the buyer will pay.

We can see that the effect of applying these criteria is that a sale on credit is usually recognised *before* the cash is received. Thus, the total sales revenue figure shown in the income statement may include sales transactions for which the cash has yet to be received. The total sales revenue figure in the income statement for a period will often, therefore, be different from the total cash received from sales during that period.

Where goods are sold for cash rather than on credit, the revenue will normally be recognised at the point of sale. It is at this point that all the criteria will usually be met. For cash sales, there will be no difference in timing between reporting sales revenue and cash received.

Real World 3.2 sets out the revenue recognition criteria for one well-known manufacturing and retail business which specialises in healthcare products.

Real World 3.2

Selling point

Revenue comprises sales and services to external customers (excluding VAT and other sales taxes). Consideration received from customers is recorded as revenue only when the group has completed full performance in respect of that consideration.

In respect of the Boots loyalty scheme, the Advantage Card, when points are issued to customers the retail value of those points expected to be redeemed is deferred. When the points are used by the customer they are recorded as revenue.

Sales of gift vouchers are included in revenue only when the vouchers are redeemed.

Source: Boots Group plc Annual Report 2006.

Long-term contracts

Some contracts, both for goods and for services, can last for more than one accounting period. If the business providing the goods or service were to wait until the contract is fulfilled before recognising revenue, the income statement could give a misleading impression of the wealth generated in the various accounting periods covered by the contract. This is a particular problem for businesses that undertake major long-term contracts, where a single contract could represent a large proportion of their total activities.

Construction contracts

Construction contracts often extend over a long period of time. Suppose a customer enters into a contract with a builder to build a new factory that will take three years to complete. In such a situation, it is possible to recognise revenue *before* the factory is completed provided that the building work can be broken down into a number of stages and each stage can be measured reliably. Let us assume that building the factory could be broken down into the following stages:

Stage 1 – clearing and levelling the land and putting in the foundations.
Stage 2 – building the walls.

Stage 3 – putting on the roof.

Stage 4 – putting in the windows and completing all the interior work.

Each stage can be awarded a separate price with the total for all the stages being equal to the total contract price for the factory. This means that, as each stage is completed, the builder can recognise the price for that stage as revenue and bill the customer accordingly.

If the builder were to wait until the factory was completed before recognising revenue, the income statement covering the final year of the contract would recognise all the revenue and the income statements for each preceding year would recognise no revenue. This would give a misleading impression as it would not reflect the work done during each period.

Real World 3.3 sets out the revenue recognition criteria for one large construction business.

Real World 3.3

Tracking revenue

Jarvis plc is a business operating in the area at road and rail infrastructure renewal, facilities Management and plant hire. The point at which revenue on long-term contracts is recognised by the business is as follows:

> When the outcome of a long-term contract can be estimated reliably, contract revenue is recognised by reference to the degree of completion of each contract, based on the amounts certified and to be certified by the customer.

Source: Jarvis plc Annual Report and Accounts 2006, p. 43.

Services

Revenue from contracts for services may also be recognised in stages. Suppose a consultancy business has a contract to install a new computer system for the government, which will take several years to complete. Revenue can be recognised *before* the contract is completed as long as the contract can be broken down into stages and the particular stages of completion can be measured reliably. This is really the same approach as that used in the construction contract mentioned above.

Sometimes a continuous service is provided to a customer; for example, a telecommunications business may provide open access to the internet to those who subscribe to the service. In this case, revenue is usually recognised as the service is rendered. Benefits from providing the service are usually assumed to flow evenly over time and so revenue is recognised evenly over the subscription period.

Where it is not possible to break down a service into particular stages of completion, or to assume that benefits from providing the service accrue evenly over time, revenue will not usually be recognised until the service is fully completed. A solicitor handling a house purchase for a client would be one such example.

Real World 3.4 provides an example of how one major business recognises revenue from providing services.

Real World 3.4

Broadcasting revenue

British Sky Broadcasting Group plc is a major satellite broadcaster that generates various forms of revenue. Here are the ways in which some of its revenues are recognised:

- Pay-per-view revenues – when the event (movie or football match) is viewed.
- Direct-to-home subscription services – as the services are provided.
- Cable revenues – as the services are provided.
- Advertising revenues – when the advertising is broadcast.
- Installations and digibox revenues – when the services have been provided.

Source: British Sky Broadcasting Group plc Annual Report and Accounts 2005, p. 45.

When a service is provided, there will normally be a timing difference between the recognition of revenue and the receipt of cash. Revenue for providing services is often recognised *before* the cash is received, just like the sale of goods on credit. However, there are occasions when it is the other way around, usually because the business demands payment before providing the service.

Activity 3.3

Can you think of any examples of where cash may be demanded in advance of a service being provided? (*Hint*: Try to think of services that you may use.)

Examples of where cash is received in advance of the service being provided may include:

- rent received from letting premises
- telephone line rental charges
- TV licence (BBC) or subscription (for example, Sky) fees
- subscriptions received for the use of health clubs or golf clubs.

You may have thought of others.

Recognising expenses

 Having decided on the point at which revenue is recognised, we can now turn to the issue of the recognition of expenses. The **matching convention** in accounting is designed to provide guidance concerning the recognition of expenses. This convention states that expenses should be matched to the revenue that they helped to generate. In other words, the expenses that are associated with a particular revenue must be taken into account in the income statement for the same accounting period as that in which that revenue is included in the total sales revenue figure. Applying this convention may mean that a particular expense reported in the income statement for a period may not be the same figure as the cash paid for that item during the period. The expense reported might be either more or less than the cash paid during the period. Let us consider two examples that illustrate this point.

When the expense for the period is more than the cash paid during the period

Example 3.4

Domestic Ltd sells household electrical appliances. It pays its sales staff a commission of 2 per cent of sales revenue generated. Total sales revenue for last year amounted to £300,000. This will mean that the commission to be paid in respect of the sales for the year will be £6,000. However, by the end of the period, the amount of sales commission that had actually been paid to staff was £5,000. If the business reported only the amount paid, it would mean that the income statement would not reflect the full expense for the year. This would contravene the *matching convention* because not all of the expenses associated with the revenue of the year would have been matched in the income statement. This will be remedied as follows:

- Sales commission expense in the income statement will include the amount paid plus the amount outstanding (that is, £6,000 = £5,000 + £1,000).

- The amount outstanding (£1,000) represents an outstanding liability at the balance sheet date and will be included under the heading **accrued expenses**, or 'accruals', in the balance sheet. As this item will have to be paid within 12 months of the balance sheet date, it will be treated as a current liability.

- The cash will already have been reduced to reflect the commission paid (£5,000) during the period.

These points are illustrated in Figure 3.2.

Figure 3.2   Accounting for sales commission

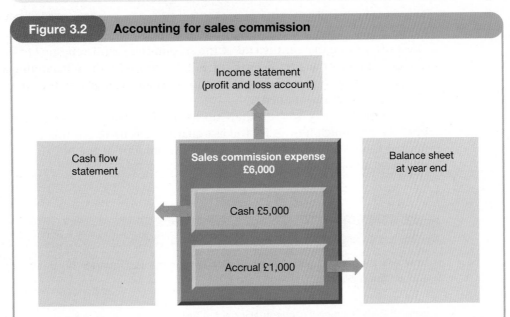

This illustrates the main points of Example 3.4. We can see that the sales commission expense of £6,000 (which appears in the income statement) is made up of a cash element £5,000 and an accrued element £1,000. The cash element appears in the cash flow statement and the accrued element will appear as a year-end liability in the balance sheet.

In principle, all expenses should be matched to the period in which the sales revenue to which they relate is reported. However, it is sometimes difficult to match certain expenses to sales revenue in the same precise way that we have matched sales commission to sales revenue. It is unlikely, for example, that electricity charges incurred can be linked directly to particular sales in this way. As a result, the electricity charges incurred by, say, a retailer would be matched to the *period* to which they relate. Example 3.5 illustrates this.

Example 3.5

Domestic Ltd has reached the end of its accounting year and has only paid electricity for the first three quarters of the year (amounting to £1,900). This is simply because the electricity company has yet to send out bills for the quarter that ends on the same date as Domestic Ltd's year end. The amount of Domestic Ltd's bill for the last quarter is £500. In this situation, the amount of the electricity expense outstanding is dealt with as follows:

- Electricity expense in the income statement will include the amount paid, plus the amount of the bill for the last quarter (that is, £1,900 + £500 = £2,400) in order to cover the whole year.
- The amount of the outstanding bill (£500) represents a liability at the balance sheet date and will be included under the heading 'accruals' or 'accrued expenses' in the balance sheet. This item would normally have to be paid within 12 months of the end of the accounting year and will, therefore, be treated as a current liability.
- The cash will already have been reduced to reflect the electricity paid (£1,900) during the period.

This treatment will have the desired effect of increasing the electricity expense to the correct figure for the year in the income statement. It will also have the effect of showing that, at the end of the accounting year, Domestic Ltd owed the amount of the last quarter's electricity bill. Dealing with the outstanding amount in this way reflects the dual aspect of the item and will ensure that the balance sheet equation is maintained.

Domestic Ltd may wish to draw up its income statement before it is able to discover how much it owes for the last quarter's electricity. In this case it is quite normal to make a reasonable estimate of the amount of the bill and to use this estimated amount as described above.

Activity (3.4)

How will the payment of the electricity bill for the last quarter be dealt with in the accounting records of Domestic Ltd?

When the electricity bill is eventually paid, it will be dealt with as follows:

- Reduce cash by the amount of the bill.
- Reduce the amount of the accrued expense as shown on the balance sheet by the same amount.

If an estimated figure is used and there is a slight error in the estimate, a small adjustment (either negative or positive depending on the direction of the error) can be made to the following year's expense. Dealing with the estimation error in this way is not strictly correct, but the amount is likely to be insignificant.

Activity 3.5

Can you think of other expenses for a retailer, apart from electricity charges, that cannot be linked directly to sales revenue and for which matching will therefore be done on a time basis?

You may have thought of the following examples:

- rent and rates
- insurance
- interest payments
- licence fees payable.

This is not an exhaustive list. You may have thought of others.

When the amount paid during the year is more than the full expense for the period

It is not unusual for a business to be in a situation where it has paid more during the year than the full expense for that year. Example 3.6 illustrates how we deal with this.

Example 3.6

Images Ltd, an advertising agency, normally pays rent for its premises quarterly in advance (on 1 January, 1 April, 1 July and 1 October). On the last day of the last accounting year (31 December), it paid the next quarter's rent (£4,000) to the following 31 March, which was a day earlier than required. This would mean that a total of five quarters' rent was paid during the year. If Images Ltd reports all of the cash paid as an expense in the income statement, this would be more than the full expense for the year. This would contravene the matching convention because a higher figure than the expenses associated with the revenue of the year would appear in the income statement.

The problem is overcome by dealing with the rental payment as follows:

- Show the rent for four quarters as the appropriate expense in the income statement (that is, $4 \times £4,000 = £16,000$).
- The cash (that is, $5 \times £4,000 = £20,000$) would already have been paid during the year.
- Show the quarter's rent paid in advance (£4,000) as a prepaid expense under assets in the balance sheet. (The prepaid expense will appear as a current asset in the balance sheet, under the heading **prepaid expenses** or 'prepayments'.)

In the next accounting period, this prepayment will cease to be an asset and will become an expense in the income statement of that period. This is because the rent prepaid relates to that period and will be 'used up' during that period.

These points are illustrated in Figure 3.3.

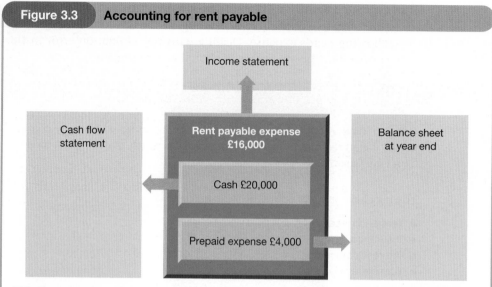

Figure 3.3 Accounting for rent payable

This illustrates the main points of Example 3.6. We can see that the rent expense of £16,000 (which appears in the income statement) is made up of four quarters' rent at £4,000 per quarter. This is the amount that relates to the period and is 'used up' during the period. The cash paid of £20,000 (which appears in the cash flow statement) is made up of the cash paid during the period, which is five quarters at £4,000 per quarter. Finally, the prepayment of £4,000 (which appears on the balance sheet) represents the payment made on 31 December and relates to the next financial year.

 In practice, the treatment of accruals and prepayments will be subject to the **materiality convention** of accounting. This convention states that, where the amounts involved are immaterial, we should consider only what is reasonable. This may mean that an item will be treated as an expense in the period in which it is paid, rather than being strictly matched to the revenue to which it relates. For example, a business may find that, at the end of an accounting period, a bill of £5 has been paid for stationery that has yet to be delivered. For a business of any size, the time and effort involved in recording this as a prepayment would not be justified by the little effect that this would have on the measurement of profit or financial position. The amount would, therefore, be treated as an expense when preparing the income statement for the current period and ignored in the following period.

Profit, cash and accruals accounting

As we have just seen, revenue does not usually represent cash received and expenses are not the same as cash paid. As a result, the profit figure (that is, total revenue minus total expenses) will not normally represent the net cash generated during a period. It is therefore important to distinguish between profit and liquidity. Profit is a measure of achievement, or productive effort, rather than a measure of cash generated. Although making a profit will increase wealth, as we have already seen in Chapter 2, cash is only one form in which that wealth may be held.

 The above points are reflected in the **accruals convention** of accounting, which asserts that profit is the excess of revenue over expenses for a period, not the excess of cash receipts over cash payments. Leading on from this, the approach to accounting that is based on the accruals convention is frequently referred to as **accruals accounting**. Thus, the balance sheet and the income statement are both prepared on the basis of accruals accounting. The cash flow statement, on the other hand, is not, as it simply deals with cash receipts and payments.

Depreciation

→ The expense of **depreciation**, which appeared in the income statement in Activity 3.1, requires further explanation. Most non-current assets do not have a perpetual existence. They are eventually used up in the process of generating revenue for the business. In essence, depreciation is an attempt to measure that portion of the cost (or fair value) of a non-current asset that has been used up in generating the revenue recognised during a particular period. The depreciation charge is considered to be an expense of the period to which it relates. Depreciation tends to be relevant both to tangible non-current assets (property, plant and equipment) and to intangible non-current assets. We should be clear that the principle is the same for both types of non-current asset. We shall deal with each of these two in turn.

Tangible non-current assets (property, plant and equipment)

To calculate a depreciation charge for a period, four factors have to be considered:

- the cost (or fair value) of the asset
- the useful life of the asset
- the residual value of the asset
- the depreciation method.

The cost (or fair value) of the asset

The cost of an asset will include all costs incurred by the business to bring the asset to its required location and to make it ready for use. Thus, in addition to the costs of acquiring the asset, any delivery costs, installation costs (for example, setting up a new machine) and legal costs incurred in the transfer of legal title (for example, in purchasing property) will be included as part of the total cost of the asset. Similarly, any costs incurred in improving or altering an asset in order to make it suitable for its intended use within the business will also be included as part of the total cost.

Activity 3.6

Andrew Wu (Engineering) Ltd bought a new motor car for its marketing director. The invoice received from the motor car supplier revealed the following:

	£
New BMW 325i	26,350
Delivery charge	80
Alloy wheels	660
Sun roof	200
Petrol	30
Number plates	130
Road fund licence	165
	27,615
Part exchange – Reliant Robin	(1,000)
Amount outstanding	26,615

Activity 3.6 continued

What is the total cost of the new car that will be treated as part of the business's property, plant and equipment?

The cost of the new car will be as follows:

	£
New BMW 325i	26,350
Delivery charge	80
Alloy wheels	660
Sun roof	200
Number plates	130
	27,420

This cost includes delivery charges and number plates, as they are a necessary and integral part of the asset. Improvements (alloy wheels and sun roof) are also regarded as part of the total cost of the motor car. The petrol and road fund licence, however, represent costs of operating the asset rather than a part of the total cost of acquiring it and making it ready for use: hence these amounts will be charged as an expense in the period incurred (although part of the cost of the licence may be regarded as a prepaid expense in the period incurred).

The part-exchange figure shown is part payment of the total amount outstanding and so is not relevant to a consideration of the total cost.

The fair value of an asset was defined in Chapter 2 as the exchange value that could be obtained in an arm's-length transaction. We have already seen that assets may be revalued to fair value only if this can be measured reliably. When a revaluation is carried out, all items within the same class must be revalued and revaluations must be kept up to date.

The useful life of the asset

A tangible non-current asset has both a *physical life* and an *economic life*. The physical life will be exhausted through the effects of wear and tear and/or the passage of time. It is possible, however, for the physical life to be extended considerably through careful maintenance, improvements and so on. The economic life is decided by the effects of technological progress and by changes in demand. After a while, the benefits of using the asset may be less than the costs involved. This may be because the asset is unable to compete with newer assets, or because it is no longer relevant to the needs of the business. The economic life of a non-current tangible asset may be much shorter than its physical life. For example, a computer may have a physical life of eight years and an economic life of three years.

It is the economic life that will determine the expected useful life for the purpose of calculating depreciation. Forecasting the economic life, however, may be extremely difficult in practice: both the rate at which technology progresses and shifts in consumer tastes can be swift and unpredictable.

Residual value (disposal value)

When a business disposes of a tangible non-current asset that may still be of value to others, some payment may be received. This payment will represent the **residual value**, or *disposal value*, of the asset. To calculate the total amount to be depreciated, the residual value must be deducted from the cost of the asset. The likely amount to be received on disposal can, once again, be difficult to predict. The best guide is often past experience of similar assets sold.

Depreciation method

Once the amount to be depreciated (that is, the cost, or fair value, of the asset less any residual value) has been estimated, the business must select a method of allocating this depreciable amount between the accounting periods covering the asset's useful life. Although there are various ways in which the total depreciation may be allocated and, from this, a depreciation charge for each period derived, there are really only two methods that are commonly used in practice.

The first of these is known as the **straight-line method**. This method simply allocates the amount to be depreciated evenly over the useful life of the asset. In other words, an equal amount of depreciation is charged for each year the asset is held.

Example 3.7

To illustrate this method, consider the following information:

Cost of machine	£40,000
Estimated residual value at the end of its useful life	£1,024
Estimated useful life	4 years

To calculate the depreciation charge for each year, the total amount to be depreciated must be calculated. This will be the total cost less the estimated residual value: that is, £40,000 – £1,024 = £38,976. Having done this, the annual depreciation charge can be derived by dividing the amount to be depreciated by the estimated useful life of the asset of four years. The calculation is therefore:

$$\frac{£38,976}{4} = £9,744$$

Thus, the annual depreciation charge that appears in the income statement in relation to this asset will be £9,744 for each of the four years of the asset's life.

The amount of depreciation relating to the asset will be accumulated for as long as the asset continues to be owned by the business. This accumulated depreciation figure will increase each year as a result of the annual depreciation amount charged to the income statement. This accumulated amount will be deducted from the cost of the asset on the balance sheet. At the end of the second year, for example, the accumulated depreciation will be £9,744 × 2 = £19,488, and the asset details will appear on the balance sheet as follows:

	£
Machine at cost	40,000
Accumulated depreciation	(19,488)
	20,512

The balance of £20,512 shown above is referred to as the **carrying amount** (sometimes also known as the **written-down value** or **net book value**) of the asset. It represents that portion of the cost (or fair value) of the asset that has still to be charged as an expense (written off) in future years. It must be emphasised that this figure does not represent the current market value, which may be quite different.

The straight-line method derives its name from the fact that the carrying amount of the asset at the end of each year, when plotted against time, will result in a straight line, as shown in Figure 3.4.

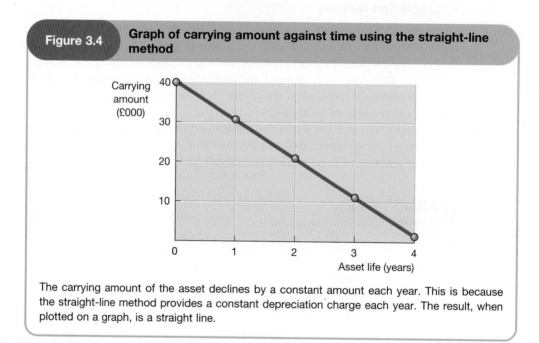

| Figure 3.4 | Graph of carrying amount against time using the straight-line method |

The carrying amount of the asset declines by a constant amount each year. This is because the straight-line method provides a constant depreciation charge each year. The result, when plotted on a graph, is a straight line.

The second approach to calculating depreciation for a period, found in practice, is referred to as the **reducing-balance method**. This method applies a fixed percentage rate of depreciation to the carrying value of an asset each year. The effect of this will be high annual depreciation charges in the early years and lower charges in the later years. To illustrate this method, let us take the same information used in Example 3.7. It can be shown that using a fixed percentage of 60 per cent of the carrying amount to determine the annual depreciation charge will have the effect of reducing the carrying amount to £1,024 after four years.

The calculations will be as follows:

	£
Cost of machine	40,000
Year 1 Depreciation charge (60%* of cost)	(24,000)
Carrying amount	16,000
Year 2 Depreciation charge (60% of carrying amount)	(9,600)
Carrying amount	6,400
Year 3 Depreciation charge (60% of carrying amount)	(3,840)
Carrying amount	2,560
Year 4 Depreciation charge (60% of carrying amount)	(1,536)
Residual value	1,024

* See the following box for an explanation of how to derive the fixed percentage.

Deriving the fixed percentage

Deriving the fixed percentage to be applied requires the use of the following formula:

$$P = (1 - \sqrt[n]{R/C}) \times 100\%$$

where: P = the depreciation percentage

n = the useful life of the asset (in years)

R = the residual value of the asset

C = the cost, or fair value, of the asset.

The fixed percentage rate will, however, be given in all examples used in this text.

We can see that the pattern of depreciation is quite different for the two methods. If we plot the carrying amount of the asset, which has been derived using the reducing-balance method, against time, the result will be as shown in Figure 3.5.

Figure 3.5	Graph of carrying amount against time using the reducing-balance method

Under the reducing-balance method, the carrying amount of an asset falls by a larger amount in the earlier years than in the later years. This is because the depreciation charge is based on a fixed-rate percentage of the carrying amount.

Activity 3.7

Assume that the machine used in the example above was owned by a business that made a profit before depreciation of £20,000 for each of the four years in which the asset was held.

Calculate the profit for the business for each year under each depreciation method, and comment on your findings.

Activity 3.7 continued

Your answer should be as follows:

Straight-line method

	(a) Profit before depreciation £	(b) Depreciation £	(a – b) Profit £
Year 1	20,000	9,744	10,256
Year 2	20,000	9,744	10,256
Year 3	20,000	9,744	10,256
Year 4	20,000	9,744	10,256

Reducing-balance method

	(a) Profit before depreciation £	(b) Depreciation £	(a – b) Profit/(loss) £
Year 1	20,000	24,000	(4,000)
Year 2	20,000	9,600	10,400
Year 3	20,000	3,840	16,160
Year 4	20,000	1,536	18,464

The straight-line method of depreciation results in a constant profit figure over the four-year period. This is because both the profit before depreciation and the depreciation charge are constant over the period. The reducing-balance method, however, results in a changing profit figure over time, despite the fact that in this example the pre-depreciation profit is the same each year. In the first year a loss is reported, and thereafter a rising profit is reported.

Although the *pattern* of profit over the four-year period will be quite different, depending on the depreciation method used, the *total* profit for the period (£41,024) will remain the same. This is because both methods of depreciating will allocate the same amount of total depreciation (£38,976) over the four-year period. It is only the amount allocated *between years* that will differ.

In practice, the use of different depreciation methods may not have such a dramatic effect on profits as suggested in Activity 3.7. Where a business replaces some of its assets each year, the total depreciation charge calculated under the reducing-balance method will reflect a range of charges (from high through to low), as assets will be at different points in the replacement cycle. This could mean that each year's total depreciation charge may not be significantly different from the total depreciation charge that would be derived under the straight-line method.

Selecting a depreciation method

How does a business choose which depreciation method to use for a particular asset? The answer is the one that best matches the depreciation expense to the pattern of economic benefits that the asset provides. Where these benefits are provided evenly over time (buildings, for example), the straight-line method is usually appropriate. Where assets lose their efficiency (such as certain types of machinery), the benefits provided will decline over time and so the reducing-balance method may be more appropriate. Where the pattern of economic benefits provided by the asset is uncertain, the straight-line method is normally chosen.

There is an international financial reporting standard (or international accounting standard) to deal with the depreciation of property, plant and equipment. As we shall see in Chapter 5, the purpose of accounting standards is to narrow areas of accounting difference and to ensure that information provided to users is transparent and comparable. The relevant standard endorses the view that the depreciation method chosen should reflect the pattern of economic benefits provided but does not specify particular methods to be used. It states that the useful life, depreciation method and residual values of non-current assets should be reviewed at least annually and adjustments made where appropriate.

Real World 3.5 sets out the depreciation policies of Thorntons plc.

Real World 3.5

Depreciation policies in practice

Thorntons plc, the manufacturer and retailer of confectionery, uses the straight-line method to depreciate nearly all its non-current assets. In practice, this appears to be the most widely used method of depreciation. The financial statements for the year ended 30 June 2006 show the period over which different classes of tangible non-current assets are depreciated as follows:

In equal annual instalments

Factory freehold premises	50 years
Short leasehold land and buildings	Period of the lease
Retail fixtures and fittings	5 years
Retail equipment	4 to 5 years
Retail store improvements	Up to 10 years
Other equipment and vehicles	3 to 7 years
Manufacturing plant and machinery	12 to 15 years
Computer licenses and software	3 to 5 years

We can see that there are wide variations in the expected useful lives of the various non-current assets held.

Source: Thorntons plc Annual Report and Accounts 2006, p. 24.

The approach taken to calculating depreciation is summarised in Figure 3.6.

Depreciating intangible assets

Where an intangible asset has a finite life, the approach taken for the depreciation (or *amortisation* as it is usually called with intangibles) is broadly the same as that for property, plant and equipment (tangible non-current assets). The asset is amortised (depreciated) over its useful life and the amortisation method used should reflect the pattern of benefits provided. Some differences arise, however, because of the valuation problems surrounding these assets. Intangible assets are normally reported at cost rather than their fair value. They are rarely revalued because there is usually no active

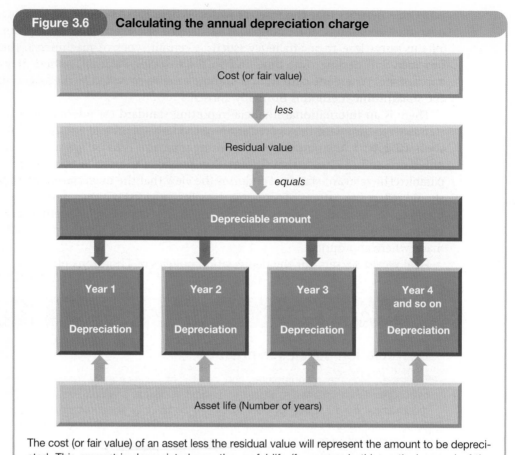

Figure 3.6 Calculating the annual depreciation charge

The cost (or fair value) of an asset less the residual value will represent the amount to be depreciated. This amount is depreciated over the useful life (four years in this particular case) of the asset using an appropriate depreciation method.

market from which to establish fair values. For similar reasons, the residual value of an intangible asset is normally assumed to be zero.

We saw in Chapter 2 that some intangible assets, which may include acquired goodwill, have an indefinite useful life. These assets are not amortised but instead are tested for impairment at least annually. While intangible assets with finite lives and property, plant and equipment are also subject to impairment testing, this will only occur when there is some indication that impairment has taken place.

Depreciation and the replacement of non-current assets

There seems to be a misunderstanding in the minds of some people that the purpose of depreciation is to provide the funds for the replacement of an asset when it reaches the end of its useful life. However, this is not the purpose of depreciation as conventionally defined. It was mentioned earlier that depreciation represents an attempt to allocate the cost, or fair value (less any residual value), of an asset over its expected useful life. The resulting depreciation charge in each accounting period represents an expense, which is then used in the calculation of profit for the period. Calculating the depreciation charge for a period is therefore necessary for the proper measurement of financial performance, and must be done whether or not the business intends to replace the asset in the future.

If there is an intention to replace the asset, the depreciation charge in the income statement will not ensure that liquid funds are set aside by the business specifically for this purpose. Although the effect of a depreciation charge is to reduce profit, and therefore to reduce the amount available for withdrawal by the owners, the amounts retained within the business as a result may be invested in ways that are unrelated to the replacement of the specific asset.

Depreciation and judgement

When reading the above sections on depreciation, it may have struck you that accounting is not as precise and objective as is sometimes suggested. There are areas where subjective judgement is required, and depreciation provides a good illustration of this.

Activity 3.8

What kinds of judgements must be made to calculate a depreciation charge for a period?

You may have thought of the following:

● the expected residual or disposal value of the asset
● the expected useful life of the asset
● the choice of depreciation method.

Making different judgements on these matters would result in a different pattern of depreciation charges over the life of the asset, and therefore in a different pattern of reported profits. However, underestimations or overestimations that are made in relation to the above will be adjusted for in the final year of an asset's life, and so the total depreciation charge (and total profit) over the asset's life will not be affected by estimation errors.

Real World 3.6 describes the effect of extending the useful life of property, plant and equipment on the short-term profits of one large business.

Real World 3.6

Sports massage

JJB Sports plc, a leading retailer, reported interim financial results for the six months ended 30 June 2005 that caused some disquiet among investors and analysts. The business changed the estimates for the useful life of its property, plant and equipment when calculating depreciation. It explained that this was due to new requirements to adopt International Financial Reporting Standards (IFRSs) when preparing financial statements. The article below, however, suggests that not everyone believed this.

JJB massages results to boost profits

High street retailer JJB Sports massaged last week's disappointing interim results by changing its depreciation calculations, in order to boost flagging profits by £4.3m.

Real World 3.6 continued

Analysts admitted that they were caught on the hop, as the company reported a 35.8% drop in operating profits from £27.4m to £17.6m for six months ended June 2005 on revenues down 6% to £340.4m. Operating profits would have plummeted even further to £14.3m had the company not changed its accounting for depreciation. 'The company explained the change as coming out of its IFRS conversion review, but it was clearly there for other reasons,' said Teather & Greenwood retail analyst Sanjay Vidyarthi.

JJB said that an impairment review ahead of its IFRS transition had forced a rethink on the carrying value of property, plant and equipment.

It concluded that these items had useful economic lives that more closely matched the length of the short-term lease of the property, rather than the 10-year economic life, which had formed the basis of the depreciation charge in previous accounting periods.

Richard Ratner, head of equity research at Seymour Pierce, said: 'They said the way they had depreciated assets previously was not correct but I haven't seen any other companies make this kind of change.'

JJB's share price fell from 168.2p before the results to 164.7p at the end of last week.

Source: 'JJB massages results to boost profits', Accountancy Age, 20 October 2005, p. 3.

Activity 3.9

Sally Dalton (Packaging) Ltd bought a machine for £40,000. At the end of its useful life of four years, the amount received on sale was £4,000. When the asset was bought the business received two estimates of the likely residual value of the asset, which were: (a) £8,000, and (b) zero.

Show the pattern of annual depreciation charges over the four years and the total depreciation charges for the asset under each of the two estimates. The straight-line method should be used to calculate the annual depreciation charges.

The depreciation charge, assuming estimate (a), will be £8,000 a year (that is, [£40,000 − 8,000]/4). The depreciation charge, assuming estimate (b), will be £10,000 a year (that is, £40,000/4). As the actual residual value is £4,000, estimate (a) will lead to underdepreciation of £4,000 (that is, £8,000 − £4,000) over the life of the asset, and estimate (b) will lead to overdepreciation of £4,000 (that is, £0 − £4,000). These under- and overestimations will be dealt with in year 4.

The pattern of depreciation and total depreciation charges will therefore be:

		Estimate	
		(a)	(b)
Year		£	£
1	Annual depreciation	8,000	10,000
2	Annual depreciation	8,000	10,000
3	Annual depreciation	8,000	10,000
4	Annual depreciation	8,000	10,000
		32,000	40,000)
4	Under/(over)depreciation	4,000	(4,000)
	Total depreciation	36,000	36,000

The final adjustment for underdepreciation of an asset is often referred to as 'loss (or deficit) on sale of non-current asset', as the amount actually received is less than the residual value. Similarly, the adjustment for overdepreciation is often referred to as 'profit (or surplus) on sale of non-current asset'.

Costing inventories

The way in which we measure the cost of inventories (or stock) is important because the cost of inventories sold during a period will affect the calculation of profit and the remaining inventories held at the end of the period will affect the portrayal of financial position in the balance sheet. In the previous chapter, we saw that historic cost is often the basis for reporting assets, and so it is tempting to think that determining the cost of inventories held is very straightforward. However, in a period of *changing prices*, the costing of inventories can be a problem.

A business must determine the cost of the inventories sold during the period and the cost of the inventories remaining at the end of the period. To do this, some assumption must be made about the way in which the inventories are physically handled. The assumption made need have nothing to do with how the inventories are *actually* handled; it is concerned only with providing useful accounting information.

Two common assumptions used are:

- **first in, first out (FIFO)** – the earliest inventories held are the first to be used;
- **last in, first out (LIFO)** – the latest inventories held are the first to be used.

Another approach to deriving the cost of inventories is to assume that inventories entering the business lose their separate identity, and any issues of inventories reflect the average cost of the inventories that are held. This is the **weighted average cost (AVCO)** method, where the weights used in deriving the average cost figures are the quantities of each batch of inventories bought. Example 3.8 provides a simple illustration of the way in which each method is applied.

Example 3.8

A business that supplies coal to factories has the following transactions during a period:

		Tonnes	Cost/tonne
1 May	Opening inventories	1,000	£10
2 May	Bought	5,000	£11
3 May	Bought	8,000	£12
		14,000	
6 May	Sold	(9,000)	
	Closing inventories	5,000	

First in, first out (FIFO)

Using the first in, first out approach, the first 9,000 tonnes of coal are treated as if these are the ones to be sold. This will consist of the opening inventories (1,000 tonnes), the purchases made on 2 May (5,000 tonnes) and some of the purchases made on 3 May

(3,000 tonnes). The remainder of the 3 May purchases (5,000 tonnes) will comprise the closing inventories. Thus we have:

	Cost of sales			Closing inventories		
	Tonnes	Cost/tonne £	Total £000	Tonnes	Cost/tonne £	Total £000
1 May	1,000	10	10.0			
2 May	5,000	11	55.0			
3 May	3,000	12	36.0	5,000	12	60.0
Cost of sales			101.0	Closing inventories		60.0

Last in, first out (LIFO)

Using the last in, first out approach, the later purchases will be treated as if these are the first to be sold. This is the 3 May purchases (8,000 tonnes) and some of the 2 May purchases (1,000 tonnes). The earlier purchases (the rest of the 2 May purchase and the opening inventories) will comprise the closing inventories. Thus we have:

	Cost of sales			Closing inventories		
	Tonnes	Cost/tonne £	Total £000	Tonnes	Cost/tonne £	Total £000
3 May	8,000	12	96.0			
2 May	1,000	11	11.0	4,000	11	44.0
1 May				1,000	10	10.0
Cost of sales			107.0	Closing inventories		54.0

Weighted average cost (AVCO)

Using this approach, a weighted average cost will be determined that will be used to derive both the cost of goods sold and the cost of the remaining inventories held. This simply means that the total cost of the opening inventories, the 2 May and 3 May purchases, are added together and divided by the total number of tonnes to obtain the weighted average cost per tonne. Both the cost of sales and closing inventories values are based on that average cost per tonne. Thus we have:

	Purchases		
	Tonnes	Cost/tonne £	Total £000
1 May	1,000	10	10.0
2 May	5,000	11	55.0
3 May	8,000	12	96.0
	14,000		161.0

Average cost = £161,000/14,000 = £11.5 per tonne

	Cost of sales			Closing inventories	
Tonnes	Cost/tonne £	Total £000	Tonnes	Cost/tonne £	Total £000
9,000	11.5	103.5	5,000	11.5	57.5

Activity 3.10

Suppose the 9,000 tonnes of inventories in Example 3.8 were sold for £15 per tonne.

(a) Calculate the gross profit for the period under each of the three methods.
(b) What observations concerning the portrayal of financial position and performance can you make about each method when prices are rising?

Your answer should be along the following lines:

(a) Gross profit calculation:

	FIFO £000	LIFO £000	AVCO £000
Sales revenue (9,000 @ £15)	135.0	135.0	135.0
Cost of sales	(101.0)	(107.0)	(103.5)
Gross profit	34.0	28.0	31.5
	£000	£000	£000
Closing inventories figure	60.0	54.0	57.5

(b) The above figures reveal that FIFO will give the highest gross profit during a period of rising prices. This is because sales revenue is matched with the earlier (and cheaper) purchases. LIFO will give the lowest gross profit because sales revenue is matched against the more recent (and dearer) purchases. The AVCO method will normally give a figure that is between these two extremes.

The closing inventories figure in the balance sheet will be highest with the FIFO method. This is because the cost of goods still held will be based on the more recent (and dearer) purchases. LIFO will give the lowest closing inventories figure as the goods held will be based on the earlier (and cheaper) purchases. Once again, the AVCO method will normally give a figure that is between these two extremes.

Activity 3.11

Assume that prices in Activity 3.10 are falling rather than rising. How would your observations concerning the portrayal of financial performance and position be different for the various costing methods?

→

Activity 3.11 continued

When prices are falling, the position of FIFO and LIFO is reversed. FIFO will give the lowest gross profit as sales revenue is matched against the earlier (and dearer) goods bought. LIFO will give the highest gross profit as sales revenue is matched against the more recent (and cheaper) goods bought. AVCO will give a cost of sales figure between these two extremes. The closing inventories figure in the balance sheet will be lowest under FIFO as the cost of inventories will be based on the more recent (and cheaper) purchases. LIFO will provide the highest closing inventories figure and AVCO will provide a figure between the two extremes.

The different costing methods will only have an effect on the reported profit from one year to the next. The figure derived for closing inventories will be carried forward and matched with sales revenue in a later period. Thus, if the cheaper purchases of inventories are matched to sales revenue in the current period, it will mean that the dearer purchases will be matched to sales revenue in a later period. Over the life of the business, therefore, the total profit will be the same whichever costing method has been used.

Inventories – some further issues

We saw in Chapter 2 that the convention of prudence requires that inventories be valued at the lower of cost and net realisable value. (The net realisable value of inventories is the estimated selling price less any further costs that may be necessary to complete the goods and any costs involved in selling and distributing the goods.) This rule may mean that the valuation method applied to inventories (cost or net realisable value) will switch each year depending on which of cost and net realisable value is the lower. In practice, however, the cost of the inventories held is usually below the current net realisable value – particularly during a period of rising prices. It is, therefore, the cost figure that will normally appear in the balance sheet.

Activity 3.12

Can you think of any circumstances where the net realisable value will be lower than the cost of inventories held, even during a period of generally rising prices?

The net realisable value may be lower where:

- goods have deteriorated or become obsolete;
- there has been a fall in the market price of the goods;
- the goods are being used as a 'loss leader';
- bad buying decisions have been made.

There is an international financial reporting standard that deals with inventories. It states that the cost of inventories should normally be determined using either FIFO or AVCO. The LIFO approach is not an acceptable method to use. The standard also requires the 'lower of cost or net realisable value' rule to be used.

Real World 3.7 sets out the costing methods of two large businesses.

Real World 3.7

Costing inventories in practice

Tate and Lyle plc, the sugar and other starch-based food processor, reports inventories on either a 'first in, first out' basis or weighted average costs basis.

British-American Tobacco, the cigarette manufacturer, uses weighted average cost only.

Sources: Tate and Lyle plc Annual Report 2006, p. 75; and British-American Tobacco Directors Report and Accounts 2005, p. 33.

→   Costing inventories and depreciation provide two examples where the **consistency convention** must be applied. This convention holds that once a particular method of accounting is selected, it should be applied consistently over time. Thus, it would not be acceptable to switch from, say, FIFO to AVCO between periods (unless exceptional circumstances make it appropriate). The purpose of this convention is to help users make valid comparisons of performance and position from one period to the next.

Activity 3.13

Reporting inventories in the financial statements provides a further example of the need to apply subjective judgement. For the inventories of a retail business, what are the main areas where judgement is required?

The main areas are:

● the choice of cost method (FIFO, LIFO, AVCO);
● deducing the net realisable value figure for inventories held.

Dealing with trade receivables' problems

We have seen that, when businesses sell goods or services on credit, revenue will often be recognised before the customer pays the amounts owing. Recording the dual aspect of a credit sale will involve:

● increasing sales revenue;
● increasing trade receivables (debtors);

by the amount of the revenue from the credit sale.

With this type of sale there is always the risk that the customer will not pay the amount due, however reliable they might have appeared to be at the time of the sale.

When it becomes reasonably certain that the customer will never pay, the debt owed is considered to be 'bad' and this must be taken into account when preparing the financial statements.

Activity (3.14)

When preparing the financial statements, what would be the effect on the income statement and on the balance sheet, of not taking into account the fact that a debt is bad?

The effect would be to overstate the assets (trade receivables) on the balance sheet and to overstate profit in the income statement, as the revenue (which has been recognised) will not result in any future benefit.

To provide a more realistic picture of financial performance and position, the **bad debt** must be 'written off'. This will involve:

- reducing the trade receivables;
- increasing expenses (by creating an expense known as 'bad debts written off');

by the amount of the bad debt.

The matching convention requires that the bad debt is written off in the same period as the sale that gave rise to the debt is recognised.

Note that, when a debt is bad, the accounting response is not simply to cancel the original sale. If this were done, the income statement would not be so informative. Reporting the bad debts as an expense can be extremely useful in assessing management performance.

At the end of the accounting period, it may not be possible to identify with reasonable certainty all the bad debts that have been incurred during the period. It may be that some trade receivables appear doubtful, but only at some later point in time will the true position become clear. The uncertainty that exists does not mean that, when preparing the financial statements, we should ignore the possibility that some of the trade receivables outstanding will eventually prove to be bad. It would not be prudent to do so, nor would it comply with the need to match expenses to the period in which the associated sale is recognised. As a result, the business will normally try to identify all those trade receivables that, at the end of the period, can be classified as doubtful (that is, there is a possibility that they may eventually prove to be bad). This can be done by examining individual accounts of trade receivables or by taking a proportion of the total trade receivables outstanding based on past experience.

Once a figure has been derived, an expense known as **allowances for trade receivables** can be created. This will be:

- shown as an expense in the income statement, and
- deducted from the total trade receivables figure in the balance sheet.

By doing this, full account is taken, in the appropriate accounting period, of those trade receivables where there is a risk of non-payment. This accounting treatment of these trade receivables will be in addition to the treatment of bad debts described above.

Example 3.9 illustrates the reporting of bad debts and allowances for trade receivables.

Example 3.9

Desai Enterprises had trade receivables of £350,000 outstanding at the end of the accounting year to 30 June 2007. Investigation of these trade receivables revealed that £10,000 would probably be irrecoverable and that a further £30,000 were doubtful of being recoverable.

Relevant extracts from the income statement for that year would be as follows:

Income statement (extracts) for the year ended 30 June 2007

	£
Bad debts written off	10,000
Allowances for trade receivables	30,000

Balance sheet (extracts) as at 30 June 2007

	£
Trade receivables	340,000*
Allowances for trade receivables	(30,000)
	310,000

* That is, £350,000 – £10,000 irrecoverable trade receivables.

The allowances for trade receivables figure is, of course, an estimate, and it is quite likely that the actual amount of trade receivables that prove to be bad will be different from the estimate. Let us say that, during the next accounting period, it was discovered that, in fact, £26,000 of the trade receivables considered doubtful proved to be irrecoverable. These trade receivables must now be written off as follows:

● reduce trade receivables by £26,000, and
● reduce allowances for trade receivables by £26,000.

However, allowances for trade receivables of £4,000 will remain. This amount represents an overestimate made when creating the allowance as at 30 June 2007. As the allowance is no longer needed, it should be eliminated. Remember that the allowance was made by creating an expense in the income statement for the year to 30 June 2007. As the expense was too high, the amount of the overestimate should be 'written back' in the next accounting period. In other words, it will be treated as revenue for the year to 30 June 2008. This will mean:

● reducing the allowances for trade receivables by £4,000, and
● increasing revenue by £4,000.

Ideally, of course, the amount should be written back to the 2007 income statement; however, it is too late to do this. At the end of of the year to 30 June 2008, not only will 2007's overestimate be written back but a new allowance should be created to take account of the trade receivables arising from 2008's credit sales that are considered doubtful.

Activity (3.15)

Clayton Conglomerates had trade receivables of £870,000 outstanding at the end of the accounting year to 31 March 2006. The chief accountant believed that £40,000 of those trade receivables were irrecoverable and that a further £60,000 were doubtful of being recoverable. In the subsequent year, it was found that an over-pessimistic estimate of those trade receivables considered doubtful had been made and that only a further £45,000 of trade receivables had actually proved to be bad.

Show the relevant extracts in the income statement for both 2006 and 2007 to report the bad debts written off and the allowances for trade receivables. Also show the relevant balance sheet extract as at 31 March 2006.

Your answer should be as follows:

Income statement (extracts) for the year ended 31 March 2006

	£
Bad debts written off	40,000
Allowances for trade receivables	60,000

Income statement (extracts) for the year ended 31 March 2007

	£
Allowances for trade receivables written back (revenue)	15,000

(*Note*: This figure will usually be netted off against any allowances for trade receivables created in respect of 2007.)

Balance sheet (extracts) as at 31 March 2006

	£
Trade receivables	830,000
Allowances for trade receivables	(60,000)
	770,000

Activity (3.16)

Bad debts and allowances for trade receivables are two further examples where judgement is needed to derive an appropriate expense figure. What will be the effect of different judgements concerning the appropriate amount of bad debts expense and allowances for trade receivables expense on the profit for a particular period and on the total profit reported over the life of the business?

Judgement is often required in deriving a figure for bad debts incurred during a period. There may be situations where views will differ concerning whether or not a debt is irrecoverable. The decision concerning whether or not to write off a bad debt will have an effect on the expenses for the period and, hence, the reported profit. However, over the life of the business the total reported profit would not be affected, as incorrect judgements in one period will be adjusted for in a later period.

Suppose that a debt of £100 was written off in a period and that, in a later period, the amount owing was actually received. The increase in expenses of £100 in the period in which the bad debt was written off would be compensated for by an increase in revenue of £100 when the amount outstanding was finally received (bad debt recoverable). If, on the other hand, the amount owing of £100 was never written off in the first place, the profit for the two periods would not be affected by the bad debt adjustment and would, therefore, be different – but the total profit for the two periods would be the same.

A similar situation would apply where there are differences in judgements concerning allowances for trade receivables.

Real World 3.8 shows the effect of bad debts on the banking sector.

Real World 3.8

Household debt adds to rise in bank write-offs

FT

Banks were forced to write off record amounts of bad debts last year, Bank of England figures are expected to show this week. The figures, to be published on Thursday, are likely to increase concern about soaring levels of consumer debt and, in particular, the willingness of banks to offer large loans to poorer households.

The data are expected to show that write-offs in the fourth quarter of 2004 reached a record level of more than £6bn for the year as a whole. The previous record for bad debt write-offs occurred in the early 1990s when Britain was mired in a recession.

The banks' write-offs, which have risen sharply since 2001, are largely a result of consumer rather than corporate bad debts.

Credit card lending, in particular, has been a problem, with write-offs more than trebling since 1995 to more than 3 per cent by the end of 2003.

Simon Walker, head of retail banking at accountants KPMG, said most of the rise in write-offs could be attributed to the decision of banks to go 'more downmarket' as they expanded their credit card lending books.

Write-offs of lending to individuals because of increased write-offs of credit card debt have risen from £100m a decade ago to nearly £2bn now.

The increase has driven up the percentage of household write-offs accounted for by credit card debt from less than 20 per cent in 1993 to nearly 50 per cent now.

The boom in lending has generally been profitable for the banks despite sharp rises in bad debts.

Write-offs on mortgage debts have declined and remain at modest levels. Secured lending, such as mortgages, is less likely to be written off since banks can possess the property if the loan cannot be repaid.

Rising house prices have also reduced the amount of debt outstanding after a property is repossessed and sold, thereby cutting the amounts a bank would need to write off.

Source: 'Household debt adds to rise in bank write-offs', Simon Briscoe, *Financial Times*, 28 March 2005, FT.com.

Let us now try to bring together some of the points that we have raised in this chapter through a self-assessment question.

Self-assessment question 3.1

TT and Co. is a new business that started trading on 1 January 2006. The following is a summary of transactions that occurred during the first year of trading:

1 The owners introduced £50,000 of capital, which was paid into a bank account opened in the name of the business.
2 Premises were rented from 1 January 2006 at an annual rental of £20,000. During the year, rent of £25,000 was paid to the owner of the premises.
3 Rates (a tax on business premises) were paid during the year as follows:

For the period 1 January 2006 to 31 March 2006	£500
For the period 1 April 2006 to 31 March 2007	£1,200

4 A delivery van was bought on 1 January 2006 for £12,000. This is expected to be used in the business for four years and then to be sold for £2,000.
5 Wages totalling £33,500 were paid during the year. At the end of the year, the business owed £630 of wages for the last week of the year.
6 Electricity bills for the first three quarters of the year were paid totalling £1,650. After 31 December 2006, but before the financial statements had been finalised for the year, the bill for the last quarter arrived showing a charge of £620.
7 Inventories totalling £143,000 were bought on credit.
8 Inventories totalling £12,000 were bought for cash.
9 Sales revenue on credit totalled £152,000 (cost of sales £74,000).
10 Cash sales revenue totalled £35,000 (cost of sales £16,000).
11 Receipts from trade receivables totalled £132,000.
12 Payments to trade payables totalled £121,000.
13 Van running expenses paid totalled £9,400.

At the end of the year it was clear that a trade receivable who owed £400 would not be able to pay any part of the debt. The business uses the straight-line method for depreciating non-current assets.

Required:

Prepare a balance sheet as at 31 December 2006 and an income statement for the year to that date. (Use the outline financial statements produced below to help you.)

TT and Co.
Balance sheet as at 31 December 2006

	£
Non-current assets	
Delivery van	
Accumulated depreciation	
	____
	____
Current assets	
Inventories	
Trade receivables	
Prepaid expenses	
Cash	
	____
Total Assets	____
	____

Capital (owner's equity)
Original
Profit   _____
                                                           _____

Current liabilities
Trade payables
Accrued expenses   _____
                                                           _____

Total equity and liabilities   _____

Income statement for the year ended 31 December 2006

                                                           £

Sales revenue
Cost of goods sold   _____
Gross profit
Rent
Rates
Wages
Electricity
Bad debts
Van expenses
Van depreciation   _____
Profit for the year   _____

The answer to this question can be found at the back of the book on pages 694–5.

Interpreting the income statement

When an income statement is presented to users it is sometimes the case that the only item that will concern them will be the final profit figure, or *bottom line* as it is sometimes called. Although the profit figure is a primary measure of performance, and its importance is difficult to overstate, the income statement contains other information that should also be of interest. To evaluate business performance effectively, it is important to find out how the final profit figure was derived. Thus the level of sales revenue, the nature and amount of expenses incurred, and the profit in relation to sales revenue are important factors in understanding the performance of the business over a period. The analysis and interpretation of financial statements is considered in detail in Chapter 7.

Summary

The main points of this chapter may be summarised as follows.

The income statement (profit and loss account)
- Measures and reports how much profit (loss) has been generated over a period.
- Profit (loss) for the period is the difference between the total revenue and total expenses for the period.

- Links the balance sheets at the beginning and end of an accounting period.
- The income statement of a retail business will first calculate gross profit, then add any additional revenue and then deduct any overheads for the period. The final figure derived is the profit (loss) for the period.
- Gross profit represents the difference between the sales revenue for the period and the cost of sales.

Expenses and revenue

- Cost of sales may be identified by either matching the cost of each sale to the particular sale or by adjusting the goods bought during the period to take account of opening and closing inventories.
- The classification of expenses is often a matter of judgement, although there are rules for businesses that trade as limited companies.
- Revenue is recognised when the amount of revenue can be measured reliably and it is probable that the economic benefits will be received.
- Where there is a sale of goods, there is an additional criterion that ownership and control must pass to the buyer before revenue can be recognised.
- Revenue can be recognised after partial completion provided a particular stage of completion can be measured reliably.
- The matching convention states that expenses should be matched to the revenue that they help generate.
- A particular expense reported in the income statement may not be the same as the cash paid. This will result in some adjustment for accruals or prepayments.
- The materiality convention states that where the amounts are immaterial, we should consider only what is expedient.
- 'Accruals accounting' is preparing the income statement and balance sheet following the accruals convention, which says that profit = revenue – expenses (not cash receipts – cash payments).

Depreciation of non-current assets

- Depreciation requires a consideration of the cost (or fair value), useful life and residual value of an asset. It also requires a consideration of the method of depreciation.
- The straight-line method of depreciation allocates the amount to be depreciated evenly over the useful life of the asset.
- The reducing-balance method applies a fixed percentage rate of depreciation to the written-down value of an asset each year.
- The depreciation method chosen should reflect the pattern of benefits associated with the asset.
- Depreciation is an attempt to allocate the cost (or fair value), less the residual value, of an asset over its useful life. It does not provide funds for replacement of the asset.

Costing inventories

- The way in which we derive the cost of inventories is important in the calculation of profit and the presentation of financial position.
- The first in, first out (FIFO) method approaches matters as if the earliest inventories held are the first to be used.
- The last in, first out (LIFO) method approaches matters as if the latest inventories are the first to be used.
- The weighted average cost (AVCO) method applies an average cost to all inventories used.
- When prices are rising, FIFO gives the lowest cost of sales figure and highest closing inventories figure and LIFO gives the highest cost of sales figure and the lowest

closing inventories figure. AVCO gives figures for cost of sales and closing inventories that lie between FIFO and LIFO.

- When prices are falling, the positions of FIFO and LIFO are reversed.
- Inventories are shown at the lower of cost and net realisable value.
- When a particular method of accounting, such as an inventories costing method, is selected, it should be applied consistently over time.

Bad debts

- Where it is reasonably certain that a credit customer will not pay, the debt is regarded as 'bad' and written off.
- Where it is doubtful that a credit customer will pay, an allowances for trade receivables expense should be created.

MyAccountingLab **Now check your progress in your personal Study Plan**

 Key terms

profit p. 72	**depreciation** p. 87
revenue p. 72	**residual value** p. 89
expense p. 72	**straight-line method** p. 89
income statement p. 72	**carrying amount** p. 90
accounting period p. 73	**written-down value** p. 90
gross profit p. 74	**net book value** p. 90
operating profit p. 75	**reducing-balance method** p. 90
profit for the year p. 75	**first in, first out (FIFO)** p. 97
cost of sales p. 76	**last in, first out (LIFO)** p. 97
matching convention p. 82	**weighted average cost (AVCO)** p. 97
accrued expenses p. 83	
prepaid expenses p. 85	**consistency convention** p. 101
materiality convention p. 86	**bad debt** p. 102
accruals convention p. 86	**allowances for trade receivables** p. 102
accruals accounting p. 86	

Further reading

If you would like to explore the topics covered in this chapter in more depth, we recommend the following books:

Corporate Financial Accounting and Reporting, *Sutton T.*, 2nd edn, Financial Times Prentice Hall, 2004, chapters 2, 8, 9 and 10.

Financial Accounting and Reporting, *Elliott B. and Elliott J.*, 11th edn, Financial Times Prentice Hall, 2006, chapters 2, 16, 18 and 19.

International Financial Reporting Standards in Depth, *Kirk R.J.*, CIMA Publishing, 2005, chapters 2 and 3.

KPMG's Practical Guide to International Financial Reporting Standards, *KPMG*, 3rd edn, Thomson, 2006, sections 3.2, 3.3 and 3.8.

Review questions

Answers to these questions can be found at the back of the book on page 775.

3.1 'Although the income statement is a record of past achievement, the calculations required for certain expenses involve estimates of the future.' What is meant by this statement? Can you think of examples where estimates of the future are used?

3.2 'Depreciation is a process of allocation and not valuation.' What do you think is meant by this statement?

3.3 What is the convention of consistency? Does this convention help users in making a more valid comparison between businesses?

3.4 'An asset is similar to an expense.' Do you agree?

Exercises

Exercises 3.6 to 3.8 are more advanced than 3.1 to 3.5. Those with coloured numbers have answers at the back of the book, starting on page 712.

If you wish to try more exercises, visit the students' side of the Companion Website.

3.1 You have heard the following statements made. Comment critically on them.

(a) 'Capital only increases or decreases as a result of the owners putting more cash into the business or taking some out.'
(b) 'An accrued expense is one that relates to next year.'
(c) 'Unless we depreciate this asset we shall be unable to provide for its replacement.'
(d) 'There is no point in depreciating the factory building. It is appreciating in value each year.'

3.2 Singh Enterprises has an accounting year to 31 December and uses the straight-line method of depreciation. On 1 January 2004 the business bought a machine for £10,000. The machine had an expected useful life of four years and an estimated residual value of £2,000. On 1 January 2005 the business bought another machine for £15,000. This machine had an expected useful life of five years and an estimated residual value of £2,500. On 31 December 2006 the business sold the first machine bought for £3,000.

Required:
Show the relevant income statement extracts and balance sheet extracts for the years 2004, 2005 and 2006.

3.3 The owner of a business is confused, and comes to you for help. The financial statements for the business, prepared by an accountant, for the last accounting period revealed an increase in profit of £50,000. However, during the accounting period the bank balance declined by £30,000. What reasons might explain this apparent discrepancy?

3.4 Spratley Ltd is a builders' merchant. On 1 September the business had, as part of its inventories, 20 tonnes of sand at a cost of £18 per tonne and at a total cost of £360. During the first week in September, the business bought the following amounts of sand:

September	Tonnes	Cost per tonne £
2	48	20
4	15	24
6	10	25

On 7 September the business sold 60 tonnes of sand to a local builder.

Required:
Calculate the cost of goods sold and the closing inventories from the above information using the following costing methods:

(a) first in, first out
(b) last in, first out
(c) weighted average cost.

3.5 Fill in the values (a) to (f) in the following table on the assumption that there were no opening balances involved.

	Relating to period		At end of period	
	Paid/Received £	Expense/Revenue for period £	Prepaid £	Accruals/Deferred revenues £
Rent payable	10,000	a	1,000	
Rates and insurance	5,000	b		1,000
General expenses	c	6,000	1,000	
Loan interest payable	3,000	2,500	d	
Salaries	e	9,000		3,000
Rent receivable	f	1,500		1,500

3.6 The following is the balance sheet of TT and Co. at the end of its first year of trading (from Self-assessment question 3.1):

TT and Co.
Balance sheet as at 31 December 2006

	£
Non-current assets	
Property, plant and equipment	
Delivery van at cost	12,000
Depreciation	(2,500)
	9,500
Current assets	
Inventories	65,000
Trade receivables	19,600
Prepaid expenses*	5,300
Cash	750
	90,650
Total assets	100,150
Capital (owners' equity)	
Original	50,000
Retained profit	26,900
	76,900
Current liabilities	
Trade payables	22,000
Accrued expenses†	1,250
	23,250
Total equity and liabilities	100,150

* The prepaid expenses consisted of rates (£300) and rent (£5,000).
† The accrued expenses consisted of wages (£630) and electricity (£620).

During 2007, the following transactions took place:

1 The owners withdrew capital in the form of cash of £20,000.
2 Premises continued to be rented at an annual rental of £20,000. During the year, rent of £15,000 was paid to the owner of the premises.
3 Rates on the premises were paid during the year as follows: for the period 1 April 2007 to 31 March 2008 £1,300.
4 A second delivery van was bought on 1 January 2007 for £13,000. This is expected to be used in the business for four years and then to be sold for £3,000.
5 Wages totalling £36,700 were paid during the year. At the end of the year, the business owed £860 of wages for the last week of the year.
6 Electricity bills for the first three quarters of the year and £620 for the last quarter of the previous year were paid totalling £1,820. After 31 December 2007, but before the accounts had been finalised for the year, the bill for the last quarter arrived showing a charge of £690.
7 Inventories totalling £67,000 were bought on credit.
8 Inventories totalling £8,000 were bought for cash.
9 Sales revenue on credit totalled £179,000 (cost £89,000).
10 Cash sales revenue totalled £54,000 (cost £25,000).
11 Receipts from trade receivables totalled £178,000.
12 Payments to trade payables totalled £71,000.
13 Van running expenses paid totalled £16,200.

The business uses the straight-line method for depreciating non-current assets.

Required:
Prepare a balance sheet as at 31 December 2007 and an income statement for the year to that date.

3.7   The following is the balance sheet of WW Associates as at 31 December 2005:

Balance sheet as at 31 December 2005

	£
Non-current assets	
Machinery	25,300
Current assets	
Inventories	12,200
Trade receivables	21,300
Prepaid expenses (rates)	400
Cash	8,300
Total Assests	67,500
Capital (owners' equity)	
Original	25,000
Retained profit	23,900
	48,900
Current liabilities	
Trade payables	16,900
Accrued expenses (wages)	1,700
	18,600
Total equity and liabilities	67,500

During 2006, the following transactions took place:

1   The owners withdrew capital in the form of cash of £23,000.
2   Premises were rented at an annual rental of £20,000. During the year, rent of £25,000 was paid to the owner of the premises.
3   Rates on the premises were paid during the year for the period 1 April 2006 to 31 March 2007 and amounted to £2,000.
4   Some machinery (a non-current asset), which was bought on 1 January 2005 for £13,000, has proved to be unsatisfactory. It was part-exchanged for some new machinery on 1 January 2006, and WW Associates paid a cash amount of £6,000. The new machinery would have cost £15,000 had the business bought it without the trade-in.
5   Wages totalling £23,800 were paid during the year. At the end of the year, the business owed £860 of wages.
6   Electricity bills for the four quarters of the year were paid totalling £2,700.
7   Inventories totalling £143,000 were bought on credit.
8   Inventories totalling £12,000 were bought for cash.
9   Sales revenue on credit totalled £211,000 (cost £127,000).
10   Cash sales revenue totalled £42,000 (cost £25,000).
11   Receipts from trade receivables totalled £198,000.
12   Payments to trade payables totalled £156,000.
13   Van running expenses paid totalled £17,500.

The business uses the reducing-balance method of depreciation for non-current assets at the rate of 30 per cent each year.

Required:

Prepare a balance sheet as at 31 December 2006 and an income statement (profit and loss account) for the year to that date.

3.8 The following is the income statement for Nikov and Co. for the year ended 31 December 2006, along with information relating to the preceding year.

Income statement for the year ended 31 December

	2006 £000	2005 £000
Sales revenue	420.2	382.5
Cost of sales	(126.1)	(114.8)
Gross profit	294.1	267.7
Salaries and wages	(92.6)	(86.4)
Selling and distribution costs	(98.9)	(75.4)
Rent and rates	(22.0)	(22.0)
Bad debts written off	(19.7)	(4.0)
Telephone and postage	(4.8)	(4.4)
Insurance	(2.9)	(2.8)
Motor vehicle expenses	(10.3)	(8.6)
Depreciation – Delivery van	(3.1)	(3.3)
– Fixtures and fittings	(4.3)	(4.5)
Operating profit	35.5	56.3
Loan interest	(4.6)	(5.4)
Profit for the year	30.9	50.9

Required:

Analyse the performance of the business for the year to 31 December 2006 in so far as the information allows.

Accounting for limited companies (1)

Introduction

Most businesses in the UK, except the very smallest, operate in the form of limited companies. More than 2 million limited companies now exist and they account for the majority of UK business activity and employment. The economic significance of this type of business is not confined to the UK; it can be seen in many of the world's developed countries.

In this chapter we consider the nature of limited companies and how they differ from sole proprietorship businesses and partnerships. We examine the ways in which the owners provide finance as well as the rules governing the way in which limited companies must account to their owners and to other interested parties. We shall also see how the financial statements, which were discussed in the previous two chapters, are prepared for this type of business.

Learning outcomes

When you have completed this chapter, you should be able to:

● Discuss the nature of the limited company.

● Explain the role of directors of limited companies.

● Describe the main features of the owners' claim in a limited company.

● Explain how the income statement and balance sheet of a limited company differ in detail from that of sole proprietorships and partnerships.

 Remember to create your own personalised Study Plan

The main features of limited companies

Legal nature

Let us begin our examination of limited companies by discussing their legal nature. A **limited company** has been described as an artificial person that has been created by law. This means that a company has many of the rights and obligations that 'real' people have. It can, for example, sue or be sued by others and can enter into contracts in its own name. This contrasts sharply with other types of businesses, such as sole proprietorships and partnerships (that is, unincorporated businesses), where it is the owner(s) rather than the business that must sue, enter into contracts and so on, because the business has no separate legal identity.

With the rare exceptions of those that are created by Act of Parliament or by Royal Charter, all UK companies are created (or *incorporated*) by registration. To create a company the person or persons (usually known as *promoters*) wishing to create it, fill in a few simple forms and pay a modest registration fee. After having ensured that the necessary formalities have been met, the Registrar of Companies, a government official, enters the name of the new company on the Registry of Companies. Thus, in the UK, companies can be formed very easily and cheaply (for about £100).

Companies may be owned by just one person, but most have more than one owner and some have many owners. The owners are usually known as *members* or *shareholders*. The ownership of a company is normally divided into a number, frequently a large number, of **shares**, each of equal size. Each owner, or shareholder, owns one or more shares in the company. Large companies typically have a very large number of shareholders. For example, at 31 March 2006, BT Group plc, the telecommunications business, had nearly 1.4 million different shareholders.

As a limited company has its own legal identity, it is regarded as being quite separate from those that own and manage it. This fact leads to two important features of the limited company: perpetual life and limited liability. These are explained below.

Just before we leave the topic of the legal separateness of owners and the company, however, it is worth emphasising that this has no connection with the business entity convention of accounting, which we discussed in Chapter 2. This accounting convention applies equally well to all business types, including sole proprietorships and partnerships where there is certainly no legal distinction between the owner(s) and the business.

Perpetual life

A company is normally granted a perpetual existence and so will continue even where an owner of some, or even all, of the shares in the company dies. The shares of the deceased person will simply pass to the beneficiary of his or her estate. The granting of perpetual existence means that the life of a company is quite separate from the lives of those individuals who own or manage it. It is not, therefore, affected by changes in ownership that arise when individuals buy and sell shares in the company.

Though a company may be granted a perpetual existence when it is first formed, it is possible for either the shareholders or the courts to bring this existence to an end. When this is done, the assets of the company are sold off to meet outstanding liabilities. Any surplus arising from the sale will then be used to pay the shareholders. Shareholders may agree to end the life of a company where it has achieved the purpose for which it was formed or where they feel that the company has no real future. The courts may bring the life of a company to an end where creditors have applied to the courts for this to be done because they have not been paid amounts owing.

Where shareholders agree to end the life of a company, it is referred to as a 'voluntary liquidation'. **Real World 4.1** describes the demise of one company by this method.

Real World 4.1

Monotub Industries in a spin as founder gets Titan for £1   **FT**

Monotub Industries, maker of the Titan washing machine, yesterday passed into corporate history with very little ceremony and with only a whimper of protest from minority shareholders.

At an extraordinary meeting held in a basement room of the group's West End headquarters, shareholders voted to put the company into voluntary liquidation and sell its assets and intellectual property to founder Martin Myerscough for £1. (The shares in the company were at one time worth 650p each.)

The only significant opposition came from Giuliano Gnagnatti who, along with other shareholders, has seen his investment shrink faster than a wool twin-set on a boil wash.

The not-so-proud owner of 100,000 Monotub shares, Mr Gnagnatti, the managing director of an online retailer . . . described the sale of Monotub as a 'free gift' to Mr Myerscough. This assessment was denied by Ian Green, the chairman of Monotub, who said the closest the beleaguered company had come to a sale was an offer for £60,000 that gave no guarantees against liabilities, which are thought to amount to £750,000.

The quiet passing of the washing machine, eventually dubbed the Titanic, was in strong contrast to its performance in many kitchens.

Originally touted as the 'great white goods hope' of the washing machine industry with its larger capacity and removable drum, the Titan ran into problems when it kept stopping during the spin cycle, causing it to emit a loud bang and leap into the air.

Summing up the demise of the Titan, Mr Green said: 'Clearly the machine had some revolutionary aspects, but you can't get away from the fact that the machine was faulty and should not have been launched with those defects.'

The usually vocal Mr Myerscough, who has promised to pump £250,000 into the company and give Monotub shareholders £4 for every machine sold, refused to comment on his plans for the Titan or reveal who his backers were. But . . . he did say that he intended to 'take the Titan forward'.

Source: 'Monotub Industries in a spin as founder gets Titan for £1', Lisa Urquhart, *Financial Times*, 23 January 2003, FT.com.

Limited liability

Since the company is a legal person in its own right, it must take responsibility for its own debts and losses. This means that once the shareholders have paid what they have agreed to pay for the shares, their obligation to the company, and to the company's creditors, is satisfied. Thus shareholders can limit their losses to the amount that they have paid, or agreed to pay, for their shares. This is of great practical importance to potential shareholders since they know that what they can lose, as part owners of the business, is limited.

Contrast this with the position of sole proprietors or partners. They cannot 'ring fence' assets that they do not want to put into the business. If a sole proprietary or partnership business finds itself in a position where liabilities exceed the business assets, the law gives unsatisfied creditors the right to demand payment out of what the sole proprietor or partner may have regarded as 'non-business' assets. Thus the sole proprietor or partner could lose everything – house, car, the lot. This is because the law sees Jill, the sole proprietor, as being the same as Jill the private individual. The shareholder, by contrast, can lose only the amount committed to that company. Legally, the business operating as a limited company, in which Jack owns shares, is not the same as Jack himself. This is true even if Jack were to own all of the shares in the company.

Real World 4.2 gives an example of a well-known case where the shareholders of a particular company were able to avoid any liability to those that had lost money as a result of dealing with the company.

Real World 4.2

Carlton and Granada 1 – Nationwide Football League 0

Two television broadcasting companies, Carlton and Granada, each owned 50 per cent of a separate company, ITV Digital (formerly ON Digital). ITV Digital signed a contract to pay the Nationwide Football League (in effect the three divisions of English football below the Premiership) more than £89m on both 1 August 2002 and 1 August 2003 for the rights to broadcast football matches over three seasons. ITV Digital was unable to sell enough subscriptions for the broadcasts and collapsed because it was unable to meet its liabilities. The Nationwide Football League tried to force Carlton and Granada (ITV Digital's only shareholders) to meet the ITV Digital's contractual obligations. It was unable to do so because the shareholders could not be held legally liable for the amounts owing.

Carlton and Granada merged into one business in 2003, but at the time of ITV Digital were two independent companies.

Activity 4.1

The fact that shareholders can limit their losses to that which they have paid, or have agreed to pay, for their shares is of great practical importance to potential shareholders.
   Can you think of any practical benefit to a private-sector economy, in general, of this ability of shareholders to limit losses?

Business is a risky venture – in some cases very risky. People with money to invest will usually be happier to do so when they know the limit of their liability. By giving investors limited liability, new businesses are more likely to be formed and existing ones are likely to find it easier to raise more finance. This is good for the private-sector economy and may ultimately lead to the generation of greater wealth for society as a whole.

Although **limited liability** has this advantage to the providers of capital (the shareholders), it is not necessarily to the advantage of all others who have a stake in the business, like the Nationwide Football League clubs (see Real World 4.2). Limited liability is attractive to shareholders because they can, in effect, walk away from the unpaid debts of the company if their contribution has not been sufficient to meet those debts. This is likely to make any individual, or another business, that is considering entering into a contract, wary of dealing with the limited company. This can be a real problem for smaller, less established companies. Suppliers may insist on cash payment before delivery of goods or the rendering of a service. Alternatively, they may require a personal guarantee from a major shareholder that the debt will be paid before allowing trade credit. In the latter case, the supplier circumvents the company's limited liability status by demanding the personal liability of an individual. Larger, more established companies, on the other hand, tend to have built up the confidence of suppliers.

Legal safeguards

Various safeguards exist to protect individuals and businesses contemplating dealing with a limited company. These include the requirement to indicate limited liability status in the name of the company. By doing this, an alert is issued to prospective suppliers and lenders.

A further safeguard is the restrictions placed on the ability of shareholders to withdraw their investment from the company. These restrictions are designed to prevent shareholders from protecting their own investment and, as a result, leaving lenders and suppliers in an exposed position. We consider this point in more detail later in the chapter.

Finally, limited companies are required to produce annual financial statements (income statement, balance sheet and cash flow statement), and make them publicly available. This means that anyone interested can gain an impression of the financial performance and position of the company. The form and content of these statements are considered in some detail later in the chapter.

Public and private companies

When a company is registered with the Registrar of Companies, it must be registered either as a public or as a private company. The main practical difference between these is that a **public company** can offer its shares for sale to the general public, but a **private company** is restricted from doing so. A public limited company must signal its status to all interested parties by having the words 'public limited company', or its abbreviation 'plc' in its name. For a private limited company, the word 'limited' or 'Ltd' must appear as part of its name.

Private limited companies tend to be smaller businesses where the ownership is divided among relatively few shareholders who are usually fairly close to one another – for example, a family company. Numerically, there are vastly more private limited companies in the UK than there are public ones. Of the 2.1 million UK limited companies now in existence, only 11,500 (representing 0.5 per cent of the total) are public limited companies. Figure 4.1 shows the trend in the numbers of public and private limited companies in recent years.

Since individual public companies tend to be larger, they are often economically more important. In some industry sectors, such as banking, insurance, oil refining and grocery retailing, they are completely dominant. Although some large private limited companies exist, many are little more than the vehicle through which one-person businesses operate.

Figure 4.1 **Number of private and public limited companies registered, 2001 to 2006**

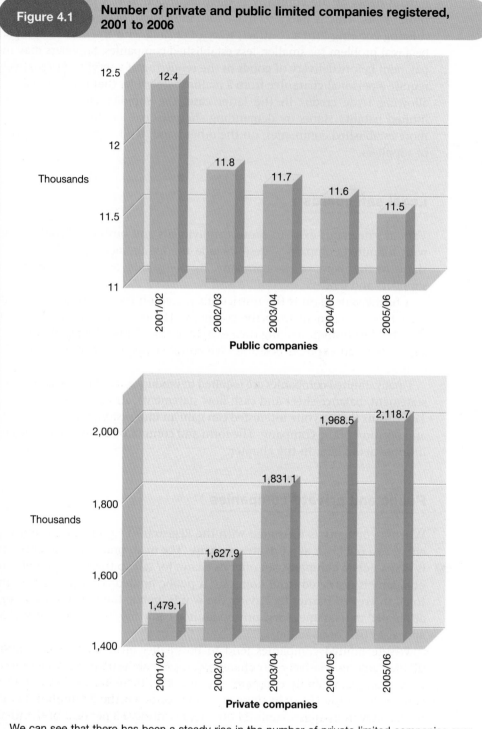

We can see that there has been a steady rise in the number of private limited companies over the five-year period. This has been matched by a gradual decline in the number of public limited companies.

Source: www.companieshouse.gov.uk.

Real World 4.3 reveals the extent of market dominance of public limited companies in one particular business sector.

Real World 4.3

A big slice of the market

The grocery sector is dominated by four large players: Tesco, Sainsbury, Morrisons and Asda. The first three are public limited companies and the fourth, Asda, is owned by a large US public company, Wal-Mart. Figure 4.2 shows the share of the grocery market enjoyed by each.

Figure 4.2   **Market share of the four largest grocers: 12 weeks to 16 July 2006**

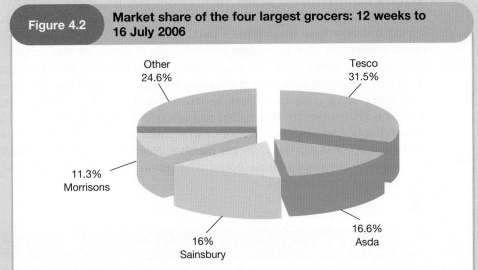

The diagram above shows that Tesco had by far the largest market share and that the four largest grocers, when taken together, had more than 75 per cent of the total market during the period.

Source: www.sharecast.com, 26 July 2006.

Taxation

Another consequence of the legal separation of the limited company from its owners is that companies must be accountable to the tax authorities for tax on their profits and gains. This leads to the reporting of tax in the financial statements of limited companies. The charge for tax is shown in the income statement (profit and loss account). The tax charge for a particular year is based on that year's profit. Since only 50 per cent of a company's tax liability is due for payment during the year concerned, the other 50 per cent will appear on the end-of-year balance sheet as a short-term liability. This will be illustrated a little later in the chapter. The tax position of companies contrasts with that of sole proprietorships and partnerships, where tax is levied not on the business but on the owner(s). Thus tax does not impact on the financial statements of unincorporated businesses, but is an individual matter between the owner(s) and the tax authorities.

Companies are charged **corporation tax** on their profits and gains. The percentage rates of tax tend to vary from year to year, but have recently been 30 per cent for larger companies and 19 per cent for smaller companies. These rates of tax are levied on the company's taxable profit, which is not necessarily the same as the profit shown on the income statement. This is because tax law does not, in every respect, follow the normal accounting rules. Generally, however, the taxable profit and the company's accounting profit are pretty close to one another.

Transferring share ownership: the role of the Stock Exchange

The point has already been made that shares in a company may be transferred from one owner to another. The desire of some shareholders to sell their shares, coupled with the desire of others to buy those shares, has led to the existence of a formal market in which shares can be bought and sold. The London Stock Exchange, and similar organisations around the world, provide a marketplace in which shares in public companies may be bought and sold. Share prices are determined by the laws of supply and demand, which are, in turn, determined by investors' perceptions of the future economic prospects of the companies concerned. Only the shares of certain companies (*listed* companies) may be traded on the London Stock Exchange. About 1,300 UK companies are listed. This represents only 1 in about 1,600 of all UK companies (public and private) and about 1 in 9 public limited companies. However, many of these 1,300 listed companies are massive. Nearly all of the 'household name' UK businesses (for example, Tesco, Boots, BT, Cadbury Schweppes, Vodafone, BP, and so on) are listed companies.

Activity 4.2

If, as has been pointed out earlier, the change in ownership of shares does not directly affect the particular company, why do many public companies actively seek to have their shares traded in a recognised market?

The main reason is that investors are generally very reluctant to pledge their money unless they can see some way in which they can turn their investment back into cash. In theory, the shares of a particular company may be very valuable because the company has bright prospects. However, unless this value is capable of being turned into cash, the benefit to the shareholders is dubious. After all, we cannot spend shares; we generally need cash.

This means that potential shareholders are much more likely to be prepared to buy new shares from the company (thereby providing the company with new finance) where they can see a way of liquidating their investment (turning it into cash), as and when they wish. Stock exchanges provide the means of liquidation.

Although the buying and selling of 'second-hand' shares does not provide the company with cash, the fact that the buying and selling facility exists will make it easier for the company to raise new share capital when it needs to do so.

Managing a company

A limited company may have legal personality, but it is not a human being capable of making decisions and plans about the business and exercising control over it. People must undertake these management tasks. The most senior level of management of a company is the board of directors.

→ The shareholders elect **directors** (by law there must be at least one director for a private limited company and two for a public limited company) to manage the company on a day-to-day basis on behalf of those shareholders. In a small company, the board may be the only level of management and consist of all of the shareholders. In larger companies, the board may consist of ten or so directors out of many thousands of shareholders. Indeed, directors are not even required to be shareholders. Below the board of directors of the typical large company could be several layers of management comprising thousands of people.

→ In recent years, the issue of **corporate governance** has generated much debate. The term is used to describe the ways in which companies are directed and controlled. The issue of corporate governance is important because, with larger companies, those who own the company (that is, the shareholders) are usually divorced from the day-to-day control of the business. The shareholders employ the directors to manage the company for them. Given this position, it may seem reasonable to assume that the best interests of shareholders will guide the directors' decisions. However, in practice this does not always occur. The directors may be more concerned with pursuing their own interests, such as increasing their pay and 'perks' (such as expensive motor cars, overseas visits and so on) and improving their job security and status. As a result, a conflict can occur between the interests of shareholders and the interests of directors.

Where directors pursue their own interests at the expense of the shareholders, there is clearly a problem for the shareholders. However, it may also be a problem for society as a whole. If shareholders feel that their funds are likely to be mismanaged, they will be reluctant to invest. A shortage of funds will mean fewer investments can be made and the costs of funds will increase as businesses compete for what funds are available. Thus, a lack of concern for shareholders can have a profound effect on the performance of individual companies and, with this, the health of the economy. To avoid these problems, most competitive market economies have a framework of rules to help monitor and control the behaviour of directors.

These rules are usually based around three guiding principles:

- *Disclosure*. This lies at the heart of good corporate governance. An OECD report (see the reference at the end of the chapter for details) summed up the benefits of disclosure as follows:

  > Adequate and timely information about corporate performance enables investors to make informed buy-and-sell decisions and thereby helps the market reflect the value of a corporation under present management. If the market determines that present management is not performing, a decrease in stock [share] price will sanction management's failure and open the way to management change.

- *Accountability*. This involves defining the roles and duties of the directors and establishing an adequate monitoring process. In the UK, company law requires that the directors of a business act in the best interests of the shareholders. This means, among other things, that they must not try to use their position and knowledge to make gains at the expense of the shareholders. The law also requires larger companies to have their annual financial statements independently audited. The purpose of an independent audit is to lend credibility to the financial statements prepared by the directors. We shall take a brief look at audit in Chapter 5.

● *Fairness*. Directors should not be able to benefit from access to 'inside' information that is not available to shareholders. As a result, both the law and the Stock Exchange place restrictions on the ability of directors to buy and sell the shares of the business. One example of these restrictions is that the directors cannot buy or sell shares immediately before the announcement of the annual trading results of the business or before the announcement of a significant event such as a planned merger or the loss of the chief executive.

Strengthening the framework of rules

The number of rules designed to safeguard shareholders has increased considerably over the years. This has been in response to weaknesses in corporate governance procedures, which have been exposed through well-publicised business failures and frauds, excessive pay increases to directors and evidence that some financial reports were being 'massaged' so as to mislead shareholders. (This last point will be discussed in some detail in Chapter 5.) Some believe, however, that the shareholders must shoulder some of the blame for any weaknesses. Not all shareholders in large companies are private individuals owning just a few shares each. In fact, ownership, by market value, of the shares listed on the London Stock Exchange is dominated by investing institutions such as insurance businesses, banks and pension funds. These are often massive operations, owning large quantities of the shares of the companies in which they invest. These institutional investors employ specialist staff to manage their portfolios of shares in various companies. It has been argued that the large institutional shareholders, despite their size and relative expertise, have not been very active in corporate governance matters. Thus there has been little monitoring of directors. However, things seem to be changing. There is increasing evidence that institutional investors are becoming more proactive in relation to the companies in which they hold shares.

The Combined Code

During the 1990s there was a real effort by the accountancy profession and the London Stock Exchange to address the problems mentioned above. A Code of Best Practice on Corporate Governance emerged in 1992. This was concerned with accountability and financial reporting. In 1995, a separate code of practice emerged. This dealt with directors' pay and conditions. These two codes were revised, 'fine tuned' and amalgamated to produce the **Combined Code**, which was issued in 1998.

The Combined Code was revised in 2003, following the recommendations of the Higgs Report. These recommendations were mainly concerned with the roles of the company chairman (the senior director) and the other directors. The report was particularly concerned with the role of 'non-executive' directors. Non-executive directors do not work full time in the company, but act solely in the role of director. This contrasts with 'executive' directors who are salaried employees. For example, the finance director of most large companies is a full-time employee. This person is a member of the board of directors and, as such, takes part in the key decision making at board level. At the same time, he or she is also responsible for managing the departments of the company that act on those board decisions as far as finance is concerned.

The view reflected in the 2003 Combined Code is that executive directors can become too embroiled in the day-to-day management of the company to be able to take a broad view. It also reflects the view that, for executive directors, conflicts can arise between their own interests and those of the shareholders. The advantage of non-executive directors can be that they are much more independent of the company than are their executive colleagues. Non-executive directors are remunerated by the company for their work, but this would normally form only a small proportion of their total income. This gives them an independence that the executive directors may lack. Non-executive directors are often senior managers in other businesses or people who have had good experience of such roles.

The Combined Code, which underwent some minor modifications in 2006, has the backing of the London Stock Exchange. This means that companies listed on the London Stock Exchange are expected to comply with the requirements of the Code or must give their shareholders good reason why they do not. Failure to do one or other of these can lead to the company's shares being suspended from listing. This is an important sanction against non-compliant directors.

The Combined Code sets out a number of principles relating to such matters as the role of the directors, their relations with shareholders, and their accountability. **Real World 4.4** outlines some of the more important of these.

Real World 4.4

The Combined Code

Some of the key elements of the Combined Code are as follows:

- Every listed company should have a board of directors to lead and control the company.
- There should be a clear division of responsibilities between the chairman and the chief executive officer of the company to ensure that a single person does not have unbridled power.
- There should be a balance between executive and non-executive (who are often part-time and independent) members of the board, to ensure that small groups of individuals cannot dominate proceedings.
- The board should receive timely information that is of sufficient quality to enable them to carry out their duties.
- Appointments to the board should be the subject of rigorous, formal and transparent procedures.
- All directors should submit themselves for re-election at regular intervals, subject to satisfactory performance.
- There should be formal and transparent procedures for developing policy on directors' remuneration.
- The board has a responsibility for ensuring that a satisfactory dialogue with shareholders occurs.
- Boards should use the annual general meeting to communicate with private investors and encourage their participation.
- Institutional shareholders have a responsibility to use their votes.
- The board should publish a balanced and understandable assessment of the company's position and performance.
- Internal controls should be in place to protect the shareholders' wealth.
- Formal and transparent arrangements for applying financial reporting and internal control principles and for maintaining an appropriate relationship with auditors should be in place.

Strengthening the framework of rules has improved the quality of information available to shareholders, resulted in better checks on the powers of directors, and provided greater transparency in corporate affairs. However, rules can only be a partial answer. A balance must be struck between the need to protect shareholders and the need to encourage the entrepreneurial spirit of directors – which could be stifled under a welter of rules. This implies that rules should not be too tight and so unscrupulous directors may still find ways around them.

Activity 4.3

Can you think of ways in which the shareholders themselves may try to ensure that the directors always act in the shareholders best interests?

Two ways are commonly used in practice:

● The shareholders may insist on monitoring closely the actions of the directors and the way in which they use the resources of the company.
● The shareholders may introduce incentive plans for directors that link their pay to the share performance of the company. In this way, the interests of the directors and shareholders will become more closely aligned.

Implementing the code

A detailed study of how the various principles mentioned above are implemented is beyond the scope of this book. However, it is useful to have some idea as to how companies apply the code in practice. To achieve this, we can take a look at extracts from the statement on corporate governance made by the directors of J D Wetherspoon plc, the pub operator, which is set out in its 2006 annual report and accounts.

The first extract, which is set out in **Real World 4.5**, concerns the division of responsibilities between the chairman and the chief executive.

Real World 4.5

Divide and rule

The following table sets out the respective responsibilities of the company's two most senior officers.

Chairman's responsibility	Chief executive's responsibility
Delegated responsibility of authority to exchange contracts on behalf of the company	Develop and maintain effective management controls, planning and performance measurements
Provide advice, support and feedback to the chief executive	Develop and maintain an effective organisational structure
Support the company strategy and encourage the chief executive with development of strategy	External and internal communications, in conjunction with the chairman, on any issues facing the company

Chairman's responsibility	Chief executive's responsibility
Maintain relations with investors	Implement and monitor compliance with board policy
Chair general meetings, board meetings, operational meetings and agree board agendas	Timely and accurate reporting of the above to the board
Manage chief executive's contract, appraisal and remuneration by way of making recommendations to the remuneration committee	Recruit and manage senior managers within the business
Provide support to executive directors and senior managers of the company	Develop and maintain effective risk management and regulatory controls
Provide 'ethos' and 'vision' of the company	Maintain primary relationships with shareholders
Provide operational presence throughout the estate	Chair the management board responsible for implementing the company strategy

Source: J D Wetherspoon plc Annual Report and Accounts 2006, p. 18.

The next extract, which is set out in **Real World 4.6**, concerns the need for directors to receive timely information.

Real World 4.6

Time gentlemen, please!

Information is normally furnished to all board members in the week before a board meeting, to enable the directors to consider the issues for discussion and to request clarification or additional information.

All directors are provided with, and have full access to, information which enables them to make informed decisions on corporate and business issues, including operational and financial performance. In particular, the board receives monthly information on the financial trading performance of the company and a comprehensive finance report which includes operational highlights. All directors receive sales and margin information for the company weekly by trading unit.

Source: J D Wetherspoon plc Annual Report and Accounts 2006, p. 19.

The final extract, which is set out in **Real World 4.7**, concerns the ways in which the directors seek to protect shareholder wealth through various internal controls.

Real World 4.7

Exercising control

During the year, the company and the board continued to support and invest in resources to provide an internal audit and risk-management function. The system of internal control and risk mitigation is deeply embedded in the operations and culture of the company. The board is responsible for maintaining a sound system of internal control and reviewing its effectiveness. The function can only manage, rather than eliminate entirely, and can only provide reasonable and not absolute assurance against material misstatement or loss. Ongoing reviews and assessments took place continually throughout the year.

The company has an internal audit function which is discharged as follows:

● Adequate regular audits of the company stock (inventories)
● Unannounced visits to the retail units
● Monitoring systems which control the company cash

The company has key procedures in place as follows:

● Clearly defined authority limits and controls over cash-handling purchasing commitments and capital expenditure
● Comprehensive budgeting process, with a detailed operating plan for twelve months and a mid-term financial plan, both approved by the board
● Business results are reported weekly (for key times), with a monthly comprehensive report in full, and compared with budget
● Forecasts are prepared regularly throughout the year for review by the board
● Complex treasury instruments are not used; decisions on treasury matters are reserved by the board

The directors confirm that they have reviewed the effectiveness of the system of internal control.

Source: J D Wetherspoon plc Annual Report and Accounts 2006, p. 20.

Financing limited companies

The owners' claim

The owner's claim of a sole proprietorship is normally encompassed in one figure on the balance sheet, usually labelled 'capital'. With companies, this is usually a little more complicated, although in essence the same broad principles apply. With a company, the owners' claim is divided between shares (for example, the original investment), on the one hand, and **reserves** (that is, profits and gains subsequently made), on the other. There is also the possibility that there will be more than one type of shares and of reserves. Thus, within the basic divisions of share capital and reserves, there might well be further subdivisions. This might seem quite complicated, but we shall shortly consider the reasons for these subdivisions and all should become clearer.

The sum of share capital and reserves is commonly known as **equity**.

The basic division

When a company is first formed, those who take steps to form it (the promoters) will decide how much needs to be raised by the potential shareholders to set the company up with the necessary assets to operate. Example 4.1 acts as a basis for illustration.

Example 4.1

A group of friends get together and decide to form a company to operate an office cleaning business. They estimate that the company will need £50,000 to obtain the necessary assets to operate. Between them, they raise the cash, which they use to buy shares in the company, on 31 March 2006, with a **nominal** (or **par**) **value** of £1 each.

At this point the balance sheet of the company would be:

Balance sheet as at 31 March 2006

	£
Net assets (all in cash)	50,000
Equity	
Share capital	
50,000 shares of £1 each	50,000

The company now buys the necessary non-current assets (vacuum cleaners and so on) and inventories (cleaning materials) and starts to trade. During the first year, the company makes a profit of £10,000. This, by definition, means that the owners' claim expands by £10,000. During the year, the shareholders (owners) make no drawings of their claim, so at the end of the year the summarised balance sheet looks like this:

Balance sheet as at 31 March 2007

	£
Net assets (various assets less liabilities*)	60,000
Equity	
Share capital	
50,000 shares of £1 each	50,000
Reserves (revenue reserve)	10,000
Total equity	60,000

* We know from Chapter 2 that Assets = Capital (or Equity) + Liabilities. This can be rearranged so that Assets − Liabilities = Capital (or Equity).

The profit is shown in a reserve, known as a **revenue reserve**, because it arises from generating revenue (making sales). Note that we do not simply merge the profit with the share capital: we must keep the two amounts separate (to satisfy company law). The reason for this is that there is a legal restriction on the maximum drawings of the shareholders' claim (or payment of a **dividend**) that the owners can make. This is defined by the amount of revenue reserves, and so it is helpful to show these separately. We shall look at why there is this restriction, and how it works, a little later in the chapter.

Share capital

→ Shares represent the basic units of ownership of a business. All companies issue **ordinary shares**. Ordinary shares are often known as *equities*. The nominal value of such shares is at the discretion of the people that start up the company. For example, if the initial capital is to be £50,000, this could be two shares of £25,000 each, 5 million shares of one penny each or any other combination that gives a total of £50,000. All shares must have equal value.

Activity 4.4

The initial capital requirement for a new company is £50,000. There are to be two equal shareholders. Would you advise them to issue two shares of £25,000 each? Why?

Such large-denomination shares tend to be unwieldy. Suppose that one of the shareholders wanted to sell her shares. She would have to find one buyer. If there were shares of smaller denomination, it would be possible to sell part of the shareholding to various potential buyers. Furthermore, it would be possible to sell just part of the holding and retain a part.

In practice, £1 is the normal maximum nominal value for shares. Shares of 25 pence each and 50 pence each are probably the most common.

→ Some companies also issue other classes of shares, **preference shares** being the most common. Preference shares guarantee that *if a dividend is paid*, the preference shareholders will be entitled to the first part of it up to a maximum value. This maximum is normally defined as a fixed percentage of the nominal value of the preference shares. If, for example, a company issues 10,000 preference shares of £1 each with a dividend rate of 6 per cent, this means that the preference shareholders are entitled to receive the first £600 (that is, 6 per cent of £10,000) of any dividend that is paid by the company for a year. The excess over £600 goes to the ordinary shareholders. Normally, any undistributed profits and gains also accrue to the ordinary shareholders.

The ordinary shareholders are the primary risk takers as they are entitled to share in the profits of the company only after other claims have been satisfied, and their potential rewards reflect this risk. There are no upper limits, however, on the amount by which they may benefit. The potential rewards available to ordinary shareholders reflect the risks that they are prepared to take. Since ordinary shareholders take most of the risks, power normally resides in their hands. Usually, only the ordinary shareholders are able to vote on issues that affect the company, such as who the directors should be.

It is open to the company to issue shares of various classes – perhaps with some having unusual and exotic conditions – but in practice it is rare to find other than straightforward ordinary and preference shares. Although a company may have different classes of shares whose holders have different rights, within each class all shares must be treated equally. The rights of the various classes of shareholders, as well as other matters relating to a particular company, are contained in that company's set of rules, known as the 'articles and memorandum of association'. A copy of these rules must be lodged with the Registrar of Companies, who makes it available for inspection by the general public.

Reserves

Reserves are profits and gains that have been made by a company, which still form part of the shareholders' (owners') claim or equity. One reason that past profits and gains may not remain part of equity is that they have been paid out to shareholders (as dividends and so on). Another reason is that reserves will be reduced by the amount of any losses that the company might suffer. In the same way that profits increase equity, losses reduce it.

The shareholders' claim consists of share capital and reserves.

Activity 4.5

Are reserves amounts of cash? Can you think of a reason why this is an odd question?

To deal with the second point first, it is an odd question because reserves are a claim, or part of one, on the assets of the company, whereas cash is an asset. So reserves cannot be cash.

Reserves are classified as either revenue reserves or capital reserves. In Example 4.1 we came across one type of reserve, the revenue reserve. We should recall that this reserve represents the company's retained trading profits and gains on the disposal of non-current assets. It is worth mentioning that retained profits, or earnings, as they are often called, represent overwhelmingly the largest source of new finance for UK companies. For most companies they amount to more than share issues and borrowings combined.

 Capital reserves arise for two main reasons:

- issuing shares at above their nominal value (for example, issuing £1 shares at £1.50);
- revaluing (upwards) non-current assets.

Where a company issues shares at above their nominal value, UK law requires that the excess of the issue price over the nominal value be shown separately.

Activity 4.6

Can you think why shares might be issued at above their nominal value? (*Hint*: This would not usually happen when a company is first formed and the initial shares are being issued.)

Once a company has traded and has been successful, the shares would normally be worth more than the nominal value at which they were issued. If additional shares are to be issued to new shareholders to raise finance for further expansion, unless they are issued at a value higher than the nominal value, the new shareholders will be gaining at the expense of the original ones.

Example 4.2 shows how this works.

Example 4.2

Based on future prospects, the net assets of a company are worth £1.5m. There are currently 1 million ordinary shares in the company, each with a face (nominal) value of £1. The company wishes to raise an additional £0.6m of cash for expansion and has decided to raise it by issuing new shares. If the shares are issued for £1 each (that is 600,000 shares), the total number of shares will be:

$$1.0m + 0.6m = 1.6m$$

and their total value will be the value of the existing net assets plus the new injection of cash:

$$£1.5m + £0.6m = £2.1m$$

This means that the value of each share after the new issue will be:

$$£2.1m/1.6m = £1.3125$$

The current value of each share is:

$$£1.5m/1.0m = £1.50$$

So the original shareholders will lose:

$$£1.50 - £1.3125 = £0.1875 \text{ a share}$$

and the new shareholders will have gained

$$£1.3125 - £1.0 = £0.3125 \text{ a share}$$

The new shareholders will, no doubt, be delighted with this outcome; the original ones will not.

Things could be made fair between the two sets of shareholders described in Example 4.2 by issuing the new shares at £1.50 each. In this case it would be necessary to issue 400,000 shares to raise the necessary £0.6 million. £1 a share of the £1.50 is the nominal value and will be included with share capital in the balance sheet (£400,000 in total). The remaining £0.50 is a share premium, which will be shown as a capital reserve known as the **share premium account** (£200,000 in total).

It is not clear why UK company law insists on the distinction between nominal share values and the premium. In some other countries (for example, the United States) with similar laws governing the corporate sector, there is not the necessity of distinguishing between share capital and share premium. Instead, the total value at which shares are issued is shown as one comprehensive figure on the company balance sheet. **Real World 4.8** shows the shareholders' claim of one well-known business.

Real World 4.8

How Thorntons is funded

Thorntons plc, the chocolate maker, had the following share capital and reserves as at 24 June 2006:

	£m
Share capital (10p ordinary shares)	6,724
Share premium account	12,890
Retained earnings	12,340
Total equity	31,954

Note how the nominal share capital figure is nearly half the share premium account figure. This implies that Thorntons has issued shares at higher prices than the 10p per share nominal value. This reflects its trading success since the company was first formed. Note also how, at balance sheet values, retained earnings (profits) make up nearly 40 per cent of the total for share capital and reserves.

Source: Thorntons plc Annual Report 2006, p. 22.

Altering the nominal value of shares

The point has already been made that the promoters of a new company may make their own choice of the nominal, or par, value of the shares. This value need not be permanent. At a later date the shareholders can decide to change it.

Suppose that a company has 1 million ordinary shares of £1 each and a decision is made to change the nominal value of the shares from £1 to £0.50, in other words to halve the value. This would lead the company to issue each shareholder with a new share certificate (the shareholders' evidence of ownership of their shareholding) for exactly twice as many shares, each with half the nominal value. The result would be that each shareholder retains a holding of the same total nominal value. This process is known, not surprisingly, as splitting the shares. The opposite, reducing the number of shares and increasing their nominal value per share to compensate, is known as consolidating.

Since each shareholder would be left, after a split or consolidation, with exactly the same proportion of ownership of the company's assets as before, the process should not increase the value of the total shares held.

Activity 4.7

Why might the shareholders want to split their shares in the manner described above?

The answer is probably to avoid individual shares becoming too valuable and making them a bit unwieldy, in the way discussed in the answer to Activity 4.4. If a company trades successfully, the value of each share is likely to rise, and in time could increase to a level that makes them less marketable. Splitting would solve this problem.

Real World 4.9 gives an example of a share split by a large UK company.

Share split at Pennon

Pennon Group plc owns South West Water Ltd, the business that provides water and sewerage services to the far south west of England, and Viridor Waste Ltd, a waste management business.

In July 2006, Pennon Group plc decided to split its ordinary shares. Each share with a nominal value of 122.1p was subdivided into three new ordinary shares of 40.7p per share. This meant that each ordinary shareholder became the owner of three times as many new shares, with each share having a market value of one-third of each of the old ones. The reason given by the company was as follows:

> In recent years the price of the company's ordinary shares has risen to the point where they are now one of the most highly priced ordinary shares compared with comparator companies quoted on the London Stock Exchange. It is hoped that the share split will lead to increased market liquidity of the company's shares.

Source: Investor information, www.pennon-group.co.uk.

Bonus shares

It is always open to a company to take reserves of any kind (irrespective of whether they are capital or revenue) and turn them into share capital. This will involve transferring the desired amount from the reserve concerned to share capital and then distributing the appropriate number of new shares to the existing shareholders. New shares arising from such a conversion are known as **bonus shares**. Issues of bonus shares are quite frequently encountered in practice. Example 4.3 illustrates this aspect of share issues.

Example 4.3

The summary balance sheet of a company is as follows:

Balance sheet as at 31 March 2007

	£
Net assets (various assets less liabilities)	128,000
Equity	
Share capital	
50,000 shares of £1 each	50,000
Reserves	78,000
Total equity	128,000

The company decides that it will issue existing shareholders with one new share for every share currently owned by each shareholder. The balance sheet immediately following this will appear as follows:

Balance sheet as at 31 March 2007

	£
Net assets (various assets less liabilities)	128,000
Equity	
Share capital	
100,000 shares of £1 each (50,000 + 50,000)	100,000
Reserves (78,000 − 50,000)	28,000
Total equity	128,000

We can see that the reserves have decreased by £50,000 and share capital has increased by the same amount. Share certificates for the 50,000 ordinary shares of £1 each that have been created from reserves will be issued to the existing shareholders to complete the transaction.

Activity 4.8

A shareholder of the company in Example 4.3 owned 100 shares before the bonus issue. How will things change for this shareholder as regards the number of shares owned and the value of the shareholding?

The answer should be that the number of shares will double, from 100 to 200. Now the shareholder owns one five-hundredth of the company (that is, 200/100,000). Before the bonus issue, the shareholder also owned one five-hundredth of the company (that is, 100/50,000). The company's assets and liabilities have not changed as a result of the bonus issue and so, logically, one five-hundredth of the value of the company should be identical to what it was before. Thus, each share is worth half as much.

→ A **bonus issue** simply takes one part of the owners' claim (part of a reserve) and puts it into another part of the owners' claim (share capital). The transaction has no effect on the company's assets or liabilities, so there is no effect on shareholders' wealth.

Note that a bonus issue is not the same as a share split. A split does not affect the reserves.

Activity 4.9

Can you think of any reasons why a company might want to make a bonus issue if it has no economic consequence?

We think that there are three possible reasons:

- *Share price*. To lower the value of each share without reducing the shareholders' collective or individual wealth. This has a similar effect to share splitting.
- *Shareholder confidence*. To provide the shareholders with a 'feel-good factor'. It is believed that shareholders like bonus issues because it seems to make them better off, although in practice it should not affect their wealth.
- *Lender confidence*. Where reserves arising from operating profits and/or realised gains on the sale of non-current assets are used to make the bonus issue, it has the effect of taking part of that portion of the owners' claim that could be drawn by the shareholders,

→

Activity 4.9 continued

as drawings (or dividends), and locking it up. The amount transferred becomes part of the permanent capital base of the company. (We shall see a little later in this chapter that there are severe restrictions on the extent to which shareholders may make drawings from their claim.) An individual or business contemplating lending money to the company may insist that the dividend payment possibilities are restricted as a condition of making the loan. This point will be explained shortly.

Real World 4.10 provides an example of a bonus share issue.

Real World 4.10

Bonus shares

Workspace Group plc provides flexible business accommodation for small and medium-sized businesses. In March 2005 it made a 9-for-1 bonus issue of shares following a £15.2m capitalisation of reserves. The nominal value of a share in the company is 10p and a total of 151,955,694 new shares was issued. Following the issue, the net asset value per share was divided by ten so that year-end net asset values were adjusted from £22.40 per share to £2.24 per share.

Source: Based on information in Workspace Group plc Annual Report 2005 and at www.workspacegroup.co.uk.

Share capital jargon

Before leaving our detailed discussion of share capital, it might be helpful to clarify some of the jargon relating to shares that is used in company financial statements.

Share capital that has been issued to shareholders is known as the **issued** (or **allotted**) **share capital**. Sometimes, but not very often, a company may not require shareholders to pay the whole amount that is due to be paid for the shares at the time of issue. This may happen where the company does not need the money all at once. Some money would normally be paid at the time of issue and the company would 'call' for further instalments until the shares were **fully paid**. That part of the total issue price that has been 'called' is known as the **called-up share capital**. That part that has been called and paid is known as the **paid-up share capital**.

Raising share capital

Once the company has made its initial share issue to start business (usually soon after the company is first formed) it may decide to make further issues of new shares. These may be:

- *Rights issues*, that is issues made to existing shareholders, in proportion to their existing shareholding.
- *Public issues*, that is issues made to the general investing public.
- *Private placings*, that is issues made to selected individuals who are usually approached and asked if they would be interested in taking up new shares.

During its lifetime a company may use all three of these approaches to raising funds through issuing new shares (although only public companies can make appeals to the general public). These approaches will be discussed in detail in Chapter 15.

Borrowings

Most companies borrow money to supplement that raised from share issues and ploughed-back profits. Company borrowing is often on a long-term basis, perhaps on a ten-year contract. Lenders may be banks and other professional providers of loan finance. Many companies raise loan finance in such a way that small investors, including private individuals, are able to lend small amounts. This is particularly the case with the larger, Stock Exchange listed, companies and involves their making a **loan notes** issue, which, though large in total, can be taken up in small slices by individual investors, both private individuals and investing institutions, such as pension funds and insurance companies. In some cases, these slices of loans can be bought and sold through the Stock Exchange. This means that investors do not have to wait the full term of the loan to obtain repayment, but can sell their slice of the loan to another would-be lender at intermediate points in the term of the loan. Loan notes are often known as *loan stock* or *debentures*.

Some of the features of loan notes financing, particularly the possibility that the loan notes may be traded on the Stock Exchange, can lead to a confusion that loan notes are shares by another name. We should be clear that this is not the case. It is the shareholders who own the company and, therefore, who share in its losses and profits. Holders of loan notes lend money to the company under a legally binding contract that normally specifies the rate of interest, the interest payment dates and the date of repayment of the loan itself. Usually, long-term loans are secured on assets of the company.

Long-term financing of companies can be depicted as in Figure 4.3.

| Figure 4.3 | Sources of long-term finance for a typical limited company |

Companies derive their long-term financing needs from three sources: new share issues, retained profit and long-term borrowings. For a typical company, the sum of the first two (jointly known as 'equity finance') exceeds the third. Retained profit usually exceeds either of the other two in terms of the amount of finance raised in most years.

It is important to the prosperity and stability of a company that it strikes a suitable balance between finance provided by the shareholders (equity) and from borrowing. This topic will be explored in Chapter 7. Equity and loan notes are, of course, not the only forms of finance available to a company. In Chapter 15, we consider other sources of finance available to businesses, including companies.

Real World 4.11 shows the long-term borrowings of Rolls-Royce plc, the engine-building business, at 31 December 2005.

Real World 4.11

Borrowing at Rolls-Royce

The following extract from the annual financial statements of Rolls-Royce plc sets out the sources of the company's long-term borrowing as at 31 December 2005.

	£m
Unsecured	
Bank loans	4
$6^3/8$% Notes 2007	354
$7^3/8$% Notes 2016	200
5.84% Notes 2010	107
6.38% Notes 2013	134
6.55% Notes 2015	49
$4^1/2$% Notes 2011	524
Other loans 2009 (interest rates nil)	1
Secured	
Bank loans	71
Obligations under finance leases payable:	
Between one and two years	5
Between two and five years	8
After five years	1
	1,458
Repayable	
Between one and two years – by instalments	49
– otherwise	–
Between two and five years – by instalments	11
– otherwise	354
After five years – by instalments	29
– otherwise	1,015
	1,458

Source: Rolls-Royce plc Annual Report and Accounts 2005, note 18.

Note the large number of sources from which the company borrows. This is typical of most large companies and probably reflects a desire to exploit all available means of raising finance, each of which may have some advantages and disadvantages. 'Secured' in this context means that the lender would have the right, should Rolls-Royce fail to meet its interest and/or capital repayment obligations, to seize a specified asset of the business (probably some land) and use it to raise the sums involved. Normally, a lender would accept a lower rate of interest where the loan is secured as there is less risk involved. It should be said that whether a loan to a company like Rolls-Royce is secured or unsecured is usually pretty academic. It is unlikely that such a large and profitable company would fail to meet its obligations.

'Finance leases' are, in effect, arrangements where Rolls-Royce needs the use of a non-current asset (such as an item of machinery) and, instead of buying the asset itself, it arranges for a financier to buy the asset. The financier then leases it to the business, probably for the entire economic life of the asset. Though legally it is the financier who owns the asset, from an accounting point of view the essence of the arrangement is that, in effect, Rolls-Royce has borrowed cash from the financier to buy the asset. Thus, the asset appears among the business's non-current assets and the financial obligation to the financier is shown here as long-term borrowing. This is a good example of how accounting tries to report the economic *substance* of a transaction, rather than its strict legal *form*. Finance leasing is a fairly popular means of raising long-term funds.

Chapter 15 considers in some detail the factors that a business must consider when deciding how to finance its operations.

Withdrawing equity

Companies are legally obliged to distinguish between that part of the shareholders equity which may be withdrawn and that part which may not. The withdrawable part consists of profits arising from trading and from the disposal of non-current assets. It is represented in the balance sheet by *revenue reserves*.

It is important to appreciate that the total revenue reserves appearing in the balance sheet is rarely the total of all trading profits and profits on disposals of non-current assets generated by the company. This total will normally have been reduced by at least one of the following three factors:

● corporation tax paid on those profits
● any dividends paid
● any losses from trading and the disposal of non-current assets.

The non-withdrawable part consists of profits arising from shareholders buying shares in the company and from upward revaluations of assets still held. It is represented in the balance sheet by *share capital and capital reserves*.

The law does not specify how large the non-withdrawable part of a particular company's shareholders' equity should be. However, when seeking to impress prospective lenders and credit suppliers, the larger this part, the better. Those considering doing business with the company must be able to see from the company's balance sheet how large it is.

Activity 4.10

Why are limited companies required to distinguish different parts of their shareholders' claim whereas sole proprietorship and partnership businesses are not?

The reason stems from the limited liability that company shareholders enjoy but which owners of unincorporated businesses do not. If a sole proprietor or partner withdraws all of the owners' claim, or even an amount in excess of this, the position of the lenders and credit suppliers of the business is not weakened since they can legally enforce their claims against the sole proprietor or partner as an individual. With a limited company, the business and the owners are legally separated and such right to enforce claims against individuals does not exist. To protect the company's lenders and credit suppliers, however, the law insists that the shareholders cannot normally withdraw a specific part of their claim.

Let us now look at another example.

Example 4.4

The summary balance sheet of a company at a particular date is as follows:

Balance sheet

	£
Total assets	43,000
Equity	
Share capital	
20,000 shares of £1 each	20,000
Reserves (revenue)	23,000
Total equity	43,000

A bank has been asked to make a £25,000 long-term loan to the company. If the loan were to be made, the balance sheet immediately following would appear as follows:

Balance sheet (after the loan)

	£
Total assets (£43,000 + £25,000)	68,000
Equity	
Share capital	
20,000 shares of £1 each	20,000
Reserves (revenue)	23,000
	43,000
Non-current liability	
Borrowings – Loan	25,000
Total equity and liabilities	68,000

As things stand, there are assets to a total balance sheet value of £68,000 to meet the bank's claim of £25,000. It would be possible and perfectly legal, however, for the company to pay a dividend (withdraw part of their claim) of £23,000. The balance sheet would then appear as follows:

Balance sheet

	£
Total assets (£68,000 – £23,000)	45,000
Equity	
Share capital	
20,000 shares of £1 each	20,000
Reserves [revenue (£23,000 – £23,000)]	–
	20,000
Non-current liabilities	
Borrowings – Loan	25,000
Total equity and liabilities	45,000

This leaves the bank in a very much weaker position, in that there are now total assets with a balance sheet value of £45,000 to meet a claim of £25,000. Note that the difference between the amount of the borrowings (bank loan) and the total assets equals the capital and reserves total. Thus, the capital and reserves represent a margin of safety for lenders and suppliers. The larger the amount of the owners' claim withdrawable by the shareholders, the smaller is the potential margin of safety for lenders and suppliers.

As we have already seen, the law says nothing about how large the margin of safety must be. It is up to each company to decide what is appropriate.

As a practical footnote to Example 4.4, it is worth pointing out that long-term lenders would normally seek to secure a loan against an asset of the company, such as land. This, as we have seen, would give the lender the right to seize the asset concerned, sell it and satisfy the repayment obligation, should the company default.

Activity 4.11

Would you expect a company to pay all of its revenue reserves as a dividend? What factors might be involved with a dividend decision?

It would be rare for a company to pay all of its revenue reserves as a dividend: the fact that it is legally possible does not necessarily make it a good idea. Most companies see ploughed-back profits as a major – usually *the* major – source of new finance. The factors that influence the dividend decision are likely to include:

- the availability of cash to pay a dividend; it would not be illegal to borrow to pay a dividend, but it would be unusual and, possibly, imprudent;
- the needs of the business for finance for new investment;
- the expectations of shareholders concerning the amount of dividends to be paid.

You may have thought of others.

The law states, however, that shareholders cannot, under normal circumstances, withdraw that part of their claim that is represented by shares and capital reserves. This means that potential lenders and credit suppliers know the maximum amount of the shareholders' equity that can be withdrawn. Figure 4.4 shows the important division between that part of the shareholders' equity which can be withdrawn as a dividend and that part which cannot.

Earlier in this chapter, the point was made that a potential lender may insist that some revenue reserves are converted to bonus shares (or capitalised) to increase the margin of safety as a condition of granting the loan.

If we refer back to Real World 4.8, we can see that Thorntons plc could legally have paid a dividend of £12,340m on 24 June 2006, which is the amount of its revenue reserves. For several reasons, including the fact that this represented nearly 40 per cent of the balance sheet value of the company's net assets, no such dividend was paid.

Figure 4.4 **Availability for dividends of various parts of the shareholders' claim**

Total equity finance of limited companies consists of share capital, capital reserves and revenue reserves. Only the revenue reserves (which arise from realised profits and gains) can be used to fund a dividend. In other words, the maximum legal dividend is the amount of the revenue reserves.

Activity 4.12

Can you think of any circumstances where the non-withdrawable part of a company's capital could be reduced, without contravening the law?

It can be reduced as a result of the company sustaining trading losses, or losses on disposal of non-current assets, which exceed the withdrawable amount of shareholders' equity. It cannot be reduced by shareholders making withdrawals.

Though payment of a cash dividend is the standard way for shareholders to withdraw equity from a company, it is not the only way. Provided that certain conditions are met, it is perfectly legal for a company to redeem some of its shares or to buy some of its shares from particular shareholders and cancel them. These conditions are generally not difficult to meet for profitable companies.

The main financial statements

As we might expect, the financial statements of a limited company are, in essence, the same as those of a sole proprietor. There are, however, some differences of detail, and we shall now consider these. Example 4.5 sets out the income statement (profit and loss account) and balance sheet of a limited company.

Example 4.5

Da Silva plc
Income statement for the year ended 31 December 2006

	£m
Revenue	840
Cost of sales	(520)
Gross profit	320
Wages and salaries	(98)
Heat and light	(18)
Rent and rates	(24)
Motor-vehicle expenses	(20)
Insurance	(4)
Printing and stationery	(12)
Depreciation	(45)
Audit fee	(4)
Operating profit	95
Interest payable	(10)
Profit before taxation	85
Taxation	(24)
Profit for the year	61

Balance sheet as at 31 December 2006

	£m
Non-current assets	
Property, plant and equipment	203
Intangible assets	100
	303
Current assets	
Inventories	65
Trade receivables	112
Cash	36
	213
Total assets	516
Equity	
Ordinary shares of £0.50 each	200
Share premium account	30
Other reserves	50
Retained earnings	25
	305
Non-current liabilities	
Borrowings	100
Current liabilities	
Trade payables	99
Taxation	12
	111
Total equity and liabilities	516

Perhaps the most striking thing about these statements is their similarity to those of sole proprietors; the differences are small. Let us now go through and pick up these differences.

The income statement

There are a few features in the income statement that need consideration.

Profit

We can see that, following the calculation of operating profit, two further measures of profit are shown.

 ● The first of these is the **profit before taxation**. Interest charges are deducted from the operating profit to derive this figure. In the case of a sole proprietor or partnership business, the income statement would end here.

 ● The second measure of profit is the **profit for the year**. As the company is a separate legal entity, it is liable to pay tax (known as corporation tax) on the profits generated. (This contrasts with the sole proprietor business where it is the owner rather than the business that is liable for the tax on profits, as we saw earlier in the chapter.) This measure of profit represents the amount that is available for the shareholders.

Audit fee

Companies beyond a certain size are required to have their financial statements audited by an independent firm of accountants, for which a fee is charged. As we shall see in Chapter 5, the purpose of the audit is to lend credibility to the financial statements. Although it is also open to sole proprietors and partnerships to have their financial statements audited, relatively few do, so this is an expense that is most often seen in the income statement of a company.

The balance sheet

The main points for consideration in the balance sheet are as follows.

Taxation

The amount that appears as part of the current liabilities represents 50 per cent of the tax on the profit for the year 2006. It is, therefore, 50 per cent (£12m) of the charge that appears in the income statement (£24m); the other 50 per cent (£12m) will already have been paid. The unpaid 50 per cent will be paid shortly after the balance sheet date. These payment dates are set down by law.

Other reserves

This will include any reserves that are not separately identified on the face of the balance sheet. It may include a *general reserve*, which normally consists of trading profits that have been transferred to this separate reserve for reinvestment ('ploughing back') into the operations of the company. In theory, there is no reason to set up a separate reserve for this purpose. The trading profits could remain unallocated and so swell the retained earnings of the company. It is not entirely clear why directors decide to make transfers to general reserves, since the profits concerned remain part of the revenue reserves, and are, therefore, still available for dividend. The most plausible explanation seems to be that directors feel that placing profits in a separate reserve indicates an intention to invest the funds, represented by the reserve, permanently in the company and, therefore, not to use them to pay a dividend. Of course, the retained earnings appearing on the balance sheet are also a reserve, but that fact is not indicated in its title.

Dividends

It has already been mentioned that dividends represent drawings by the shareholders of the company. Dividends are paid out of the revenue reserves of the company and should be deducted from these reserves (usually retained earnings) when preparing the balance sheet. Shareholders are often paid an annual dividend, which may be paid by the company in two parts. An 'interim' dividend may be paid part way through the year and a 'final' dividend shortly after the year end.

Dividends declared by the directors during the year but still unpaid at the year end *may* appear as a liability in the balance sheet. To be recognised as a liability, however, they must be properly authorised before the balance sheet date. This normally means that the dividend must be approved by the shareholders.

Large companies tend to have a clear and consistent policy towards the payment of dividends. Any change in the policy provokes considerable interest and is usually interpreted by shareholders as a signal of the directors' views concerning the future. For example, an increase in dividends may be taken as a signal from the directors' that future prospects are bright: a higher dividend being seen as tangible evidence of their confidence. **Real World 4.12** provides an example of a dividend payment that may well have been interpreted in this way.

Real World 4.12

MyTravel set to resume dividend

FT

MyTravel, the tour operator formerly known as Airtours, has marked a return to financial good health by signaling that it would resume dividend payments for the first time since it fell into financial difficulties in 2001. The group's improved performance was led by MyTravel's UK business, which has returned to growth after a dismal few years.

The gains in UK performance offset declines at MyTravel's North American operations, which were hit by the effects of Hurricane Wilma.

My Travel came close to collapse four years ago when a series of accounting errors and profit warnings caused the shares to tumble.

But the tour operator has completed a long restructuring, overhauling its management, cutting costs and changing its revenue recognition policies. Yesterday it said that advance bookings for this summer were outperforming the market.

Source: 'MyTravel set to resume its dividend', FT.com, 14 March 2006.

Accounting for groups of companies

Most large businesses, including nearly all of the well-known ones, operate not as a single company but as a group of companies. In these circumstances, one company (the **parent** or **holding company**) is able to control various subsidiary companies, normally by owning more than 50 per cent of their shares. Many larger businesses have numerous subsidiary companies, with each subsidiary operating some aspect of the group's activities. The reasons why many businesses operate in the form of groups include:

● a desire for each part of the business to have its own limited liability, so that financial problems in one part of a business cannot have an adverse effect on other parts;

- an attempt to make each part of the business have some sense of independence and autonomy and, perhaps, to create or perpetuate a market image of a smaller independent business.

Each company within a group will prepare its own independent annual financial statements. The law also requires, however, that the parent company prepares **consolidated** or **group financial statements**. These group financial statements amalgamate the financial statements of all of the group members. Thus, the group income statement includes the total revenue figure for all group companies, the balance sheet includes the property, plant and equipment for all group companies, and so on. This means that the group financial statements will look like the financial statements of the parent company had it owned and operated all of the assets of the business directly instead of through subsidiary companies.

Given the above, it may not be possible to detect whether the business operates through a single company or through a large number of subsidiaries simply by looking at a set of group financial statements. Only by referring to the heading at the top of each statement, which should mention the word 'consolidated' or 'group', might we find this out. In many cases, however, one or two items will be reported that are peculiar to group financial statements. These items are:

- *Goodwill arising on consolidation.* This occurs when a parent acquires a subsidiary from previous owners and pays more for the subsidiary than the value of the subsidiary's individual assets (net of liabilities) appear to be worth. This excess may represent such things as the value of a good reputation that the new subsidiary already has in the market, or the value of its having a loyal and skilled workforce.

  Goodwill arising on consolidation will appear as an intangible non-current asset on the group balance sheet.

- *Minority or outsiders' interests.* One of the principles followed when preparing group financial statements is that all of the revenue, expenses, assets, liabilities and cash flows of each subsidiary are reflected to their full extent in the group financial statements. This is true whether or not the parent owns all of the shares in each subsidiary, provided that the parent has control. Control normally means owning more than 50 per cent of the subsidiary's ordinary shares. Where not all of the shares are owned by the parent, the investment of those shareholders in the subsidiary, other than the parent company, appears as part of the shareholders' equity in the group balance sheet. This shows that, although the net assets of the group are being financed mainly by the parent company's shareholders, 'outside' shareholders also finance a part. Similarly, the group income statement reflects the fact that not all of the net profit of the group is attributable to the shareholders of the parent company; a part of it is attributable to the 'outside' shareholders.

Example 4.6 shows how the balance sheet of Major plc and its subsidiary is drawn up. Note that the group balance sheet closely resembles that of an individual company.

Example 4.6

Major plc has just bought, from the previous shareholders, 45m (out of 60m) ordinary shares in Minor plc, paying £75m for them. The remaining 15m Minor plc shares are owned by other shareholders. These shareholders are now referred to by Major plc as the 'minority'. Minor plc is now a subsidiary of Major plc and, as is clear from Major plc's balance sheet, its only subsiduary company.

The balance sheets of the two companies immediately following the **takeover** of Minor plc by Major plc were as follows:

	Major plc £m	Minor plc £m
Non-current assets		
Property, plant and equipment	63	67
Intangible – 45 million shares in Minor plc	75	
	138	67
Current assets		
Inventories	37	21
Trade receivables	22	12
Cash	16	2
	75	35
Total assets	213	102
Equity		
Ordinary shares of £1 each	100	60
Reserves	60	20
	160	80
Non-current liabilities		
Borrowings – Loan notes	35	13
Current liabilities		
Trade payables	18	9
Total equity and liabilities	213	102

As would be normal practice, the balance sheet of the subsidiary (Minor plc) has been revised so that the values of the individual assets is based on *fair values*, rather than what Minor plc originally paid for them. Fair values are those that would be agreed as the selling price between a buyer and a seller, both of whom are knowledgable and willing. In this particuar context, they probably equate to the values that Major plc would have placed on the individual tangible assets when assessing Minor plc's value.

If a balance sheet for the group were to be drawn up immediately following the takeover, it would be as follows:

	Major plc and its subsidiary £m
Non-current assets	
Property, plant and equipment (63 + 67)	130
Intangible – Goodwill [75 − ($^{45}/_{60}$ × 80)]	15
	145
Current assets	
Inventories (37 + 21)	58
Trade receivables (22 + 12)	34
Cash (16 + 2)	18
	110
Total assets	245
Equity	
Ordinary shares of £1 each	100
Reserves	60
Equity attributable to equity holders of the parent	160
Minority interests ($^{15}/_{60}$ × 80)	20
Total equity	180
Non-current liabilities	
Borrowings – Loan notes (35 + 13)	48
Current liabilities	
Trade payables (18 + 9)	27
Total equity and liabilities	245

Note that all of the items, except two, in the group balance sheet are simply the two figures for the item concerned added together. This is despite the fact that Major plc owns only three-quarters of the shares of Minor plc. The logic of group financial statements is that if the parent owns enough shares to control its subsidiary, all of the subsidiary's assets and claims should be reflected on the group balance sheet.

As we have seen, there are two exceptions to this approach: goodwill and minority interests.

Goodwill is simply the excess of what Major paid for the shares over their fair value, based on tangible assets. Major plc bought 45 million of 60 million shares, paying £75m. According to Minor plc's balance sheet, this was net assets (non-current and current assets, less current and non-current liabilities) of £80m. So Major plc paid £75m for £60m (that is, $^{45}/_{60} \times$ £80m) of net assets – an excess of £15m usually referred to as 'goodwill arising on consolidation'. This asset is seen as being the value of a loyal workforce, a regular and profitable customer base, and so on, that a new business setting up would not have. The relevant International Financial Reporting Standard (IFRS 3) demands that goodwill be reviewed at least annually: if its value has been impaired, it must be written down to the lower value.

Minority interests take account of the fact that, although Major plc may control all of the assets and liabilities of Minor plc, it only provides the equity finance for three-quarters of them. The other quarter, £20m (that is, $^{15}/_{60} \times$ £80m), is still provided by shareholders in Minor plc, other than Major plc.

Example 4.7 shows the income statement of Major plc and its subsidiary (Minor plc) for the first year following the takeover. As with the balance sheet, the various revenue and expense figures are simply the individual figures for each company added together. The minority interest figure (£2m) represents $^{15}/_{60} \times$ the after-tax profit of Minor plc, which is assumed to be £8m.

Example 4.7

Income statement for the first year

	£m
Revenue	123
Cost of sales	(56)
Gross profit	67
Administration expenses	(28)
Distribution expenses	(9)
Profit before tax	30
Taxation	(12)
Profit for the year	18
Attributable to:	
Equity holders of the parent	16
Minority interests	2
	18

Self-assessment question 4.1

The summarised balance sheet of Dev Ltd is as follows:

Balance sheet as at 31 December 2006

	£
Net assets (various assets less liabilities)	235,000
Equity	
Share capital: 100,000 shares of £1 each	100,000
Share premium account	30,000
Revaluation reserve	37,000
Retained earnings	68,000
Total equity	235,000

Required:

(a) Without any other transactions occurring at the same time, the company made a 1-for-5 rights share issue at £2 per share payable in cash. This means that each shareholder was offered one share for every five already held. All shareholders took up their rights. Immediately afterwards, the company made a 1-for-2 bonus issue. Show the balance sheet immediately following the bonus issue, assuming that the directors wanted to retain the maximum dividend payment potential for the future.

(b) Explain what external influence might cause the directors to choose not to retain the maximum dividend payment possibilities.

(c) Show the balance sheet immediately following the bonus issue, assuming that the directors wanted to retain the *minimum* dividend payment potential for the future.

(d) What is the maximum dividend that could be paid before and after the events described in (a) if the minimum dividend payment potential is achieved?

(e) Lee owns 100 shares in Dev Ltd before the events described in (a). Assuming that the net assets of the company have a value equal to their balance sheet value, show how these events will affect Lee's wealth.

(f) Looking at the original balance sheet of Dev Ltd, shown above, what four things do we know about the company's status and history that are not specifically stated on the balance sheet?

The answer to this question can be found at the back of the book on page 695.

Summary

The main points of this chapter may be summarised as follows.

Main features of a limited company

- It is an artificial person that has been created by law.
- It has a separate life to its owners and is granted a perpetual existence.
- It must take responsibility for its own debts and losses but its owners are granted limited liability.
- A public company can offer its shares for sale to the public; a private company cannot.
- It is governed by a board of directors, which is elected by the shareholders.
- Corporate governance is a major issue, various scandals have led to the emergence of the Combined Code.

Financing the limited company

- The share capital of a company can be of two main types: ordinary shares and preference shares.
- Ordinary shares (equities) are the main risk takers and are given voting rights; they form the backbone of the company.
- Preference shares are given a right to a fixed dividend before ordinary shareholders receive a dividend.
- Reserves are profits and gains made by the company and form part of the ordinary shareholders' claim.
- Borrowings provide another major source of finance.

Share issues

- Bonus shares are issued to existing shareholders when part of the reserves of the company is converted into share capital.
- Rights issues give existing shareholders the right to buy new shares in proportion to their existing holding.
- Public issues are made direct to the investing public generally.
- Private placings are share issues to particular investors.
- The shares of public companies may be bought and sold on a recognised stock exchange.

Reserves

- Reserves are of two types: revenue reserves and capital reserves.
- Revenue reserves arise from trading profits and from realised profits on the sale of non-current assets.
- Capital reserves arise from the issue of shares above their nominal value or from the upward revaluation of non-current assets.
- Revenue reserves can be withdrawn as dividends by the shareholders whereas capital reserves, normally, cannot.

Financial statements of limited companies

- The financial statements of limited companies are based on the same principles as those of sole proprietorship and partnership businesses. However, there are some differences in detail.

- The income statement has three measures of profit displayed after the gross profit figure: operating profit, net profit before tax and net profit for the year.

- The income statement also shows audit fees and corporation tax on profits for the year.

- Any unpaid tax and unpaid, but authorised, dividends will appear in the balance sheet as current liabilities.

- The share capital plus the reserves will be shown as 'equity'.

Groups of companies

- Parent companies are required to produce group financial statements incorporating the results of all companies controlled by the parent.

- A group balance sheet is prepared by adding like items of assets and liabilities based on 'fair values' together, as if all of the trading is undertaken through the parent company.

- A 'goodwill arising on consolidation' figure often emerges in the group balance sheet.

- Where the parent does not own all of the shares of each subsidiary, a minority interest figure will appear in the balance sheet, representing the outside shareholders' investment.

- A group income statement is drawn up following similar logic to that applied to the group balance sheet.

- The group income statement will contain a minority interest figure if not all subsidiaries are fully owned by the parent, which represents the outside shareholders' share of the group profit.

MyAccountingLab   **Now check your progress in your personal Study Plan**

Key terms

limited company p. 116	capital reserves p. 131
shares p. 116	share premium account p. 132
limited liability p. 118	bonus shares p. 134
public company p. 119	bonus issue p. 135
private company p. 119	issued share capital p. 136
corporation tax p. 122	allotted share capital p. 136
director p. 123	fully paid shares p. 136
corporate governance p. 123	called-up share capital p. 136
Combined Code p. 124	paid-up share capital p. 136
reserves p. 128	loan notes p. 137
equity p. 128	profit before taxation p. 144
nominal value p. 129	profit for the year p. 144
par value p. 129	parent/holding company p. 145
revenue reserve p. 129	consolidated/group financial
dividend p. 129	statements p. 146
ordinary shares p. 130	takeover p. 146
preference shares p. 130	

Reference

Corporate Governance: Improving competitiveness and access to capital in global markets, report by Business Sector Advisory Group on Corporate Governance, Organisation for Economic Co-operation and Development (OECD), 1998, p. 14.

Further reading

If you would like to explore the topics covered in this chapter in more depth, we recommend the following books:

Corporate Financial Accounting and Reporting, *Sutton T.*, 2nd edn, Financial Times Prentice Hall, 2004, chapters 6 and 12.

Financial Accounting and Reporting, *Elliott B. and Elliott J.*, 11th edn, Financial Times Prentice Hall, 2006, chapters 5, 6, 8, and 21–23.

KPMG's Practical Guide to International Financial Reporting Standards, *KPMG*, 3rd edn, Thomson, 2006, section 2.5.

Review questions

Answers to these questions can be found at the back of the book on pages 775–6.

4.1 How does the liability of a limited company differ from the liability of a real person, in respect of amounts owed to others?

4.2 Some people are about to form a company, as a vehicle through which to run a new business. What are the advantages to them of forming a private limited company rather than a public one?

4.3 What is a reserve? Distinguish between a revenue reserve and a capital reserve.

4.4 What is a preference share? Compare the main features of a preference share with those of

(a) an ordinary share, and
(b) loan notes.

Exercises

Exercises 4.6 to 4.8 are more advanced than 4.1 to 4.5. Those with **coloured numbers** have answers at the back of the book, starting on page 715.

If you wish to try more exercises, visit the students' side of the Companion Website.

4.1 Comment on the following quote:

> Limited companies can set a limit on the amount of debts that they will meet. They tend to have reserves of cash, as well as share capital and they can use these reserves to pay dividends to the shareholders. Many companies have preference as well as ordinary shares. The preference shares give a guaranteed dividend. The shares of many companies can be bought and sold on the Stock Exchange, and shareholders selling their shares can represent a useful source of new capital to the company.

4.2 Comment on the following quotes:

(a) 'Bonus shares increase the shareholders' wealth because, after the issue, they have more shares, but each one of the same nominal value as they had before.'
(b) 'By law, once shares have been issued at a particular nominal value, they must always be issued at that value in any future share issues.'
(c) 'By law, companies can pay as much as they like by way of dividends on their shares, provided that they have sufficient cash to do so.'
(d) 'Companies do not have to pay tax on their profits because the shareholders have to pay tax on their dividends.'

4.3 Briefly explain each of the following expressions that you have seen in the financial statements of a limited company:

(a) dividend
(b) audit fee
(c) share premium account.

4.4 Iqbal Ltd started trading on 1 January 2002. During the first five years of trading, the following occurred:

Year ended 31 December	Trading profit/ (loss) £	Profit/(loss) on sale of non-current assets £	Upward revaluation of non-current assets £
2002	(15,000)	–	–
2003	8,000	–	10,000
2004	15,000	5,000	–
2005	20,000	(6,000)	–
2006	22,000	–	–

Required:
Assume that the company paid the maximum legal dividend each year. Under normal circumstances, how much would each year's dividend be?

4.5 Da Silva plc's outline balance sheet as at a particular date was as follows:

	£m
Net assets (assets less liabilities)	72
Equity	
£1 ordinary shares	40
General reserve	32
Total equity	72

The directors made a 1-for-4 bonus issue, immediately followed by a 1-for-4 rights issue at a price of £1.80 per share.

Required:
Show the balance sheet of Da Silva plc immediately following the two share issues.

4.6 Presented below is a draft set of simplified financial statements for Pear Limited for the year ended 30 September 2006.

Income statement for the year ended 30 September 2006

	£000
Revenue	1,456
Cost of sales	(768)
Gross profit	688
Salaries	(220)
Depreciation	(249)
Other operating costs	(131)
Operating profit	88
Interest payable	(15)
Profit before taxation	73
Taxation at 30%	(22)
Profit for the year	51

Balance sheet as at 30 September 2006

	£000
Non-current assets	
Property, plant and equipment	
Cost	1,570
Depreciation	(690)
	880
Current assets	
Inventories	207
Trade receivables	182
Cash at bank	21
	410
Total assets	1,290
Equity	
Share capital	300
Share premium account	300
Retained earnings at beginning of year	104
Profit for year	51
	755
Non-current liabilities	
Borrowings (10% loan repayable 2009)	300
Current liabilities	
Trade payables	88
Other payables	20
Taxation	22
Borrowings (bank overdraft)	105
	235
Total equity and liabilities	1,290

The following information is available:

1 Depreciation has not been charged on office equipment with a carrying amount of £100,000. This class of assets is depreciated at 12 per cent a year using the reducing balance method.
2 A new machine was purchased, on credit, for £30,000 and delivered on 29 September 2006 but has not been included in the financial statements. (Ignore depreciation.)
3 A sales invoice to the value of £18,000 for September 2006 has been omitted from the financial statements. (The cost of sales figure is stated correctly.)
4 A dividend of £25,000 had been approved by the shareholders before 30 September 2006, but was unpaid at that date. This is not reflected in the financial statements.
5 The interest payable on the debenture for the second half-year was not paid until 1 October 2006 and has not been included in the financial statements.
6 An allowance for receivables is to be made at the level of 2 per cent of receivables.
7 An invoice for electricity to the value of £2,000 for the quarter ended 30 September 2006 arrived on 4 October and has not been included in the financial statements.
8 The charge for taxation will have to be amended to take account of the above information. Make the simplifying assumption that tax is payable shortly after the end of the year, at the rate of 30 per cent of the profit before tax.

Required:
Prepare a revised set of financial statements for the year ended 30 September 2006 incorporating the additional information in 1 to 8 above. (Work to the nearest £1,000.)

4.7 Presented below is a draft set of financial statements for Chips Limited.

Chips Limited
Income statement for the year ended 30 June 2006

	£000
Revenue	1,850
Cost of sales	(1,040)
Gross profit	810
Depreciation	(220)
Other operating costs	(375)
Operating profit	215
Interest payable	(35)
Profit before taxation	180
Taxation	(60)
Profit for the year	120

Balance sheet as at 30 June 2006

	Cost £000	Depreciation £000	£000
Non-current assets			
Property, plant and equipment			
Buildings	800	(112)	688
Plant and equipment	650	(367)	283
Motor vehicles	102	(53)	49
	1,552	(532)	1,020
Current assets			
Inventories			950
Trade receivables			420
Cash at bank			16
			1,386
Total assets			2,406
Equity			
Ordinary shares of £1, fully paid			800
Reserves at 1 July 2005			248
Profit for the year			120
			1,168
Non-current liabilities			
Borrowings (secured 10% loan)			700
Current liabilities			
Trade payables			361
Other payables			117
Taxation			60
			538
Total equity and liabilities			2,406

The following additional information is available:

1 Purchase invoices for goods received on 29 June 2006 amounting to £23,000 have not been included. This means that the cost of sales figure in the income statement has been understated.

2 A motor vehicle costing £8,000 with depreciation amounting to £5,000 was sold on 30 June 2006 for £2,000, paid by cheque. This transaction has not been included in the company's records.

3 No depreciation on motor vehicles has been charged. The annual rate is 20 per cent of cost at the year end.

4 A sale on credit for £16,000 made on 1 July 2006 has been included in the financial statements in error. The cost of sales figure is correct in respect of this item.

5 A half-yearly payment of interest on the secured loan due on 30 June 2006 has not been paid.

6 The tax charge should be 30 per cent of the reported profit before taxation. Assume that it is payable, in full, shortly after the year end.

Required:

Prepare a revised set of financial statements incorporating the additional information in 1 to 6 above. (Work to the nearest £1,000.)

4.8 Rose Limited operates a small chain of retail shops that sell high-quality teas and coffees. Approximately half of sales are on credit. Abbreviated and unaudited financial statements are given below:

Rose Limited

Income statement for the year ended 31 March 2006

	£000
Revenue	12,080
Cost of sales	(6,282)
Gross profit	5,798
Labour costs	(2,658)
Depreciation	(625)
Other operating costs	(1,003)
Operating profit	1,512
Interest payable	(66)
Net profit before tax	1,446
Taxation	(434)
Net profit for the year	1,012

Balance sheet as at 31 March 2006

	£000
Non-current assets	2,728
Current assets	
Inventories	1,583
Receivables	996
Cash	26
	2,605
Total assets	5,333
Equity	
Share capital (50p shares, fully paid)	750
Share premium	250
Retained earnings	1,468
	2,468
Non-current liabilities	
Borrowings – Secured loan (2011)	300
Current liabilities	
Trade payables	1,118
Other payables	417
Tax	434
Borrowings – Overdraft	596
	2,565
Total equity and liabilities	5,333

Since the unaudited financial statements for Rose Limited were prepared, the following information has become available:

1 An additional £74,000 of depreciation should have been charged on fixtures and fittings.
2 Invoices for credit sales on 31 March 2006 amounting to £34,000 have not been included; cost of sales is not affected.
3 Allowances for receivables should be provided at a level of 2 per cent of receivables at the year end.
4 Inventories, which had been purchased for £2,000, have been damaged and are unsaleable. This is not reflected in the financial statements.
5 Fixtures and fittings to the value of £16,000 were delivered just before 31 March 2006, but these assets were not included in the financial statements and the purchase invoice had not been processed.
6 Wages for Saturday-only staff, amounting to £1,000, have not been paid for the final Saturday of the year. This is not reflected in the financial statements.
7 Tax is payable at 30 per cent of net profit after tax. Assume that it is payable shortly after the year end.

Required:

Prepare revised financial statements for Rose Limited for the year ended 31 March 2006, incorporating the information in 1 to 7 above. (Work to the nearest £1,000.)

Accounting for limited companies (2)

Introduction

This chapter continues our examination of the financial statements of limited companies. We begin by identifying the legal responsibilities of directors and then go on to discuss the main sources of accounting rules governing published financial statements. Although a detailed consideration of these accounting rules is beyond the scope of this book, the key rules that shape the form and content of the published financial statements are discussed. We also consider the efforts made to ensure that these rules are underpinned by a coherent framework of principles.

The increasing complexity of business and the added demands for information by financial report users have led to the publication of a number of additional financial reports. This chapter considers two of these, namely the segmental financial report and the operating and financial review. These reports aim to provide users with a more complete picture of financial performance and position.

Despite the proliferation of accounting rules and the increasing supply of financial information to users of financial reports, concerns have been expressed over the quality of some of those published reports. This chapter ends by considering some well-publicised accounting scandals and the problem of creative accounting.

Learning outcomes

When you have completed this chapter, you should be able to:

- Describe the responsibilities of directors and auditors concerning the annual financial statements provided to shareholders and others.

- Identify the main sources of regulation affecting the financial statements of limited companies.

- Discuss the framework of principles for accounting.

- Prepare an income statement, balance sheet and statement of changes in equity for a limited company in accordance with International Financial Reporting Standards.

- Explain the purpose of the segmental report and the operating and financial review and describe their main features.

- Discuss the threat posed by creative accounting to the quality of published financial statements.

 Remember to create your own personalised Study Plan

The directors' duty to account

With most large companies, it is not possible for all shareholders to be involved in the management of the company, nor do most of them wish to be involved. Instead, they appoint directors to act on their behalf. This separation of ownership from day-to-day control creates the need for directors to be accountable for their stewardship (management) of the company's assets. Thus, the law requires that directors:

- maintain appropriate accounting records;
- prepare annual financial statements and a directors' report, and make these available to all shareholders and to the public at large.

The financial statements are made available to the public by submitting a copy to the Companies Registry (Department of Trade and Industry), which allows anyone who wishes to do so to inspect them. In addition, listed companies are required to publish their financial statements on their website.

Activity 5.1

Why does the law require directors to account in this way and who benefits from these requirements?

We thought of the following benefits and beneficiaries:

- *To inform and protect shareholders.* If shareholders do not receive information about the performance and position of their investment, they will have problems in appraising their investment. Under these circumstances, they would probably be reluctant to invest and this, in turn, would affect the functioning of the private sector. Any society with a significant private sector needs to encourage equity investment.
- *To inform and protect suppliers of labour, goods, services and finance, particularly those supplying credit (loans) or goods and services on credit.* Individuals and organisations would be reluctant to engage in commercial relationships, such as supplying goods or lending money, where a company does not provide information about its financial health. The fact that a company has limited liability increases the risks involved in dealing with the company. An unwillingness to engage in commercial relationships with limited companies will, once again, affect the functioning of the private sector.
- *To inform and protect society more generally.* Some companies exercise enormous power and influence in society generally, particularly on a geographically local basis. For example, a particular company may be the dominant employer and purchaser of commercial goods and services in a particular town or city. Legislators have tended to take the view that society has the right to information about the company and its activities.

The need for accounting rules

If we accept the need for directors to prepare and publish financial statements, we must also accept the need for a framework of rules concerning how these statements are prepared and presented. Without rules, there is a much greater risk that unscrupulous directors will adopt policies and practices that portray an unrealistic view of financial health. There is also a much greater risk that the financial statements will not be comparable over time or with those of other companies. These risks are likely to undermine the integrity of financial statements in the eyes of users.

Users must, however, be realistic about what can be achieved through regulation. Problems of manipulation and of concealment can still occur even within a highly regulated environment and some examples of both will be considered later in the chapter. The scale of these problems, however, should be reduced. Problems of comparability can also still occur, as accounting is not a precise science. Judgements and estimates must be made when preparing financial statements, and these may hinder comparisons. Furthermore, no two companies are identical and the accounting policies adopted may vary between companies for valid reasons.

Sources of accounting rules

In recent years there has been a trend towards the internationalisation of business, which seems set to continue. This trend has led to calls for the international harmonisation of accounting rules to help both users and companies. Harmonisation should help investors and other users of financial statements by making it easier to compare the performance and position of different companies operating in different countries. It should help companies with international operations by reducing the time and cost of producing financial statements: different sets of financial statements would no longer have to be prepared to comply with the rules of different countries.

The International Accounting Standards Board (IASB) is an independent body which is at the forefront of the move towards harmonisation. The Board, which is based in the UK, is dedicated to developing a single set of high quality, global accounting rules that provide transparent and comparable information in financial statements.

 These rules, which are known as **International Accounting Standards** or **International Financial Reporting Standards**, deal with key issues such as:

- what information should be disclosed;
- how information should be presented;
- how assets should be valued;
- how profit should be measured.

The overriding requirement for financial statements prepared according to IASB standards is to provide a fair representation of the company's financial position, financial performance and cash flows. There is a presumption that this fair representation will be achieved where the financial statements are drawn up in accordance with the various IASB standards that have been issued.

The authority of the IASB was given a huge boost when the European Commission adopted a regulation requiring nearly all stock exchange listed companies of EU member states to prepare their financial statements according to IASB standards for accounting periods commencing on or after 1 January 2005. Although non-listed UK companies are not currently required to adopt IASB standards, they have the option to do so. Many informed observers believe, however, that IASB standards will soon become a requirement for all UK companies.

The EU regulation overrides any laws in force in member states that could either hinder or restrict compliance with IASB standards. The ultimate aim is to achieve a single framework of accounting rules for companies from all member states. The EU recognises that this will be achieved only if individual governments do not add to the requirements imposed by the various IASB standards. Thus, it seems that accounting rules developed within individual EU member countries will eventually disappear. For the time being, however, the EU accepts that the governments of member states may need to impose additional disclosures for some corporate governance matters and regulatory requirements. In the UK, company law requires disclosure relating to various corporate governance issues. There is, for example, a requirement to disclose details of directors' remuneration in the published financial statements, which goes beyond anything required by IASB standards. Furthermore, the Financial Services Authority (FSA), in its role as the UK (Stock Exchange) listing authority, imposes rules on Stock Exchange listed companies. These include the requirement to publish a condensed set of interim (half-year) financial statements in addition to the annual financial statements. (These statements are not required by the IASB, although there is a standard providing guidance on their content and structure.)

Figure 5.1 sets out the main sources of accounting rules for Stock Exchange listed companies discussed above. While company law and the FSA still play an important role, in the longer term IASB standards seem set to become the sole source of company accounting rules.

Figure 5.1 Sources of external accounting rules for a UK public limited company listed on the London Stock Exchange

International Financial Reporting Standards provide the basic framework of accounting rules for nearly all Stock Exchange listed companies. These rules are augmented by company law and by the Financial Services Authority (FSA) in its role as the UK listing authority.

Real World 5.1 provides a list of standards that have been issued, or adopted, by the IASB to give an idea of the range of topics that are covered.

Real World 5.1

International standards

The following is a list of the International Accounting Standards (IASs) or International Financial Reporting Standards (IFRSs) in issue as at 1 August 2006. (The latter term is used for standards issued from 2003 onwards.) Several standards have been issued and subsequently withdrawn, which explains the gaps in the numerical sequence. In addition, several have been revised and reissued.

IAS 1   Presentation of Financial Statements
IAS 2   Inventories
IAS 7   Cash Flow Statements
IAS 8   Accounting Policies, Changes in Accounting Estimates and Errors
IAS 10   Events after the Balance Sheet Date
IAS 11   Construction Contracts
IAS 12   Income Taxes
IAS 14   Segment Reporting
IAS 15   Information Reflecting the Effects of Changing Prices
IAS 16   Property, Plant and Equipment
IAS 17   Leases
IAS 18   Revenue
IAS 19   Employee Benefits
IAS 20   Accounting for Government Grants and Disclosure of Government Assistance
IAS 21   The Effects of Changes in Foreign Exchange Rates
IAS 23   Borrowing Costs
IAS 24   Related Party Transactions
IAS 26   Accounting and Reporting by Retirement Benefit Plans
IAS 27   Consolidated and Separate Financial Statements
IAS 28   Investments in Associates
IAS 29   Financial Reporting in Hyperinflationary Economies
IAS 30   Disclosures in the Financial Statements of Banks and Similar Financial
           Institutions
IAS 31   Interests in Joint Ventures
IAS 32   Financial Investments: Disclosure and Presentation
IAS 33   Earnings per Share
IAS 34   Interim Financial Reporting
IAS 35   Discontinuing Operations
IAS 36   Impairment of Assets
IAS 37   Provisions, Contingent Liabilities and Contingent Assets
IAS 38   Intangible Assets
IAS 39   Financial Instruments: Recognition and Measurement
IAS 40   Investment Property
IAS 41   Agriculture
IFRS 1   First-time Adoption of International Financial Reporting Standards
IFRS 2   Share-based Payments
IFRS 3   Business Combinations
IFRS 4   Insurance Contracts
IFRS 5   Non-current Assets Held for Sale and Discontinued Operations
IFRS 6   Exploration for and Evaluation of Mineral Resources

Source: Insights into IFRS, KPMG, Thomson, 2006.

The IASB has promised a period of stability over the short term, with no new major standards becoming effective until 2009. This should ease the transition to international standards and allow countries to amend their laws where necessary. The IASB, however, has an ambitious agenda and significant changes are likely to occur over the longer term.

Presenting the financial statements

Now that we have gained an impression of the sources of rules affecting limited companies, let us turn our attention to the main rules to be followed in the presentation of financial statements. We shall focus on the IASB rules and, in particular, those contained in IAS 1 *Presentation of Financial Statements*. This standard is very important as it sets out the structure and content of financial statements and the principles to be followed in preparing these statements.

According to IAS 1, the financial statements consist of:

- an income statement
- a balance sheet
- a statement of changes in equity
- a cash flow statement
- notes on accounting policies and other explanatory notes.

We shall discuss each of these below but, before doing so, we should be clear as to what is the main consideration when preparing these statements.

Fair representation

The overriding requirement is for the financial statements to provide a fair representation of the company's financial position, financial performance and cash flows. There is a presumption that this will be achieved where the financial statements are drawn up in accordance with the various IASB standards that have been issued. It is only in very rare circumstances that compliance with a standard would not result in a fair representation of the financial health of a company.

Activity 5.2

IAS 1 does not say that the overriding requirement is for the financial statements to show a 'correct' or an 'accurate' presentation of financial health. Why, in your opinion, does it not use those words? (*Hint*: Think of depreciation of non-current assets.)

Accounting can never really be said to be 'correct' or 'accurate' as these words imply that there is a precise value that any asset, claim, revenue or expense could have. This is simply not true in many, if not most, cases.

Depreciation provides a good example. The annual depreciation expense is based on judgements about the future concerning the expected useful life and residual value of an asset. If all relevant factors are taken into account and reasonable judgements are applied, it may be possible to achieve a fair representation of the amount of the cost or fair value of the asset that is consumed for a particular period. However, a precise figure for depreciation for a period cannot be achieved.

Income statement

Although the format of the income statement is not prescribed, IAS 1 sets out the *minimum* information to be presented on the face of income statement. These items include:

- revenue
- finance costs
- gains or losses on the sale of assets or settlement of liabilities arising from discontinued operations
- tax expense
- profit or loss.

The standard makes it clear, however, that further items should be shown on the face of the income statement where they are relevant to an understanding of performance. For example, if a business is badly affected by flooding, and inventories are destroyed as a result, the cost of the flood damage should be shown.

As a further aid to understanding, all material expenses must be separately disclosed. However, they need not be shown on the face of the income statement: they can appear in the notes to the financial statements. The sorts of material items that may require separate disclosure include:

- write-down of inventories to net realisable value
- write-down or disposal of property, plant and equipment
- disposal of investments
- restructuring costs
- discontinuing operations
- litigation settlements.

This is not an exhaustive list and, in practice, other material expenses may require separate disclosure.

The standard suggests two possible ways in which expenses can be presented on the face of the income statement. Expenses can be presented either according to their nature, such as depreciation, employee expenses and so on, or according to business functions, such administrative activities and distribution.

So far in this book, expenses have been broadly set out according to their nature. Example 5.1, however, shows how expenses may be presented according to business functions.

Example 5.1

Degas plc
Income statement for the year ended 31 May 2007

	£000
Revenue	690
Cost of sales	(330)
	360
Distribution costs	(102)
Administrative expenses	(115)
Other expenses	(14)
Operating profit	129
Finance costs	(20)
Profit before tax	109
Taxation	24
Profit for the period	85

The choice between the two ways of presenting expenses should depend on which the directors believe will provide the more relevant and reliable information. The second of these two ways, which is illustrated above, shows how much of the revenue generated was absorbed by particular functions and may provide a better impression of the efficiency of the business. However, it is not always easy to attribute costs to particular functional areas, particularly where facilities and other resources are being shared. If this second approach is adopted, additional information concerning the nature of the expenses, including depreciation charges and employee costs, must also be shown. This is because this kind of information can be useful in predicting future cash flows.

Balance sheet

Again, IAS 1 does not prescribe the format of this financial statement but does set out the *minimum* information that should be presented on the face of the balance sheet. This includes the following:

- property, plant and equipment
- investment property
- intangible assets
- financial assets (such as shares and loan notes of other companies held)
- inventories
- trade and other receivables
- cash and cash equivalents
- trade and other payables
- provisions
- financial liabilities (excluding payables and provisions shown above)
- tax liabilities
- issued share capital and reserves (equity).

Additional information should be also shown where it is relevant to an understanding of the financial position of the business.

The standard requires that normally a distinction be made on the balance sheet between current assets and non-current assets and between current liabilities and non-current liabilities. However, where a company considers that more reliable and relevant information will be presented by ordering the items according to their liquidity, it is permitted to do this.

The sub-classification of some of the items shown above may be necessary, either to comply with particular standards or because of their size or nature. For example, sub-classifications are required for certain assets such as property, plant and equipment and inventories as well as for provisions and reserves. In addition, details of share capital, such as the number of issued shares and their par value, must also be shown. However, to avoid cluttering up the balance sheet, this additional information can be shown in the notes.

Statement of changes in equity

→   The **statement of changes in equity** aims to help users to understand the changes in share capital and reserves that took place during the period. It reconciles the capital and reserves figures at the beginning of the period with those at the end of the period.

immediately preceding period) be provided. The comparative figures enable users to assess the current figure for a particular item against its counterpart for the previous period.

The standard provides support for three key accounting conventions when preparing the financial statements. These are:

- going concern
- accruals (except for the cash flow statement)
- consistency.

These conventions were covered in Chapters 2 and 3.

To improve the transparency of financial statements, the standard states that:

- offsetting liabilities against assets, or expenses against income, is not allowed. Thus it is not acceptable, for example, to offset a bank overdraft against a positive bank balance (where the company has both); and
- material items must be shown separately.

The framework of principles

In Chapters 2 and 3 we came across various accounting conventions such as prudence, historic cost and going concern. These conventions were developed as a practical response to particular problems that were confronted when preparing financial statements. They have stood the test of time and are still of value to preparers today. However, they do not provide, and were never designed to provide, a framework of principles to guide the development of financial statements. As we grapple with increasingly complex financial reporting problems, the need to have a sound understanding of *why* we account for things in a particular way becomes more pressing. Knowing *why* we account, rather than simply *how* we account, is vital if we are to improve the quality of financial statements.

In recent years, much effort has been expended in various countries, including the UK, to develop a clear **framework of principles** that will guide us in the development of accounting. Such a framework should provide clear answers to such fundamental questions as:

- Who are the main users of financial statements?
- What is the purpose of financial statements?
- What qualities should financial information possess?
- What are the main elements of financial statements?
- How should these elements be defined, recognised and measured?

If these questions can be answered, accounting rule makers, such as the IASB, will be in a stronger position to identify best practice and to develop more coherent rules. This should, in turn, increase the credibility of financial reports in the eyes of users. It may even help reduce the possible number of rules, because some issues may be resolved by reference to the application of general principles rather than by the generation of further rules.

The IASB framework

The quest for a framework of accounting principles began in earnest in the 1970s when the Financial Accounting Standards Board (FASB) in the US devoted a very large amount of time and resources to this endeavour. This resulted in a broad framework of principles, which other rule-making bodies, including the IASB, have drawn upon when developing their own frameworks.

The IASB has produced the *Framework for the Preparation and Presentation of Financial Statements*, which begins by discussing the main user groups and their needs. This is well-trodden territory and the various groups and needs identified are broadly in line with those set out in the sections on this topic in Chapter 1. The framework goes on to identify the objective of financial statements, which is

> to provide information about the financial position, performance and changes in financial position of an enterprise that is useful to a wide range of users in making economic decisions.

This reflects the mainstream view and is similar to the objective of financial statements that others have developed in recent years.

The IASB framework sets out the qualitative characteristics that make financial statements useful. The main characteristics identified are relevance, reliability, comparability and understandability, all of which were discussed in Chapter 1. The framework also identifies the main elements of financial statements. These are assets, liabilities, equity, income and expense; and a definition of each element is provided. The definitions adopted hold no surprises and are similar to those adopted by other rule-making bodies and to those discussed earlier, in Chapters 2 and 3.

The IASB framework identifies different valuation bases in use but does not indicate a preference for a particular valuation method. It simply notes that historic cost is the most widely used method of valuation (although fair values are now increasingly used in International Financial Reporting Standards). Finally, the framework discusses the type of capital base that a business should try to maintain. It includes a discussion of the two main types of capital base – financial capital and physical capital – but, again, expresses no preference as to which should be maintained. The IASB framework does not have the same legal status as an IASB standard. Nevertheless, it offers guidance for dealing with accounting issues, particularly where no relevant accounting standard exists.

Overall, the IASB framework has provoked little debate and the principles and definitions adopted appear to enjoy widespread acceptance. There has been some criticism, mainly from academics, that the framework is really a descriptive document and does not provide theoretical underpinning to the financial statements. There has also been some criticism of the definitions of the elements of the financial statements. However, these criticisms have not sparked any major controversies.

The auditors' role

 Shareholders are required to elect a qualified and independent person or, more usually, a firm to act as **auditors**. The auditors' main duty is to report whether, in their opinion, the financial statements do what they are supposed to do, namely to show a true and fair view of the financial performance, position and cash flows of the company by complying with the relevant accounting rules. To be able to form such an opinion, auditors must scrutinise both the annual financial statements and the evidence upon which they are based. The auditors' opinion must be included with the financial statements sent to the shareholders and to the Registrar of Companies.

The relationship between the shareholders, the directors and the auditors is illustrated in Figure 5.2. This shows that the shareholders elect the directors to act on their behalf, in the day-to-day running of the company. The directors are then required to

Figure 5.2   The relationship between the shareholders, the directors and the auditors

The directors are appointed by the shareholders to manage the company on the shareholders' behalf. The directors are required to report each year to the shareholders, principally by means of financial statements, on the company's performance, position and cash flows. To give greater confidence in the statements, the shareholders also appoint auditors to investigate the reports and to express an opinion on their reliability.

'account' to the shareholders on the performance, position and cash flows of the company, on an annual basis. The shareholders also elect auditors, whose role it is to give the shareholders an independent view of the truth and fairness of the financial statements prepared by the directors.

Directors' report

In addition to preparing the financial statements, the law requires the directors to prepare an annual report to shareholders and other interested parties. This report contains information of both a financial and a non-financial nature and goes beyond that which is contained in the financial statements. The information disclosed covers a variety of topics, including details of share ownership, details of directors and their financial interests in the company, employment policies, and charitable and political donations. The auditors do not carry out an audit of the **directors' report**. However, they will check to see that the information in the report is consistent with that contained in the audited financial statements.

Segmental financial reports

Most large businesses are engaged in a variety of activities, with each activity having its own levels of risk, growth and profitability. Information relating to each type of business activity, however, is normally aggregated in the financial statements to provide an overall picture of financial performance and position. This aggregation (that is, adding together) of information makes it difficult to undertake comparisons over time or between businesses. Some idea of the range and scale of the various business activities must be gained for a proper assessment of financial health.

Where a business operates in different geographical markets, the same arguments apply. Markets in different countries or regions may have different levels of risk, profitability and growth which will be obscured by aggregation. The impact on a business of changes in such factors as the political climate, inflation or exchange rates relating to a particular country, or geographical region, cannot be assessed unless the degree of exposure to the country, or region, is known.

To undertake any meaningful analysis of financial performance and position, it is usually necessary to disaggregate the information contained within the financial statements. By breaking down the financial information according to business activities and/or geographical markets, we can evaluate the relative risks and profitability of each segment and make useful comparisons with other businesses or other business segments. We can also see the trend of performance for each segment over time and so determine more accurately the likely growth prospects for the business as a whole. We should also be able to assess more easily the impact on the overall business, of changes in market conditions relating to particular activities.

Disclosure of information relating to the performance of each segment may also help to improve the efficiency of the business by keeping managers on their toes. Business segments that are performing poorly will be revealed and this should put pressure on managers to take corrective action. In addition, where a business segment has been sold, the shareholders will be better placed to assess the wisdom of the managers' decision.

Segmental reporting rules

An IASB standard (IAS 14 *Segment Reporting*) requires listed companies to disclose segmental information according to each business segment *and* to each geographical region. Both forms of segmentation are regarded as important to users. A business segment, for the purposes of the standard, is a part of the business that can be separately identified and which provides an individual product or service, or a group of related products or services. A geographical segment is a part of the business that can be separately identified and which provides products or services within a particular economic environment. The environment may comprise a region within a country, a country or a group of countries. One problem that must be confronted when identifying geographical segments is whether the business should be segmented according to where the *operations* are located or where the *markets* are located. The relevant standard allows either approach to be used but states that the choice should be based on the way in which the business is organised and structured.

To be reported separately, a business or geographical segment must be of significant size. This means that it must account for 10 per cent or more of the business's revenue, or operating results or total revenue. A segment that does not meet this size threshold may be combined with other segments, shown as an allocated item, or separately reported despite its size.

For reporting purposes, it is necessary to establish whether it is

- the products or services offered; or
- the geographical regions in which the company operates

that has the bigger impact on the risks and returns of the company.

It is for the directors to decide which has the bigger impact and is, therefore, the primary segment. The way in which a business is organised and structured should provide a useful indicator.

Identifying which is the primary and which the secondary segments is important because the disclosure requirements are greater for the former.

Segmental disclosure

The following are the main items of information that should be disclosed for the primary segments:

- revenue, distinguishing between revenue from external customers and revenue from other segments of the business;
- total assets;
- capital expenditure for the period;
- depreciation, impairments and other non-cash items;
- segment operating result (that is, segment revenue less segment operating expenses); and
- total liabilities.

For secondary segments, only the first three items identified above need be disclosed.

Example 5.3 provides an illustrative **segmental financial report** for a business where the business segments are the primary segments. Following the example, we shall discuss some of the key points that are raised.

Example 5.3

Goya plc
Segmental report for the year ended 30 June 2007

	Publishing	Film making	Eliminations	Consolidation (Total)
	£m	£m	£m	£m
Revenue				
External sales	150	200		
Inter-segment sales	20	10	(30)	
Total revenue	170	210	(30)	350
Result				
Segment result	15	19	(2)	32
Unallocated expenses				14
Operating profit				18
Interest expense				(6)
Net profit before tax				12
Corporation tax				(3)
Profit for the year				9
Other information				
Segment assets	74	86		160
Unallocated assets				32
Consolidated total assets				192
Segment liabilities	24	21		45
Unallocated liabilities				30
Consolidated total liabilities				75
Capital expenditure	10	8		
Depreciation	15	21		

We can see that information relating to each segment is shown as well as information relating to the business as a whole. Revenue from both external and inter-segment sales for each segment appear separately; however, only the combined external sales revenue for the segments appear in the far right-hand column. This is because the revenue from inter-segment sales will cancel one another out when calculating the revenue for the business as a whole. Similarly, the combined operating profit of each segment *less* the inter-segment profit will appear as the operating profit for the business as a whole.

Unallocated expenses appearing in the above report are those which are not attributable to a particular segment or which cannot be allocated to a segment on any reasonable basis. Note that these expenses have not been apportioned between the two segments but have been deducted from the results of the business as a whole.

Activity 5.4

What kinds of items do you think may appear as unallocated expenses?

These items may include:

- head office expenses
- research and development costs
- marketing expenses
- finance charges.

You may have thought of others.

Unallocated assets and liabilities are those which are not attributable to a particular segment or which cannot be allocated to a particular segment on any reasonable basis. Head office buildings may provide an example of such an unallocated asset and loan capital may provide an example of an unallocated liability.

A similar layout to the report shown above can be used to show geographical segments, where they are regarded as the primary segments.

Problems of segmental reporting

There are various problems associated with preparing segmental reports, not least of which is the problem of identifying a segment. The relevant standard mentions some of the factors that should be taken into account when identifying segments; however, a fair amount of judgement by the directors will often be required. Although this may be the only sensible course of action, it does mean that comparisons between businesses may still be difficult because of different judgements being applied within different companies.

Many segments do not operate in a completely independent manner and there may be a significant amount of sales between segments. If this is the case, the **transfer price** of the goods or services between segments can have a substantial impact on the reported profits of each segment. (The transfer price is the price at which sales are made between different segments of the company.) Indeed, it may be possible to manipulate profit figures for each segment through the use of particular transfer pricing policies.

For this reason, the International Financial Reporting Standard requires that the basis for inter-segment transfers must be disclosed.

Finally, there may be problems where expenses incurred relate to more than one business segment. The way in which these costs are treated may vary between businesses and so may hinder comparisons.

Self-assessment question 5.1

Segmental information relating to J Baxter plc, which has operations in three different countries, for the year to 30 April 2007 is shown below.

	UK £m	France £m	Italy £m	Eliminations £m	Consolidation £m
Revenue					
External sales	230	180	360		
Inter-segment sales	40	20	30	(90)	
Total revenue	270	200	390	(90)	770
Result					
Segment result	34	30	8	(6)	66
Unallocated expenses					18
Operating profit					48
Interest expense					(16)
Corporation tax					(6)
Profit for the year					26
Other information					
Segment assets	129	150	116		395
Unallocated assets					36
Consolidated total assets					431
Segment liabilities	35	28	22		85
Unallocated liabilities					40
Consolidated total liabilities					125
Capital expenditure	20	15	35		
Depreciation	28	35	11		

Required:
Analyse the performance of each of the business segments for the year and comment on your results.

The answer to this question can be found at the back of the book on page 697.

Narrative reporting

A business, particularly a large business, may have extremely complex organisational arrangements, financing methods and operating characteristics. To portray financial performance and position faithfully, the published financial statements must reflect this complexity. As a result, these statements may well be difficult to understand and to interpret. To help users gain a clearer picture, a narrative report may be produced to accompany the financial statements. This report will provide a commentary on the business and its financial results.

The UK Accounting Standards Board (ASB) has issued a reporting statement (RS 1), mainly aimed at listed companies, for an **operating and financial review (OFR)**. The OFR is a narrative report which aims to provide a balanced and comprehensive examination of:

- the performance of the business during the year and its position at the end of the year;
- the key trends and factors affecting performance and position during the year as well as those which are likely to affect future performance and position.

The OFR is meant to reflect the directors' views of the business and should complement as well as supplement the financial statements.

Activity 5.5

What are the main characteristics concerning quality that information contained within the OFR should possess? (*Hint*: Think back to Chapter 1.)

To be useful, the information should contain the characteristics for accounting information in general, which we identified in Chapter 1. Thus the information should be relevant, understandable, reliable and comparable. The fact that we are dealing with narrative information does not alter the need for these characteristics to be present.

A further requirement of the OFR is comprehensiveness. This means that it should include all significant information that will help assess business performance. Thus, information that places the business in an unfavourable light should not be omitted.

The OFR framework

The framework for an OFR, rests on the disclosure of four key elements of a business:

1 the nature of the business
2 business performance
3 resources, risks and relationships
4 financial position.

Each of these elements is discussed below.

1 The nature of the business

This element will include a description of the environment within which the business operates. It is a potentially wide area and may include a commentary on products sold, business processes, business structure and competitive position. A commentary on the legal, economic and social environment may also be included.

The objectives of the business and the strategy adopted to achieve those objectives should also be discussed. **Real World 5.2** reveals how one well-known business describes in its OFR the strategy that has been adopted.

Real World 5.2

Tesco's strategy

The 2006 annual report of Tesco plc includes a 17-page OFR, which provides a lot of information about its business and its financial results. The strategy of the business is described in the OFR as follows:

> Tesco has a well-established and consistent strategy for growth, which is strengthening the core business and driving our expansion into new markets. This four-part strategy was laid down in 1997 and it has been the foundation of Tesco's success in recent years. Its objectives are:
>
> - to grow the core business
> - to become a successful international retailer
> - to be as strong in non-food as in food, and
> - to develop retailing services – such as Tesco Personal Finance, Telecoms and tesco.com

Source: Tesco plc Annual Report 2006, p. 1.

Key performance indicators (KPIs) used by the directors to assess whether the strategy is effective should be included in the OFR. These KPIs quantify the factors that are critical to the success of the business and are often a mixture of financial and non-financial measures. Key financial measures may relate to sales revenue growth, profit, total shareholder return, dividends and so on. Key non-financial measures may relate to market share, employee satisfaction, product quality, supplier satisfaction and so on.

2 Business performance

This element will examine the development and performance of the business for both the year under review and the future. It should include any factors affecting performance, such as changes in market conditions or the launch of new products or services. It should also examine trends and factors that may affect future prospects. Real World 5.3 provides an extract from Tesco's OFR, which describes plans that have significant potential to affect future prospects.

Real World 5.3

Foreign parts

In line with the strategy mentioned above, Tesco plc has become increasingly international in its focus. Future growth in international activities is planned to be significant, as stated in the following extract from Tesco's 2006 OFR:

> At the end of February [2006], our international operations were trading from 814 stores, including 341 hypermarkets, with a total of 32.8m sq.ft. of selling space. Almost 56% of Group sales area is now in International. . . . We plan to open 396 new stores in the current year [2006/07], adding 6.6m sq.ft. of selling area.

Source: Tesco plc Annual Report 2006, p. 8.

3 Resources, risks and relationships

The OFR should describe the resources of the business and how they are managed. The resources identified should include any items not reflected in the balance sheet. These items will, of course, vary between businesses but may include corporate reputation, patents, trademarks, brand names, market position and the quality of employees.

The OFR should also include a description of the main risks and uncertainties facing the business and the ways in which the directors deal with them. **Real World 5.4** reveals how Tesco plc comments on one important risk in its OFR.

Real World 5.4

Risky business

In its 2006 OFR, Tesco plc identifies more than twenty forms of risk that the business must consider. These cover a wide range and include competition, financial, environmental, product safety, terrorism and currency risks. The risk posed by competitors is described as follows:

> The retail industry is highly competitive. The Group competes with a wide variety of retailers of varying sizes, and faces increased competition from UK retailers, as well as international operators, here and overseas. Failure to compete with competitors on areas including price, product range, quality and service could have an adverse effect on the Group's financial results.
>
> We aim to have a broad appeal in price, range and store format in a way that allows us to compete in different markets. We track performance against a range of measures that customers tell us are critical to their shopping trip experience. We constantly monitor customer perceptions of ourselves and our competitors to ensure that we can respond quickly if we need to.

Source: Tesco plc Annual Report 2006, p. 14.

This element also requires a commentary on key relationships with stakeholders, apart from shareholders, that may affect the performance of the business and its value. The stakeholders may include customers, suppliers, employees, contractors and lenders as well as other businesses with which the business has strategic alliances. **Real World 5.5** reveals how, in its 2006 OFR, Tesco plc describes its relationship with its customers.

Real World 5.5

Every little helps

> Our customers have told us what they want from an 'every little helps' shopping trip and this year 12,000 of them attended our Customer Question Times to offer ideas on how we can improve. Clubcard also helps us to understand what our customers want, whilst allowing us to thank them for shopping with us – this year we gave away £320m in Clubcard vouchers.
>
> We don't always get it right but we try to make their shopping trip as easy as possible, reduce prices where we can to help them spend less and give them the convenience of shopping where and when they want – in small stores, large stores or on-line.

Source: Tesco plc Annual Report 2006, p. 14.

4 Financial position

This final element of the OFR framework should describe events that have influenced the financial position of the business during the year and those that are likely to affect the business in the future. It should also include a discussion of the capital structure, cash flows and liquidity of the company. **Real World 5.6** reveals how Tesco plc comments on its cash flows.

Real World 5.6

Tesco's cash

Tesco's 2006 OFR contains the following comment concerning its cash flows:

> The Group generated net cash of £165m during the year, benefiting from strong cash flow from operating activities of £3.4bn and the net proceeds of £346m from our property joint venture with Concensus. Within this, £239m of cash was released from working capital, which was £199m lower than last year. This was mainly due to a smaller rise in trade creditors [payables] than last year (last year's increase was exceptionally large and the change in International year end reduced trade creditors), higher non-food stocks (linked to global sourcing) and increased debtors (resulting from advance rent on new leasehold stores in Korea).

Source: Tesco plc Annual Report 2006, p. 4.

This final element should also comment on the treasury policy of the business. Treasury policy is concerned with such matters as managing cash, obtaining finance and managing relationships with financial institutions. Possible areas for discussion may include major financing transactions and the effects of interest charges or interest rate changes on current or future results. **Real World 5.7** shows how, in its 2006 OFR, Tesco plc comments on major new funding arrangements during the year and its debt position at the end of the year.

Real World 5.7

Funding Tesco

Tesco plc finances its operations by a combination of retained profits, share issues, leases and borrowing of different forms. The 2006 OFR includes the following:

> New funding of £529m was arranged during the year, including a net £484m from property joint ventures and £45m from medium-term notes (MTNs). We renewed our €10bn MTN programme on 28 February 2006. At the year end, net debt was £4.5bn (last year £3.9bn) and the average debt maturity was six years (last year eight years).

Source: Tesco plc Annual Report 2006, p. 16.

The business review and RS 1

Recent legislation requires all companies (except small companies) to include a business review as part of the directors' report. This is a narrative report, which for listed companies in particular, covers much of the ground discussed above. As the form that a business review should take is not clearly specified, directors of larger companies are likely to look to RS 1 for guidance.

Summary financial statements

We saw earlier that the directors must provide each shareholder with a copy of the annual financial statements. For large companies, these financial statements can be extremely detailed and complicated: along with the accompanying notes they may extend over many pages. It is possible, however, for the directors to provide a summarised version of the full financial statements as an alternative. The main advantages of providing summarised financial statements are that:

- many shareholders do not wish to receive the full version because they may not have the time, interest or skill necessary to be able to gain much from it;
- directors could improve their communication with their shareholders by providing something closer to the needs of many shareholders;
- reproducing and posting copies of the full version is expensive and a waste of resources where particular shareholders do not wish to receive it.

→ Many large companies send all of their private shareholders a copy of the **summary financial statements**, with a clear message that the full versions are available on request. The full version is, however, required for filing with the Registrar of Companies.

Creative accounting

Despite the proliferation of accounting rules and the independent checks that are imposed, concerns over the quality of published financial statements surface from time to time. Some directors apply particular accounting policies or structure particular transactions in such a way as to portray a picture of financial health that is in line with what they would like users to see rather than what is a true and fair view of financial
→ position and performance. This practice is referred to as **creative accounting** and it poses a major problem for accounting rule makers and for society generally.

Activity 5.6

Why might the directors of a company engage in creative accounting?

There are many reasons, and these include:

- to get around restrictions (for example, to report sufficient profit to pay a dividend);
- to avoid government action (for example, the taxation of excessive profits);
- to hide poor management decisions;
- to achieve sales revenue or profit targets, thereby ensuring that performance bonuses are paid to the directors;
- to attract new share capital or loan capital by showing a healthy financial position;
- to satisfy the demands of major investors concerning levels of return.

Creative accounting methods

The ways in which unscrupulous directors can manipulate the financial statements are many and varied. However, they usually involve adopting unorthodox practices for reporting key elements of the financial statements such as revenue, expenses, assets and liabilities. They may also involve the use of complicated or obscure transactions in an attempt to hide the underlying economic reality. The manipulation carried out may be designed to bend the rules or may be designed to break the rules. Below we consider some of the more important ways in which rules may be bent or broken.

Overstating revenue

Some creative accounting methods are designed to overstate the revenue for a period. These methods often involve the early recognition of sales revenue or the reporting of sales transactions that have no real substance. **Real World 5.8** provides examples of both types of revenue manipulation.

Real World 5.8

Overstating revenue

Hollow swaps: telecoms companies sell useless fibre optic capacity to each other in order to generate revenues on their income statements. Example: Global Crossing.

Channel stuffing: a company floods the market with more products than its distributors can sell, artificially boosting its sales. SSL, the condom maker, shifted £60 million in excess inventories on to trade customers. Also known as 'trade loading'.

Round tripping: also known as 'in-and-out trading'. Used to notorious effect by Enron. Two or more traders buy and sell energy among themselves for the same price and at the same time. Inflates trading volumes and makes participants appear to be doing more business than they really are.

Pre-dispatching: goods such as carpets are marked as 'sold' as soon as an order is placed. . . . This inflates sales and profits.

Note that some of the techniques used, such as round tripping, may inflate the sales revenue for a period but will not inflate reported profits. Nevertheless, this may still benefit the business. Sales revenue growth has become an important yardstick of performance for some investors and can affect the value they place on the business.

Source: 'Dirty laundry: how companies fudge the numbers', *The Times*, Business Section, 22 September 2002.

The manipulation of revenue has been at the heart of many of the accounting scandals recently exposed. Given its critical role in the measurement of performance, this is, perhaps, not surprising. **Real World 5.9** provides an example of the impact of the early recognition of revenue on the financial results of one well-known business.

Real World 5.9

Not to be copied

One case of overstating revenue is alleged to have been carried out by the Xerox Corporation, a large US company and a leading player in the photocopying business. It is alleged that the company brought forward revenues in order to improve reported profits as its fortunes declined in the late 1990s. These revenues related to copier equipment sales, particularly in Latin America. To correct for the overstatement of revenues, Xerox had to restate its equipment sales revenue figures for a five-year period. The result was a reversal in reported revenues of a staggering $6.4bn, although $5.1bn was reallocated to other revenues as a result. This restatement was one of the largest in US corporate history.

In June 2002 the company paid a fine of $10m but denied any wrongdoing.

Sources: Based on information in 'Can't tell the scandals without a scorecard', *Wall Street Journal Europe*, October 2003, p. A5; and 'Xerox acts to put itself on a firmer footing', FT.com, 28 June 2002.

Massaging expenses

Some creative accounting methods focus on the manipulation of expenses. Those expenses that rely on directors' estimates of the future or their choice of accounting policy are particularly vulnerable to manipulation.

Activity 5.7

Can you identify the kind of expenses where the directors make estimates or choices in the ways described?

These include certain expenses that we discussed in Chapter 3, such as:

● depreciation of property, plant and equipment
● amortisation of intangible assets, such as goodwill
● inventories costing methods
● allowances for receivables.

By changing estimates about the future (for example, the useful life or residual value of an asset), or by changing accounting policies (for example, switching from FIFO to AVCO), it may be possible to derive an expense figure, and consequently a profit figure, that suits the directors.

The incorrect capitalisation of expenses may also be used as a means of manipulation. This involves treating expenses as if they were amounts incurred to acquire or develop non-current assets, rather than amounts consumed during the period. Businesses that build their own assets are often best placed to undertake this form of malpractice.

Activity 5.8

What would be the effect on the profits and total assets of a business of incorrectly capitalising expenses?

Both would be artificially inflated. Reported profits would increase because expenses would be reduced. Total assets would be increased because the expenses would be incorrectly treated as non-current assets.

Real World 5.10 provides an example of one business that capitalised expenses on a huge scale.

Real World 5.10

Sorry – wrong numbers

One particularly notorious case of capitalising expenses is alleged to have occurred in the financial statements of WorldCom (now renamed MCI). This company, which is a large US telecommunications business, is alleged to have overstated profits by treating certain operating expenses, such as basic network maintenance, as capital expenditure. This happened over a fifteen-month period during 2001 and 2002. To correct for this overstatement, profits had to be reduced by a massive $3.8bn.

Source: Based on two personal views on WorldCom posted on the FT.com site, 27 June 2002.

Concealing 'bad news'

Some creative accounting methods focus on the concealment of losses or liabilities. The financial statements can look much healthier if these can somehow be eliminated. One way of doing this is to create a 'separate' entity that will take over the losses or liabilities.

Real World 5.11 describes how one large business concealed losses and liabilities.

Real World 5.11

For a very special purpose

Perhaps the most well-known case of concealment of losses and liabilities concerned the Enron Corporation. This was a large US energy business that used 'special purpose entities' (SPEs) as a means of concealment. SPEs were used by Enron to rid itself of problem assets that were falling in value, such as its broadband operations. In addition, liabilities were transferred to these entities to help Enron's balance sheet look healthier. The company had to keep its gearing ratios (the relationship between borrowing and equity) within particular limits to satisfy credit-rating agencies and SPEs were used to achieve this. The SPEs used for concealment purposes were not independent of the company and should have been consolidated in the balance sheet of Enron, along with their losses and liabilities.

When these, and other accounting irregularities, were discovered in 2001, there was a restatement of Enron's financial performance and position to reflect the consolidation of the SPEs, which had previously been omitted. As a result of this restatement, the company recognised $591m in losses over the preceding four years and an additional $628m worth of liabilities at the end of 2000.

The company collapsed at the end of 2001.

Source: 'The rise and fall of Enron', C. W. Thomas, *Journal of Accountancy*, vol. 194, no. 3, 2002. This article represents the opinions of the author, which are not necessarily those of the Texas Society of Certified Public Accountants.

Overstating assets

Finally, creative accounting may involve the overstatement of asset values. This may involve revaluing the assets using figures that are higher than their fair market values. It may also involve the capitalising of costs that should have been written off as expenses, as described earlier.

Real World 5.12 describes how one large business went much further by reporting assets that simply did not exist.

Real World 5.12

When things go sour

Parmalat, a large Italian dairy-and-food business, announced in December 2003 that a bank account held in the Cayman Islands with the Bank of America did not have, as had been previously reported, a balance of €3.95bn. The fake balance turned out to be part of a web of deception: it had simply been 'invented' in order to help offset more than $16 billion

Real World 5.12 continued

of outstanding borrowings. According to Italian prosecutors, the business had borrowed heavily on the strength of fictitious sales revenues.

A Cayman Islands subsidiary, which was supposed to hold the fake bank balance, engaged in fictitious trading in an attempt to conceal the true nature of the deception. This included the supply of 300,000 tones of milk powder from a fake Singapore-based business to a Cuban business through the subsidiary.

Source: 'How it all went so sour', P. Gumbel, Time Europe Magazine, 21 November 2004.

Checking for creative accounting

When examining the financial statements of a business, a number of checks may be carried out on the financial statements to help gain a feel for their reliability. These can include checks to see whether:

- the reported profits are significantly higher than the operating cash flows for the period, which may suggest that profits have been overstated;
- the corporation tax charge is low in relation to reported profits, which may suggest, again, that profits are overstated, although there may be other, more innocent explanations;
- the valuation methods used for assets held are based on historic cost or fair values, and if the latter approach has been used why and how the fair values were determined;
- there have been any changes in accounting policies over the period, particularly in key areas such as revenue recognition, inventories valuation and depreciation;
- the accounting policies adopted are in line with those adopted by the rest of the industry;
- the auditors' report gives a 'clean bill of health' to the financial statements; and
- the 'small print', that is the notes to the financial statements, is not being used to hide significant events or changes.

Real World 5.13 describes the emphasis that one analyst places on this particular check.

Real World 5.13

Taking note   **FT**

Alistair Hodgson, investment manager at private client stockbroker Pilling and Co says:

> I almost look at the notes more than I look at the main figures at first. The notes tend to hold the key to anything that looks strange. I look to pick out things that the auditor has told the company to declare – the kind of thing they might not want to declare, but they have got to do so in order to make the accounts honest.

Source: 'It pays to read between the lines', FT.com 17 September 2005.

Some checks may be carried out to provide confirmation of positive financial health. These may include checks to see whether:

- the business is paying increased dividends;
- the directors are buying shares in the business.

Although the various checks described are useful, they cannot be used to guarantee the reliability of the financial statements. Some creative accounting practices may be very deeply seated and may go undetected for years.

Creative accounting and economic growth

A few years ago there was a wave of creative accounting scandals, particularly in the US but also in Europe; however, it seems that this wave has now subsided. The quality of financial statements is improving and, it is to be hoped, trust among investors and others is being restored. As a result of the actions taken by various regulatory bodies and by accounting rule makers, creative accounting has become a more risky and difficult process for those who attempt it. However, it will never disappear completely and a further wave of creative accounting scandals may occur in the future.

The recent wave coincided with a period of strong economic growth, and during good economic times, investors and auditors become less vigilant. Thus, the opportunity to manipulate the figures becomes easier. We must not, therefore, become too complacent. Things may change again when we next experience a period of strong growth.

Summary

The main points of this chapter may be summarised as follows.

Directors' duty

- The directors have a duty to:
  - maintain appropriate accounting records;
  - prepare and publish financial statements and a directors' report.

The need for accounting rules

- Accounting rules are necessary to:
  - avoid unacceptable accounting practices;
  - improve the comparability of financial statements.

Accounting rules

- The International Accounting Standards Board (IASB) has become an important source of rules.
- Company law and the London Stock Exchange are also sources of rules for UK companies.

Presenting financial statements

- IAS 1 sets out the structure and content of financial statements.
- It identifies five financial statements: the income statement, balance sheet, statement of changes in equity, cash flow statement and explanatory notes.

- The overriding consideration is to provide a fair representation of the financial health of a company and this will normally be achieved by adherence to relevant IASB standards.
- IAS 1 identifies information to be shown in the various financial statements.
- It also identifies some of the principles to be followed in preparing the statements.

Framework of principles

- This helps to underpin accounting rules.
- The IASB framework identifies and discusses: the users of financial statements, the objective of financial statements, the qualitative characteristics of financial statements, the elements of financial statements, different valuation bases, and different capital maintenance bases.
- The IASB framework draws on earlier work by other rule-making bodies.

Other statutory reports

- The auditors' report provides an opinion by an independent auditor concerning whether the financial statements provide a true and fair view of the financial health of a business.
- The directors' report contains information of a financial and a non-financial nature, which goes beyond that contained in the financial statements.

Additional financial reports

- Segmental reports disaggregate information on the financial statements to help achieve a better understanding of financial health.
- Companies can be segmented according to products or services and according to geographical operations.
- An IASB standard requires certain information relating to each segment to be shown.
- Identifying a segment and allocating costs between segments can raise problems.
- An operating and financial review (OFR) discusses the nature and objectives of the business, the development and performance of the business both in the period and in the future, the resources, risks and key relationships of the business and the financial position of the business both during the period and in the future.
- In the UK, the ASB has issued a reporting standard on the preparation of an OFR.
- Summary financial statements are available to investors who do not require the full set of financial statements.

Creative accounting

- Despite the accounting rules in place there have been examples of creative accounting by directors.
- This involves using accounting practices to show what the directors would like users to see rather than what is a fair representation of reality.
- There are various checks that can be carried out to the financial statements to see whether creative accounting practices may have been used.

MyAccountingLab *Now check your progress in your personal Study Plan*

Key terms

International Accounting Standards
  p. 161
International Financial Reporting
Standards   p. 161
statement of changes in equity
  p. 166
framework of principles   p. 169
auditor   p. 170

directors' report   p. 171
segmental financial report   p. 173
transfer price   p. 174
operating and financial review (OFR)
  p. 176
summary financial statements   p. 180
creative accounting   p. 180

Further reading

If you would like to explore the topics covered in this chapter in more depth, we recommend the following books:

Corporate Financial Accounting and Reporting, *Sutton T.*, 2nd edn, Financial Times Prentice Hall, 2004, chapters 6 and 7.

Financial Accounting and Reporting, *Elliott B. and Elliott J.*, 11th edn, Financial Times Prentice Hall, 2006, chapters 5–8.

Insights into IFRS, *KPMG*, 3rd edn, Thomson, 2006, sections 3.1, 4.1 and 5.2.

Operating and Financial Review, *Accounting Standards Board*, ASB, May 2005.

Review questions

Answers to these questions can be found at the back of the book on pages 776–7.

5.1 'Searching for an agreed framework of principles for accounting rules is likely to be a journey without an ending'. Discuss.

5.2 The size of annual financial reports published by limited companies has increased steadily over the years. Can you think of any reasons, apart from the increasing volume of accounting regulation, why this has occurred?

5.3 What problems does a user of segmental financial statements face when seeking to make comparisons between businesses?

5.4 'An OFR should not be prepared by accountants but should be prepared by the board of directors.' Why should this be the case?

Exercises

Exercises 5.6 to 5.8 are more advanced than 5.1 to 5.5. Those with coloured numbers have answers at the back of the book, starting on page 717.

If you wish to try more exercises, visit the students' side of the Companion Website.

5.1 It has been suggested that too much information might be as bad as too little information for users of annual reports. Explain.

5.2 What problems are likely to be encountered when preparing summary financial statements for shareholders?

5.3 The following information was extracted from the financial statements of I. Ching (Booksellers) plc for the year to 31 December 2006:

	£m
Interest payable	40
Cost of sales	460
Distribution costs	110
Revenue	943
Administration expenses	212
Other expenses	25

Note: Corporation tax is calculated at 25% of the profit available to shareholders.

Required:
Prepare an income statement for the year ended 31 December 2006 that is set out in accordance with the requirements of IAS 1 *Presentation of Financial Statements*.

5.4 Manet plc had the following share capital and reserves as at 30 June 2006:

	£m
Share capital (£0.25 ordinary shares)	250
Share premium account	50
Revaluation reserve	120
Currency translation reserve	15
Retained earnings	380
Total equity	815

During the year to 30 June 2007, the company revalued its freehold land upwards by £30m and made a loss on foreign exchange translation of £5m. The company made a profit after tax from operations of £160m during the year and the dividend payout was 50% of the profit available to shareholders.

Required:

Prepare a statement of changes in equity in accordance with the requirements of IAS 1 *Presentation of Financial Statements*.

5.5 Professor Myddleton argues that accounting standards should be limited to disclosure requirements and should not impose rules on companies as to how to measure particular items in the financial statements. He states:

> The volume of accounting instructions is already high. If things go on like this, where will we be in 20 or 30 years time? On balance I conclude we would be better off without any standards on accounting measurement. There could still be some disclosure requirements for listed companies, though probably less than now.

Do you agree with this idea? Discuss. (*Note*: This issue has not been directly covered in the chapter, but you should be able to use your knowledge to try to come up with some points on both sides of the argument.)

5.6 The following is the segment reports of Tora plc, which manufactures and sells three main classes of product, for the year ended 31 December 2006.

	Paper £m	Plastic £m	Metal £m	Eliminations £m	Consolidation £m
Revenue					
External sales	420	280	140		
Inter-segment sales	20	10	15	(45)	
Total revenue	440	290	155	(45)	840
Result					
Segment result	80	65	45	(6)	184
Unallocated expenses					38
					146
Interest expense					(14)
Corporation tax					(26)
Profit for the year					106
Other information					
Segment assets	350	650	226		1,226
Unallocated assets					146
Consolidated total assets					1,372
Segment liabilities	55	150	42		247
Unallocated liabilities					60
Consolidated total liabilities					307
Capital expenditure	10	–	15		25
Depreciation	72	130	70		272

Required:

Analyse the performance of each of the business segments for the year and comment on your results.

5.7 Obtain a copy of an operating and financial review of two companies within the same industry. Compare the usefulness of each. In answering this question you should consider the extent to which the OFRs incorporate the recommendations made by the Accounting Standards Board.

5.8 The following information has been extracted from the segmental report for 2006 of Carpetright plc, a leading carpet retailer.

Segmental analysis

The Group's primary reporting segment is geographic, as this is the basis on which the Group is organised and managed. The Group does not report a secondary segment on the basis of business operations because business operations throughout the Group are the same. The geographical sectors are: United Kingdom & Republic of Ireland ('UK & RoI'), and Poland, Belgium and The Netherlands ('Rest of Europe'). Central costs are incurred principally in the UK and are immaterial. As such these costs are included within the UK & RoI segment. Segment revenue, expense, result, assets and liabilities include transfers between geographical segments. Such transfers are priced at arm's length and are eliminated on consolidation.

Analysis by geography:

	2006			2005		
	UK & RoI	Rest of Europe	Group	UK & RoI	Rest of Europe	Group
	£m	£m	£m	£m	£m	£m
Gross Revenue	400.7	53.7	454.4	411.8	53.3	465.1
Inter-segment revenue	(3.0)	–	(3.0)	(2.6)	–	(2.6)
Segment Revenue						
(by origin and destination)	397.7	53.7	451.4	409.2	53.3	462.5
Gross profit	241.2	29.7	270.9	245.2	27.8	273.0
Operating profit before exceptional items	55.1	3.6	58.7	60.4	3.0	63.4
Segment result: operating profit after exceptional items	62.6	3.6	66.2	71.4	3.0	74.4
Net interest payable			(2.0)			(1.9)
Profit before taxation			64.2			72.5
Taxation			(20.1)			(23.2)
Profit for the financial period			44.1			49.3
Other non-cash expenses:						
Depreciation of property, plant and equipment	9.9	2.2	12.1	9.5	2.3	11.8
Depreciation of investment property	0.1	0.3	0.4	–	–	–
Amortisation of intangible assets	1.1	–	1.1	0.4	–	0.4
Impairment of goodwill	–	–	–	0.5	–	0.5
Share-based payments	0.4	–	0.4	0.2	–	0.2

	2006			2005		
	UK & RoI	Rest of Europe	Group	UK & RoI	Rest of Europe	Group
	£m	£m	£m	£m	£m	£m
Segment Assets:						
Gross assets (by origin and destination)	163.1	74.8	237.9	151.9	64.2	216.1
Inter-segment balances	(0.4)	–	(0.4)	(4.0)	–	(4.0)
Total segment assets	162.7	74.8	237.5	147.9	64.2	212.1
Segment Liabilities:						
Gross liabilities (by origin and destination)	110.0	15.0	125.0	100.9	15.8	116.7
Inter-segment balances	–	(0.4)	(0.4)	–	(4.0)	(4.0)
Total segment liabilities	110.0	14.6	124.6	100.9	11.8	112.7
Capital Expenditure:						
Capital expenditure (by origin and destination)	30.8	4.3	35.1	23.6	9.5	33.1

Source: Carpetright plc Annual Report and Accounts 2006.

Required:

Analyse the performance of each of the major segments in so far as the information allows.

Measuring and reporting cash flows

Introduction

This chapter is devoted to the third major financial statement identified in Chapter 2: the cash flow statement. This statement reveals the movements of cash over a period and the effect of these movements on the cash position of the business. It is an important financial statement because cash is vital to the survival of a business. Without cash, no business can operate.

In this chapter we shall see how the cash flow statement is prepared and how the information that it contains may be interpreted. We shall also see why the deficiencies of the income statement in revealing cash flows over time make a separate cash flow statement necessary.

The cash flow statement is being considered after the chapter on limited companies because the format of the statement requires an understanding of this type of business. Limited companies are required to provide a cash flow statement, as well as the more traditional income statement and balance sheet, for shareholders and other interested parties.

Learning outcomes

When you have completed this chapter, you should be able to:

● Discuss the crucial importance of cash to a business.

● Explain the nature of the cash flow statement and discuss how it can be helpful in identifying cash flow problems.

● Prepare a cash flow statement.

● Interpret a cash flow statement.

MyAccountingLab Remember to create your own personalised Study Plan

The cash flow statement (or statement of cash flows)

The cash flow statement is a fairly recent addition to the set of financial statements sent to shareholders and to others. There used to be no regulation requiring companies to produce more than an income statement and a balance sheet. The prevailing view seems to have been that any financial information required would be contained within these two statements. This view may have been based partly on the assumption that if a business were profitable, it would also have plenty of cash. Although in the very long run this is likely to be true, it is not necessarily true in the short to medium term.

We have already seen in Chapter 3 that the income statement sets out the revenue and expenses, rather than the cash receipts and cash payments, for the period. Thus, profit (loss), which represents the difference between the revenue and expenses for the period, may have little or no relation to the cash generated for the period. To illustrate this point, let us take the example of a business making a sale (a revenue). This may well lead to an increase in wealth and will be reflected in the income statement. However, if the sale is made on credit, no cash changes hands – at least not at the time of sale. Instead, the increase in wealth is reflected in another asset: an increase in trade receivables. Furthermore, if an item of inventories is the subject of the sale, wealth is lost to the business through the reduction in inventories. This means an expense is incurred in making the sale, which will be shown in the income statement. Once again, however, no cash has changed hands at the time of sale. For such reasons, the profit and the cash generated for a period will rarely go hand in hand.

The following activity helps to underline how profit and cash for a period may be affected differently by particular transactions or events.

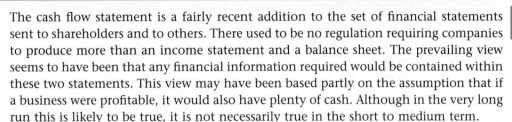

Activity 6.1

The following is a list of business/accounting events. In each case, state the effect (increase, decrease or no effect) on both profit and cash:

		Effect	
		on profit	on cash
1	Repayment of borrowings	_____	_____
2	Making a sale on credit	_____	_____
3	Buying a current asset on credit	_____	_____
4	Receiving cash from a credit customer (trade receivable)	_____	_____
5	Depreciating a non-current asset	_____	_____
6	Buying some inventories for cash	_____	_____
7	Making a share issue for cash	_____	_____

You should have come up with the following:

		Effect	
		on profit	on cash
1	Repayment of borrowings	none	decrease
2	Making a sale on credit	increase	none
3	Buying a current asset on credit	none	none
4	Receiving cash from a credit customer (trade receivable)	none	increase
5	Depreciating a non-current asset	decrease	none
6	Buying some inventories for cash	none	decrease
7	Making a share issue for cash	none	increase

Activity 6.1 continued

The reasons for these answers are as follows:

1 Repaying borrowings requires that cash be paid to the lender. Thus two figures in the balance sheet will be affected, but not the income statement.
2 Making a sale on credit will increase the sales revenue figure (and a profit or a loss, unless the sale was made for a price that precisely equalled the expenses involved). No cash will change hands at this point, however.
3 Buying a current asset on credit affects neither the cash balance nor the profit figure.
4 Receiving cash from a receivable increases the cash balance and reduces the credit customer's balance. Both of these figures are on the balance sheet. The income statement is unaffected.
5 Depreciating a non-current asset means that an expense is recognised. This causes the value of the asset, as it is recorded on the balance sheet, to fall by an amount equal to the amount of the expense. No cash is paid or received.
6 Buying some inventories for cash means that the value of the inventories will increase and the cash balance will decrease by a similar amount. Profit is not affected.
7 Making a share issue for cash increases the owners' claim and increases the cash balance; profit is unaffected.

It is clear from the above that if we are to gain an insight to cash movements over time, the income statement is not the answer. Instead we need a separate financial statement. This fact has become widely recognised in recent years, and in 1991 a UK financial reporting standard, FRS 1, emerged that required all but the smallest companies to produce and publish a cash flow statement. This standard has been superseded for many companies from 2005 by the International Accounting Standard IAS 7. The two standards have broadly similar requirements. This chapter follows the provisions of IAS 7.

Why is cash so important?

It is worth asking why cash is so important. After all, cash is just an asset that the business needs to help it to function. In that sense, it is no different from inventories or non-current assets.

The reason for the importance of cash is that people and organisations will not normally accept other than cash in settlement of their claims against the business. If a business wants to employ people, it must pay them in cash. If it wants to buy a new non-current asset to exploit a business opportunity, the seller of the asset will normally insist on being paid in cash, probably after a short period of credit. When businesses fail, it is their inability to find the cash to pay the amounts owed that really pushes them under.

These factors lead to cash being the pre-eminent business asset. It is the one that analysts tend to watch most carefully when trying to assess the ability of businesses to survive and/or to take advantage of commercial opportunities as they arise. The fact that cash and profits do not always go hand in hand is illustrated in **Real World 6.1**. This explains how Eurotunnel, the cross-channel business between England and France, continues to struggle to achieve profit, yet generates positive cash flows.

Real World 6.1

Cash flows under the channel

FT

Richard Shirrefs [Eurotunnel's chief executive] called for a shift from 'a stable equilibrium of failure to a stable equilibrium of success'.

The company, which last restructured its long term debt in 2003, proposes to shift to a lower price, higher volume model for tunnel usage. Access rates for train operators would be reduced to entice them to introduce more services to more destinations, such as Amsterdam, and to encourage greater freight traffic.

Eurotunnel progressed its own plans for freight on Monday, announcing it expected to start a traction business in 2005 and that a platform designed to accept continental gauge freight trains would begin operations at Folkestone at the same time.

Mr Shirrefs said taxpayers had invested £10bn and industry £15bn in the tunnel and associated infrastructure and: 'We need to get all that infrastructure working . . . neither investor nor taxpayer is getting value'.

Last year was a difficult one for Eurotunnel with reduced cross channel passenger flows bringing fare competition from ferry operators.

The company's operating revenue was down 5 per cent at £566m and its operating profit down 18 per cent at £170m. With interest payments of £318m, the underlying loss was up 40 per cent at £148m. However, it maintained a positive cash flow of £290m, down from £307m in 2002.

Source: Extracts from 'Eurotunnel takes £1.3bn impairment charge', Toby Shelley, FT.com, 9 February 2004.

The main features of the cash flow statement

The cash flow statement is a summary of the cash receipts and payments over the period concerned. All payments of a particular type, for example cash payments to acquire additional non-current assets or other investments, are added together to give just one figure that appears in the statement. The net total of the statement is the net increase or decrease of the cash (and cash equivalents) of the business over the period. The statement is basically an analysis of the business's cash (and cash equivalents) movements for the period.

A definition of cash and cash equivalents

IAS 7 defines cash as notes and coins in hand and deposits in banks and similar institutions that are accessible to the business on demand. Cash equivalents are short-term, highly liquid investments that are readily convertible to known amounts of cash and which are subject to an insignificant risk of changes of value. Cash equivalents are held for the purpose of meeting short-term cash commitments rather than for investment or other purposes.

Activity 6.2 should clarify the types of items that fall within the definition of 'cash equivalents'.

Activity 6.2

At the end of its accounting period, Zeneb plc's balance sheet included the following items:

1 *A bank deposit account where one month's notice of withdrawal is required*. This deposit was made because the business has a temporary cash surplus that it will need to use in the short term for operating purposes;
2 *Ordinary shares in Jones plc (a Stock Exchange listed business)*. These were acquired because the business has a temporary cash surplus and Zeneb plc's directors believed that the share represented a good short-term investment. The funds invested will need to be used in the short term for operating purposes.
3 *A bank deposit account that is withdrawable instantly*. This represents an investment of surplus funds that are not seen as being needed in the short term.
4 *An overdraft on the business's bank current account.*

Which (if any) of these four items would be included in the figure for cash and cash equivalents?

Your response should have been as follows:

1 A cash equivalent because the deposit is part of the business's normal cash management activities and there is little doubt about how much cash will be obtained when the deposit is withdrawn.
2 Not a cash equivalent. Although the investment was made as part of normal cash management, there is a significant risk that the amount expected (hoped for!) when the shares are sold may not actually be forthcoming.
3 Not a cash equivalent because this represents an investment rather than a short-term surplus amount of cash.
4 This is cash itself, though a negative amount of it. The only exception to this classification would be where the business is financed in the longer term by an overdraft, when it would be part of the financing of the business.

As can be seen from the responses to Activity 6.2, whether a particular item falls within the definition of cash and cash equivalent depends on two factors:

- the nature of the item; and
- why it has arisen.

In practice, it is not usually difficult to decide whether an item is a cash equivalent.

The relationship between the primary financial statements

The cash flow statement is now accepted, along with the income statement, the statement of changes in equity and the balance sheet, as a primary financial statement. The relationship between the four statements is shown in Figure 6.1. The balance sheet reflects the combination of assets (including cash) and claims (including the owners' claim) of the business *at a particular point in time*. The cash flow statement, the income statement and the statement of changes in equity explain the *changes over a period* to two of the items in the balance sheet. The cash flow statement explains the changes to cash. The income statement, together with the statement of changes in equity, explains changes to the owners' claim (equity).

Figure 6.1 The relationship between the balance sheet, the income statement, the statement of changes in equity and the cash flow statement

The balance sheet shows the position, at a particular point in time, of the business's assets and claims. The income statement explains how, over a period between two balance sheets, the owners' claim figure in the first balance sheet has altered as a result of trading operations. The statement of changes in equity explains how the owners' claim has altered, through non-trading actions, to become the owners' claim (equity) figure in the second balance sheet. The cash flow statement also looks at changes over the accounting period, but this statement explains the alteration in the cash (and cash equivalent) balances from the first to the second of the two consecutive balance sheets.

The form of the cash flow statement

The standard layout of the cash flow statement is summarised in Figure 6.2. Explanations of the terms used in the cash flow statement are given below.

Cash flows from operating activities

This is the net inflow or outflow from trading operations, after tax and financing costs. It is equal to the sum of cash receipts from trade receivables, and cash receipts from cash sales where relevant, less the sums paid to buy inventories, to pay rent, to pay wages and so on. From this are also deducted payments for interest on the business's borrowings, corporation tax and dividends paid.

Note that it is the amounts of cash received and paid during the period that feature in the cash flow statement, not the revenue and expenses for that period. It is, of course, the income statement that deals with the revenue and expenses. Similarly the tax and dividend payments that appear in the cash flow statement are those made in the period of the statement. Companies normally pay tax on their profits in four equal instalments. Two of these are during the year concerned, and the other two are during the following year. Thus by the end of each accounting year, one half of the tax will have been paid and the remainder will be a current liability at the end of the year, to be paid off during the following year. During any particular year, therefore, the tax payment would normally equal 50 per cent of the previous year's tax charge and 50 per cent of that of the current year.

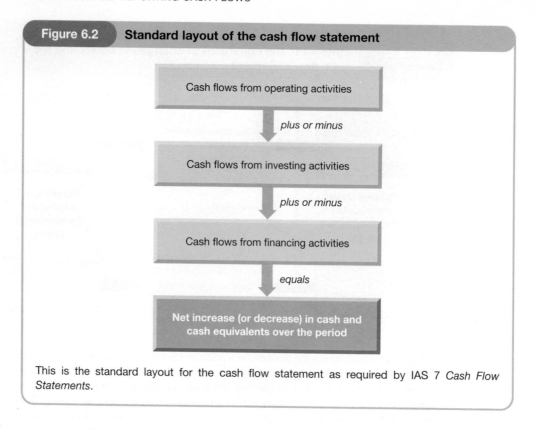

Figure 6.2 **Standard layout of the cash flow statement**

This is the standard layout for the cash flow statement as required by IAS 7 *Cash Flow Statements*.

The net figure for this section is intended to indicate the net cash flows for the period that arose from normal day-to-day trading activities after taking account of the tax that has to be paid on them and the cost of servicing the finance (equity and borrowings) needed to support them.

Cash flows from investing activities

This section of the statement is concerned with cash payments made to acquire additional non-current assets and with cash receipts from the disposal of non-current assets. These non-current assets will tend to be the usual items such as buildings and machinery. They might also be loans made by the business or shares in another company bought by the business.

This section also includes receipts from investments (loans and equity investments) made outside the business. These receipts are interest on loans made by the business and dividends from shares in other companies that are owned by the business.

This section shows the net cash flows from making new investments and/or disposing of existing ones.

Cash flows from financing activities

This part of the statement is concerned with the long-term financing of the business. So here we are considering borrowings (other than very short term) and finance from share issues. This category is concerned with repayment/redemption of finance as well as with the raising of it. It is permissible under IAS 7 to include dividend payments made by the business here, as an alternative to including them in 'Cash flows from operating activities' (above).

This section shows the net cash flows from raising and/or paying back long-term finance.

Net increase or decrease in cash and cash equivalents

The total of the statement must, of course, be the net increase or decrease in cash and cash equivalents over the period covered by the statement.

The effect on a business's cash and cash equivalents of its various activities is shown in Figure 6.3. The activities that affect cash are analysed in the same way as is required by IAS 7. As explained in the diagram, the arrows show the *normal* direction of cash flow for the typical healthy, profitable business in a typical year.

Figure 6.3 **Diagrammatical representation of the cash flow statement**

Various activities of the business each have their own effect on its cash and cash equivalent balances, either positive (increasing them) or negative (reducing them). The net increase or decrease in the cash and cash equivalent balances over a period will be the sum of these individual effects, taking account of the direction (cash in or cash out) of each activity.

Note that the direction of the arrow shows the *normal* direction of the cash flow in respect of each activity. In certain circumstances, each of these arrows could be reversed in direction.

The normal direction of cash flows

Normally 'operating activities' provide positive cash flows, that is, they help to increase the business's cash resources. In fact, for most UK businesses, in most time periods, cash generated from day-to-day trading, even after deducting tax, interest and dividends, is overwhelmingly the most important source of new finance.

Activity 6.3

Last year's cash flow statement for Angus plc showed a negative cash flow from operating activities. What could be the reason for this, and should the business's management be alarmed by it? (*Hint:* We think that there are two broad possible reasons for a negative cash flow.)

The two reasons are:

- The business is unprofitable. This leads to more cash being paid out to employees, suppliers of goods and services, interest and so on, than is received from receivables in respect of sales. This would be particularly alarming, because a major expense for most businesses is depreciation of non-current assets. Since depreciation does not lead to a cash flow, it is not considered in 'net cash inflows from operating activities'. Thus, a negative operating cash flow might well indicate a very much larger trading loss – in other words, a significant loss of the business's wealth; something to concern management.

Activity 6.3 continued

- The other reason might be less alarming. A business that is expanding its activities (level of sales revenue) would tend to spend quite a lot of cash relative to the amount of cash coming in from sales. This is because it will probably be expanding its assets (non-current and current) to accommodate the increased demand. For example, a business may well have to have inventories in place before additional sales can be made. Even when the additional sales are made, those sales would normally be made on credit, with the cash inflow lagging behind the sale. All of this means that, in the first instance, in cash flow terms, the business would not necessarily benefit from the additional sales revenue. This would be particularly likely to be true of a new business, which would be expanding inventories and other assets from zero. Expansion typically causes cash flow strains for the reasons just explained. This can be a particular problem because the business's increased profitability might encourage a feeling of optimism, which could lead to lack of attention being paid to the cash flow problem.

Investing activities typically cause net negative cash flows. This is because many types of non-current asset wear out, and many that do not wear out become obsolete. Also, businesses tend to seek to expand their asset base. When a business sells some non-current assets, the sale will give rise to positive cash flows, but in net terms the cash flows are normally negative with cash spent on new assets outweighing that received from disposal of old ones.

Financing can go in either direction, depending on the financing strategy at the time. Since businesses seek to expand, there is a general tendency for this area to lead to cash coming into the business rather than leaving it.

Real World 6.2 shows the summarised cash flow statement of Tesco plc, the UK-based supermarket.

Real World 6.2

Cashing in

The published summarised cash flow statement for Tesco plc for the six months to 26 August 2006 shows the cash flows of the business under each of the headings described above.

Summarised cash flow statement for the half year to 26 August 2006

	£m
Net cash from operating activities	1,319
Net cash used in investing activities	(1,109)
Net cash used in financing activities	(124)
Net increase in cash and cash equivalents	86
Cash and cash equivalents at beginning of period	1,325
Effects of foreign exchange rate changes [*]	(21)
Cash and cash equivalents at end of period	1,390

* This adjustment is required because transactions are undertaken by the business in different currencies and movements in exchange rates can lead to gains or losses.

Source: Adapted from www.tescocorporate.com.

As we shall see shortly, more detailed information under each of the main headings is provided when a cash flow statement for a full year is prepared.

Preparing the cash flow statement

Deducing net cash flows from operating activities

The first section of the cash flow statement is the 'cash flows from operating activities'. There are two methods that can be used to derive this figure: the direct method and the indirect method.

The direct method

→ The **direct method** involves an analysis of the cash records of the business for the period, picking out all payments and receipts relating to operating activities. These are summarised to give the total figures for inclusion in the cash flow statement. Done on the computer, this would be a simple matter, but not many businesses adopt this approach.

The indirect method

→ The **indirect method** is the more popular method. It relies on the fact that, broadly, sales revenue gives rise to cash inflows, and expenses give rise to outflows. This means that the profit for the year figure will be closely linked to the net cash inflows from operating activities. Since businesses have to produce an income statement in any case, information from it can be used as a starting point to deduce the cash flows from operating activities.

Of course, within a particular accounting period, profit for the year will not normally equal the net cash inflows from operating activities. We saw in Chapter 3 that, when sales are made on credit, the cash receipt occurs some time after the sale. This means that sales revenue made towards the end of an accounting year will be included in that year's income statement, but most of the cash from those sales will flow into the business, and should be included in the cash flow statement, in the following year. Fortunately it is easy to deduce the cash received from sales if we have the relevant income statement and balance sheets, as we shall see in Activity 6.4.

Activity 6.4

How can we deduce the cash inflows from sales using the income statement and balance sheet for the business?

The balance sheet will tell us how much was owed in respect of credit sales at the beginning and end of the year (trade receivables). The income statement tells us the sales revenue figure. If we adjust the sales revenue figure by the increase or decrease in trade receivables over the year, we deduce the cash from sales for the year.

Example 6.1

The sales revenue figure for a business for the year was £34m. The trade receivables totalled £4m at the beginning of the year, but had increased to £5m by the end of the year.

Basically, the trade receivables figure is affected by sales revenue and cash receipts. It is increased when a sale is made and decreased when cash is received from a credit customer. If, over the year, the sales revenue and the cash receipts had been equal, the beginning-of-year and end-of-year trade receivables figures would have been equal. Since the trade receivables figure increased, it must mean that less cash was received than sales revenues were made. Thus the cash receipts from sales must be £33m (that is, 34 − (5 − 4)).

Put slightly differently, we can say that as a result of sales, assets of £34m flowed into the business during the year. If £1m of this went to increasing the asset of trade receivables, this leaves only £33m that went to increase cash.

The same general point is true in respect of nearly all of the other items that are taken into account in deducing the operating profit figure. The exception is depreciation. This is not necessarily associated with any movement in cash during the accounting period.

All of this means that we can take the profit before taxation (that is, the profit after interest but before taxation) for the year, add back the depreciation and interest expense charged in arriving at that profit, and adjust this total by movements in inventories, trade receivables and payables. If we then go on to deduct payments made during the accounting period for taxation, interest on borrowings and dividends, we have the net cash from operating activities.

Example 6.2

The relevant information from the financial statements of Dido plc for last year is as follows:

	£m
Profit before taxation (after interest)	122
Depreciation charged in arriving at profit before taxation	34
Interest expense	6
At the beginning of the year	
Inventories	15
Trade receivables	24
Trade payables	18
At the end of the year	
Inventories	17
Trade receivables	21
Trade payables	19

The following further information is available about payments during last year:

	£m
Taxation paid	32
Interest paid	5
Dividends paid	9

The cash flow from operating activities is derived as follows:

	£m	£m
Profit before taxation (after interest)		122
Add Depreciation	34	
Interest expense	6	40
		162
Less Increase in inventories (17 – 15)		(2)
Add Decrease in trade receivables (21 – 24)	3	
Increase in trade payables (19 – 18)	1	4
Cash generated from operations		164
Less Interest paid	5	
Taxation paid	32	
Dividends paid	9	46
Net cash from operating activities		118

Thus, the net increase in working capital, as a result of trading, was £162m. Of this, £2m went into increased inventories. More cash was received from trade receivables than sales revenues were made, and less cash was paid to trade payables than purchases of goods and services on credit. Both of these had a favourable effect on cash, which increased by £164m. When account was taken of the payments for interest, tax and dividends, the net cash flow from operating activities was £118m (inflow).

Note that we needed to adjust the profit before taxation (after interest) by the depreciation and interest expenses to derive the profit before depreciation, interest and taxation.

The indirect method of deducing the net cash flow from operating activities is summarised in Figure 6.4.

Activity 6.5

The relevant information from the financial statements of Pluto plc for last year is as follows:

	£m
Profit before taxation (after interest)	165
Depreciation charged in arriving at operating profit	41
Interest expense	21
At the beginning of the year:	
Inventories	22
Trade receivables	18
Trade payables	15
At the end of the year:	
Inventories	23
Trade receivables	21
Trade payables	17

Activity 6.5 continued

The following further information is available about payments during last year:

	£m
Taxation paid	49
Interest paid	25
Dividends paid	28

What figure should appear in the cash flow statement for 'Cash flows from operating activities'?

Net cash inflows from operating activities:

	£m	£m
Profit before taxation (after interest)		165
Add Depreciation	41	
Interest expense	21	62
		227
Less Increase in inventories (23 – 22)	1	
Increase in trade receivables (21 – 18)	3	(4)
Add Increase in trade payables (17 – 15)		2
Cash generated from operations		225
Less Interest paid	25	
Taxation paid	49	
Dividends paid	28	(102)
Net cash from operating activities		123

Deducing the other areas of the cash flow statement

We can now go on to take a look at the preparation of a complete cash flow statement through Example 6.3.

Example 6.3

Torbryan plc's income statement for the year ended 31 December 2007 and the balance sheets as at 31 December 2006 and 2007 are as follows:

Income statement for the year ended 31 December 2007

	£m
Revenue	576
Cost of sales	(307)
Gross profit	269
Distribution expenses	(65)
Administrative expenses	(26)
	178
Other operating income	21
Operating profit	199
Interest receivable	17
	216
Interest payable	(23)
Profit before taxation	193
Taxation	(46)
Profit for the year	147

Figure 6.4   **The indirect method of deducing the net cash flows from operating activities**

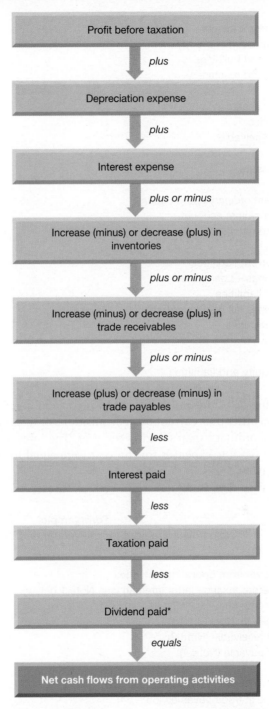

Determining the net cash from operating activities firstly involves adding back the depreciation and the interest expense to the profit before taxation. Next, adjustment is made for increases or decreases in inventories, trade receivables and trade payables. Lastly, cash paid for interest, taxation and dividends is deducted.

* Note that dividends could alternatively be included under the heading 'Cash flows from financing activities'.

Balance sheets as at 31 December 2006 and 2007

	2006 £m	2007 £m
Non-current assets		
Property, plant and equipment		
Land and buildings	241	241
Plant and machinery	309	325
	550	566
Current assets		
Inventories	44	41
Trade receivables	121	139
	165	180
Total assets	715	746
Equity		
Called-up ordinary share capital	150	200
Share premium account	–	40
Retained earnings	26	123
	176	363
Non-current liabilities		
Borrowings – Loan notes	400	250
Current liabilities		
Borrowings (all bank overdraft)	68	56
Trade payables	55	54
Taxation	16	23
	139	133
Total equity and liabilities	715	746

During 2007, the business spent £95m on additional plant and machinery. There were no other non-current-asset acquisitions or disposals. A dividend of £50m was paid on ordinary shares during the year. The interest receivable revenue and the interest payable expenses for the year were equal to the cash inflow and outflow respectively.

The cash flow statement would be as follows:

Torbryan plc
Cash flow statement for the year ended 31 December 2007

	£m	£m
Cash flows from operating activities		
Profit before taxation (after interest) (see Note 1 below)		193
Adjustments for:		
Depreciation (Note 2)		79
Interest receivable (Note 3)		(17)
Interest payable (Note 4)		23
		278
Increase in trade receivables (139 – 121)		(18)
Decrease in trade payables (55 – 54)		(1)
Decrease in inventories (44 – 41)		3
Cash generated from operations		262
Interest paid		(23)
Taxation paid (Note 5)		(39)
Dividend paid		(50)
Net cash from operating activities		150

Cash flows from investing activities

Payments to acquire tangible non-current assets	(95)	
Interest received (Note 3)	17	
Net cash used in investing activities		(78)

Cash flows from financing activities

Repayments of loan notes (Note 6)	(150)	
Issue of ordinary shares (Note 7)	90	
Net cash used in financing activities		(60)
Net increase in cash and cash equivalents		12
Cash and cash equivalents at 1 January 2007 (Note 8)		(68)
Cash and cash equivalents at 31 December 2007		(56)

To see how this relates to the cash of the business at the beginning and end of the year it can be useful to provide a reconciliation as follows:

Analysis of cash and cash equivalents during the year ended 31 December 2007

	£m
Overdraft balance at 1 January 2007	(68)
Net cash inflow	12
Overdraft balance at 31 December 2007	(56)

Notes:

1 This is simply taken from the income statement for the year.
2 Since there were no disposals, the depreciation charges must be the difference between the start and end of the year's plant and machinery (non-current assets) values, adjusted by the cost of any additions.

	£m
Carrying amount at 1 January 2007	309
Additions	95
	404
Depreciation (balancing figure)	(79)
Carrying amount at 31 December 2007	325

3 Interest receivable must be taken away to work towards the profit before crediting it, because it is not part of operations but of investing activities. The cash inflow from this source appears under the 'Cash flows from investing activities' heading.
4 Interest payable expense must be taken out, by adding it back to the profit figure. We subsequently deduct the cash paid for interest payable during the year. In this case the two figures are identical.
5 Taxation is paid by companies 50 per cent during their accounting year and 50 per cent in the following year. Thus the 2007 payment would have been half the tax on the 2006 profit (that is, the figure that would have appeared in the current liabilities at the end of 2006), plus half of the 2007 taxation charge (that is, $16 + (1/2 \times 46) = 39$). Probably the easiest way to deduce the amount paid during the year to 31 December 2007 is by following this approach:

	£m
Taxation owed at start of the year (from the balance sheet as at 31 December 2006)	16
Taxation charge for the year (from the income statement)	46
	62
Less Taxation owed at the end of the year (from the balance sheet as at 31 December 2007)	(23)
Taxation paid during the year	39

This follows the logic that if we start with what the business owed at the beginning of the year, add the increase in what was owed as a result of the current year's taxation charge and then deduct what was owed at the end, the resulting figure must be what was paid during the year.

6 It has been assumed that the loan notes were redeemed for their balance sheet value. This is not, however, always the case.
7 The share issue raised £90m, of which £50m went into the share capital total on the balance sheet and £40m into share premium.
8 There were no 'cash equivalents', just cash (though negative).

What does the cash flow statement tell us?

The cash flow statement tells us how the business has generated cash during the period and where that cash has gone. Since cash is properly regarded as the lifeblood of just about any business, this is potentially very useful information.

Tracking the sources and uses of cash over several years could show financing trends that a reader of the statements could use to help to make judgements about the likely future behaviour of the business.

Looking specifically at the cash flow statement for Torbryan plc, in Example 6.3, we can see the following:

- Net cash flow from operations was strong, much larger than the profit for the year figure, after taking account of the dividend paid. This would be expected because depreciation is deducted in arriving at profit. There was a general tendency for working capital to absorb some cash. This would not be surprising had there been an expansion of activity (sales revenue) over the year. From the information supplied, we do not know whether there was an expansion or not. (We have only one year's income statement.)
- There were net outflows of cash for investing activities, but this would not be unusual. Many items of property, plant and equipment have limited lives and need to be replaced with new ones. The expenditure during the year was not out of line with the depreciation expense for the year, which is what we might expect.
- There was a fairly major outflow of cash to redeem some borrowings, partly offset by the proceeds of a share issue. This presumably represents a change of financing strategy. Together with the ploughed-back profit from trading, there has been a significant shift in the equity/borrowings balance.

Real World 6.3 indicates the importance of the cash flow statement in analysing the health of one well-known business.

Real World 6.3

Watching the cash flows

FT

When WaterfordWedgwood reports its annual results today, brokers will be focused not just on the income statement of the crystal and porcelain manufacturer, or the balance sheet – the traditional windows on the health of a company – but on the cash flow statement.

Brokers, in particular, are looking for signs of improvement in the working capital position – the company's ability to squeeze more cash from suppliers, to get paid earlier by its customers and reduce the amount of costly product held in its warehouses or elsewhere in the supply chain.

The signs are mixed. The company this month warned that profits for the period to March 31 would be €12m (£8m) or 15 per cent shy of what it had been predicting in January.

It cited difficulties at its German porcelain subsidiary. It was also hit when US stores did not restock after the Christmas sales.

The poorer trading means inventories levels should be lower. On the other hand, there is less cash generated to pay down the debt. . . .

Going forward, the big challenge is to extract more cash from the businesses. Accenture, the consultant, has been asked to look at the issue.

> John Sheehan, at NCB stockbrokers, anticipates big inventories write-offs. 'The real issue is can they do this without saturating the market and hurting the brand?' he asks.
>
> On the manufacturing side, the company is adopting a twin approach, outsourcing the manufacturing to cheaper locations while harnessing big-name designers to appeal to a younger consumer.
>
> *Source*: 'WaterfordWedgwood face some intense questions over its cash flow', *Financial Times*, 17 June 2004, FT.com.

Real World 6.4 looks at the cash flow statement of an emerging business, LiDCO Group plc, that is experiencing negative cash flows as it seeks to establish a profitable market for its products.

 Real World 6.4

Not losing heart

LiDCO Group plc is a smaller business whose shares are listed on the Alternative Investment Market (AIM). AIM is a section of the London Stock Exchange that specialises in providing a market for the shares of smaller up and coming businesses. We shall discuss AIM in Chapter 15.

LiDCO makes highly sophisticated equipment for monitoring the hearts of cardiac patients, typically in hospitals and clinics. The business was started by four doctors and scientists. It has spent £6.8m over ten years developing its products, obtaining registration for their use from both the UK and US authorities and creating manufacturing facilities.

LiDCO's cash flow statement for the year to 31 January 2006 was as follows:

	£000	£000
Cash flows from operating activities		
Profit before taxation	(2,127)	
Depreciation	440	
Decrease in inventories	25	
Increase in trade receivables	(307)	
Decrease in trade payables	130	
		(1,839)
Cash flows from investing activities		
Payments to acquire tangible non-current assets	(55)	
Payments to acquire intangible non-current assets	(362)	
Interest received	42	
Net cash inflow from investing activities		(375)
Cash flows from financing activities		
Issue of ordinary share capital	203	
Convertible loan	1,355	
Net cash inflow from financing activities		1,558
Net decrease in cash and cash equivalents		(656)

To put these figures into context, the sales revenue for the year was £3,421,000. This means that the net cash outflow from operating activities was equal to over 50 per cent of the revenue figure. Such cash flow profiles are fairly typical of 'high-tech' businesses that have enormous start-up costs to bring their products to the market in sufficient quantities to yield a profit. Of course, not all such businesses achieve this, but LiDCO seems confident of success.

Source: Information taken from LiDCO Group plc Annual Report 2006 and AIM company profile, www.londonstockexchange.com.

Self-assessment question 6.1

Touchstone plc's income statements for the years ended 31 December 2006 and 2007 and the balance sheets as at 31 December 2006 and 2007 are as follows:

Income statements for the years ended 2006 and 2007

	2006 £m	2007 £m
Revenue	173	207
Cost of sales	(96)	(101)
Gross profit	77	106
Distribution expenses	(18)	(20)
Administrative expenses	(24)	(26)
	35	60
Other operating income	3	4
Operating profit	38	64
Interest payable	(2)	(4)
Profit before taxation	36	60
Taxation	(8)	(16)
Profit for the year	28	44

Balance sheets as at 31 December 2006 and 2007

	2005 £m	2006 £m
Non-current assets		
Property, plant and equipment		
Land and buildings	94	110
Plant and machinery	53	62
	147	172
Current assets		
Inventories	25	24
Treasury bills (short-term investments)	–	15
Trade receivables	16	26
Cash at bank and in hand	4	4
	45	69
Total assets	192	241
Equity		
Called-up ordinary share capital	100	100
Retained earnings	30	56
	130	156
Non-current liabilities		
Borrowings – Loan notes (10%)	20	40
Current liabilities		
Trade payables	38	37
Taxation	4	8
	42	45
Total equity and liabilities	192	241

Included in 'cost of sales', 'distribution costs' and 'administration expenses', depreciation was as follows:

	2006 £m	2007 £m
Land and buildings	5	6
Plant and machinery	6	10

There were no non-current asset disposals in either year.

The interest payable expense equalled the cash payment made during the year.

Dividends were paid on ordinary shares of £14m during 2006 and £18m during 2007.

The Treasury bills represent a short-term investment of funds that will be used shortly in operations. There is insignificant risk that this investment will lose value.

Required:

Prepare a cash flow statement for the business for 2007.

The answer to this question can be found at the back of the book on pages 689–901.

Summary

The main points of this chapter may be summarised as follows:

The need for a cash flow statement

- Cash is important because no business can operate without it.
- The cash flow statement is specifically designed to reveal movements in cash over a period.
- Cash movements cannot be readily detected from the income statement, which focuses on revenue and expenses rather than on cash receipts and cash payments.
- Profit (loss) and cash generated for the period are rarely equal.
- The cash flow statement is a primary financial statement, along with the income statement, balance sheet and statement of changes in equity.

Preparing the cash flow statement

- The layout of the statement contains three categories of cash movement:
  - cash flows from operating activities;
  - cash flows from investing activities;
  - cash flows from financing activities.
- The total of the cash movements under these three categories will provide the net increase or decrease in cash and cash equivalents for the period.
- A reconciliation can be undertaken to check that the opening balance of cash and cash equivalents plus the net increase (decrease) for the period equals the closing balance.

Calculating the cash generated from operations

- The net cash flows from operating activities can be derived by either the direct method or the indirect method.

- The direct method is based on an analysis of the cash records for the period, whereas the indirect method uses information contained within the income statement and balance sheets of the business.

- The indirect method takes the net operating profit for the period, adds back any depreciation charge and then adjusts for changes in inventories, receivables and payables during the period.

Interpreting the cash flow statement

- The cash flow statement shows the main sources and uses of cash.

- Tracking the cash movements over several periods may reveal financing and investing patterns and may help predict future management action.

 Now check your progress in your personal Study Plan

→ **Key terms**

direct method   p. 201   indirect method   p. 201

Further reading

If you would like to explore the topics covered in this chapter in more depth, we recommend the following books:

Corporate Financial Accounting and Reporting, *Sutton, T.*, 2nd edn, Financial Times Prentice Hall, 2004, chapters 6 and 18.

Financial Accounting and Reporting, *Elliott B. and Elliott J.*, 11th edn, Financial Times Prentice Hall, 2006, chapter 27.

KPMG's Practical Guide to International Financial Reporting Standards, *KPMG*, 3rd edn, Thomson, 2006, section 2.4.

Review questions

Answers to these questions can be found at the back of the book on pages 777–8.

6.1 The typical business outside the service sector has about 50 per cent more of its resources tied up in inventories than in cash, yet there is no call for a 'inventories flow statement' to be prepared. Why is cash regarded as more important than inventories?

6.2 What is the difference between the direct and indirect methods of deducing cash generated from operations?

6.3 Taking each of the categories of the cash flow statement in turn, in which direction would you normally expect the cash flow to be? Explain your answer.

(a) Cash flows from operating activities.
(b) Cash flows from investing activities.
(c) Cash flows from financing activities.

6.4 What causes the profit for the year not to equal the net cash inflow?

Exercises

Exercises 6.3 to 6.8 are more advanced than 6.1 and 6.2. Those with **coloured numbers** have answers at the back of the book, starting on page 720.

If you wish to try more exercises, visit the students' side of the Companion Website.

6.1 How will each of the following events ultimately affect the amount of cash?

(a) An increase in the level of inventories.
(b) A rights issue of ordinary shares.
(c) A bonus issue of ordinary shares.
(d) Writing off part of the value of some inventories.
(e) The disposal of a large number of the business's shares by a major shareholder.
(f) Depreciating a non-current asset.

6.2 The following information has been taken from the financial statements of Juno plc for last year and the year before last:

	Year before last £m	Last year £m
Operating profit	156	187
Depreciation charged in arriving at operating profit	47	55
Inventories held at the end of:	27	31
Receivables at the end of:	24	23
Payables at the end of:	15	17

Required:
What is the cash generated from the operations figure for Juno plc for last year?

6.3   Torrent plc's income statement for the year ended 31 December 2007 and the balance sheets as at 31 December 2006 and 2007 are as follows:

Income statement

	£m
Revenue	623
Cost of sales	(353)
Gross profit	270
Distribution expenses	(71)
Administrative expenses	(30)
	169
Rental income	27
Operating profit	196
Interest payable	(26)
Profit before taxation	170
Taxation	(36)
Profit for the year	134

Balance sheets as at 31 December 2006 and 2007

	2006 £m	2007 £m
Non-current assets		
Property, plant and equipment		
Land and buildings	310	310
Plant and machinery	325	314
	635	624
Current assets		
Inventories	41	35
Trade receivables	139	145
	180	180
Total assets	815	804
Equity		
Called-up ordinary share capital	200	300
Share premium account	40	–
Revaluation reserve	69	9
Retained earnings	123	197
	432	506
Non-current liabilities		
Borrowings – Loan notes	250	150
Current liabilities		
Borrowings (all bank overdraft)	56	89
Trade payables	54	41
Taxation	23	18
	133	148
Total equity and liabilities	815	804

During 2007, the business spent £67m on additional plant and machinery. There were no other non-current asset acquisitions or disposals.

There was no share issue for cash during the year. The interest payable expense was equal in amount to the cash outflow. A dividend of £60m was paid.

Required:

Prepare the cash flow statement for Torrent plc for the year ended 31 December 2007.

6.4 Chen plc's income statements for the years ended 31 December 2006 and 2007 and the balance sheets as at 31 December 2006 and 2007 are as follows:

Income statement

	2006 £m	2007 £m
Revenue	207	153
Cost of sales	(101)	(76)
Gross profit	106	77
Distribution expenses	(22)	(20)
Administrative expenses	(20)	(28)
Operating profit	64	29
Interest payable	(4)	(4)
Profit before taxation	60	25
Taxation	(16)	(6)
Profit for the year	44	19

Balance sheets as at 31 December 2006 and 2007

	2006 £m	2007 £m
Non-current assets		
Property, plant and equipment		
Land and buildings	110	130
Plant and machinery	62	56
	172	186
Current assets		
Inventories	24	25
Trade receivables	26	25
Cash at bank and in hand	19	–
	69	50
Total assets	241	236
Equity		
Called-up ordinary share capital	100	100
Retained earnings	56	57
	156	157
Non-current liabilities		
Borrowings – Loan notes (10%)	40	40
Current liabilities		
Borrowings (all bank overdraft)	–	2
Trade payables	37	34
Taxation	8	3
	45	39
Total equity and liabilities	241	236

Included in 'cost of sales', 'distribution costs' and 'administrative expenses', depreciation was as follows:

	2006 £m	2007 £m
Land and buildings	6	10
Plant and machinery	10	12

There were no non-current asset disposals in either year. The amount of cash paid for interest equalled the expense in both years. Dividends were paid totalling £18m in each year.

Required:

Prepare a cash flow statement for the business for 2007.

6.5 The following are the financial statements for Nailsea plc for the years ended 30 June 2006 and 2007:

Income statement for years ended 30 June

	2006 £m	2007 £m
Revenue	1,230	2,280
Operating expenses	(722)	(1,618)
Depreciation	(270)	(320)
Operating profit	238	342
Interest payable	–	(27)
Profit before taxation	238	315
Taxation	(110)	(140)
Profit for the year	128	175

Balance sheets as at 30 June

	2006 £m	2007 £m
Non-current assets		
Property, plant and equipment (at carrying amount)		
Land and buildings	1,500	1,900
Plant and machinery	810	740
	2,310	2,640
Current assets		
Inventories	275	450
Trade receivables	100	250
Bank	–	118
	375	818
Total assets	2,685	3,458
Equity		
Share capital (fully paid £1 shares)	1,400	1,600
Share premium account	200	300
Retained profits	828	958
	2,428	2,858
Non-current liabilities		
Borrowings – 9% Loan notes (repayable 2011)	–	300
Current liabilities		
Borrowings (all bank overdraft)	32	–
Trade payables	170	230
Taxation	55	70
	257	300
Total equity and liabilities	2,685	3,458

There were no disposals of non-current assets in either year. Dividends were paid in 2006 and 2007 of £40m and £45m, respectively.

Required:

Prepare a cash flow statement for Nailsea plc for the year ended 30 June 2007.

6.6 The following financial statements for Blackstone plc are a slightly simplified set of published accounts. Blackstone plc is an engineering business that developed a new range of products in 2005. These products now account for 60 per cent of its turnover.

Income statement for the years ended 31 March

	Notes	2006 £m	2007 £m
Revenue		7,003	11,205
Cost of sales		(3,748)	(5,809)
Gross profit		3,255	5,396
Operating expenses		(2,205)	(3,087)
Operating profit		1,050	2,309
Interest payable	1	(216)	(456)
Profit before taxation		834	1,853
Taxation		(210)	(390)
Profit for the year		624	1,463

Balance sheets as at 31 March

	Notes	2006 £m	2007 £m
Non-current assets			
Property, plant and equipment	2	4,300	7,535
Intangible assets	3	–	700
		4,300	8,235
Current assets			
Inventories		1,209	2,410
Trade receivables		641	1,173
Cash at bank		123	–
		1,973	3,583
Total assets		6,273	11,818
Equity			
Share capital		1,800	1,800
Share premium		600	600
Capital reserves		352	352
Retained profits		685	1,748
		3,437	4,500
Non-current liabilities			
Borrowings – Bank loan (repayable 2011)		1,800	3,800
Current liabilities			
Trade payables		931	1,507
Taxation		105	195
Borrowings (all bank overdraft)		–	1,816
		1,036	3,518
Total equity and liabilities		6,273	11,818

Notes:
1 The expense and the cash outflow for interest payable are equal.
2 The movements in property, plant and equipment during the year are set out below.

	Land and buildings £m	Plant and machinery £m	Fixtures and fittings £m	Total £m
Cost				
At 1 April 2006	4,500	3,850	2,120	10,470
Additions	–	2,970	1,608	4,578
Disposals	–	(365)	(216)	(581)
At 31 March 2007	4,500	6,455	3,512	14,467
Depreciation				
At 1 April 2006	1,275	3,080	1,815	6,170
Charge for year	225	745	281	1,251
Disposals	–	(305)	(184)	(489)
At 31 March 2007	1,500	3,520	1,912	6,932
Carrying amount				
At 31 March 2007	3,000	2,935	1,600	7,535

3 Intangible assets represent the amounts paid for the goodwill of another engineering business acquired during the year.

4 Proceeds from the sale of non-current assets in the year ended 31 March 2007 amounted to £54m.

5 Dividends were paid on ordinary shares of £300m in 2006 and £400m in 2007.

Required:

Prepare a cash flow statement for Blackstone plc for the year ended 31 March 2007. (*Hint*: A loss (deficit) on disposal of non-current assets is simply an additional amount of depreciation and should be dealt with as such in preparing the cash flow statement.)

6.7 Simplified financial statements for York plc are as follows:

York plc
Income statement for the year ended 30 September 2007

	£m
Revenue	290.0
Cost of sales	(215.0)
Gross profit	75.0
Operating expenses (Note 1)	(62.0)
Operating profit	13.0
Interest payable (Note 2)	(3.0)
Profit before taxation	10.0
Taxation	(2.6)
Profit for the year	7.4

Balance sheet at 30 September

	2006 £m	2007 £m
Non-current assets (Note 4)	80.0	85.0
Current assets		
Inventories and trade receivables	119.8	122.1
Cash at bank	9.2	16.6
	129.0	138.7
Total assets	209.0	223.7
Equity		
Share capital	35.0	40.0
Share premium account	30.0	30.0
Reserves	31.0	34.9
	96.0	104.9
Non-current liabilities		
Borrowings	32.0	35.0
Current liabilities		
Trade payables	80.0	82.5
Taxation	1.0	1.3
	81.0	83.8
Total equity and liabilities	209.0	223.7

Notes:

1 Operating expenses include depreciation of £13m and a surplus of £3.2m on the sale of non-current assets.
2 The expense and the cash outflow for interest payable are equal.
3 A dividend of £3.5m was paid during 2007.
4 Non-current asset costs and depreciation:

	Cost £m	Accumulated depreciation £m	Carrying amount £m
At 1 October 2006	120.0	40.0	80.0
Disposals	(10.0)	(8.0)	(2.0)
Additions	20.0		20.0
Depreciation		13.0	(13.0)
At 30 September 2007	130.0	45.0	85.0

Required:
Prepare a cash flow statement for York plc for the year ended 30 September 2007.

6.8 The balance sheets of Axis plc as at 31 December 2006 and 2007 and the income statement for the year ended 31 December 2007 were as follows:

Balance sheet as at 31 December

	2006		2007	
	£m	£m	£m	£m
Non-current assets				
Property, plant and equipment				
Land and building at cost	130		130	
Accumulated depreciation	(30)	100	(32)	98
Plant and machinery at cost	70		80	
Accumulated depreciation	(17)	53	(23)	57
		153		155
Current assets				
Inventories		25		24
Trade receivables		16		26
Short-term investments		–		12
Cash at bank and in hand		–		7
		41		69
Total assets		194		224
Equity				
Share capital		100		100
Retained earnings		36		40
		136		140
Non-current liabilities				
Borrowings – 10% loan notes		20		40
Current liabilities				
Trade payables		31		36
Taxation		7		8
		38		44
Total equity and liabilities		194		224

Income statement for the year ended 31 December 2007

	£m
Revenue	173
Cost of sales	(96)
Gross profit	77
Interest receivable	2
	79
Sundry operating expenses	(24)
Deficit on sale of non-current asset	(1)
Depreciation – buildings	(2)
– plant	(16)
Operating profit	36
Interest payable	(2)
Profit before taxation	34
Taxation	(16)
Profit for the year	18

During the year, plant (a non-current asset) costing £15m and with accumulated depreciation of £10m was sold.

The short-term investments were government securities, where there was little or no risk of loss of value.

The expense and the cash outflow for interest payable were equal.

During 2007 a dividend of £14m was paid.

Required:

Prepare a cash flow statement for Axis plc for the year ended 31 December 2007.

Analysing and interpreting financial statements

Introduction

In this chapter we shall consider the analysis and interpretation of the financial statements discussed in Chapters 2, 3 and 6. We shall see how financial (or accounting) ratios can help in assessing the financial health of a business. We shall also consider the problems that are encountered when applying this technique.

Financial ratios can be used to examine various aspects of financial position and performance and are widely used for planning and control purposes. As we shall see in later chapters, they can be very helpful to managers in a wide variety of decision areas, such as profit planning, pricing, working-capital management, financial structure and dividend policy.

Learning outcomes

When you have completed this chapter, you should be able to:

● Identify the major categories of ratios that can be used for analysis purposes.

● Calculate important ratios for assessing the financial performance and position of a business, and explain the significance of the ratios calculated.

● Discuss the limitations of ratios as a tool of financial analysis.

● Discuss the use of ratios in helping to predict financial failure.

 Remember to create your own personalised Study Plan

Financial ratios

Financial ratios provide a quick and relatively simple means of assessing the financial health of a business. A ratio simply relates one figure appearing in the financial statements to some other figure appearing there (for example, operating profit in relation to capital employed) or, perhaps, to some resource of the business (for example, operating profit per employee, sales revenue per square metre of selling space, and so on).

Ratios can be very helpful when comparing the financial health of different businesses. Differences may exist between businesses in the scale of operations, and so a direct comparison of, say, the operating profit generated by each business may be misleading. By expressing operating profit in relation to some other measure (for example, capital [or funds] employed), the problem of scale is eliminated. A business with an operating profit of, say, £10,000 and capital employed of £100,000 can be compared with a much larger business with an operating profit of, say, £80,000 and sales revenue of £1,000,000 by the use of a simple ratio. The operating profit to capital employed ratio for the smaller business is 10 per cent (that is, (10,000/100,000) × 100%) and the same ratio for the larger business is 8 per cent (that is, (80,000/1,000,000) × 100%). These ratios can be directly compared whereas comparison of the absolute operating profit figures would be less meaningful. The need to eliminate differences in scale through the use of ratios can also apply when comparing the performance of the same business over time.

By calculating a small number of ratios it is often possible to build up a good picture of the position and performance of a business. It is not surprising, therefore, that ratios are widely used by those who have an interest in businesses and business performance. Although ratios are not difficult to calculate, they can be difficult to interpret, and so it is important to appreciate that they are really only the starting point for further analysis.

Ratios help to highlight the financial strengths and weaknesses of a business, but they cannot, by themselves, explain why those strengths or weaknesses exist or why certain changes have occurred. Only a detailed investigation will reveal these underlying reasons. Ratios tend to enable us to know which questions to ask, rather than provide the answers.

Ratios can be expressed in various forms, for example as a percentage or as a proportion. The way that a particular ratio is presented will depend on the needs of those who will use the information. Although it is possible to calculate a large number of ratios, only a few, based on key relationships, tend to be helpful to a particular user. Many ratios that could be calculated from the financial statements (for example, rent payable in relation to current assets) may not be considered because there is no clear or meaningful relationship between the two items.

There is no generally accepted list of ratios that can be applied to the financial statements, nor is there a standard method of calculating many ratios. Variations in both the choice of ratios and their calculation will be found in practice. However, it is important to be consistent in the way in which ratios are calculated for comparison purposes. The ratios that we shall discuss here are those that are widely used. They are popular because many consider them to be among the more important for decision-making purposes.

Financial ratio classifications

Ratios can be grouped into categories, each of which relates to a particular aspect of financial performance or position. The following broad categories provide a useful basis for explaining the nature of the financial ratios to be dealt with. There are five of them:

- *Profitability*. Businesses generally exist with the primary purpose of creating wealth for their owners. Profitability ratios provide an insight to the degree of success in achieving this purpose. They express the profit made (or figures bearing on profit, such as sales revenue or overheads) in relation to other key figures in the financial statements or to some business resource.
- *Efficiency*. Ratios may be used to measure the efficiency with which particular resources have been used within the business. These ratios are also referred to as *activity* ratios.
- *Liquidity*. It is vital to the survival of a business that there are sufficient liquid resources available to meet maturing obligations (that is, amounts owing that must be paid in the near future). Some liquidity ratios examine the relationship between liquid resources held and amounts due for payment in the near future.
- *Financial gearing*. This is the relationship between the contribution to financing the business made by the owners of the business and the amount contributed by others, in the form of loans. The level of gearing has an important effect on the degree of risk associated with a business, as we shall see. Gearing is, therefore, something that managers must consider when making financing decisions. Gearing ratios tend to highlight the extent to which the business uses borrowings.
- *Investment*. Certain ratios are concerned with assessing the returns and performance of shares in a particular business from the perspective of shareholders who are not involved with the management of the business.

The analyst must be clear *who* the target users are and *why* they need the information. Different users of financial information are likely to have different information needs, which will in turn determine the ratios that they find useful. For example, shareholders are likely to be interested in their returns in relation to the level of risk associated with their investment. Profitability, investment and gearing ratios will, therefore, be of particular interest. Long-term lenders are concerned with the long-term viability of the business and, to help them to assess this, the profitability and gearing ratios of the business are also likely to be of particular interest. Short-term lenders, such as suppliers of goods and services on credit, may be interested in the ability of the business to repay the amounts owing in the short term. As a result, the liquidity ratios should be of interest.

We shall consider ratios falling into each of the five categories (profitability, efficiency, liquidity, gearing and investment) a little later in the chapter.

The need for comparison

Merely calculating a ratio will not tell us very much about the position or performance of a business. For example, if a ratio revealed that the business was generating £100 in sales revenue per square metre of counter space, it would not be possible to deduce from this information alone whether this particular level of performance was good, bad or indifferent. It is only when we compare this ratio with some 'benchmark' that the information can be interpreted and evaluated.

Can you think of any bases that could be used to compare a ratio you have calculated from the financial statements of a particular period?
We feel that there are three sensible possibilities.

You may have thought of the following bases:

- past periods for the same business
- similar businesses for the same or past periods
- planned performance for the business.

We shall now take a closer look at these three in turn.

Past periods

By comparing the ratio we have calculated with the same ratio, but for a previous period, it is possible to detect whether there has been an improvement or deterioration in performance. Indeed, it is often useful to track particular ratios over time (say, five or ten years) to see whether it is possible to detect trends. The comparison of ratios from different periods brings certain problems, however. In particular, there is always the possibility that trading conditions were quite different in the periods being compared. There is the further problem that, when comparing the performance of a single business over time, operating inefficiencies may not be clearly exposed. For example, the fact that sales revenue per employee has risen by 10 per cent over the previous period may at first sight appear to be satisfactory. This may not be the case, however, if similar businesses have shown an improvement of 50 per cent for the same period. Finally, there is the problem that inflation may have distorted the figures on which the ratios are based. Inflation can lead to an overstatement of profit and an understatement of asset values.

Similar businesses

In a competitive environment, a business must consider its performance in relation to that of other businesses operating in the same industry. Survival may depend on the ability to achieve comparable levels of performance. A useful basis for comparing a particular ratio, therefore, is the ratio achieved by similar businesses during the same period. This basis is not, however, without its problems. Competitors may have different year ends, and therefore trading conditions may not be identical. They may also have different accounting policies, which can have a significant effect on reported profits and asset values (for example, different methods of calculating depreciation or valuing inventories). Finally, it may be difficult to obtain the financial statements of competitor businesses. Sole proprietorships and partnerships, for example, are not obliged to make their financial statements available to the public. In the case of limited companies, there is a legal obligation to do so. However, a diversified business may not provide a breakdown of activities that is sufficiently detailed to enable analysts to compare the activities with those of other businesses.

Planned performance

Ratios may be compared with the targets that management developed before the start of the period under review. The comparison of planned performance with actual performance may therefore be a useful way of revealing the level of achievement attained. However, the planned levels of performance must be based on realistic assumptions if they are to be useful for comparison purposes.

Planned performance is likely to be the most valuable benchmark for the managers to assess their own business. Businesses tend to develop planned ratios for each aspect of their activities. When formulating its plans, a business may usefully take account of its own past performance and that of other businesses. There is no reason, however, why a particular business should seek to achieve either its own previous performance or that of other businesses. Neither of these may be seen as an appropriate target.

Analysts outside the business do not normally have access to the business's plans. For these people, past performance and the performances of other, similar, businesses may be the only practical benchmarks.

Calculating the ratios

Probably the best way to explain financial ratios is through an example. Example 7.1 provides a set of financial statements from which we can calculate important ratios.

Example 7.1

The following financial statements relate to Alexis plc, which operates a whole-sale carpet business:

Balance sheets as at 31 March

	2006 £m	2007 £m
Non-current assets		
Property, plant and equipment (at cost less depreciation)		
Land and buildings	381	427
Fixtures and fittings	129	160
	510	587
Current assets		
Inventories at cost	300	406
Trade receivables	240	273
Cash at bank	4	–
	544	679
Total assets	1,054	1,266
Equity		
£0.50 ordinary shares (Note 1)	300	300
Retained earnings	263	234
	563	534
Non-current liabilities		
Borrowings – 9% loan notes (secured)	200	300
Current liabilities		
Trade payables	261	354
Taxation	30	2
Short-term borrowings (all bank overdraft)	–	76
	291	432
Total equity and liabilities	1,054	1,266

Income statements for the year ended 31 March

	2006 £m	2007 £m
Revenue (Note 2)	2,240	2,681
Cost of sales (Note 3)	(1,745)	(2,272)
Gross profit	495	409
Operating expenses	(252)	(362)
Operating profit	243	47
Interest payable	(18)	(32)
Profit before taxation	225	15
Taxation	(60)	(4)
Profit for the year	165	11

Cash flow statement for the year ended 31 March

	2006 £m	2006 £m	2007 £m	2007 £m
Cash flows from operating activities				
Net profit, after interest, before taxation	225		15	
Adjustments for:				
Depreciation	26		33	
Interest expense	18		32	
	269		80	
Increase in inventories	(59)		(106)	
Increase in trade receivables	(17)		(33)	
Increase in trade payables	58		93	
Cash generated from operations	251		34	
Interest paid	(18)		(32)	
Taxation paid	(63)		(32)	
Dividend paid	(40)		(40)	
Net cash from/(used in) operating activities		130		(70)
Cash flows from investing activities				
Payments to acquire property, plant and equipment	(77)		(110)	
Net cash used in investing activities		(77)		(110)
Cash flows from financing activities				
Issue of loan notes	–		100	
Net cash from financing activities		–		100
Net increase in cash and cash equivalents		53		(80)
Cash and cash equivalents at start of year				
Cash/(overdraft)		(49)		4
Cash and cash equivalents at end of year				
Cash/(overdraft)		4		(76)

Notes:

1 The market value of the shares of the business at the end of the year was £2.50 for 2006 and £1.50 for 2007.
2 All sales and purchases are made on credit.
3 The cost of sales figure can be analysed as follows:

	2006 £m	2007 £m
Opening inventories	241	300
Purchases (Note 2)	1,804	2,378
	1,045	2,678
Closing inventories	(300)	(406)
Cost of sales	1,745	2,272

4 A dividend of £40m had been paid to the shareholders in respect of each of the years.
5 The business employed 13,995 staff at 31 March 2006 and 18,623 at 31 March 2007.
6 The business expanded its capacity during 2007 by setting up a new warehouse and distribution centre in the north of England.
7 At 1 April 2005, the total of equity stood at £438m and the total of equity and non-current liabilities stood at £638m.

A brief overview

Before we start our detailed look at the ratios for Alexis plc (in Example 7.1), it is helpful to take a quick look at what information is obvious from the financial statements. This will usually pick up some issues that the ratios may not be able to identify. It may also highlight some points that could help us in our interpretation of the ratios. Starting at the top of the balance sheet, the following points can be noted:

- *Expansion of non-current assets.* These have increased by about 15 per cent (from £510m to £587m). Note 5 mentions a new warehouse and distribution centre, which may account for much of the additional investment in non-current assets. We are not told when this new facility was established, but it is quite possible that it was well into the year. This could mean that not much benefit was reflected in terms of additional sales revenue or cost saving during 2007. Sales revenue, in fact, expanded by about 20 per cent (from £2,240m to £2,681m), greater than the expansion in non-current assets.

- *Major expansion in the elements of working capital.* Inventories increased by about 35 per cent, trade receivables by about 14 per cent and trade payables by about 36 per cent between 2006 and 2007. These are major increases, particularly in inventories and payables (which are linked because the inventories are all bought on credit – see Note 2).

- *Reduction in the cash balance.* The cash balance fell from £4m (in funds) to a £76m overdraft, between 2006 and 2007. The bank may be putting the business under pressure to reverse this, which could raise difficulties.

- *Apparent debt capacity.* Comparing the non-current assets with the long-term borrowings implies that the business may well be able to offer security on further borrowing. This is because potential lenders usually look at the value of assets that can be offered as security when assessing loan requests. Lenders seem particularly attracted to land and, to a lesser extent, buildings as security. For example, at 31 March 2007, non-current assets had a balance sheet value of £587m, but long-term borrowing was only £300m (though there was also an overdraft of £76m). Balance sheet values are not normally, of course, market values. On the other hand, land and buildings tend to have a market value higher than their balance sheet value due to inflation in property values.

- *Lower operating profit.* Though sales revenue expanded by 20 per cent between 2006 and 2007, both cost of sales and operating expenses rose by a greater percentage, leaving both gross profit and, particularly, operating profit massively reduced. The level of staffing, which increased by about 33 per cent (from 13,995 to 18,623 employees), may have greatly affected the operating expenses. (Without knowing when the additional employees were recruited during 2007, we cannot be sure of the effect on operating expenses.) Increasing staffing by 33 per cent must put an enormous strain on management, at least in the short term. It is not surprising, therefore that 2007 was not successful for the business.

Having had a quick look at what is fairly obvious without calculating the normal ratios, we shall now go on to calculate and interpret them.

Profitability

The following ratios may be used to evaluate the profitability of the business:

- return on ordinary shareholders' funds
- return on capital employed
- operating profit margin
- gross profit margin.

We shall now look at each of these in turn.

Return on ordinary shareholders' funds (ROSF)

→ The **return on ordinary shareholders' funds ratio** compares the amount of profit for the period available to the owners, with the owners' average stake in the business during that same period. The ratio (which is normally expressed in percentage terms) is as follows:

$$\text{ROSF} = \frac{\text{Profit for the year (net profit) less any preference dividend}}{\text{Ordinary share capital} + \text{Reserves}} \times 100$$

The profit for the year (less preference dividend (if any)) is used in calculating the ratio, as this figure represents the amount of profit that is left for the owners.

In the case of Alexis plc, the ratio for the year ended 31 March 2006 is:

$$\text{ROSF} = \frac{165}{(438 + 563)/2} \times 100 = 33.0\%$$

Note that, when calculating the ROSF, the average of the figures for ordinary shareholders' funds as at the beginning and at the end of the year has been used. It is preferable to use an average figure as this is likely to be more representative. This is because the shareholders' funds did not have the same total throughout the year, yet we want to compare it with the profit earned during the whole period. We know, from Note 7, that the total of the shareholders' funds at 1 April 2005 was £438m. By a year later, however, it had risen to £563m, according to the balance sheet as at 31 March 2006.

The easiest approach to calculating the average amount of shareholders' funds is to take a simple average based on the opening and closing figures for the year. This is often the only information available, as is the case with Example 7.1. Averaging in this way is generally valid for all ratios that combine a figure for a period (such as profit for the year) with one taken at a point in time (such as shareholders' funds).

Where not even the beginning-of-year figure is available, it is usually acceptable to use just the year-end figure, provided that this approach is consistently adopted.

Activity (7.2)

Calculate the ROSF for Alexis plc for the year to 31 March 2007.

The ratio for 2007 is:

$$\text{ROSF} = \frac{11}{(563 + 534)/2} \times 100 = 2.0\%$$

Broadly, businesses seek to generate as high a value as possible for this ratio, provided that it is not achieved at the expense of potential future returns by, for example, taking on more risky activities. In view of this, the 2007 ratio is very poor by any standards; a bank deposit account will yield a better return than this. We need to try to find out why things went so badly wrong in 2007. As we look at other ratios, we should find some clues.

Return on capital employed (ROCE)

The **return on capital employed ratio** is a fundamental measure of business performance. This ratio expresses the relationship between the operating profit generated during a period and the average long-term capital invested in the business during that period.

The ratio is expressed in percentage terms and is as follows:

$$ROCE = \frac{Operating\ profit}{Share\ capital + Reserves + Non\text{-}current\ liabilities} \times 100$$

Note, in this case, that the profit figure used is the operating profit (that is, the net profit *before* interest and taxation), because the ratio attempts to measure the returns to all suppliers of long-term finance before any deductions for interest payable on borrowings, or payments of dividends to shareholders, are made.

For the year to 31 March 2006, the ratio for Alexis plc is:

$$ROCE = \frac{243}{(638 + 763)/2} \times 100 = 34.7\%$$

ROCE is considered by many to be a primary measure of profitability. It compares inputs (capital invested) with outputs (operating profit). This comparison is vital in assessing the effectiveness with which funds have been deployed. Once again, an average figure for capital employed may be used where the information is available.

Activity 7.3

Calculate the ROCE for Alexis plc for the year to 31 March 2007.

For 2007, the ratio is:

$$ROCE = \frac{47}{(763 + 834)/2} \times 100 = 5.9\%$$

This ratio tells much the same story as ROSF; namely a poor performance, with the return on the assets being less than the rate that the business has to pay for most of its borrowed funds (that is, 10 per cent for the loan notes).

Real World 7.1 shows how financial ratios are used by businesses as a basis for setting profitability targets.

Real World 7.1

Targeting profitability

The ROCE ratio is widely used by businesses when establishing targets for profitability. These targets are sometimes made public and here are some examples:

De Vere Hotels and Leisure Ltd, the UK hotels business has a target for a 10 per cent ROCE by 2006/07.

BSkyB plc, the satelite broadcaster has a target ROCE of 15 per cent by 2011 for its broadband operation.

Sources: 'De Vere is prepared to sell more assets', M. Garrahan, *Financial Times*, 12 July 2004; and 'BSkyB/triple play', FT.com, 12 July 2006.

Real World 7.2 provides some insight to the levels of ROCE achieved by UK businesses.

Real World 7.2

Achieving profitability

UK businesses reported an average ROCE of 14.4 per cent for the first quarter of 2006, equalling the 2005 rate. This was the highest level of ROCE since the Office of National Statistics first kept records.

Service sector businesses were much the more successful with an average ROCE of 19.9 per cent, compared with 6.6 per cent among manufacturers. In fact, manufacturers' average ROCE had fallen from 9.9 per cent in 2005.

Source: Information taken from 'Services companies see record return on capital but manufacturing struggles', Chris Giles, *Financial Times*, 5 July 2006.

Operating profit margin

→ The **operating profit margin ratio** relates the operating profit for the period to the sales revenue during that period. The ratio is expressed as follows:

$$\text{Operating profit margin} = \frac{\text{Operating profit}}{\text{Sales revenue}} \times 100$$

The operating profit (that is, net profit before interest and taxation) is used in this ratio as it represents the profit from trading operations before the interest payable expense is taken into account. This is often regarded as the most appropriate measure of operational performance, when used as a basis of comparison, because differences arising from the way in which the business is financed will not influence the measure.

For the year ended 31 March 2006, Alexis plc's operating profit margin ratio is:

$$\text{Operating profit margin} = \frac{243}{2,240} \times 100 = 10.8\%$$

This ratio compares one output of the business (operating profit) with another output (sales revenue). The ratio can vary considerably between types of business. For example, supermarkets tend to operate on low prices and, therefore, low operating profit margins. This is done in an attempt to stimulate sales and thereby increase the total amount of operating profit generated. Jewellers, on the other hand, tend to have high operating profit margins but have much lower levels of sales volume. Factors such as the degree of competition, the type of customer, the economic climate and industry characteristics (such as the level of risk) will influence the operating profit margin of a business. This point is picked up again later in the chapter.

Activity 7.4

Calculate the operating profit margin for Alexis plc for the year to 31 March 2007.

The ratio for 2007 is:

$$\text{Operating profit margin} = \frac{47}{2,681} \times 100 = 1.8\%$$

Once again, a very weak performance compared with that of 2006. Whereas in 2006 for every £1 of sales revenue an average of 10.8p (that is, 10.8 per cent) was left as operating profit, after paying the cost of the carpets sold and other expenses of operating the business, for 2007 this had fallen to only 1.8p for every £1. It seems that the reason for the poor ROSF and ROCE ratios was partially, perhaps wholly, a high level of expenses relative to sales revenue. The next ratio should provide us with a clue as to how the sharp decline in this ratio occurred.

Real World 7.3 describes how one well-known business intends to increase its operating profit margin over time.

Real World 7.3

Increasing the operating profit margin

Toyota, the Japanese car maker, soon to overtake General Motors of the USA as the world's leader, is targeting a 10 per cent operating profit margin.

Source: 'Nissan's empty products pipeline', M. Sanchanta, *Financial Times*, 6 November 2006.

Gross profit margin

The **gross profit margin ratio** relates the gross profit of the business to the sales revenue generated for the same period. Gross profit represents the difference between sales revenue and the cost of sales. The ratio is therefore a measure of profitability in buying (or producing) and selling goods before any other expenses are taken into account. As cost of sales represents a major expense for many businesses, a change in this ratio can have a significant effect on the 'bottom line' (that is, the profit for the year). The gross profit margin ratio is calculated as follows:

$$\text{Gross profit margin} = \frac{\text{Gross profit}}{\text{Sales revenue}} \times 100$$

For the year to 31 March 2006, the ratio for Alexis plc is:

$$\text{Gross profit margin} = \frac{495}{2,240} \times 100 = 22.1\%$$

Activity 7.5

Calculate the gross profit margin for Alexis plc for the year to 31 March 2007.

The ratio for 2007 is:

$$\text{Gross profit margin} = \frac{409}{2,681} \times 100 = 15.3\%$$

The decline in this ratio means that gross profit was lower *relative* to sales revenue in 2007 than it had been in 2006. Bearing in mind that:

Gross profit = Sales revenue – Cost of sales (or cost of goods sold)

this means that cost of sales was higher *relative* to sales revenue in 2007, than in 2006. This could mean that sales prices were lower and/or that the purchase cost of goods sold had increased. It is possible that both sales prices and goods sold prices had reduced, but the former at a greater rate than the latter. Similarly they may both have increased, but with sales prices having increased at a lesser rate than the cost of the goods sold.

Clearly, part of the decline in the operating profit margin ratio is linked to the dramatic decline in the gross profit margin ratio. Whereas, after paying for the carpets sold, for each £1 of sales revenue 22.1p was left to cover other operating expenses and leave an operating profit in 2006, this was only 15.3p in 2007.

The profitability ratios for the business over the two years can be set out as follows:

	2006	2007
	%	%
ROSF	33.0	2.0
ROCE	34.7	5.9
Operating profit margin	10.8	1.8
Gross profit margin	22.1	15.3

Activity 7.6

What do you deduce from a comparison of the declines in the operating profit and gross profit margin ratios?

It occurs to us that the decline in the operating profit margin was 9 per cent (that is, 10.8 per cent to 1.8 per cent), whereas that of the gross profit margin was only 6.8 per cent (that is, from 22.1 per cent to 15.3 per cent). This can only mean that operating expenses were greater, compared with sales revenue in 2007, than they had been in 2006. The declines in both ROSF and ROCE were caused partly, therefore, by the business incurring higher inventories purchasing costs relative to sales revenue and partly through higher operating expenses to sales revenue. We would need to compare these ratios with the planned levels for them before we could usefully assess the business's success.

The analyst must now carry out some investigation to discover what caused the increases in both cost of sales and operating expenses, relative to sales revenue, from 2006 to 2007. This will involve checking on what has happened with sales and inventories prices over the two years. Similarly, it will involve looking at each of the individual areas that make up operating expenses to discover which ones were responsible for the increase, relative to sales revenue. Here, further ratios, for example, staff expenses (wages and salaries) to sales revenue, could be calculated in an attempt to isolate the cause of the change from 2006 to 2007. In fact, as we discussed when we took an overview of the financial statements, the increase in staffing may well account for most of the increase in operating expenses.

Real World 7.4 shows how one well-known international business is seeking to improve its ROCE.

Real World 7.4

Lazy assets raise the ROCE at Shell

During 2003 Shell, the oil business (The 'Shell' Transport and Trading Company plc) disposed of $4bn of what it called 'lazy assets'. These are assets that the business felt were not earning their keep and were holding the ROCE below the target range of 13 to 15 per cent. The business had also identified a further $3bn of assets that could be 'improved', so that they could also boost the business's ROCE.

Source: Based on information in 'Shell disposals of $4 billion double initial estimate', Toby Shelley, FT.com, 22 December 2003.

Efficiency

Efficiency ratios examine the ways in which various resources of the business are managed. The following ratios consider some of the more important aspects of resource management:

- average inventories turnover period
- average settlement period for trade receivables
- average settlement period for trade payables
- sales revenue to capital employed
- sales revenue per employee.

We shall now look at each of these in turn.

Average inventories turnover period

Inventories often represent a significant investment for a business. For some types of business (for example, manufacturers), inventories may account for a substantial proportion of the total assets held (see Real World 16.1, page 617). The **average inventories turnover period ratio** measures the average period for which inventories are being held. The ratio is calculated as follows:

$$\text{Average inventories turnover period} = \frac{\text{Average inventories held}}{\text{Cost of sales}} \times 365$$

The average inventories for the period can be calculated as a simple average of the opening and closing inventories levels for the year. However, in the case of a highly seasonal business, where inventories levels may vary considerably over the year, a monthly average may be more appropriate.

In the case of Alexis plc, the inventories turnover period for the year ended 31 March 2006 is:

$$\text{Average inventories turnover period} = \frac{(241 + 300)/2}{1,745} \times 365 = 56.6 \text{ days}$$

This means that, on average, the inventories held are being 'turned over' every 56.6 days. So, a carpet bought by the business on a particular day would, on average, have been sold about eight weeks later. A business will normally prefer a short inventories turnover period to a long one, because holding inventories has a cost, for example the opportunity cost of the funds tied up. When judging the amount of inventories to carry, the business must consider such things as the likely demand for the inventories, the possibility of supply shortages, the likelihood of price rises, the amount of storage space available and the perishability/susceptibility to obsolescence of the inventories. The management of inventories will be considered in more detail in Chapter 16.

This ratio is sometimes expressed in terms of months rather than days. Multiplying by 12 rather than 365 will achieve this.

Activity 7.7

Calculate the average inventories turnover period for Alexis plc for the year ended 31 March 2007.

The ratio for 2007 is:

$$\text{Average inventories turnover period} = \frac{(300 + 406)/2}{2,272} \times 365 = 56.7 \text{ days}$$

The inventories turnover period is virtually the same in both years.

Average settlement period for trade receivables

A business will usually be concerned with amount of funds tied up in trade receivables and try to keep this to a minimum. The speed of payment can have a significant effect on the business's cash flow. The **average settlement period for trade receivables ratio** calculates how long, on average, credit customers take to pay the amounts that they owe to the business. The ratio is as follows:

$$\text{Average settlement period for trade receivables} = \frac{\text{Trade receivables}}{\text{Credit sales revenue}} \times 365$$

A business will normally prefer a shorter average settlement period to a longer one as, once again, funds are being tied up that may be used for more profitable purposes. Although this ratio can be useful, it is important to remember that it produces an *average* figure for the number of days for which debts are outstanding. This average may be badly distorted by, for example, a few large customers who are very slow or very fast payers.

Since all sales made by Alexis plc are on credit, the average settlement period for trade receivables for the year ended 31 March 2006 is:

$$\text{Average settlement period for trade receivables} = \frac{240}{2,240} \times 365 = 39.1 \text{ days}$$

As no figure for opening trade receivables is available, only the year-end figure is used. This is common practice for calculating any ratio where averaging would be desirable but is impossible because of lack of the opening value.

Activity 7.8

Calculate the average settlement period for Alexis plc's trade receivables for the year ended 31 March 2007. (To be consistent with the 2006 calculation, use the year-end trade receivables figure rather than an average figure.)

The ratio for 2007 is:

$$\text{Average settlement period for trade receivables} = \frac{273}{2,681} \times 365 = 37.2 \text{ days}$$

On the face of it, this reduction in the settlement period is welcome. It means that less cash was tied up in trade receivables for each £1 of sales revenue in 2007 than in 2006. Only if the reduction were achieved at the expense of customer goodwill or a high direct financial cost might the desirability of the reduction be questioned. For example, the reduction may have been due to chasing customers too vigorously or as a result of incurring higher expenses, such as discounts allowed to customers who pay quickly.

Average settlement period for trade payables

→ The **average settlement period for trade payables ratio** measures how long, on average, the business takes to pay those who have supplied goods and services on credit. The ratio is calculated as follows:

$$\text{Average settlement period for trade payables} = \frac{\text{Trade payables}}{\text{Credit purchases}} \times 365$$

This ratio provides an average figure, which, like the average settlement period for trade receivables ratio, can be distorted by the payment period for one or two large suppliers.

As trade payables provide a free source of finance for the business, it is perhaps not surprising that some businesses attempt to increase their average settlement period for trade payables. However, such a policy can be taken too far and result in a loss of goodwill of suppliers. We shall return to the issues concerning the management of trade receivables and trade payables in Chapter 16.

For the year ended 31 March 2006, Alexis plc's average settlement period for trade payables is:

$$\text{Average settlement period for trade payables} = \frac{261}{1,804} \times 365 = 52.8 \text{ days}$$

Once again, the year-end figure rather than an average figure for trade payables has been used in the calculations.

Activity (7.9)

Calculate the average settlement period for trade payables for Alexis plc for the year ended 31 March 2007. (For the sake of consistency, use a year-end figure for trade payables.)

The ratio for 2007 is:

$$\text{Average settlement period for trade payables} = \frac{354}{2,378} \times 365 = 54.3 \text{ days}$$

There was an increase, between 2006 and 2007, in the average length of time that elapsed between buying inventories and services and paying for them. On the face of it, this is beneficial because the business is using free finance provided by suppliers. If, however, this is leading to a loss of supplier goodwill that could have adverse consequences for Alexis plc, it is not necessarily advantageous.

Sales revenue to capital employed

→ The **sales revenue to capital employed ratio** (or asset turnover ratio) examines how effectively the assets of the business are being used to generate sales revenue. It is calculated as follows:

$$\frac{\text{Sales revenue to}}{\text{capital employed ratio}} = \frac{\text{Sales revenue}}{\text{Share capital} + \text{Reserves} + \text{Non-current liabilities}}$$

Generally speaking, a higher asset turnover ratio is preferred to a lower one. A higher ratio will normally suggest that assets are being used more productively in the generation of revenue. However, a very high ratio may suggest that the business is 'overtrading on its assets', that is, it has insufficient assets to sustain the level of sales revenue achieved. (Overtrading will be discussed in more detail later in the chapter.) When comparing this ratio for different businesses, factors such as the age and condition of assets held, the valuation bases for assets and whether assets are leased or owned outright can complicate interpretation.

A variation of this formula is to use the total assets less current liabilities (which is equivalent to long-term capital employed) in the denominator (lower part of the fraction). The identical result is obtained.

For the year ended 31 March 2006 this ratio for Alexis plc is:

$$\text{Sales revenue to capital employed} = \frac{2,240}{(638 + 763)/2} = 3.20 \text{ times}$$

Activity (7.10)

Calculate the sales revenue to capital employed ratio for Alexis plc for the year ended 31 March 2007.

The sales revenue to capital employed ratio for the 2007 is:

$$\text{Sales revenue to capital employed} = \frac{2,681}{(763 + 834)/2} = 3.36 \text{ times}$$

This seems to be an improvement, since in 2007 more sales revenue was being generated for each £1 of capital employed (£3.36) than was the case in 2006 (£3.20). Provided that overtrading is not an issue and that the additional sales are generating an acceptable profit, this is to be welcomed.

Sales revenue per employee

→ The **sales revenue per employee ratio** relates sales revenue generated to a particular business resource, that is, labour. It provides a measure of the productivity of the workforce. The ratio is:

$$\text{Sales revenue per employee} = \frac{\text{Sales revenue}}{\text{Number of employees}}$$

Generally, businesses would prefer to have a high value for this ratio, implying that they are using their staff efficiently.

For the year ended 31 March 2006, the ratio for Alexis plc is:

$$\text{Sales revenue per employee} = \frac{£2,240\text{m}}{13,995} = £160,057$$

Activity 7.11

Calculate the sales revenue per employee for Alexis plc for the year ended 31 March 2007.

The ratio for 2007 is:

$$\text{Sales revenue per employee} = \frac{£2,681\text{m}}{18,623} = £143,962$$

This represents a fairly significant decline and probably one that merits further investigation. As we discussed previously, the number of employees had increased quite notably (by about 33 per cent) during 2007 and the analyst will probably try to discover why this had not generated sufficient additional sales revenue to maintain the ratio at its 2006 level. It could be that the additional employees were not appointed until late in the year ended 31 March 2007.

The efficiency, or activity, ratios may be summarised as follows:

	2006	2007
Average inventories turnover period	56.6 days	56.7 days
Average settlement period for trade receivables	39.1 days	37.2 days
Average settlement period for trade payables	52.8 days	54.3 days
Sales revenue to capital employed (asset turnover)	3.20 times	3.36 times
Sales revenue per employee	£160,057	£143,962

Activity (7.12)

What do you deduce from a comparison of the efficiency ratios over the two years?

We feel that maintaining the inventories turnover period at the 2006 level might be reasonable, though whether this represents a satisfactory period can probably only be assessed by looking at the business's planned inventories period. The inventories holding period for other businesses operating in carpet retailing, particularly those regarded as the market leaders, may have been helpful in formulating the plans. On the face of things, a shorter receivables collection period and a longer payables payment period are both desirable. On the other hand, these may have been achieved at the cost of a loss of the goodwill of customers and suppliers, respectively. The increased asset turnover ratio seems beneficial, provided that the business can manage this increase. The decline in the sales revenue per employee ratio is undesirable but, as we have already seen, is probably related to the dramatic increase in the level of staffing. As with the inventories turnover period, these other ratios need to be compared with the planned standard of efficiency.

Relationship between profitability and efficiency

In our earlier discussions concerning profitability ratios, we saw that return on capital employed (ROCE) is regarded as a key ratio by many businesses. The ratio is:

$$\text{ROCE} = \frac{\text{Operating profit}}{\text{Long-term capital employed}} \times 100$$

where long-term capital comprises share capital plus reserves plus long-term borrowings. This ratio can be broken down into two elements, as shown in Figure 7.1. The first ratio is the operating profit margin ratio, and the second is the sales revenue to capital employed (asset turnover) ratio, both of which we discussed earlier.

Figure 7.1 **The main elements of the ROCE ratio**

The ROCE ratio can be divided into two elements: operating profit to sales revenue and sales revenue to capital employed. By analysing ROCE in this way, we can see the influence of both profitability and efficiency on this important ratio.

By breaking down the ROCE ratio in this manner, we highlight the fact that the overall return on funds employed within the business will be determined both by the profitability of sales and by efficiency in the use of capital.

Example 7.2

Consider the following information, for last year, concerning two different businesses operating in the same industry:

	Antler plc	Baker plc
Operating profit	£20m	£15m
Average long-term capital employed	£100m	£75m
Sales revenue	£200m	£300m

The ROCE for each business is identical (20 per cent). However, the manner in which that return was achieved by each business was quite different. In the case of Antler plc, the operating profit margin is 10 per cent and the sales revenue to capital employed ratio is 2 times (so ROCE = 10% × 2 = 20%). In the case of Baker plc, the operating profit margin is 5 per cent and the sales revenue to capital employed ratio is 4 times (and so ROCE = 5% × 4 = 20%).

Example 7.2 demonstrates that a relatively high sales revenue to capital employed ratio can compensate for a relatively low operating profit margin. Similarly, a relatively low sales revenue to capital employed ratio can be overcome by a relatively high operating profit margin. In many areas of retail and distribution (for example, supermarkets and delivery services), the operating profit margins are quite low but the ROCE can be high, provided that the assets are used productively (that is, low margin, high turnover).

Activity 7.13

Show how the ROCE ratio for Alexis plc can be analysed into the two elements for each of the years 2006 and 2007. What conclusions can you draw from your figures?

	ROCE =	Operating profit margin	×	Sales revenue to capital employed
2006	34.7%	10.8%		3.20
2007	5.9%	1.8%		3.36

As we can see, the relationship between the three ratios holds for Alexis plc for both years. The small apparent differences arise because the three ratios are stated here only to one or two decimal places.

Although the business was more effective at generating sales revenue (sales revenue to capital employed ratio increased) in 2007 than in 2006, in 2007 it fell well below the level necessary to compensate for the sharp decline in the effectiveness of each sale (operating profit margin). As a result, the 2007 ROCE was well below the 2006 value.

Liquidity

Liquidity ratios are concerned with the ability of the business to meet its short-term financial obligations. The following ratios are widely used:

- current ratio
- acid test ratio
- operating cash flows to maturing obligations.

These three will now be considered.

Current ratio

→ The **current ratio** compares the 'liquid' assets (that is, cash and those assets held that will soon be turned into cash) of the business with the current liabilities. The ratio is calculated as follows:

$$\text{Current ratio} = \frac{\text{Current assets}}{\text{Current liabilities}}$$

Some people seem to believe that there is an 'ideal' current ratio (usually 2 times or 2:1) for all businesses. However, this fails to take into account the fact that different types of business require different current ratios. For example, a manufacturing business will often have a relatively high current ratio because it is necessary to hold inventories of finished goods, raw materials and work-in-progress. It will also normally sell goods on credit, thereby giving rise to trade receivables. A supermarket chain, on the other hand, will have a relatively low ratio, as it will hold only fast-moving inventories of finished goods and all of its sales will be made for cash (no credit sales). (See Real World 16.1 on page 617.)

The higher the ratio, the more liquid the business is considered to be. As liquidity is vital to the survival of a business, a higher current ratio might be thought to be preferable to a lower one. If a business has a very high ratio, however, it may be that funds are tied up in cash or other liquid assets and are not, therefore, being used as productively as they might otherwise be.

As at 31 March 2006, the current ratio of Alexis plc is:

$$\text{Current ratio} = \frac{544}{291} = 1.9 \text{ times (or 1.9:1)}$$

Activity (7.14)

Calculate the current ratio for Alexis plc as at 31 March 2007.

The ratio as at 31 March 2007 is:

$$\text{Current ratio} = \frac{679}{432} = 1.6 \text{ times (or 1.6:1)}$$

Although this is a decline from 2006 to 2007, it is not necessarily a matter of concern. The next ratio may provide a clue as to whether there seems to be a problem.

Acid test ratio

→ The **acid test ratio** is very similar to the current ratio, but it represents a more stringent test of liquidity. It can be argued that, for many businesses, inventories cannot be converted into cash quickly. (Note that, in the case of Alexis plc, the inventories turnover period was about 57 days in both years (see page 234).) As a result, it may be better to exclude this particular asset from any measure of liquidity. The acid test ratio is a variation of the current ratio, but excluding inventories.

The minimum level for this ratio is often stated as 1.0 times (or 1:1; that is, current assets (excluding inventories) equals current liabilities). In many highly successful businesses that are regarded as having adequate liquidity, however, it is not unusual for the acid test ratio to be below 1.0 without causing particular liquidity problems. (See Real World 16.1 on page 617.)

The acid test ratio is calculated as follows:

$$\text{Acid test ratio} = \frac{\text{Current assets (excluding inventories)}}{\text{Current liabilities}}$$

The acid test ratio for Alexis plc as at 31 March 2006 is:

$$\text{Acid test ratio} = \frac{544 - 300}{291} = 0.8 \text{ times (or 0.8:1)}$$

We can see that the 'liquid' current assets do not quite cover the current liabilities, so the business may be experiencing some liquidity problems.

Activity 7.15

Calculate the acid test ratio for Alexis plc as at 31 March 2007.

The ratio as at 31 March 2006 is:

$$\text{Acid test ratio} = \frac{679 - 406}{432} = 0.6 \text{ times}$$

The 2007 ratio is significantly below that for 2006. The 2007 level may well be a cause for concern. The rapid decline in this ratio should lead to steps being taken, at least, to stop further decline.

Cash generated from operations to maturing obligations

→ The **cash generated from operations to maturing obligations ratio** compares the cash generated from operations (taken from the cash flow statement) with the current liabilities of the business. It provides a further indication of the ability of the business to meet its maturing obligations. The ratio is expressed as:

$$\frac{\text{Cash generated from operations}}{\text{to maturing obligations}} = \frac{\text{Cash generated from operations}}{\text{Current liabilities}}$$

The higher this ratio, the better the liquidity of the business. This ratio has the advantage over the current ratio that the operating cash flows for a period usually provide a more reliable guide to the liquidity of a business than do the current assets held at the balance sheet date. Alexis plc's ratio for the year ended 31 March 2006 is:

$$\text{Cash generated from operations to maturing obligations ratio} = \frac{251}{291} = 0.9 \text{ times}$$

This ratio indicates that the operating cash flows for the period are not quite sufficient to cover the current liabilities at the end of the period.

Activity (7.16)

Calculate the cash generated from operations to maturing obligations ratio for Alexis plc for the year ended 31 March 2007.

$$\text{Cash generated from operations to maturing obligations ratio} = \frac{34}{432} = 0.1 \text{ times}$$

This ratio shows an alarming decline in the ability of the business to meet its maturing obligations from its operating cash flows. This confirms that liquidity is a real cause for concern for the business.

The liquidity ratios for the two-year period may be summarised as follows:

	2006	2007
Current ratio	1.9	1.6
Acid test ratio	0.8	0.6
Cash generated from operations to maturing obligations	0.9	0.1

Activity (7.17)

What do you deduce from the liquidity ratios set out above?

Although it is probably not really possible to make a totally valid judgement without knowing the planned ratios, there appears to have been a worrying decline in liquidity. This is indicated by all three of these ratios. The most worrying is in the last ratio because it shows that the ability of the business to generate cash from trading operations has declined, relative to the short-term debts, from 2006 to 2007. The apparent liquidity problem may, however, be planned, short term and linked to the expansion in non-current assets and staffing. It may be that when the benefits of the expansion come on stream, liquidity will improve. On the other hand, short-term claimants may become anxious when they see signs of weak liquidity. This anxiety could lead to steps being taken to press for payment, and this could cause problems for Alexis plc.

Financial gearing

→ **Financial gearing** occurs when a business is financed, at least in part, by borrowing instead of by finance provided by the owners (the shareholders) as equity. A business's level of gearing (that is, the extent to which it is financed from sources that require a fixed return) is an important factor in assessing risk. Where a business borrows, it takes on a commitment to pay interest charges and make capital repayments. Where the borrowing is heavy, this can be a significant financial burden; it can increase the risk of the business becoming insolvent. Nevertheless, most businesses are geared to some extent.

Given the risks involved, we may wonder why a business would want to take on gearing (that is, to borrow). One reason may be that the owners have insufficient funds, so the only way to finance the business adequately is to borrow from others. Another reason is that gearing can be used to increase the returns to owners. This is possible provided the returns generated from borrowed funds exceed the cost of paying interest. Example 7.3 illustrates this point.

Example 7.3

The long-term capital structures of two new businesses, Lee Ltd and Nova Ltd, are as follows:

	Lee Ltd £	Nova Ltd £
£1 ordinary shares	100,000	200,000
10% loan notes	200,000	100,000
	300,000	300,000

In their first year of operations, they each make an operating profit (that is, profit before interest and taxation) of £50,000. The tax rate is 30 per cent of the profit before taxation after interest.

Lee Ltd would probably be considered relatively highly geared, as it has a high proportion of borrowed funds in its long-term capital structure. Nova Ltd is much lower geared. The profit available to the shareholders of each business in the first year of operations will be:

	Lee Ltd £	Nova Ltd £
Operating profit	50,000	50,000
Interest payable	(20,000)	(10,000)
Profit before taxation	30,000	40,000
Taxation (30%)	(9,000)	(12,000)
Profit for the year (available to ordinary shareholders)	21,000	28,000

The return on ordinary shareholders' funds (ROSF) for each business will be:

Lee Ltd

$$\frac{21,000}{100,000} \times 100 = 21\%$$

Nova Ltd

$$\frac{28,000}{200,000} \times 100 = 14\%$$

We can see that Lee Ltd, the more highly geared business, has generated a better ROSF than Nova Ltd. This is despite the fact that the ROCE (return on capital employed) is identical for both businesses (that is, (£50,000/£300,000) × 100 = 16.7%).

Note that at the £50,000 level of operating profit, the shareholders of both Lee Ltd and Nova Ltd benefit from gearing. Were the two businesses totally reliant on equity financing, the profit for the year (after taxation profit) would be £35,000 (that is, £50,000 less 30 per cent taxation), giving an ROSF of 11.7 per cent (that is, £35,000/£300,000). Both businesses generate higher ROSFs than this as a result of financial gearing.

An effect of gearing is that returns to shareholders become more sensitive to changes in operating profits. For a highly geared business, a change in operating profits will lead to a proportionately greater change in the ROSF ratio.

Activity (7.18)

Assume that the operating profit was 20 per cent higher for each business than stated above (that is, an operating profit of £60,000). What would be the effect of this on ROSF?

The revised profit available to the shareholders of each business in the first year of operations will be:

	Lee Ltd	Nova Ltd
	£	£
Operating profit	60,000	60,000
Interest payable	(20,000)	(10,000)
Profit before taxation	40,000	50,000
Taxation (30%)	(12,000)	(15,000)
Profit for the year (available to ordinary shareholders)	28,000	35,000

The ROSF for each business will now be:

Lee Ltd
$$\frac{28,000}{100,000} \times 100 = 28\%$$

Nova Ltd
$$\frac{35,000}{200,000} \times 100 = 17.5\%$$

We can see that for Lee Ltd, the higher-geared business, the returns to shareholders have increased by one-third (from 21 per cent to 28 per cent), whereas for the lower-geared business, Nova Ltd, the benefits of gearing are less pronounced, increasing by only one-quarter (from 14 per cent to 17.5 per cent). The effect of gearing can of course, work in both directions. So, for a highly geared business, a small decline in operating profit will bring about a much greater decline in the returns to shareholders.

The reason that gearing tends to be beneficial to shareholders is that interest rates for borrowings are low by comparison with the returns that the typical business can earn. On top of this, interest expenses are tax deductible, in the way shown in Example 7.3 and Activity 7.17, making the effective cost of borrowing quite cheap. It is debatable whether the apparent low interest rates really are beneficial to the shareholders. Some argue that since borrowing increases the risk to shareholders, there is a hidden cost of borrowing. What are not illusory, however, are the benefits to the shareholders of the tax deductibility of loan interest.

The effect of gearing is like that of two intermeshing cogwheels of unequal size (see Figure 7.2). The movement in the larger cog (operating profit) causes a more than proportionate movement in the smaller cog (returns to ordinary shareholders). The subject of gearing is discussed further in Chapter 15.

Two ratios are widely used to assess gearing:

- gearing ratio
- interest cover ratio.

Gearing ratio

→ The **gearing ratio** measures the contribution of long-term lenders to the long-term capital structure of a business:

Figure 7.2   The effect of financial gearing

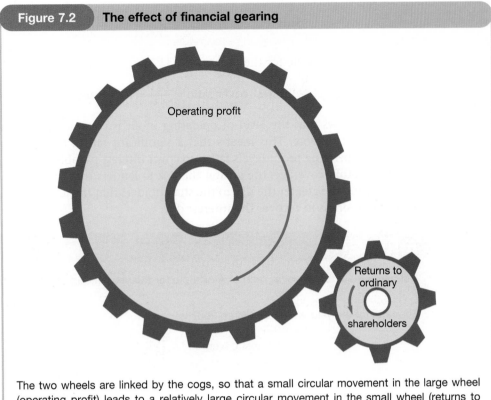

The two wheels are linked by the cogs, so that a small circular movement in the large wheel (operating profit) leads to a relatively large circular movement in the small wheel (returns to ordinary shareholders).

$$\text{Gearing ratio} = \frac{\text{Long-term (non-current) liabilities}}{\text{Share capital + Reserves + Long-term (non-current) liabilities}} \times 100$$

The gearing ratio for Alexis plc, as at 31 March 2006, is:

$$\text{Gearing ratio} = \frac{200}{(563 + 200)} \times 100 = 26.2\%$$

This ratio reveals a level of gearing that would not normally be considered to be very high.

Activity 7.19

Calculate the gearing ratio of Alexis plc as at 31 March 2007.

The ratio as at 31 March 2007 is:

$$\text{Gearing ratio} = \frac{300}{(534 + 300)} \times 100 = 36.0\%$$

This ratio reveals a substantial increase in the level of gearing over the year.

Interest cover ratio

The **interest cover ratio** measures the amount of operating profit available to cover interest payable. The ratio may be calculated as follows:

$$\text{Interest cover ratio} = \frac{\text{Operating profit}}{\text{Interest payable}}$$

The ratio for Alexis plc for the year ended 31 March 2006 is:

$$\text{Interest cover ratio} = \frac{243}{18} = 13.5 \text{ times}$$

This ratio shows that the level of operating profit is considerably higher than the level of interest payable. This means that a significant fall in operating profit could occur before operating profit levels failed to cover interest payable. The lower the level of operating profit coverage, the greater the risk to lenders that interest payments will not be met, and the greater the risk to the shareholders that the lenders will take action against the business to recover the interest due.

Activity 7.20

Calculate the interest cover ratio of Alexis plc for the year ended 31 March 2007.

The ratio for the year ended 31 March 2007 is:

$$\text{Interest cover ratio} = \frac{47}{32} = 1.5 \text{ times}$$

Real World 7.5 shows how Tesco plc the UK and, increasingly, international supermarket chain was able to use financial gearing to boost ROSF in the early 2000s.

Real World 7.5

Changing gear at Tesco

Figure 7.3 plots the ROSF, ROCE and interest cover ratios over the period 2000 to 2006.

Figure 7.3   The effect of financial gearing at Tesco plc, 2000 to 2006

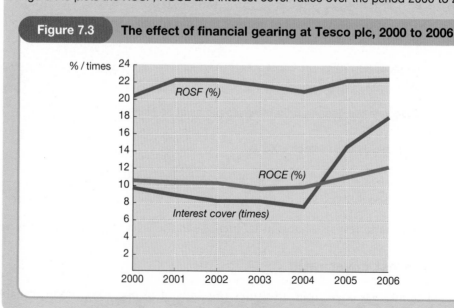

Tesco was able to boost returns to shareholders (ROSF), despite the business not producing a better ROCE (which reduced slightly between 1999 and 2003). This was achieved as a result of increasing financial gearing (as measured by interest cover) over that period. After 2004, Tesco started to reduce gearing again. Now ROSF continued to increase, but as a result of increasing ROCE.

Source: Based on information contained in Tesco plc Annual Reports from 2003 to 2006.

Alexis plc's gearing ratios are:

	2006	2007
Gearing ratio	26.2%	36.0%
Interest cover ratio	13.5 times	1.5 times

Activity 7.21

What do you deduce from a comparison of Alexis plc's gearing ratios over the two years?

The gearing ratio altered significantly. This is mainly due to the substantial increase in long-term lenders to the financing of the business.

The interest cover ratio has declined dramatically from a position where operating profit covered interest 13.5 times in 2006, to one where operating profit covered interest only 1.5 times in 2007. This was partly caused by the increase in borrowings in 2007, but mainly caused by the dramatic decline in profitability in that year. The later situation looks hazardous; only a small decline in future profitability in 2007 would leave the business with insufficient operating profit to cover the interest payments. The gearing ratio at 31 March 2007 would not necessarily be considered to be very high for a business that was trading successfully. It is the low profitability that is the problem.

Without knowing what the business planned these ratios to be, it is not possible to reach a valid conclusion on Alexis plc's gearing.

Real World 7.6 provides some evidence concerning the gearing of listed businesses.

Real World 7.6

The gearing of listed businesses

Larger listed businesses tend to have higher levels of gearing than smaller ones. A Bank of England report on the financing of small businesses found that the average level of gearing among smaller listed businesses was 27 per cent compared with 37 per cent for the top 350 listed businesses. Over recent years the level of borrowing by larger listed businesses has risen steadily (Tesco plc – see Real World 7.5 – provides an example of this) whereas the level of borrowing for smaller listed businesses has remained fairly stable. This difference in gearing levels between larger and smaller businesses flies in the face of conventional wisdom.

Recent government investigations have found that smaller listed businesses often find it hard to attract investors. Many large institutional investors, who dominate the stock market, are not interested in the shares of smaller listed businesses because the amount of investment required is too small. As a result, shares in smaller businesses are less marketable. In such circumstances, it may be imagined that smaller businesses would

Real World 7.6 continued

become more reliant on borrowing and so would have higher levels of gearing than larger businesses. However, this is clearly not the case.

Although smaller businesses increase the level of shareholder funds by paying relatively low dividends and retaining more profits, they tend to be less profitable than larger businesses. So, higher retained profits do not seem to explain this phenomenon satisfactorily.

The only obvious factors that could explain this difference between smaller and larger businesses are the level of tax relief on interest on borrowings, and borrowing capacity. Broadly, larger businesses pay tax at a higher rate than their smaller counterparts. This means that the tax benefits of borrowing tend to be greater per £ of interest paid for larger businesses than for smaller ones. It may well be that larger businesses can borrow at lower interest rates than smaller ones, if only because they tend to borrow larger sums and so economies of scale may apply. Also, larger businesses tend to be less likely to get into financial difficulties than smaller ones, so they may be able to borrow at lower interest rates.

Source: Adapted from 'Small companies surprise on lending', *Financial Times*, 25 April 2003.

Investment ratios

There are various ratios available that are designed to help investors assess the returns on their investment. The following are widely used:

- dividend payout ratio
- dividend yield ratio
- earnings per share
- operating cash flow per share
- price/earnings ratio.

Dividend payout ratio

 The **dividend payout ratio** measures the proportion of earnings that a business pays out to shareholders in the form of dividends. The ratio is calculated as follows:

$$\text{Dividend payout ratio} = \frac{\text{Dividends announced for the year}}{\text{Earnings for the year available for dividends}} \times 100$$

In the case of ordinary shares, the earnings available for dividend will normally be the profit for the year (that is, the net profit after taxation) less any preference dividends relating to the year. This ratio is normally expressed as a percentage.

The dividend payout ratio for Alexis plc for the year ended 31 March 2006 is:

$$\text{Dividend payout ratio} = \frac{40}{165} \times 100 = 24.2\%$$

The information provided by this ratio is often expressed slightly differently as the **dividend cover ratio**. Here the calculation is:

$$\text{Dividend cover ratio} = \frac{\text{Earnings for the year available for dividend}}{\text{Dividend announced for the year}}$$

In the case of Alexis plc (for 2006) it would be 165/40 = 4.1 times. That is to say, the earnings available for dividend cover the actual dividend by just over four times.

→

Activity (7.22)

Calculate the dividend payout ratio of Alexis plc for the year ended 31 March 2007.

The ratio for 2007 is:

$$\text{Dividend payout ratio} = \frac{40}{11} \times 100 = 363.6\%$$

This would normally be considered to be a very alarming increase in the ratio over the two years. Paying a dividend of £40m in 2007 would probably be regarded as very imprudent.

Dividend yield ratio

→ The **dividend yield ratio** relates the cash return from a share to its current market value. This can help investors to assess the cash return on their investment in the business. The ratio, expressed as a percentage is:

$$\text{Dividend yield} = \frac{\text{Dividend per share}/(1 - t)}{\text{Market value per share}} \times 100$$

where t is the 'dividend tax credit' rate of income tax. This requires some explanation. In the UK, investors who receive a dividend from a business also receive a tax credit. As this tax credit can be offset against any tax liability arising from the dividends received, the dividends are effectively issued net of income tax, at the dividend tax credit rate.

Investors may wish to compare the returns from shares with the returns from other forms of investment. As these other forms of investment are often quoted on a 'gross' (that is, pre-tax) basis it is useful to 'gross up' the dividend to make comparison easier. We can achieve this by dividing the **dividend per share** by $(1 - t)$, where t is the

→ 'dividend tax credit' rate of income tax.

Using the 2007/08 dividend tax credit rate of 10 per cent, the dividend yield for Alexis plc for the year ended 31 March 2006 is:

$$\text{Dividend yield} = \frac{0.067^*/(1 - 0.10)}{2.50} \times 100 = 3.0\%$$

* Dividend proposed/number of shares = 40/(300 × 2) = £0.067 dividend per share (the 300 is multiplied by 2 because they are £0.50 shares).

Activity (7.23)

Calculate the dividend yield for Alexis plc for the year ended 31 March 2007.

The ratio for 2007 is:

$$\text{Dividend yield} = \frac{0.067^*/(1 - 0.10)}{1.50} \times 100 = 4.9\%$$

* 40/(300 × 2) = £0.067.

Earnings per share

→ The **earnings per share (EPS)** ratio relates the earnings generated by the business, and available to shareholders, during a period to the number of shares in issue. For equity (ordinary) shareholders, the amount available will be represented by the profit for the year (net profit after taxation) less any preference dividend, where applicable. The ratio for equity shareholders is calculated as follows:

$$\text{Earnings per share} = \frac{\text{Earnings available to ordinary shareholders}}{\text{Number of ordinary shares in issue}}$$

In the case of Alexis plc, the earnings per share for the year ended 31 March 2006 is as follows:

$$\text{EPS} = \frac{£165m}{600m} = 27.5p$$

Many investment analysts regard the EPS ratio as a fundamental measure of share performance. The trend in earnings per share over time is used to help assess the investment potential of a business's shares. Although it is possible to make total profit rise through ordinary shareholders investing more in the business, this will not necessarily mean that the profitability *per share* will rise as a result.

It is not usually very helpful to compare the EPS of one business with that of another. Differences in capital structure (for example, in the nominal value of shares issued) can render any such comparison meaningless. However, it can be very useful to monitor the changes that occur in this ratio for a particular business over time.

Activity (7.24)

Calculate the earnings per share of Alexis plc for the year ended 31 March 2007.

The ratio for 2007 is:

$$\text{EPS} = \frac{£11m}{600m} = 1.8p$$

Cash generated from operations per share

It can be argued that, in the short term at least, cash generated from operations (found in the cash flow statement) provides a better guide to the ability of a business to pay dividends and to undertake planned expenditures than the earnings per share figure. The
→ **cash generated from operations (CGO) per ordinary share ratio** is calculated as follows:

$$\text{Cash generated from operations per share} = \frac{\text{Cash generated from operations less preference dividend (if any)}}{\text{Number of ordinary shares in issue}}$$

The ratio for Alexis plc for the year ended 31 March 2006 is as follows:

$$\text{CGO per share} = \frac{£251m}{600m} = 41.8p$$

Calculate the CGO per ordinary share for Alexis plc for the year ended 31 March 2007.

The ratio for 2007 is:

$$\text{CGO per share} = \frac{£34m}{600m} = 5.7p$$

There has been a dramatic decrease in this ratio over the two-year period.

Note that, for both years, the CGO per share for Alexis plc is higher than the earnings per share. This is not unusual. The effect of adding back depreciation to derive the CGO figures will often ensure that a higher figure is derived.

Price/earnings (P/E) ratio

→ The **price/earnings ratio** relates the market value of a share to the earnings per share. This ratio can be calculated as follows:

$$\text{P/E ratio} = \frac{\textbf{Market value per share}}{\textbf{Earnings per share}}$$

The P/E ratio for Alexis plc as at 31 March 2006 is:

$$\text{P/E ratio} = \frac{£2.50}{27.5p^*} = 9.1 \text{ times}$$

* The EPS figure (27.5p) was calculated on page 250.

This ratio reveals that the capital value of the share is 9.1 times higher than its current level of earnings. The ratio is a measure of market confidence in the future of a business. The higher the P/E ratio, the greater the confidence in the future earning power of the business and, consequently, the more investors are prepared to pay in relation to the earnings stream of the business.

P/E ratios provide a useful guide to market confidence concerning the future and they can, therefore, be helpful when comparing different businesses. However, differences in accounting policies between businesses can lead to different profit and earnings per share figures, and this can distort comparisons.

Calculate the P/E ratio of Alexis plc as at 31 March 2007.

The ratio for 2007 is:

$$\text{P/E ratio} = \frac{£1.50}{1.8p} = 83.3 \text{ times}$$

The investment ratios for Alexis plc over the two-year period are as follows:

	2006	2007
Dividend payout ratio	24.2%	363.6%
Dividend yield ratio	3.0%	4.9%
Earnings per share	27.5p	1.8p
Cash generated from operations per share	41.8p	5.7p
P/E ratio	9.1 times	83.3 times

Activity (7.27)

What do you deduce from the investment ratios set out above?
   Can you offer an explanation why the share price has not fallen as much as it might have done, bearing in mind the very poor (relative to 2006) trading performance in 2007?

We thought that, although the EPS has fallen dramatically and the dividend payment for 2007 seems very imprudent, the share price seems to have held up remarkably well (fallen from £2.50 to £1.50, see page 226). This means that dividend yield and P/E value for 2007 look better than those for 2006. This is an anomaly of these two ratios, which stems from using a forward-looking value (the share price) in conjunction with historic data (dividends and earnings). Share prices are based on investors' assessments of the business's future. It seems with Alexis plc that, at the end of 2007, the 'market' was not happy with the business, relative to 2006. This is evidenced by the fact that the share price had fallen by £1 a share. On the other hand, the share price has not fallen as much as profit for the year. It appears that investors believe that the business will perform better in the future than it did in 2007. This may well be because they believe that the large expansion in assets and employee numbers that occurred in 2007 will yield benefits in the future; benefits that the business was not able to generate during 2007.

Real World 7.7 gives some information about the shares of several large, well-known UK businesses. This type of information is provided on a daily basis by several newspapers, notably the *Financial Times*.

Real World 7.7

Market statistics for some well-known businesses

The following data was extracted from the *Financial Times* on 11 November 2006, relating to the previous day's trading of the shares of some well-known businesses on the London Stock Exchange:

Share	Price	Chng	2006 High	Low	Y'ld	P/E	Volume 000s
BP	598	−3.5	723.08	558.5	3.6	11.2	101,930
J D Wetherspoon	646.5	+19	646.5	317	0.7	27.3	419
BSkyB	551	−3	578	471.19	2.2	18.3	7,677
Marks and Spencer	702	–	716.50	477.19	2	19.9	19,533
Rolls-Royce	461.25	+2.75	496.75	373	1.6	9.4	3,823
Vodafone	134.50	+0.50	138.38	107.37	4.5	9.8	353,257

The column headings are as follows:

Price   Mid-market price in pence (that is, the price midway between buying and selling price) of the shares at the end of 10 November 2006.

Chng   Gain or loss in the mid-market price during 10 November 2006.

High/Low   Highest and lowest prices reached by the share during the year.

Y'ld   Gross dividend yield, based on the most recent year's dividend and the current share price.

P/E   Price/earnings ratio, based on the most recent year's (after-tax) profit for the year and the current share price.

Volume   The number of shares (in thousands) that were bought/sold on 10 November 2006.

So, for example for BP, the oil business:

- the shares had a mid-market price of £5.98 each at the close of Stock Exchange trading on 10 November 2006;
- the shares had decreased in price by 3.5 pence during trading on 10 November;
- the shares had highest and lowest prices during 2006 of £7.2308 and £5.585, respectively.
- the shares had a dividend yield, based on the 10 November price (and the dividend for the most recent year) of 3.6 per cent.
- the shares had a P/E ratio, based on the 10 November price (and the after-taxation earnings per share for the most recent year) of 11.2.
- During trading in the shares on 10 November, 101,930,000 of the business's shares had changed hands from one investor to another.

Real World 7.8 shows how investment ratios can vary between different industry sectors.

Real World 7.8

How investment ratios vary between industries

Investment ratios can vary significantly between businesses and between industries. To give some indication of the range of variations that occur, the average dividend yield ratios and average P/E ratios for listed businesses in twelve different industries are shown in Figures 7.4 and 7.5, respectively.

These dividend yield ratios are calculated from the current market value of the shares and the most recent year's dividend paid.

Some industries tend to pay out lower dividends than others, leading to lower dividend yield ratios. The average for all Stock Exchange listed businesses was (as is shown in Figure 7.4) 2.93, but there is a wide variation with Real Estate at 1.74 and Banks at 4.14.

Pharmaceutical businesses tend to invest heavily in developing new drugs, hence their tendency to pay low dividends compared with their share prices. Some of the inter-industry differences in the dividend yield ratio can be explained by the nature of the calculation of the ratio. The prices of shares at any given moment are based on expectations of their economic futures; dividends are actual past events. A business that had a good

Real World 7.8 continued

Figure 7.4   **Average dividend yield ratios for businesses in a range of industries**

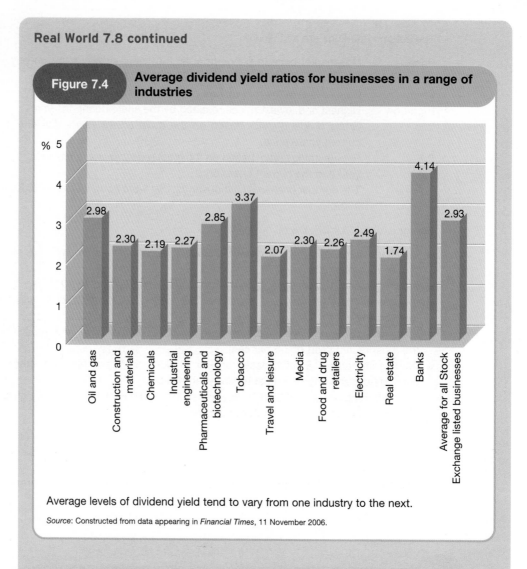

Average levels of dividend yield tend to vary from one industry to the next.

Source: Constructed from data appearing in *Financial Times*, 11 November 2006.

trading year recently may have paid a dividend that, in the light of investors' assessment on the business's economic future, may be high (a high dividend yield).

These P/E ratios are calculated from the current market value of the shares and the most recent year's earnings per share (EPS).

Businesses that have a high share price relative to their recent historic earnings have high P/E ratios. This may be because their future is regarded as economically bright, which may be the result of investing heavily in the future at the expense of recent profits (earnings). On the other hand, high P/Es also arise where businesses have recent low earnings but investors believe that their future is brighter. The average for all Stock Exchange listed businesses was 14.01, but Oil and Gas was as low as 10.89 and Food and Drug Retailers as high as 26.18.

Many larger businesses publish certain key financial ratios as part of their annual reports to help users identify significant trends. These ratios typically cover several years' activities. **Real World 7.10** shows part of the table of 'key performance measures' of Marks and Spencer plc (M&S), the well-known UK high street store.

Real World 7.10

Key performance measures of Marks and Spencer plc

		2006 52 weeks	2005 52 weeks	2004 53 weeks	2003 52 weeks	2002 52 weeks
Gross margin	$\frac{\text{Gross profit}}{\text{Turnover}}$	38.3%	34.7%	35.4%	34.8%	34.4%
Net margin	$\frac{\text{Operating profit}}{\text{Turnover}}$	10.9%	8.0%	9.9%	8.6%	7.7%
Net margin excluding exceptional items and asset disposals		11.0%	8.7%	10.2%	9.2%	7.1%
Profitability	$\frac{\text{Profit before tax}}{\text{Turnover}}$	9.6%	6.7%	9.4%	8.4%	8.5%
Profitability excluding exceptional items		9.6%	7.4%	9.7%	9.0%	7.9%
Earnings per share	$\frac{\text{Standard earnings}}{\text{Weighted average ordinary shares in issue}}$	31.4p	29.1p	24.2p	21.8p	5.4p
Earnings per share adjusted for exceptional items		31.5p	20.8p	24.7p	23.3p	16.3p
Dividend per share declared in respect of the year		14.0p	12.1p	11.5p	10.5p	9.5p
Dividend cover	$\frac{\text{Profit attributable to shareholders}}{\text{Dividends payable}}$	2.2×	2.9×	2.1×	2.1×	2.2×
Return on equity	$\frac{\text{Profit attributable to shareholders}}{\text{Average equity shareholders' funds}}$	52.3%	35.0%	25.2%	22.4%	11.5%

Source: Marks and Spencer plc Annual Report 2006. Reproduced by kind permission of Marks and Spencer plc. The results for 2002 have not been restated following the adoption of a number of accounting standards in 2004. Similarly, the 2002 to 2004 results have not been restated following the adoption of the International Financial Reporting Standards in 2005. This means that the results over the five years are not strictly comparable.

After many years of profitable growth, M&S suffered a decline in its fortunes during the late 1990s. This was seen by the directors, and by many independent commentators, as arising from the business allowing itself to be drawn away from its traditional areas of strength. Steps were taken to deal with the problem and the business seemed to have 'turned the corner'. M&S reached its low point in the year ended March 2001 when it incurred a significant overall loss, with an operating profit well below that achieved in 1998. The improvements in every year since 2002 are very clear. The return on equity (return on ordinary shareholders' funds) in 2006 is significantly better than for any other of the five years. Although in 2005, both the gross profit and net (operating profit) margins are lower than in 2004, they both recovered strongly in 2006. The return on equity was boosted in 2005 by the profit on disposal of the business's financial services division and a lower equity base due to M&S buying and cancelling some of its own shares.

Using ratios to predict financial failure

Financial ratios, based on current or past performance, are often used to help predict the future. However, both the choice of ratios and the interpretation of results are normally dependent on the judgement and opinion of the analyst. In recent years, however, attempts have been made to develop a more rigorous and systematic approach to the use of ratios for prediction purposes. In particular, researchers have shown an interest in the ability of ratios to predict the financial failure of a business.

By financial failure, we mean a business either being forced out of business or being severely adversely affected by its inability to meet its financial obligations. It is often referred to as 'going bust' or 'going bankrupt'. This, of course, is an area with which all those connected with the business are likely to be concerned.

Using single ratios

Many approaches that attempt to use ratios to predict future financial failure have been developed. Early research focused on the examination of ratios on an individual basis to see whether they were good or bad predictors of financial failure. Here, a particular ratio (for example the current ratio) for a business that had failed was tracked over several years leading up to the date of the failure. This was to see whether it was possible to say that the ratio had shown a trend that could have been taken as a warning sign.

Beaver (see reference 1 at the end of the chapter) carried out the first research in this area. He identified 79 businesses that had failed. He then calculated the average (mean) of various ratios for these 79 businesses, going back over the financial statements of each business for each of the ten years leading up to each one's failure. Beaver then compared these average ratios with similarly derived ratios for a sample of 79 businesses that did not fail over this period. (The research used a matched-pair design, where each failed business was matched with a non-failed business of similar size and industry type.) Beaver found that some ratios exhibited a marked difference between the failed and non-failed businesses for up to five years prior to failure. This is shown in Figure 7.7.

To explain Figure 7.7, let us take a closer look at graph (a). This plots the ratio, cash flow (presumably the operating cash flow figure, taken from the cash flow statement) divided by total debt (borrowings). For the non-failed businesses this stayed fairly steady at just below +0.45 over the period. For the failed businesses, however, this was already well below the non-failed businesses, at about +0.15, even five years before those businesses eventually failed. It then declined steadily until, by one year before the failure, it was less than −0.15. Note that the scale of the horizontal axis shows the most recent year before actual failure (Year 1) on the left and the earliest one (Year 5) on the right. The other graphs in Figure 7.7 show a similar picture for five other ratios.

| Figure 7.7 | Average (mean) ratios of failed and non-failed businesses plotted against the number of years before failure |

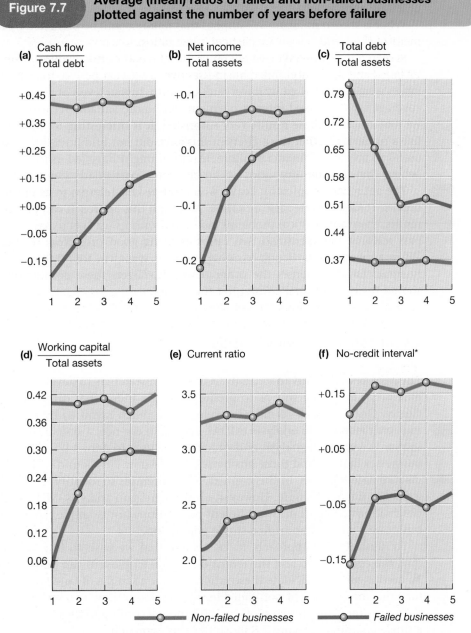

Each of the ratios (a) to (f) above indicates a marked difference in the average ratio between the sample of failed businesses and a matched sample of non-failed businesses. The vertical scale of each graph is the average value of the particular ratio for each group of businesses (failed and non-failed). The horizontal axis is the number of years before failure. Thus Year 1 is the most recent year and Year 5 the earliest of the years. For each of the six ratios, the difference between the average for the failed and the non-failed businesses can be detected five years prior to the failure of the former group.

* The no-credit interval is the same as the cash generated from operations to maturing obligations ratio discussed earlier in the chapter.

Source: Beaver (see reference 1 at the end of the chapter).

In each case there is a deteriorating average ratio for the failed businesses as the time of failure approaches.

What is shown in Figure 7.7 implies that failure could be predicted by careful assessment of the trend shown by particular key ratios.

Research by Zmijewski (see reference 2 at the end of the chapter), using a sample of 72 failed and 3,573 non-failed businesses over a six-year period, found that failed businesses were characterised by lower rates of return, higher levels of gearing, lower levels of coverage for their fixed interest payments and more variable returns on shares. While we may not find these results very surprising, it is interesting to note that Zmijewski, like a number of other researchers in this area, did not find liquidity ratios particularly useful in predicting financial failure. Intuition might have led us (wrongly it seems) to believe that the liquidity ratios would have been particularly helpful in this context.

→   The approach adopted by Beaver and Zmijewski is referred to as **univariate analysis** because it looks at one ratio at a time. Although this approach can produce interesting results, there are practical problems associated with its use. Let us say, for example, that past research has identified two ratios as being good predictors of financial failure. When applied to a particular business, however, it may be found that one ratio predicts financial failure whereas the other does not. Given these conflicting signals, how should the decision maker interpret the results?

Using combinations of ratios

The weaknesses of univariate analysis have led researchers to develop models that combine ratios in such a way as to produce a single index that can be interpreted more clearly. One approach to model development, much favoured by researchers, applies
→   **multiple discriminate analysis** (MDA). This is, in essence, a statistical technique that is similar to regression analysis and which can be used to draw a boundary between those businesses that fail and those businesses that do not. This boundary is referred to as the
→   **discriminate function**. In this context, MDA attempts to identify those factors likely to influence financial failure. However, unlike regression analysis, MDA assumes that the observations come from two different populations (for example, failed and non-failed businesses) rather than from a single population.

To illustrate this approach, let us assume that we wish to test whether two ratios (say, the current ratio and the return on capital employed) can help to predict failure. To do this, we can calculate these ratios, first for a sample of failed businesses and then for a matched sample of non-failed businesses. From these two sets of data we can produce a scatter diagram that plots each business according to these two ratios to produce a single coordinate. Figure 7.8 illustrates this approach.

Using the observations plotted on the diagram, we try to identify the boundary between the failed and the non-failed businesses. This is the diagonal line in Figure 7.8.

We can see that those businesses that fall below and to the left of the line are predominantly failed and those that fall to the right are predominantly non-failed ones. Note that there is some overlap between the two populations. The boundary produced is unlikely, in practice, to eliminate all errors. Some businesses that fail may fall on the side of the boundary with non-failed businesses, and the other way round as well. However, the analysis will *minimise* the misclassification errors.

The boundary shown in Figure 7.8 can be expressed in the form:

$$Z = a + (b \times \textbf{Current ratio}) + (c \times \text{ROCE})$$

Figure 7.8   **Scatter diagram showing the distribution of failed and non-failed businesses**

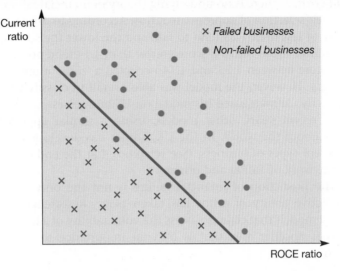

The distribution of failed and non-failed businesses is based on two ratios. The line represents a boundary between the samples of failed and non-failed businesses. Although there is some crossing of the boundary, the boundary represents the line that minimises the problem of misclassifying particular businesses.

where *a* is a constant and *b* and *c* are weights to be attached to each ratio. A weighted average or total score (*Z*) is then derived. The weights given to the two ratios will depend on the slope of the line and its absolute position.

Z score models

Altman (see reference 3 at the end of the chapter) was the first to develop a model (in 1968), using financial ratios, that was able to predict financial failure. In 2000 he revised that model. In fact, the revisions necessary to make the model effective in present times were quite minor. Altman's revised model, the *Z* score model, is based on five financial ratios and is as follows:

$$Z = 0.717a + 0.847b + 3.107c + 0.420d + 0.998e$$

where *a* = Working capital/Total assets
     b = Accumulated retained profits/Total assets
     c = Operating profit/Total assets
     d = Book (balance sheet) value of ordinary and preference shares/Total liabilities at book (balance sheet) value
     e = Sales revenue/Total assets

In developing and revising this model, Altman carried out experiments using a paired sample of failed businesses and non-failed businesses and collected relevant data for each business for five years prior to failure. He found that the model represented by the formula above was able to predict failure for up to two years before it occurred.

However, the predictive accuracy of the model became weaker the longer the time before the date of the actual failure.

The ratios used in this model were identified by Altman through a process of trial and error, as there is no underlying theory of financial failure to help guide researchers in their selection of appropriate ratios. According to Altman, those businesses with a Z score of less than 1.23 tend to fail, and the lower the score the greater the probability of failure. Those with a Z score greater than 4.14 tend not to fail. Those businesses with a Z score between 1.23 and 4.14 occupied a 'zone of ignorance' and were difficult to classify. However, the model was able overall to classify 91 per cent of the businesses correctly. Altman based his model on US businesses.

In recent years, other models, using a similar approach, have been developed throughout the world. In the UK, Taffler has developed separate Z score models for different types of business. (See reference 4 at the end of the chapter for a discussion of the work of Taffler and others.)

The prediction of financial failure is not the only area where research into the predictive ability of ratios has taken place. Researchers have also developed ratio-based models that claim to assess the vulnerability of a business to takeover by another. This is another area that is of vital importance to all those connected with the business.

Limitations of ratio analysis

Although ratios offer a quick and useful method of analysing the position and perform-ance of a business, they are not without their problems and limitations. Some of the more important limitations are described below.

Quality of financial statements

It must always be remembered that ratios are based on financial statements, and the results of ratio analysis are dependent on the quality of these underlying statements. Ratios will inherit the limitations of the financial statements on which they are based. A significant example of this arises from the application of the prudence convention to internally generated intangible non-current assets (as compared with purchased ones). This convention tends to lead to assets of considerable value, such as goodwill and brand names, being excluded from the balance sheet. This can mean that ratios such as ROSF, ROCE and the gearing ratio fail to take account of these assets.

There is also the problem of deliberate attempts to make the financial statements misleading. We discussed this problem of *creative accounting* in Chapter 5.

Inflation

A persistent, though recently less severe, problem, in most western countries is that the financial results of businesses can be distorted as a result of inflation. One effect of inflation is that the balance sheet values of assets held for any length of time may bear little relation to current values. Generally speaking, the balance sheet value of assets will be understated in current terms during a period of inflation as they are usually recorded at their original cost (less any amounts written off for depreciation). This means that comparisons, either between businesses or between periods, will be hindered. A difference in, say, ROCE may simply be owing to the fact that assets in one of the balance sheets being compared were acquired more recently (ignoring the effect of depreciation on the asset values). Another effect of inflation is to distort the measurement of profit. Sales revenue for a period is often matched against costs from an earlier period because there is often a time lag between acquiring a particular resource and using it to help generate sales revenue. For example, inventories may be acquired in one period and sold in a later period. During a period of inflation, this will mean that the expense does not reflect current prices. The cost of sales figure is usually based on the historic cost of the inventories concerned. As a result, expenses will be understated in the income statement and this, in turn, means that profit will be overstated. One effect of this will be to distort the profitability ratios discussed earlier.

The restricted vision of ratios

It is important not to rely exclusively on ratios, thereby losing sight of information contained in the underlying financial statements. As we saw earlier in the chapter, some items reported in these statements can be vital in assessing position and performance. For example, the total sales revenue, capital employed and profit figures may be useful in assessing changes in absolute size that occur over time, or differences in scale between businesses. Ratios do not provide such information. When comparing one figure with another, ratios measure *relative* performance and position, and therefore provide only part of the picture. When comparing two businesses, therefore, it will often be useful to assess the absolute size of profits, as well as the relative profitability of each business. For example, Business A may generate £1m operating profit and have a ROCE of 15 per cent, and Business B may generate £100,000 operating profit and have a ROCE of 20 per cent. Although Business B has a higher level of *profitability*, as measured by ROCE, it generates lower total operating profits.

The basis for comparison

We saw earlier that if ratios are to be useful they require a basis for comparison. Moreover, it is important that the analyst compares like with like. However, no two businesses are identical, and the greater the differences between the businesses being compared, the greater the limitations of ratio analysis. Also, when comparing businesses, differences in such matters as accounting policies, financing methods (gearing levels) and financial year ends will add to the problems of evaluation.

Balance sheet ratios

Because the balance sheet is only a 'snapshot' of the business at a particular moment in time, any ratios based on balance sheet figures, such as the liquidity ratios, may not be representative of the financial position of the business for the year as a whole. For example, it is common for a seasonal business to have a financial year end that coincides with a low point in business activity. As a result, inventories and trade receivables may be low at the balance sheet date, and so the liquidity ratios may also be low. A more representative picture of liquidity can only really be gained by taking additional measurements at other points in the year.

Real World 7.11 points out another way in which ratios are limited.

Real World 7.11

Remember, it's people that really count . . .

Lord Weinstock (1924–2002) was an influential industrialist whose management style and philosophy helped to shape management practice in many UK businesses. During his long and successful reign at GEC plc, a major engineering business, Lord Weinstock relied heavily on financial ratios to assess performance and to exercise control. In particular, he relied on ratios relating to sales revenue, expenses, trade receivables, profit margins and inventories turnover. However, he was keenly aware of the limitations of ratios and recognised that, ultimately, people produce profits.

In a memo written to GEC managers he pointed out that ratios are an aid to good management rather than a substitute for it. He wrote:

> The operating ratios are of great value as measures of efficiency but they are only the measures and not efficiency itself. Statistics will not design a product better, make it for a lower cost or increase sales. If ill-used, they may so guide action as to diminish resources for the sake of apparent but false signs of improvement.
>
> Management remains a matter of judgement, of knowledge of products and processes and of understanding and skill in dealing with people. The ratios will indicate how well all these things are being done and will show comparison with how they are done elsewhere. But they will tell us nothing about how to do them. That is what you are meant to do.

Source: Extract from *Arnold Weinstock and the Making of GEC*, S. Aris (Aurum Press, 1998), published in *The Sunday Times*, 22 February 1998, p. 3.

Summary

The main points of this chapter may be summarised as follows.

Ratio analysis

- Compares two related figures, usually both from the same set of financial statements.
- Is an aid to understanding what the financial statements really mean.
- Is an inexact science so results must be interpreted cautiously.
- Past periods, the performance of similar businesses and planned performance are often used to provide benchmark ratios.
- A brief overview of the financial statements can often provide insights that may not be revealed by ratios and/or may help in the interpretation of them.

Profitability ratios – concerned with effectiveness at generating profit

- Return on ordinary shareholders' funds (ROSF).
- Return on capital employed (ROCE).
- Operating profit margin.
- Gross profit margin.

Efficiency ratios – concerned with efficiency of using assets/resources

- Average inventories turnover period.
- Average settlement period for trade receivables.
- Average settlement period for trade payables.
- Sales revenue to capital employed.
- Sales revenue per employee.

Liquidity ratios – concerned with the ability to meet short-term obligations

- Current ratio.
- Acid test ratio.
- Cash generated from operations to maturing obligations.

Gearing ratios – concerned with relationship between equity and debt financing

- Gearing ratio.
- Interest cover ratio.

Investment ratios – concerned with returns to shareholders

- Dividend payout ratio.
- Dividend yield ratio.
- Earnings per share.
- Cash generated from operations per share.
- Price/earnings ratio.

Trend analysis

- Individual ratios can be tracked (for example, plotted on a graph) to detect trends.

Ratios as predictors of financial failure

- Univariate analysis – looking at just one ratio over time in an attempt to predict financial failure.
- Multiple discriminate analysis – looking at several ratios, put together in a model, over time in an attempt to predict financial failure – Z scores.

Limitations of ratio analysis

- Ratios are only as reliable as the financial statements from which they derive.
- Inflation can distort the information.
- Ratios have restricted vision.
- It can be difficult to find a suitable benchmark (for example, another business) as comparator.
- Some ratios could mislead due to the 'snapshot' nature of the balance sheet.

MyAccountingLab   *Now check your progress in your personal Study Plan*

Key terms

return on ordinary shareholders'
  funds ratio (ROSF) p. 228
return on capital employed ratio
  (ROCE) p. 229
operating profit margin ratio p. 230
gross profit margin ratio p. 231
average inventories turnover period
  ratio p. 233
average settlement period for trade
  receivables ratio p. 234
average settlement period for trade
  payables ratio p. 235
sales revenue to capital employed
  ratio p. 236
sales revenue per employee ratio
  p. 237
current ratio p. 240
acid test ratio p. 241

cash generated from operations to
  maturing obligations ratio p. 241
financial gearing p. 242
gearing ratio p. 244
interest cover ratio p. 245
dividend payout ratio p. 248
dividend cover ratio p. 248
dividend yield ratio p. 249
dividend per share p. 249
earnings per share p. 250
cash generated from operations per
  ordinary share ratio p. 250
price/earnings ratio p. 251
overtrading p. 256
univariate analysis p. 262
multiple discriminate analysis p. 262
discriminate function p. 262

References

1 'Financial ratios as predictors of failure', *Beaver W.H.*, Empirical Research in Accounting: Selected studies, a supplement to the Journal of Accounting Research, 1966, pp. 71–111.

2 'Predicting corporate bankruptcy: an empirical comparison of the extent of financial distress models', *Zmijewski M.E.*, Research paper, State University of New York, 1983.

3 'Predicting financial distress of companies: revisiting the Z-score and Zeta models', *Altman E.I.*, Working paper, New York University, June 2000.

4 'Predicting corporate failure: empirical evidence for the UK', *Neophytou E., Charitou A. and Charalamnous C.*, Working Paper 01-173, Department of Accounting and Management Science, University of Southampton, 2001.

Further reading

If you would like to explore the topics covered in this chapter in more depth, we recommend the following books:

Corporate Financial Accounting and Reporting, *Sutton T.*, 2nd edn, Financial Times Prentice Hall, 2004, chapter 19.

Financial Accounting and Reporting, *Elliott B. and Elliott J.*, 11th edn, Financial Times Prentice Hall, 2006, chapters 28 and 29.

Financial Reporting and Analysis, *Revsine L., Collins D. and Bruce Johnson W.*, 3rd edn, Prentice Hall, 2005, chapter 5.

Financial Statement Analysis, *Wild J., Subramanyam K. and Halsey R.*, 9th edn, McGraw-Hill, 2006, chapters 8, 9 and 11.

Review questions

Answers to these questions can be found at the back of the book on page 778.

7.1 Some businesses operate on a low operating profit margin (for example, a supermarket chain). Does this mean that the return on capital employed from the business will also be low?

7.2 What potential problems arise for the external analyst from the use of balance sheet figures in the calculation of financial ratios?

7.3 Two businesses operate in the same industry. One has an inventories turnover period that is longer than the industry average. The other has an inventories turnover period that is shorter than the industry average. Give three possible explanations for each business's inventories turnover period ratio.

7.4 Identify and discuss three reasons why the P/E ratio of two businesses operating within the same industry may differ.

Exercises

Exercises 7.5 to 7.8 are more advanced than 7.1 to 7.4. Those with coloured numbers have answers at the back of the book, starting on page 725.

If you wish to try more exercises, visit the students' side of the Companion Website.

7.1 I. Jiang (Western) Ltd has recently produced its financial statements for the current year. The directors are concerned that the return on capital employed (ROCE) had decreased from 14 per cent last year to 12 per cent for the current year.

The following reasons were suggested as to why this reduction in ROCE had occurred:

(i)   an increase in the gross profit margin;
(ii) a reduction in sales revenue;
(iii) an increase in overhead expenses;
(iv) an increase in amount of inventories held;
(v)   the repayment of some borrowings at the year end; and
(vi) an increase in the time taken for credit customers (trade receivables) to pay.

Required:
Taking each of these six suggested reasons in turn, state, with reasons, whether each of them could lead to a reduction in ROCE.

7.2 Amsterdam Ltd and Berlin Ltd are both engaged in retailing, but they seem to take a different approach to it according to the following information:

Ratio	Amsterdam Ltd	Berlin Ltd
Return on capital employed (ROCE)	20%	17%
Return on ordinary shareholders' funds (ROSF)	30%	18%
Average settlement period for trade receivables	63 days	21 days
Average settlement period for trade payables	50 days	45 days
Gross profit margin	40%	15%
Operating profit margin	10%	10%
Average inventories turnover period	52 days	25 days

Required:

Describe what this information indicates about the differences in approach between the two businesses. If one of them prides itself on personal service and one of them on competitive prices, which do you think is which and why?

7.3 Conday and Co. Ltd has been in operation for three years and produces antique reproduction furniture for the export market. The most recent set of financial statements for the business is set out as follows:

Balance sheet as at 30 November

	£000
Non-current assets	
Property, plant and equipment (Cost less depreciation)	
Land and buildings	228
Plant and machinery	762
	990
Current assets	
Inventories	600
Trade receivables	820
	1,420
Total assets	2,410
Equity	
Ordinary shares of £1 each	700
Retained earnings	365
	1,065
Non-current liabilities	
Borrowings – 9% loan notes (Note 1)	200
Current liabilities	
Trade payables	665
Taxation	48
Short-term borrowings (all bank overdraft)	432
	1,145
Total equity and liabilities	2,410

Income statement for the year ended 30 November

	£000
Revenue	2,600
Cost of sales	(1,620)
Gross profit	980
Selling and distribution expenses (Note 2)	(408)
Administration expenses	(194)
Operating profit	378
Finance expenses	(58)
Profit before taxation	320
Taxation	(95)
Profit for the year	225

Notes:

1 The loan notes are secured on the freehold land and buildings.
2 Selling and distribution expenses include £170,000 in respect of bad debts.
3 A dividend of £160,000 was paid on the ordinary shares during the year.

4 The directors have invited an investor to take up a new issue of ordinary shares in the business at £6.40 each making a total investment of £200,000. The directors wish to use the funds to finance a programme of further expansion.

Required:
(a) Analyse the financial position and performance of the business and comment on any features that you consider to be significant.
(b) State, with reasons, whether or not the investor should invest in the business on the terms outlined.

7.4 The directors of Helena Beauty Products Ltd have been presented with the following abridged financial statements:

Helena Beauty Products Ltd
Income statement for the year ended 30 September

	2006		2007	
	£000	£000	£000	£000
Sales revenue		3,600		3,840
Cost of sales				
Opening inventories	320		400	
Purchases	2,240		2,350	
	2,560		2,750	
Closing inventories	(400)	(2,160)	(500)	(2,250)
Gross profit		1,440		1,590
Expenses		(1,360)		(1,500)
Profit		80		90

Balance sheet as at 30 September

	2006	2007
	£000	£000
Non-current assets		
Property, plant and equipment	1,900	1,860
Current assets		
Inventories	400	500
Trade receivables	750	960
Cash at bank	8	4
	1,158	1,464
Total assets	3,058	3,324
Equity		
£1 ordinary shares	1,650	1,766
Reserves	1,018	1,108
	2,668	2,874
Current liabilities	390	450
Total equity and liabilities	3,058	3,324

Required:
Using six ratios, comment on the profitability (three ratios) and efficiency (three ratios) of the business as revealed by the statements shown above.

7.5 Threads Limited manufactures nuts and bolts, which are sold to industrial users. The abbreviated financial statements for 2006 and 2007 are as follows:

Income statements for the year ended 30 June

	2006 £000	2007 £000
Revenue	1,180	1,200
Cost of sales	(680)	(750)
Gross profit	500	450
Operating expenses	(200)	(208)
Depreciation	(66)	(75)
Operating profit	234	167
Interest	(–)	(8)
Profit before taxation	234	159
Taxation	(80)	(48)
Profit for the year	154	111

Balance sheets as at 30 June

	2006 £000	2007 £000
Non-current assets		
Property, plant and equipment	702	687
Current assets		
Inventories	148	236
Trade receivables	102	156
Cash	3	4
	253	396
Total assets	955	1,083
Equity		
Ordinary share capital of £1 (fully paid)	500	500
Retained earnings	256	295
	756	795
Non-current liabilities		
Borrowings – Bank loan	–	50
Current liabilities		
Trade payables	60	76
Other payables and accruals	18	16
Taxation	40	24
Short-term borrowings (all bank overdraft)	81	122
	199	238
Total equity and liabilities	955	1,083

Dividends were paid on ordinary shares of £70,000 and £72,000 in respect of 2006 and 2007, respectively.

Required:
(a) Calculate the following financial ratios for *both* 2006 and 2007 (using year-end figures for balance sheet items):
  (i)   return on capital employed
  (ii)   operating profit margin
  (iii)   gross profit margin
  (iv)   current ratio
  (v)   acid test ratio
  (vi)   settlement period for trade receivables
  (vii)   settlement period for trade payables
  (viii) inventories turnover period.

(b) Comment on the performance of Threads Limited from the viewpoint of a business considering supplying a substantial amount of goods to Threads Limited on usual trade credit terms.

7.6 Bradbury Ltd is a family-owned clothes manufacturer based in the south west of England. For a number of years the chairman and managing director was David Bradbury. During his period of office, sales revenue had grown steadily at a rate of 2–3 per cent each year. David Bradbury retired on 30 November 2006 and was succeeded by his son Simon. Soon after taking office, Simon decided to expand the business. Within weeks he had successfully negotiated a five-year contract with a large clothes retailer to make a range of sports and leisurewear items. The contract will result in an additional £2m in sales revenue during each year of the contract. To fulfil the contract, Bradbury Ltd acquired new equipment and premises.

Financial information concerning the business is given below:

Income statements for the year ended 30 November

	2006 £000	2007 £000
Revenue	9,482	11,365
Operating profit	914	1,042
Interest charges	(22)	(81)
Profit before taxation	892	961
Taxation	(358)	(386)
Profit for the year	534	575

Balance sheets as at 30 November

	2006 £000	2007 £000
Non-current assets		
Property, plant and equipment		
Premises at cost	5,240	7,360
Plant and equipment (net)	2,375	4,057
	7,615	11,417
Current assets		
Inventories	2,386	3,420
Trade receivables	2,540	4,280
	4,926	7,700
Total assets	12,541	19,117
Equity		
Share capital	2,000	2,000
Reserves	7,813	8,268
	9,813	10,268
Non-current liabilities		
Borrowing – Loans	1,220	3,675
Current liabilities		
Trade payables	1,157	2,245
Taxation	179	193
Short-term borrowings (all bank overdraft)	172	2,736
	1,508	5,174
Total equity and liabilities	12,541	19,117

Dividends of £120,000 were paid on ordinary shares in respect of each of the two years.

Required:

(a) Calculate, for each year (using year-end figures for balance sheet items), the following ratios:

(i) operating profit margin

(ii) return on capital employed

(iii) current ratio

(iv) gearing ratio

(v) days trade receivables (settlement period)

(vi) sales revenue to capital employed.

(b) Using the above ratios, and any other ratios or information you consider relevant, comment on the results of the expansion programme.

7.7 The financial statements for Harridges Ltd are given below for the two years ended 30 June 2006 and 2007. Harridges Limited operates a department store in the centre of a small town.

Harridges Ltd
Income statement for the years ended 30 June

	2006 £000	2007 £000
Sales revenue	2,600	3,500
Cost of sales	(1,560)	(2,350)
Gross profit	1,040	1,150
Wages and salaries	(320)	(350)
Overheads	(260)	(200)
Depreciation	(150)	(250)
Operating profit	310	350
Interest payable	(50)	(50)
Profit before taxation	260	300
Taxation	(105)	(125)
Profit for the year	155	175

Balance sheet as at 30 June

	2006 £000	2007 £000
Non-current assets		
Property, plant and equipment	1,265	1,525
Current assets		
Inventories	250	400
Trade receivables	105	145
Cash at bank	380	115
	735	660
Total assets	2,000	2,185
Equity		
Share capital: £1 shares fully paid	490	490
Share premium	260	260
Retained earnings	350	450
	1,100	1,200
Non-current liabilities		
Borrowings – 10% loan notes	500	500
Current liabilities		
Trade payables	300	375
Other payables	100	110
	400	485
Total equity and liabilities	2,000	2,185

Dividends were paid on ordinary shares of £65,000 and £75,000 in respect of 2006 and 2007, respectively.

Required:

(a) Choose and calculate eight ratios that would be helpful in assessing the performance of Harridges Ltd. Use end-of-year values and calculate ratios for both 2006 and 2007.

(b) Using the ratios calculated in (a) and any others you consider helpful, comment on the business's performance from the viewpoint of a prospective purchaser of a majority of shares.

7.8 Genesis Ltd was incorporated in 2004 and has grown rapidly over the past three years. The rapid rate of growth has created problems for the business, which the directors have found difficult to deal with. Recently, a firm of management consultants has been asked to help the directors to overcome these problems.

In a preliminary report to the board of directors, the management consultants state: 'Most of the difficulties faced by the business are symptoms of an underlying problem of overtrading.'

The most recent financial statements of the business are set out below:

Balance sheet as at 31 October 2007

	£000	£000
Non-current assets		
Property, plant and equipment		
Land and buildings at cost	530	
Accumulated depreciation	(88)	442
Fixtures and fittings at cost	168	
Accumulated depreciation	(52)	116
Motor vans at cost	118	
Accumulated depreciation	(54)	64
		622
Current assets		
Inventories		128
Trade receivables		104
		232
Total assets		854
Equity		
Ordinary £0.50 shares		60
General reserve		50
Retained earnings		74
		184
Non-current liabilities		
Borrowings – 10% loan notes (secured)		120
Current liabilities		
Trade payables		184
Taxation		8
Short-term borrowings (all bank overdraft)		358
		550
Total equity and liabilities		854

Income statement for the year ended 31 October 2007

	£000	£000
Revenue		1,640
Cost of sales		
Opening inventories	116	
Purchases	1,260	
	1,376	
Closing inventories	(128)	(1,248)
Gross profit		392
Selling and distribution expenses		(204)
Administration expenses		(92)
Operating profit		96
Interest payable		(44)
Profit before taxation		52
Taxation		(16)
Profit for the year		36

All purchases and sales were on credit.

A dividend was paid during the year on ordinary shares of £4,000.

Required:

(a) Explain the term 'overtrading' and state how overtrading might arise for a business.

(b) Discuss the kinds of problem that overtrading can create for a business.

(c) Calculate and discuss *five* financial ratios that might be used to establish whether the business is overtrading.

(d) State the ways in which a business may overcome the problem of overtrading.

PART 2

Management accounting

8 Relevant costs for decision making

9 Cost–volume–profit analysis

10 Full costing

11 Costing and pricing in a competitive environment

12 Budgeting

13 Accounting for control

Part 2 deals with the area of accounting usually known as 'management accounting' or 'managerial accounting'. This area is concerned with providing information to help managers to manage the business: it is intended to help them to plan, to make decisions and to ensure that plans are achieved.

It is difficult to overestimate the extent to which management accounting, and with it the role of the management accountant, has changed in recent times. The advance of the computer has had an enormous influence. Information technology (IT) has released the management accountant from much of the routine work associated with preparation of management accounting reports and has provided the opportunity to take a more proactive role within the business. This has led to the management accountant becoming part of the management team and, therefore, directly involved in planning and decision making.

At the same time, it has become increasingly obvious that businesses must be customer focused, outward looking and orientated towards value creation (as discussed in Chapter 1). This more strategic approach to management has required the management accountant to provide the types of information to managers that would have been unthought of, for the typical business, until fairly recently.

These new dimensions to the management accountant's role have implications for the kinds of skills required to operate effectively. In particular, certain 'soft' skills are needed, such as interpersonal skills for working as part of an effective team and communication skills to help influence the attitudes and behaviour of others.

→ Through working as part of a cross-functional team, the management accountant should gain a greater awareness of strategic and operational matters and an increased understanding of the information needs of managers. This is likely to have a positive effect on the design and development of management accounting systems. We should therefore see increasing evidence that management accounting systems are being designed to fit the particular structure and processes of the business rather than the other way round. By participating in planning, decision making and control of the business as well as providing management accounting information for these purposes, the management accountant plays a key role in achieving the objectives of the business. It is a role that should add value to the business and improve its competitive position.

Part 2 begins with a consideration of the basics of financial decision making. The first chapter in this part, Chapter 8, deals with how we identify information that is relevant to a particular decision. In practice, we may be confronted with a large volume of financial information and we must be able to discriminate between that which is relevant to a particular decision and that which can be ignored. Unless we can do this, we run the risk of making poor decisions. Chapter 9 continues our examination of the basics by considering the relationship between costs, volume of activity and profit. We shall see that an understanding of this relationship can be helpful in developing plans and in making a variety of decisions. This chapter incorporates an examination of break-even analysis, which is concerned with deducing the volume of activity at which the sales revenue equals the costs incurred so that neither profit nor loss is made by the activity. Knowledge of the break-even figure can be useful in assessing the degree of risk associated with the operations.

In Chapter 10 we look at how businesses can determine the full cost of each unit of their output. By 'full cost' we mean the figure that takes account of all of the costs of producing a product or service. This includes not just those costs that are directly caused by the unit of output, but also those, like rent and administrative costs, which are indirectly involved. This topic is continued in Chapter 11, where we consider some recent developments in determining the full cost of a product or service. In this chapter we also consider how a business can set prices for its output and how costs can be controlled.

Chapter 12 deals with the way in which businesses convert their general objectives and long-term plans into workable short-term plans or budgets. Budgets are an important feature of business life and we shall be looking at the budgeting process in some detail. We shall examine the purpose of budgets and the way in which budgets are prepared. In Chapter 13 we consider how, after the period of the budget, the actual performance can be compared with the budgeted performance. This is done to assess performance and to help identify the reasons for any failure to meet budget targets. By finding out what has gone wrong, managers may be able to put things right for the future. The chapter concludes with a discussion of the impact of budgets on the attitudes and behaviour of managers.

CHAPTER 8

Relevant costs for decision making

Introduction

This chapter considers the identification and use of costs in making management decisions. These decisions should be made in a way that will promote the business's achievement of its strategic objective. We shall see that not all of the costs that appear to be linked to a particular business decision are relevant to it. It is important to distinguish carefully between costs (and revenues) that are relevant and those that are not. Failure to do this could well lead to bad decisions being made. The principles outlined here provide the basis for much of the rest of the book.

Learning outcomes

When you have completed this chapter, you should be able to:

- Define and distinguish between relevant costs, outlay costs and opportunity costs.
- Identify and quantify the costs that are relevant to a particular decision.
- Use relevant costs to make decisions.
- Set out the analysis in a logical form so that the conclusion may be communicated to managers.

 MyAccountingLab *Remember to create your own personalised Study Plan*

What is meant by 'cost'?

→ Let us begin by asking, 'What is meant by cost?' The answer to this question may seem, at first sight, very obvious. Many people might say that **cost** is how much was paid for an item of goods being supplied or a service being provided. However, the following activity illustrates that the definition of cost is not always as obvious as might at first be thought.

Activity 8.1

You own a motor car for which you paid a purchase price of £5,000 – much below the list price – at a recent car auction. You have just been offered £6,000 for this car.

What is the cost to you of keeping the car for your own use? (*Note*: Ignore running costs and so on; consider just the 'capital' cost of the car.)

By retaining the car you are forgoing a cash receipt of £6,000. Thus, the real sacrifice, or cost, incurred by keeping the car for your own use is £6,000. Any decision that you make with respect to the car's future should logically take account of this figure. This cost is known as the 'opportunity cost' since it is the value of the opportunity forgone in order to pursue the other course of action. (In this case, the other course of action is to retain the car.)

We can see that the cost of retaining the car is not the same as the purchase price. In one sense, of course, the cost of the car in Activity 8.1 is £5,000 because that is how much was paid for it. However, this cost, which for obvious reasons is known as the
→ **historic cost**, is only of academic interest. It cannot logically ever be used to make a decision on the car's future. If we disagree with this point, we should ask ourselves how we should assess an offer of £5,500, from another person, for the car. The answer is that
→ we should compare the offer price of £5,500 with the **opportunity cost** of £6,000. This should lead us to reject the offer as it is less than the £6,000 opportunity cost. In these circumstances, it would not be logical to accept the offer of £5,500 on the basis that it was more than the £5,000 that we originally paid. (The only other figure that should concern us is the value to us, in terms of pleasure, usefulness and so on, of retaining the car. If we valued this more highly than the £6,000 opportunity cost, we should reject both offers.)

We may still feel, however, that the £5,000 is relevant here because it will help us in assessing the profitability of the decision. If we sell the car, we shall make a profit of either £500 (that is, £5,500 – £5,000) or £1,000 (that is, £6,000 – £5,000) depending on which offer we accept. Since we should seek to make the higher profit, the right decision is to sell the car for £6,000. However, we do not need to know the historic cost of the car to make the right decision. What decision should we make if the car cost us £4,000 to buy? Clearly we should still sell the car for £6,000 rather than for £5,500 as the important comparison is between the offer price and the opportunity cost. We should reach the same conclusion whatever the historic cost of the car.

To emphasise the above point, let us assume that the car cost £10,000. Even in this case the historic cost would still be irrelevant. Had we just bought a car for £10,000 and found that shortly after it is only worth £6,000, we may well be fuming with rage at our mistake, but this does not make the £10,000 a **relevant cost**. The only relevant factors in a decision whether to sell the car or to keep it are the £6,000 opportunity cost and the value of the benefits of keeping it. Thus, the historic cost can never be relevant to a future decision.

Historic cost is normally used in accounting statements, such as the balance sheet and the income statement. This is logical, however, since these statements are intended to be accounts of what has actually happened and are drawn up after the event. In the context of decision making, which is always related to the future, historic cost is always irrelevant.

To say that historic cost is an **irrelevant cost** is not to say that *the effects of having incurred that cost* are always irrelevant. The fact that we own the car, and are thus in a position to exercise choice as to how to use it, is not irrelevant.

Real World 8.1 gives an example of linked decisions made by two English football clubs: Manchester United and Chelsea.

Real world 8.1

Transferring players: a game of two halves

In August 2003, Manchester United Football Club transferred one of its midfield players, Juan Sebastian Veron, the Argentinean international, to Chelsea Football Club for a reported £15m. Manchester United had purchased the player's services two years earlier for a reported club transfer record of £28.1m. As the transfer price to Chelsea Football Club was only a little more than half of the amount originally paid, Manchester United made a huge loss on the transaction. However, the offer of £15m from Chelsea must have been greater than the sacrifice, or cost, of losing Veron's services for Manchester United to agree to the transfer. The original amount paid for the player's services should not have been an issue in arriving at the agreed transfer price.

In June 2005, Veron was the subject of another such decision when Chelsea transferred him to Inter Milan, the Italian Serie A club, for no transfer fee – a free transfer. Chelsea must have judged that it was more beneficial to the club to avoid having to pay Veron's contracted salary for the remainder of his contract than to have the player's services available to it. Again the transfer fee paid for the player should logically not have been taken into account in making this decision.

Veron played successfully in Italy for a couple of years before returning to his first club, Estudiantes de la Plata, in mid 2006.

Source: http://en.wikipedia.org.

It might be useful to formalise what we have discussed so far.

A definition of cost

Cost may be defined as the amount of resources, usually measured in monetary terms, sacrificed to achieve a particular objective.

The objective might be to retain a car, to buy a particular house, to make a particular product or to render a particular service.

Relevant costs: opportunity and outlay costs

→ We have just seen that, when we are making decisions concerning the future, **past costs** (that is, historic costs) are irrelevant. It is future opportunity costs and future
→ **outlay costs** that are of concern. An opportunity cost can be defined as the value in monetary terms of being deprived of the next best opportunity in order to pursue the particular objective. An outlay cost is an amount of money that will have to be spent to achieve that objective. We shall shortly meet plenty of examples of both of these types of future cost.

To be relevant to a particular decision, a future outlay cost, or opportunity cost, must satisfy both of the following criteria:

● *It must relate to the objectives of the business.* Most businesses have enhancing owners' (shareholders') wealth as their key strategic objective. That is to say, they are seeking to become richer (see Chapter 1). Thus, to be relevant to a particular decision, a cost must have an effect on the wealth of the business.
● *It must differ from one possible decision outcome to the next.* Only costs (and revenues) that are different between outcomes can be used to distinguish between them. Thus the reason that the historic cost of the car that we discussed earlier is irrelevant is that it is the same whichever decision is taken about the future of the car. This means that all past costs are irrelevant because what has happened in the past must be the same for all possible future outcomes.

It is not only past costs that are the same from one decision outcome to the next; some future costs may also be the same. Take, for example, a road haulage business that has decided that it will buy a new lorry and the decision lies between two different models. The load capacity, the fuel and maintenance costs are different for each lorry. The potential costs and revenues associated with these are relevant items. The lorry will require a driver, so the business will need to employ one, but a suitably qualified driver could drive either lorry equally well, for the same wage. The cost of employing the driver is thus irrelevant to the decision as to which lorry to buy. This is despite the fact that this cost is a future one.

If, however, the decision did not concern a choice between two models of lorry but rather whether to operate an additional lorry or not, the cost of employing the additional driver would be relevant, because it would then be a cost that would vary with the decision made.

Activity 8.2

A garage business has an old car that it bought several months ago. The car needs a replacement engine before it can be driven. It is possible to buy a reconditioned engine for £300. This would take seven hours to fit by a mechanic who is paid £12 an hour. At present the garage is short of work, but the owners are reluctant to lay off any mechanics or even to cut down their basic working week because skilled labour is difficult to find and an upturn in repair work is expected soon.

The garage paid £3,000 to buy the car. Without the engine it could be sold for an estimated £3,500. What is the minimum price at which the garage should sell the car with a reconditioned engine fitted?

The minimum price is the amount required to cover the relevant costs of the job. At this price, the business will make neither a profit nor a loss. Any price lower than this amount will mean that the wealth of the business is reduced. Thus, the minimum price is:

	£
Opportunity cost of the car	3,500
Cost of the reconditioned engine	300
Total	3,800

The original cost of the car is irrelevant for reasons that have already been discussed; it is the opportunity cost of the car that concerns us. The cost of the new engine is relevant because, if the work is done, the garage will have to pay £300 for the engine; but it will pay nothing if the job is not done. The £300 is an example of a future outlay cost.

The labour cost is irrelevant because the same cost will be incurred whether the mechanic undertakes the work or not. This is because the mechanic is being paid to do nothing if this job is not undertaken; thus the additional labour cost arising from this job is zero.

It should be emphasised that the garage will not seek to sell the car with its reconditioned engine for £3,800; it will attempt to charge as much as possible for it. However, any price above the £3,800 will make the garage better off financially than it would be by not undertaking the engine replacement.

Activity 8.3

Assume exactly the same circumstances as in Activity 8.2, except that the garage is quite busy at the moment. If a mechanic is to be put on the engine-replacement job, it will mean that other work that the mechanic could have done during the seven hours, all of which could be charged to a customer, will not be undertaken. The garage's labour charge is £40 an hour, although the mechanic is paid only £12 an hour.

What is the minimum price at which the garage should sell the car, with a reconditioned engine fitted, under these altered circumstances?

The minimum price is:

	£
Opportunity cost of the car	3,500
Cost of the reconditioned engine	300
Labour cost (7 × £40)	280
Total	4,080

We can see that the opportunity cost of the car and the cost of the engine are the same as in Activity 8.2 but now a charge for labour has been added to obtain the minimum price. The relevant labour cost here is that which the garage will have to sacrifice in making the time available to undertake the engine replacement job. While the mechanic is working on this job, the garage is losing the opportunity to do work for which a customer would pay £280. Note that the £12 an hour mechanic's wage is still not relevant. The mechanic will be paid £12 an hour irrespective of whether it is the engine-replacement work or some other job that is undertaken.

Activity (8.4)

A business is considering making a bid to undertake a contract. Fulfilment of the contract will require the use of two types of raw material. Quantities of both of these materials are held by the business. If it chose to, the business could sell the raw materials in their present state. All of the inventories of these two raw materials will need to be used on the contract. Information on the raw materials concerned is as follows:

Inventories item	Quantity	Historic cost	Sales value	Replacement cost
	Units	£/unit	£/unit	£/unit
A1	500	5	3	6
B2	800	7	8	10

Inventories item A1 is in frequent use in the business on a variety of work. The inventories of item B2 were bought a year ago for a contract that was abandoned. It has recently become obvious that there is no likelihood of ever using this raw material if the contract currently being considered does not proceed.

Management wishes to deduce the minimum price at which the business could undertake the contract without reducing its wealth as a result. This can be used as the baseline in deducing the bid price.

How much should be included in the minimum price in respect of the two inventories items detailed above?

The relevant costs to be included in the minimum price are:

Inventories (stock) item: A1   £6 × 500 = £3,000
                         B2   £8 × 800 = £6,400

We are told that item A1 is in frequent use and so, if it is used on the contract, it will need to be replaced. Sooner or later the business will have to buy 500 units (currently costing £6 a unit) additional to those which would have been required had the contract not been undertaken.

We are told that item B2 will never be used by the business unless the contract is undertaken. Thus, if the contract is not undertaken, the only reasonable thing for the business to do is to sell the B2. This means that if the contract is undertaken and the B2 is used, it will have an opportunity cost equal to the potential proceeds from disposal, which is £8 a unit.

Note that the historic cost information about both materials is irrelevant and this will always be the case.

Activity (8.5)

HLA Ltd is in the process of preparing a quotation for a special job for a customer. The job will have the following material requirements:

Material	Units required	Units currently held in inventories			
		Quantity held	Historic cost £/unit	Sales value £/unit	Replacement cost £/unit
P	400	0	–	–	40
Q	230	100	62	50	64
R	350	200	48	23	59
S	170	140	33	12	49
T	120	120	40	0	68

Material Q is used consistently by the business on various jobs. The business holds materials R, S and T as the result of previous overbuying. No other use (apart from this special job) can be found for R, but the 140 units of S could be used in another job as a substitute for 225 units of material V that are about to be purchased at a price of £10 a unit. Material T has no other use, it is a dangerous material that is difficult to store and the business has been informed that it will cost £160 to dispose of the material currently held.

If it chose to, the business could sell the raw materials already held in their present state.

What is the relevant cost of the materials for the job specified above?

The relevant cost is as follows:

	£
Material P	
This will have to be purchased at £40 a unit (400 × £40)	16,000
Material Q	
This will have to be replaced, therefore, the relevant price is (230 × £64)	14,720
Material R	
200 units of this are held and these could be sold. The relevant price of these is the sales revenue forgone (200 × £23)	4,600
The remaining 150 units of R would have to be purchased (150 × £59)	8,850
Material S	
This could be sold or used as a substitute for material V.	
The existing inventories could be sold for £1,680 (140 × £12). However, the saving on material V is higher and therefore should be taken as the relevant amount (225 × £10)	2,250
The remaining units of material S must be purchased (30 × £49)	1,470
A saving on disposal will be made if material T is used	(160)
Total relevant cost	**47,730**

Sunk costs and committed costs

When trying to identify relevant costs for a particular decision, we may come across the terms **sunk cost** and **committed cost**. In order to deal with such costs we need to understand what these terms mean. A sunk cost is simply another way of saying past cost and the two expressions can be used interchangeably. A committed cost is also, in effect, a past cost to the extent that an irrevocable decision has been made to incur the cost because, for example, the business has entered into a binding contract. As a result, it is more or less a past cost despite the fact that the cash may not be paid in respect of it until some point in the future. Since the business has no choice as to whether it incurs the cost or not, a committed cost can never be a relevant cost.

It is important to remember that, to be relevant, a cost must be capable of varying according to the decision made. If the business is already committed by a legally binding contract to a cost, that cost cannot vary with the decision.

Figure 8.1 summarises the relationship between relevant, irrelevant, opportunity, outlay and past costs.

Figure 8.1 **Summary of the relationship between relevant and irrelevant costs**

Note, in particular, that future outlay costs may be either relevant or irrelevant costs depending on whether they vary with the decision. Future opportunity costs and outlay costs, which vary with the decision, are relevant; future outlay costs, which do not vary with the decision, and all past costs, are irrelevant.

Activity 8.6

Past costs are irrelevant costs. Does this mean that what happened in the past is irrelevant?

No, it does not mean this. The fact that the business has an asset that it can deploy in the future is highly relevant. What is not relevant is how much it cost to acquire that asset. This point was examined in the discussion that followed Activity 8.1.

Another reason why the past is not irrelevant is that it generally – though not always – provides us with our best guide to the future. Suppose that we need to estimate the cost of doing something in the future to help us to decide whether it is worth doing. In these circumstances our own experience, or that of others, of how much it has cost to do the thing in the past may provide us with a valuable guide to how much it is likely to cost in the future.

Qualitative factors of decisions

Although businesses must look closely at the obvious financial effects when making decisions, they must also consider factors that are not directly economic. These are likely to be factors that have a broader, but less immediate, impact on the business. Ultimately, however, these factors are likely to have economic effect – that is, to affect the wealth of the business.

Activity 8.7

Activity 8.3 was concerned with the cost of putting a car into a marketable condition. Apart from whether the car could be sold for more than the relevant cost of doing this, are there any other factors that should be taken into account in making a decision as to whether or not to do the work?

We can think of three points:

- Turning away another job in order to do the engine replacement may lead to customer dissatisfaction.
- On the other hand, having the car available for sale may be useful commercially for the garage, beyond the profit that can be earned from that particular car sale. For example, having a good range of second-hand cars for sale may attract potential customers wanting to buy a car.
- There is also a more immediate economic point. It has been assumed that the only opportunity cost concerns labour (the charge-out rate for the seven hours concerned). In practice, most car repairs involve the use of some materials and spare parts. These are usually charged to customers at a profit to the garage. Any such profit from a job turned away would be lost to the garage, and this lost profit would be an opportunity cost of the engine replacement and should, therefore, be included in the calculation of the minimum price to be charged for the sale of the car.

You may have thought of additional points.

It is important to consider 'qualitative' factors carefully. They can seem unimportant because they are virtually impossible to assess in terms of their ultimate economic effect. This effect can nevertheless be very significant.

Self-assessment question (8.1)

JB Limited is a small specialist manufacturer of electronic components. Makers of aircraft, for both civil and military purposes, use much of its output. One of the aircraft makers has offered a contract to JB Limited for the supply, over the next 12 months, of 400 identical components. The data relating to the production of each component are as follows:

(i) *Material requirements*:
   3 kg of material M1 (see Note 1 below)
   2 kg of material P2 (see Note 2 below)
   1 bought-in component (part number 678) (see Note 3 below)

   Note 1: Material M1 is in continuous use by the business; 1,000 kg are currently held by the business. The original cost was £4.70/kg, but it is known that future purchases will cost £5.50/kg.

   Note 2: 1,200 kg of material P2 are currently held. The original cost of this material was £4.30/kg. The material has not been required for the past two years. Its scrap value is £1.50/kg. The only foreseeable alternative use is as a substitute for material P4 (in constant use), but this would involve further processing costs of £1.60/kg. The current cost of material P4 is £3.60/kg.

   Note 3: It is estimated that the component (part number 678) could be bought in for £50 each.

(ii) *Labour requirements*: Each component would require five hours of skilled labour and five hours of semi-skilled labour. A skilled employee is available and is currently paid £14/hour. A replacement would, however, have to be obtained at a rate of £12/hour for the work which would otherwise be done by the skilled employee. The current rate for semi-skilled work is £10/hour and an additional employee could be appointed for this work.

(iii) *General manufacturing costs*: It is JB Limited's policy to charge a share of the general costs (rent, heating and so on) to each contract undertaken at the rate of £20 for each machine hour used on the contract. If the contract is undertaken, the general costs are expected to increase as a result of undertaking the contract by £3,200.

   Spare machine capacity is available and each component would require 4 machine hours. A price of £200 per component has been offered by the potential customer.

Required:

(a) Should the contract be accepted? Support your conclusion with appropriate figures to present to management.

(b) What other factors ought management to consider that might influence the decision?

The answer to this question can be found at the back of the book on page 700.

To end the chapter, **Real World 8.2** describes another case where the decision makers, quite correctly, ignored past costs and concentrated on future options for the business concerned.

Real world 8.2

FT

£1 shop

Merchant Equity partners, a newly formed private equity group, has agreed to buy the retail arm of MFI for just £1 with a view to turning round the furniture chain and selling it on for up to £500m in five years.

The buy-out agreement will see MFI pay a 'dowry' of £75m over three years to offload the loss-making retail business, in a deal that will allow it to concentrate on its profitable Howden Joinery unit. Howden sells kitchen cabinets to the building trade and will be renamed Galiform.

The decision by MFI to pay to have the 42-year-old chain taken off its hands comes after management struggled to prevent the 200-store chain slipping deeper into distress.

Matthew Ingle, chief executive of MFI, said, 'This is a good deal if you compare the payout of £75m over three years to annual losses of £40 to £50m.'

Source: 'MFI furniture retail arm bought for £1', FT.com, 22 September 2006.

Summary

The main points in this chapter may be summarised as follows.

Cost = amount of resources, usually measured in monetary terms, sacrificed to achieve a particular objective

Relevant and irrelevant costs

- Relevant costs must:
  - relate to the objective being pursued by the business;
  - differ from one possible decision outcome to the next.
- Relevant costs therefore include:
  - opportunity costs;
  - differential future outlay costs.
- Irrelevant costs therefore include:
  - all past (or sunk) costs;
  - all committed costs;
  - non-differential outlay costs.

Qualitative factors of decisions

- Financial/economic decisions almost inevitably have qualitative aspects that financial analysis cannot really handle, despite their importance.

MyAccountingLab   *Now check your progress in your personal Study Plan*

Key terms

cost p. 280	past cost p. 282
historic cost p. 280	outlay cost p. 282
opportunity cost p. 280	sunk cost p. 286
relevant cost p. 281	committed cost p. 286
irrelevant cost p. 281	

Further reading

If you would like to explore the topics covered in this chapter in more depth, we recommend the following books:

Cost Accounting: A managerial emphasis, *Horngren C., Datar S. and Foster G.*, 12th edn, Prentice Hall, 2006, chapter 11.

Management Accounting, *Atkinson A., Banker R., Kaplan R., Young S.M. and Matsumura E.,* 5th edn, Prentice Hall, 2007, chapter 6.

Management and Cost Accounting, *Drury C.*, 6th edn, Thomson Learning, 2004, chapter 9.

Managerial Accounting, *Hilton R.*, 6th edn, McGraw-Hill/Irwin, 2005, chapter 14.

Review questions

Answers to these questions can be found the back of the book on page 779.

8.1 To be relevant to a particular decision, a cost must have two attributes. What are they?

8.2 Distinguish between a sunk cost and an opportunity cost.

8.3 Define the word 'cost' in the context of management accounting.

8.4 What is meant by the expression 'committed cost'? How do committed costs arise?

Exercises

Exercises 8.7 and 8.8 are more advanced than 8.1 to 8.6. Those with coloured numbers have answers at the back of the book, starting on page 729.

If you wish to try more exercises, visit the students' side of the Companion Website.

8.1 Lombard Ltd has been offered a contract for which there is available production capacity. The contract is for 20,000 identical items, manufactured by an intricate assembly operation, to be produced and delivered in the next few months at a price of £80 each. The specification for one item is as follows:

Assembly labour	4 hours
Component X	4 units
Component Y	3 units

There would also be the need to hire equipment, for the duration of the contract, at an outlay cost of £200,000.

The assembly is a highly skilled operation and the workforce is currently underutilised. It is the business's policy to retain this workforce on full pay in anticipation of high demand next year for a new product currently being developed. Skilled workers are paid £15 an hour.

Component X is used in a number of other subassemblies produced by the business. It is readily available. 50,000 units of component X are currently held in inventories (stock). Component Y was a special purchase in anticipation of an order that did not, in the end, materialise. It is therefore surplus to requirements, and the 100,000 units that are currently held may have to be sold at a loss. An estimate of various values for components X and Y provided by the materials planning department is as follows:

	X £/unit	Y £/unit
Historic cost	4	10
Replacement cost	5	11
Net realisable value	3	8

It is estimated that any additional relevant costs associated with the contract (beyond the above) will amount to £8 an item.

Required:

Analyse the information and advise Lombard Ltd on the desirability of the contract.

8.2   The local authority of a small town maintains a theatre and arts centre for the use of a local repertory company, other visiting groups and exhibitions. Management decisions are taken by a committee that meets regularly to review the financial statements and to plan the use of the facilities.

The theatre employs a full-time non-performing staff and a number of artistes at costs of £9,600 and £35,200 a month, respectively. The theatre mounts a new production every month for 20 performances. Other monthly costs of the theatre are as follows:

	£
Costumes	5,600
Scenery	3,300
Heat and light	10,300
A share of the administration costs of local authority	16,000
Casual staff	3,520
Refreshments	2,360

On average the theatre is half full for the performances of the repertory company. The capacity and seat prices in the theatre are:

200 seats at £24 each
500 seats at £16 each
300 seats at £12 each

In addition, the theatre sells refreshments during the performances for £7,760 a month. Programme sales cover their costs, but advertising in the programme generates £6,720 a month.

The management committee has been approached by a popular touring group which would like to take over the theatre for one month (25 performances). The group is prepared to pay half of its ticket income for the booking. It expects to fill the theatre for 10 nights and achieve two-thirds capacity on the remaining 15 nights. The prices charged are £2 less than normally applies in the theatre.

The local authority will pay for heat and light costs and will still honour the contracts of all artistes and pay the non-performing employees who will sell refreshments, programmes and so on. The committee does not expect any change in the level of refreshments or programme sales if they agree to this booking.

Note: The committee includes the share of the local authority administration costs when making profit calculations. It assumes occupancy applies equally across all seat prices.

Required:

(a)   On financial grounds should the management committee agree to the approach from the touring group? Support your answer with appropriate workings.

(b)   What other factors may have a bearing on the decision by the committee?

8.3   Andrews and Co. Ltd has been invited to tender for a contract. It is to produce 10,000 metres of an electrical cable in which the business specialises. The estimating department of the business has produced the following information relating to the contract:

● *Materials*: The cable will require a steel core, which the business buys in. The steel core is to be coated with a special plastic, also bought in, using a special process. Plastic for the covering will be required at the rate of 0.10 kg/metre of completed cable.

● *Direct labour*.   Skilled: 10 minutes/metre
                            Unskilled: 5 minutes/metre

The business already holds sufficient of each of the materials required to complete the contract. Information on the cost of the inventories is as follows:

	Steel core £/metre	Plastic £/kg
Historic cost	1.50	0.60
Current buying-in cost	2.10	0.70
Scrap value	1.40	0.10

The steel core is in constant use by the business for a variety of work that it regularly undertakes. The plastic is a surplus from a previous contract where a mistake was made and an excess quantity ordered. If the current contract does not go ahead, this plastic will be scrapped (zero proceeds).

Unskilled labour, which is paid at the rate of £7.50 an hour, will need to be taken on specifically to undertake the contract. The business is fairly quiet at the moment which means that a pool of skilled labour exists that will still be employed at full pay of £12 an hour to do nothing if the contract does not proceed. The pool of skilled labour is sufficient to complete the contract.

Required:

Indicate the minimum price at which the contract could be undertaken such that the business would be neither better nor worse off as a result of doing it.

8.4   SJ Services Ltd has been asked to quote a price for a special contract to render a service that will take the business one week to complete. Information relating to labour for the contract is as follows:

Grade of labour	Hours required	Basic rate/hour
Skilled	27	£12
Semi-skilled	14	£9
Unskilled	20	£7

A shortage of skilled labour means that the necessary staff to undertake the contract would have to be moved from other work that is currently yielding an excess of sales revenue over labour and other costs of £8 an hour.

Semi-skilled labour is currently being paid at semi-skilled rates to undertake unskilled work. If the relevant members of staff are moved to work on the contract, unskilled labour will have to be employed for the week to replace them.

The unskilled labour actually needed to work on the contract will be specifically employed for the week of the contract.

All labour is charged to contracts at 50 per cent above the rate paid to the employees, so as to cover the contract's fair share of the business's general costs (rent, heating and so on). It is estimated that these general costs will increase by £50 as a result of undertaking the contract.

Undertaking the contract will require the use of a specialised machine for the week. The business owns such a machine, which it depreciates at the rate of £120 a week. This machine is currently being hired out to another business at a weekly rental of £175 on a week-by-week contract.

To derive the above estimates, the business has had to spend £300 on a specialised study. If the contract does not proceed, the results of the study can be sold for £250.

An estimate of the contract's fair share of the business's rent is £150 a week.

Required:

Deduce the minimum price at which SJ Services Ltd could undertake the contract such that it would be neither better nor worse off as a result of undertaking it.

8.5 A business in the food industry is currently holding 2,000 tonnes of material in bulk storage. This material deteriorates with time, and so in the near future it needs to be repackaged for sale or sold in its present form.

The material was acquired in two batches: 800 tonnes at a price of £40 a tonne and 1,200 tonnes at a price of £44 a tonne. The current market price of any additional purchases is £48 a tonne. If the business were to dispose of the material, it could sell any quantity but only for £36 a tonne; it does not have the contacts or reputation to command a higher price.

Repackaging this bulk material may be undertaken to develop either Product A or Product X. No weight loss occurs with repackaging, that is, one tonne of material will make one tonne of A or X. For Product A, there is an additional cost of £60 a tonne, after which it will sell for £105 a tonne. The marketing department estimates that 500 tonnes could be sold in this way.

In the development of Product X, the business incurs additional costs of £80 a tonne for repackaging. A market price for X is not known and no minimum price has been agreed. The management is currently engaged in discussions over the minimum price that may be charged for Product X in the current circumstances. Management wants to know the relevant cost per tonne for Product X so as to provide a basis for negotiating a profitable selling price for the product.

Required:
Identify the relevant cost per tonne for Product X, given sales volumes of X of:
(a) up to 1,500 tonnes
(b) over 1,500 tonnes, up to 2,000 tonnes
(c) over 2,000 tonnes.

Explain your answer.

8.6 A local education authority is faced with a predicted decline in the demand for school places in its area. It is believed that some schools will have to close in order to remove up to 800 places from current capacity levels. The schools that may face closure are referenced as A, B, C or D. Their details are as follows:

- *School A* (capacity 200) was built 15 years ago at a cost of £1.2m. It is situated in a 'socially disadvantaged' community area. The authority has been offered £14m for the site by a property developer.
- *School B* (capacity 500) was built 20 years ago and cost £1m. It was renovated only two years ago at a cost of £3m to improve its facilities. An offer of £8m has been made for the site by a business planning a shopping complex in this affluent part of the town.
- *School C* (capacity 600) cost £5m to build five years ago. The land for this school is rented from a local business for an annual cost of £300,000.
- *School D* (capacity 800) cost £7m to build eight years ago. Last year £1.5m was spent on an extension. The school has considerable grounds, which are currently used for sporting events. This factor makes it popular with developers, who have recently offered £9m for the site.

In the accounting system, the local authority depreciates non-current (fixed) assets based on 2 per cent a year on the original cost. It also differentiates between one-off, large items of capital expenditure or revenue, and annually recurring items.

The land rented for School C is based on a 100-year lease. If the school closes, the property reverts immediately to the owner. If School C is not closed, it will require a £3m investment to improve safety at the school.

If School D is closed, it will be necessary to pay £1.8m to adapt facilities at other schools to accommodate the change.

The local authority has a central staff, which includes administrators for each school costing £200,000 a year for each school, and a chief education officer costing £80,000 a year in total.

Required:

(a) Prepare a summary of the relevant cash flows (costs and revenues, relative to not making any closures) under the following options:

   (i)   closure of D only

   (ii) closure of A and B

   (iii) closure of A and C.

Show separately the one-off effects and annually recurring items, rank the options open to the local authority, and briefly interpret your answer. (*Note:* Various approaches are acceptable provided that they are logical.)

(b) Identify and comment on any two different types of irrelevant cost contained in the information given in the question.

(c) Discuss other factors that might have a bearing on the decision.

8.7 Rob Otics Ltd, a small business that specialises in building electronic-control equipment, has just received an order from a customer for eight identical robotic units. These will be completed using Rob Otic's own labour force and factory capacity. The product specification prepared by the estimating department shows the following:

- Material and labour requirements for each robotic unit:

  Component X   2 per unit

  Component Y   1 per unit

  Component Z   4 per unit

- Other miscellaneous items:

  Assembly labour   25 hours per unit (but see below)

  Inspection labour   6 hours per unit

As part of the costing exercise, the business has collected the following information:

- *Component X.* This item is normally held by the business as it is in constant demand. The 10 units currently held were invoiced to Rob Otics at £150 a unit, but the sole supplier has announced a price rise of 20 per cent effective immediately. Rob Otics has not yet paid for the items currently held.
- *Component Y.* 25 units are currently held. This component is not normally used by Rob Otics but the units currently held are because of a cancelled order following the bankruptcy of a customer. The units originally cost the business £4,000 in total, although Rob Otics has recouped £1,500 from the liquidator. As Rob Otics can see no use for it, the finance director proposes to scrap the 25 units (zero proceeds).
- *Component Z.* This is in regular use by Rob Otics. There is none in inventories but an order is about to be sent to a supplier for 75 units, irrespective of this new proposal. The supplier charges £25 a unit on small orders but will reduce the price to £20 a unit for all units on any order over 100 units.
- Other miscellaneous items. These are expected to cost £250 in total.

Assembly labour is currently in short supply in the area and is paid at £10 an hour. If the order is accepted, all necessary labour will have to be transferred from existing work, and other orders will be lost. It is estimated that for each hour transferred to this contract £38 will be lost (calculated as lost sales revenue £60, less materials £12 and labour £10). The production director suggests that, owing to a learning process, the time taken to make each unit will reduce, from 25 hours to make the first one, by one hour a unit made.

Inspection labour can be provided by paying existing personnel overtime which is at a premium of 50 per cent over the standard rate of £12 an hour.

When the business is working out its contract prices, it normally adds an amount equal to £20 for each assembly hour to cover its general costs (such as rent and electricity). To the resulting total, 40 per cent is normally added as a profit mark-up.

Required:

(a) Prepare an estimate of the minimum price that you would recommend Rob Otics Ltd to charge for the proposed contract, and provide explanations for any items included.

(b) Identify any other factors that you would consider before fixing the final price.

8.8 A business places substantial emphasis on customer satisfaction and, to this end, delivers its product in special protective containers. These containers have been made in a department within the business. Management has recently become concerned that this internal supply of containers is very expensive. As a result, outside suppliers have been invited to submit tenders for the provision of these containers. A quote of £250,000 a year has been received for a volume that compares with current internal supply.

An investigation into the internal costs of container manufacture has been undertaken and the following emerges:

(i) The annual cost of material is £120,000, according to the stores records maintained, at actual historic cost. Three-quarters (by cost) of this represents material that is regularly stocked and replenished. The remaining 25 per cent of the material cost is a special foaming chemical that is not used for any other purpose. There are 40 tonnes of this chemical currently held. It was bought in bulk for £750 a tonne. Today's replacement price for this material is £1,050 a tonne but it is unlikely that the business could realise more than £600 a tonne if it had to be disposed of owing to the high handling costs and special transport facilities required.

(ii) The annual labour cost is £80,000 for this department; however, most are casual employees or recent starters, and so, if an outside quote were accepted, little redundancy would be payable. There are, however, two long-serving employees who would each accept as a salary £15,000 a year until they reached retirement age in two years' time.

(iii) The department manager has a salary of £30,000 a year. The closure of this department would release him to take over another department for which a vacancy is about to be advertised. The salary, status and prospects are similar.

(iv) A rental charge of £9,750 a year, based on floor area, is allocated to the containers department. If the department were closed, the floor space released would be used for warehousing and, as a result, the business would give up the tenancy of an existing warehouse for which it is paying £15,750 a year.

(v) The plant cost £162,000 when it was bought five years ago. Its market value now is £28,000 and it could continue for another two years, at which time its market value would have fallen to zero. (The plant depreciates evenly over time.)

(vi) Annual plant maintenance costs are £9,900 and allocated general administrative costs £33,750 for the coming year.

Required:

Calculate the annual cost of manufacturing containers for comparison with the quote using relevant figures for establishing the cost or benefit of accepting the quote. Indicate any assumptions or qualifications you wish to make.

Cost-volume-profit analysis

Introduction

This chapter is concerned with the relationship between volume of activity, costs and profit. Broadly, costs can be analysed as those that are fixed, relative to the volume of activity, and those that vary with the volume of activity. We shall consider how we can use knowledge of this relationship to make decisions and to assess risk, particularly in the context of short-term decisions. This will help the business to work towards its strategic objectives. This continues the theme of Chapter 8, but in this chapter we shall be looking at situations where a whole class of costs – fixed costs – can be treated as being irrelevant for decision-making purposes.

Learning outcomes

When you have completed this chapter, you should be able to:

- Distinguish between fixed costs and variable costs and use this distinction to explain the relationship between costs, volume and profit.

- Prepare a break-even chart and deduce the break-even point for some activity.

- Discuss the weaknesses of break-even analysis.

- Demonstrate the way in which marginal analysis can be used when making short-term decisions.

MyAccountingLab   *Remember to create your own personalised Study Plan*

The behaviour of costs

We saw in the previous chapter that costs represent the resources that have to be sacrificed to achieve a business objective. The objective may be to make a particular product, to provide a particular service, to operate a particular hospital for a month, and so on. The costs incurred by a business may be classified in various ways and one important way is according to how they behave in relation to changes in the volume of activity. There are costs that:

● are fixed (stay the same) when changes occur to the volume of activity; and
● vary according to the volume of activity.

 These are known as **fixed costs** and **variable costs** respectively.

A restaurant manager's salary would normally provide an example of a fixed cost of operating the restaurant. The cost to the restaurant of buying the raw food would be a typical variable cost.

We shall see in this chapter that knowledge of how much of each type of cost is associated with some particular activity can be of great value to the decision maker.

Fixed costs

The way in which fixed costs behave can be shown by preparing a graph that plots the fixed costs of a business against the level of activity, as in Figure 9.1. The distance 0F represents the amount of fixed costs, and this stays the same irrespective of the volume of activity.

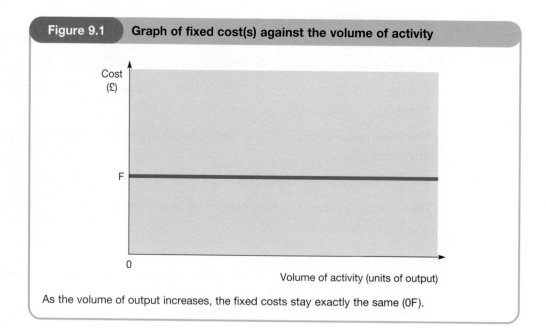

Figure 9.1 **Graph of fixed cost(s) against the volume of activity**

As the volume of output increases, the fixed costs stay exactly the same (0F).

Activity 9.1

Can you give some examples of costs that are likely to be fixed for a hairdressing salon?

We came up with the following:

- rent
- insurance
- cleaning costs
- staff salaries.

These costs seem likely to be the same irrespective of the number of customers having their hair cut or styled.

Staff salaries and wages seem sometimes to be assumed automatically to be variable costs. In practice, they tend to be fixed. People are generally not paid according to the volume of output, and it is not normal to dismiss staff when there is a short-term downturn in activity. If there is a long-term downturn, or at least if it looks that way to management, redundancies may occur, with fixed-cost savings. This, however, is true of all costs. If there is seen to be a likely reduction in demand, the business may decide to close some branches and make rental cost savings. Thus 'fixed' does not mean set in stone for all time; it usually means fixed over the short to medium term.

There are circumstances in which labour costs are variable (for example, where employees are paid according to how much output they produce), but this is unusual.

It is important to be clear that 'fixed', in this context, means only that the cost is not altered by changes in the volume of activity. Fixed costs are likely to be affected by inflation. If rent (a typical fixed cost) goes up because of inflation, a fixed cost will have increased, but not because of a change in the volume of activity.

Similarly, the level of fixed costs does not stay the same, irrespective of the time period involved. Fixed costs are almost always *time-based*: that is, they vary with the length of time concerned. The rental charge for two months is normally twice that for one month. Thus fixed costs normally vary with time, but (of course) not with the volume of output. We should note that when we talk of fixed costs being, say, £1,000, we must add the period concerned, say, £1,000 a month.

Activity 9.2

Do fixed costs stay the same irrespective of the volume of output, even where there is a massive rise in that volume?
    Think in terms of the rent cost for the hairdressing business.

In fact, the rent is only fixed over a particular range (known as the 'relevant' range). If the number of people wanting to have their hair cut by the business increased, and the business wished to meet this increased demand, it would eventually have to expand its physical size. This might be achieved by opening an additional branch, or perhaps by moving the existing business to larger premises nearby. It may be possible to cope with relatively minor increases in activity by using existing space more efficiently, or by having longer opening hours. If activity continued to expand, increased rent charges would seem inevitable, however.

In practice, the situation described in Activity 9.2 would look something like Figure 9.2.

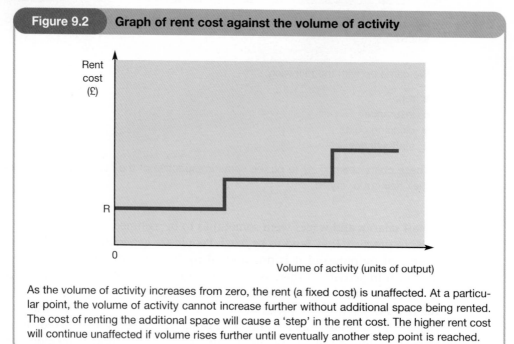

Figure 9.2 **Graph of rent cost against the volume of activity**

As the volume of activity increases from zero, the rent (a fixed cost) is unaffected. At a particular point, the volume of activity cannot increase further without additional space being rented. The cost of renting the additional space will cause a 'step' in the rent cost. The higher rent cost will continue unaffected if volume rises further until eventually another step point is reached.

At lower volumes of activity, the rent cost shown in Figure 9.2 would be 0R. As the volume of activity expands, the accommodation becomes inadequate and further expansion requires an increase in premises and, therefore, cost. This higher level of accommodation provision will enable further expansion to take place. Eventually, additional costs will need to be incurred if further expansion is to occur. Fixed costs that behave like this are often referred to as **stepped fixed costs**.

Variable costs

We saw earlier that variable costs are costs that vary with the volume of activity. In a manufacturing business, for example, this would include raw materials used.

Variable costs can be represented graphically as in Figure 9.3. At zero volume of activity the variable cost is zero. The cost increases in a straight line as activity increases.

Activity 9.3

Can you think of some examples of variable costs in the hairdressing business?

We can think of a couple:

● lotions and other materials used;
● laundry costs to wash towels used to dry customers' hair.

As with many types of business activity, variable costs of hairdressers tend to be relatively light in comparison with fixed costs, that is, fixed costs tend to make up the bulk of total costs.

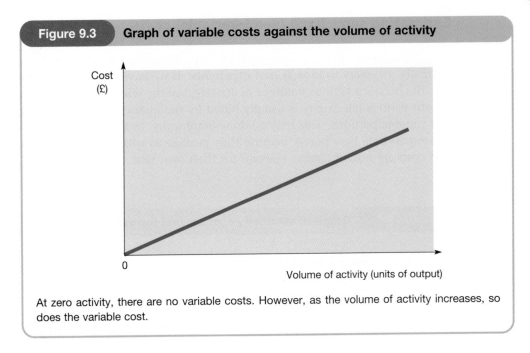

Figure 9.3   **Graph of variable costs against the volume of activity**

At zero activity, there are no variable costs. However, as the volume of activity increases, so does the variable cost.

The straight line for variable cost on the graph implies that the variable cost will normally be the same per unit of activity, irrespective of the volume of activity concerned. We shall consider the practicality of this assumption a little later in this chapter.

Semi-fixed (semi-variable) costs

In some cases, costs have an element of both fixed and variable cost. These can be described as **semi-fixed (semi-variable) costs**. An example might be the electricity cost for the hairdressing business. Some of this will be for heating and lighting, and this part is probably fixed, at least until the volume of activity expands to a point where longer opening hours or larger premises are necessary. The other part of the cost will vary with the volume of activity. Here we are talking about such things as power for hairdryers and so on.

Activity 9.4

Can you suggest another cost for a hairdressing business that is likely to be semi-fixed (semi-variable)?

We thought of telephone charges for landlines. These tend to have a rental element, which is fixed, and there may also be certain calls that have to be made irrespective of the volume of activity involved. However, increased business would be likely to lead to the need to make more telephone calls and so to increased call charges.

Estimating semi-fixed (semi-variable) costs

Usually, it is not obvious how much of each element a particular cost contains. It is normally necessary to look at past experience. If we have data on what the electricity cost has been for various volumes of activity, say the relevant data over several three-month periods (electricity is usually billed by the quarter), we can estimate the fixed and variable portions. This may be done graphically, as shown in Figure 9.4. We tend to use past data here purely because they provide us with an estimate of future costs; past costs are not, of course, relevant for their own sake.

Figure 9.4	Graph of electricity cost against the volume of activity

Here the electricity bill for a time period (for example, three months) is plotted against the volume of activity for that same period. This is done for a series of periods. A line is then drawn that best 'fits' the various points on the graph. From this line we can then deduce both the cost at zero activity (the fixed element) and the slope of the line (the variable element).

Each of the dots in Figure 9.4 is the electricity charge for a particular quarter plotted against the volume of activity (probably measured in terms of sales revenue) for the same quarter. The diagonal line on the graph is the *line of best fit*. This means that this was the line that best seemed (to us, at least) to represent the data. A better estimate can usually be made using a statistical technique (*least squares regression*), which does not involve drawing graphs and making estimates. In practice though, it probably makes little difference which approach is taken.

From the graph we can say that the fixed element of the electricity cost is the amount represented by the vertical distance from the origin at zero (bottom left-hand corner) to the point where the line of best fit crosses the vertical axis of the graph. The variable cost per unit is the amount that the graph rises for each increase in the volume of activity.

By breaking down semi-fixed costs in this way into their fixed and variable elements we are left with just two types of cost: fixed costs and variable costs.

Now that we have considered the nature of fixed and variable costs, we can go on to do something useful with that knowledge: carry out a **break-even analysis**.

Finding the break-even point

If, in respect of a particular activity, we know the total fixed costs for a period and the total variable cost per unit, we can produce a graph like the one shown in Figure 9.5.

Figure 9.5　Graph of total cost against volume of activity

The bottom part of the graph represents the fixed-cost element. To this is added the wedge-shaped top portion, which represents the variable costs. The two parts together represent total cost. At zero activity, the variable costs are zero, so total costs equal fixed costs. As activity increases so does total cost, but only because variable costs increase. We are assuming that there are no steps in the fixed costs.

The bottom part of Figure 9.5 shows the fixed cost area. Added to this is the variable cost, the wedge-shaped portion at the top of the graph. The uppermost line represents the total cost at any particular volume of activity. This total is the vertical distance between the graph's horizontal axis and the uppermost line for the particular volume of activity concerned. Logically, the total cost at zero activity is the amount of the fixed costs. This is because, even where there is nothing going on, the business will still be paying rent, salaries and so on, at least in the short term. The fixed cost is augmented by the amount of the relevant variable costs, to give the total cost, as the volume of activity increases.

If we take this total cost graph in Figure 9.5, and superimpose on it a line representing total revenue for each volume of activity, we obtain the **break-even chart**. This is shown in Figure 9.6.

Note in Figure 9.6 that, at zero volume of activity (zero sales), there is zero sales revenue. The profit (loss), which is the difference between total sales revenue and total cost, for some volume of activity is the vertical distance between the total sales revenue line and the total cost line at that particular volume of activity. Where the volume of activity is at **break-even point (BEP)**, there is no vertical distance between these two lines (total sales revenue equals total costs) and so there is no profit or loss; that is, the activity *breaks even*. Where the volume of activity is below BEP, a loss will be incurred

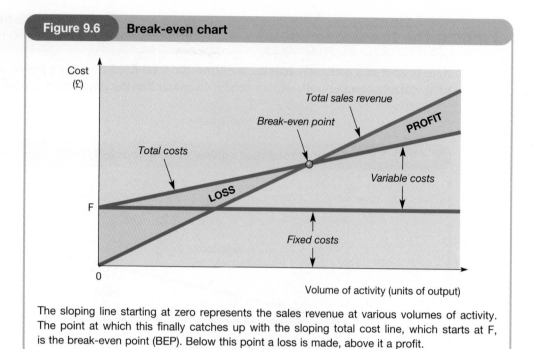

Figure 9.6 **Break-even chart**

The sloping line starting at zero represents the sales revenue at various volumes of activity. The point at which this finally catches up with the sloping total cost line, which starts at F, is the break-even point (BEP). Below this point a loss is made, above it a profit.

because total costs exceed total sales revenue. Where the business operates at a volume of activity above BEP, there will be a profit because total sales revenue will exceed total costs. The further below BEP, the higher the loss: the further above BEP, the higher the profit.

As may be imagined, deducing BEPs by graphical means is a laborious business. However, since the relationships in the graph are all linear (that is, the lines are all straight), it is easy to calculate the BEP.

We know that at BEP (but not at any other point):

> **Total sales revenue = Total costs**

(At all other points except the BEP, either total sales revenue will exceed total cost or the other way round. Only at BEP are they equal.) That is,

> **Total sales revenue = Fixed costs + Total variable costs**

If we call the number of units of output at BEP b, then

$$b \times \text{Sales revenue per unit} = \text{Fixed costs} + (b \times \text{Variable costs per unit})$$

so:

$$(b \times \text{Sales revenue per unit}) - (b \times \text{Variable costs per unit}) = \text{Fixed costs}$$

and:

$$b \times (\text{Sales revenue per unit} - \text{Variable costs per unit}) = \text{Fixed costs}$$

giving:

$$b = \frac{\text{Fixed costs}}{\text{Sales revenue per unit} - \text{Variable costs per unit}}$$

If we look back at the break-even chart in Figure 9.6, this seems logical. The total cost line starts off at point F, higher than the starting point for the total sales revenue line (zero) by amount F (the amount of the fixed costs). Because the sales revenue per unit is greater than the variable cost per unit, the sales revenue line will gradually catch up with the total cost line. The rate at which it will catch up is dependent on the relative steepness of the two lines and the amount that it has to catch up (the fixed costs). Bearing in mind that the slopes of the two lines are the variable cost per unit and the selling price per unit, the above equation for calculating b looks perfectly logical.

Although the BEP can be calculated quickly and simply, as shown, it does not mean that the graphical approach of the break-even chart is without value. The chart shows the relationship between cost, volume and profit over a range of output and in a form that can easily be understood by non-financial managers. The break-even chart can therefore be a useful device for explaining this relationship.

Example 9.1

Cottage Industries Ltd makes baskets. The fixed costs of operating the workshop for a month total £500. Each basket requires materials that cost £2. Each basket takes one hour to make, and the business pays the basket makers £10 an hour. The basket makers are all on contracts such that if they do not work for any reason, they are not paid. The baskets are sold to a wholesaler for £14 each.

What is the BEP for basket making for the business?

The BEP (in number of baskets) is:

$$BEP = \frac{Fixed\ costs}{(Sales\ revenue\ per\ unit - Variable\ costs\ per\ unit)}$$

$$= \frac{£500}{£14 - (£2 + £10)}$$

$$= 250\ baskets\ per\ month$$

Note that the BEP must be expressed with respect to a period of time.

Real World 9.1 shows information on the BEPs of three well-known businesses.

Real World 9.1

BE at BA, Ryanair and easyJet

Commercial airlines seem to pay a lot of attention to their BEPs and their 'load factors', that is, their actual level of activity. Figure 9.7 shows the BEP and load factor for three well-known airlines operating from the UK. British Airways (BA) is a traditional airline. Ryanair and easyJet both are 'no frills' carriers, which means that passengers receive lower levels of service in return for lower fares. All three operate flights within the UK and from the UK to other European countries. Only BA operates flights beyond Europe. We can see that all three airlines are making operating profits as each has a load factor greater than its BEP.

→

Real World 9.1 continued

Figure 9.7 **Break even and load factors in the airline industry**

Source: Based on information contained in 'Ryanair alert hits shares', Jon Ashworth, *The Times*, 4 June 2003, p. 21. The data in the article are based on the year ended 31 March 2003.

Activity 9.5

Can you think of reasons why the managers of a business might find it useful to know the BEP of some activity that they are planning to undertake?

The usefulness of being able to deduce the BEP is that it makes it possible to compare the planned or expected volume of activity with the BEP and so make a judgement about risk. Planning to operate only just above the volume of activity necessary in order to break even may indicate that it is a risky venture, since only a small fall from the planned volume of activity could lead to a loss.

Activity 9.6

Cottage Industries Ltd (see Example 9.1) expects to sell 500 baskets a month. The business has the opportunity to rent a basket-making machine. Doing so would increase the total fixed costs of operating the workshop for a month to £3,000. Using the machine would reduce the labour time to half an hour per basket. The basket makers would still be paid £10 an hour.

(a) How much profit would the business make each month from selling baskets (i) assuming that the basket-making machine is not rented and (ii) assuming that it is rented?
(b) What is the BEP if the machine is rented?
(c) What do you notice about the figures that you calculate?

(a) Estimated monthly profit from basket making:

	Without the machine		With the machine	
	£	£	£	£
Sales revenue (500 × £14)		7,000		7,000
Less Materials (500 × £2)	1,000		1,000	
Labour (500 × 1 × £10)	5,000			
(500 × ½ × £10)			2,500	
Fixed costs	500		3,000	
		6,500		6,500
Profit		500		500

(b) The BEP (in number of baskets) with the machine:

$$\text{BEP} = \frac{\text{Fixed costs}}{\text{Sales revenue per unit} - \text{Variable costs per unit}}$$

$$= \frac{£3,000}{£14 - (£2 + £5)}$$

$$= 429 \text{ baskets a month}$$

The BEP without the machine is 250 baskets per month (see Example 9.1).

(c) There seems to be nothing to choose between the two manufacturing strategies regarding profit, at the estimated sales volume. There is, however, a distinct difference between the two strategies regarding the BEP. Without the machine, the actual volume of sales could fall by a half of that which is expected (from 500 to 250) before the business would fail to make a profit. With the machine, however, just a 14 per cent fall (from 500 to 429) would be enough to cause the business to fail to make a profit. On the other hand, for each additional basket sold above the estimated 500, an additional profit of only £2 (that is, £14 − (£2 + £10)) would be made without the machine, whereas £7 (that is, £14 − (£2 + £5)) would be made with the machine. (Note that knowledge of the BEP and the planned volume of activity gives some basis for assessing the riskiness of the activity.)

We shall take a closer look at the relationship between fixed costs, variable costs and break even together with any advice that we might give the management of Cottage Industries Ltd after we have briefly considered the notion of contribution.

Contribution

The bottom part of the break-even formula (sales revenue per unit less variable costs per unit) is known as the **contribution per unit**. Thus for the basket-making activity, without the machine the contribution per unit is £2, and with the machine it is £7. This can be quite a useful figure to know in a decision-making context. It is called 'contribution' because it contributes to meeting the fixed costs and, if there is any excess, it also contributes to profit.

We shall see, a little later in this chapter, how knowing the amount of the contribution generated by a particular activity can be valuable in making short-term decisions of various types, as well as being useful in the BEP calculation.

Margin of safety

→ The **margin of safety** is the extent to which the planned volume of output or sales lies above the BEP. Going back to Activity 9.6, we saw that the following situation exists:

	Without the machine (number of baskets)	With the machine (number of baskets)
Expected volume of sales	500	500
BEP	250	429
Difference (margin of safety):		
Number of baskets	250	71
Percentage of estimated volume of sales	50%	14%

Activity 9.7

What advice would you give Cottage Industries Ltd about renting the machine, on the basis of the values for margin of safety?

It is a matter of personal judgement, which in turn is related to individual attitudes to risk, as to which strategy to adopt. Most people, however, would prefer the strategy of not renting the machine, since the margin of safety between the expected volume of activity and the BEP is much greater. Thus, for the same level of return the risk will be lower without renting the machine.

The relative margins of safety are directly linked to the relationship between the selling price per basket, the variable costs per basket and the fixed costs per month. Without the machine the contribution (selling price less variable costs) per basket is £2; with the machine it is £7. On the other hand, without the machine the fixed costs are £500 a month; with the machine they are £3,000. This means that, with the machine, the contributions have more fixed costs to 'overcome' before the activity becomes profitable. However, the rate at which the contributions can overcome fixed costs is higher with the machine, because variable costs are lower. This means that one more, or one less, basket sold has a greater impact on profit than it does if the machine is not rented. The contrast between the two scenarios is shown graphically in Figures 9.8(a) and (b).

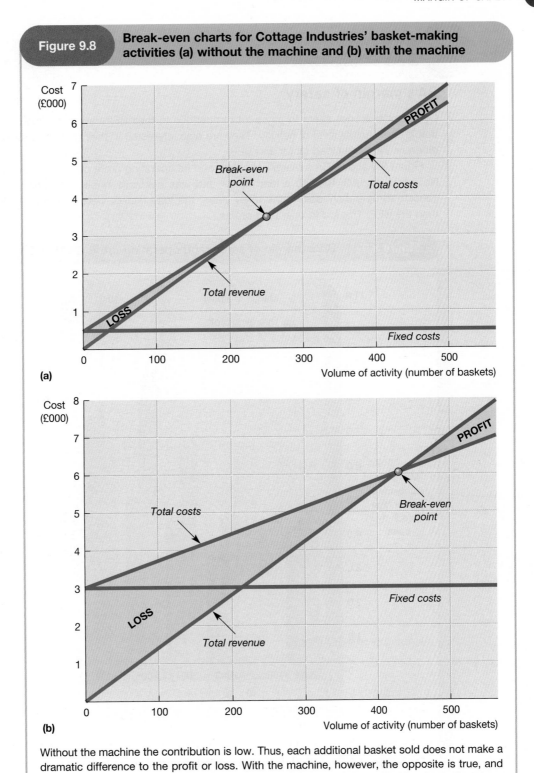

| Figure 9.8 | Break-even charts for Cottage Industries' basket-making activities (a) without the machine and (b) with the machine |

Without the machine the contribution is low. Thus, each additional basket sold does not make a dramatic difference to the profit or loss. With the machine, however, the opposite is true, and small increases or decreases in the sales volume will have a marked effect on the profit or loss.

If we look back to Real World 9.1, we can see that Ryanair had a much larger margin of safety than either BA or easyJet.

Real World 9.2 goes into more detail on the margin of safety and operating profit, over recent years, of one of the three airlines featured in Real World 9.1.

Real World 9.2

BA's margin of safety

Commercial airlines seem to pay a lot of attention to their BEPs and their 'load factors', that is, their actual level of activity. They are also interested in their margin of safety (the difference between load factor and BEP).

Figure 9.9 shows BA's margin of safety and its operating profit over a six-year period. Note that in 2002, BA had a load factor that was below its break-even point and this caused an operating loss. In the other years, the load factors were comfortably greater than the BEP. This led to operating profits.

Figure 9.9   **BA's margin of safety and operating profit, 2001 to 2006**

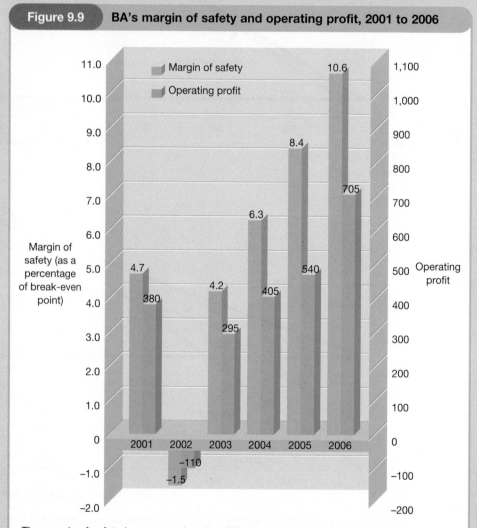

The margin of safety is expressed as the difference between the load factor and the BEP (for each year), expressed as a percentage of the BEP. Generally, the higher the margin of safety, the higher the operating profit.

Source: Derived from information contained in British Airways plc Annual Reports 2001 to 2006.

Source: British Airways plc Annual Reports 2001 to 2006.

Operating gearing

→ The relationship between contribution and fixed costs is known as **operating gearing** (or **operational gearing**). An activity with relatively high fixed costs compared with its variable costs is said to have high operating gearing. Thus, Cottage Industries Ltd has higher operating gearing using the machine than not using it. Renting the machine increases the level of operating gearing quite dramatically because it causes an increase in fixed costs, but at the same time it leads to a reduction in variable costs per basket.

Operating gearing and its effect on profit

The reason why the word 'gearing' is used in this context is that, as with intermeshing gear wheels of different circumferences, a circular movement in one of the factors (volume of output) causes a more than proportionate circular movement in the other (profit), as illustrated by Figure 9.10.

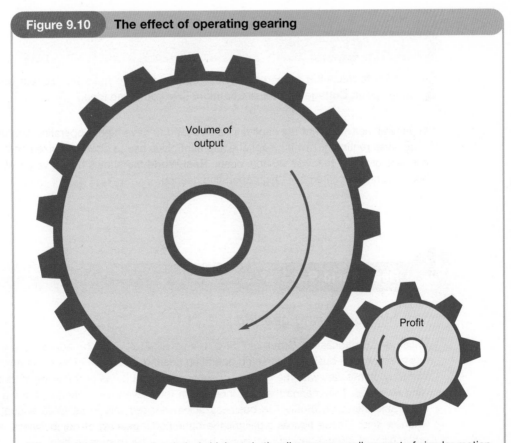

Figure 9.10 **The effect of operating gearing**

Where operating gearing is relatively high, as in the diagram, a small amount of circular motion in the volume wheel causes a relatively large amount of circular motion in the profit wheel. An increase in volume would cause a disproportionately greater increase in profit. The equivalent would also be true of a decrease in activity, however.

Increasing the level of operating gearing makes profits more sensitive to changes in the volume of activity. We can demonstrate operating gearing with Cottage Industries Ltd's basket-making activities as follows:

	Without the machine			With the machine		
Volume (number of baskets)	500	1,000	1,500	500	1,000	1,500
	£	£	£	£	£	£
Contributions*	1,000	2,000	3,000	3,500	7,000	10,500
Less Fixed costs	500	500	500	3,000	3,000	3,000
Profit	500	1,500	2,500	500	4,000	7,500

* £2 per basket without the machine and £7 per basket with it.

Note that, without the machine (low operating gearing), a doubling of the output from 500 to 1,000 units brings a trebling of the profit. With the machine (high operating gearing), doubling output causes profit to rise by eight times. At the same time, reductions in the volume of output tend to have a more damaging effect on profit where the operating gearing is higher.

Activity (9.8)

In general terms, what types of business activity tend to have the highest operating gearing? (*Hint*: Cottage Industries Ltd might give you some idea.)

In general, activities that are capital intensive tend to have higher operating gearing. This is because renting or owning capital equipment gives rise to additional fixed costs, but it can also give rise to lower variable costs. **Real World 9.3** shows how a very well-known business has benefited from high operating gearing.

Real World 9.3

Sky-high operating gearing

British Sky Broadcasting Group plc (Sky), the satellite television broadcaster, is an obvious example of a business with high operating gearing. Nearly all of its costs are fixed in that they do not vary with the number of subscribers that it has or the value of its advertising revenues. This means that any increase in total revenues is likely to have a strong favourable effect on profit. The business acknowledged this in its 2005 annual report where it said: 'These figures highlight the operational gearing of our business and the profitability of adding new subscribers', before going on to explain how an 11 per cent increase in revenue (from £3,656m to £4,048m) led to an increase of 34 per cent in operating profit (from £600m to £805m).

Source: British Sky Broadcasting Group plc Annual Report 2005, p. 5.

Profit-volume charts

→ A slight variant of the break-even chart is the **profit–volume (PV) chart**. A typical PV chart is shown in Figure 9.11.

Figure 9.11   Profit–volume chart

The sloping line is profit (loss) plotted against activity. As activity increases, so does total contribution (sales revenue less variable costs). At zero activity there are no contributions, so there will be a loss equal in amount to the total fixed costs.

The PV chart is obtained by plotting loss or profit against volume of activity. The slope of the graph is equal to the contribution per unit, since each additional unit sold decreases the loss, or increases the profit, by the sales revenue per unit less the variable cost per unit. At zero volume of activity there are no contributions, so there is a loss equal to the amount of the fixed costs. As the volume of activity increases, the amount of the loss gradually decreases until BEP is reached. Beyond BEP, profits increase as activity increases.

As we can see, the PV chart does not tell us anything not shown by the break-even chart. On the other hand, information is perhaps more easily absorbed from the PV chart. This is particularly true of the profit (loss) at any volume of activity. The break-even chart shows this as the vertical distance between the total cost and total sales revenue lines. The PV chart, in effect, combines the total sales revenue and total variable cost lines, which means that profit (or loss) is directly readable.

The economist's view of the break-even chart

So far in this chapter we have treated all the relationships as linear – that is, all of the lines in the graphs have been straight. This is typically the approach taken in management accounting, though it may not be strictly valid.

Consider, for example, the variable cost line in the break-even chart; accountants would normally treat this as being a straight line. Strictly, however, the line should probably not be straight because at high levels of output **economies of scale** may be available to an extent not available at lower levels. For example, a raw material (a typical variable cost) may be able to be used more efficiently with higher volumes of activity. Similarly, the relatively large quantities of material and services bought may enable the business to benefit from bulk discounts and general power in the market-place to negotiate lower prices.

There is also a general tendency for sales revenue per unit to reduce as volume is expanded, since to sell more units of the product or service, it will probably be necessary to lower the selling price.

Economists tend to recognise that, in real life, the relationships portrayed in the break-even chart are usually non-linear. The typical economist's view of the chart is shown in Figure 9.12.

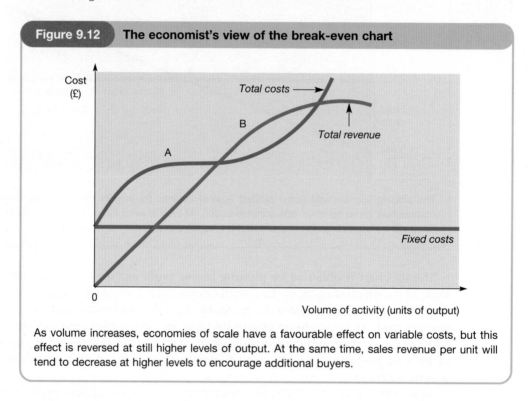

Figure 9.12   **The economist's view of the break-even chart**

As volume increases, economies of scale have a favourable effect on variable costs, but this effect is reversed at still higher levels of output. At the same time, sales revenue per unit will tend to decrease at higher levels to encourage additional buyers.

Note, in Figure 9.12, that the variable costs start to increase quite steeply with volume but, around point A, economies of scale start to take effect. After this point, further increases in volume do not cause such a large increase in variable costs for each additional unit of output. These economies of scale continue to have a benign effect on costs until a point is reached where the business will be operating towards the end of its efficient range. Here the business may have problems finding supplies of the variable-cost elements, which will normally adversely affect their price. Also, the business may find it more difficult to produce, there may be machine breakdowns and so on.

At low levels of output, sales may be made at a relatively high price per unit. To increase sales output beyond point B it may be necessary to lower the average sales price per unit.

Note how this 'curvilinear' representation of the break-even chart can easily lead to the existence of two break-even points.

Accountants justify their approach to this topic by the fact that, although the lines may not, in practice, be perfectly straight, this defect is probably not worth taking into account in most cases. This is partly because all of the information used in the analysis is based on estimates of the future. As this will inevitably be flawed, it seems point-less to be pedantic about minor approximations, such as treating the total cost and total revenue lines as straight when strictly this is not so. Only where significant economies or diseconomies of scale are involved should the non-linearity of the variable costs be taken into account. Also, for most businesses, the range of possible volumes of activity at which they are capable of operating (the **relevant range**) is pretty narrow. Over very short distances, it is perfectly reasonable to treat a curved line as being straight.

Failing to break even

Where a business fails to reach its BEP, steps must be taken to remedy the problem: there must be an increase in sales revenue or a reduction in costs, or both of these. **Real World 9.4** reveals that Ford's luxury car division is struggling to reach its BEP, leading to the possibility of Ford selling Aston Martin. Although Aston Martin is now profitable, other of Ford's luxury brands, including Jaguar, are struggling.

Real World 9.4

Trying to keep on the road

FT

Ford Motor put Aston Martin up for auction on Thursday as the troubled US carmaker began dismantling its stable of British luxury brands in the face of deep losses in its home market.

Ford has appointed an investment bank to handle the sale of the famous brand, for which it is understood to have pencilled in a price of more than $2bn – far higher than the value put on it by financial analysts. It is already in early talks with 'interested parties', Ford said, although it could retain a minority stake.

The sale comes as Ford is considering which other brands it should sell to fund restruc-turing and reduce losses at Premier Automotive Group, its luxury car unit, which lost $162m in the second quarter. The luxury division was supposed to break even this year after losing $100m last year but Ford warned in July that it would again make a loss.

Aston Martin, famous for sports cars driven by James Bond in films such as *Goldfinger* and *Thunderball* never made a profit until 2005, Ulrich Bez, chief executive, said this year. Ford took a controlling stake in 1987 and sales have increased from 46 units in 1992 to 4,500 last year.

Source: Extracts from 'Ford puts Aston Martin up for auction', James Mackintosh, FT.com, 31 August 2006.

Weaknesses of break-even analysis

As we have seen, break-even analysis can provide some useful insights to the import-ant relationship between fixed costs, variable costs and the volume of activity. It does, however, have its weaknesses. There are three general problems:

● *Non-linear relationships.* The management accountant's normal approach to break-even analysis assumes that the relationships between sales revenues, variable costs and volume are strictly straight-line ones. In real life this is unlikely to be so. This is probably not a major problem, since, as we have just seen:

- break-even analysis is normally conducted in advance of the activity actually taking place. Our ability to predict future costs, revenues and so on is somewhat limited, so what are probably minor variations from strict linearity are unlikely to be significant, compared with other forecasting errors; and

- most businesses operate within a narrow range of volume of activity; over short ranges, curved lines tend to be relatively straight;

- *Stepped fixed costs.* Most fixed costs are not fixed over all volumes of activity. They tend to be 'stepped' in the way depicted in Figure 9.2. This means that, in practice, great care must be taken in making assumptions about fixed costs. The problem is particularly heightened because most activities will involve fixed costs of various types (rent, supervisory salaries, administration costs), all of which are likely to have steps at different points.

- *Multi-product businesses.* Most businesses do not offer just one product or service. This is a problem for break-even analysis since it raises the question of the effect of additional sales of one product or service on sales of another of the business's products or services. There is also the problem of identifying the fixed costs of one particular activity. Fixed costs tend to relate to more than one activity – for example, two activities may be carried out in the same rented premises. There are ways of dividing fixed costs between activities, but these tend to be arbitrary, which calls into question the value of the break-even analysis.

Despite some problems, the notions of break-even analysis and BEP seem to be widely used. The media frequently refer to the BEP for businesses and activities. For example, there is seemingly constant discussion about Eurotunnel's BEP and whether it will ever be reached. Similarly, the number of people regularly needed to pay to watch a football team so that the club breaks even often seems to be referred to.

Real World 9.5 shows specific references to break even point for three organisations.

Real World 9.5

Breaking even is breaking out all over

Blacks breaks even

Blacks Leisure Group plc, the UK outdoor leisure business (Blacks, Millets, Freespirit and so on), is barely breaking even during 2006 despite a small increase in its sales revenue and profit margins.

Source: 'Ashley buys 29.4% of Blacks Leisure', Tom Griggs, *Financial Times*, 26 October 2006.

Superjumbo break-even point grows

German industrial group EADS is developing the Airbus A380 aircraft. The aircraft can carry up to 555 passengers on each flight. When EADS approved development of the plane in 2000, it was estimated that the business would need to sell 250 of them to break even. By 2005, the break even number had increased to 270, but by late 2006 the costs of development had increased to the point where it was estimated that it would require sales of 420 of the aircraft for it to break even. So far the business has 159 firm orders, but total sales of the aircraft are expected to be 750 over its commercial lifetime.

Source: Taken from 'Airbus raises A380 break even target', Kevin Done and Gerrit Wiesmann, *Financial Times*, 20 October 2006.

Activity 9.10

Cottage Industries Ltd (see Example 9.1 on page 305) has spare capacity in that its basket makers have some spare time. An overseas retail chain has offered the business an order for 300 baskets at a price of £13 each.

Without considering any wider issues, should the business accept the order? (Assume that the business does not rent the machine.)

Since the fixed costs will be incurred in any case, they are not relevant to this decision. All we need to do is see whether the price offered will yield a contribution. If it will, the business will be better off by accepting the contract than by refusing it.

	£
Additional revenue per unit	13
Less Additional cost per unit	12
Additional contribution per unit	1

For 300 units, the additional contribution will be £300 (that is, 300 × £1). Since no fixed cost increase is involved, irrespective of what else is happening to the business, it will be £300 better off by taking this contract than by refusing it.

As ever with decision making, there are other factors that are either difficult or impossible to quantify. These should be taken into account before reaching a final decision. In the case of Cottage Industries Ltd's decision on the overseas customer, these could include the following:

- The possibility that spare capacity will have been 'sold off' cheaply when there might be another potential customer who will offer a higher price, but, by which time, the capacity will be fully committed. It is a matter of commercial judgement how likely this will be.
- Selling the same product, but at different prices, could lead to a loss of customer goodwill. The fact that a different price will be set for customers in different countries (that is, in different markets) may be sufficient to avoid this potential problem.
- If the business is going to suffer continually from being unable to sell its full production potential at the 'usual' price, it might be better, in the long run, to reduce capacity and make fixed cost savings. Using the spare capacity to produce marginal benefits may lead to the business failing to address this issue.
- On a more positive note, the business may see this as a way of breaking into the overseas market. This is something that might be impossible to achieve if the business charges its usual price.

The most efficient use of scarce resources

It is often the level of market demand that restricts output. This is to say that it is the ability of a business to sell that will limit production, rather than the ability to produce limiting sales. In some cases, however, it is a limit on what can be produced that limits sales. Limited production might stem from a shortage of any factor of production – labour, raw materials, space, machinery and so on. Such scarce factors are often known as *key* or *limiting* factors.

The most profitable combination of products will occur where the *contribution per unit of the scarce factor* is maximised. Example 9.2 should illustrate this point.

Example 9.2

A business provides three different services, the details of which are as follows:

	Service AX107	Service AX109	Service AX220
	£	£	£
Selling price per unit	50	40	65
Variable cost per unit	(25)	(20)	(35)
Contribution per unit	25	20	30
Labour time per unit	5 hours	3 hours	6 hours

The market will take as many units of each service as can be provided, but the ability to provide the service is limited by the availability of labour, all of which needs to be skilled. Fixed costs are not affected by the choice of service provided because all three services use the same facilities.

The most profitable service is AX109 because it generates a contribution of £6.67 (£20/3) an hour. The other two generate only £5.00 each an hour (£25/5 and £30/6). So, to maximise profit, priority should be given to the production that maximises the contribution per unit of limiting factor.

Our first reaction may have been that the business should provide only service AX220, because this is the one that yields the highest contribution per unit sold. If so, we should have been making the mistake of thinking that it is the ability to sell that is the limiting factor. If the above analysis is not convincing, we can take an imaginary number of available labour hours and ask ourselves what is the maximum contribution (and, therefore, profit) that could be made by providing each service exclusively. Bear in mind that there is no shortage of anything else, including market demand, just a shortage of labour.

Activity 9.11

A business makes three different products, the details of which are as follows:

	Product B14	Product B17	Product B22
Selling price per unit (£)	25	20	23
Variable cost per unit (£)	10	8	12
Weekly demand (units)	25	20	30
Machine time per unit (hours)	4	3	4

Fixed costs are not affected by the choice of product because all three products use the same machine. Machine time is limited to 148 hours a week.

Which combination of products should be manufactured if the business is to produce the highest profit?

	B14	B17	B22
	£	£	£
Selling price per unit	25	20	23
Variable cost per unit	(10)	(8)	(12)
Contribution per unit	15	12	11
Machine time per unit	4 hours	3 hours	4 hours
Contribution per machine hour	£3.75	£4.00	£2.75
Order of priority	2nd	1st	3rd

Therefore produce:

20 units of product B17 using		60 hours
22 units of product B14 using		88 hours
		148 hours

This leaves unsatisfied the market demand for a further 3 units of product B14 and 30 units of product B22.

Activity 9.12

What steps could be contemplated that could lead to a higher level of contribution for the business in Activity 9.11?

The possibilities for improving matters that occurred to us are as follows:

● Consider obtaining additional machine time. This could mean obtaining a new machine, subcontracting the machining to another business, or perhaps squeezing a few more hours a week out of the business's own machine. Perhaps a combination of two or more of these is a possibility.
● Redesign the products in a way that requires less time per unit on the machine.
● Increase the price per unit of the three products. This might well have the effect of dampening demand, but the existing demand cannot be met at present, and it may be more profitable in the long run to make a greater contribution on each unit sold than to take one of the other courses of action to overcome the problem.

Activity 9.13

Going back to Activity 9.11, what is the maximum price that the business concerned would logically be prepared to pay to have the remaining B14s machined by a sub-contractor, assuming that no fixed or variable costs would be saved as a result of not doing the machining in-house?
    Would there be a different maximum if we were considering the B22s?

If the remaining three B14s were subcontracted at no cost, the business would be able to earn a contribution of £15 a unit, which it would not otherwise be able to gain. Therefore, any price up to £15 a unit would be worth paying to a subcontractor to undertake the machining. Naturally, the business would prefer to pay as little as possible, but anything up to £15 would still make it worthwhile subcontracting the machining.
    This would not be true of the B22s because they have a different contribution per unit; £11 would be the relevant figure in their case.

Make-or-buy decisions

Businesses are frequently confronted by the need to decide whether to produce the product or service that they sell themselves, or to buy it in from some other business. Thus, a producer of electrical appliances might decide to subcontract the manufacture of one of its products to another business, perhaps because there is a shortage of production capacity in the producer's own factory, or because it believes it to be cheaper to subcontract than to make the appliance itself.

It might just be part of a product or service that is subcontracted. For example, the producer may have a component for the appliance made by another manufacturer. In principle, there is hardly any limit to the scope of make-or-buy decisions. Virtually any part, component or service that is required in production of the main product or service, or the main product or service itself, could be the subject of a make-or-buy decision. So, for example, the personnel function of a business, which is normally performed in-house, could be subcontracted. At the same time, electrical power, which is typically provided by an outside electrical utility business, could be generated in-house.

 Obtaining services or products from a subcontractor is often called **outsourcing**.

Real World 9.7 provides an example of outsourcing by a well-known international retailer.

Real World 9.7

IBM minds the Gap IT requirements

During 2006, Gap Inc., the US-based clothing retailer, decided to subcontract or 'outsource' its IT activities to IBM. Now, instead of employing its own IT staff, Gap has a 10-year contract for IBM to run its IT facility. Gap said that it expects to improve capabilities while reducing costs.

Outsourcing this type of activity is becoming very common in the UK and elsewhere.

Source: www.ibm.com.

Example 9.3

Shah Ltd needs a component for one of its products. It can subcontract production of the component to a subcontractor who will provide the components for £20 each. The business can produce the components internally for total variable costs of £15 per component. Shah Ltd has spare capacity.

Should the component be subcontracted or produced internally?

The answer is that Shah Ltd should produce the component internally, since the variable cost of subcontracting is greater by £5 than the variable cost of internal manufacture.

Activity 9.14

Now assume that Shah Ltd (Example 9.3) has no spare capacity, so it can only produce the component internally by reducing its output of another of its products. While it is making each component, it will lose contributions of £12 from the other product.
Should the component be subcontracted or produced internally?

The answer is to subcontract.
The relevant cost of internal production of each component is:

	£
Variable cost of production of the component	15
Opportunity cost of lost production of the other product	12
	27

This is obviously more costly than the £20 per component that will have to be paid to the subcontractor.

Activity 9.15

What factors, other than the immediately financially quantifiable, would you consider when making a make-or-buy decision?

We feel that there are two major factors:

1 The general problems of subcontracting:
 (a) loss of control of quality;
 (b) potential unreliability of supply.
2 Expertise and specialisation. It is possible for most businesses, with sufficient determination, to do virtually everything in-house. This may, however, require a level of skill and facilities that most businesses neither have nor feel inclined to acquire. For example, although it is true that most businesses could generate their own electricity, their managements tend to take the view that this is better done by a specialist generator business. Specialists can often do things more cheaply, with less risk of things going wrong.

Closing or continuation decisions

It is quite common for businesses to produce separate financial statements for each department or section, to try to assess the relative effectiveness of each one.

Example 9.4

Goodsports Ltd is a retail shop that operates through three departments, all in the same premises. The three departments occupy roughly equal-sized areas of the premises. The trading results for the year just finished showed the following:

	Total	Sports equipment	Sports clothes	General clothes
	£000	£000	£000	£000
Sales revenue	534	254	183	97
Costs	(482)	(213)	(163)	(106)
Profit/(loss)	52	41	20	(9)

It would appear that if the general clothes department were to close, the business would be more profitable, by £9,000 a year, assuming last year's performance to be a reasonable indication of future performance.

When the costs are analysed between those that are variable and those that are fixed, however, the contribution of each department can be deduced and the following results obtained:

	Total	Sports equipment	Sports clothes	General clothes
	£000	£000	£000	£000
Sales revenue	534	254	183	97
Variable costs	(344)	(167)	(117)	(60)
Contribution	190	87	66	37
Fixed costs (rent and so on)	(138)	(46)	(46)	(46)
Profit/(loss)	52	41	20	(9)

Now it is obvious that closing the general clothes department, without any other developments, would make the business worse off by £37,000 (the department's contribution). The department should not be closed, because it makes a positive contribution. The fixed costs would continue whether the department were closed or not. As can be seen from the above analysis, distinguishing between variable and fixed costs, and deducing the contribution, can make the picture a great deal clearer.

Activity 9.16

In considering Goodsports Ltd (Example 9.4), we saw that the general clothes department should not be closed 'without any other developments'. What 'other developments' could affect this decision, making continuation either more attractive or less attractive?

The things that we could think of are as follows:

- Expansion of the other departments or replacing the general clothes department with a completely new activity. This would make sense only if the space currently occupied by the general clothes department could generate contributions totalling at least £37,000 a year.
- Subletting the space occupied by the general clothes department. Once again, this would need to generate a net rent greater than £37,000 a year to make it more financially beneficial than keeping the department open.
- Keeping the department open, even if it generated no contribution whatsoever (assuming that there is no other use for the space), may still be beneficial. If customers are attracted into the shop because it has general clothing, they may then buy something from one of the other departments. In the same way, the activity of a sub-tenant might attract customers into the shop. (On the other hand, it might drive them away.)

Self-assessment question 9.1

Khan Ltd can render three different types of service (Alpha, Beta and Gamma) using the same staff. Various estimates for next year have been made as follows:

	Alpha £/unit	Beta £/unit	Gamma £/unit
Selling price	30	39	20
Variable material cost	15	18	10
Other variable costs	6	10	5
Share of fixed costs	8	12	4
Staff time required (hours)	2	3	1

Fixed costs for next year are expected to total £40,000.

Required:

(a) If the business were to render only service Alpha next year, how many units of the service would it need to provide in order to break even? (Assume for this part of the question that there is no effective limit to market size and staffing level.)

(b) If the business has a maximum of 10,000 staff hours next year, in which order of preference would the three services come?

(c) If the maximum market for next year for the three services is as follows:

Alpha	3,000 units
Beta	2,000 units
Gamma	5,000 units

what quantities of which service should the business provide next year and how much profit would this be expected to yield?

The answer to this question can be found at the back of the book on page 700.

Summary

The main points in this chapter may be summarised as follows.

Behaviour of costs

- Fixed costs are those that are independent of the level of activity (for example, rent).
- Variable costs are those that vary with the level of activity (for example, raw materials).
- Semi-fixed (semi-variable) costs are a mixture of the two (for example, electricity).

Break-even analysis

- The break-even point (BEP) is the level of activity (in units of output or sales revenue) at which total costs (fixed + variable) = total sales revenue.
- Calculation of BEP is as follows:

$$\text{BEP (in units of output)} = \frac{\text{Fixed costs for the period}}{\text{Contribution per unit}}$$

- Use of knowledge of BEP for a particular activity: risk assessment.
- Contribution per unit = sales revenue per unit less variable cost per unit.

- Margin of safety = excess of planned volume of activity over BEP.
- Operating gearing = the extent to which the total costs of some activity are fixed rather than variable.
- Profit–volume (PV) chart is an alternative approach to BE chart.
- Economists tend to take a different approach to BE, taking account of economies (and diseconomies) of scale and of the fact that, generally, to be able to sell large volumes, price per unit has to be reduced.

Weaknesses of BE analysis

- Non-linear relationships.
- Stepped fixed costs.
- Multi-product businesses.

Marginal analysis (ignores fixed costs where these are not affected by the decision)

- Accepting/rejecting special contracts – consider only the effect on contributions.
- Using scarce resources – the limiting factor is most effectively used by maximising its contribution per unit.
- Make-or-buy decisions – take the action that leads to the highest total contributions.
- Closing/continuing an activity – should be assessed by net effect on total contributions.

 Now check your progress in your personal Study Plan

 Key terms

fixed costs   p. 298
variable costs   p. 298
stepped fixed costs   p. 300
semi-fixed (semi-variable) costs   p. 301
break-even analysis   p. 302
break-even chart   p. 303
break-even point (BEP)   p. 303
contribution per unit   p. 307

margin of safety   p. 308
operating gearing   p. 311
operational gearing   p. 311
profit–volume (PV) chart   p. 313
economies of scale   p. 313
relevant range   p. 315
marginal analysis   p. 318
marginal cost   p. 318
outsourcing   p. 322

Further reading

If you would like to explore the topics covered in this chapter in more depth, we recommend the following books:

Cost Accounting: A managerial emphasis, *Horngren C., Datar S. and Foster G.*, 12th edn, Prentice Hall, 2006, chapter 3.

Management and Cost Accounting, *Drury C.*, 6th edn, Thomson Learning, 2004, chapter 8.

Managerial Accounting, *Hilton R.*, 6th edn. McGraw-Hill/Irwin, 2005, chapter 8.

Review questions

Answers to these questions can be found at the back of the book on pages 779–80.

9.1 Define the terms *fixed cost* and *variable cost*. Explain how an understanding of the distinction between fixed costs and variable costs can be useful to managers.

9.2 What is meant by the *break-even point* for an activity? How is the BEP calculated? Why is it useful to know the BEP?

9.3 When we say that some business activity has *high operating gearing*, what do we mean? What are the implications for the business of high operating gearing?

9.4 If there is a scarce resource that is restricting sales, how will the business maximise its profit? Explain the logic of the approach that you have identified for maximising profit.

Exercises

Exercises 9.4 to 9.8 are more advanced than 9.1 to 9.3. Those with coloured numbers have answers at the back of the book, starting on page 731.

If you wish to try more exercises, visit the students' side of the Companion Website.

9.1 The management of a business is concerned about its inability to obtain enough fully trained labour to enable it to meet its present budget projection for its three services, Alpha, Beta and Gamma.

	Alpha £000	Beta £000	Gamma £000	Total £000
Variable costs				
Materials	6	4	5	15
Labour	9	6	12	27
Expenses	3	2	2	7
Allocated fixed costs	6	15	12	33
Total cost	24	27	31	82
Profit	15	2	2	19
Sales revenue	39	29	33	101

The amount of labour likely to be available amounts to £20,000. All of the variable labour is paid at the same hourly rate. You have been asked to prepare a statement of plans ensuring that at least 50 per cent of the budgeted sales revenues are achieved for each service, and the balance of labour is used to produce the greatest profit.

Required:

(a) Prepare a statement, with explanations, showing the greatest profit available from the limited amount of skilled labour available, within the constraint stated. *Hint*: Remember that all labour is paid at the same rate.

(b) What steps could the business take in an attempt to improve profitability, in the light of the labour shortage?

9.2   Lannion and Co. is engaged in providing and marketing a standard advice service. Summarised results for the past two months reveal the following:

	October	November
Sales (units of the service)	200	300
Sales revenue (£)	5,000	7,500
Operating profit (£)	1,000	2,200

There were no price changes of any description during these two months.

Required:

(a) Deduce the BEP (in units of the service) for Lannion and Co.

(b) State why the business might find it useful to know its BEP.

9.3   A hotel group prepares financial statements on a quarterly basis. The senior management is reviewing the performance of one hotel and making plans for next year.

The managers have in front of them the results for this year (based on some actual results and some forecasts to the end of this year):

Quarter	Sales revenue	Profit/(loss)
	£000	£000
1	400	(280)
2	1,200	360
3	1,600	680
4	800	40
Total	4,000	800

The total estimated number of visitors (guest nights) for this year is 50,000. The results follow a regular pattern; there are no unexpected cost fluctuations beyond the seasonal trading pattern shown above. The management intends to incorporate into its plans for next year an anticipated increase in unit variable costs of 10 per cent and a profit target for the hotel of £1m.

Required:

(a) Calculate the total variable and total fixed costs of the hotel for this year. Show the provisional annual results for this year in total, showing variable and fixed costs separately. Show also the revenue and costs per visitor.

(b) (i)   If there is no increase in visitors for next year, what will be the required revenue rate per hotel visitor to meet the profit target?

(ii) If the required revenue rate per visitor is not raised above this year's level, how many visitors will be required to meet the profit target?

(b) Outline and briefly discuss the assumptions that are made in typical PV or break-even analysis, and assess whether they limit its usefulness.

9.4   Motormusic Ltd makes a standard model of car radio, which it sells to car manufacturers for £60 each. Next year the business plans to make and sell 20,000 radios. The business's costs are as follows:

Manufacturing	
Variable materials	£20 per radio
Variable labour	£14 per radio
Other variable costs	£12 per radio
Fixed costs	£80,000 per year
Administration and selling	
Variable	£3 per radio
Fixed	£60,000 per year

Required:

(a) Calculate the break-even point for next year, expressed both in quantity of radios and sales value.

(b) Calculate the margin of safety for next year, expressed both in quantity of radios and sales value.

9.5 A business makes three products, A, B and C. All three products require the use of two types of machine: cutting machines and assembling machines. Estimates for next year include the following:

	A	B	C
Selling price (£/unit)	25	30	18
Sales demand (units)	2,500	3,400	5,100
Material cost (£/unit)	12	13	10
Variable production cost (£/unit)	7	4	3
Time required per unit on cutting machines (hours)	1.0	1.0	0.5
Time required per unit on assembling machines (hours)	0.5	1.0	0.5

Fixed costs for next year are expected to total £42,000. It is the business's policy for each unit of production to absorb these in proportion to its total variable costs.

The business has cutting machine capacity of 5,000 hours a year and assembling machine capacity of 8,000 hours a year.

Required:

(a) State, with supporting workings, which products in which quantities the business should plan to make next year on the basis of the above information. (*Hint*: First determine which machines will be a limiting factor (scarce resource).)

(b) State the maximum price per product that it would be worth the business paying to a subcontractor to carry out that part of the work that could not be done internally.

9.6 Darmor Ltd has three products, X, Y and Z, which require the same production facilities. Information about the production costs for one unit of its products is as follows:

	X £	Y £	Z £
Labour: Skilled	6	9	3
Unskilled	2	4	10
Materials	12	25	14
Other variable costs	3	7	7
Fixed costs	5	10	10

All labour and materials are variable costs. Skilled labour is paid £12 an hour, and unskilled labour is paid £8 an hour. All references to labour costs, above, are based on basic rates of pay. Skilled labour is scarce, which means that the business could sell more than the maximum that it is able to make of any of the three products.

Product X is sold in a regulated market, and the regulators have set a price of £30 per unit for it.

Required:

(a) State, with supporting workings, the price that must be charged for products Y and Z such that the business would find it equally profitable to make and sell any of the three products.

(b) State, with supporting workings, the maximum rate of overtime premium that the business would logically be prepared to pay its skilled workers to work beyond the basic time.

9.7 Intermediate Products Ltd produces four types of water pump. Two of these (A and B) are sold by the business. The other two (C and D) are incorporated, as components, into other of the business's products. Neither C nor D is incorporated into A or B. Costings (per unit) for the products are as follows:

	A £	B £	C £	D £
Variable materials	15	20	16	17
Variable labour	25	10	10	15
Other variable costs	5	3	2	2
Fixed costs	20	8	8	12
	£65	£41	£36	£46
Selling price (per unit)	£70	£45		

There is an outside supplier who is prepared to supply unlimited quantities of products C and D to the business, charging £40 per unit for product C and £55 per unit for product D.

Next year's estimated demand for the products, from the market (in the case of A and B) and from other production requirements (in the case of C and D) is as follows:

	Units
A	5,000
B	6,000
C	4,000
D	3,000

For strategic reasons, the business wishes to supply a minimum of 50 per cent of the above demand for products A and B.

Manufacture of all four products requires the use of a special machine. The products require time on this machine as follows:

	Hours per unit
A	0.5
B	0.4
C	0.5
D	0.3

Next year there are expected to be a maximum of 6,000 special-machine hours available. There will be no shortage of any other factor of production.

Required:

(a) State, with supporting workings and assumptions, which quantities of which products the business should plan to make next year.

(b) Explain the maximum amount that it would be worth the business paying per hour to rent a second special machine.

(c) Suggest ways, other than renting an additional special machine, that could solve the problem of the shortage of special machine time.

9.8 Gandhi Ltd renders a promotional service to small retailing businesses. There are three levels of service: the 'basic', the 'standard' and the 'comprehensive'. On the basis of past experience, the business plans next year to work at absolute full capacity as follows:

	Number of units of the service	Selling price £	Variable cost per unit £
Basic	11,000	50	25
Standard	6,000	80	65
Comprehensive	16,000	120	90

The business's fixed costs total £660,000 a year. Each service takes about the same length of time, irrespective of the level.

One of the accounts staff has just produced a report that seems to show that the standard service is unprofitable. The relevant extract from the report is as follows:

Standard service cost analysis

	£	
Selling price per unit	80	
Variable cost per unit	(65)	
Fixed cost per unit	(20)	[£660,000/(11,000 + 6,000 + 16,000)]
Net loss	(5)	

The producer of the report suggests that the business should not offer the standard service next year.

Required:

(a) Should the standard service be offered next year, assuming that the quantity of the other services could not be expanded to use the spare capacity?

(b) Should the standard service be offered next year, assuming that the released capacity could be used to render a new service, the 'nova', for which customers would be charged £75, and which would have variable costs of £50 and take twice as long as the other three services?

(c) What is the minimum price that could be accepted for the basic service, assuming that the necessary capacity to expand it will come only from not offering the standard service?

CHAPTER 10

Full costing

Introduction

In this chapter we shall examine an approach to deducing the cost of some productive activity, such as producing a unit of product (for example, a tin of baked beans), providing a unit of service (for example, a car repair) or creating a facility (for example, building a national football stadium). Full (or absorption) costing is a widely used approach that takes account of all of the costs of producing a particular unit of output. The precise approach taken tends to depend on whether each unit of output is identical to the next or whether each job has its own individual characteristics. It also tends to depend on whether the business accounts for overheads on a departmental basis. We shall look at how full (absorption) costing is carried out and consider its usefulness for management purposes.

In this chapter we consider the traditional, but still very widely used, form of full costing. In Chapter 11 we shall consider activity-based costing, which is a more recently developed approach.

Learning outcomes

When you have completed this chapter, you should be able to:

- Deduce the full (absorption) cost of a unit of output in a single-product environment.

- Deduce the full (absorption) cost of a unit of output in a multi-product environment.

- Discuss the problems of deducing full (absorption) costs in practice.

- Discuss the usefulness of full (absorption) cost information to managers.

MyAccountingLab | *Remember to create your own personalised Study Plan*

Why do managers want to know the full cost?

As we saw in Chapter 1, the only point in providing any item of accounting information is to provide one or more of the user groups with information that will help them make more informed decisions. There are broadly four areas where managers use knowledge of the full cost of their output. These are:

- *Pricing and output decisions*. Having full cost information can enable managers to make decisions on the price to be charged to customers for the business's products or services and how many to provide.
- *Exercising control*. Managers need information that will enable them to make decisions that are aimed at getting the business back on course if plans are not being met. Budgets are typically expressed in full-cost terms. This means that periodic reports that compare actual performance with budgets need to be expressed in the same full-cost terms.
- *Assessing relative efficiency*. Full cost information can enable managers to compare the cost of doing something in one way, or location, with its cost if done in a different manner or place. For example, a car manufacturer may find it useful to compare the cost of building a particular model of car in one of its plants rather than in another. This could enable the manufacturer to make a decision on where to locate future production.
- *Assessing performance*. The level of profit, or income, generated over a period is an important measure of business performance. To measure profit, or income, we need to compare sales revenue with the associated expenses. With a business that produces a product or service, a major expense will be the cost of making the product or rendering the service. Logically this is the full cost of what was sold. Measuring income provides managers (and other users) with information that can help them to make a wide range of decisions.

Later in the chapter we shall consider some of the issues surrounding these four uses.

Figure 10.1 shows the four uses of full costing information.

Figure 10.1 **Uses of full costs by managers**

Managers use full costs for four main purposes.

Now let us consider **Real World 10.1**.

Real World 10.1

Operating cost

The average cost of performing a hip replacement operation in a UK National Health Service hospital is £4,300. This represents the 'full cost' of the operation.

Source: Based on information in *Hip Replacements: An update*, National Audit Office, 17 July 2003.

This raises some points if this information is to be used in any of the ways identified above. For example, the average cost of the hip replacement operation might be used to make a decision on how many such procedures to perform next year. Where does the £4,300 figure come from? What does it include? Is it just the salary earned by the surgeon while dealing with one patient's case? Does it include an allowance for the equipment used in the operating theatre? If so, how is the value of this calculated? Should it include an allowance for the salaries of hospital administrative staff? If yes, how is this calculated? Do all hospitals calculate their full costs in the same way? If not, is the £4,300 a potentially misleading figure?

These questions, and several others, are the subject of this chapter.

What is full costing?

→ **Full cost** is the total amount of resources, usually measured in monetary terms, sacrificed to achieve a particular objective. It takes account of all resources sacrificed to achieve the objective. Thus, if the objective were to supply a customer with a product or service, all costs relating to the production of the product or provision of the service would be included as part of the full cost. To derive the full cost figure, we must accumulate the costs incurred and then assign them to the particular product or service.

→ The logic of **full costing** is that all of the costs of running a particular facility, say an office, are part of the cost of the output of that office. For example, the rent may be a cost that will not alter merely because we provide one more unit of the service. If the office were not rented, there would be nowhere for the staff, who provide the service, to work. So rent is an important element of the cost of each unit of output.

In the sections that follow, we shall first see how full costing is applied to a single-product business and then see how it is done for a multi-product one.

Single-product businesses

The simplest case for which to deduce the full cost per unit is where the business has only one product or service, that is, each unit of its production is identical. Here it is simply a question of adding up all the costs of production incurred in the period (materials, labour, rent, fuel, power and so on) and dividing this total by the total number of units of output for the period.

Activity 10.1

Fruitjuice Ltd has just one product, a sparkling orange drink that is marketed as Orange Fizz. During last month, the business produced 7,300 litres of the drink. The costs incurred were as follows:

	£
Ingredients (oranges and so on)	390
Fuel	85
Rent of premises	350
Depreciation of equipment	75
Labour	880

What is the full cost per litre of producing Orange Fizz?

The full cost figure is found by simply adding together all of the costs incurred and then dividing by the number of litres produced:

$$£(390 + 85 + 350 + 75 + 880)/7{,}300 = £0.24 \text{ per litre}$$

In practice, there can be problems in deciding exactly how much cost was incurred. In the case of Fruitjuice Ltd, for example, how is the cost of depreciation deduced? It is certainly an estimate, and so its reliability is open to question. The cost of raw materials may also be a problem. Should we use the 'relevant' cost of the raw materials (in this case, almost certainly the replacement cost), or the actual price paid for it (historic cost)? If the cost per litre is to be used for some decision-making purpose, the replacement cost is probably more logical. In practice, however, it seems that historic costs are more often used to deduce full costs.

There can also be problems in deciding precisely how many units of output there were. If making Orange Fizz is not a very fast process, some of the drink will probably be in the process of being made at any given moment. This, in turn, means that some of the costs incurred last month were for some Orange Fizz that was work in progress at the end of the month, so is not included in last month's output quantity of 7,300 litres. Similarly, part of the 7,300 litres might well have been started and incurred costs in the previous month, yet all of those litres were included in the 7,300 litres that we used in our calculation of the cost per litre. Work in progress is not a serious problem, but some adjustment for the value of opening and closing work in progress for a period needs to be made if reliable full cost information is to be obtained.

The approach to full costing, which is usually taken with identical, or near identical, units of output (of goods or services), is often referred to as **process costing**.

Multi-product businesses

Most businesses produce more than one type of product or service. In this situation, the units of output of the product, or service, will not be identical and so the approach that we used with litres of Orange Fizz in Activity 10.1 cannot be used. Although it is reasonable to assign an identical cost to units of output that are identical, it is not reasonable to do this where the units of output are obviously different. It would not be reasonable, for example, to assign the same costs to each car repair carried out by a garage, irrespective of the complexity and size of the repair.

Direct and indirect costs

To provide full cost information, we need to have a systematic approach to accumulating costs and then assigning these costs to particular units of product or service on some reasonable basis. Where units of output are not identical, the starting point is to separate costs into two categories: direct costs and indirect costs.

→ • **Direct costs.** These are costs that can be identified with specific cost units. That is to say, the effect of the cost can be measured in respect of each particular unit of output. A cost unit is one unit of whatever is having its cost determined. This is usually one unit of a product, be it a service or a manufactured item. The main examples of these are direct materials and direct labour. Thus, in costing a motor car repair by a garage, both the cost of spare parts used in the repair and the cost of the mechanic's time would be direct costs. Collecting direct costs is a simple matter of having a cost-recording system that is capable of capturing the cost of direct materials used on each job and the cost, based on the hours worked and the rate of pay, of direct workers.

→ • **Indirect costs** (or **overheads**). These are all other costs, that is, those that cannot be directly measured in respect of each particular unit of output. Thus the rent of the garage premises would be an indirect cost of a motor car repair.

→ We shall use the terms 'indirect costs' and 'overheads' interchangeably for the remainder of this book. Overheads are also sometimes known as **common costs** because they are common to all outputs of the production unit (for example, factory or department) for the period.

Activity (10.2)

A garage bases its prices on the direct costs of each job (car repair) that it carries out. How could the garage collect the direct costs (labour and materials) for a particular job?

Someone on the staff, probably the mechanic doing the work on the job, needs to record the length of time that was worked on the car by direct workers (that is, the mechanic concerned and any colleagues). Usually, direct workers are required to record how long was spent on each job. The stores staff would normally be required to keep a record of the cost of parts and materials used.

A 'job sheet' would be prepared – perhaps on the computer – for each individual job. Staff would need to get into the routine of faithfully recording all elements of direct labour and materials applied to the job.

Real World 10.2 provides some insight to the direct/indirect cost balance in practice.

Real World 10.2

Direct and indirect costs in practice

A survey of 176 fairly large UK businesses, conducted during 1999, revealed that, on average, total costs of businesses are in the following proportions:

- direct costs: 70 per cent
- indirect costs: 30 per cent.

Perhaps surprisingly, these proportions did not vary greatly between manufacturers, retailers and service businesses. The only significant variation from the 70/30 proportions was with financial and commercial businesses, which had an average 52/48 split.

Source: Based on information in Drury and Tayles (see reference 1 at the end of the chapter).

An extensive (nearly 2,000 responses) and more recent (2003) survey of management accounting practice in the US showed similar results. Like the 1999 UK survey, the US survey tended to relate to larger businesses. About 40 per cent were manufacturers and about 16 per cent financial services; the remainder were from a range of other industries. This survey revealed that, of total costs, indirect costs accounted for between:

- 34 per cent for retailers (lowest), and
- 42 per cent for manufacturers (highest),

with other industries' proportion of indirect costs falling within the 34–42 per cent range. Financial and commercial businesses showed an indirect cost percentage of 38 per cent.

Source: Ernst and Young (see reference 2 of the end of the chapter).

The differences between the UK and the US could be accounted for by a higher level of capital intensity in US industry, which would tend to increase indirect costs relative to direct ones.

Job costing

The term **job costing** is used to describe the way in which we identify the full cost per unit of output (job) where the units of output differ. To cost (that is, deduce the full cost of) a particular unit of output (job), we first identify the direct costs of the job, which, by the definition of direct costs, is fairly straightforward. We then seek to 'charge' each unit of output with a fair share of indirect costs. Put another way, cost units (products) absorb overheads. This leads to full costing also being called **absorption costing**. This is shown graphically in Figure 10.2.

Figure 10.2 The relationship between direct costs and indirect costs

The full cost of any particular job is the sum of those costs that can be measured specifically in respect of the job (direct costs) and a share of those costs that create the environment in which production (of an object or service) can take place, but which do not relate specifically to any particular job (overheads).

Activity (10.3)

Sparky Ltd is a business that employs a number of electricians. The business undertakes a range of work for its customers, from replacing fuses to installing complete wiring systems in new houses.

In respect of a particular job done by Sparky Ltd, into which category (direct or indirect) would each of the following costs fall?

1 The wages of the electrician who did the job.
2 Depreciation of the tools used by the electrician.
3 The salary of Sparky Ltd's accountant.
4 The cost of cable and other materials used on the job.
5 Rent of the premises where Sparky Ltd stores its inventories of cable and other materials.

Only the electrician's wages earned while working on the particular job and the cost of the materials used on the job are direct costs. This is because it is possible to measure how much time (and therefore the direct labour cost) was spent on the particular job and the amount of materials used (and therefore the direct material cost) in the job.

All of the other costs are general costs of running the business and, as such, must form part of the full cost of doing the job, but they cannot be directly measured in respect of the particular job.

It is important to note that whether a cost is direct or indirect depends on the item being costed – the cost objective. People sometimes refer to overheads without stating what the cost objective is; this is incorrect.

Activity (10.4)

Into which category, direct or indirect, would each of the costs listed in Activity 10.3 fall if we were seeking to find the cost of operating the entire business of Sparky Ltd for a month?

The answer is that all of them will be direct costs, since they can all be related to, and measured in respect of, running the business for a month.

Naturally, broader-reaching cost objectives, such as operating Sparky Ltd for a month, tend to include a higher proportion of direct costs than do more limited ones, such as a particular job done by Sparky Ltd. As we shall see shortly, this makes costing broader cost objectives rather more straightforward than costing narrower ones. It is generally the case that direct costs are easier to deal with than indirect ones.

Full (absorption) costing and the behaviour of costs

We saw in Chapter 9 that the full cost of doing something (or total cost, as it is usually known in the context of marginal analysis) can be analysed between the fixed and the variable elements. This is illustrated in Figure 10.3.

Figure 10.3 The relationship between fixed costs, variable costs and total costs

The total cost of a job is the sum of those costs that remain the same irrespective of the level of activity (fixed costs) and those that vary according to the level of activity (variable costs).

The similarity of what is shown in Figure 10.3 to that depicted in Figure 10.2 seems to lead some people to believe, mistakenly, that variable costs and direct costs are the same and that fixed costs and overheads are the same. This is incorrect.

The notions of fixed and variable are concerned entirely with **cost behaviour** in the face of changes in the volume of activity. Directness of costs, on the other hand, is entirely concerned with collecting together the elements that make up full cost, that is, with the extent to which costs can be measured directly in respect of particular units of output or jobs. These are two entirely different concepts. Although it may be true that there is a tendency for fixed costs to be indirect costs (overheads) and for variable costs to be direct costs, there is no link, and there are many exceptions to this tendency. For example, most activities have variable overheads. Labour is a major element of direct cost in most types of business activity but is usually a fixed cost, at least over the short term.

The relationship between the reaction of costs to volume changes (cost behaviour), on the one hand, and how costs need to be gathered to deduce the full cost (cost collection), on the other, in respect of a particular job is shown in Figure 10.4.

Figure 10.4 The relationship between direct, indirect, variable and fixed costs of a particular job

A particular job's full (or total) cost will be made up of some variable and some fixed cost elements. It will also be made up of some direct and some indirect (overhead) elements.

Total cost is the sum of direct and indirect costs. It is also the sum of fixed and variable costs. These two facts are independent of one another. Thus a particular cost may be fixed, relative to the level of output, but that fact tells us nothing about whether it is a direct or an indirect cost.

The problem of indirect costs

Distinguishing between direct and indirect costs is related only to deducing full cost in a job-costing environment, that is, where units of output differ. When we were considering costing a litre of Orange Fizz drink in Activity 10.1, whether particular elements of cost were direct or indirect was of absolutely no consequence, because all costs were shared equally between the litres of Orange Fizz. Where we have units of output that are not identical, however, we have to look more closely at the make-up of the costs to achieve a fair measure of the full cost of a particular job.

 Indirect costs of any activity must form part of the cost of each unit of output. By definition, however, they cannot be directly related to individual **cost units**. This raises a major practical issue: how are indirect costs to be apportioned to individual cost units or products?

 ## Overheads as service renderers

It is reasonable to view the overheads as rendering a service to the cost units. A legal case undertaken by a firm of solicitors for a particular client can be seen as being rendered a service by the office in which the work is done. In this sense, it is reasonable to charge each case (cost unit) with a share of the costs of running the office (rent, lighting, heating, cleaning, building maintenance and so on). It also seems reasonable to relate the charge for the 'use' of the office to the level of service that the particular case has received from the office.

The next step is the difficult one. How might the cost of running the office, which is a cost of all work done by the firm, be divided between individual cases that are not similar in size and complexity?

One possibility is sharing this overhead cost equally between each case handled by the firm within the period. Most of us would not propose this method unless the cases were close to being identical in terms of the extent to which they had 'benefited' from the overheads.

If we are not to propose equal shares, we must identify something observable and measurable about the cases that we feel provides a reasonable basis for distinguishing between one case and the next. In practice, time spent working on the cost unit or product by direct labour is the basis that is most popular. It must be stressed that this is not the 'correct' way, and it certainly is not the only way.

Job costing: a worked example

To see how job costing (as it is usually called) works, let us consider Example 10.1.

Example 10.1

Johnson Ltd, a business that provides a personal computer service to its customers, has overheads of £10,000 each month. Each month 1,000 direct labour hours are worked and charged to units of output (repairs carried out by the business). A particular repair undertaken by the business used direct materials costing £15. Direct labour worked on the repair was 3 hours and the wage rate is £16 an hour. Overheads are charged to jobs on a direct labour hour basis.

Required:
What is the full (absorption) cost of the repair?

Solution
First, let us establish the **overhead absorption (recovery) rate**, that is, the rate at which individual repairs will be charged with overheads. This is £10 (that is, £10,000/1,000) per direct labour hour.

Thus, the full cost of the repair is:

	£
Direct materials	15
Direct labour (3 × £16)	48
	63
Overheads (3 × £10)	30
Full cost of the job	93

Note, in Example 10.1, that the number of labour hours (3 hours) appears twice in deducing the full cost: once to deduce the direct labour cost and a second time to deduce the overheads to be charged to the repair. These are really two separate issues, though they are both based on the same number of labour hours.

Note also that if all of the repair jobs that are undertaken during the month are assigned overheads in a similar manner, all £10,000 of overheads will be charged to the jobs between them. Jobs that involve a lot of direct labour will be assigned a large share of overheads, and those that involve little direct labour will be assigned a small share of overheads.

Activity 10.5

Can you think of reasons why the direct labour hours basis is regarded as the most logical basis for sharing overheads between cost units?

The reasons that occurred to us are as follows:

● Large jobs should logically attract large amounts of overheads because they are likely to have been rendered more 'service' by the overheads than small ones. The length of time that they are worked on by direct labour may be seen as a rough and ready way of measuring relative size, although other means of doing this may be found – for example, relative physical size, where the cost unit is a physical object such as a manufactured product.
● Most overheads are related to time. Rent, heating, lighting, non-current asset depreciation, supervisors' and managers' salaries and loan interest, which are all typical

Activity 10.5 continued

overheads, are all more or less time based. That is to say that the overhead cost for one week tends to be about half of that for a similar two-week period. Thus, a basis of allotting overheads to jobs that takes account of the length of time that the units of output benefited from the 'service' rendered by the overheads seems logical.

● Direct labour hours are capable of being measured for each job. They will normally be measured to deduce the direct labour element of cost in any case. Thus, a direct labour hour basis of dealing with overheads is practical to apply in the real world.

It cannot be emphasised enough that there is no 'correct' way to allot overheads to jobs. Overheads (indirect costs), by definition, do not naturally relate to individual jobs. If, nevertheless, we wish to take account of the fact that overheads are part of the cost of all jobs, we must find some acceptable way of including a share of the total overheads in each job. If a particular means of doing this is accepted by those who use the full cost deduced, then the method is as good as any other method. Accounting is concerned only with providing useful information to decision makers. In practice, the method that seems to be regarded as being the most useful is the direct labour hour method. Real World 10.3 (page 346) provides some evidence of this.

Activity 10.6

Marine Suppliers Ltd undertakes a range of work, including making sails for small sailing boats on a made-to-measure basis.

The business expects to incur the following costs during the next month:

Direct labour costs	£60,000
Direct labour time	6,000 hours
Indirect labour cost	£9,000
Depreciation of machinery	£3,000
Rent and rates	£5,000
Heating, lighting and power	£2,000
Machine time	2,000 hours
Indirect materials	£500
Other miscellaneous indirect costs	£200
Direct materials cost	£3,000

The business has received an enquiry about a sail. It is estimated that the particular sail will take 12 direct labour hours to make and will require 20 square metres of sailcloth, which costs £2 per square metre.

The business normally uses a direct labour hour basis of charging overheads to individual jobs.

What is the full (absorption) cost of making the sail?

The direct costs of making the sail can be identified as follows:

	£
Direct materials (20 × £2)	40.00
Direct labour [12 × (£60,000/6,000)]	120.00
	160.00

To deduce the indirect cost element that must be added to derive the full cost of the sail, we first need to total these costs as follows:

	£
Indirect labour	9,000
Depreciation	3,000
Rent and rates	5,000
Heating, lighting and power	2,000
Indirect materials	500
Other miscellaneous indirect costs	200
Total indirect costs	19,700

Since the business uses a direct labour hour basis of charging overheads to jobs, we need to deduce the indirect cost (or overhead) recovery rate per direct labour hour. This is simply:

£19,700/6,000 = £3.28 per direct labour hour

Thus, the full cost of the sail would be expected to be:

	£
Direct materials (20 × £2)	40.00
Direct labour [12 × (£60,000/6,000)]	120.00
Indirect costs (12 × £3.28)	39.36
Full cost	199.36

Figure 10.5 shows the process for applying overheads and direct costs to the sail that was the subject of Activity 10.6.

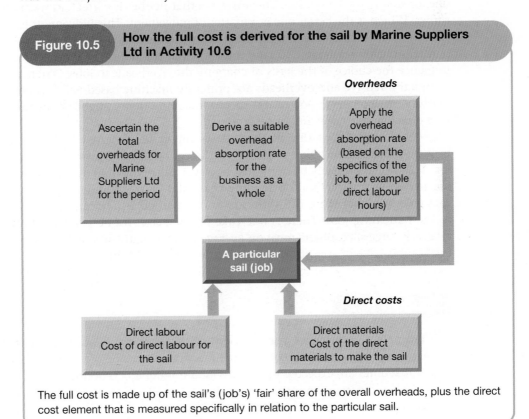

Figure 10.5   How the full cost is derived for the sail by Marine Suppliers Ltd in Activity 10.6

The full cost is made up of the sail's (job's) 'fair' share of the overall overheads, plus the direct cost element that is measured specifically in relation to the particular sail.

Activity (10.7)

Suppose that Marine Suppliers Ltd (see Activity 10.6) used a machine hour basis of charging overheads to jobs. What would be the cost of the job detailed if it was expected to take 5 machine hours (as well as 12 direct labour hours)?

The total overheads of the business will of course be the same irrespective of the method of charging them to jobs. Thus, the overhead recovery rate, on a machine hour basis, will be:

$$£19,700/2,000 = £9.85 \text{ per machine hour}$$

Thus, the full cost of the sail would be expected to be:

	£
Direct materials (20 × £2)	40.00
Direct labour [12 × (£60,000/6,000)]	120.00
Indirect costs (5 × £9.85)	49.25
Full cost	209.25

Selecting a basis for charging overheads

A question now presents itself as to which of the two costs for this sail is the correct one, or simply the better one. The answer is that neither is correct, as was pointed out earlier. Which is the better one is a matter of judgement. This judgement is concerned entirely with the usefulness of information, which is difficult to assess.

It is probably reasonable to take the view that the nature of the overheads should influence the choice of the basis of charging the overheads to jobs. Where production is capital intensive and overheads are primarily machine based (such as depreciation, machine maintenance, power and so on), machine hours might be favoured. Otherwise direct labour hours might be preferred.

It could appear that one of these bases might be preferred to the other simply because it apportions either a higher or a lower amount of overheads to a particular job. This would probably be irrational, however. Since the total overheads are the same irrespective of the method of dividing that total between individual jobs, a method that gives a higher share of overheads to one particular job must give a lower share to the remaining jobs. There is one cake of fixed size. If one person is to be given a relatively large slice, others must on average receive relatively small slices. To illustrate further this issue of apportioning overheads, consider Example 10.2.

Example 10.2

A business, that provides a service, expects to incur overheads totalling £20,000 next month. The total direct labour time worked is expected to be 1,600 hours and machines are expected to operate for a total of 1,000 hours.

During the next month, the business expects to do just two large jobs. Information concerning each job is as follows:

	Job 1	Job 2
Direct labour hours	800	800
Machine hours	700	300

Required:

How much of the total overheads will be charged to each job if overheads are to be charged on:

(a) a direct labour hour basis; and
(b) a machine hour basis?

What do you notice about the two sets of figures that you calculate?

Solution

(a) *Direct labour hour basis*

Overhead recovery rate = £20,000/1,600 = £12.50 per direct labour hour.

Job 1:   £12.50 × 800 = £10,000
Job 2:   £12.50 × 800 = £10,000

(b) *Machine hour basis*

Overhead recovery rate = £20,000/1,000 = £20.00 per machine hour.

Job 1:   £20.00 × 700 = £14,000
Job 2:   £20.00 × 300 = £6,000

It is clear from these calculations that the total of the overheads charged to jobs is the same (that is, £20,000) whichever method is used. So, whereas the machine hour basis gives Job 1 a higher share than the direct labour hour basis, the opposite is true for Job 2.

It is not practical to charge overheads on one basis to one job and on the other basis to the other job. This is because either total overheads will not be fully charged to the jobs, or the jobs will be overcharged with overheads. For example, using the direct labour hour method for Job 1 (£10,000) and the machine hour basis for Job 2 (£6,000) will mean that only £16,000 of a total £20,000 of overheads will be charged to jobs. As a result, the objective of full (absorption) costing, which is to charge all overheads to jobs done, will not be achieved. In this particular case, if selling prices are based on full costs, the business may not charge high enough prices to cover all of its costs.

Figure 10.6 shows the effect of the two different bases of charging overheads to Jobs 1 and 2.

Activity (10.8)

The point was made above that it would normally be irrational to prefer one basis of charging overheads to jobs simply because it apportions either a higher or a lower amount of overheads to a particular job. This is because the total overheads are the same irrespective of the method of charging the total to individual jobs. Can you think of any circumstances where it would not necessarily be so irrational?

Activity 10.8 continued

This might apply where, for a particular job, a customer has agreed to pay a price based on full cost plus an agreed fixed percentage for profit. Here it would be beneficial to the producer for the total cost of the job to be as high as possible. This would be relatively unusual, but in the past public sector organisations, particularly central and local government departments, have entered into contracts to have work done with the price to be deduced on a cost-plus basis after the work has been completed. Such contracts are rare these days, probably because they are open to abuse in the way described. Usually, contract prices are agreed in advance, typically in conjunction with competitive tendering.

Figure 10.6	**The effect of different bases of charging overheads to jobs in Example 10.2**

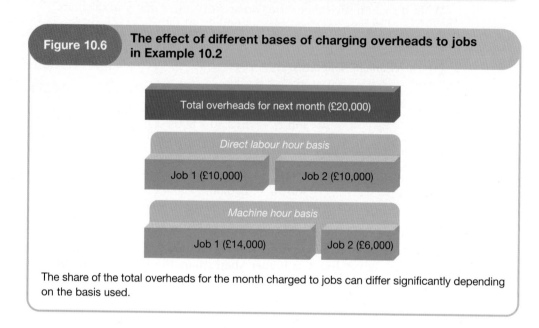

The share of the total overheads for the month charged to jobs can differ significantly depending on the basis used.

Real World 10.3 provides some insight to the basis of overhead recovery in practice.

Real World 10.3

Overhead recovery rates in practice

A survey of 303 UK manufacturing businesses, published in 1993, showed that the direct labour hour basis of charging overheads to cost units was overwhelmingly the most popular, used by 73 per cent of the respondents to the survey. Where the work has a strong labour element this seems reasonable, but the survey also showed that 68 per cent of businesses used this basis for automated activities. It is surprising that direct labour hours should have been used as the basis of charging overheads in an environment dominated by machines and machine-related costs.

Although this survey is not very recent and applied only to manufacturing businesses, in the absence of other information it provides some impression of what happens in practice. There is no reason to believe that current practice is very different from that which applied at the beginning of the 1990s.

Source: Based on information in Drury *et al.* (see reference 3 at the end of the chapter).

Segmenting the overheads

As we have just seen, charging the same overheads to different jobs on different bases is not possible. It is possible, however, to charge one segment of the total overheads on one basis and another segment (or other segments) on another basis (or bases).

Activity 10.9

Taking the same business as in Example 10.2, on closer analysis we find that of the overheads totalling £20,000 next month, £8,000 relate to machines (depreciation, maintenance, rent of the space occupied by the machines, and so on) and the remaining £12,000 to more general overheads. The other information about the business is exactly as it was before.

How much of the total overheads will be charged to each job if the machine-related overheads are to be charged on a machine hour basis and the remaining overheads are charged on a direct labour hour basis?

Direct labour hour basis

> Overhead recovery rate = £12,000/1,600 = £7.50 per direct labour hour

Machine hour basis

> Overhead recovery rate = £8,000/1,000 = £8.00 per machine hour

Overheads charged to jobs

	Job 1 £	Job 2 £
Direct labour hour basis:		
£7.50 × 800	6,000	
£7.50 × 800		6,000
Machine hour basis:		
£8.00 × 700	5,600	
£8.00 × 300		2,400
Total	11,600	8,400

We can see from this that the expected overheads of £20,000 are charged in total.

Segmenting the overheads in this way may well be seen as providing a better basis of charging overheads to jobs. This is quite often found in practice, usually by dividing a business into separate 'areas' for costing purposes, charging overheads differently from one area to the next, according to the nature of the work done there.

Remember that there is no correct basis of charging overheads to jobs, so our frequent reference to the direct labour and machine hour bases should not be taken to imply that these are the correct methods. However, it should be said that these two methods do have something to commend them and are popular in practice. As we have already seen, a sensible method does need to identify something about each job that can be measured and which distinguishes it from other jobs. There is also a lot to be said for methods that are concerned with time, because most overheads are time related.

Dealing with overheads on a departmental basis

In general, as we saw in Chapter 1, all but the smallest businesses are divided into departments. Normally, each department deals with a separate activity. The reasons for dividing a business into departments include the following:

- Many businesses are too large and complex to be managed as a single unit. It is usually more practical to operate each business as a series of relatively independent units (departments) with each one having its own manager.
- Each department normally has its own area of specialism and is managed by a specialist.
- Each department can have its own accounting records that enable its performance to be assessed. This can lead to greater management control and motivation among the staff.

As is shown in Real World 10.4 (page 350), most businesses charge overheads to cost units on a department-by-department basis. They do this in the expectation that it will give rise to a more useful way of charging overheads. It is probably often the case that it does not lead to any great improvement in the usefulness of the resulting full costs. Although it may not be of enormous benefit in many cases, it is probably not an expensive exercise to apply overheads on a departmental basis. Since costs are collected by each department for other purposes (particularly control), to apply overheads on a department-by-department basis is a relatively simple matter.

Example 10.3 looks at how the departmental approach to deriving full costs works in a service-industry context.

Example 10.3

Autosparkle Ltd offers a motor vehicle paint-respray service. The jobs that it undertakes range from painting a small part of a saloon car, usually following a minor accident, to a complete respray of a double-decker bus.

Each job starts life in the preparation department, where it is prepared for the paintshop department. In the preparation department the job is worked on by direct workers, in most cases taking some direct materials from the stores with which to treat the old paintwork to render the vehicle ready for respraying. Thus the job will be charged with direct materials, direct labour and with a share of the preparation department's overheads. The job then passes into the paintshop department, already valued at the costs that it picked up in the preparation department.

In the paintshop, the staff draw direct materials (mainly paint) from the stores and direct workers spend time respraying the job, using sophisticated spraying apparatus as well as working by hand. So, in the paintshop, the job is charged with direct materials, direct labour plus a share of that department's overheads. The job now passes into the finishing department, valued at the cost of the materials, labour and overheads that it accumulated in the first two departments.

In the finishing department, jobs are cleaned and polished ready to go back to the customers. Further direct labour and, in some cases, materials are added. All jobs also pick up a share of that department's overheads. The job, now complete, passes back to the customer.

Figure 10.7 shows graphically how this works for a particular job.

Figure 10.7 A cost unit (Job A) passing through Autosparkle Ltd's process

As the particular paint job passes through the three departments, where work is carried out on it, the job 'gathers' costs of various types.

The basis of charging overheads to jobs (for example, direct labour hours) might be the same for all three departments, or it might be different from one department to another. It is possible that spraying apparatus costs dominate the paintshop costs, so that department's overheads might well be charged to jobs on a machine hour basis. The other two departments are probably labour intensive, so that direct labour hours may be seen as being appropriate there.

The passage of the job through the departments, picking up costs as it goes, can be compared to a snowball being rolled across snow: as it rolls, it picks up more and more snow.

 Where costs are dealt with departmentally, each department is known as a **cost centre.** This can be defined as some physical area or some activity or function for which costs are separately identified. Charging direct costs to jobs, in a departmental system, is exactly the same as where the whole business is one single cost centre. It is simply a matter of keeping a record of:

● the number of hours of direct labour worked on the particular job and the grade of labour, assuming that there are different grades with different rates of pay;
● the cost of the direct materials taken from stores and applied to the job; and
● any other direct costs, for example some subcontracted work, associated with the job.

This record keeping will normally be done departmentally in a departmental system.

It is obviously necessary to break down the production overheads of the entire business on a departmental basis. This means that the total overheads of the business must be divided between the departments such that the sum of the departmental overheads equals the overheads for the entire business. By charging all of their overheads to jobs, the departments will, between them, charge all of the overheads of the business to jobs. **Real World 10.4** provides an indication of the number of different cost centres that businesses tend to use in practice.

Real World 10.4

Cost centres in practice

It is not unusual for businesses to have several cost centres. Figure 10.8 shows the results of a recent survey by Drury and Tayles of 186 larger UK businesses involved in various activities.

Figure 10.8   **Analysis of the number of cost centres within a business**

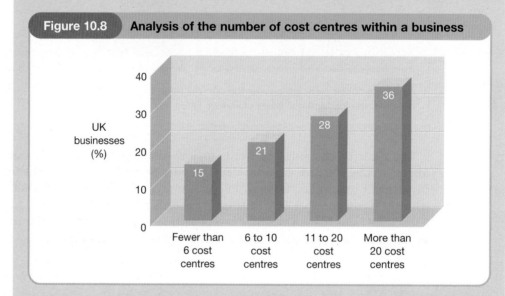

We can see from the diagram that 85 per cent of businesses surveyed had six or more cost centres and that 36 per cent of businesses had more than twenty cost centres. Though not shown on the diagram, 3 per cent of businesses surveyed had a single cost centre (that is, there was a business-wide or overall overhead rate used). Clearly, businesses that deal with overheads on a business-wide basis are rare.

Source: Based on information in Drury and Tayles (see reference 4 at the end of the chapter).

 For purposes of cost assignment, it is necessary to distinguish between **product cost centres** (or departments) and **service cost centres** (or departments). Product cost centres are departments in which jobs are worked on by direct workers and/or where direct materials are added. Here jobs can be charged with a share of their overheads. The preparation, paintshop and finishing departments discussed in Example 10.3 are all examples of product cost centres.

Activity (10.10)

Can you guess what the definition of a service cost centre is?
Can you think of an example of a service cost centre?

A service cost centre is one where no direct costs are involved. It renders a service to other cost centres. Examples include:

● General administration
● Accounting
● Stores
● Maintenance
● Personnel
● Catering.

All of these render services to product cost centres and, possibly, to other service cost centres.

Service cost centre costs must be charged to product cost centres and become part of the product cost centres' overheads so that those overheads can be recharged to jobs. This must be done so that all of the overheads of the business find their way into the cost of the jobs. If this is not done, the 'full' cost derived will not really be the full cost of the jobs.

Logically, the costs of a service cost centre should be charged to product cost centres on the basis of the level of service provided to the product cost centre concerned. For example, a production department that has a lot of machine maintenance carried out relative to other production departments should be charged with a larger share of the maintenance department's costs than should those other product cost centres.

The process of dividing overheads between departments is as follows:

→ ● **Cost allocation**. Allocate costs that are specific to the departments. These are costs that relate to, and are specifically measurable in respect of, individual departments, that is, they are direct costs of running the department. Examples include:
  – salaries of indirect workers whose activities are wholly within the department, for example the salary of the departmental manager;
  – rent, where the department is housed in its own premises for which rent can be separately identified;
  – electricity, where it is separately metered for each department.

→ ● **Cost apportionment**. Apportion the more general overheads to the departments. These are overheads that relate to more than one department, perhaps to them all. These would include:
  – rent, where more than one department is housed in the same premises;
  – electricity, where it is not separately metered;
  – salaries of cleaning staff who work in a variety of departments.

  These costs would be apportioned to departments on the basis of the extent to which each department benefits from the overhead concerned. For example, the rent cost might be apportioned on the basis of the square metres of floor area occupied by each department. With electricity used to power machinery the basis of apportionment might be the level of mechanisation of each department. As with charging overheads to individual jobs, usefulness is the issue; there is no correct basis of apportioning general overheads to departments.

● Having totalled, allocated and apportioned costs to all departments, it is now necessary to apportion the total costs of service cost centres to production departments. Logically, the basis of apportionment should be the level of service rendered by the individual service department to the individual production department. With personnel department costs, for example, the basis of apportionment might be the number of staff in each production department, because it could be argued that the higher the number of staff, the more benefit the production department has derived from the personnel department. This is, of course, rather a crude approach. A particular production department may have severe personnel problems and a high staff turnover rate, which may make it a user of the personnel service that is way out of proportion to the number of staff in the production department.

The final total for each product cost centre is that cost centre's overheads. These can be charged to jobs as they pass through. The process of applying overheads to cost units on a departmental basis is shown in Figure 10.9.

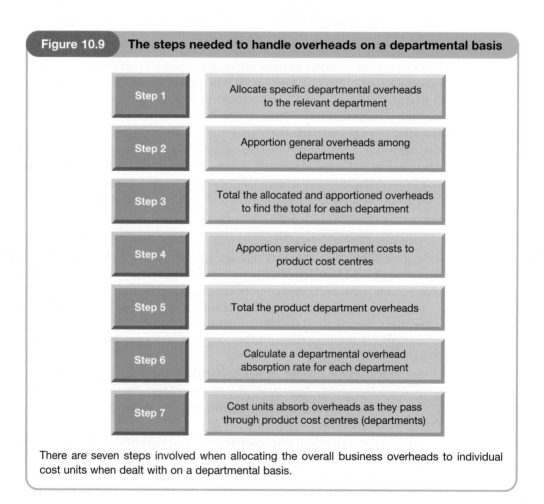

Figure 10.9 **The steps needed to handle overheads on a departmental basis**

Step 1	Allocate specific departmental overheads to the relevant department
Step 2	Apportion general overheads among departments
Step 3	Total the allocated and apportioned overheads to find the total for each department
Step 4	Apportion service department costs to product cost centres
Step 5	Total the product department overheads
Step 6	Calculate a departmental overhead absorption rate for each department
Step 7	Cost units absorb overheads as they pass through product cost centres (departments)

There are seven steps involved when allocating the overall business overheads to individual cost units when dealt with on a departmental basis.

We shall now consider Example 10.4, which deals with overheads on a departmental basis.

Example 10.4

A business consists of four departments:

1 preparation department
2 machining department
3 finishing department
4 general administration (GA) department.

The first three are product cost centres and the last renders a service to the other three. The level of service rendered is thought to be roughly in proportion to the number of employees in each production department.

Overhead costs, and other data, for next month are expected to be as follows:

	£000
Rent	10,000
Electricity to power machines	3,000
Electricity for heating and lighting	800
Insurance of premises	200
Cleaning	600
Depreciation of machines	2,000

Salaries of each of the indirect workers are as follows:

	£000
Preparation department	200
Machining department	240
Finishing department	180
General administration department	180

The general administration department has a staff consisting of only indirect workers (including managers). The other departments have both indirect workers (including managers) and direct workers. There are 100 indirect workers within each of the four departments and none does any 'direct' work.

Each direct worker is expected to work 160 hours next month. The number of direct workers in each department is:

	Hours
Preparation department	600
Machining department	900
Finishing department	500

Machining department direct workers are paid £12 an hour; other direct workers are paid £10 an hour.

All of the machinery is in the machining department. Machines are expected to operate for 120,000 hours next month.

The floorspace (in square metres) occupied by the departments is as follows:

	Sq m
Preparation department	16,000
Machining department	20,000
Finishing department	10,000
General administration department	2,000

→ Deducing the overheads can be done, department by department, using a schedule, as follows:

	£000	Total £000	Prep'n £000	Mach'g £000	Fin'g £000	GA £000
Allocated costs:						
Machine power		3,000		3,000		
Machine depreciation		2,000		2,000		
Indirect salaries		800	200	240	180	180
Apportioned costs:						
Rent	10,000					
Heating and lighting	800					
Insurance of premises	200					
Cleaning	600					
Apportioned by floor area		11,600	3,867	4,833	2,417	483
Departmental overheads		17,400	4,067	10,073	2,597	663
Reapportion GA costs by number of staff (including the indirect workers)			202	288	173	(663)
		17,400	4,269	10,361	2,770	–

Activity (10.11)

Assume that the machining department overheads (in Example 10.4) are to be charged to jobs on a machine hour basis, but that the direct labour hour basis is to be used for the other two departments. What will be the full (absorption) cost of a job with the following characteristics?

	Preparation	Machining	Finishing
Direct labour hours	10	7	5
Machine hours	–	6	–
Direct materials (£)	85	13	6

(*Hint*: This should be tackled as if each department were a separate business, then departmental costs added together for the job so as to arrive at the total full cost.)

First, we need to deduce the overhead recovery rates for each department:
   Preparation department (direct labour hour based):

$$\frac{£4,269,000}{600 \times 160} = £44.47$$

Machining department (machine hour based):

$$\frac{£10,361,000}{120,000} = £86.34$$

Finishing department (direct labour hour based):

$$\frac{£2,770,000}{500 \times 160} = £34.63$$

The cost of the job is as follows:

	£	£
Direct labour:		
Preparation department (10 × £10)	100.00	
Machining department (7 × £12)	84.00	
Finishing department (5 × £10)	50.00	
		234.00
Direct materials:		
Preparation department	85.00	
Machining department	13.00	
Finishing department	6.00	
		104.00
Overheads:		
Preparation department (10 × £44.47)	444.70	
Machining department (6 × £86.34)	518.04	
Finishing department (5 × £34.63)	173.15	
		1,135.89
Full cost of the job		1,473.89

Activity (10.12)

The manufacturing costs for Buccaneers Ltd for next year are expected to be as follows:

	£000
Direct materials:	
Forming department	450
Machining department	100
Finishing department	50
Direct labour:	
Forming department	180
Machining department	120
Finishing department	75
Indirect materials:	
Forming department	40
Machining department	30
Finishing department	10
Administration department	10
Indirect labour:	
Forming department	80
Machining department	70
Finishing department	60
Administration department	60
Maintenance costs:	50
Rent and rates	100
Heating and lighting	20
Building insurance	10
Machinery insurance	10
Depreciation of machinery	120
Total manufacturing costs	1,645

Activity 10.12 continued

The following additional information is available:

(i) All direct labour is paid £6 an hour for all hours worked.
(ii) The administration department renders personnel and general services to the production departments.
(iii) The area of the premises in which the business manufactures amounts to 50,000 sq m, divided as follows:

	Sq m
Forming department	20,000
Machining department	15,000
Finishing department	10,000
Administration department	5,000

(iv) The maintenance employees are expected to divide their time between the production departments as follows:

	%
Forming department	15
Machining department	75
Finishing department	10

(v) Machine hours are expected to be as follows:

	Hours
Forming department	5,000
Machining department	15,000
Finishing department	5,000

On the basis of this information:

(a) Allocate and apportion overheads to the three production departments.
(b) Deduce overhead recovery rates for each department using two different bases for each department's overheads.
(c) Calculate the full cost of a job with the following characteristics:

Direct labour hours:	
Forming department	4 hours
Machining department	4 hours
Finishing department	1 hour
Machine hours:	
Forming department	1 hour
Machining department	2 hours
Finishing department	1 hour
Direct materials:	
Forming department	£40
Machining department	£9
Finishing department	£4

Use whichever of the two bases of overhead recovery, deduced in (b), that you consider the more appropriate.

(d) Explain why you consider the basis used in (c) to be the more appropriate.

(a) Overheads can be allocated and apportioned as follows:

Cost	Basis of appor't	Total £000	Forming £000	Machining £000	Finishing £000	Admin. £000
Indirect materials	Specifically allocated	90	40	30	10	10
Indirect labour	Specifically allocated	270	80	70	60	60
Maintenance	Staff time	50	7.5	37.5	5	–
Rent/rates	100					
Heat/light	20					
Bldgs insurance	10					
	Area	130	52	39	26	13
Machine insurance	10					
Machine dep'n	120					
	Machine hours	130	26	78	26	–
		670	205.5	254.5	127	83
Admin.	Direct labour		39.84	26.56	16.6	(83)
		670	245.34	281.06	143.6	–

Note: Direct costs are not included in the above because they are allocated *directly* to jobs.

(b) Overhead recovery rates are as follows:

Basis 1: direct labour hours

$$\text{Forming} = \frac{£245,340}{180,000/6} = £8.18 \text{ per direct labour hour}$$

$$\text{Machining} = \frac{£281,060}{120,000/6} = £14.05 \text{ per direct labour hour}$$

$$\text{Finishing} = \frac{£143,600}{75,000/6} = £11.49 \text{ per direct labour hour}$$

Basis 2: machine hours

$$\text{Forming} = \frac{£245,340}{5,000} = £49.07 \text{ per machine hour}$$

$$\text{Machining} = \frac{£281,060}{15,000} = £18.74 \text{ per machine hour}$$

$$\text{Finishing} = \frac{£143,600}{5,000} = £28.72 \text{ per machine hour}$$

(c) Full cost of job – on direct labour hour basis of overhead recovery

	£	£
Direct labour cost (9 × £6)		54.00
Direct materials (£40 + £9 + £4)		53.00
Overheads:		
Forming (4 × £8.18)	32.72	
Machining (4 × £14.05)	56.20	
Finishing (1 × £11.49)	11.49	100.41
Full cost		£207.41

Activity 10.12 continued

(d) The reason for using the direct labour hour basis rather than the machine hour basis was that labour is more important, in terms of the number of hours applied to output, than is machine time. Strong arguments could have been made for the use of the alternative basis; certainly, a machine hour basis could have been justified for the machining department.

It would be possible, and it may be reasonable, to use one basis in respect of one department's overheads and a different one for those of another department. For example, machine hours could have been used for the machining department and a direct labour hours basis for the other two.

Batch costing

The production of many types of goods and services (particularly goods) involves producing in a batch of identical, or nearly identical, units of output, but where each batch is distinctly different from other batches. For example, a theatre may put on a production whose nature (and therefore costs) is very different from that of other productions. On the other hand, ignoring differences in the desirability of the various types of seating, all of the individual units of output (tickets to see the production) are identical.

In these circumstances, we should normally deduce the cost per ticket by using a job costing approach (taking account of direct and indirect costs and so on) to find the cost of mounting the production and then we should simply divide this by the expected number of tickets to be sold to find the cost per ticket. This is known as **batch costing**.

Figure 10.10 shows the process for deriving the cost of one cost unit (product) in a batch.

| Figure 10.10 | **Deriving the cost of one cost unit where production is in batches** |

The full cost of the batch, derived on a 'job-costing' basis

divided by

The number of cost units (products) in the batch

equals

The full cost of one cost unit (product)

The cost for the batch is derived using a job costing basis and this is divided by the number in the batch to determine the cost for each cost unit.

Full (absorption) cost as the break-even price

We should recognise that, if all goes according to plan (so that direct costs, overheads and the basis of charging overheads, for example direct labour hours, prove to be as expected), then selling the output for its full cost should cause the business to break even exactly. Therefore, whatever profit (in total) is loaded on to full cost to set actual selling prices will, if plans are achieved, result in that level of profit being earned for the period.

The forward-looking nature of full (absorption) costing

Although deducing full costs can be done after the work has been completed, it is often done in advance. In other words, costs are frequently predicted. Where, for example, full costs are needed as a basis on which to set selling prices, it is usually the case that prices need to be set before the customer will accept the job being done. Even where no particular customer has been identified, some idea of the ultimate price will need to be known before the business will be able to make a judgement as to whether potential customers will buy the product, and in what quantities. There is a risk, of course, that the actual outcome will differ from that which was predicted. If this occurs, corrections are subsequently made to the full costs originally calculated.

Self-assessment question 10.1

Hector and Co. Ltd has been invited to tender for a contract to produce 1,000 clothes hangers. The following information relates to the contract.

- *Materials*: The clothes hangers are made of metal wire covered with a padded fabric. Each hanger requires 2 m of wire and 0.5 sq m of fabric.
- *Direct labour*: Skilled: 10 minutes per hanger
  Unskilled: 5 minutes per hanger.

The business already holds sufficient of each of the materials required to complete the contract. Information on the cost of the materials is as follows:

	Metal wire £/m	Fabric £/sq m
Historic cost	2.20	1.00
Current buying-in cost	2.50	1.10
Scrap value	1.70	0.40

The metal wire is in constant use by the business for a range of its products. The fabric has no other use for the business and is scheduled to be scrapped.

Unskilled labour, which is paid at the rate of £7.50 an hour, will need to be taken on specifically to undertake the contract. The business is fairly quiet at the moment, which means that a pool of skilled labour exists that will still be employed at full pay of £12.00 an hour to do nothing if the contract does not proceed. The pool of skilled labour is sufficient to complete the contract.

The business charges jobs with overheads on a direct labour hour basis. The production overheads of the entire business for the month in which the contract will be undertaken are estimated at £50,000. The estimated total direct labour hours that will be worked are 12,500. The business tends not to alter the established overhead recovery rate

→

Self-assessment question 10.1 continued

to reflect increases or reductions to estimated total hours arising from new contracts. The total overhead cost is not expected to increase as a result of undertaking the contract.

The business normally adds 12.5 per cent profit loading to the job cost to arrive at a first estimate of the tender price.

Required:
(a) Price this job on a traditional job-costing basis.
(b) Indicate the minimum price at which the contract could be undertaken such that the business would be neither better nor worse off as a result of doing it.

The answer to this question can be found at the back of the book on page 701.

Using full (absorption) cost information

We saw at the beginning of the chapter that full (absorption) cost information may be used for four main purposes. Now that we have seen how full costs are deduced, let us consider in more detail how this information may be used.

- *Pricing and output decisions.* Full costs can be used as the starting point for determining prices. An amount is simply added to the full cost of a product or service for profit in order to derive the selling price. The amount of profit is often calculated as a percentage of the full (absorption) cost figure. This approach to pricing is known as **cost-plus pricing**.

  Garages carrying out vehicle repairs typically operate in this way. Solicitors and accountants often use this approach as well. Where there is a competitive market, however, it is not possible to set prices on a cost-plus basis. Businesses will usually have to accept the price that the market is prepared to pay. Thus they are usually *price takers* rather than *price makers*. The prices that businesses are able to sell their output will usually be a major determinant of the quantity that they make available to the market. We shall take a closer look at pricing and its relationship to costs and output in Chapter 11.

- *Exercising control.* Full (absorption) costs seem often to be used as the basis of budgeting and comparing actual outcomes with budgets, enabling action to be taken to exercise control. It can be useful in this context, though care needs to be taken to try to ensure that individual managers are not being held responsible for costs, say overhead costs, that they are unable control. This point will be raised again in Chapter 11, where we consider another approach to dealing with overheads in full costing. We shall look at budgeting and control in some detail in Chapters 12 and 13.

- *Assessing relative efficiency.* Full costs seem to be used as the basis of comparing relative efficiency in terms of the comparative cost of doing similar things. For example, the costs of carrying out a standard surgical operation may be compared on the basis of full cost between one hospital and another. The objective of this may well be to identify the cheaper hospital in order to encourage the other hospital to adopt the same approach.

  As we saw in Chapters 8 and 9, including all costs (as full costing does) can lead to incorrect decisions. It is necessary to identify the costs that are strictly relevant to a decision and ignore the rest, be they direct or indirect in the full-costing context.

Similarly, comparing the full cost of doing something, particularly when the two things are being done in different organisations, can be confusing and can lead to poor decisions.

● *Assessing performance.* The conventional approach to measuring a business's income for a period requires that expenses be matched with the sales revenue to which they relate *in the same accounting period*. Thus, where a service is partially rendered in one accounting period but the revenue is recognised in the next, or where manufactured inventories are made in one period but sold in the next, the full cost (including an appropriate share of overheads) must be carried from the first accounting period to the second one.

Deducing full cost is important because, unless we know the full cost of work done in one period that is sold in the next, the profit figures for each of the two periods concerned will be meaningless. Managers and others will not have a reliable means of assessing the effectiveness of the business as a whole, or the effectiveness of its individual parts.

A little later on we shall take a quick look at an alternative approach to income measurement which does not use full costs.

The way in which full cost information is used to measure income can be illustrated by Example 10.5.

Example 10.5

During the accounting year that ended on 31 December last year, IT Modules Ltd developed a special piece of computer software for a customer, Kingsang Ltd. At the beginning of this year, after having a series of tests successfully completed by a subcontractor, the software was passed to Kingsang Ltd. IT Modules' normal practice (and typical of most businesses) is to take account of sales revenue when the product passes to the customer. The sale price of the Kingsang software was £45,000.

During last year, subcontract work costing £3,500 was used in developing the Kingsang software and 1,200 hours of direct labour, costing £24,300, were worked on it. The business uses a direct labour hour basis of charging overheads to jobs, which is believed to be fair because most of its work is labour intensive. The total production overheads for the business for last year were £77,000, and the total direct labour hours worked were 22,000. Testing the Kingsang software this year cost £1,000.

How much profit or loss did IT Modules make on the Kingsang software during last year? How much profit or loss did it make on the software during this year? At what value should IT Modules have included the software on its balance sheet at the end of last year so that the correct profit will be recorded for each of the two years?

Solution
The answers to these questions are as follows.

● No profit or loss was made during last year. This is because of IT Modules' (and the generally accepted) approach to recognising revenues (sales) and the need to match expenses with the revenues to which they relate. The costs incurred during last year are carried forward to this year, which is the year of sale.

→

● As the sale is recognised this year, the costs of developing the software is treated as expenses in this year. These costs will include a reasonable share of overheads. Were IT Modules to draw up a 'mini' income statement for the Kingsang contract for this year, it would be as follows:

Kingsang software	£	£
Sales price		45,000
Costs:		
Direct labour	(24,300)	
Subcontract	(3,500)	
Overheads [1,200 × (£77,000/22,000)]	(4,200)	
Total incurred last year	(32,000)	
Testing cost	(1,000)	
Total cost		(33,000)
This year's profit from the software		12,000

● The software needs to be shown as an asset of the business (valued at £32,000) in the balance sheet as at 31 December last year. It represents the work in progress that is carried forward to this year.

 ## Criticisms of full (absorption) costing

Full costing has been criticised because, in practice, it tends to use past costs and to restrict its consideration of future costs to outlay costs. It can be argued that past costs are irrelevant, irrespective of the purpose for which the information is to be used. This is basically because it is not possible to make decisions about the past, only about the future. Advocates of full costing would argue, however, that it provides a useful guide to long-run average cost.

Despite the criticisms that are made of full costing, it is, according to research evidence, very widely practised. An International Accounting Standard (IAS2 *Inventories*) requires that all inventories, including work in progress, be valued at full cost in the published financial reports. This fact demands the use of full costing. As a result virtually all businesses that have work in progress and/or inventories of finished goods at the end of their financial periods apply full costing for income measurement purposes. (This will include the many service providers that tend to have work in progress.) Whether they use full cost information for other purposes, is not clear.

Full (absorption) costing versus variable costing

An alternative to full (absorption) costing is **variable costing**, which we discussed in Chapter 9. We may recall that this approach distinguishes between fixed and variable costs and this distinction may be helpful when making short-term decisions. Where a business divides its costs between fixed and variable, it will measure its income differently from that described above. A variable costing approach will include only variable costs, including any variable overheads, as part of the cost of the goods or service. Fixed costs, whether direct or indirect, are treated as costs of the period in which they are incurred. Part of the philosophy of variable costing is that no fixed costs are linked to cost units in the way that they tend to be with full costing. Thus any inventories of finished products or work in progress that is carried from one accounting period to the next, are valued only on the basis of their variable costs.

As we have seen, full costing includes in product costs, not only the direct costs (whether fixed or variable) but also a 'fair' share of the overheads (both fixed and variable) that were incurred during the time that the product was being made or developed.

To illustrate the effect of this difference in approach, let us consider Example 10.6.

Example 10.6

IT Modules Ltd's (Example 10.5) direct labour and overheads are all fixed costs, so the only variable cost associated with developing the Kingsang software last year was the subcontract cost (£3,500). Under variable costing:

- All of IT Modules' overheads for last year, including the £4,200 absorbed by the software with the full-costing approach plus the direct labour relating to the Kingsang software, will be treated as an expense of last year and appear in last year's income statement along with all of the other fixed costs incurred during last year.
- The expenses of the subcontract cost brought forward plus the testing cost should be set against the revenue of £45,000 this year. This year's expenses will include all of the fixed costs incurred during this year.
- The software will be shown as an asset of the business (valued at £3,500) in the balance sheet as at 31 December last year.

Taking the Kingsang Ltd software job alone, the profit reported between the two years would be very different.

Which method is better?

In most practical circumstances, profits from one year to the next, for the business as a whole, would not be greatly affected by the choice of costing approach. Although, as we saw in Example 10.6, the reported profit/(loss) for an individual product can be greatly affected by the choice of costing method, the choice between full and variable costing may not make very much difference overall. If the level of fixed costs stays broadly the same from one year to the next and there are similar amounts of inventories and work in progress at year ends, reported profit will be similar for the two methods. This is because the same amount of fixed costs will be treated as an expense each year. In the case of variable costing, all fixed costs will originate from the current year, while, in the case of full costing, some will originate from past years.

Variable costing proponents might argue that the variable costing approach simplifies accounting procedures since fewer costs are carried forward. Perhaps most importantly, they would argue that only variable costs are relevant to decision makers (as we discussed in Chapters 8 and 9) and that considering fixed costs obscures the issue.

Proponents of full (absorption) costing might counter that full costing provides a fairer measure of profit, job by job. Furthermore, in the long run, all costs can be avoided, and so to concentrate on only those that can be avoided in the short term (the variable costs) could be misleading.

In practice management accountants can prepare their income statements taking either, or even both, approaches. We have already seen, however, that accounting rules insist that a full costing approach is taken when preparing published financial statements.

Real World 10.5 provides some indication of the extent that variable costing is used in practice.

Real world 10.5

Variable costing in practice

A recent survey of 41 UK manufacturing businesses found that 68 per cent of them used a variable costing approach to management reporting.

Many would find this surprising. It seemed to be widely believed that the requirement for financial statements in published annual reports to be in full cost terms has led those businesses to use a full cost approach for management reporting as well. This, however, seems not to be the case.

Source: Dugdale *et al.* (see reference 5 at the end of the chapter).

Summary

The main points in this chapter may be summarised as follows.

Full (absorption) cost = the total amount of resources sacrificed to achieve a particular objective.

Uses of full (absorption) cost information
- Pricing and output decisions.
- Exercising control.
- Assessing relative efficiency.
- Income measurement.

Single-product businesses
- Where all the units of output are identical, the full cost can be calculated as follows:

$$\text{Cost per unit} = \frac{\text{Total cost of output}}{\text{Number of units produced}}$$

Multi-product businesses – job costing
- Where units of output are not identical, it is necessary to divide the costs into two categories: direct costs and indirect costs.
- Direct costs = costs that can be identified with specific cost units (for example, labour of a garage mechanic, in relation to a particular job).
- Indirect costs (overheads) = costs that cannot be directly measured in respect of a particular job (for example, the rent of a garage).

- Full (absorption) cost = direct cost + indirect cost.
- Direct/indirect is not linked to variable/fixed.
- Indirect costs are difficult to relate to individual cost units. Arbitrary bases are used and there is no single correct method.
- Traditionally, indirect costs are seen as the costs of providing a 'service' to cost units.
- Direct labour hour basis of applying indirect costs to cost units is the most popular in practice.

Dealing with overheads on a departmental basis

- Indirect costs can be segmented, usually on a departmental basis. Each department has its own overhead recovery rate.
- Each department is a separate cost centre, that is, an area, activity or function for which costs are separately collected.
- Overheads must be allocated or apportioned to cost centres.
- Service cost centre costs must then be apportioned to product cost centres and product cost centre overheads absorbed by cost units (jobs).

Batch costing

- A variation of job costing where each job consists of a number of identical (or near identical) cost units:

$$\text{Cost per unit} = \frac{\text{Cost of the batch (direct + indirect)}}{\text{Number of units in the batch}}$$

Break-even price and full (absorption) costing

- If the full (absorption) cost is charged as the sales price and things go according to plan, the business will break even.

Criticisms of full (absorption) costing

- Full cost information is seen by some as not very useful because it can be backward looking: it includes information irrelevant to decision making, but excludes some relevant information.

Full (absorption) costing versus variable costing

- With full costing all costs, fixed and variable, are included in product costs and treated as expenses when the product is sold.
- With variable costing, only the variable product costs are linked to the products in this way; fixed costs are treated as an expense of the period in which they were incurred.
- Variable costing tends to be more straightforward and, according to proponents, more relevant for decision making.
- Supporters of full costing argue that it gives a more complete measure of the income generated from the sale of each unit of the product.

MyAccountingLab Now check your progress in your personal Study Plan

Key terms

full cost p. 334	**cost unit** p. 340
full costing p. 334	**overhead absorption (recovery) rate**
process costing p. 335	p. 341
direct costs p. 336	**cost centre** p. 349
indirect costs p. 336	**product cost centre** p. 350
overheads p. 336	**service cost centre** p. 350
common costs p. 336	**cost allocation** p. 351
job costing p. 337	**cost apportionment** p. 351
absorption costing p. 337	**batch costing** p. 358
cost behaviour p. 339	**cost-plus pricing** p. 360
total cost p. 340	**variable costing** p. 362

References

1 Cost Systems Design and Profitability Analysis in UK Manufacturing Companies, *Drury C. and Tayles M.*, CIMA Publishing, 2000.

2 2003 Survey of Management Accounting, *Ernst and Young*, Ernst and Young, 2003.

3 A Survey of Management Accounting Practices in UK Manufacturing Companies, *Drury C., Braund S., Osborne P. and Tayles M.*, Chartered Association of Certified Accountants, 1993.

4 'Profitability analysis in UK organisations', *Drury C. and Tayles M.*, British Accounting Review, December 2006.

5 Contemporary Management Accounting Practices in UK Manufacturing, *Dugdale D., Jones C. and Green S.*, CIMA Research Publication, vol. 1, no. 13, 2005.

Further reading

If you would like to explore the topics covered in this chapter in more depth, we recommend the following books:

Cost Accounting: A managerial emphasis, *Horngren C., Foster G. and Datar S.*, 12th edn, Prentice Hall, 2006, chapter 4.

Management Accounting, *Atkinson A., Kaplan R., Young S.M. and Matsumura E.*, 5th edn, Prentice Hall, 2007, chapter 3.

Management and Cost Accounting, *Drury C.*, 6th edn, Thomson Learning, 2004, chapters 3, 4 and 5.

Managerial Accounting, *Hilton R.*, 6th edn, McGraw-Hill/Irwin, 2005, chapters 2 and 3.

Review questions

Answers to these questions can be found at the back of the book on pages 780–1.

10.1 What problem does the existence of work in progress cause in process costing?

10.2 What is the point of distinguishing direct costs from indirect ones? Why is this not necessary in process costing environments?

10.3 Are direct costs and variable costs the same thing? Explain your answer.

10.4 It is sometimes claimed that the full cost of pursuing some objective represents the long-run break-even selling price. Why is this said, and what does it mean?

Exercises

Exercises 10.4 to 10.8 are more advanced than 10.1 to 10.3. Those with **coloured numbers** have answers at the back of the book, starting on page 734.

If you wish to try more exercises, visit the students' side of the Companion Website.

10.1 Bodgers Ltd, a business that provides a market research service, operates a job costing system. Towards the end of each financial year, the overhead recovery rate (the rate at which overheads will be absorbed by jobs) is established for the forthcoming year.

Required:
(a) Why does the business bother to predetermine the recovery rate in the way outlined?
(b) What steps will be involved in predetermining the rate?
(c) What problems might arise with using a predetermined rate?

10.2 Athena Ltd is an engineering business doing work for its customers to their particular requirements and specifications. It determines the full cost of each job taking a 'job costing' approach, accounting for overheads on a departmental basis. It bases its prices to customers on this full cost figure. The business has two departments: a machining department, where each job starts, and a fitting department, which completes all of the jobs. Machining department overheads are charged to jobs on a machine hour basis and those of the fitting department on a direct labour hour basis. The budgeted information for next year is as follows:

Heating and lighting	£25,000	(allocated equally between the two departments)
Machine power	£10,000	(all allocated to the machining department)
Direct labour	£200,000	(£150,000 allocated to the fitting department and £50,000 to the machining department. All direct workers are paid £10 an hour)
Indirect labour	£50,000	(apportioned to the departments in proportion to the direct labour cost)
Direct materials	£120,000	(all applied to jobs in the machining department)
Depreciation	£30,000	(all relates to the machining department)
Machine time	20,000 hours	(all worked in the machining department)

Required:

(a) Prepare a statement showing the budgeted overheads for next year, analysed between the two departments. This should be in the form of three columns: one for the total figure for each type of overhead and one column each for the two departments, where each type of overhead is analysed between the two departments. Each column should also show the total of overheads for the year.

(b) Derive the appropriate rate for charging the overheads of each department to jobs (that is, a separate rate for each department).

(c) Athena Ltd has been asked by a customer to specify the price that it will charge for a particular job that will, if the job goes ahead, be undertaken early next year. The job is expected to use direct materials costing Athena Ltd £1,200, to need 50 hours of machining time, 10 hours of machining department direct labour and 20 hours of fitting department direct labour. Athena Ltd charges a profit loading of 20% to the full cost of jobs to determine the selling price.

Show workings to derive the proposed selling price for this job.

10.3 Pieman Products Ltd makes road trailers to the precise specifications of individual customers. The following are predicted to occur during the forthcoming year, which is about to start:

Direct materials cost	£50,000
Direct labour costs	£160,000
Direct labour time	16,000 hours
Indirect labour cost	£25,000
Depreciation of machine	£8,000
Rent and rates	£10,000
Heating, lighting and power	£5,000
Indirect materials	£2,000
Other indirect costs	£1,000
Machine time	3,000 hours

All direct labour is paid at the same hourly rate.

A customer has asked the business to build a trailer for transporting a racing motorcycle to races. It is estimated that this will require materials and components that will cost £1,150. It will take 250 direct labour hours to do the job, of which 50 will involve the use of machinery.

Required:

Deduce a logical cost for the job, and explain the basis of dealing with overheads that you propose.

10.4 Promptprint Ltd, a printing business, has received an enquiry from a potential customer for the quotation of a price for a job. The pricing policy of the business is based on the plans for the next financial year shown below.

	£
Sales revenue (billings to customers)	196,000
Materials (direct)	(38,000)
Labour (direct)	(32,000)
Variable overheads	(2,400)
Advertising (for business)	(3,000)
Depreciation	(27,600)
Administration	(36,000)
Interest	(8,000)
Profit (before taxation)	49,000

A first estimate of the direct costs for the particular job is:

Direct materials: £4,000
Direct labour: £3,600

Required:
(a) Prepare a recommended price for the job based on the plans, commenting on your method, ignoring the information given in the Appendix (below).
(b) Comment on the validity of using financial plans in pricing, and recommend any improvements you would consider desirable for the pricing policy used in (a).
(c) Incorporate the effects of the information shown in the Appendix (below) into your estimates of direct material costs, explaining any changes you consider it necessary to make to the above direct material cost of £4,000.

Appendix to Exercise 10.4
Based on historic costs, direct material costs were computed as follows:

	£
Paper grade 1	1,200
Paper grade 2	2,000
Card (zenith grade)	500
Inks and other miscellaneous items	300
	4,000

Paper grade 1 is regularly used by the business. Enough of this paper to complete the job is currently held. Because it is imported, it is estimated that if it is used for this job, a new purchase order will have to be placed shortly. Sterling has depreciated against the foreign currency by 25% since the last purchase.

Paper grade 2 is purchased from the same source as grade 1. The business holds exactly enough of it for the job, but this was bought in for a special order. This order was cancelled, although the defaulting customer was required to pay £500 towards the cost of the paper. The accountant has offset this against the original cost to arrive at the figure of £2,000 shown above. This paper is rarely used and, due to its special chemical coating, will be unusable if it is not used on the job in question.

The card is another specialist item currently held by the business. There is no use foreseen and it would cost £750 to replace if required. However, the inventories controller had planned to spend £130 on overprinting to use the card as a substitute for other materials costing £640.

Inks and other items are in regular use in the print shop.

10.5 Bookdon plc manufactures three products, X, Y and Z, in two production departments: a machine shop and a fitting section; it also has two service departments: a canteen and a machine maintenance section. Shown below are next year's planned production data and manufacturing costs for the business.

	X	Y	Z
Production	4,200 units	6,900 units	1,700 units
Direct materials	£11/unit	£14/unit	£17/unit
Direct labour:			
Machine shop	£6/unit	£4/unit	£2/unit
Fitting section	£12/unit	£3/unit	£21/unit
Machine hours	6 hr/unit	3 hr/unit	4 hr/unit

Planned overheads are as follows:

	Machine shop	Fitting section	Canteen	Machine maintenance section	Total
Allocated overheads	£27,660	£19,470	£16,600	£26,650	£90,380
Rent, rates, heat and light					£17,000
Dep'n and insurance of equipment					£25,000
Additional data:					
Gross book value of equipment	£150,000	£75,000	£30,000	£45,000	
Number of employees	18	14	4	4	
Floorspace occupied	3,600 sq m	1,400 sq m	1,000 sq m	800 sq m	

All machining is carried out in the machine shop. It has been estimated that approximately 70% of the machine maintenance section's costs are incurred servicing the machine shop and the remainder servicing the fitting section.

Required:
(a) Calculate the following planned overhead absorption rates:
   (i)   A machine hour rate for the machine shop.
   (ii) A rate expressed as a percentage of direct wages for the fitting section.
(b) Calculate the planned full cost per unit of Product X.

10.6 Shown below is an extract from next year's plans for a business manufacturing three products, A, B and C, in three production departments.

	A	B	C
Production	4,000 units	3,000 units	6,000 units
Direct material cost	£7/unit	£4/unit	£9/unit
Direct labour requirements:			
Cutting department:			
Skilled operatives	3 hr/unit	5 hr/unit	2 hr/unit
Unskilled operatives	6 hr/unit	1 hr/unit	3 hr/unit
Machining department	½ hr/unit	¼ hr/unit	⅓ hr/unit
Pressing department	2 hr/unit	3 hr/unit	4 hr/unit
Machine requirements:			
Machining department	2 hr/unit	1½ hr/unit	2½ hr/unit

The skilled operatives employed in the cutting department are paid £16 an hour and the unskilled operatives are paid £10 an hour. All the operatives in the machining and pressing departments are paid £12 an hour.

	Production departments			Service departments	
	Cutting	Machining	Pressing	Engineering	Personnel
Planned total overheads	£154,482	£64,316	£58,452	£56,000	£34,000
Service department – costs incurred for the benefit of other departments:					
Engineering services	20%	45%	35%	–	–
Personnel services	55%	10%	20%	15%	–

The business operates a full absorption costing system.

Required:
Derive the total planned cost of:

(a) One completed unit of Product A.
(b) One incomplete unit of Product B, which has been processed by the cutting and machining departments but which has not yet been passed into the pressing department.

10.7 Consider this statement:
'In a job costing system, it is necessary to divide up the business into departments. Fixed costs (or overheads) will be collected for each department. Where a particular fixed cost relates to the business as a whole, it must be divided between the departments. Usually this is done on the basis of area of floor space occupied by each department relative to the entire business. When the total fixed costs for each department have been identified, this will be divided by the number of hours that were worked in each department to deduce an overhead recovery rate. Each job that was worked on in a department will have a share of fixed costs allotted to it according to how long it was worked on. The total cost for each job will therefore be the sum of the variable costs of the job and its share of the fixed costs. It is essential that this approach is taken in order to deduce a selling price for the business's output.'

Required:
Prepare a table of two columns. In the first column you should show any phrases or sentences in the above statement with which you do not agree, and in the second column you should show your reason for disagreeing with each one.

10.8 Many businesses charge overheads to jobs on a departmental basis.

Required:
(a) What is the advantage that is claimed for charging overheads to jobs on a departmental basis, and why is it claimed?
(b) What circumstances need to exist to make a difference to a particular job whether overheads are charged on a business-wide basis or on a departmental basis. (Note that the answer to this part of the question is not specifically covered in the chapter. You should, nevertheless, be able to deduce the reason from what you know.)

CHAPTER 11

Costing and pricing in a competitive environment

Introduction

In recent years we have seen major changes in the business world, including deregulation, privatisation, the growing expectations of shareholders and the impact of new technology. These have led to a much more fast-changing and competitive environment that has radically altered the way in which businesses are managed. In this chapter, we consider some of the management accounting techniques that have been developed to help businesses maintain their competitiveness in this new era.

We begin by considering the impact of this new environment on the full-costing approach that we considered in Chapter 10. We shall see that activity-based costing, which is a development of the traditional full-costing approach, takes a much more enquiring, much less accepting attitude towards overheads. We shall also examine some recent approaches to costing that can help lower costs and, therefore, increase the ability of a business to compete on price.

Management accounting embraces both financial and non-financial measures and, in this chapter, we shall consider the increasing importance of non-financial measures in managing a business. These include the Balanced Scorecard approach, which seeks to integrate financial and non-financial measures into a framework for the achievement of business objectives.

We shall go on to consider the idea of shareholder value, which has been a 'hot' issue among managers in recent years. Many leading businesses now claim that the quest for shareholder value is the driving force behind strategic and operational decisions. In this chapter we consider what the term 'shareholder value' means and we shall look at one of the main methods of measuring shareholder value.

Lastly, we shall see how, in theory and in practice, a business can use costing information to aid pricing decisions. This will pick up some of the points on relevant cost and cost–volume–profit relationships that we considered in Chapters 8 and 9.

Learning outcomes

When you have completed this chapter, you should be able to:

● Discuss the nature and practicalities of activity-based costing.

● Explain how new developments such as total life-cycle costing and target costing can be used to control costs.

● Discuss the importance of non-financial measures of performance in managing a business and the way in which the Balanced Scorecard attempts to integrate financial and non-financial measures.

● Explain the term 'shareholder value' and describe the role of EVA® in measuring and delivering shareholder value.

● Explain the theoretical underpinning of pricing and discuss the issues involved in reaching a pricing decision in real-world situations.

MyAccountingLab   **Remember to create your own personalised Study Plan**

Costing and the changed business environment

Costing and pricing in the traditional way

The traditional and still widely used approach to product costing and pricing was developed around the time of the Industrial Revolution, when industry was characterised by:

● *Direct-labour-intensive and direct-labour-paced production.* Labour was at the heart of production. Where machinery was used, it was to support the efforts of direct labour, and the speed of production was dictated by direct labour.
● *A low level of overheads relative to direct costs.* Little was spent on power, personnel services, machinery (leading to low depreciation charges) and other areas typical of the overheads of modern businesses.
● *A relatively uncompetitive market.* Transport difficulties, limited industrial production worldwide and a lack of knowledge by customers of competitors' prices meant that businesses could prosper without being too scientific in costing and pricing their output. Customers tended to accept what the supplier offered, rather than demanding precisely what they wanted.

Since overheads at that time represented a relatively small element of total costs, it was acceptable and practical to deal with them in a fairly arbitrary manner. Little effort was devoted to controlling the cost of overheads because the benefits of better control were relatively small, particularly compared with the benefits from firmer control of direct labour and material costs. It was also reasonable to charge overheads to individual jobs on a direct labour hour basis. Most of the overheads were incurred directly in support of direct labour: providing direct workers with a place to work, heating and lighting that workplace, employing people to supervise the direct workers, and so on. Direct workers, perhaps aided by machinery, carried out all production.

At that time, service industries were a relatively unimportant part of the economy and would have largely consisted of self-employed individuals. These individuals would probably have been uninterested in trying to do more than work out a rough hourly/daily rate for their time and to try to base prices on this.

Costing and pricing in the new environment

In recent years, the world of industrial production has fundamentally altered. Most of it is now characterised by:

● *Capital-intensive and machine-paced production.* Machines are at the heart of much production, including service provision. Most labour supports the efforts of machines, for example technically maintaining them. Also, machines often dictate the pace of production.

● *A high level of overheads relative to direct costs.* Modern businesses tend to have very high depreciation, servicing and power costs. There are also high costs of a nature scarcely envisaged in the early days of industrial production, such as personnel and staff training costs. At the same time, there are very low (sometimes no) direct labour costs. Although direct material cost often remains an important element of total cost, more efficient production methods lead to less waste and, therefore, less total material cost, again tending to make overheads more dominant.

● *A highly competitive, international market.* Production, much of it highly sophisticated, is carried out worldwide. Transport, including fast airfreight, is relatively cheap. Fax, telephone and, particularly, the internet ensure that potential customers can quickly and cheaply find the prices of a range of suppliers. Markets now tend to be highly price competitive. Customers increasingly demand products custom made to their own requirements. This means that businesses need to know their product costs with a greater degree of accuracy than historically has been the case. Businesses also need to take a considered and informed approach to pricing their output.

In the UK, as in many developed countries, service industries now dominate the economy, employing the great majority of the workforce and producing most of the value of productive output. Although there are many self-employed individuals supplying services, many service providers are vast businesses such as banks, insurance companies and cinema operators. For most of these larger service providers, the activities closely resemble modern manufacturing activity. They too are characterised by high capital intensity, overheads dominating direct costs and a competitive international market.

Activity-based costing

In Chapter 10 we considered the traditional approach to job/batch costing (deriving the full cost of output where one unit/batch of output differs from another). This approach is to collect, for each job/batch, those costs that can be unequivocally linked to, and measured in respect of, the particular job/batch (direct costs). All other costs (overheads) are thrown into a pool of costs and charged to individual jobs/batches according to some formula. As we saw in Chapter 10, survey evidence indicates that this formula has usually been on the basis of the number of direct labour hours worked on each particular job/batch.

In the past, overhead recovery rates (that is, rates at which overheads are absorbed by jobs/batches) were typically of a much lower value for each direct labour hour than the rate paid to direct workers as wages or salaries. It is now, however, becoming increasingly common for overhead recovery rates to be between five and ten times the hourly rate of pay, because overheads are now much more significant and the direct labour input much less so. When production is dominated by direct labour paid, say, £8 an hour, it might be reasonable to have an overhead recovery rate of, say, £1 an hour. When, however, direct labour plays a relatively small part in production, to have overhead recovery rates of, say, £50 for each direct labour hour is likely to lead to very arbitrary costing. Even a small change in the amount of direct labour worked on a job/batch could massively affect the total cost deduced. This is not because the direct worker is very highly paid, but because of the effect of the direct labour change on the overhead loading. Also, overheads are still typically charged on a direct labour hour basis even though those overheads may not be particularly closely related to direct labour.

An alternative approach to full costing

As a result of changes in the business environment, the whole question of overheads, what causes them and how they are charged to jobs/batches, has been receiving much closer attention. Historically, businesses have been content to accept that overheads exist and, therefore, for product costing purposes they must be dealt with in as practical a way as possible. In recent years, however, there has been an increasing acceptance of the fact that overheads do not just happen; they must be caused by something. To illustrate this point, let us consider Example 11.1.

Example 11.1

Modern Producers Ltd has, like virtually all manufacturers, a storage area that is set aside for its inventories of finished goods. The costs of running the stores include a share of the factory rent and other establishment costs, such as heating and lighting. They also include the salaries of staff employed to look after the inventories and the cost of financing the inventories held in the stores.

The business has two product lines: A and B. Product A tends to be made in small batches, and low levels of finished inventories are held. The business prides itself on its ability to supply Product B in relatively large quantities instantly. As a consequence, most of the space in the finished goods store is filled with finished Product Bs ready to be despatched immediately an order is received.

Traditionally, the whole cost of operating the stores would have been treated as a general overhead and included in the total of overheads charged to batches, probably on a direct labour hour basis. This means that when assessing the cost of Products A and B, the cost of operating the stores has fallen on them according to the number of direct labour hours worked on each one; a factor that has nothing to do with storage.

In fact, most of the stores cost should be charged to Product B, since this product causes (and benefits from) the stores cost much more than does Product A. Failure to account more precisely for the cost of running the stores is masking the fact that Product B is not as profitable as it seems to be. It may even be leading to losses as a result of the relatively high stores-operating cost that it causes. So far, much of this cost has been charged to Product A without regard to the fact that Product A causes little of it.

What drives the costs?

Realisation that overheads do not just occur, but that they are caused by activities –
such as holding products in stores – that 'drive' the costs, is at the heart of **activity-
based costing (ABC)**. The traditional approach is that direct labour hours are the **cost
driver**, which probably used to be true. ABC recognises that this is often not the case.

There is a basic philosophical difference between the traditional and the ABC
approaches. Traditionally we tend to think of overheads as *rendering a service to cost
units*, the cost of which must be charged to those units. ABC sees overheads as being
caused by activities, and so it is the cost units that cause the activities that must be
charged with the costs that they cause.

Activity 11.1

Can you think of any other purpose that identification of the cost drivers serves, apart
from deriving more accurate costs?

Identification of the activities that cause costs puts management in a position where it may
well be able to control them more effectively.

It is not always easy to see how and why some overhead costs have arisen. This has
traditionally made them more difficult to control than direct labour and material costs.
If, however, an analysis of overheads can identify the cost drivers, questions can be
asked about whether the activity driving certain costs is necessary at all, and whether
the cost justifies the benefit. In Example 11.1, it may well be a good marketing policy
that Product B can be supplied immediately from inventories, but this causes a cost
that should be recognised and assessed against the benefit.

Adopting ABC requires that most overheads can be analysed and the cost drivers
identified. This means that it might be possible to gain much clearer insights about the
overhead costs that are caused, activity by activity, so that fairer and more accurate
product costs can be identified, and costs can be controlled more effectively.

Cost pools

Under ABC, an overhead **cost pool** is established for each cost driver in which all of
the costs caused by that driver are placed. So, the business in Example 11.1 would
create a cost pool for operating the stores. All costs associated with this activity would
be allocated to that cost pool. The total costs in that pool would then be allocated to
output (Products A and B, in this case), using the cost driver identified, according to
the extent to which each unit of output 'drove' those costs.

Example 11.2

The management accountant at Modern Producers Ltd (Example 11.1) has estimated that the costs of running the finished goods stores for next year will be
£90,000. This will be the amount allocated to the 'finished goods stores cost pool'.

It is estimated that each Product A will spend an average of one week in the
stores before being sold. With Product B, the equivalent period is four weeks.

Both products are of roughly similar size and have similar storage needs. It is felt, therefore, that the quantity of each product and the period spent in the stores ('product weeks') are the cost drivers.

It is estimated that, next year, 50,000 Product As and 25,000 Product Bs will pass through the stores. So the total number of 'product weeks' in store will be:

Product A (50,000 × 1 week)	50,000
B (25,000 × 4 weeks)	100,000
	150,000

The stores cost for each 'product week' is given by

$$£90,000/150,000 = £0.60$$

Therefore each Product A will be charged with £0.60 for finished stores costs, and each Product B with £2.40 (that is, £0.60 × 4).

Allocating overhead costs to cost pools, as is necessary with ABC, contrasts with the traditional approach, where the overheads are normally allocated to production departments (cost centres). In both cases, however, the overheads are then charged to cost units (goods or services). The two different approaches are illustrated in Figure 11.1.

With the traditional approach, overheads are apportioned to product departments (cost centres). Each department would then derive an overhead recovery rate, typically overheads per direct labour hour. Overheads would then be applied to units of output according to how many direct labour hours were worked on them.

With ABC, the overheads are analysed into cost pools, with one cost pool for each cost driver. The overheads are then charged to units of output, through activity cost driver rates (for example, £0.60 per 'product week' for the stores cost in Example 11.2). These rates are an attempt to represent the extent to which each cost unit is believed to cause the particular part of the overheads.

Cost pools are much the same as cost centres, except that cost pools are linked to a particular *activity* (operating the stores in Examples 11.1 and 11.2), rather than being more general, as is the case with cost centres in traditional product costing.

ABC and service industries

Much of our discussion of ABC has concentrated on manufacturing industry, perhaps because early users of ABC were manufacturing businesses. In fact, ABC is possibly even more relevant to service industries because, in the absence of a direct material element, a service business's total costs are likely to be largely made up of overheads. There is certainly evidence that ABC has been adopted more readily by businesses that sell services rather than goods, as we shall see later.

Activity 11.2

What is the difference in the way in which direct costs are accounted for when using ABC, relative to their treatment taking a traditional approach to full costing?

The answer is no difference at all. ABC is concerned only with the way in which overheads are charged to jobs to derive the full cost.

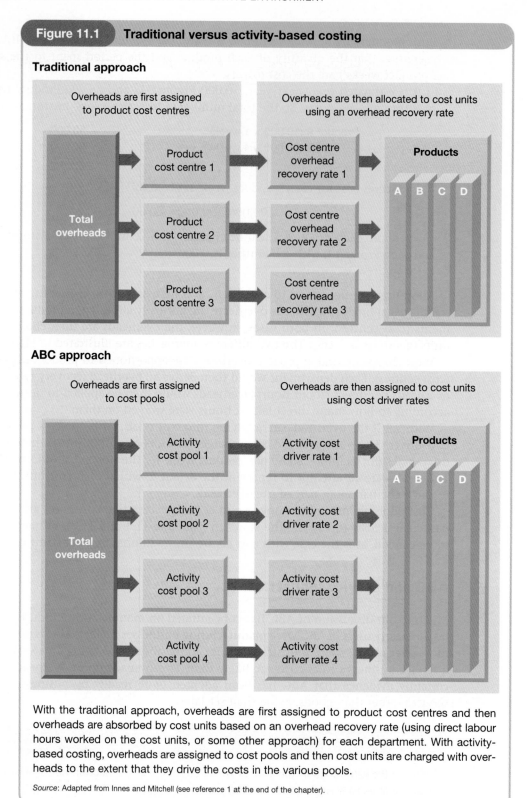

Figure 11.1 Traditional versus activity-based costing

With the traditional approach, overheads are first assigned to product cost centres and then overheads are absorbed by cost units based on an overhead recovery rate (using direct labour hours worked on the cost units, or some other approach) for each department. With activity-based costing, overheads are assigned to cost pools and then cost units are charged with overheads to the extent that they drive the costs in the various pools.

Source: Adapted from Innes and Mitchell (see reference 1 at the end of the chapter).

Example 11.3 provides an example of activity-based costing and brings together the points that have been raised so far.

Example 11.3

Comma Limited manufactures two types of Sprizzer: Standard and Deluxe. Each product requires the incorporation of a difficult-to-handle special part (one of them for a Standard and four for a Deluxe). Both of these products are made in batches (large batches for Standards and small ones for Deluxes). Each new batch requires that the production facilities are 'set up'.

Details of the two products are:

	Standard	Deluxe
Annual sales volume	12,000 units	12,000 units
Sales price per unit	£65	£87
Batch size	1,000 units	50 units
Direct labour time per unit	2 hours	2½ hours
Direct labour rate per hour	£8	£8
Direct material cost per unit	£22	£32
Number of special parts per unit	1	4
Number of set-ups per batch	1	3
Number of separate material issues from stores per batch	1	1
Number of sales invoices issued per year	50	240

In recent months, Comma Limited has been trying to persuade customers who buy the Standard to purchase the Deluxe instead. An analysis of overhead costs for Comma Limited has provided the following information.

Overhead analysis	£	Cost driver
Set-up costs	73,200	Number of set-ups
Special part handling costs	60,000	Number of special parts
Customer invoicing costs	29,000	Number of invoices
Material handling costs	63,000	Number of batches
Other overheads	108,000	Labour hours

Required:

(a) Calculate the profit per unit and the gross profit margin ratio (gross profit/sales revenue × 100%) for Standard and Deluxe Sprizzers using:
   (i) the traditional direct-labour-hour-based absorption of overheads; and
   (ii) activity-based costing methods.
(b) Comment on the managerial implications for Comma Limited of the results in (a) above.

Solution

Using the traditional full (absorption) costing approach that we considered in Chapter 10, the overhead costs are added together and an overhead recovery rate deduced as follows:

Overheads	£
Set-up costs	73,200
Special part handling costs	60,000
Customer invoicing costs	29,000
Material handling costs	63,000
Other overheads	108,000
	333,200

$$\text{Overhead recovery rate} = \frac{\text{Total overheads}}{\text{Number of direct labour hours}}$$

$$= \frac{333,200}{54,000}$$

$$= £6.17 \text{ per hour}$$

The total cost per unit of each type of Sprizzer is calculated by adding the direct costs to the overhead costs per unit. The overhead costs per unit are calculated by multiplying the number of direct labour hours spent on the product (2 hours for each Standard and $2\frac{1}{2}$ hours for each Deluxe) by the overhead recovery rate calculated above. Hence:

	Standard £	Deluxe £
Direct costs:		
Labour	16.00	20.00
Material	22.00	32.00
Indirect costs:		
Overheads (£6.17 per hour)	12.34	15.43
Total cost per unit	50.34	67.43

The gross profit margin ratio is calculated as follows:

	Standard (per unit) £	Deluxe (per unit) £
Selling price	65.00	87.00
Total cost (see above)	50.34	67.43
Gross profit	14.66	19.57
Gross profit margin ratio (gross profit/sales revenue) × 100%	22.55%	22.49%

Using the ABC costing approach, the activity cost driver rate will be calculated as follows:

Overhead cost pool	Driver	(a) Standard driver volume	(b) Deluxe driver volume	(c) Total driver volume (a + b)	(d) Costs £	(e) Driver rate (d/c) £
Set-up	Set-ups per batch	12	720	732	73,200	100
Special part	Special parts per unit	12,000	48,000	60,000	60,000	1
Customer invoices	Invoices per year	50	240	290	29,000	100
Material handling	Number of batches	12	240	252	63,000	250
Other overheads	Labour hours	24,000	30,000	54,000	108,000	2

The activity-based costs are derived as follows:

Overhead cost pool	(f) Total costs Standard (a × e) £	(g) Total costs Deluxe (b × e) £	Unit costs Standard (f/12,000) £	Unit costs Deluxe (g/12,000) £
Set-up	1,200	72,000	0.10	6.00
Special part	12,000	48,000	1.00	4.00
Customer invoices	5,000	24,000	0.42	2.00
Material handling	3,000	60,000	0.25	5.00
Other overheads	48,000	60,000	4.00	5.00
Total overheads			5.77	22.00

The total cost per unit is calculated as follows:

	Standard £/unit	Deluxe £/unit
Direct costs:		
Labour	16.00	20.00
Material	22.00	32.00
Indirect costs:		
Overheads (see above)	5.77	22.00
Total cost per unit	43.77	74.00

The gross profit margin ratio is calculated as follows:

	Standard £/unit	Deluxe £/unit
Selling price	65.00	87.00
Total cost (see above)	43.77	74.00
Profit	21.23	13.00
Gross profit margin ratio (gross profit/sales revenue) × 100%	32.67%	14.94%

The figures show that, under the traditional approach, the gross profit margins are broadly equal between the two approaches. However, the ABC approach shows that the Standard product is far more profitable. Hence, the business should reconsider its policy of trying to persuade customers to switch to the Deluxe product.

Criticisms of ABC

Critics of ABC argue that analysing overheads in order to identify cost drivers is time-consuming and costly, and that the benefit of doing so, in terms of more accurate product costing and the potential for cost control, does not justify the cost of carrying out the analysis. This cost–benefit issue is portrayed in Figure 1.2 (page 10).

ABC is also criticised for the same reason that full costing is generally criticised, which is that it does not provide relevant information for decision making. The point was made in Chapter 10 that full costing tends to use past costs and to ignore opportunity costs. Since past costs are always irrelevant in decision making and opportunity costs can be significant, full costing information is an expensive irrelevance. In contrast, advocates of full costing claim that it *is* relevant, in that it provides a long-run average cost, whereas 'relevant costing', which we considered in Chapter 8, relates only to the specific circumstances of the short term. The use of ABC, rather than the traditional approach to product costing, does not affect the validity of this irrelevance argument.

Even if ABC-derived product costs were not really helpful (and many would argue that they are helpful), identifying the activities that cause the costs may still be well worth doing. As was pointed out above, knowing what drives the costs may make cost control more effective.

Real World 11.1 shows how ABC came to be used at the Royal Mail.

Real World 11.1

Delivering ABC

Early in the 2000s the publicly-owned Royal Mail adopted ABC and used it to find the cost of making postal deliveries. Royal Mail identified 340 activities that gave rise to costs and created a cost pool and identified a cost driver for each of these.

Roger Tabour, Royal Mail's Enterprise Systems Programme Director, explained: 'A new regulatory and competitive environment, plus a down-turned economy, led management to seek out more reliable sources of information on performance and profitability', and this led to the introduction of ABC.

The Royal Mail is a public-sector organisation that is subject to supervision by Postcomm, the UK-government appointed regulatory body. The government requires the Royal Mail to operate on a commercial basis and to make profits.

Source: www.sas.com.

Real World 11.2 provides some indication of the extent to which ABC is used in practice.

Real World 11.2

ABC in practice

A survey of large UK businesses in 1999 revealed that, on average, 15 per cent of businesses fully use an ABC approach to dealing with full costing. A further 8 per cent use it partially. The remaining 77 per cent do not use ABC at all. Even so, there was a surprising range in the level of usage of ABC from industry to industry (see Figure 11.2). It is particularly surprising that so few manufacturing businesses use ABC. The survey showed that it tends to be larger businesses that adopt ABC.

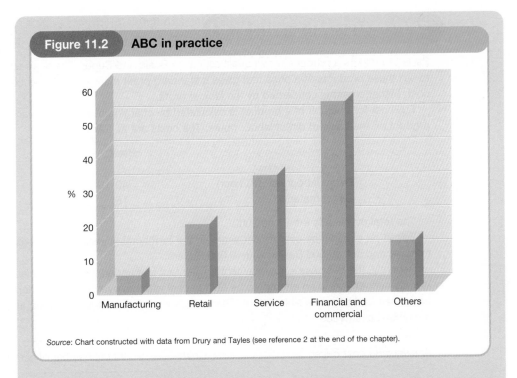

Figure 11.2   **ABC in practice**

Source: Chart constructed with data from Drury and Tayles (see reference 2 at the end of the chapter).

There is some evidence of a decrease in the use of ABC in the late 1990s. A different survey of large UK businesses (conducted by Innes, Mitchell and Sinclair) in 1999, repeated a 1994 survey conducted by the same researchers. They found the following:

	1994	*1999*
	%	%
Currently using ABC	21.0	17.5
Currently considering using ABC	29.6	20.3
Rejected using ABC after assessing it	13.3	15.3

Thus, it seems that both as to current and potential usage of ABC, the method was less popular in 1999 than it had been five years previously.

Source: Innes *et al.* (see reference 3 at the end of the chapter).

A survey of 960 large businesses throughout the world was conducted by Rigby and Bilodeau (R and B) in 2004. About 20 per cent of these businesses were in North America, 30 per cent in Europe, 30 per cent in Asia-Pacific and 10 per cent in Latin America, with the remaining 10 per cent elsewhere.

The survey showed that 52 per cent of businesses used ABC in 2004. This seems at odds with both the Drury and Tayles and the Innes *et al.* findings (above). Explanations of the differences may be as follows:

- The R and B survey was worldwide, whereas the other two related to UK businesses. UK businesses may not use ABC as much as overseas businesses.
- The R and B survey is much more recent than the other two. The Innes *et al.* survey showed a diminishing use of ABC over time, but this may be consistent with the R and B survey. R and B surveyed similar businesses each year starting in 1993. They found a steady rate of usage of ABC of about 50 per cent over this period, except during the four years 1998 to 2002. During that period its popularity fell, so that in 2000 only about 30 per cent of the businesses surveyed used it. Its popularity then recovered. The Innes *et al.* second survey was conducted in 1999.

Source: Rigby and Bilodeau (see reference 4 at the end of the chapter).

Self-assessment question (11.1)

Psilis Ltd makes a product in two qualities, called Basic and Super. The business is able to sell these products at a price that gives a standard profit mark-up of 25 per cent of full cost. Management is concerned by the lack of profit.

Full cost for one unit of a product is calculated by charging overheads to each type of product on the basis of direct labour hours. The costs are as follows:

	Basic	Super
	£	£
Direct labour (all £10/hour)	40	60
Direct material	15	20

The total overheads are £1,000,000.

Based on experience over recent years, in the forthcoming year the business expects to make and sell 40,000 Basics and 10,000 Supers.

Recently, the business's management accountant has undertaken an exercise to try to identify cost drivers in an attempt to be able to deal with the overheads on a more precise basis than had been possible before. This exercise has revealed the following analysis of the annual overheads:

Activity (and cost driver)	Cost	Annual number of activities		
	£000	Total	Basic	Super
Number of machine set-ups	280	100	20	80
Number of quality-control inspections	220	2,000	500	1,500
Number of sales orders processed	240	5,000	1,500	3,500
General production (machine hours)	260	500,000	350,000	150,000
Total	1,000			

The management accountant explained the analysis of the £1,000,000 overheads as follows:

- The two products are made in relatively small batches, so that the amount of the finished product held in inventories is negligible. The Supers are made in very small batches because their demand is relatively low. Each time a new batch is produced, the machines have to be reset by skilled staff. Resetting for Basic production occurs about 20 times a year and for Supers about 80 times: about 100 times in total. The cost of employing the machine-setting staff is about £280,000 a year. It is clear that the more set-ups that occur, the higher the total set-up costs; in other words, the number of set-ups is the factor that drives set-up costs.
- All production has to be inspected for quality and this costs about £220,000 a year. The higher specifications of the Supers mean that there is more chance that there will be quality problems. Thus the Supers are inspected in total 1,500 times annually, whereas the Basics need only about 500 inspections. The number of inspections is the factor that drives these costs.
- Sales order processing (dealing with customers' orders, from receiving the original order to despatching the products) costs about £240,000 a year. Despite the larger amount of Basic production, there are only 1,500 sales orders each year because the Basics are sold to wholesalers in relatively large-sized orders. The Supers are sold mainly direct to the public by mail order, usually in very small-sized orders. It is believed that the number of orders drives the costs of processing orders.

Required:
(a) Deduce the full cost of each of the two products on the basis used at present and, from these, deduce the current selling price.
(b) Deduce the full cost of each product on an ABC basis, taking account of the management accountant's recent investigations.
(c) What conclusions do you draw? What advice would you offer the management of the business?

The answer to this question can be found at the back of the book on pages 702–3.

Other approaches to cost management

The increasingly competitive environment in which modern businesses operate is leading to greater effort being applied in trying to manage costs. Businesses need to keep costs to a minimum so that they can supply goods and services at a price that customers will be prepared to pay and, at the same time, generate a level of profit necessary to meet the businesses' objectives of enhancing shareholder wealth. We have just seen how ABC can help manage costs. We shall now go on to outline some other techniques that have recently emerged in an attempt to meet these goals of competitiveness and profitability. These can be used in conjunction with ABC.

Total (or whole) life-cycle costing

The total (or whole) life cycle of a product or service can be divided into three phases. These are:

1 The *pre-production phase*. During this first phase, research and development of the product or service, as well as market research, is carried out. The product or service is created and so is the means of production or delivery. The phase culminates in setting up the necessary production or delivery facilities and carrying out the initial advertising and promotion.
2 The *production phase* comes next and involves making and selling the product or providing the service to customers.
3 The *post-production phase* comes last. During this phase, any costs necessary to correct faults arising with products or services sold (after-sales service) are incurred. There may also be the costs of closing production at the end of the product's or service's life cycle, such as the cost of decommissioning production facilities. Since after-sales service will tend to arise from as early as the first product or service being sold and probably, therefore, well before the last one is sold, this phase would typically overlap the manufacturing/service-rendering phase.

Businesses may consider environmental costs, as well as the more obvious financial costs, that are involved in the life of a product. The total life cycle is shown in Figure 11.3.

In some types of business, particularly those engaged in an advanced-manufacturing environment, it is estimated that a very high proportion (as much as 80 per cent) of the total costs that will be incurred over the total life of a particular product are either incurred or committed at the pre-production phase. For example, a motor-car

---

Figure 11.3   **The total (whole) life-cycle of a product or service**

Total life cycle of a product or service

Research and development, production set-up, pre-production marketing costs — Pre-production phase

Manufacturing and marketing costs — Production phase

After-sales service and production facility decommissioning costs — Post-production phase

From the producer's viewpoint, the life of a product can be seen as having three distinct phases. During the first the product is developed and everything is prepared so that production and marketing can start. Next comes production and sales. Lastly, dealing with post-production activities is undertaken.

---

manufacturer, when designing, developing and setting up production of a new model, incurs or commits a high proportion of the total costs that will be incurred on that model during the whole of its life. Not only are pre-production costs specifically incurred during this phase, but the need to incur particular costs during the production phase is also established. This is because the design will incorporate features that will lead to particular manufacturing costs. Once the design of the car has been finalised and the manufacturing plant set up, it may be too late to 'design out' a costly feature without incurring another large cost.

Activity (11.3)

A decision taken at the design stage could well commit the business to costs after the manufacture of the product has taken place. Can you suggest a potential cost that could be built in at the design stage that will show itself after the manufacture of the product?

After-sales service costs could be incurred as a result of some design fault. Once the manufacturing facilities have been established, it may not be economic to revise the design but merely to deal with the problem through after-sales service procedures.

→   **Total life-cycle costing** seeks to focus management's attention on the fact that it is not just during the production phase that attention needs to be paid to cost management. By the start of the production phase it is too late to try to manage a large element of the product's, or service's, total life-cycle cost. Efforts need to be made to assess the costs of alternative designs.

There needs to be a review of the product or service over its entire life cycle, which could be a period of twenty years or more. Traditional management accounting, however, tends to be concerned with assessing performance over periods of just one year or less.

Real World 11.3 provides some idea of the extent to which total life-cycle costing is used in practice.

Real World 11.3

Total (whole) life-cycle costing in practice

A survey of management accounting practice in the US was conducted in 2003. Nearly 2,000 businesses replied to the survey. These tended to be larger businesses, of which about 40 per cent were manufacturers and about 16 per cent financial services; the remainder were across a range of other industries.

The survey revealed that 22 per cent extensively use a total life-cycle approach to cost control, with a further 37 per cent considering using the technique in the future.

Although the survey relates to the US, in the absence of UK evidence it provides some insight to what is likely also to be practised in the UK and elsewhere in the developed world.

Source: Ernst and Young (see reference 5 at the end of the chapter).

Real World 11.4 shows how a well-known international car maker uses total life-cycle costing.

Real World 11.4

Total life-cycle costing at Renault

According to Renault, the French motor vehicle manufacturer;

The life of a vehicle is long and comprises several phases:

Design: Creating a vehicle
Manufacturing: Extracting and producing materials, manufacturing and assembling the components, and then the whole vehicle
Distribution: Transition between the vehicle's departure from the production plant and its purchase by a customer
Vehicle service life: The use by the motorist, the longest phase
Recycling.

These phases make up the life cycle. Why the word 'cycle'? Because the end of a vehicle's service life is factored in right from the design phase.

Source: www.renault.com.

Note that Renault divides the *production phase* into two sections: manufacturing and distribution. It also divides the *post-production phase* into vehicle service life and recycling.

Target costing

With traditional cost-plus pricing, costs are totalled for a product or service and a percentage is added for profit to arrive at a selling price. We saw in Chapter 10 that this is not a very practical basis on which to price output for many businesses – certainly not those operating in a price-competitive market. The cost-plus price may well be totally unacceptable to the market. (We shall take another look at this later in this chapter.)

 Target costing approaches the problem from the other direction. First, with the help of market research or other means, a unit selling price and sales volume are established.

From the unit selling price is taken an appropriate amount for profit to meet the business's profit objective. The remaining amount is the target cost, which may well be less than the 'current' cost; thus there may be a 'cost gap'. Efforts are then made to bridge this gap, that is, to provide the service or product in a way that will enable the target cost to be met. These efforts may involve revising the design, finding more efficient means of production or requiring suppliers of goods and services to supply more cheaply.

Target costing is seen as a part of a total life-cycle costing approach, in that cost savings are sought at a very early stage in the life cycle, during the pre-production phase.

Real World 11.5 indicates the level of usage of target costing. This shows quite a low level of usage in both the UK and US. In contrast, survey evidence shows that target costing is very widely used by Japanese manufacturing businesses.

Real World 11.5

Target costing in practice on both sides of the Atlantic

The survey by Drury *et al.* suggests that target costing is not much used by UK businesses: 22 per cent of respondents never use this approach and only 26 per cent use it often or always.

Source: Drury et al. (see reference 6 at the end of the chapter).

The Ernst and Young survey of management accounting practice in the US, conducted in 2003, revealed that 27 per cent of respondents use target costing extensively, with a further 41 per cent considering using the technique in the future.

Source: Ernst and Young (see reference 5 at the end of the chapter).

Activity 11.4

Although target costing seems effective, it has its problems. Can you suggest what these problems might be?

There seem to be three main problem areas:

- It can lead to various conflicts – for example, between the business and its suppliers and between staff within the business.
- It can cause a great deal of stress for employees who are trying to meet target costs that are sometimes extremely difficult to achieve.
- Although, in the end, ways may be found to meet a target cost (through product or service redesign, negotiating lower prices with suppliers and so on), the whole process can be very expensive.

Costing quality control

Such is the importance that customers place on quality that businesses must ensure their output is of a high quality. In a competitive environment, failure to deliver quality will often lead customers to go to another supplier in the future. Businesses need to establish procedures that promote the quality of their output, either by preventing quality problems in the first place or by dealing with them when they occur. These procedures have a cost. It has been estimated that these **quality costs** can amount to up to 30 per cent of total processing costs. These costs tend to be incurred during the *production phase* of the product life cycle and are seen as falling into four main categories:

- *Prevention costs.* These are involved with procedures to try to prevent products being produced that are not up to the required quality. Such procedures might include staff training on quality issues. Some types of prevention costs might be incurred during the *pre-production phase* of the product life cycle, where the production process could be designed in such a way as to avoid quality problems with the output.
- *Appraisal costs.* These are concerned with monitoring raw materials, work in progress and finished products to try to avoid substandard production from reaching the customer.
- *Internal failure costs.* These include the costs of rectifying substandard products before they pass to the customer and the costs of scrap arising from quality failures.
- *External failure costs.* These are involved with rectifying quality problems with products that have passed to the customer. There is also the cost to the business of its loss of reputation from having passed substandard products to the customer.

Figure 11.4 sets these out in diagram form.

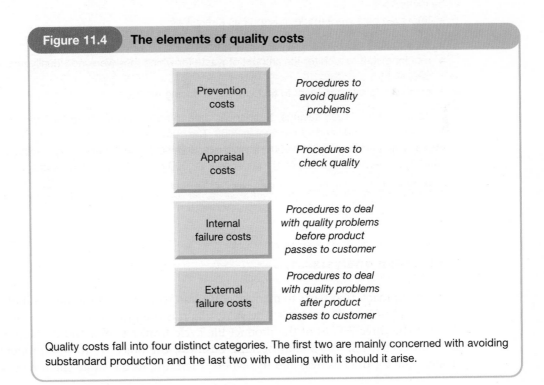

| Figure 11.4 | The elements of quality costs |

Prevention costs — Procedures to avoid quality problems

Appraisal costs — Procedures to check quality

Internal failure costs — Procedures to deal with quality problems before product passes to customer

External failure costs — Procedures to deal with quality problems after product passes to customer

Quality costs fall into four distinct categories. The first two are mainly concerned with avoiding substandard production and the last two with dealing with it should it arise.

Kaizen costing

 Kaizen costing is linked to total life-cycle costing and focuses on cost saving during the production phase. Since this is a relatively late stage in the life cycle (from a cost control point of view), only relatively small cost savings can be made in the production phase. Also, the major production-phase cost savings should already have been made through target costing. The Japanese word *kaizen* implies 'small changes'. The application of the *kaizen* costing approach implies continuous improvement, in terms of cost saving, throughout the production phase.

With *kaizen* costing, efforts are made to reduce the unit manufacturing cost of the particular product or service under review, if possible taking it below the unit cost in the previous period. Target percentage reductions can be set. Usually, production workers are encouraged to identify ways of reducing costs. This is something that the 'hands-on' experience of those workers may enable them to do. Even though the scope to reduce costs is limited at the production stage, valuable savings can still be made.

Real World 11.6 explains how a major UK manufacturer used *kaizen* costing to advantage.

 Real World 11.6

Kaizen costing is part of the package

Kappa Packaging is a major UK packaging business. It has a factory at Stalybridge where it makes, among other things, packaging (cardboard cartons) for glass bottles containing alcoholic drinks. In 2002, Kappa introduced a new approach to reducing the amount of waste paper and cardboard. Before this, the business wasted 14.6 per cent of its raw materials used. This figure was taken as the base against which improvements would be measured.

Improvements were made at Kappa as a result of:

● making staff more aware of the waste problem;
● requiring staff to monitor the amount of waste for which they were individually responsible; and
● establishing a *kaizen* team to find ways of reducing waste.

As a result of *kaizen* savings, Kappa was able to reduce waste from 14.6 per cent to 13.1 per cent in 2002 and 11 per cent in 2003. The business estimates that each 1 per cent waste saving was worth £110,000 a year. So by the end of 2003, Kappa was saving about £400,000 a year, relative to 2001, that is, over £2,000 per employee each year.

Source: Taken from 'Accurate measurement of process waste leads to reduced costs', www.envirowise.gov.uk, 2003.

Value chain analysis

 Another approach that seeks to manage costs, and which recognises the total life-cycle concept, is **value chain analysis**. The value chain is the linking sequence of activities, through the three phases of the product life cycle from research and development to after-sales activities. In a wealth-seeking business, the objective for the product is to create value for the business and its owners. Each link in the value chain represents a particular activity. All of the activities will lead to a cost. Ideally, each link should add value to the product, making the product more valuable to the customer. Any links in the chain that fail to add value should be examined very critically. The purpose of this examination is to assess whether the particular link could be eliminated completely or, at least, have its cost reduced.

An example of a typical non-value-added activity is inspection of the completed product or service by a quality controller. This activity does not add value to the product or service, yet it adds cost. This inspection cost might well be capable of being reduced, or even completely eliminated. The introduction of a 'quality' culture in the business could lead to all output being reliable and not needing to be inspected. This is a development that many modern businesses have achieved.

An example of a value-added activity would be the rendering of a service to a customer for which the customer is prepared to pay more than it cost.

Real World 11.7 provides an example of how non-value-added activities may help transform the nature of the business.

Real World 11.7

Driving in a different direction

In the US, the big three car makers, General Motor, Ford and Chrysler, have suffered from intense competition for market share. They have responded by re-examining all aspects of their businesses in order to save costs and to eliminate non-value-creating activities. They have standardised components across vehicle platforms and brands and have streamlined their purchasing systems so that they deal with fewer suppliers. In the future, they are expected to collaborate strongly with key suppliers over the engineering aspects of cars to explore whether further costs may be saved. It is predicted that this will lead to greater pressure for suppliers to assume responsibility for engineering. This part of the car makers' task will be passed down the 'value chain' so that, ultimately, car makers may simply market and design cars.

Source: Based on information in 'Parts companies feel knock-on effect', FT.com, 4 March 2003.

Real World 11.8 gives some indication of the extent that value chain analysis is used in practice.

Real World 11.8

Value chain analysis in practice

The Ernst and Young survey of management accounting practice in the US, conducted in 2003, revealed that 27 per cent of respondents use value chain analysis extensively, with a further 47 per cent considering using the technique in the future.

Source: Ernst and Young (see reference 5 at the end of the chapter).

Benchmarking

 Benchmarking is an activity – usually a continuing one – where a business, or one of its divisions, seeks to emulate a successful business or division and so achieve a similar level of success. The successful business or division provides a benchmark against which the business can measure its own performance, as well as examples of approaches that can lead to success. Sometimes the benchmark business will help with the activity, but even where no co-operation is given, outside observers can still learn a lot about what makes that business successful.

Real Worlds 11.9 and **11.10** outline the use of benchmarking in practice in the UK, in the public and private sectors respectively.

Real World 11.9

Benchmarking in local government

The Audit Commission is a public body that has a statutory right to investigate public sector organisations and report on the extent to which those organisations provide value for money to the public.

In the context of local government, the Commission sees benchmarking as one way of assessing value for money. It has been doing this since the 1980s, and so while bench-marking may be seen as a recent innovation for businesses, it has a fairly long history in the public sector.

Since the Commission has legal powers, it has been able to insist that the various local government authorities provide information to enable a comprehensive benchmarking operation to take place. Contrast this with the private sector where benchmarking between businesses is difficult because there is no compulsion. Businesses are reluctant to divulge commercially sensitive information to other businesses with which they may be in competition. Often, the best that can be achieved in the private sector is for businesses to benchmark internally, with one division or department comparing itself with another part of the same business.

Real World 11.10

Benchmarking at Saint-Gobain

Saint-Gobain, the France-based business, is the largest glass maker in the world. It operates in 49 different countries through a large number of glass-making plants. Glass for motor vehicles is a major part of its output.

Saint-Gobain's plants are benchmarked against one another, with each being assessed against the best one for the particular feature under consideration. The features that are the subject of benchmarking include:

- safety
- quality of the output
- production cost.

Source: Information taken from 'Factory of the year: Saint-Gobain', Lucy Smy, FT.com, 21 September 2005.

Real World 11.11 gives an indication of the extent that benchmarking is used in practice.

Real World 11.11

Benchmarking in practice

The Ernst and Young survey of management accounting practice in the US, conducted in 2003, revealed that 53 per cent of respondents benchmark extensively, with a further 36 per cent considering using the technique in the future. The Rigby and Bilodeau survey in 2004 of businesses across the world showed that 73 per cent of them used benchmarking and that a similar percentage had done so since 1993. The difference between the results of these two surveys may be accounted for by the fact that the second study seemed just to ask if the technique was used at all, whereas the first asked whether businesses used it extensively.

Sources: Ernst and Young (see reference 5 at the end of the chapter), and Rigby and Bilodeau (see reference 4 at the end of the chapter).

Non-financial measures of performance

Financial measures have long been regarded as the most important measures for a business. They provide us with a valuable means of summarising and evaluating business achievement, and there is no serious doubt about the continued importance of financial measures in this role. However, in recent years there has been increasing recognition that financial measures alone will not provide managers with the information that they require to manage a business effectively. Non-financial measures should also be used to help gain a deeper understanding of the business and to achieve business objectives.

Financial measures portray various aspects of business achievement (for example, sales revenue, profits, return on capital employed) that can help managers determine whether the business is increasing the wealth of its owners. This is vitally important in an increasingly competitive environment, but managers also need to understand what particular things drive the creation of wealth. These **value drivers**, as they are often called, may be such things as employee satisfaction, customer loyalty and the level of product innovation. Often, they do not lend themselves to financial measurement, though non-financial measures may be used to arrive at some indirect means of assessment.

Activity 11.5

How might we measure the following?

(a) Employee satisfaction
(b) Customer loyalty
(c) The level of product innovation.

Activity 11.5 continued

(a) *Employee satisfaction* may be measured through the use of an employee survey. This could examine attitudes towards various aspects of the job, the degree of autonomy that is permitted, the level of recognition and reward received, the level of participation in decision making, the degree of support received in carrying out tasks, and so on. Less direct measures of satisfaction may include employee turnover rates and employee productivity; however, other factors may have a significant influence on these measures.

(b) *Customer loyalty* may be measured through the proportion of total sales generated from existing customers, the number of repeat sales made to customers, the percentage of customers renewing subscriptions or other contracts, and so on.

(c) *The level of product innovation* may be measured through the number of innovations during a period compared with those of competitors, the percentage of sales revenue attributable to recent product innovations, the number of innovations that are brought successfully to market, the number of patents developed and so on.

Real World 11.12 gives an example of a well-known international business that focuses a lot of attention on non-financial measures.

Real World 11.12

Non-financial measures at Pepsi

Pepsi Cola attaches considerable importance to non-financial measures when assessing the success of the business. This is reflected in the fact that managers' bonuses are linked to meeting targets based on non-financial measures, as well as more conventional financial measures. The non-financial measures include:

● market-oriented measures, based on quality, customer attitudes and market share (known as marketplace profit and loss account); and
● employee motivation, based on regular surveys.

Source: Based on information in 'The marketing route to value', *Financial Times*, 14 October 2002.

Financial measures are normally 'lag' indicators, in so far as they tell us about outcomes. In other words, they measure the consequences arising from management decisions that were made earlier. Non-financial measures can also be used as lag indicators of course. They can, however, also be used as 'lead' indicators by focusing on those things that drive the creation of wealth. It is argued that if we measure changes in these value drivers, we may be able to predict changes in future financial performance. For example, we may find from experience that if, during a particular period, there is a 10 per cent fall in the level of product innovation, this will lead to a 20 per cent fall in sales value over the following three periods. In this case, the levels of product innovation can be regarded as a lead indicator that can alert managers to a future decline in sales unless corrective action is taken.

The Balanced Scorecard

One of the most impressive attempts to integrate the use of financial and non-financial measures has been the **Balanced Scorecard**, developed by Robert Kaplan and David

Norton (see reference 7 at the end of the chapter). The Balanced Scorecard is both a management system and a measurement system. In essence, it provides a framework that translates the aims and objectives of a business into a series of key performance measures and targets. This framework is intended to make the strategy of the business more coherent by tightly linking it to particular targets and initiatives. As a result, managers should be able to see more clearly whether the objectives that have been set have actually been achieved.

The Balanced Scorecard approach involves setting objectives and developing appropriate measures and targets in four main areas:

- *Financial*. This area will specify the financial returns required by shareholders and may involve the use of financial measures such as return on capital employed, net profit margin and percentage sales revenue growth.
- *Customer*. This area will specify the kind of customer and/or markets the business wishes to serve and will establish appropriate measures such as customer satisfaction and new customer growth levels.
- *Internal business process*. This area will specify those business processes (for example, innovation, types of operation and after-sales service) that are important to the success of the business and will establish appropriate measures such as percentage of sales from new products, time to market for new products, product cycle times, and speed of response to customer complaints.
- *Learning and growth*. This area will specify the kinds of people, the systems and the procedures that are necessary to deliver long-term business growth. This area is often the most difficult for the development of appropriate measures. However, examples of measures may include employee motivation, employee skills profiles and information systems capabilities.

These four areas are shown in Figure 11.5.

The Balanced Scorecard approach does not prescribe the particular objectives, measures or targets that a business should adopt; this is a matter for the individual business to decide upon. There are differences between businesses in terms of technology employed, organisational structure, management philosophy and business environment, so each business should develop objectives and measures that reflect its unique circumstances. The Balanced Scorecard simply sets out the framework for developing a coherent set of objectives for the business and for ensuring that these objectives are then linked to specific targets and initiatives.

A Balanced Scorecard will be prepared for the business as a whole or, in the case of large, diverse businesses, for each strategic business unit. However, having prepared an overall scorecard, it is then possible to prepare a Balanced Scorecard for each sub-unit, such as a department, within the business. Thus, the Balanced Scorecard approach can cascade down the business and can result in a pyramid of Balanced Scorecards that are linked to the 'master' Balanced Scorecard through an alignment of the objectives and measures employed.

Although a very large number of measures, both financial and non-financial, exist and so could be used in a Balanced Scorecard, only a handful of measures should be employed. A maximum of twenty measures will normally be sufficient to enable the factors that are critical to the success of the business to be captured. (If a business has come up with more than twenty measures, it is usually because the managers have not thought hard enough about what the key measures really are.) The key measures developed should be a mix of lagging indicators (those relating to outcomes) and lead indicators (those relating to the things that drive performance).

| Figure 11.5 | The Balanced Scorecard – for translating a strategy into operational processes |

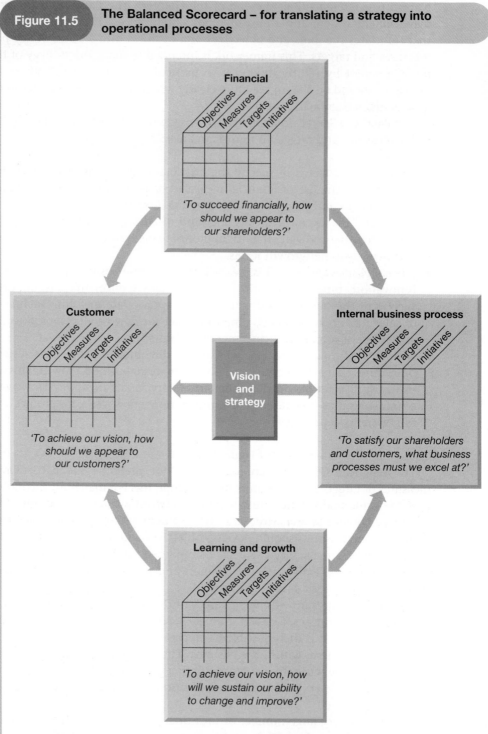

There are four main areas covered by the Balanced Scorecard. Note that, for each area, a fundamental question must be addressed. By answering these questions, managers should be able to develop the key objectives of the business. Once this has been done, suitable measures and targets can be developed that are relevant to those objectives. Finally, appropriate management initiatives will be developed to achieve the targets set.

Source: Kaplan and Norton (see reference 7 at the end of the chapter).

Figure 11.6 shows the cause and effect relationship between the investment in staff development and the business's financial objectives.

Figure 11.6   The cause-and-effect relationship

The investment in staff development is linked through a cause-and-effect relationship to the financial objectives of the business.

Although the Balanced Scorecard employs measures across a wide range of business activity, it does not seek to dilute the importance of financial measures and objectives. In fact, the opposite is true. Kaplan and Norton (see reference 7 at the end of the chapter) emphasise the point that a Balanced Scorecard must reflect a concern for the financial objectives of the business and so measures and objectives in the other three areas that have been identified must ultimately be related back to the financial objectives. There must be a clear cause-and-effect relationship. So, for example, an investment in staff development (in the learning and growth area) may lead to improved levels of after-sales service (internal business process area), which, in turn, may lead to higher

Activity 11.6

Do you think this is a rather hard-nosed approach to dealing with staff development? Should staff development always have to be justified in terms of the financial results achieved?

This approach may seem rather hard-nosed. However, Kaplan and Norton argue that unless this kind of link between staff development and increased financial returns can be demonstrated, managers are likely to become cynical about the benefits of staff development and so the result may be that there will be no investment in staff.

levels of customer satisfaction (customer area) and, ultimately, higher sales revenues and profits (financial area).

We may wonder why this framework is referred to as a *Balanced* Scorecard. According to Kaplan and Norton there are various reasons. First, it is because it aims to strike a balance between *external* measures relating to customers and shareholders, and *internal* measures relating to business process, learning and growth. Secondly, it aims to strike a balance between the measures that portray *outcomes* (lag indicators) and measures that help *predict future performance* (lead indicators). Finally, the framework aims to strike a balance between *hard* financial measures and *soft* non-financial measures.

It is possible to adapt the Balanced Scorecard to fit the needs of the particular business. **Real World 11.13** shows how this has been done by one large UK business.

Real World 11.13

Safety first

Jarvis plc provides infrastructure support services and is engaged in sectors, such as public transport, where safety is of the utmost importance. It has therefore added a fifth element of 'safety' to its Balanced Scorecard. The following extract has been taken from its 2005 annual report.

> A rigorous balanced business scorecard approach to performance has been developed and driven right through the core businesses. This approach is not just about ensuring the highest levels of company performance but also about embedding a stronger culture of social responsibility throughout the business.
>
> The Jarvis Balanced Scorecard measures:
>
> - safety – the number one priority: employee safety, operational safety and environmental protection;
> - learning and growth – innovation, employee development, staff satisfaction;
> - customer satisfaction – quality of service, cost to customer, customer relationships;
> - internal business processes – delivery, operational capability and efficiency, process improvement; and
> - finance – cash, business growth and business sustainability.
>
> Balanced Scorecard measures are entirely linked to the Jarvis business plan and the new approach has been driven through the organisation by way of workshops attended by all members of staff.

Source: Jarvis plc Annual Report and Accounts 2005, p. 69.

Real World 11.14 shows how one large UK business has successfully adopted the Balanced Scorecard and how this has affected its staff. The business is Wolseley plc, which owns several chains of outlets selling to the building trade and DIY customers, including Build Centers and Plumb Centers.

Real World 11.14

Building a Balanced Scorecard   **FT**

Mel Keeley and his staff at the Build Center in Romford, to the east of London, have little time for lofty management theories. They are too busy meeting customer demand for bricks and mortar.

Being at the front line, however, they are the very employees that Wolseley, the international building products group, had to bring on board when it launched a performance measurement system modelled on the Balanced Scorecard, which covers a mix of financial and non-financial targets.

'When it was first presented to us, we were a bit sceptical,' admits Mr Keeley, whose 15 staff supply local builders and DIY enthusiasts with construction materials, interiors and electrical hire equipment.

The highly acquisitive FTSE-100 group introduced the system in its UK 'heavyside' division to improve performance by binding newer and older businesses together with a common culture and objectives. The Balanced Scorecard offsets the traditional bias towards purely financial measures by incorporating factors such as customer satisfaction and staff motivation.

Wolseley realised from the start that if it failed to win over those at the sharp end, the project would be pointless. 'We always had in mind that we were going to be delivering this to hard-nosed branch managers,' says Adrian Barden, UK managing director, who introduced the programme when he was in charge of the division. 'It had to be meaningful and easy to understand and measure, otherwise they would rubbish it.'

Branch managers as well as senior executives were involved in the working party that began designing the programme in late 2001. The team spent several months deciding on the key elements of the business and how to measure them. They settled on 17, from financial indicators such as return on capital employed and sales growth to non-financial measures such as customer satisfaction, branch safety and purchases from preferred suppliers.

To communicate to the branches how they were doing on each measure, the team devised a traffic light system. They discarded references to a 'Balanced Scorecard' in favour of 'R2G' (red-to-green) – shorthand for the drive to improve performance from unacceptable (red) or acceptable (amber) to excellent (green). Results were sent to the branches each month.

'As the results started to come back and we started to hit green and see what it was doing to our branches, we got more and more enthusiastic about it,' says Mr Keeley. 'It keeps you focused on all the major parts of the branch and the business. There are times when you're really busy and you take your eye off a certain aspect of it. This highlights it straightaway.'

Wolseley has done better than most at using a Balanced Scorecard system to achieve its objectives, according to Andy Neely, professor of operations strategy and performance at Cranfield School of Management. 'Its implementation is one of the most robust and effective that I have ever seen,' says Prof Neely, who is completing a study of the scheme for the Advanced Institute for Management Research (AIM).

'There's a lot of rhetoric about the Balanced Scorecard, which says: "If you implement this, you'll move from number three to number one in your industry". Of course it's much more complex. It's the people at the front line, the customer service people, who have to improve the quality of service. If you don't give them data in a form that allows them to understand what to do differently, it's not very helpful.'

Prof Neely compared 156 Wolseley branches using R2G with a control group of 156 plumbing branches that did not use the system. He picked the nearest Plumb Center branches in each case, on average 4.5 km away, controlling for the month, the weather and market demand.

Following the launch of R2G, the build branches showed a statistically significant increase in sales and gross profits compared to the plumb branches. Within the Build division, however, some branches produced better financial results than others. They were the ones that also performed better on non-financial measures such as customer retention.

In other words, some branches were more enthusiastic than others about wooing customers, suppliers and staff under the scheme, and this produced better financial results. To find out why attitudes to these less tangible aspects of performance varied, Prof Neely interviewed 40 managers.

His initial findings show that most reacted well to the scheme. Some came up with creative ways to boost non-financial performance, for example by allocating staff to contact builders who had not visited the branch for a while and persuade them to come back. These managers were asked to share their ideas with other branches.

Real World 11.14 continued

A few branch managers remained sceptical about the scheme and one admitted he had 'never taken a blind bit of notice of it'. This was despite bonuses initially being linked to the scheme's success. Some managers had reservations about measures being too complex or outside their control.

Wolseley's experience demonstrates how a Balanced Scorecard system can improve financial performance. Mr Barden says the company has similar schemes in other divisions, such as the US lumber business, but only uses it where appropriate.

The emphasis now is on giving branch managers a deeper understanding of how the non-financial elements affect performance.

Certain conditions seem to be necessary to maintain improvements in performance: the programme must have commitment from the top; it must be tailored to the needs of the business; it should be adaptable to changing conditions; and it should incorporate incentives, preferably for all staff.

During the evaluation, Wolseley stopped linking managers' and employees' bonuses directly to success in achieving green scores. The link is due to be re-established in August. Mr Keeley, the Romford branch manager, says it proved an important reward, particularly to employees. 'It created a lot more interest within the branch.'

Source: Extracts from 'How to put ideas to work', Alison Maitland, FT.com, 23 May 2006.

As a footnote to our consideration of the Balanced Scorecard, **Real World 11.15** provides an interesting analogy with aeroplane pilots limiting themselves to just one control device.

(UN)Real World 11.15

Fear of flying

Kaplan and Norton invite you to imagine the following conversation between you and the pilot of a jet aeroplane in which you are flying:

Q: I'm surprised to see you operating the plane with only a single instrument. What does it measure?

A: Airspeed. I'm really working on airspeed this flight.

Q: That's good. Airspeed certainly seems important. But what about altitude? Wouldn't an altimeter be helpful?

A: I worked on altitude for the last few flights and I've gotten pretty good on it. Now I have to concentrate on proper airspeed.

Q: But I notice you don't even have a fuel gauge. Wouldn't that be useful?

A: You're right; fuel is significant, but I can't concentrate on doing too many things well at the same time. So on this flight I'm focusing on airspeed. Once I get to be excellent at airspeed, as well as altitude, I intend to concentrate on fuel consumption on the next set of flights.

The point they are trying to make (apart from warning you against flying with a pilot like this) is that to fly an aeroplane, which is a complex activity, a wide range of navigation instruments is required. A business, however, can be even more complex to manage than an aeroplane and so a wide range of measures, both financial and non-financial, is necessary. Reliance on financial measures is not enough and so the Balanced Scorecard aims to provide managers with a more complete navigation system.

Source: Kaplan and Norton (see reference 7 at the end of the chapter).

Measuring shareholder value

Traditional measures of financial performance have been subject to much criticism in recent years and new measures have been advocated to guide and to assess strategic management decisions. In this section we shall consider one such measure, which is based on the idea of increasing shareholder value. Before examining this method, we shall first consider why increasing shareholder value is regarded as the ultimate financial objective of a business.

The quest for shareholder value

For some years, shareholder value has been a 'hot' issue among managers. Many leading businesses now claim that the quest for shareholder value is the driving force behind their strategic and operational decisions. As a starting point, we shall consider what is meant by the term 'shareholder value'.

In simple terms, shareholder value is about putting the needs of shareholders at the heart of management decisions. It is argued that shareholders invest in a business with a view to increasing their wealth. This means generating financial returns that are high in relation to the associated risks. As managers are appointed by the shareholders to act on their behalf, management decisions and actions should therefore reflect a concern for enhancing shareholders' wealth. Though the business may have other 'stakeholder' groups, such as employees, customers and suppliers, it is the shareholders that are usually seen as the pre-eminent group.

This, of course, is not a new idea. As we discussed in Chapter 1, increasing shareholders' wealth is assumed to be the key objective of a business. However, not everyone accepts this idea. Some believe that a balance must be struck between the competing claims of the various stakeholders. A debate concerning the merits of each viewpoint is beyond the scope of this book; however, it is worth pointing out that, in recent years, the business environment has radically changed.

In the past, shareholders have been accused of being too passive and of accepting too readily the profits and dividends that managers have delivered. However, this has changed. Shareholders are now much more assertive, and, as owners of the business, are in a position to insist that their needs are given priority. Since the 1980s we have witnessed the deregulation and globalisation of business, as well as enormous changes in technology. The effect has been to create a much more competitive world. This has meant not only competition for products and services but also competition for funds. Businesses must now compete more strongly for shareholder funds and so must offer competitive rates of return.

Thus, self-interest may be the most powerful reason for managers to commit themselves to improving shareholders' wealth. If they do not do this, there is a real risk that shareholders will either replace them with managers who will, or shareholders will allow the business to be taken over by another business that has managers who are more focused on the shareholders' economic welfare.

How can shareholder value be created?

Creating shareholder value involves a four-stage process. The first stage is to set objectives for the business that recognise the central importance of enhancing shareholders' wealth. This will set a clear direction for the business. The second stage is to establish an appropriate means of measuring the value that has been generated for shareholders. For reasons that we shall discuss later, the traditional methods of measuring returns to shareholders are inadequate for this purpose. The third stage is to manage the business in such a manner as to ensure that shareholder wealth is enhanced. This means setting demanding targets and then achieving them through the best possible use of resources, the use of incentive systems and the embedding of a shareholder value culture throughout the business. The final stage is to measure the shareholder returns over a period of time to see whether the objectives are being achieved.

Figure 11.7 shows the shareholder value creation process.

Figure 11.7 **The four-stage process for creating shareholder value**

Set objectives that recognise the supremacy of shareholders

Select an appropriate measure of shareholder return

Generate shareholder returns through focused management

Measure shareholder returns to see whether the objectives are being achieved

There are four stages in the process required to create shareholder value.

The need for new measures

Given a commitment to increase shareholder value, we must select an appropriate measure that will help us assess the returns to shareholders over time. It is argued that the traditional methods for measuring shareholder returns are seriously flawed and so should not be used for this purpose.

Activity (11.7)

What are the traditional methods of measuring shareholder returns?

The traditional approach is to use accounting profit or some ratio that is based on accounting profit, such as return on shareholders' funds or earnings per share.

There are broadly four problems with using accounting profit, or a ratio based on profit, to assess shareholder returns. These are:

- *Profit is measured over a relatively short period of time* (usually one year). However, when we talk about enhancing shareholder wealth, we are concerned with improving returns over the *long term*. It has been suggested that using profit as the key measure will run the risk that managers will take decisions that improve performance in the short term, but which may have an adverse effect on long-term performance. For example, profits may be increased in the short term by cutting back on staff training and research expenditure. However, this type of expenditure may be vital to long-term survival.

- *Risk is ignored.* A fundamental business reality is that there is a clear relationship between the level of returns achieved and the level of risk that must be taken to achieve those returns. The higher the level of returns required, the higher the level of risk that must be taken to achieve the returns. A management strategy that produces an increase in profits can reduce shareholder value if the increase in profits achieved is not commensurate with the increase in the level of risk. Thus, profit alone is not enough.

- *Accounting profit does not take account of all of the costs of the capital invested by the business.* The conventional approach to measuring profit will deduct the cost of borrowings (that is, interest charges) in arriving at net profit, but there is no similar deduction for the cost of shareholder funds. (Any dividends paid, which are part of the return to shareholders, are deducted after arriving at the net profit figure.) Critics of the conventional approach point out that a business will not make a profit, in an economic sense, unless it covers the cost of all funds invested, including shareholder funds. Unless this done, the business will operate at a loss and so shareholder value will be reduced.

- *Accounting profit reported by a business can vary according to the particular accounting policies that have been adopted.* The way that accounting profit is measured can vary from one business to another. Some businesses adopt a very conservative approach, which would be reflected in particular accounting policies such as immediately treating some intangible assets (for example, research and development and goodwill) as expenses ('writing them off') rather than retaining them on the balance sheet as assets. Similarly, the use of the reducing-balance method of depreciation (which means high depreciation charges in the early years) can reduce profit in those early years.

Businesses that adopt less conservative accounting policies would report higher profits in the early years of owning depreciating assets. Writing off intangible assets over a long time period (or perhaps, not writing off intangible assets at all), or the use of the straight-line method of depreciation, will have this effect. In addition, there may be some businesses that adopt particular accounting policies or carry out particular transactions in a way that paints a picture of financial health that is in line with what those who prepared the financial statements would like shareholders and other users to see, rather than what is a true and fair view of financial performance and position. This practice, known as 'creative accounting', was discussed in Chapter 5 (page 180). It has been a major problem for accounting rule makers, for society generally and for those trying to measure the creation of shareholder value.

Economic value added (EVA®)

 Economic value added (EVA®) has been developed and trademarked by a US management consultancy firm, Stern Stewart. However, EVA® is based on the idea of economic profit, which has been around for many years. The measure reflects the point made earlier that, for a business to be profitable in an economic sense, it must generate returns that exceed the required returns of investors. It is not enough simply to make an accounting profit, because this measure does not take full account of the returns required by investors.

EVA® indicates whether or not the returns generated exceed the required returns by investors. The formula is as follows:

$$EVA® = NOPAT - (R \times C)$$

where: NOPAT = net operating profit after tax
  R = required returns of investors
  C = capital invested (that is, the net assets of the business).

Only when EVA® is positive can we say that the business is increasing shareholder wealth. The higher the EVA®, the greater the increase in shareholder wealth.

Activity 11.8

Can you suggest what managers might do in order to increase EVA®? (*Hint*: Use the formula shown above as your starting point.)

The formula suggests that in order to increase EVA®, managers may try to do the following:

- Increase NOPAT. This may be done either by reducing expenses or by increasing sales revenue.
- Reduce capital invested by using assets more efficiently. This means selling off any assets that are not generating adequate returns and investing in assets that are generating a satisfactory NOPAT.
- Reduce the required rates of return for investors. This may be achieved by changing the capital structure in favour of loan capital (which tends to be cheaper to service than share capital). However, this strategy can create problems.

Real World 11.16 sets out the EVA® measures for one major international business.

Real World 11.16

EVA®-lite

SABMiller is one of the world's largest brewers, with operations in over 40 countries. Among its portfolio of branded beers is the well-known Miller Lite. Each year, the business measures economic value added and publishes this information in its annual reports. Below are its EVA® measures for the period 2003 to 2005.

	2005 US$m	2004 US$m	2003 US$m
Net operating profit after tax	1,593	1,243	837
Capital charge	(1,088)	(1,002)	(773)
EVA®	505	241	64
Required returns for investors	8.75%	8.75%	9.0%

We can see that the business has achieved a dramatic increase in EVA® over the three-year period.

Source: SABMiller Annual Reports 2004 and 2005.

EVA® relies on conventional financial statements (income statement and balance sheet) to measure the wealth created for shareholders. However, the NOPAT and capital figures shown on these statements are used only as a starting point. They have to be adjusted because of the problems and limitations of conventional measures. According to Stern Stewart, the major problem is that profit and capital are understated because of the conservative bias in accounting measurement.

Profit is understated as a result of judgemental write-offs (such as goodwill written off or research and development expenditure written off) and as a result of excessive provisions being created (such as allowances for receivables). Both of these stem from taking an unrealistically pessimistic view of the value of some of the business's assets.

Capital is also understated because assets are reported at their original cost (less amounts written off for depreciation and so on), which can produce figures considerably below current market values. In addition, certain assets, such as internally generated goodwill and brand names, are omitted from the financial statements because no external transactions have occurred.

Stern Stewart has identified more than 100 adjustments that could be made to the conventional financial statements in order to eliminate the conservative bias. However, it is believed that, in practice, only a handful of adjustments will usually have to be made to the accounting figures of any particular business. Unless an adjustment is going to have a significant effect on the calculation of EVA® it is really not worth making. The adjustments made should reflect the nature of the particular business. Each business is unique and so must customise the calculation of EVA® to its particular circumstances. (This aspect of EVA® can be seen either as indicating flexibility or as being open to manipulation depending on whether you support this measure.)

The most common adjustments that have to be made are:

- *Research costs and similar costs.* In theory, these costs should be written off (treated as an expense) over time as they provide benefit to the business. In practice, however, they are usually written off in the period in which they are incurred. This means that any amounts written off immediately should be added back to the assets on the balance sheet, thereby increasing invested capital, and then written off over time.

- *Goodwill.* Goodwill may be written off over time. However, Stern Stewart suggests leaving goodwill on the balance sheet. One argument in favour of this treatment is that goodwill is really a 'catch-all' that includes intangible items such as brand names and reputation that have infinite lives. Thus any amounts written off should be added back to assets.

- *Restructuring costs.* This item can be viewed as an investment in the future rather than an expense to be written off. Supporters of EVA® argue that, by restructuring, the business is better placed to meet future challenges, and so any amounts incurred should be added back to assets.

- *Marketable investments.* Investments in shares and loan capital are not included as part of the capital invested in the business. This is because the income from marketable investments is not included in the calculation of operating profit. (Income from this source will be added in the income statement *after* operating profit has been calculated.)

Let us now consider a simple example to show how EVA® may be calculated.

Example 11.4

Scorpio plc was established two years ago and has produced the following balance sheet and income statement at the end of the second year of trading.

Balance sheet as at the end of the second year

	£m	£m
Non-current assets		
Goodwill	24.0	
Plant and equipment	56.0	
Motor vehicles	12.4	
Marketable investments	6.6	99.0
Current assets		
Inventories	34.5	
Trade receivables	29.3	
Cash	2.1	65.9
Total assets		164.9
Equity		
Share capital	60.0	
Reserves	23.7	83.7
Non-current liabilities		
Borrowings – Loan notes		50.0
Current liabilities		
Trade payables	29.4	
Taxation	1.8	31.2
Total equity and liabilities		164.9

Income statement for the second year

	£m
Revenue	148.6
Cost of sales	(76.2)
Gross profit	72.4
Wages	(24.5)
Depreciation of plant and equipment	(8.8)
Goodwill written off	(4.0)
Marketing costs	(22.5)
Allowance for trade receivables (doubtful debts)	(4.5)
Operating profit	8.1
Income from investments	0.4
	8.5
Interest payable	(0.5)
Profit before taxation	8.0
Restructuring costs	(2.0)
Profit before taxation	6.0
Taxation	(1.8)
Profit for the year	4.2

Discussions with the finance director reveal the following:

1 Goodwill was purchased during the first year of trading when another business was acquired. The goodwill cost £32.0m and this amount is being written off over an eight-year period (starting in the first year of the business).

2 Marketing costs relate to the launch of a new product. The benefits of the marketing campaign are expected to last for a three-year period (including this most recent year).

3 The allowance for trade receivables (doubtful debts) was created this year and the amount of the provision is very high. A more realistic figure for the provision would be £2.0m.

4 Restructuring costs were incurred as a result of a collapse in a particular product market. By restructuring the business, benefits are expected to flow for an infinite period.

5 The business has a required rate of return for investors of 10 per cent a year.

The first step in calculating EVA® is to adjust the net operating profit after taxation to take account of the various points revealed from the discussion with the finance director. The revised figure is calculated as follows:

NOPAT adjustment

	£m	£m
Operating profit		8.1
Taxation		(1.8)
		6.3
EVA® adjustments (to be added back to profit)		
Goodwill (Note 1)	4.0	
Marketing costs ($^2/_3$ × 22.5) (Note 2)	15.0	
Excess allowance for trade receivables (doubtful debts)	2.5	21.5
Adjusted NOPAT		27.8

The next step is to adjust the net assets (as represented by share capital and reserves and loan notes) to take account of the points revealed.

Adjusted net assets (or capital invested)

	£m	£m
Net assets according to the balance sheet (83.7 + 50)		133.7
Add		
Goodwill adjustment (Note 1)	8.0	
Marketing costs (Note 2)	15.0	
Allowance for trade receivables (doubtful debts)	2.5	
Restructuring costs (Note 3)	2.0	27.5
		161.2
Less		
Marketable investments (Note 4)		6.6
Adjusted net assets		154.6

Notes:

1 The goodwill adjustment takes account of the fact that there was a £4.0m write-off in years 1 and 2.

2 The marketing costs represent two years' benefits added back ($^2/_3$ × £22.5m).

3 The restructuring costs are added back to the net assets as they provide benefits over an infinite period. (Note that they were not added back to the operating profit, as these costs were deducted *after* arriving at operating profit in the income statement.)

4 The marketable investments do not form part of the operating assets of the business and the income from these investments is not part of the operating income.

Activity (11.9)

Can you work out the EVA® for the second year of the business in Example 11.4?

EVA® can be calculated as follows:

$$EVA® = NOPAT - (R \times C)$$
$$= £27.8m - (10\% \times £154.6m)$$
$$= £12.3m \text{ (to one decimal place)}$$

Thus, we can see that the business increased shareholder wealth during the year.

The main advantage of this measure is the discipline to which managers are subjected as a result of the charge for capital that has been invested. Before any increase in shareholder wealth can be recognised, an appropriate deduction is made for the use of business resources. Thus EVA® encourages managers to use these resources efficiently. Where managers are focused simply on increasing profits, there is a danger that the resources used to achieve any increase in profits will not be taken into proper account.

Real World 11.17 provides an example of the use of EVA® by a well-known German business in an attempt to generate shareholder value.

Real World 11.17

VW changes gear

Following a change in top management, the German car maker VW has begun to focus more attention on controlling its capital spending. In particular, research and development expenditure is seen as a key area to be contained. The size of the problem is partly illustrated by the fact that the first-half-year results for 2003 showed that the cash flow from auto operations was €1bn less than needed to cover the €3.9bn of investment and research and development expenditure. In the drive to contain capital spending, performance measures such as return on sales revenue are being abandoned in favour of performance measures that focus on the profitable use of capital. One effect of this change is that bonuses of managers are to be linked to EVA® to encourage them to reduce their capital requirements.

Source: Based on information in 'VW signals passing of the age of engineers', FT.com, 7 September 2003.

Real World 11.18 gives some indication of the extent of the usage of value-based management (of which EVA® is an example) in the US.

Real World 11.18

The extent of the use of value-based management in practice

The Ernst and Young survey of management accounting practice in the US, conducted in 2003, revealed that 52 per cent of respondents use value-based management, with a further 40 per cent considering using this approach in the future.

Source: Ernst and Young (see reference 5 at the end of the chapter).

Pricing

As we saw in Chapter 10, full costs can be used as a basis for setting prices for the business's output. We also saw that it can be criticised in that role. In this section we are going to take a closer look at pricing. We shall begin by considering some theoretical aspects of the subject before going on to look at some more practical issues, particularly the role of management accounting information in pricing decisions.

Economic theory

In most market conditions, the price charged by a business will determine the number of units sold. This is shown graphically in Figure 11.8.

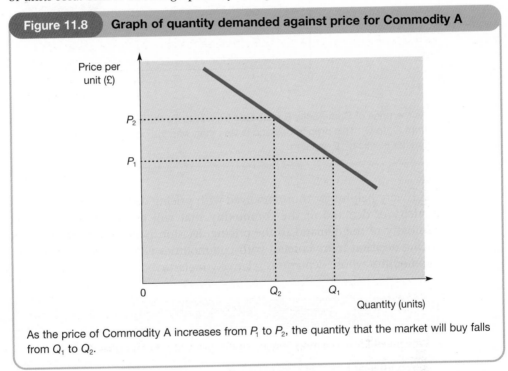

Figure 11.8 Graph of quantity demanded against price for Commodity A

As the price of Commodity A increases from P_1 to P_2, the quantity that the market will buy falls from Q_1 to Q_2.

Figure 11.8 shows the number of units of output that the market would demand at various prices. As price increases, the less willing are people to buy the commodity (call it Commodity A). At a relatively low price a unit (P_1), the quantity of units demanded by the market (Q_1) is fairly high. When the price is increased to P_2, the demand decreases to Q_2. The graph shows a linear (straight-line) relationship between the price and demand. In practice, the relationship, though broadly similar, may not be quite so straightforward.

Not all commodities show exactly the same slope of line. Figure 11.9 shows the demand/price relationship for Commodity B, a different commodity from the one depicted in Figure 11.8.

Although a rise in price of Commodity B, from P_1 to P_2, causes a fall in demand, the fall in demand is much smaller than is the case for Commodity A with a similar rise in price. As a result, we say that Commodity A has a higher **elasticity of demand** than Commodity B. Demand for A reacts much more dramatically (stretches more) to price changes than does demand for B. Elastic demand tends to be associated with commodities that are not essential, perhaps because there is a ready substitute.

Figure 11.9   **Graph of quantity demanded against price for Commodity B**

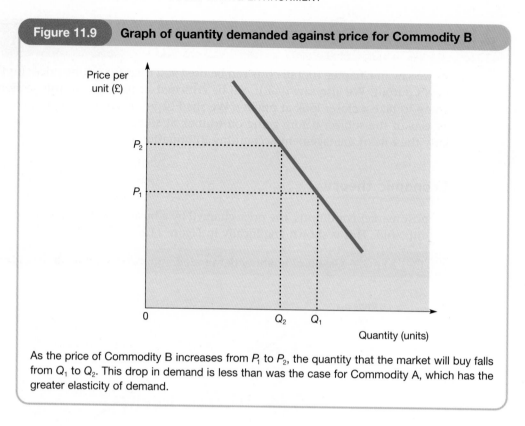

As the price of Commodity B increases from P_1 to P_2, the quantity that the market will buy falls from Q_1 to Q_2. This drop in demand is less than was the case for Commodity A, which has the greater elasticity of demand.

It is very helpful for those involved with pricing decisions to have some feel for the elasticity of demand of the commodity that will be the subject of a decision. The sensitivity of the demand to the pricing decision is obviously much greater (and the pricing decision more crucial) with commodities whose demand is elastic than with commodities whose demand is relatively inelastic.

Activity (11.10)

Which would be the more elastic of the following commodities?

- A particular brand of chocolate bar
- Mains electricity supply.

A branded chocolate bar seems likely to have a fairly *elastic* demand. This is for several reasons, including the following:

- Few buyers of the bar would feel that chocolate bars are essentials.
- Other chocolate bars, probably quite similar to the one in question, will be easily available.

Mains electricity probably has a relatively *inelastic* demand. This is because:

- Many users of electricity would find it very difficult to manage without fuel of some description.
- For neither household nor business users of electricity is there an immediate, practical substitute. For some uses of electricity – for example, powering machinery – there is probably no substitute. Even for a purpose such as heating, where there are substitutes such as gas and oil, it may be impractical to switch to the substitute because gas and oil heating appliances are not immediately available and are costly to acquire.

Real World 11.19 provides an insight to price elasticity and the pharmaceutical industry.

Real World 11.19

The price of drugs

GlaxoSmithKline plc (GSK) is a leading pharmaceutical business based in the UK. In recent years it has been under pressure, along with other major pharmaceutical businesses, to provide low-priced drugs to developing countries to help combat life-threatening diseases such as Aids and malaria. Although the business has gone some way to meet this challenge, Mr Garnier, the chief executive of GSK, has hinted that the business may make even greater cuts in the price of drugs for developing countries. He believes that the price of drugs in these countries is elastic and has argued that 'price elasticity means substantial cuts could trigger greater volumes'.

Source: Based on information in 'Garnier outlines four-point plan to help GSK's health', FT.com, 30 December 2005.

Real World 11.20 looks at another business's experience of price elasticity.

Real World 11.20

Elasticity of demand at Disney World depends on where the customers live

Disney World, the world-famous theme park in Florida, US, experiences different price elasticity for entry to the park between local residents and those coming from further afield. Disney World has found that demand from local residents is much more affected by price increases than is the case with others. It offers discounts of up to 50 per cent for Florida residents because it finds that, at the lower price, they tend to visit the park more than once. Those coming greater distances tend to visit only once almost irrespective of the price of admission.

Source: Information taken from 'Go figure . . .', Tim Harford, FT.com, 21 October 2005.

As we saw in Chapter 1, the objective of most businesses is to enhance the wealth of their owners. Broadly speaking, this will be best achieved by seeking to maximise profits, that is, having the largest possible difference between total costs and total revenues. Thus, prices should be set in a way that is likely to have this effect. To be able to do this, the managers need to have some insight to the way in which costs and prices relate to volume of output.

Figure 11.10 shows the relationship between cost and volume of output, which we have already met in Chapter 9.

The figure shows that the total cost of providing a particular commodity (Service X) increases as the quantity of output increases. It is shown here as a straight line. In practice it may be curved, either curving upwards (tending to become closer to the vertical) or flattening out (tending to become closer to the horizontal). The figure assumes that the marginal cost of each unit is constant over the range shown.

Figure 11.10 Graph of total cost against quantity (volume) of output of Service X

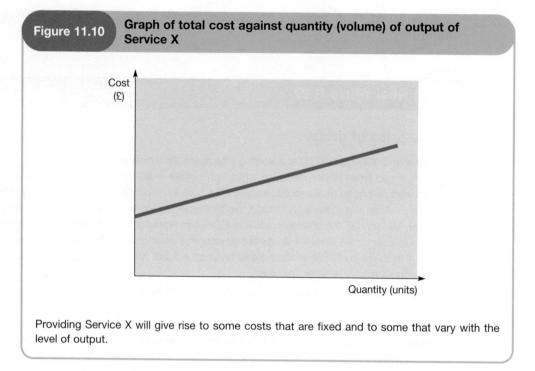

Providing Service X will give rise to some costs that are fixed and to some that vary with the level of output.

Activity 11.11

What general effect would tend to cause the total cost line in Figure 11.10 to (a) curve towards the vertical, and (b) curve towards the horizontal? (You may recall that we considered this issue in Chapter 9.)

(a) Curving towards the vertical would mean that the marginal cost (additional cost of making one more) of each successive unit of output would become greater. This would probably imply that increased activity would be causing a shortage of supply of some factor of production, which had the effect of increasing cost prices. This might be caused by a shortage of labour, meaning that overtime payments would need to be made to encourage people to work the hours necessary for increased production. It might also/alternatively be caused by a shortage of raw materials. Perhaps normal supplies were exhausted at lower levels of output and more expensive sources had to be used to expand output.

(b) Curving towards the horizontal might be caused by the business being able to exploit the economies of scale at higher levels of output, making the marginal cost of each successive unit of output cheaper. Perhaps higher volumes of output enable division of labour or more mechanisation. Possibly, suppliers of raw materials offer better deals for larger orders.

Figure 11.11 shows the total sales revenue against quantity of Service X sold. The total sales revenue increases as the quantity of output increases, but only up to a certain point.

Figure 11.11 — Graph of total sales revenue against quantity (volume) sold of Service X

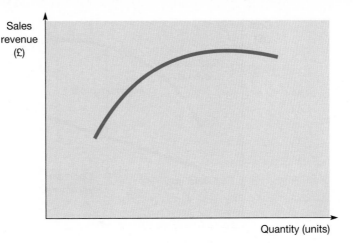

As more units of Service X are sold, the total sales revenue initially increases, but at a declining rate. This is because, in order to persuade people to buy increasing quantities, the price must be reduced. Eventually the price will have to be reduced so much to encourage additional sales that the total sales revenue will fall as the number of units sold increases.

Activity 11.12

What does Figure 11.11 suggest about the average price for a unit of Service X as the number of units sold increases?

The graph suggests that, to sell more units, the price must be lowered, meaning that the average price for each unit of output reduces as the volume sold increases. As we discussed earlier in this section, this is true of most markets found in practice.

Figure 11.11 implies that there will come a point where, to make increased sales, prices will have to be reduced by so much that total sales revenue will not increase; it may even reduce.

In Chapter 9, when we considered break-even analysis, we assumed a steady price per unit over the range that we were considering. Now we are saying that, in practice, it does not work like this. How can these two positions be reconciled? The answer is that, when we dealt with break-even analysis we were considering only a relatively small range of output, namely from zero sales revenue to the break-even point. It may well be that over a small range, particularly at low levels of output, a constant sales price per unit is a reasonable assumption. That is to say that, to the left of the curve in Figure 11.10 there may be a straight line from zero up to the start of the curve.

There is nothing in break-even analysis that demands that the assumption about steady selling prices is made, but making it does mean that the analysis is very straightforward.

Figure 11.12 combines information about total sales revenue and total cost for Service X over a range of output levels.

Figure 11.12 Graph of total sales revenue and total cost against quantity (volume) of output of Service X

Profit is the vertical distance between the total cost and total sales revenue lines. For a wealth-maximising business, the optimum level of sales will occur when this is at a maximum.

The total sales revenue increases, but at a decreasing rate, and the total cost of production increases as the quantity of output increases. The maximum profit is made where the total sales revenue and total cost lines are vertically furthest apart. At the left-hand end of the graph we are clearly above break-even point because the total sales revenue line has already gone above the total cost line. At the lower levels of volume of sales and output, the total sales revenue line is climbing faster than the total cost line. The business will wish to keep expanding output as long as this continues to be the case, because profit is the vertical distance between the two lines. A point will be reached where the total sales revenue line flattens towards the horizontal to such an extent that further expansion will reduce profit.

The point at which profit is maximised is where the two lines stop diverging, that is, the point at which the two lines are climbing at exactly the same rate. Thus we can say that profit is maximised at the point where:

Marginal sales revenue = Marginal cost of production

that is:

$$\begin{bmatrix} \text{Increase in total sales} \\ \text{revenue from selling} \\ \text{one more unit} \end{bmatrix} = \begin{bmatrix} \text{Increase in total costs} \\ \text{that will result from} \\ \text{selling one more unit} \end{bmatrix}$$

To see how this approach can be applied, consider Example 11.5.

Example 11.5

A schedule of predicted total sales revenue and total costs at various levels of provision for Service Y is shown in columns (a) and (c) of the table.

Quantity of output Units	(a) Total sales revenue £	(b) Marginal sales revenue £	(c) Total cost £	(d) Marginal cost £	(e) Profit/(loss) £
0	0		0		0
1	1,000	1,000	2,300	2,300	(1,300)
2	1,900	900	2,600	300	(700)
3	2,700	800	2,900	300	(200)
4	3,400	700	3,200	300	200
5	4,000	600	3,500	300	500
6	4,500	500	3,800	300	700
7	4,900	400	4,100	300	800
8	5,200	300	4,400	300	800
9	5,400	200	4,700	300	700
10	5,500	100	5,000	300	500

Column (b) is deduced by taking the total sales revenue for one less unit sold from the total sales revenue at the sales level under consideration (column (a)). For example, the marginal sales revenue of the fifth unit of the service sold (£600) is deduced by taking the total sales revenue for four units sold (£3,400) away from the total sales revenue for five units sold (£4,000).

Column (d) is deduced similarly, but using total cost figures from column (c). Column (e) is found by deducting column (c) from column (a).

It can be seen by looking at the profit/(loss) column that the maximum profit occurs with an output of seven or eight units (£800). Thus the maximum output should be eight units of the service. This is the point where marginal cost and marginal revenue are equal (at £300).

Figure 11.13 shows the total cost and total revenue for Service Y in Example 11.5.

Figure 11.13   The cost and sales revenue curves for Service Y (Example 11.5)

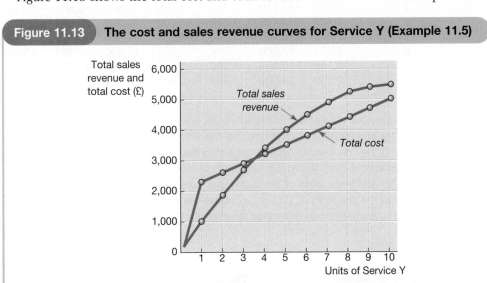

The profit (or loss) at any particular level of activity (sales of the service) is the difference between the total sales revenue and the total cost. On the graph, the vertical distance between the two curves gives this. Note that the highest profit occurs where the marginal cost equals the marginal sales revenue, that is, where the two curves run parallel to one another.

Activity (11.13)

Specialist Ltd makes a very specialised machine that is sold to manufacturing businesses. The business is about to commence production of a new model of machine for which facilities exist to produce a maximum of 10 machines each week. To assist management in a decision on the price to charge for the new machine, two pieces of information have been collected:

- *Manufacturing costs.* Fixed costs associated with manufacture of the machine are estimated at £3,000 a week. Since the work is highly labour intensive and labour is in short supply, unit variable costs are expected to be progressive. The manufacture of one machine each week is expected to have a variable cost of £1,100, but each additional machine produced will increase the variable cost for the entire output by £100 a machine. For example, if the output were three machines a week, the variable cost for each machine (for all three machines) would be £1,300.
- It is the policy of the business always to charge the same price for its entire output of a particular model.

What is the most profitable level of output of the new machine?

Output (number of machines)	Unit sales revenue £	Total sales revenue £	Marginal sales revenue £	Unit variable cost £	Total variable cost £	Total cost £	Marginal cost £	Profit/ (loss) £
0	0	0	0	0	0	3,000	3,000	(3,000)
1	2,900	2,900	2,900	1,100	1,100	4,100	1,100	(1,200)
2	2,800	5,600	2,700	1,200	2,400	5,400	1,300	200
3	2,700	8,100	2,500	1,300	3,900	6,900	1,500	1,200
4	2,600	10,400	2,300	1,400	5,600	8,600	1,700	1,800
5	2,500	12,500	2,100	1,500	7,500	10,500	1,900	2,000
6	2,400	14,400	1,900	1,600	9,600	12,600	2,100	1,800
7	2,300	16,100	1,700	1,700	11,900	14,900	2,300	1,200
8	2,200	17,600	1,500	1,800	14,400	17,400	2,500	200
9	2,100	18,900	1,300	1,900	17,100	20,100	2,700	(1,200)
10	2,000	20,000	1,100	2,000	20,000	23,000	2,900	(3,000)

An output of five machines each week will maximise profit at £2,000 a week.

The additional cost of producing the fifth machine compared with the cost of producing the first four (£1,900) is just below the marginal revenue (the amount by which the total revenue from five machines exceeds that from selling four (£2,100)).

The additional cost of producing the sixth machine compared with the cost of producing the first five (£2,100) is just above the marginal revenue (the amount by which the total revenue from six machines exceeds that from selling five (£1,900)).

Some practical considerations

Despite the analysis in Activity 11.13, in practice, the answer of five machines a week may prove not to be the best answer. This might be for various reasons:

- Demand is notoriously difficult to predict, even assuming no changes in the environment.

- The effect of sales of the new machine on the other of the business's products may mean that the machine cannot be considered in isolation. Five machines a week may be the optimum level of output if sales were being taken from a rival business or a new market were being created, but possibly not in other circumstances.
- Costs are difficult to estimate.
- Since labour is in short supply, the relevant labour cost should probably include an element for opportunity cost.
- The level of sales volume is derived on the assumption that short-run profit maximisation is the goal of the business. Unless this is consistent with wealth enhancement in the longer term, it may not be in the business's best interests.

These points highlight some of the weaknesses of the theoretical approaches to pricing, particularly the fact that costs and demands are difficult to predict. It would be wrong, however, to dismiss the theory. The fact that the theory does not work perfectly in practice does not mean that it cannot offer helpful insights to the nature of markets, how profit relates to volume, and the notion of an optimum level of output.

Full cost (cost-plus) pricing

Now that we have considered pricing theory, let us return to the subject of using full cost as the basis for setting prices. We saw in Chapter 10 that one of the reasons why some businesses deduce full costs is to base selling prices on them. This is a perfectly logical approach. If a business charges the full cost of its output as a selling price, the business will, in theory, break even, because the sales revenue will exactly cover all of the costs. Charging something above full cost will yield a profit.

 If a **full cost (cost-plus) pricing** approach is to be taken, an issue that must be addressed is the level of profit that is required from each unit sold. This must logically be based on the total profit that is required for the period. Normally, businesses seek to enhance their wealth through trading. The extent to which they expect to do this is normally related to the amount of wealth that is invested to promote wealth enhancement. Businesses tend to seek to produce a particular percentage increase in wealth. In other words, businesses seek to generate a target return on capital employed. It seems logical, therefore, that the profit loading on full cost should reflect the business's target profit and that the target should itself be based on a target return on capital employed.

Activity (11.14)

A business has just completed a service job whose full cost has been calculated at £112. For the current period, the total costs (direct and indirect) are estimated at £250,000. The profit target for the period is £100,000.

Suggest a selling price for the job.

If the profit is to be earned by jobs in proportion to their full cost, then the profit for each pound of full cost must be £0.40 (that is, £100,000/250,000). Thus, the target profit on the job must be:

£0.40 × 112 = £44.80

This means that the target price for the job must be:

£112 + £44.80 = £156.80

Other ways could be found for apportioning a share of profit to jobs – for example, direct labour or machine hours. Such bases may be preferred where it is believed that these factors are better representatives of effort and, therefore, profitworthiness. It is clearly a matter of judgement as to how profit is apportioned to units of output.

Price makers and price takers

An obvious problem with cost-plus pricing is that the market may not agree with the price. Put another way, cost-plus pricing takes no account of the market demand function (the relationship between price and quantity demanded, which we considered above). A business may fairly deduce the full cost of some product and then add what might be regarded as a reasonable level of profit, only to find that a rival producer is offering a similar product for a much lower price, or that the market simply will not buy at the cost-plus price.

Most suppliers are not strong enough in the market to dictate pricing. Most are 'price takers' not 'price makers'. They must accept the price offered by the market or they do not sell any of their products. Cost-plus pricing may be appropriate for price makers, but it has less relevance for price takers.

Real World 11.21 illustrates how adopting a cost-plus approach to pricing may lead to a situation where falling demand leads to price rises, which, in turn lead to falling demand.

Real World 11.21

A vicious circle in the library

Librarians have long complained about the price rises of academic journals and Derek Haan chairman and chief executive of Elsevier Science, which publishes more than 1,600 journals, admits that journal price inflation has been a problem for the industry. He says the problem is due to falling subscription numbers as more readers make photocopies or use interlibrary lending. With fewer subscribers to share the cost of each publication, publishers have to increase prices. To stay within budgets, libraries start cancelling titles, which creates a vicious circle of dwindling subscriber numbers, soaring prices and reduced collections. Naturally, with fixed budgets, there is significant price elasticity of demand as far as the libraries are concerned.

Source: Adapted from 'Case Study: Elsevier', FT.com, 19 June 2002.

Use of cost-plus information by price takers

The cost-plus price is not entirely useless to price takers, however. When contemplating entering a market, knowing the cost-plus price will give useful information. It will tell the price taker whether it can profitably enter the market. As we have seen, the full cost can be seen as a long-run break-even selling price. If entering a market means that this break-even price, plus an acceptable profit, cannot be achieved, then the business might be better to stay out. Having a breakdown of the full cost may put the business in a position to examine where costs might be capable of being cut in order to bring the full cost plus profit within a figure acceptable to the market.

It is not necessary for a business to dominate a particular market for it to be a price maker. Many small businesses are, to some extent, price makers. This tends to be where buyers find it difficult to make clear distinctions between the prices offered by various

suppliers. An example of this might be a car repair. Although it may be possible to obtain a series of binding estimates for the work from various garages, most people would not normally do so. As a result, garages normally charge cost-plus prices for car repairs.

In its 'pure' sense, cost-plus pricing implies that the seller sets the price which is then accepted by the customer – often with the price not established until after the subject of the sale has been passed to the customer, for example a car repair or some work done by a firm of accountants. Sometimes, however, cost-plus is used as a basis of negotiating a price in advance, which then becomes the fixed price. This is often the case with contracts with central or local government departments. Typically, with such public contracts, the price is determined by competitive tendering. Here each potential supplier offers a price for which it will perform the subject of the contract and the department concerned selects the supplier offering the lowest price, subject to quality safeguards. In some cases, however, particularly where only one supplier is capable of doing the work, a fixed cost-plus approach is used.

Cost-plus is also often the approach taken when monopoly suppliers of public utility services are negotiating with the government-appointed regulator to agree a price which they are legally allowed to charge their customers. For example, the UK mains water suppliers, when agreeing the prices that they can charge customers, argue their case with Ofwat, the water industry regulator, on the basis of cost-plus information.

Real World 11.22 considers the extent to which cost-plus pricing seems to be used in practice.

Real World 11.22

Cost-plus pricing in practice

The 1999 survey of fairly large UK businesses by Drury and Tayles (see reference 2 at the end of the chapter) revealed that cost-plus pricing is used by 60 per cent of businesses. Of that 60 per cent, not all use it to set the price of all of the business's sales, however. The 60 per cent breaks down as follows:

% of sales revenue accounted for by cost-plus pricing	% of businesses
1 to 20	26
21 to 50	11
51 to 100	23
	60

Thus, for example, 26 per cent of all businesses responding to the survey used a cost-plus approach to pricing for between 1 per cent and 20 per cent of their total sales revenue.

It is difficult to interpret these data to reach a general conclusion, but it is fair to say that cost-plus is an important approach to pricing in the UK.

The 1993 survey by Drury *et al.* (see reference 6 at the end of the chapter) indicated that 39 per cent of respondents used the cost-plus approach to most of their pricing decisions. This might indicate that the cost-plus approach was more popular in 1993 than in 1999, when only 23 per cent of respondents used it for more than 50 per cent of their output.

A more recent study by Guilding *et al.* (see reference 8 at the end of the chapter) surveyed 267 large UK and Australian businesses during the period 1999 to 2002. Their finding were broadly as follows:

→

Real World 11.22 continued

- Cost-plus is regarded as important in determining selling prices by most of the businesses, but many businesses use it for only a small percentage of their total sales.
- Retailers base most of their sales prices on their costs. This is not surprising; we might expect that retailers add a mark-up to their cost prices to arrive at selling prices.
- Retailers and service businesses (both financial services and others) attach more importance to cost-plus pricing than do manufacturers and others.
- Cost-plus pricing tends to be more important in industries where competition is most intense. This is, perhaps surprising because we might have expected less 'price makers' in more competitive markets.
- The extent of the importance of cost-plus pricing seems to have nothing to do with the size of the business. We might have imagined that larger businesses would have more power in the market and be more likely to be price makers, but the evidence does not support this. The reason could be that many larger businesses are, in effect, groups of smaller businesses. These smaller subsidiaries may not be bigger players in their markets than are small independent businesses. Also, cost-plus pricing tends to be particularly important in retailing and service businesses, where many businesses are quite small.

Pricing on the basis of relevant/marginal cost

The relevant/marginal cost approach deduces the minimum price for which the business can offer the product for sale. This minimum price will leave the business better off as a result of making the sale than it would have been had it pursued the next best opportunity instead. We considered the more general approach to relevant cost pricing in Chapter 8. In Chapter 9, we looked at the more restricted case of relevant cost pricing: **marginal cost pricing**. Here it is assumed that fixed costs will not be affected by the decision to produce and, therefore, only the variable cost element need be considered.

It would normally be the case that a relevant/marginal cost approach would be used only where there is not the opportunity to sell at a price that will cover the full cost. The business can sell at any price above the marginal cost and still be better off simply because it happens to find itself in the position that certain costs will be incurred in any case.

Activity (11.15)

A commercial aircraft is due to take off in one hour's time with 20 seats unsold. What is the minimum price at which these seats could be sold such that the airline would be no worse off as a result?

The answer is that any price above the additional cost of one more passenger, caused by people occupying the previously unsold seats, would represent an acceptable minimum. If there are no such costs, the minimum price is zero.

This is not to say that the airline will seek to charge the minimum price; it will presumably seek to charge the highest price that the market will bear. The fact that the market will not bear the full cost, plus a profit margin, should not, in principle, be sufficient for the airline to refuse to sell seats.

In practice, airlines are major users of a relevant/marginal costing approach. They often offer low-priced tickets for off-peak travel, where there are not sufficient customers willing to pay 'normal' prices. By insisting on a Saturday stopover for return tickets, they tend to exclude 'business' travellers, who are probably forced to travel but for whom a Saturday stopover may be unattractive. UK train operators often offer substantial discounts for off-peak travel, particularly through 'Saver' and 'Supersaver' tickets. Similarly, hotels often charge very low rates for off-peak rooms. A hotel mainly used by business travellers may well offer very low room rates for Friday and Saturday occupancy.

Relevant/marginal pricing must be regarded as a short-term or limited approach that can be adopted because a business finds itself in a particular position, for example having spare aircraft seats. Ultimately, if the business is to be profitable, all costs must be covered by sales revenue.

Activity (11.16)

When we considered marginal costing in Chapter 9, we identified three problems with its use. Can you remember what these problems are?

The three problems are as follows:

- The possibility that spare capacity will be sold off cheaply when there is another potential customer who will offer a higher price, but who cannot be found before the capacity is fully committed. It is a matter of commercial judgement as to how likely this will be. With Activity 11.15, would an hour before take-off be sufficiently close for the airline to be fairly confident that no 'normal' passenger will come forward to buy a seat?
- The problem that selling the same product but at different prices could lead to a loss of customer goodwill. Would a 'normal' passenger be happy to be told by another passenger that the latter had bought his or her ticket very cheaply compared with the normal price?
- If the business is going to suffer continually from being unable to sell its full production potential at the 'normal' price, it might be better, in the long run, to reduce capacity and make fixed-cost savings. Using the spare capacity to produce marginal benefits may lead to the business failing to address this issue. Would it be better for the airline to operate smaller aircraft or to have fewer flights – either of these leading to fixed-cost savings – than to sell off surplus seats at marginal prices?

Real World 11.23 provides an unusual example where humanitarian issues are the driving force for adopting marginal pricing.

Real World 11.23

Drug prices in developing countries

It was mentioned in Real World 11.19 (page 411) that large pharmaceutical businesses have recently been under considerable pressure to provide cheap drugs to developing countries. It has been suggested that life-saving therapeutic drugs should be sold to these countries at a price that is close to their marginal cost. Indeed the Department for

Real World 11.23 continued

International Development would like to see HIV drugs sold at marginal cost in the poorest countries. However, a number of obstacles to such a pricing policy have been identified:

- It may lead to customer revolts in the West (the 'loss of customer goodwill' referred to above).
- There is a concern that the drugs may not reach their intended patients and could be re-exported to western countries. A major cost of producing a new drug is the research and development costs incurred, and marginal costs of production are usually very low. Thus, a selling price based on marginal cost is likely to be considerably lower than the (full-cost) selling price in the West. This, it is feared, may lead to the cheap drugs provided leaking back into the West. Acquiring drugs at a price near to their marginal cost and reselling them at a figure close to the selling price in the West offers unscrupulous individuals an opportunity to make huge profits.
- The concern that compensation for any adverse consequences that may arise from the drugs sold will be sought in courts in the West, thereby creating the risk of huge payouts.

The above problems are not insurmountable and are not the only problems surrounding this issue, but they do appear to have slowed progress towards a speedier response to a humanitarian crisis.

Sources: Based on information in 'Drug pricing is a social problem', R. Epstein, FT.com, 16 June 2005; 'Pressure builds to cut price of HIV medicines', FT.com, 11 March 2006; and 'Patent nonsense', *Financial Times*, 24 August 2001.

Target pricing

We saw earlier in the chapter (page 388) that, as the starting point of the target costing approach to cost management, a target selling price needs to be identified. Using market research and so on, a target unit selling price and a planned sales volume are set. This is the combination of price and quantity demanded that the business would derive from its estimation of the product's demand function (see page 409). Thus the target price is the market-determined price that the business seeks to meet, in terms of costs and profit margin.

Pricing strategies

Costs and the market-demand function are not the only determinants of price. Businesses often employ pricing strategies that, in the short term, may not maximise profit. They do this in the expectation that they will gain in the long term. An example of such a strategy is **penetration pricing**. Here, the product is sold relatively cheaply in order to sell in quantity and to gain a large share of the market. This would tend to have the effect of dissuading competitors from entering the market. Subsequently, once the business has established itself as the market leader, prices would be raised to more profitable levels. By its nature, penetration pricing usually applies to new products.

In a number of countries, certainly in the UK, supermarkets have established service stations (vehicle fuel retailers) on their sites. Here they have offered fuel at a discount to prices offered by other fuel retailers. Consequently the supermarkets have an increasing share of this market. There is probably also an element of 'loss leader' pricing where the supermarkets use cheap fuel prices to encourage customers on to their sites in the hope that this leads to sales of other products.

→   **Price skimming** is almost the opposite of penetration pricing. It seeks to exploit the notion that the market can be stratified according to resistance to price. Here a new product is initially priced highly and sold only to those buyers in the stratum that is fairly unconcerned by high prices. Once this stratum of the market is saturated, the price is lowered to attract the next stratum. The price is gradually lowered as each stratum is saturated. This strategy tends only to be able to be used where there is some significant barrier to entry for other potential suppliers, such as patent protection.

DVD players provide a good example of a price skimming strategy. When they first emerged in the 1990s, DVD players would typically cost over £400. They can now be bought for less than £100. Advancing technology, the economies of scale and increasing competition have undoubtedly contributed to this fall in price, but price skimming almost certainly was a major factor. Certain customers would have regarded a DVD player as a 'must-have' product. These 'early adopters' would have been prepared to pay a high price to have one. Once the early adopters had bought their DVD player, the price was gradually reduced, until we reached today's price.

The initial high price can help to recover research and development and production set-up costs quickly. It can also keep demand within manageable levels while production capacity is being built up.

Televisions, CD players, home computers and mobile telephones are also examples of where a price-skimming strategy has been applied.

Summary

The main points of this chapter may be summarised as follows.

Activity-based costing is an approach to dealing with overheads (in full costing) that treats all costs as being caused or 'driven' by activities. Advocates argue that it is more relevant to the modern commercial environment than is the traditional approach.

- Identification of the cost drivers can lead to more relevant indirect cost treatment in full costing.
- Identification of the cost drivers can also lead to better control of overheads.
- Critics argue that ABC is time-consuming and expensive to apply – not justified by the possible improvement in the quality of information.

Total (whole) life-cycle costing takes account of all of the costs incurred over a product's entire life.

- The life cycle of a product can be broken down into three phases: pre-production, production and post-production.
- A high proportion of costs is incurred and/or committed during the pre-production phase.
- Target costing attempts to reduce costs so that the market price covers the cost plus an acceptable profit.
- Ensuring quality output has costs, known as *quality costs*, typically divided into four aspects: prevention costs, appraisal costs, internal failure costs and external failure costs.

- *Kaizen* costing attempts to reduce costs at the production stage.
- Since most costs will have been saved at the pre-production phase and through target costing, only small cost savings are likely to be possible.
- Benchmarking attempts to emulate a successful aspect of, for example, another business or division.
- Value chain analysis involves analysing the various activities in the product life cycle to identify and to try to eliminate non-value-added activities.

Non-financial measures of performance

- The Balanced Scorecard is a management tool that uses financial and non-financial measures to assess progress towards objectives.
- It has four aspects: financial, customer, internal business process, and learning and growth.
- It encourages a balanced approach to managing the business.

Value-based management

- Shareholder value is seen as the key objective of most businesses.
- One approach used to measure shareholder value is economic value added (EVA®).
- Economic value added is a means of measuring whether the returns generated by the business exceed the required returns of investors.

$$\text{EVA}^{®} = \text{NOPAT} - (R \times C)$$

where: NOPAT = net operating profit after tax

R = required returns from investors

C = capital invested (that is, the net assets of the business).

Pricing output

- In theory, profit is maximised where the price is such that:

    Marginal sales revenue = Marginal cost of production

- Elasticity of demand indicates the sensitivity of demand to price changes.
- Full cost (cost-plus) pricing takes the full cost and adds a mark up for profit.
    - it is popular;
    - the market may not accept the price (most businesses are 'price takers');
    - it can provide a useful benchmark.
- Relevant/marginal cost pricing, takes the relevant/marginal cost and adds a mark-up for profit.
    - it can be useful in the short term, but in the longer term it may be better to charge a full cost plus price.
- Target sales prices are those established as the first step in the target costing process. They are determined by the market.
- Various pricing strategies can be used, including:
    - penetration pricing;
    - price skimming.

MyAccountingLab | *Now check your progress in your personal Study Plan*

Key terms

activity-based costing (ABC) p. 376	**value driver** p. 393
cost driver p. 376	**Balanced Scorecard** p. 394
cost pool p. 376	**economic value added**® p. 403
total life-cycle costing p. 386	**elasticity of demand** p. 409
target costing p. 388	**full cost (cost-plus) pricing** p. 417
quality costs p. 389	**marginal cost pricing** p. 420
kaizen **costing** p. 390	**penetration pricing** p. 422
value chain analysis p. 390	**price skimming** p. 423
benchmarking p. 392	

References

1 **Activity Based Costing – A review with case studies**, *Innes J. and Mitchell F.*, CIMA Publishing, 1990.

2 **Cost Systems Design and Profitability Analysis in UK Companies**, *Drury C. and Tayles M.*, CIMA Publishing, 2000.

3 'Activity-based costing in the UK's largest companies', *Innes J., Mitchell F. and Sinclair D.*, **Management Accounting Research**, vol. 11, no. 3, 2000.

4 **The Bain 2005 Management Tool Study**, *Rigby D. and Bilodeau B.*, Bain & Company.

5 **2003 Survey of Management Accounting**, *Ernst and Young*, Ernst and Young, 2003.

6 **A Survey of Management Accounting Practices in UK Manufacturing Companies**, *Drury C., Braund S., Osborne P. and Tayles M.*, Chartered Association of Certified Accountants, 1993.

7 **The Balanced Scorecard**, *Kaplan R. and Norton D.*, Harvard Business School Press, 1996.

8 'An empirical investigation of the importance of cost-plus pricing', *Guilding C., Drury C. and Tayles M.*, **Management Auditing Journal**, vol. 20, no. 2, 2005.

Further reading

If you would like to explore the topics covered in this chapter in more depth, we recommend the following books:

Cost Accounting: A managerial emphasis, *Horngren C., Foster G. and Datar S.*, 12th edn, Prentice Hall, 2006, chapters 5 and 12.

Management Accounting, *Atkinson A., Kaplan R., Young S.M. and Matsumura E.*, 5th edn, Prentice Hall, 2007, chapters 4, 6, 7 and 9.

Management and Cost Accounting, *Drury C.*, 6th edn, Thomson Learning, 2004, chapters 10 and 11.

Managerial Accounting, *Hilton R.*, McGraw-Hill/Irwin, 2005, chapters 5, 6, 7 and 15.

Review questions

Answers to these questions can be found at the back of the book on pages 781–2.

11.1 How does activity-based costing differ from the traditional approach? What is the underlying difference in the philosophy of each of them?

11.2 The use of activity-based costing in helping to deduce full costs has been criticised. What has tended to be the basis of this criticism?

11.3 What is meant by elasticity of demand? How does knowledge of the elasticity of demand affect pricing decisions?

11.4 According to economic theory, at what point is profit maximised? Why is it at this point?

Exercises

Exercises 11.6 to 11.8 are more advanced than 11.1 to 11.5. Those with **coloured numbers** have answers at the back of the book, starting on page 739.

If you wish to try more exercises, visit the students' side of the Companion Website.

11.1 Woodner Ltd provides a standard service. It is able to provide a maximum of 100 units of this service each week. Experience shows that at a price of £100, no units of the service would be sold. For every £5 below this price, the business is able to sell 10 more units. For example, at a price of £95, 10 units would be sold, at £90, 20 units would be sold, and so on. The business's fixed costs total £2,500 a week. Variable costs are £20 a unit over the entire range of possible output. The market is such that it is not feasible to charge different prices to different customers.

Required:
What is the most profitable level of output of the service?

11.2 It appears from research evidence that a cost-plus approach influences pricing decisions in practice. What is meant by cost-plus pricing and what are the problems of using this approach?

11.3 Kaplan plc makes a range of suitcases of various sizes and shapes. There are 10 different models of suitcase produced by the business. In order to keep inventories (stock) of finished suitcases to a minimum, each model is made in a small batch. Each batch is costed as a separate job and the cost for each suitcase deduced by dividing the batch cost by the number of suitcases in the batch.

At present, the business derives the cost of each batch using a traditional job-costing approach. Recently, however, a new management accountant has been appointed who is advocating the use of activity-based costing (ABC) to deduce the cost of the batches. The management accountant claims that ABC leads to much more reliable and relevant costs and that it has other benefits.

Required:
(a) Explain how the business deduces the cost of each suitcase at present.
(b) Discuss the purposes to which the knowledge of the cost for each suitcase, deduced on a traditional basis, can be put and how valid the cost is for the purpose concerned.

(c) Explain how ABC could be applied to costing the suitcases, highlighting the differences between ABC and the traditional approach.

(d) Explain what advantages the new management accountant probably believes ABC to have over the traditional approach.

11.4 Comment critically on the following statements that you have overheard:

(a) 'To maximise profit you need to sell your output at the highest price.'

(b) 'Elasticity of demand deals with the extent to which costs increase as demand increases.'

(c) 'Provided that the price is large enough to cover the marginal cost of production, the sale should be made.'

(d) 'According to economic theory, profit is maximised where total cost equals total revenue.'

(e) 'Price skimming is charging low prices for the output until you have a good share of the market, and then putting up your prices.'

Explain clearly all technical terms.

11.5 Comment critically on the following statements that you have overheard:

(a) 'Direct labour hours are the most appropriate basis to use to charge overheads to jobs in the modern manufacturing environment where people are so important.'

(b) 'Activity-based costing is a means of more accurately accounting for direct labour cost.'

(c) 'Activity-based costing cannot really be applied to the service sector because the "activities" that it seeks to analyse tend to be related to manufacturing.'

(d) '*Kaizen* costing is an approach where great efforts are made to reduce the costs of developing a new product and setting up its production processes.'

(e) 'Benchmarking is an approach to job costing where each direct worker keeps a record of the time spent on each job on his or her workbench before it is passed on to the next direct worker or into finished inventories (stock) stores.'

11.6 The GB Company manufactures a variety of electric motors. The business is currently operating at about 70 per cent of capacity and is earning a satisfactory return on investment.

International Industries (II) has approached the management of GB with an offer to buy 120,000 units of an electric motor. II manufactures a motor that is almost identical to GB's motor, but a fire at the II plant has shut down its manufacturing operations. II needs the 120,000 motors over the next four months to meet commitments to its regular customers; II is prepared to pay £19 each for the motors, which it will collect from the GB plant.

GB's product cost, based on current planned cost for the motor, is:

	£
Direct materials	5.00
Direct labour (variable)	6.00
Manufacturing overhead	9.00
Total	20.00

Manufacturing overhead is applied to production at the rate of £18.00 per direct labour hour. This overhead rate is made up of the following components:

	£
Variable factory overhead	6.00
Fixed factory overhead – direct	8.00
– allocated	4.00
Applied manufacturing overhead rate	18.00

Additional costs usually incurred in connection with sales of electric motors include sales commissions of 5 per cent and freight expense of £1.00 a unit.

In determining selling prices, GB adds a 40 per cent mark-up to product costs. This provides a suggested selling price of £28 for the motor. The marketing department, however, has set the current selling price at £27.00 to maintain market share. The order would, however, require additional fixed factory overhead of £15,000 a month in the form of supervision and clerical costs. If management accepts the order, 30,000 motors will be manufactured and delivered to II each month for the next four months.

Required:

(a) Prepare a financial evaluation showing the impact of accepting the International Industries order. What is the minimum unit price that the business's management could accept without reducing its operating profit?

(b) State clearly any assumptions contained in the analysis of (a) above and discuss any other organisational or strategic factors that GB should consider.

11.7 Sillycon Ltd is a business engaged in the development of new products in the electronics industry. Subtotals on the spreadsheet of planned overheads reveal:

	Electronics department	Testing department	Service department
Overheads – Variable (£000)	1,200	600	700
– Fixed (£000)	2,000	500	800
Planned activity: Direct labour hours ('000)	800	600	

For the purposes of reallocation of service department's overheads, it is agreed that variable overheads vary with the direct labour hours worked in each department. Fixed overheads of the service department are to be reallocated on the basis of maximum practical capacity of the two departments, which is the same for each.

The business has a long-standing practice of marking up full manufacturing costs by between 25 per cent and 35 per cent in order to establish selling prices.

One new product, which is in a final development stage, is hoped to offer some improvement over competitors' products, which are currently marketed at between £110 and £130 each. Product development engineers have determined that the direct material content is £7 a unit. The product will take 4 labour hours in the electronics department and 3 hours in testing. Hourly labour rates are £10 and £6, respectively.

Management estimates that the fixed costs that would be specifically incurred in relation to the product are: supervision £13,000, depreciation of a recently acquired machine £100,000 and advertising £37,000 a year. These fixed costs are included in the table given above.

Market research indicates that the business could expect to obtain and hold about 25 per cent of the market or, optimistically, 30 per cent. The total market is estimated at 20,000 units.

Note: It may be assumed that the existing plan has been prepared to cater for a range of products and no single product decision will cause the business to amend it.

Required:

(a) Prepare a summary of information that would help with the pricing decision. Such information should include marginal cost and full cost implications after allocation of service department overheads.

(b) Explain and elaborate on the information prepared.

11.8 A business manufactures refrigerators for domestic use. There are three models: Lo, Mid and Hi. The models, their quality and their price are aimed at different markets.

Product costs are computed on a blanket overhead-rate basis using a labour hour method. Prices as a general rule are set based on cost plus 20 per cent. The following information is provided:

	Lo	Mid	Hi
Material cost (£/unit)	25	62.5	105
Direct labour hours (per unit)	½	1	1
Budget production/sales (units)	20,000	1,000	10,000

The budgeted overheads for the business amount to £4,410,000. Direct labour is costed at £8 an hour.

The business is currently facing increasing competition, especially from imported goods. As a result, the selling price of Lo has been reduced to a level that produces very little profit margin. To address this problem, an activity-based costing approach has been suggested. The overheads are examined and these are grouped around main business activities of machining (£2,780,000), logistics (£590,000) and establishment (£1,040,000) costs. It is maintained that these costs could be allocated based respectively on cost drivers of machine hours, material orders and space, to reflect the use of resources in each of these areas. After analysis, the following proportionate statistics are available related to the total volume of products:

	Lo	Mid	Hi
	%	%	%
Machine hours	40	15	45
Material orders	47	6	47
Space	42	18	40

Required:
(a) Calculate for each product the full cost and selling price determined by:
   (i) The original costing method.
   (ii) The activity-based costing method.
(b) What are the implications of the two systems of costing in the situation given?
(c) What business/strategic options exist for the business in the light of the new information?

CHAPTER 12

Budgeting

Introduction

Budgets are an important tool for management planning and control. In this chapter we shall consider the role and nature of budgets, we shall also see how budgets are prepared. Preparing budgets relies on an understanding of the financial statements (balance sheet and income statement) that we considered in Chapters 2 and 3. It also picks up on many of the issues relating to the behaviour of costs and full costing, topics that we explored in Chapters 9 and 10 respectively.

Budgets do not exist in a vacuum; they are an integral part of a planning framework that is adopted by well-run businesses. To understand fully the nature of budgets we must, therefore, understand the planning framework within which they are set. The chapter begins with a discussion of this framework and then goes on to consider detailed aspects of the budgeting process.

We shall be considering budgeting mainly in the context of private-sector businesses. It must be emphasised, however, that budgeting is also almost universally practised in the public and voluntary (charities) sectors. The principles and approaches to budgeting are identical for all types of organisation, though some of the details may vary.

Learning outcomes

When you have completed this chapter, you should be able to:

- Define a budget and show how budgets, strategic objectives and strategic plans are related.

- Explain the budgeting process and the interlinking of the various budgets within the business.

- Indicate the uses of budgeting and construct various budgets, including the cash budget, from relevant data.

- Discuss the criticisms that are made of budgeting.

 Remember to create your own personalised Study Plan

How budgets link with strategic plans and objectives

It is vital that businesses develop plans for the future. Whatever a business is trying to achieve, it is unlikely to come about unless its managers are clear what the future direction of the business is going to be. The development of plans involves five key steps:

1 *Establish mission and objectives*. The **mission statement** is a statement of broad intent. See Real World 1.5 (page 26) for the mission statement of J. Sainsbury plc, the supermarket business. Strategic objectives are more specific and, often, quantifiable goals.
2 *Undertake a position analysis*. This is to assess where the business is currently placed relative to where it wants to be, as defined by its objectives.
3 *Identify and assess the strategic options*. Here the business considers the various ways in which it might move from where it is now (identified in step 2) to where it wants to be (identified in step 1).
4 *Select strategic options*. This involves selecting what seems to be the best of the courses of action or strategies (identified in step 3) and formulating a strategic plan. The plan is normally broken down into a series of plans, one for each element of the business. These plans are the budgets. A **budget** is a business plan for the short term – typically one year. It is likely to be expressed mainly in financial terms and its role is to convert the strategic plans into actionable blueprints for the immediate future. Budgets will define precise targets concerning such things as:
   - cash receipts and payments
   - sales volumes and revenues, broken down into amounts and prices for each of the products or services provided by the business
   - detailed inventories requirements
   - detailed labour requirements
   - specific production requirements.
5 *Perform, review and control*. Here the business pursues the budgets derived in step 4. By comparing the actual outcome with the budgets, managers can see if things are going according to plan. Action would be taken to exercise control where actual performance appears not to be matching the budgets.

Activity 12.1

The approach described in step 3, above, suggests that managers will systematically collect information and then carefully evaluate all the options available. Do you think this is what managers really do?

In practice, managers may not be as rational and capable as implied in the process described. Individuals may find it difficult to handle a wealth of information relating to a wide range of options. To avoid becoming overloaded, they may restrict their range of possible options and/or discard some information. Managers may also adopt rather simple approaches to evaluating the mass of information provided. These approaches might not lead to the best decisions being made.

Clearly, the relationship between the mission, strategic objectives, strategic plans and budgets is that the mission, once set, is likely to last for quite a long time – perhaps throughout the life of the business. The objectives are also fairly long-term goals.

A series of strategic plans identifies how each objective is to be pursued and budgets identify how the strategic plan is to be fulfilled.

An analogy might be found in terms of a student enrolling on a course of study. His or her mission might be to have a happy and fulfilling life. A key strategic objective flowing from this mission might be to embark on a career that will be rewarding in various ways. He or she might have identified the particular study course as the most effective way to work towards this objective. Successfully completing the course would then be the strategic plan. In working towards this strategic plan, passing a particular stage of the course might be identified as the target for the forthcoming year. This short-term target is analogous to the budget. Having achieved the 'budget' for the first year, the budget for the second year becomes passing the second stage.

Collecting information on performance and exercising control

However well planned the activities of a business might be, they will come to nothing unless steps are taken to try to achieve them in practice. The process of making planned events actually occur is known as **control**. This is part of step 5 (above).

Control can be defined as compelling events to conform to plan. This definition is valid in any context. For example, when we talk about controlling a motor car, we mean making the car do what we plan that it should do. In a business context, management accounting is very useful in the control process. This is because it is possible to state plans in accounting terms (as budgets). Since it is also possible to state *actual* outcomes in the same terms, making comparison between actual and planned outcomes is a relatively simple matter. Where actual outcomes are at variance with budgets, this variance should be highlighted by accounting information. Managers can then take steps to get the business back on track towards the achievement of the budgets. We shall be looking quite closely at the control aspect of budgeting in Chapter 13.

It should be emphasised that planning (including budgeting) is the responsibility of managers rather than accountants. Although management accountants play a major role in the planning process, by supplying relevant information to managers and by contributing to decision making as part of the management team, they should not dominate the process. In practice, it seems that the budgeting aspect of planning is in danger of being dominated by accountants, perhaps because most budgets are expressed in financial terms. However, managers are failing in their responsibilities if they allow this to happen.

Figure 12.1 shows the planning and control process in diagrammatic form.

Time horizon of plans and budgets

The setting of strategic plans is typically performed as a major exercise about every five years and budgets are usually set annually for the forthcoming year. It need not necessarily be the case that strategic plans are set for five years and that budgets are set for one year: it is up to the management of the business concerned. Businesses involved in certain industries – say, information technology – may feel that five years is too long a planning period since new developments can, and do, occur virtually overnight. Such businesses may feel that a planning horizon of two or three years is more feasible. Similarly, a budget need not be set for one year, although this appears to be a widely used time horizon.

| Figure 12.1 | The planning and control process |

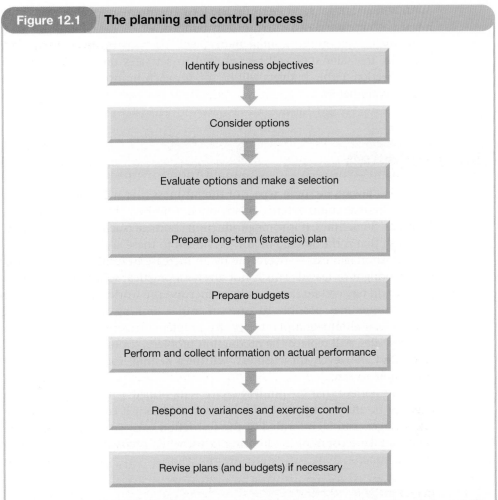

Once the objectives of the business have been determined, the various options that can fulfil these objectives must be considered and evaluated and a strategic plan derived. The budget is a short-term financial plan for the business that is prepared within the framework of the strategic plan. Control can be exercised through the comparison of budgeted and actual performance. Where a significant divergence emerges, some form of corrective action should be taken. If the budget figures prove to be based on incorrect assumptions about the future, it might be necessary to revise the budget.

Activity 12.2

Can you think of any reason why most businesses prepare detailed budgets for the forthcoming year, rather than for a shorter or longer period?

The reason is probably that a year represents a long enough time for the budget preparation exercise to be worthwhile, yet short enough into the future for detailed plans to be capable of being made. As we shall see later in this chapter, the process of formulating budgets can be a time-consuming exercise, but there are economies of scale – for example, preparing the budget for the next year would not normally take twice as much time and effort as preparing the budget for the next six months.

An annual budget sets targets for the forthcoming year for all aspects of the business. It is usually broken down into monthly budgets, which define monthly targets. Indeed, in many instances, the annual budget will be built up from monthly figures. For example, the sales staff will be required to set sales targets for each month of the budget period. Other budgets will be set, for each month of the budget period, as we shall explain below.

Limiting factors

There will always be some aspect of the business that will stop it achieving its objectives to the maximum extent. This is often a limited ability of the business to sell its products. Sometimes, it is some production shortage (such as labour, materials or plant capacity) that is the **limiting factor**, or, linked to these, a shortage of funds. Often, production shortages can be overcome by an increase in funds – for example, more plant can be bought or leased. This is not always a practical solution because no amount of money will buy certain labour skills or increase the world supply of some raw material.

It is sometimes possible to ease an initial limiting factor: for example, subcontracting can eliminate a plant capacity problem. This means that some other factor, perhaps sales, will replace the production problem, though at a higher level of output. Ultimately, however, the business will hit a ceiling; some limiting factor will prove impossible to ease.

It is important that the limiting factor is identified. Ultimately, most, if not all, budgets will be affected by the limiting factor, and so if it can be identified at the outset, all managers can be informed of the restriction early in the process. This will enable them to take account of the limiting factor when preparing the budgets.

Budgets and forecasts

As we have seen, a budget may be defined as a business plan for the short term. Budgets are, to a great extent, expressed in financial terms. Note, particularly, that a budget is a *plan*, not a forecast. To talk of a plan suggests an intention or determination to achieve the targets; **forecasts** tend to be predictions of the future state of the environment.

Clearly, forecasts are helpful to the planner/budget setter. If, for example, a reputable forecaster has forecast the number of new cars to be purchased in the UK during next year, it will be valuable for managers in a car manufacturing business to take account of this forecast figure when setting next year's sales budgets. However, a forecast and a budget are distinctly different.

Periodic and continual budgets

Budgeting can be undertaken on a periodic or a continual basis. A **periodic budget** is prepared for a particular period (usually one year). Managers will agree the budget for the year and then allow the budget to run its course. Although it may be necessary to revise the budget on occasions, the budget is prepared just once during each financial year. A **continual budget**, as the name suggests, is continually updated. We have seen that an annual budget will normally be broken down into smaller time intervals (usually monthly periods) to help control the activities of a business. A continual budget will add a new month to replace the month that has just passed, thereby ensuring that, at all times, there will be a budget for a full planning period. Continual budgets are also referred to as **rolling budgets**.

Activity 12.3

What do you think are the advantages and disadvantages of each form of budgeting?

Periodic budgeting will usually take less time and effort to prepare and will therefore be less costly. However, as time passes, the budget period shortens and towards the end of the financial year managers will be working to a very short planning period. Continual budgeting, on the other hand, will ensure that managers always have a full year's budget to help them make decisions. It is claimed that continual budgeting ensures that managers plan throughout the year rather than just once each year. In this way it encourages a forward-looking attitude. However, there is a danger that budgeting will become a mechanical exercise, as managers may not have time to step back from their other tasks each month and consider the future carefully. It may be unreasonable to expect managers continually to take this future-oriented perspective.

How budgets link to one another

A business will prepare more than one budget for a particular period. Each budget prepared will relate to a specific aspect of the business. It is generally considered that the ideal situation is that there should be a separate budget for each person who is in a managerial position, no matter how junior. The contents of all of the individual budgets will be summarised in **master budgets** consisting usually of a budgeted income statement and balance sheet. The cash flow statement (in summarised form) is considered by some to be a third master budget.

Figure 12.2 illustrates the interrelationship and interlinking of individual budgets, in this particular case using a manufacturing business as an example.

The sales budget is usually the first budget to be prepared (at the left of Figure 12.2), as this tends to determine the overall level of activity for the forthcoming period. This is because sales demand is probably the most common limiting factor (see above). The level of sales would tend to dictate the finished inventories requirement, though it would also be dictated by the policy of the business on the amount of finished products that it holds in inventories. The requirement for finished inventories would define the required production levels, which would, in turn, dictate the requirements of the individual production departments or sections. The demands of manufacturing, in conjunction with the business's policy on how long it holds raw materials before they enter production, define the raw materials inventories budget. The purchases budget will be dictated by the materials inventories budget, which will, in conjunction with the policy of the business on taking credit from suppliers, dictate the trade payables budget. One of the determinants of the cash budget will be the trade payables budget; another will be the trade receivables budget, which itself derives, through the business's policy on credit periods granted to credit customers, from the sales budget. Cash will also be affected by overheads and direct labour costs (themselves linked to production) and by capital expenditure. The factors that affect policies on matters such as inventories holding and trade receivables collection and trade payables payment periods will be discussed in some detail in Chapter 16.

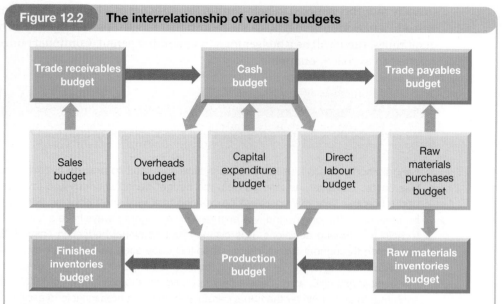

Figure 12.2 **The interrelationship of various budgets**

This is the interrelationship between budgets in a manufacturing business. The starting point is usually the sales budget. The expected level of sales frequently defines the overall level of activity for the business; the other budgets will be drawn up in accordance with this. Thus the sales budget will largely define the finished inventories requirements and from this we can define the production requirements and so on.

A manufacturing business has been used as the example in Figure 12.2 simply because it has all of the types of budgets found in practice. Service businesses have similar arrangements of budgets, but obviously do not have inventories' budgets. All of the issues relating to budgets apply equally well to all types of business.

It may prove to be the case that it is not sales demand that limits activities. Assuming that the budgeting process takes the order just described, it might be found in practice that there is some constraint other than sales demand. For example, the production capacity of the business may be incapable of meeting the necessary levels of output to match the sales budget for one or more months. In this case, it might be reasonable to look at the ways of overcoming the problem. As a last resort, it might be necessary to revise the sales budget to a lower level to enable production to meet the target.

Activity 12.4

Can you think of any ways in which a short-term shortage of production facilities of a manufacturer might be overcome?

We thought of the following:

- Higher production in previous months and stockpiling to meet periods of higher demand.
- Increasing production capacity, perhaps by working overtime and/or acquiring (buying or leasing) additional plant.
- Subcontracting some production.
- Encouraging potential customers to change the timing of their buying by offering discounts or other special terms during the months that have been identified as quiet.

You might well have thought of other approaches.

There will be the horizontal relationships between budgets, which we have just looked at, but there will usually be vertical ones as well. For example, the sales budget may be broken down into a number of subsidiary budgets, perhaps one for each regional sales manager. The overall sales budget will be a summary of the subsidiary ones. The same may be true of virtually all of the other budgets, most particularly the production budget.

Figure 12.3 shows the vertical relationship for the sales budgets for a business. The business has four geographical sales regions, each one the responsibility of a separate manager who is probably located in the region concerned. Each regional manager is responsible to the overall sales manager for the business. The overall sales budget is the sum of the budgets for the four sales regions.

Figure 12.3   The vertical relationship between budgets

Overall sales budget

| Sales budget North region | Sales budget South region | Sales budget East region | Sales budget West region |

This business manages its sales through four geographical areas. The overall sales budget for the business as a whole is the sum of the four regional sales budgets.

Although sales are often managed on a geographical basis and so their budgets reflect this, sales may be managed on some other basis. For example, a business that sells a range of products may manage sales on a product-type basis, with a specialist manager responsible for each type of product. For example, an insurance business may have separate sales managers, and so separate sales budgets, for life insurance, household insurance, motor insurance and so on. Very large businesses may even have separate product-type managers for each geographical region. Each of these managers would have a separate budget, and these would combine to form the overall sales budget for the business as a whole.

All of the operating budgets that we have just reviewed have to be consistent with the overall short-term plans laid out in the master budget, that is, the budgeted income statement and balance sheet.

How budgets help managers

Budgets are generally regarded as having five areas of usefulness. These are:

- *Budgets tend to promote forward thinking and the possible identification of short-term problems.* We saw above that a shortage of production capacity might be identified during the budgeting process. Making this discovery in good time could leave a number of means of overcoming the problem open to exploration. If the potential production problem is picked up early enough, all of the suggestions in the answer to Activity 12.4 and, possibly, other ways of overcoming the problem can be explored. Early identification of the potential problem gives managers time for calm and rational consideration of the best way of overcoming it. The best solution to the potential problem may be feasible only if action can be taken well in advance. This would be true of all of the suggestions made in the answer to Activity 12.4.

- *Budgets can be used to help co-ordination between the various sections of the business.* It is crucially important that the activities of the various departments and sections of the business are linked so that the activities of one are complementary to those of another. For example, the activities of the purchasing/procurement department of a manufacturing business should dovetail with the raw materials needs of the production departments. If this is not the case, production could run out of raw materials, leading to expensive production stoppages. Possibly just as undesirable, excessive amounts of raw materials could be bought, leading to large and unnecessary inventories holding costs. We shall see how this co-ordination tends to work in practice later in this chapter.

- *Budgets can motivate managers to better performance.* Having a stated task can motivate managers and staff in their performance. It is a well-established view that to tell managers to do their best is not very motivating, but to define a required level of achievement for each manager is more likely to be so. It is felt that managers will be better motivated by being able to relate their particular role in the business to the overall business objectives. Since budgets are directly derived from these objectives, budgeting makes this possible. It is clearly not possible to allow managers to operate in an unconstrained environment. Having to operate in a way that matches the goals of the business is a price of working in an effective organisation. We shall consider the role of budgets as motivators in Chapter 13.

- *Budgets can provide a basis for a system of control.* As mentioned earlier in the chapter, control is concerned with ensuring that events conform to plans. If senior management wishes to control and monitor the performance of more junior staff, it needs some yardstick against which the performance can be measured and assessed. It is possible to compare current performance with past performance or perhaps with what happens in another business. However, the most logical yardstick is usually planned performance. If there is information available concerning the actual performance for a period, and this can be compared with the planned performance, then a basis for control will have been established. Such a basis will enable the use of **management by exception**, a technique where senior managers can spend most of their time dealing with those staff or activities that have failed to achieve the budget (the exceptions). This means that senior managers do not have to spend too much time on those that are performing well. It also allows junior managers to exercise self-control. By knowing what is expected of them and what they have actually achieved, they can assess how well they are performing and take steps to correct matters where they are failing to achieve. We shall consider the effect of making plans and being held accountable for their achievement in Chapter 13.

- *Budgets can provide a system of authorisation* for managers to spend up to a particular limit. Some activities (for example, staff development and research expenditure) are allocated a fixed amount of funds at the discretion of senior management. This provides the authority to spend.

Figure 12.4 shows the benefits of budgets in diagrammatic form.

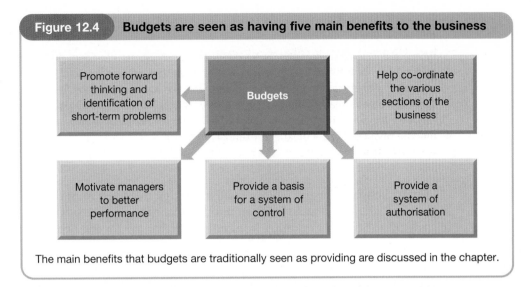

Figure 12.4 — Budgets are seen as having five main benefits to the business

The main benefits that budgets are traditionally seen as providing are discussed in the chapter.

The following three activities pick up issues that relate to some of the uses of budgets.

Activity 12.5

The third point on the above list of the uses of budgets (motivation) implies that managers are set stated tasks. Do you think there is a danger that requiring managers to work towards such predetermined targets will stifle their skill, flair and enthusiasm?

If the budgets are set in such a way as to offer challenging yet achievable targets, the manager is still required to show skill, flair and enthusiasm. There is the danger, however, that if targets are badly set (either unreasonably demanding or too easy to achieve), they will become a demotivating force and will fail to exploit the talents of managers.

Activity 12.6

The fourth point on the above list of the uses of budgets (control) implies that current management performance is compared with some yardstick. What is wrong with comparing actual performance with past performance, or the performance of others, in an effort to exercise control?

There is no automatic reason to believe that what happened in the past, or is happening elsewhere, represents a sensible target for the current year of a particular business. Considering what happened last year, and in other businesses, may help in the formulation of plans, but past events and the performance of others should not automatically be seen as the target.

Activity 12.7

The five identified uses of budgets can conflict with one another on occasions. Can you think of a possible conflict between the budget as a means of control and the budget as a system of authorisation?

Activity 12.7 continued

Where a budget is being used as a system of authorisation, managers may be motivated to spend to the limit of their budget, even though this may be wasteful. This may occur where the managers are not allowed to carry over unused funds to the next budget period or if they believe that the budget for the next period will be reduced because not all the funds for the current period were spent. The wasting of resources in this way conflicts with the role of budgets as a means of exercising control.

Conflict between the different uses will mean that managers must decide which particular uses for budgets should be given priority; managers must be prepared, if necessary, to trade off the benefits resulting from one particular use for the benefits of another.

The budget-setting process

Budgeting is such an important area for businesses, and other organisations, that it tends to be approached in a fairly methodical and formal way. This usually involves a number of steps, as described below.

Step 1: Establish who will take responsibility

It is usually seen as crucial that those responsible for the budget-setting process have real authority within the business.

Activity 12.8

Why is it crucial that those responsible for the budget-setting process have real authority?

One of the crucial aspects of the process is establishing co-ordination between budgets so that the plans of one department match, and are complementary to, those of other departments. This usually requires compromise where adjustment of initial budgets must be undertaken. This, in turn, means that someone on the board of directors (or its equivalent) has to be closely involved; only people of this rank are likely to have the necessary authority to force departmental managers to compromise.

→ Quite commonly, a **budget committee** is formed to supervise and take responsibility for the budget-setting process. This committee usually includes a senior representative of most of the functional areas of the business – marketing, production, personnel and so on.

→ Often, a **budget officer** is appointed to carry out the technical tasks of the committee, or to supervise others carrying them out. Not surprisingly, given their technical expertise in the activity, accountants are often required to take the role of budget officer.

Step 2: Communicate budget guidelines to relevant managers

Budgets are intended to be the short-term plans that seek to work towards the achievement of strategic plans and to the overall objectives of the business. It is therefore important that, in drawing up budgets, managers are well aware of what the strategic plans are and how the forthcoming budget period is intended to work towards them. Managers also need to be made well aware of the commercial/economic environment in which they will be operating. It is the responsibility of the budget committee to see that managers have all the necessary information.

Step 3: Identify the key, or limiting, factor

As we saw earlier in the chapter (page 434), there will be a limiting factor that will restrict the business from achieving its objectives to the maximum extent. It can be very helpful if the limiting factor is identified at the earliest stage in the budget-setting process.

Step 4: Prepare the budget for the area of the limiting factor

The limiting factor will determine the overall level of activity for the business. The limiting-factor budget will quite often be the sales budget since the ability to sell is frequently the limiting factor that simply cannot be eased. (When discussing the interrelationship of budgets earlier in the chapter, we started with the sales budget for this reason.) As we have seen, sales demand is not always the limiting factor.

Real World 12.1 looks at the methods favoured by businesses of different sizes to determine their sales budgets.

Real World 12.1

Sources of the sales budget in practice

Determining the future level of sales can be a difficult problem. In practice, a business may rely on the judgements of sales staff, statistical techniques or market surveys (or some combination of these) to arrive at a sales budget. A survey of UK manufacturing businesses provides the following insights concerning the use of such techniques and methods.

	All respondents	Small businesses	Large businesses
Number of respondents	281	47	46
	%	%	%
Technique:			
Statistical forecasting	31	19	29
Market research	36	13	54
Subjective estimates based on sales staff experience	85	97	80

We can see that the most popular approach by far is the opinion of sales staff. We can also see that there are differences between large and small businesses, particularly concerning the use of market surveys. This evidence is now pretty old, but in the absence of more up-to-date research it provides some idea of how businesses determine their sales targets.

Source: Drury *et al*. (see reference 1 at the end of the chapter).

Step 5: Prepare draft budgets for all other areas

The other budgets are prepared, complementing the budget for the area of the limiting factor. In all budget preparation, the computer has become an indispensable tool. Much of the work of preparing budgets is repetitive and tedious, yet the resultant budget has to be a reliable representation of the actual plans made. Computers are ideally suited to such tasks whereas human beings are not. It is often the case that budgets have to be redrafted several times because of some minor alteration, and computers do this without complaint.

There are two broad approaches to setting individual budgets. The *top-down approach* is where the senior management of each budget area originates the budget targets, perhaps discussing them with lower levels of management and, as a result, refining them before the final version is produced. With the *bottom-up approach*, the targets are fed upwards from the lowest level. For example, junior sales managers will be asked to set their own sales targets, which then become incorporated into the budgets of higher levels of management until the overall sales budget emerges.

Where the bottom-up approach is adopted, it is usually necessary to haggle and negotiate at different levels of authority to reach agreement. This may be because the plans of some departments do not fit in with those of others or because the targets set by junior managers are not acceptable to their superiors. This approach seems rarely to be found in practice.

Activity (12.9)

What are the advantages and disadvantages of each type of budgeting approach?

The bottom-up approach allows greater involvement of managers in the budgeting process and this, in turn, may increase the level of commitment to the targets set. It also allows the business to draw more fully on the local knowledge and expertise of its managers. However, this approach can be time consuming and may result in some managers setting undemanding targets for themselves in order to have an easy life.

The top-down approach enables senior management to communicate plans to employees and to co-ordinate the activities of the business more easily. It may also help in establishing more demanding targets for managers. However, the level of commitment to the budget may be lower as many of those responsible for achieving the budgets will have been excluded from the budget-setting process.

There will be further discussion of the benefits of participation in target setting in Chapter 13.

Step 6: Review and co-ordinate budgets

A business's budget committee must at this stage review the various budgets and satisfy itself that the budgets complement one another. Where there is a lack of co-ordination, steps must be taken to ensure that the budgets mesh. Since this will require that at least one budget must be revised, this activity normally benefits from a diplomatic approach. Ultimately, however, the committee may be forced to assert its authority and insist that alterations are made.

Step 7: Prepare the master budgets

The master budgets are the budgeted income statement and budgeted balance sheet (and perhaps a summarised budgeted cash flow statement). All of the information required to prepare these statements should be available from the individual budgets that have already been prepared. The budget committee usually undertakes the task of preparing the master budgets.

Step 8: Communicate the budgets to all interested parties

The formally agreed budgets are now passed to the individual managers who will be responsible for their implementation. This is, in effect, senior management formally communicating to the other managers the targets that they are expected to achieve.

Step 9: Monitor performance relative to the budget

Much of the budget-setting activity will have been pointless unless each manager's actual performance is compared with planned performance, which is embodied in the budget. This issue is examined in detail in Chapter 13.

Real World 12.2 shows how the UK-based international engineering and support services business Babcock International Group plc undertakes its budgeting process.

Real World 12.2

Budgeting at Babcock

According to its annual report, Babcock International Group has the following arrangements for budgeting:

> Comprehensive budgeting systems are in place to develop budgets and medium term financial plans. The budgets are subject to review by central management prior to submission to the Board for approval. Updated forecasts for the year are prepared on a regular basis. Actual performance is compared each month with budgets, forecasts and the prior year with written commentary on significant variances from approved plans.

Source: Babcock International Group plc Annual Report 2006, p. 32.

The steps in the budget-setting process are shown in diagrammatic form in Figure 12.5.

Using budgets in practice

There is quite a lot of recent survey evidence that reveals the extent to which budgeting is used by businesses in practice. **Real World 12.3** reviews some of this evidence and shows that most businesses prepare and use budgets.

Real World 12.3

Budgeting in practice

A recent survey of 41 UK manufacturing businesses found that 40 of the 41 prepare budgets.

Source: Dugdale *et al.* (see reference 2 at the end of the chapter).

Another recent survey of UK businesses, but this time businesses involved in the food and drink sector, found that virtually all of them use budgets.

Source: Abdel-Kader and Luther (see reference 3 at the end of the chapter).

Figure 12.5 **Steps in the budget-setting process**

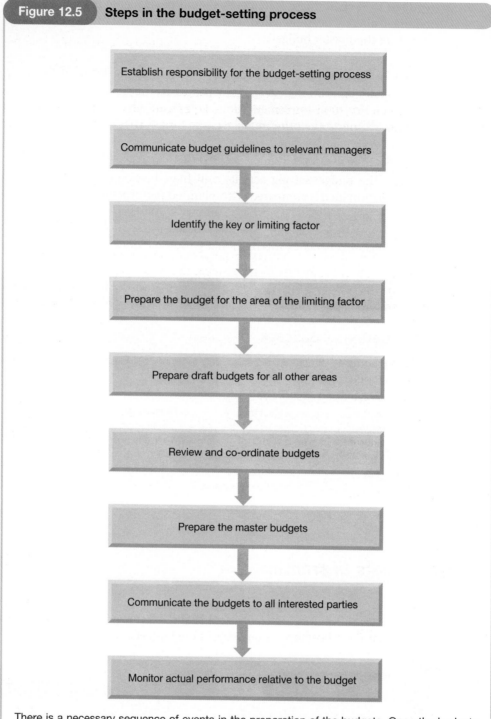

There is a necessary sequence of events in the preparation of the budgets. Once the budgets are prepared, they are communicated to all interested parties and, in due course, actual performance is monitored in relation to the targets set out in the budgets.

Real World 12.3 continued

A survey of management accounting practice in the US was conducted in 2003. Nearly 2,000 businesses replied to the survey. These tended to be larger businesses, of which about 40 per cent were manufacturers and about 16 per cent financial services; the remainder were across a range of other industries.

The survey revealed that 75 per cent use operational budgeting extensively, with a further 16 per cent considering using the technique in the future.

Source: Ernst and Young (see reference 4 at the end of the chapter).

Although these three surveys relate to UK and US businesses, they provide some insights about what is likely also to be practice elsewhere in the developed world.

A fairly recent survey of budgeting practice in small and medium-sized enterprises (SMEs) (see **Real World 12.4**) revealed that not all such businesses fully use budgeting. It seems that some smaller businesses prepare budgets only for what they see as key areas. The budget that is most frequently prepared by such businesses is the sales budget, followed by the budgeted income statement and the overheads budget. Perhaps surprisingly, the cash budget is prepared by less than two-thirds of the small businesses surveyed.

Real World 12.4

Preparation of budgets in SMEs

A study of budgeting practice in small and medium-sized enterprises (SMEs) revealed that the most frequently prepared budget is the sales budget, followed by the budgeted income statement and the overheads budget (see Figure 12.6).

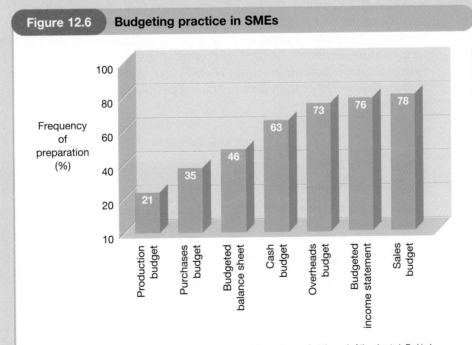

Figure 12.6   Budgeting practice in SMEs

Source: Reproduced from Figure 16 on p. 22 of Chittenden *et al*. (see reference 5 at the end of the chapter). By kind permission of the authors.

Incremental and zero-base budgeting

Traditionally, much budget setting has been on the basis of what happened last year, with some adjustment for any changes in factors that are expected to affect the forthcoming budget period (for example, inflation). This approach is sometimes known as **incremental budgeting**; it is often used for 'discretionary' budgets, such as research and development and staff training, where the **budget holder** (the manager responsible for the budget) is allocated a sum of money to be spent in the area of activity concerned. They are referred to as **discretionary budgets** because the sum allocated is normally at the discretion of senior management. These budgets are very common in local and central government (and in other public bodies), but are also used in commercial businesses to cover certain types of activity.

Discretionary budgets are often used for activities where these is no clear relationship between inputs (resources applied) and outputs (benefits). Compare this with, say, a raw materials usage budget in a manufacturing business, where the amount of material used and, therefore, the amount of funds involved, is clearly related to the level of production and, ultimately, to sales volumes. It is easy for discretionary budgets to eat up funds with no clear benefit being derived. Often only proposed increases in these budgets are closely scrutinised.

Zero-base budgeting (ZBB) rests on the philosophy that all spending needs to be justified. Thus, when establishing, say, the training budget each year, it is not automatically accepted that training courses should be financed in the future simply because they were undertaken this year. The training budget will start from a zero base (that is no resources at all) and will be increased above zero only if a good case can be made. Top management will need to be convinced that the proposed activities represent 'value for money'.

ZBB encourages managers to adopt a more questioning approach to their areas of responsibility. To justify the allocation of resources, they are often forced to think carefully about the particular activities and the ways in which they are undertaken. This questioning approach should result in a more efficient use of business resources. With an increasing portion of the total costs of most businesses being in areas where the link between outputs and inputs is not always clear, and where commitment of resources is discretionary rather than demonstrably essential to production, ZBB is increasingly relevant.

Activity 12.10

Can you think of any disadvantages of using ZBB? How might any disadvantages be partially overcome?

The principal problems with ZBB are:

- It is time consuming and therefore expensive to undertake.
- Managers whose sphere of responsibility is subjected to ZBB can feel threatened by it.

The benefits of a ZBB approach can be gained to some extent – perhaps at not too great a cost – by using the approach on a selective basis. For example, a particular budget area could be subjected to ZBB-type scrutiny only every third or fourth year. In any case, if ZBB is used more frequently, there is the danger that managers will use the same arguments each year to justify their activities. The process will simply become a mechanical exercise and the benefits will be lost. For a typical business, some areas are likely to benefit from ZBB more than others. ZBB could, in these circumstances, be applied only to those areas that will benefit from it, and not to the others. The areas that are most likely to benefit from ZBB are discretionary spending ones, such as training, advertising, and research and development.

If senior management is aware of the potentially threatening nature of this form of budgeting, care can be taken to apply ZBB with sensitivity. However, in the quest for cost control and value for money, the application of ZBB can result in some tough decisions being made.

Real World 12.5 provides some insight to the extent that ZBB is used in practice.

Real World 12.5

ZBB is not food and drink to many businesses

The 2001 survey of businesses in the UK food and drink sector found that ZBB is not much used by them. Only 48 per cent ever use it and only 16 per cent use it 'often' or 'very often'.

ZBB is, however most appropriate with 'spending' budgets, such as training, advertising and so on, which probably represent a minority for the types of business in this survey.

Source: Abdel-Kader and Luther (see reference 3 at the end of the chapter).

Preparing the cash budget

We shall now look in some detail at how the various budgets used by the typical business are prepared, starting with the cash budget and then looking at the others. It is helpful for us to start with the cash budget because:

- it is a key budget (some observers see it as a 'master budget' – along with the budgeted income statement and balance sheet); most economic aspects of a business are reflected in cash sooner or later, so that for a typical business, the cash budget reflects the whole business more than any other single budget;
- very small, unsophisticated businesses (for example, a corner shop) may feel that full-scale budgeting is not appropriate to their needs, but almost certainly they should prepare a cash budget as a minimum (despite the survey evidence mentioned in Real World 12.4).

Since budgets are documents that are to be used only internally by a business, their style is a question of management choice and will vary from one business to the next. However, as managers, irrespective of the business, are likely to be using budgets for similar purposes, some consistency of approach tends to be found. In most businesses, the cash budget will probably possess the following features:

1 The budget period would be broken down into sub-periods, typically months.
2 The budget would be in columnar form, with one column for each month.
3 Receipts of cash would be analysed under various headings and a total for each month's receipts shown.
4 Payments of cash would be analysed under various headings and a total for each month's payments shown.
5 The surplus of total cash receipts over payments, or of payments over receipts, for each month would be identified.
6 The running cash balance would be identified. This would be achieved by taking the balance at the end of the previous month and adjusting it for the surplus or deficit of receipts over payments for the current month.

Typically, all of the pieces of information in points 3 to 6 above would be useful to management for one reason or another.

Probably the best way to deal with this topic is through an example.

Example 12.1

Vierra Popova Ltd is a wholesale business. The budgeted income statements for each of the next six months are as follows:

	Jan £000	Feb £000	Mar £000	Apr £000	May £000	June £000
Sales revenue	52	55	55	60	55	53
Cost of goods sold	30	31	31	35	31	32
Salaries and wages	10	10	10	10	10	10
Electricity	5	5	4	3	3	3
Depreciation	3	3	3	3	3	3
Other overheads	2	2	2	2	2	2
Total expenses	50	51	50	53	49	50
Profit for the month	2	4	5	7	6	3

The business allows all of its customers one month's credit (this means, for example, that cash from January sales will be received in February). Sales revenue during December totalled £60,000.

The business plans to maintain inventories at their existing level until some time in March, when they are to be reduced by £5,000. Inventories will remain at this lower level indefinitely. Inventories purchases are made on one month's credit. December purchases totalled £30,000. Salaries, wages and 'other overheads' are paid in the month concerned. Electricity is paid quarterly in arrears in March and June. The business plans to buy and pay for a new delivery van in March. This will cost a total of £15,000, but an existing van will be traded in for £4,000 as part of the deal.

The business expects to have £12,000 in cash at the beginning of January.

The cash budget for the six months ending in June will look as follows:

	Jan £000	Feb £000	Mar £000	Apr £000	May £000	June £000
Receipts						
Trade receivables (Note 1)	60	52	55	55	60	55
Payments						
Trade payables (Note 2)	30	30	31	26	35	31
Salaries and wages	10	10	10	10	10	10
Electricity			14			9
Other overheads	2	2	2	2	2	2
Van purchase	–	–	11	–	–	–
Total payments	42	42	68	38	47	52
Cash surplus	18	10	(13)	17	13	3
Opening balance (Note 3)	12	30	40	27	44	57
Closing balance	30	40	27	44	57	60

Notes:

1 The cash receipts from trade receivables lag a month behind sales because customers are given a month in which to pay for their purchases. So, December sales will be paid for in January, and so on.

2 In most months, the purchases of inventories will equal the cost of goods sold. This is because the business maintains a constant level of inventories. For inventories to remain constant at the end of each month, the business must replace exactly the amount that has been used. During March, however, the business plans to reduce its inventories by £5,000. This means that inventories purchases will be lower than inventories usage in that month. The payments for inventories purchases lag a month behind purchases because the business expects to be allowed a month to pay for what it buys.

3 Each month's cash balance is the previous month's figure plus the cash surplus (or minus the cash deficit) for the current month. The balance at the start of January is £12,000 according to the information provided earlier.

4 Depreciation does not give rise to a cash payment. In the context of profit measurement (in the income statement), depreciation is a very important aspect. Here, however, we are interested only in cash.

Activity (12.11)

Looking at the cash budget of Vierra Popova Ltd, what conclusions do you draw and what possible course of action do you recommend regarding the cash balance over the period concerned?

There appears to be a fairly large cash balance, given the size of the business, and it seems to be increasing. Management might give consideration to putting some of the cash into an income-yielding deposit. Alternatively, it could be used to expand the trading activities of the business by, for example, increasing the investment in non-current (fixed) assets.

Activity 12.12

Vierra Popova Ltd (Example 12.1) now wishes to prepare its cash budget for the second six months of the year. The budgeted income statements for each month of the second half of the year are as follows:

	July £000	Aug £000	Sept £000	Oct £000	Nov £000	Dec £000
Sales revenue	57	59	62	57	53	51
Cost of goods sold	32	33	35	32	30	29
Salaries and wages	10	10	10	10	10	10
Electricity	3	3	4	5	6	6
Depreciation	3	3	3	3	3	3
Other overheads	2	2	2	2	2	2
Total expenses	50	51	54	52	51	50
Profit for the month	7	8	8	5	2	1

The business will continue to allow all of its customers one month's credit.

It plans to increase inventories from the 30 June level by £1,000 each month until, and including, September. During the following three months, inventories levels will be decreased by £1,000 each month.

Inventories purchases, which had been made on one month's credit until the June payment, will, starting with the purchases made in June, be made on two months' credit.

Salaries, wages and 'other overheads' will continue to be paid in the month concerned. Electricity is paid quarterly in arrears in September and December.

At the end of December, the business intends to pay off part of some borrowings. This payment is to be such that it will leave the business with a cash balance of £5,000 with which to start next year.

Prepare the cash budget for the six months ending in December. (Remember that any information you need that relates to the first six months of the year, including the cash balance that is expected to be brought forward on 1 July, is given in Example 12.1.)

The cash budget for the six months ended 31 December is:

	July £000	Aug £000	Sept £000	Oct £000	Nov £000	Dec £000
Receipts						
Trade receivables	53	57	59	62	57	53
Payments						
Trade payables (Note 1)	–	32	33	34	36	31
Salaries and wages	10	10	10	10	10	10
Electricity	–	–	10	–	–	17
Other overheads	2	2	2	2	2	2
Borrowings repayment (Note 2)	–	–	–	–	–	131
Total payments	12	44	55	46	48	191
Cash surplus	41	13	4	16	9	(138)
Opening balance	60	101	114	118	134	143
Closing balance	101	114	118	134	143	5

Notes:
1 There will be no payment to trade payables in July because the June purchases will be made on two months' credit and will therefore be paid in August. The July purchases, which will equal the July cost of sales figure plus the increase in inventories made in July, will be paid for in September, and so on.
2 The amount of the borrowings repayment is simply the amount that will cause the balance at 31 December to be £5,000.

Preparing other budgets

Though each one will have its own particular features, other budgets will tend to follow the same sort of pattern as the cash budget, that is, they will show inflows and outflows during each month and the opening and closing balances in each month.

Example 12.2

To illustrate some of the other budgets, we shall continue to use the example of Vierra Popova Ltd that we considered in Example 12.1. To the information given there, we need to add the fact that the inventories balance at 1 January was £30,000.

Show the trade receivables, trade payables and inventories budgets for the six months.

Solution

Trade receivables budget

This would normally show the planned amount owing from credit sales to the business at the beginning and at the end of each month, the planned total sales revenue for each month and the planned total cash receipts from receivables. The layout would be something like the following:

	Jan £000	Feb £000	Mar £000	Apr £000	May £000	June £000
Opening balance	60	52	55	55	60	55
Add Sales revenue	52	55	55	60	55	53
	112	107	110	115	115	108
Less Cash receipts	60	52	55	55	60	55
Closing balance	52	55	55	60	55	53

The opening and closing balances represent the amount that the business plans to be owed (in total) by credit customers (trade receivables) at the beginning and end of each month, respectively.

Trade payables budget

Typically this shows the planned amount owed to suppliers by the business at the beginning and at the end of each month, the planned purchases for each month and the planned total cash payments to trade payables. The layout would be something like the following:

	Jan £000	Feb £000	Mar £000	Apr £000	May £000	June £000
Opening balance	30	30	31	26	35	31
Add Purchases	30	31	26	35	31	32
	60	61	57	61	66	63
Less Cash payment	30	30	31	26	35	31
Closing balance	30	31	26	35	31	32

The opening and closing balances represent the amount planned to be owed (in total) by the business to suppliers (trade payables), at the beginning and end of each month respectively.

Inventories budget
This would normally show the planned amount of inventories to be held by the business at the beginning and at the end of each month, the planned total inventories purchases for each month and the planned total monthly inventories usage. The layout would be something like the following:

	Jan £000	Feb £000	Mar £000	Apr £000	May £000	June £000
Opening balance	30	30	30	25	25	25
Add Purchases	30	31	26	35	31	32
	60	61	56	60	56	57
Less Inventories used	30	31	31	35	31	32
Closing balance	30	30	25	25	25	25

The opening and closing balances represent the amount of inventories, at cost, planned to be held by the business at the beginning and end of each month respectively.

A *raw materials inventories budget*, for a manufacturing business, would follow a similar pattern, with the 'inventories usage' being the cost of the inventories put into production. A *finished inventories budget* for a manufacturer would also be similar to the above, except that 'inventories manufactured' would replace 'purchases'. A manufacturing business would normally prepare both a raw materials inventories budget and a finished inventories budget. Both of these would typically be based on the full cost of the inventories (that is, including overheads). There is no reason why the inventories should not be valued on the basis of either variable cost or direct costs, should managers feel that this would provide more useful information.

The inventories budget will normally be expressed in financial terms, but may also be expressed in physical terms (for example, kg or metres) for individual inventories items.

Note how the trade receivables, trade payables and inventories budgets in Example 12.2 link to one another, and to the cash budget for the same business in Example 12.1. Note particularly that the following rows of figures are identified:

- purchases in the trade payables budget and the inventories budget are identical;
- cash payments in the trade payables budget and the cash budget are identical;
- cash receipts in the trade receivables budget and the cash budget are identical.

Other values would link different budgets in a similar way. For example, the row of sales revenue figures in the trade receivables budget would be identical to the sales revenue figures that will be found in the sales budget. This is how the linking (co-ordination), which was discussed earlier in this chapter, is achieved.

Activity 12.13

Have a go at preparing the trade receivables budget for Vierra Popova Ltd for the six months from July to December (see Activity 12.12).

The trade receivables budget for the six months ended 31 December is:

	July £000	Aug £000	Sept £000	Oct £000	Nov £000	Dec £000
Opening balance (Note 1)	53	57	59	62	57	53
Add Sales revenue (Note 2)	57	59	62	57	53	51
	110	116	121	119	110	104
Less Cash receipts (Note 3)	53	57	59	62	57	53
Closing balance (Note 4)	57	59	62	57	53	51

Notes:
1 The opening trade receivables figure is the previous month's sales revenue figure (sales are on one month's credit).
2 The sales revenue is the current month's figure.
3 The cash received each month is equal to the previous month's sales revenue figure.
4 The closing balance is equal to the current month's sales revenue figure.

Note that if we knew any three of the four figures each month, we could deduce the fourth.
    This budget could be set out in any manner that would have given the sort of information that management would require in respect of planned levels of trade receivables and associated transactions.

Activity 12.14

Have a go at preparing the trade payables budget for Vierra Popova Ltd for the six months from July to December (see Activity 12.12). (*Hint*: Remember that the trade payables' payment period alters from the June purchases onwards.)

The trade payables budget for the six months ended 31 December is:

Activity 12.14 continued

	July £000	Aug £000	Sept £000	Oct £000	Nov £000	Dec £000
Opening balance	32	65	67	70	67	60
Add Purchases	33	34	36	31	29	28
	65	99	103	101	96	88
Less Cash payments	–	32	33	34	36	31
Closing balance	65	67	70	67	60	57

This, again, could be set out in any manner that would have given the sort of information that management would require in respect of planned levels of trade payables and associated transactions.

Activity-based budgeting

Activity-based budgeting (ABB) applies the philosophy of activity-based costing (ABC), which we discussed in Chapter 11, to planning and control through budgets. We should recall that ABC recognises that it is activities that cause, or 'drive', costs. If the cost-driving activities can be identified, ascertaining the cost of the output of a business can be achieved with greater accuracy. This should lead to more accurate budgeting and so it will become more reasonable to expect budget holders to meet the projected cost of planned levels of activity. Control through budgets should therefore be more achievable in an ABB environment. In addition costs become easier to manage simply because their cause is known.

It is a central feature of budgeting that those who are responsible for meeting a particular budget (budget holders) should have control over the events that affect performance in their area. Ensuring that this is always the case can be problematical. For example, a decision made at a senior level to increase the volume of activity for the business might lead to an increase in the costs for a particular junior manager, that takes those costs above the budgeted level. The junior manager might be held responsible for the cost increase, yet the volume change was beyond that manager's control. In other words, the costs are driven by activities not controlled by the manager who is being held accountable for those costs.

ABB seeks to generate budgets in such a way that the manager who has control over the cost drivers is accountable for the costs that are caused.

Real World 12.6 provides some indication of the extent that ABB is used in practice.

Real World 12.6

ABB is not often on the menu

The 2001 survey of UK food and drink businesses found that ABB is not much used by them. Only 19 per cent use it 'often' or 'very often'. Not surprisingly, businesses that use ABC are much more likely to use ABB as well.

Interestingly, ABB seems to be used by more businesses than use ABC for product costing. This implies that the 'activity-based' approach is more used in cost management than in determining product costs.

Source: Abdel-Kader and Luther (see reference 3 at the end of the chapter).

Non-financial measures in budgeting

The efficiency of internal operations and customer satisfaction levels have become of critical importance to businesses striving to survive in an increasingly competitive environment. Non-financial performance indicators have an important role to play in assessing performance in such key areas as customer/supplier delivery times, set-up times, defect levels and customer satisfaction levels.

There is no reason why budgeting need be confined to financial targets and measures. As we saw in Chapter 11 (page 393), non-financial measures can also be used as the basis for targets. They can also be incorporated into the budgeting process and reported alongside the financial targets for the business.

Budgets and management behaviour

All accounting statements and reports are intended to affect the behaviour of one or another group of people. Budgets are intended to affect the behaviour of managers, for example to encourage them to work towards the business's objectives and to do this in a co-ordinated manner.

Whether budgets are effective and how they can be made more effective are crucial issues for managers. We shall examine this topic in detail in the next chapter, after we have seen how budgets can be used to help managers to exercise control.

Self-assessment question 12.1

Antonio Ltd has planned production and sales for the next nine months as follows:

	Production Units	Sales Units
May	350	350
June	400	400
July	500	400
August	600	500
September	600	600
October	700	650
November	750	700
December	750	800
January	750	750

During the period, the business plans to advertise in order to generate these increases in sales. Payments for advertising of £1,000 and £1,500 will be made in July and October, respectively.

The selling price per unit will be £20 throughout the period. Forty per cent of sales are normally made on two months' credit. The other 60 per cent are settled within the month of the sale.

Raw materials will be held for one month before they are taken into production. Purchases of raw materials will be on one month's credit (buy one month, pay the next). The cost of raw materials is £8 per unit of production.

Self-assessment question 12.1 continued

Other direct production expenses, including labour, are £6 per unit of production. These will be paid in the month concerned.

Various production overheads, which during the period to 30 June had run at £1,800 a month, are expected to rise to £2,000 each month from 1 July to 31 October. These are expected to rise again from 1 November to £2,400 a month and to remain at that level for the foreseeable future. These overheads include a steady £400 each month for depreciation. Overheads are planned to be paid 80 per cent in the month of production and 20 per cent in the following month.

To help to meet the planned increased production, a new item of plant will be bought and delivered in August. The cost of this item is £6,600; the contract with the supplier will specify that this will be paid in three equal amounts in September, October and November.

Raw materials inventories are planned to be 500 units on 1 July. The balance at the bank on the same day is planned to be £7,500.

Required:

(a) Draw up the following for the six months ending 31 December:
   (i) A raw materials inventories budget, showing both physical quantities and financial values.
   (ii) A trade payables budget.
   (iii) A cash budget.
(b) The cash budget reveals a potential cash deficiency during October and November. Can you suggest any ways in which a modification of plans could overcome this problem?

The answer to this question can be found at the back of the book on pages 703–4.

Who needs budgets?

Until recently it would have been a heresy to suggest that budgeting was not of central importance to any business. The benefits of budgeting, mentioned earlier in this chapter, have been widely recognised and the vast majority of businesses prepare annual budgets. However, there is increasing concern that, in today's highly dynamic and competitive environment, budgets may actually be harmful to the achievement of business objectives. This has led a small but growing number of businesses to abandon traditional budgets as a tool of planning and control.

Various charges have been levelled against the conventional budgeting process, including the following:

- Budgets cannot deal with a fast-changing environment and that they are often out of date even before the start of the budget period.
- Budgets focus too much management attention on the achievement of short-term financial targets. Instead, managers should focus on the things that create value for the business (for example, innovation, building brand loyalty, responding quickly to competitive threats).
- Budgets reinforce a 'command and control' structure that concentrates power in the hands of senior managers and prevents junior managers from exercising autonomy. This may be particularly true where a top-down approach, that allocates budgets to

managers, is being used. Where managers feel constrained, attempts to retain and recruit able managers can be difficult.

- Budgeting takes up an enormous amount of management time that could be better used. In practice, budgeting can be a lengthy process that may involve much negotiation, reworking and updating. However, this may add little to the achievement of business objectives.

- Budgets are based around business functions (sales, marketing, production). However, to achieve the business's objectives, the focus should be on business processes that cut across functional boundaries and reflect the needs of the customer.

- Budgets encourage incremental thinking by using a 'last year plus x per cent' approach to planning. This can inhibit the development of 'break-out' strategies that may be necessary in a fast-changing environment.

- Budgets can protect costs rather than lower costs. In some cases, a fixed budget for an activity, such as research and development, is allocated to a manager. If the amount is not spent, the budget may be taken away and, in future periods, the budget for this activity may be either reduced or eliminated. Such a response to unused budget allocations can encourage managers to spend the whole of the budget, irrespective of need, in order to protect the allocations they receive.

- Budgets promote 'sharp' practice among managers. In order to meet budget targets, managers may try to negotiate lower sales targets or higher cost allocations than they feel is really necessary. This helps them to build some 'slack' into the budgets and so meeting the budget becomes easier (see reference 6 at the end of the chapter).

Although, some believe that many of the problems identified can be solved by better budgeting systems such as activity-based budgeting and zero-base budgeting, others believe that a more radical solution is required.

Beyond conventional budgeting

As we have just seen, some businesses have abandoned budgeting in recent years, though they still recognise the need for forward planning. No one seriously doubts that there must be appropriate systems in place to steer a business towards its objectives. It is claimed, however, that the systems adopted should reflect a broader, more integrated approach to planning. The new systems that have been implemented are often based around a 'leaner' financial planning process that is more closely linked to other measurement and reward systems. Emphasis is placed on the use of rolling forecasts, key performance indicators (such as market share, customer satisfaction and innovations) and/or 'scorecards' (like the Balanced Scorecard, which we met in Chapter 11) that identify both financial and non-financial targets to be achieved over the long term and short term. These are often very demanding ('stretch') targets, based on benchmarks that have been set by world-class businesses.

The new 'beyond budgeting' model promotes a more decentralised, participative approach to managing the business. It is claimed that the traditional hierarchical management structure, where decision making is concentrated at the higher levels of the hierarchy, encourages a culture of dependency where meeting the budget targets set by senior managers is the key to managerial success. This traditional structure is replaced by a network structure where decision making is devolved to 'front-line' managers. In the new structure a more open, questioning attitude among employees is encouraged.

There is a sharing of knowledge and best practice, and protective behaviour by managers is discouraged. In addition, rewards are linked to targets based on improvement in relative performance rather than to meeting the budget. It is claimed that this new approach allows greater adaptability to changing conditions, increases performance and increases motivation among staff.

Figure 12.7 sets out the main differences between the traditional and 'beyond budgeting' planning models.

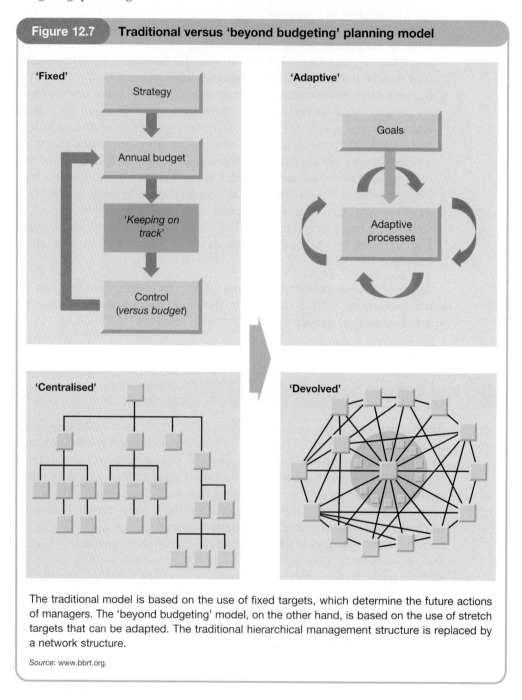

Figure 12.7   Traditional versus 'beyond budgeting' planning model

The traditional model is based on the use of fixed targets, which determine the future actions of managers. The 'beyond budgeting' model, on the other hand, is based on the use of stretch targets that can be adapted. The traditional hierarchical management structure is replaced by a network structure.

Source: www.bbrt.org.

Real World 12.7 reveals the experience of one business that decided to abandon conventional budgets.

Real World 12.7

Volvo abandons budgets

Jeremy Hope and Robin Fraser are at the forefront of those who argue that budgeting systems have an adverse effect on the ability of businesses to compete effectively. The following is a short case study of Volvo Cars that they have written.

New steering mechanisms at Volvo Cars

Following losses in 1990 to 1992 and a small profit in 1993, Volvo Cars decided to make a number of important changes, one of which was to adopt a radically different approach to managing the business. But senior managers were quick to realise that such an approach was unlikely to be successful in the longer term unless they tackled the problems of the budgeting and planning process that encouraged the old mindset of compliance and control. As Ole Johannesson, VP finance, explains, 'the budget and long-range planning systems are no longer efficient when the business environment is changing more and more rapidly. Today we need a process that enables us to react not only immediately but even beforehand'. In 1994 there was no budget requested by the Group company, AB Volvo, from operating units for the forthcoming year, 1995. As Johannesson notes, 'we recognised the extent of the cultural change needed. We wanted less and less of order-giving, victims of circumstance, administration, checking, reactive positions, functional ties and hierarchical thinking, and more and more of creating opportunities, communication, development, confidence-building, proactive positions, network ties, and process thinking.' Since that time Volvo Cars has built a highly advanced management model that has helped it face the intense competitive pressures that are endemic to the world car market.

Volvo reckoned that its previous planning, budgeting and control processes absorbed around 20 per cent of total management time. By abandoning these processes and managing in a different way, managers have not only saved significant costs but they now have more time to focus on strategy, action planning and beating the competition. This is a battle not tied to an annual cycle, but is waged continuously month by month and quarter by quarter. Strategy and forecasts are reviewed and updated several times a year with four distinct cycles apparent. Each month a 'flash' forecast is prepared covering the next three months; each quarter a two-year rolling forecast is updated; and each year sees a revised four-year and ten-year strategic plan. While targets are broad-brush and comprise a number of key performance indicators, there is more time spent on developing action plans to support them. Monthly reports to the board include financial information (actual month, actual year-to-date, forecast remainder of year, revised forecast for total years, and last year-to-date) and a number of key performance indicators such as market share, order intake, customer satisfaction, product costs, dealer profitability, warranty costs, fault frequency, and total ownership cost (all where possible compared with the competition). Four years after dismantling the budgeting process there is now a strong 'responsibility' and 'no blame' culture at Volvo Cars.

According to Ole Johannesson, 'managers now know that they mustn't come to meetings with problems, but with explanations about what they've done to solve them.' The management accountants now spend more time collecting a whole range of measurement data but, more importantly, they see their role as one of analysing and interpreting the data so that operating managers can take the appropriate action. Indeed the whole emphasis is on 'actions' rather than 'problems'. Volvo has transformed itself into an action-oriented company in which decisions are made by people at the appropriate level to meet changing conditions. This has contributed to Volvo's remarkable turnaround. It now ranks as the sixteenth largest motor vehicle manufacturer in the world, but in terms of profitability it is second only to Ford on profits, on sales revenue and assets.

Source: Hope and Fraser (see reference 7 at the end of the chapter), p. 17.

Note: Since this case study was written, Volvo has become part of the Ford Motor Company. It is possible that the success of the business led Ford to acquire Volvo.

It is perhaps too early to predict whether the trickle of businesses that are now seeking an alternative to budgets will turn into a flood. However, it is clear that in today's highly competitive environment a business must be flexible and responsive to changing conditions. Management systems that in any way hinder these attributes will not survive.

Long live budgets!

It is worth remembering that, despite the criticisms, budgeting remains a very widely used technique. Real Worlds 12.3 and 12.4 provide evidence for this. There is also evidence that the criticisms of budgeting are not too widely shared. **Real World 12.8** is an account of a round-table discussion at a Better Budgeting forum held in London in March 2004. This was attended by representatives of 32 large organisations, including BAA (the airport operator), the BBC, Ford Motors, Sainsbury (the supermarket business) and Unilever (the household goods group).

Real World 12.8

Alive and kicking

The report of the Better Budgeting forum discussions said:

> If you were to believe all that has been written in recent years, you'd be forgiven for thinking that budgeting is on its way to becoming extinct. Various research reports allude to the widespread dissatisfaction with the bureaucratic exercise in cost cutting that budgeting is accused of having become. Budgets are pilloried as being out of touch with the needs of modern business and accused of taking too long, costing too much and encouraging all sorts of perverse behaviour.
>
> Yet if there was one conclusion to emerge from the day's discussions it was that budgets are in fact alive and well. Not only did all the organisations present operate a formal budget, but all bar two had no interest in getting rid of it. Quite the opposite – although aware of the problems it can cause, the participants by and large regarded the budgeting system and the accompanying processes as indispensable.

Later in the report, in what could have been a reference to Volvo's use of 'rolling forecasts' (see Real World 12.7), it said:

> It quickly became obvious that, as one participant put it, 'one man's budget is another man's rolling forecast'. What people refer to when they talk about budgeting could in reality be very different things.

This presumably meant that businesses that abandon 'budgets' reintroduce them under another name.

Source: CIMA/ICAEW (see reference 8 at the end of the chapter).

In the next chapter we shall look in some detail at how budgets can be adapted for use as devices for exercising management control.

Summary

The main points of this chapter may be summarised as follows.

A budget is a short-term business plan, mainly expressed in financial terms.

- Budgets are the short-term means of working towards the business's objectives.
- They are usually prepared for a one-year period with sub-periods of a month.
- There is usually a separate budget for each key area.

Uses of budgets

- Promote forward thinking.
- Help co-ordinate the various aspects of the business.
- Motivate performance.
- Provide the basis of a system of control.
- Provide a system of authorisation.

Budget-setting process

- Establish who will take responsibility.
- Communicate guidelines.
- Identify key factor.
- Prepare budget for key factor area.
- Prepare draft budgets for all other areas.
- Review and co-ordinate.
- Prepare master budgets (income statement and balance sheet).
- Communicate the budgets to interested parties.
- Monitor performance relative to budget.

Preparing budgets

- There is no standard style – practicality and usefulness are the key issues.
- They are usually prepared in columnar form, with a column for each month (or similarly short period).
- Each budget must link (co-ordinate) with others.

Criticisms of budgets

- Cannot deal with rapid change.
- Focus on short-term financial targets, rather than value creation.
- Encourage a 'top-down' management style.
- Time consuming.
- Based around traditional business functions and do not cross boundaries.
- Encourage incremental thinking (last year's figure, plus *x* per cent).
- Protect rather than lower costs.
- Promote 'sharp' practice among managers.
- Budgeting is widely regarded as useful and extensively practised despite the criticisms.

 Now check your progress in your personal Study Plan

Key terms

mission statement p. 431	management by exception p. 438
budget p. 431	budget committee p. 440
control p. 432	budget officer p. 440
limiting factor p. 434	incremental budgeting p. 446
forecast p. 434	budget holder p. 446
periodic budget p. 434	discretionary budget p. 446
continual budget p. 434	zero-base budgeting (ZBB) p. 446
rolling budget p. 435	activity-based budgeting (ABB)
master budget p. 435	p. 454

References

1 **A Survey of Management Accounting Practices in UK Manufacturing Companies**, *Drury C., Braund S., Osborne P. and Tayles M.*, Chartered Association of Certified Accountants, 1993.

2 **Contemporary Management Accounting Practices in UK Manufacturing**, *Dugdale D., Jones C. and Green S.*, CIMA Research Publication, vol. 1, no. 13, 2005.

3 **An Empirical Investigation of the Evolution of Management Accounting Practices**, *Abdel-Kader M. and Luther R.*, Working paper no. 04/06, University of Essex, October 2004.

4 **2003 Survey of Management Accounting**, *Ernst and Young*, Ernst and Young, 2003.

5 **Financial Management and Working Capital Practices in UK SMEs**, *Chittenden F., Poutziouris P. and Michaelis N.*, Manchester Business School, 1998.

6 **Beyond budgeting**, www.beyondbudgeting.plus.com.

7 'Beyond budgeting', *Hope J. and Fraser R.*, **Management Accounting**, January 1999.

8 **Better Budgeting**, *CIMA/ICAEW*, Chartered Institute of Management Accountants and The Faculty of Finance and Management, Institute of Chartered Accountants in England and Wales, March 2004.

Further reading

If you would like to explore the topics covered in this chapter in more depth, we recommend the following books:

Cost Accounting: **A managerial emphasis**, *Horngren C., Datar S. and Foster G.*, 12th edn, Prentice Hall, 2006, chapter 6.

Management Accounting, *Atkinson A., Kaplan R., Young S.M. and Matsumura E.*, 5th edn, Prentice Hall, 2007, chapter 10.

Management and Cost Accounting, *Drury C.*, 6th edn, Thomson Learning, 2004, chapter 15.

Managerial Accounting, *Hilton R.*, 6th edn, McGraw-Hill/Irwin, 2005, chapter 9.

Review questions

Answers to these questions can be found at the back of the book on pages 782–3.

12.1 Define a budget. How is a budget different from a forecast?

12.2 What were the five uses of budgets that were identified in the chapter?

12.3 What do budgets have to do with control?

12.4 What is a budget committee? What purpose does it serve?

Exercises

Exercises 12.5 to 12.8 are more advanced than 12.1 to 12.4. Those with **coloured numbers** have answers at the back of the book, starting on page 743.

If you would like to try more exercises, visit the students' side of the Companion Website.

12.1 Daniel Chu Ltd, a new business, will start production on 1 April, but sales will not start until 1 May. Planned sales for the next nine months are as follows:

	Sales Units
May	500
June	600
July	700
August	800
September	900
October	900
November	900
December	800
January	700

The selling price of a unit will be a consistent £100 and all sales will be made on one month's credit. It is planned that sufficient finished goods inventories for each month's sales should be available at the end of the previous month.

Raw materials purchases will be such that there will be sufficient raw materials inventories available at the end of each month precisely to meet the following month's planned production. This planned policy will operate from the end of April. Purchases of raw materials will be on one month's credit. The cost of raw material is £40 a unit of finished product.

The direct labour cost, which is variable with the level of production, is planned to be £20 a unit of finished production. Production overheads are planned to be £20,000 each month, including £3,000 for depreciation. Non-production overheads are planned to be £11,000 a month, of which £1,000 will be depreciation.

Various non-current assets costing £250,000 will be bought and paid for during April.

Except where specified, assume that all payments take place in the same month as the cost is incurred.

The business will raise £300,000 in cash from a share issue in April.

Required:

Draw up the following for the six months ending 30 September:

(a) A finished inventories budget, showing just physical quantities.
(b) A raw materials inventories budget showing both physical quantities and financial values.
(c) A trade payables budget.
(d) A trade receivables budget.
(e) A cash budget.

12.2 You have overheard the following statements:

(a) 'A budget is a forecast of what is expected to happen in a business during the next year.'
(b) 'Monthly budgets must be prepared with a column for each month so that you can see the whole year at a glance, month by month.'
(c) 'Budgets are OK but they stifle all initiative. No manager worth employing would work for a business that seeks to control through budgets.'
(d) 'Activity-based budgeting is an approach that takes account of the planned volume of activity in order to deduce the figures to go into the budget.'
(e) 'Any sensible person would start with the sales budget and build up the other budgets from there.'

Required:

Critically discuss these statements, explaining any technical terms.

12.3 A nursing home, which is linked to a large hospital, has been examining its budgetary control procedures, with particular reference to overhead costs.

The level of activity in the facility is measured by the number of patients treated in the budget period. For the current year, the budget stands at 6,000 patients and this is expected to be met.

For months 1 to 6 of this year (assume 12 months of equal length), 2,700 patients were treated. The actual variable overhead costs incurred during this six-month period are as follows:

Expense	£
Staffing	59,400
Power	27,000
Supplies	54,000
Other	8,100
Total	148,500

The hospital accountant believes that the variable overhead costs will be incurred at the same rate during months 7 to 12 of the year.

Fixed overhead costs are budgeted for the whole year as follows:

Expense	£
Supervision	120,000
Depreciation/financing	187,200
Other	64,800
Total	372,000

Required:

(a) Present an overheads budget for months 7 to 12 of the year. You should show each expense, but should not separate individual months. What is the total overhead cost for each patient that would be incorporated into any statistics?

(b) The home actually treated 3,800 patients during months 7 to 12, the actual variable over-heads were £203,300, and the fixed overheads were £190,000. In summary form, examine how well the home exercised control over its overheads.

(c) Interpret your analysis and point out any limitations or assumptions.

12.4 Linpet Ltd is to be incorporated on 1 June. The opening balance sheet of the business will then be as follows:

Assets	£
Cash at bank	60,000
Share capital (£1 ordinary shares)	60,000

During June, the business intends to make payments of £40,000 for a leasehold property, £10,000 for equipment and £6,000 for a motor vehicle. The business will also purchase initial trading inventories costing £22,000 on credit.

The business has produced the following estimates:

(i)   Sales revenue for June will be £8,000 and will increase at the rate of £3,000 a month until September. In October, sales revenue will rise to £22,000 and in subsequent months will be maintained at this figure.

(ii) The gross profit percentage on goods sold will be 25 per cent.

(iii) There is a risk that supplies of trading inventories will be interrupted towards the end of the accounting year. The business therefore intends to build up its initial level of inventories (£22,000) by purchasing £1,000 of inventories each month in addition to the monthly purchases necessary to satisfy monthly sales requirements. All purchases of inventories (including the initial inventories) will be on one month's credit.

(iv) Sales revenue will be divided equally between cash and credit sales. Credit customers are expected to pay two months after the sale is agreed.

(v)   Wages and salaries will be £900 a month. Other overheads will be £500 a month for the first four months and £650 thereafter. Both types of expense will be payable when incurred.

(vi) Eighty per cent of sales revenue will be generated by salespeople who will receive 5 per cent commission on sales revenue. The commission is payable one month after the sale is agreed.

(vii) The business intends to purchase further equipment in November for £7,000 cash.

(viii) Depreciation is to be provided at the rate of 5 per cent a year on freehold property and 20 per cent a year on equipment. (Depreciation has not been included in the overheads mentioned in (v) above.)

Required:

(a) State why a cash budget is required for a business.

(b) Prepare a cash budget for Linpet Ltd for the six-month period to 30 November.

12.5 Lewisham Ltd manufactures one product line: the Zenith. Sales of Zeniths over the next few months are planned to be as follows:

1 *Demand*

	Units
July	180,000
August	240,000
September	200,000
October	180,000

Each Zenith sells for £3.

2 *Receipts from sales.* Credit customers are expected to pay as follows:

- 70 per cent during the month of sale
- 28 per cent during the following month.

The remaining trade receivables are expected to go bad (that is, to be uncollectable). Credit customers who pay in the month of sale are entitled to deduct a 2 per cent discount from the invoice price.

3 *Finished goods inventories.* Inventories of finished goods are expected to be 40,000 units at 1 July. The business's policy is that, in future, the inventories at the end of each month should equal 20 per cent of the following month's planned sales requirements.

4 *Raw materials inventories.* Inventories of raw materials are expected to be 40,000 kg on 1 July. The business's policy is that, in future, the inventories at the end of each month should equal 50 per cent of the following month's planned production requirements. Each Zenith requires 0.5 kg of the raw material, which costs £1.50/kg. Raw materials purchases are paid in the month after purchase.

5 *Labour and overheads.* The direct labour cost of each Zenith is £0.50. The variable overhead element of each Zenith is £0.30. Fixed overheads, including depreciation of £25,000, total £47,000 a month. All labour and overheads are paid during the month in which they arise.

6 *Cash in hand.* At 1 August the business plans to have a bank balance (in funds) of £20,000.

Required:

Prepare the following budgets:

(a) Finished inventories budget (expressed in units of Zenith) for each of the three months July, August and September.

(b) Raw materials inventories budget (expressed in kilograms of the raw material) for the two months July and August.

(c) Cash budget for August and September.

12.6 Newtake Records Ltd owns a chain of 14 shops selling DVDs and CDs. At the beginning of June the business had an overdraft of £35,000 and the bank had asked for this to be eliminated by the end of November. As a result, the directors have recently decided to review their plans for the next six months.

The following plans were prepared for the business some months earlier:

	May £000	June £000	July £000	Aug £000	Sept £000	Oct £000	Nov £000
Sales revenue	180	230	320	250	140	120	110
Purchases	135	180	142	94	75	66	57
Administration expenses	52	55	56	53	48	46	45
Selling expenses	22	24	28	26	21	19	18
Taxation payment				22			
Finance payments	5	5	5	5	5	5	5
Shop refurbishment	–	–	14	18	6	–	–

Notes:

(i) The inventories level at 1 June was £112,000. The business believes it is preferable to maintain a minimum inventories level of £40,000 of goods over the period to 30 November.

(ii) Suppliers allow one month's credit. The first three months' purchases are subject to a contractual agreement, which must be honoured.

(iii) The gross profit margin is 40 per cent.

(iv) All sales proceeds are received in the month of sale. However, 50 per cent of customers pay with a credit card. The charge made by the credit card business to Newtake Records Ltd is 3 per cent of the sales revenue value. These charges are in addition to the selling expenses identified above. The credit card business pays Newtake Records Ltd in the month of sale.

(v) The business has a bank loan, which it is paying off in monthly instalments of £5,000. The interest element represents 20 per cent of each instalment.

(vi) Administration expenses are paid when incurred. This item includes a charge of £15,000 each month in respect of depreciation.

(vii) Selling expenses are payable in the following month.

Required (working to the nearest £1,000):

(a) Prepare a cash budget for the six months ending 30 November which shows the cash balance at the end of each month.

(b) Compute the inventories levels at the end of each month for the six months to 30 November.

(c) Prepare a budgeted income statement for the whole of the six months period ending 30 November. (A monthly breakdown of profit is *not* required.)

(d) What problems is Newtake Records Ltd likely to face in the next six months? Can you suggest how the business might deal with these problems?

12.7 Prolog Ltd is a small wholesaler of high-powered computers for scientific research. It has in recent months been selling 50 machines a month at a price of £2,000 each. These machines cost £1,600 each. A new model has just been launched and this is expected to offer greatly enhanced performance. Its selling price and cost will be the same as for the old model. From the beginning of January, sales are planned to increase at a rate of 20 machines each month until the end of June, when sales will amount to 170 units a month. They are planned to continue at that level thereafter. Operating costs including depreciation of £2,000 a month are planned as follows:

	January	February	March	April	May	June
Operating costs (£000)	6	8	10	12	12	12

Prolog expects to receive no credit for operating costs. Additional shelving for storage will be bought, installed and paid for in April, costing £12,000. Corporation tax of £25,000 is due at the end of March. Prolog anticipates that trade receivables will amount to two months' sales revenue. To give its customers a good level of service, Prolog plans to hold enough inventories at the end of each month to fulfil anticipated demand from customers in the following month. The computer manufacturer, however, grants one month's credit to Prolog. Prolog Ltd's balance sheet appears below.

Balance sheet at 31 December

	£000	£000
Non-current assets		80
Current assets		
Inventories	112	
Trade receivables	200	
Cash	–	312
Total assets		392
Equity		
Share capital (25p ordinary shares)	10	
Retained profit	177	187
Current liabilities		
Trade payables	112	
Taxation	25	
Overdraft	68	205
Total equity and liabilities		392

Required:
(a) Prepare a cash budget for Prolog Ltd showing the cash balance or required overdraft for the six months ending 30 June.
(b) State briefly what further information a banker would require from Prolog Ltd before granting additional overdraft facilities for the anticipated expansion of sales.

12.8 Brown and Jeffreys, a West Midlands business, makes one standard product for use in the motor trade. The product, known as the Fuel Miser, for which the business holds the patent, when fitted to the fuel system of production model cars has the effect of reducing petrol consumption.

Part of the production is sold direct to a local car manufacturer, which fits the Fuel Miser as an optional extra to several of its models and the rest of the production is sold through various retail outlets, garages and so on.

Brown and Jeffreys assemble the Fuel Miser, but all three components are manufactured by local engineering businesses. The three components are codenamed A, B and C. One Fuel Miser consists of one of each component.

The planned sales for the first seven months of the forthcoming accounting period, by channels of distribution and in terms of Fuel Miser units, are as follows:

	Jan	Feb	Mar	Apr	May	June	July
Manufacturers	4,000	4,000	4,500	4,500	4,500	4,500	4,500
Retail, and so on	2,000	2,700	3,200	3,000	2,700	2,500	2,400
	6,000	6,700	7,700	7,500	7,200	7,000	6,900

The following further information is available:

(i) There will be inventories of finished units at 1 January of 7,000 Fuel Misers.
(ii) The inventories of raw materials at 1 January will be:
  A 10,000 units
  B 16,500 units
  C 7,200 units
(iii) The selling price of Fuel Misers is to be £10 each to the motor manufacturer and £12 each to retail outlets.

(iv) The maximum production capacity of the business is 7,000 units a month. There is no possibility of increasing this output.

(v) Assembly of each Fuel Miser will take 10 minutes of direct labour. Direct labour is paid at the rate of £7.20 an hour during the month of production.

(vi) The components are each expected to cost the following:

A   £2.50

B   £1.30

C   £0.80

(vii) Indirect costs are to be paid at a regular rate of £32,000 each month.

(viii) The cash at the bank at 1 January will be £2,620.

The planned sales volumes must be met and the business intends to pursue the following policies for as many months as possible, consistent with meeting the sales targets:

- Finished inventories at the end of each month are to equal the following month's total sales to retail outlets, and half the total of the following month's sales to the motor manufacturer.
- Raw materials at the end of each month are to be sufficient to cover production requirements for the following month. The production for July will be 6,800 units.
- Suppliers of raw materials are to be paid during the month following purchase. The payment for January will be £21,250.
- Customers will pay in the month of sale, in the case of sales to the motor manufacturer, and the month after sale, in the case of retail sales. Retail sales during December were 2,000 units at £12 each.

Required:

Prepare the following budgets in monthly columnar form, both in terms of money and units (where relevant), for the six months of January to June inclusive:

(a) Sales budget.*

(b) Finished inventories budget (valued at direct cost).†

(c) Raw materials inventories budget (one budget for each component).†

(d) Production budget (direct costs only).*

(e) Trade receivables budget.†

(f) Trade payables budget.†

(g) Cash budget.†

* The sales and production budgets should merely state each month's sales or production in units and in money terms.

† The other budgets should all seek to reconcile the opening balance of inventories, receivables, payables or cash with the closing balance through movements of the relevant factors over the month.

CHAPTER 13

Accounting for control

Introduction

In this chapter we shall deal with the role of budgets in management control. We, therefore, continue some of the themes that we discussed in Chapter 12. We shall consider how a budget can be used to help control a business, and we shall see that, by collecting information on actual performance and comparing it with a revised budget, it is possible to identify those activities that are under control and those that are not. Budgets are designed to influence the behaviour of managers and we shall explore some of the issues relating to budgets and management behaviour. We shall also take a look at standard costing and its relationship with budgeting. We shall see that standards provide the building blocks for budgets.

Learning outcomes

When you have completed this chapter, you should be able to:

- Discuss the role and limitations of budgets for performance evaluation and control.

- Undertake variance analysis and discuss possible reasons for the variances calculated.

- Discuss the issues that should be taken into account when designing an effective system of budgetary control.

- Explain the nature, role and limitations of standard costing.

MyAccountingLab | *Remember to create your own personalised Study Plan*

Budgeting for control

In Chapter 12 we saw that budgets provide a useful basis for exercising control over a business. Control involves making events conform to a plan and, since the budget is a short-term plan, making events conform to it is an obvious way to try to control the business. We saw in Chapter 12 that, for most businesses, the routine is as shown in Figure 13.1.

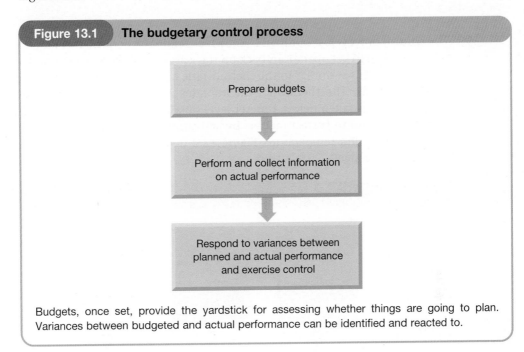

Figure 13.1 **The budgetary control process**

Prepare budgets

Perform and collect information on actual performance

Respond to variances between planned and actual performance and exercise control

Budgets, once set, provide the yardstick for assessing whether things are going to plan. Variances between budgeted and actual performance can be identified and reacted to.

If plans are drawn up sensibly, we have a basis for exercising control over the business. We must, however, measure actual performance in the same terms as those in which the budget is stated. If they are not in the same terms, valid comparison will not be possible.

Exercising control involves finding out where and why things did not go according to plan and then seeking ways to put them right for the future. One reason why things may not have gone according to plan is that the budget targets were unachievable. In this case, it may be necessary to revise the budgets for future periods so that targets become achievable.

This last point should not be taken to mean that budget targets can simply be ignored if the going gets tough; rather that they should be adaptable. Unrealistic budgets cannot form a basis for exercising control and little can be gained by sticking with them. Budgets may become unrealistic for a variety of reasons, including unexpected changes in the commercial environment (for example, an unexpected collapse in demand for services of the type that the business provides).

By having a system of budgetary control, decision making and responsibility can be delegated to junior management, yet senior management can still retain control. This is because senior managers can use the budgetary control system to find out which junior managers are meeting targets and therefore working towards achieving the objectives of the business. (We should remember that budgets are the short-term plans for achieving the business's objectives.) This enables a **management-by-exception**

environment to be created where senior management can focus on areas where things are not going according to plan (the exceptions – it is to be hoped). Junior managers who are performing to budget can be left to get on with their jobs.

Evidence (including that shown in Real World 13.2 on page 483) suggests that this approach is widely used by businesses in practice.

Types of control

→ The control process just outlined is known as **feedback control**. Its main feature is that steps are taken to get operations back on track as soon as there is a signal that they have gone wrong. This is similar to the thermostatic control that is a feature of most central heating systems. The thermostat incorporates a thermometer that senses when the temperature has fallen below a preset level (analogous to the budget). The thermostat then takes action to correct matters by activating the heating device that restores the required minimum temperature. Figure 13.2 depicts the stages in a feedback control system using budgets.

Figure 13.2   **Feedback control**

When a comparison of actual and budgeted performance shows a divergence, steps can be taken to get performance back to plan. If the plan needs revising, this can be done.

→   There is an alternative type of control, known as **feedforward control**. Here predictions are made as to what can go wrong and steps taken to avoid any undesirable outcome. The preparation of budgets, which we discussed in Chapter 12, provides an example of this type of control. Preparing a particular budget may reveal a problem that will arise unless the business changes its plans. For example, preparing the cash budget may reveal that if the original plans are followed there will be a negative cash balance for part of the budget period. Having identified the problem, the plans can then be revised to deal with it.

We can see that feedforward controls try to anticipate future problems whereas feedback controls react to problems that have already occurred. Budgeting embraces both forms of control. Preparing a budget is a form of feedforward control whereas comparing the budget with actual results is a form of feedback control. Generally speaking, feedforward controls are preferable: things are less likely to go wrong in the first place if steps have been taken to anticipate problems and plan accordingly. It is not always possible, however, to establish effective feedforward controls.

Variances from budget

The main financial objective of most businesses is to enhance their owners' (shareholders') wealth. Since profit is the net increase in wealth from business operations, the most important budget target to meet is the profit target. We shall therefore take this as our starting point when comparing the budget with the actual results. Example 13.1 shows the budgeted and actual income statement for Baxter Ltd for the month of May.

Example 13.1

The following are the budgeted and actual income statements for Baxter Ltd, a manufacturing business, for the month of May:

	Budget	Actual
Output (production and sales)	1,000 units	900 units
	£	£
Sales revenue	100,000	92,000
Raw materials	(40,000) (40,000 metres)	(36,900) (37,000 metres)
Labour	(20,000) (2,500 hours)	(17,500) (2,150 hours)
Fixed overheads	(20,000)	(20,700)
Operating profit	20,000	16,900

From these figures it is clear that the budgeted profit was not achieved. As far as May is concerned, this is a matter of history. However, the business (or at least one aspect of it) is out of control. Senior management must discover where things went wrong during May and try to ensure that these mistakes are not repeated in later months. It is not enough to know that things went wrong overall. We need to know where and why. The approach taken is to compare the budgeted and actual figures for the various items (sales, raw materials and so on) in the above statement.

Activity 13.1

Can you see any problems in comparing the various items (sales, raw materials and so on) for the budget and the actual performance of Baxter Ltd in order to draw conclusions as to which aspects were out of control?

The problem is that the actual level of output was not as budgeted. The actual level of output was 10 per cent less than budget. This means that we cannot, for example, say that there was a labour cost saving of £2,500 (that is, £20,000 – £17,500) and conclude that all is well in that area.

Flexing the budget

One practical way to overcome our difficulty is to 'flex' the budget to what it would have been had the planned level of output been 900 units rather than 1,000 units. **Flexing the budget** simply means revising it, assuming a different volume of output.

To exercise control, the budget is usually flexed to reflect the volume that actually occurred, where this is higher or lower than that originally planned. This means that we need to know which revenues and costs are fixed and which are variable relative to the volume of output. Once we know this, flexing is a simple operation. We shall assume that sales revenue, material cost and labour cost vary strictly with volume. Fixed overheads, by definition, will not. Whether, in real life, labour cost does vary with the volume of output is not so certain, but it will serve well enough as an assumption for our purposes. Were labour costs actually fixed, we should simply take this into account in the flexing process.

On the basis of our assumptions regarding the behaviour of revenues and costs, the flexed budget would be as follows:

	Flexed budget
Output (production and sales)	900 units
	£
Sales revenue	90,000
Raw materials	(36,000) (36,000 metres)
Labour	(18,000) (2,250 hours)
Fixed overheads	(20,000)
Operating profit	16,000

This is simply the original budget, with the sales revenue, raw materials and labour cost figures scaled down by 10 per cent (the same factor as the actual output fell short of the budgeted one).

Putting the original budget, the flexed budget and the actual for May together, we obtain the following:

	Original budget	Flexed budget	Actual
Output (production and sales)	1,000 units	900 units	900 units
	£	£	£
Sales revenue	100,000	90,000	92,000
Raw materials	(40,000)	(36,000) (36,000m)	(36,900) (37,000m)
Labour	(20,000)	(18,000) (2,250 hr)	(17,500) (2,150 hr)
Fixed overheads	(20,000)	(20,000)	(20,700)
Operating profit	20,000	16,000	16,900

Flexible budgets enable us to make a more valid comparison between the budget (using the flexed figures) and the actual results. Key differences, or variances, between budgeted and actual results for each aspect of the business's activities can then be calculated. In the rest of this section, we consider some of the variances that may be calculated.

Sales volume variance

It may seem as if we are saying that it does not matter if there are volume shortfalls, because we just revise the budget and carry on as if all is well. However, this is not the case, because losing sales generally means losing profit. The first point we must pick up, therefore, is the loss of profit arising from the loss of sales of 100 units of the product.

Activity 13.2

What will be the loss of profit arising from the sales volume shortfall, assuming that everything except sales volume was as planned?

The answer is simply the difference between the original and flexed budget profit figures. The only difference between these two profit figures is the volume of sales; everything else was the same. Thus the figure is £4,000 (that is, £20,000 – £16,000).

As we saw in Chapter 9, when we considered the relationship between cost, volume and profit, selling one unit less will result in one less contribution to profit. The contribution is sales revenue less variable cost. We can see from the original budget that the unit sales revenue is £100 (that is, £100,000/1,000), raw materials cost is £40 a unit (that is, £40,000/1,000) and labour cost is £20 a unit (that is, £20,000/1,000). Thus the contribution is £40 a unit (that is, £100 – [£40 + £20]).

If, therefore, 100 units of sales are lost, £4,000 (that is, 100 × £40) of contributions, and therefore profit, is forgone. This would be an alternative means of finding the sales volume variance, rather than taking the difference between the original and flexed budget profit figures. Once we have produced the flexed budget, however, it is generally easier to compare the two profit figures.

The difference between the original and flexed budget profit figures is called the *sales volume variance*. In this case, it is an **adverse variance** because, taken alone, it has the effect of making the actual profit lower than that which was budgeted. A variance that has the effect of increasing profit above that which is budgeted is known as a **favourable variance**. We can therefore say that a **variance** is the effect of that factor (taken alone) on the budgeted profit. When looking at some particular aspect, such as sales volume, we assume that all other factors went according to plan. This is shown in Figure 13.3.

> **Sales volume variance**
> The difference between the operating profit, as shown in the original budget, and the operating profit, as shown in the flexed budget for the period.

Activity 13.3

What else does the senior management of Baxter Ltd need to know about the May sales volume variance?

It needs to know why the volume of sales fell below the budgeted figure. Only by discovering this information will management be in a position to try to see that it does not occur again.

Who should be held accountable for this sales volume variance? The answer is probably the sales manager, who should know precisely why this has occurred. This is

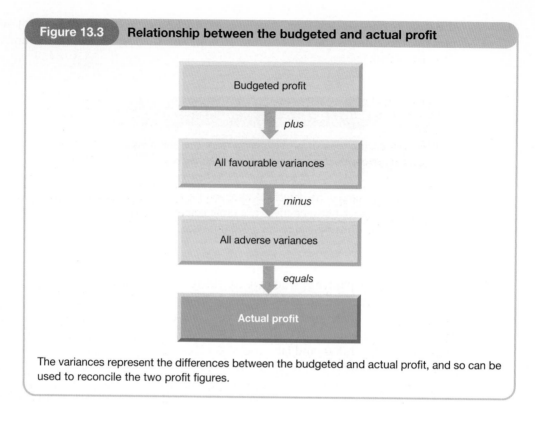

Figure 13.3 Relationship between the budgeted and actual profit

The variances represent the differences between the budgeted and actual profit, and so can be used to reconcile the two profit figures.

not the same as saying, however, that it was the sales manager's fault. The problem may have been that the business failed to produce the budgeted quantities so that not enough items were available to sell. Nevertheless, the sales manager should know the reason for the problem.

The budget and actual figures for Baxter Ltd for *June* are given in Activity 13.4 and will be used as the basis for a series of activities that provide an opportunity to calculate and assess the variances. We shall continue to use the *May* figures for explaining the variances.

Note that the business had budgeted for a higher level of output for *June* than it did for *May*.

Activity 13.4

	Budget for June	Actual for June
Output (production and sales)	1,100 units	1,150 units
	£	£
Sales revenue	110,000	113,500
Raw materials	(44,000) (44,000 metres)	(46,300) (46,300 metres)
Labour	(22,000) (2,750 hours)	(23,200) (2,960 hours)
Fixed overheads	(20,000)	(19,300)
Operating profit	24,000	24,700

Try flexing the June budget, comparing it with the original June budget, and so find the sales volume variance.

Output (production and sales)	*Flexed budget* 1,150 units
	£
Sales revenue	115,000
Raw materials	(46,000) (46,000 metres)
Labour	(23,000) (2,875 hours)
Fixed overheads	(20,000)
Operating profit	26,000

The sales volume variance is £2,000 (favourable) (that is, £26,000 – £24,000). It is favourable because the original budget profit was lower than the flexed budget profit. This arises from more sales actually being made than were budgeted.

By dealing with the sales volume variance, we have picked up the profit difference caused by any variation between the budgeted and the actual volumes of sales. This means that, for the remainder of our analysis of the difference between the budgeted and actual profits, we can ignore the original budget. We can focus exclusively on the differences between the figures in the flexed budget and the actual figures.

Each of the revenue and cost items appearing in the income statement (that is, sales revenue, raw materials, labour and fixed overheads) will now be examined in turn.

Sales price variance

Sales price variance
The difference between the actual sales revenue figure for the period and the sales revenue figure as shown in the flexed budget.

Starting with the sales revenue figure, we can see that, for *May*, there is a difference of £2,000 (favourable) between the flexed budget and the actual figures. This can only arise from higher prices being charged than were envisaged in the original budget, because any variance arising from the volume difference has already been 'stripped out' in the flexing process. This price difference is known as the *sales price variance*. Higher sales prices will, all other things being equal, mean more profit. So there is a favourable variance.

Activity 13.5

Using the figures in Activity 13.4, what is the sales price variance for June?

The sales price variance for *June* is £1,500 (adverse) (that is, £115,000 – £113,500). Actual sales prices, on average, must have been lower than those budgeted. The actual price averaged £98.70 (that is, £113,500/1,150) whereas the budgeted price was £100. Selling output at a lower price than that budgeted will have an adverse effect on profit, hence an adverse variance.

Let us now move on to look at the cost variances, starting with materials variances.

Materials variances

Total direct materials variance
The difference between the actual direct materials cost and the direct materials cost according to the flexed budget (budgeted usage for the actual output).

Direct materials usage variance
The difference between the actual quantity of direct materials used and the quantity of direct materials according to the flexed budget (budgeted usage for actual output). This quantity is multiplied by the budgeted direct materials cost for one unit of the direct materials.

In *May*, there was an overall or *total direct materials variance* of £900 (adverse) (that is, £36,900 – £36,000). It is adverse because the actual materials cost was higher than the budgeted one, which has an adverse effect on operating profit.

Who should be held accountable for this variance? The answer depends on whether the difference arises from excess usage of the raw material, in which case it is the production manager, or whether it is a higher-than-budgeted cost per metre being paid, in which case it is the responsibility of the buying manager. Fortunately, we can go beyond this total variance to examine the effect of changes in both usage and cost. We can see from the figures that in *May* there was a 1,000 metre excess usage of the raw material (that is, 37,000 metres – 36,000 metres). All other things being equal, this alone would have led to a profit shortfall of £1,000, since clearly the budgeted cost per metre is £1. The £1,000 (adverse) variance is known as the *direct materials usage variance*. Normally, this variance would be the responsibility of the production manager.

Activity 13.6

Using the figures in Activity 13.4, what was the direct material usage variance for June?

The direct material usage variance for June was £300 (adverse) (that is, (46,300 metres – 46,000 metres) × £1). It is adverse because more material was used than was budgeted for an output of 1,150 units. Excess usage of material will tend to reduce profit.

Direct materials price variance
The difference between the actual cost of the direct material used and the direct materials cost allowed (actual quantity of material used at the budgeted direct material cost).

The other aspect of direct materials is the *direct materials price variance*. Here we simply take the actual cost of materials used and compare it with the cost that was allowed, given the quantity used. In *May* the actual cost of direct materials used was £36,900, whereas the allowed cost of the 37,000 metres was £37,000. Thus we have a favourable variance of £100. Paying less than the budgeted cost will have a favourable effect on profit, hence a favourable variance.

Activity 13.7

Using the figures in Activity 13.4, what was the direct materials price variance for June?

The direct materials price variance for June was zero (that is, £46,300 – (46,300 × £1)).

As we have just seen, the total direct materials variance is the sum of the usage variance and the price variance. This is illustrated in Figure 13.4.

Figure 13.4   Relationship between the total, usage and price variances for direct materials

The total direct materials variance is the sum of the direct materials usage variance and the price variance, and can be analysed into those two.

Labour variances

Total direct labour variance
The difference between the actual direct labour cost and the direct labour cost according to the flexed budget (budgeted direct labour hours for the actual output).

Direct labour efficiency variance
The difference between the actual direct labour hours worked and the number of direct labour hours according to the flexed budget (budgeted direct labour hours for the actual output). This figure is multiplied by the budgeted direct labour rate for one hour.

Direct labour variances are similar in form to those for direct materials. The *total direct labour variance* for *May* was £500 (favourable) (that is, £18,000 – £17,500). It is favourable because £500 less was spent on labour than was budgeted for the actual level of output achieved.

Again, this information is not particularly helpful, and needs to be analysed further, since the responsibility for the rate of pay lies primarily with the personnel manager whereas the number of hours taken to complete a particular quantity of output is the responsibility of the production manager.

The *direct labour efficiency variance* compares the number of hours that would be allowed for the achieved level of production with the actual number of hours. It then costs this difference at the allowed hourly rate. Thus, for *May*, it was (2,250 hours – 2,150 hours) × £8 = £800 (favourable). We know that the budgeted hourly rate is £8 because the original budget shows that 2,500 hours were budgeted to cost £20,000. The variance is favourable because fewer hours were used than would have been allowed for the actual level of output. Working more quickly would tend to lead to higher profit.

Activity 13.8

Using the figures in Activity 13.4, what was the direct labour efficiency variance for June?

The direct labour efficiency variance for June was £680 (adverse) (that is, (2,960 hours – 2,875 hours) × £8). It is adverse because the work took longer than the budget allowed and so will have an adverse effect on profit.

Direct labour rate variance
The difference between the actual cost of the direct labour hours worked and the direct labour cost allowed (actual direct labour hours worked at the budgeted labour rate).

The *direct labour rate variance* compares the actual cost of the hours worked with the allowed cost. For 2,150 hours worked in *May*, the allowed cost would be £17,200 (that is, 2,150 × £8). So, the direct labour rate variance is £300 (adverse) (that is, £17,500 – £17,200).

Activity 13.9

Using the figures in Activity 13.4, what was the direct labour rate variance for June?

The direct labour rate variance for June was £480 (favourable) (that is, (2,960 × £8) – £23,200). It is favourable because a lower rate was paid than the budgeted one. Paying a lower wage rate will have a favourable effect on profit.

Fixed overhead variance

The final area is that of overheads. In our example, we have assumed that all of the overheads are fixed. Variable overheads certainly exist in practice, but they have been omitted here simply to restrict the amount of detailed coverage. Variances involving variable overheads are similar in style to labour and material variances.

Fixed overhead spending variance
The difference between the actual fixed overhead cost and the fixed overhead cost, according to the flexed (and the original) budget.

The *fixed overhead spending variance* is simply the difference between the flexed (or original – they will be the same) budget and the actual figures. For *May*, this was £700 (adverse) (that is, £20,700 – £20,000). It is adverse because more overheads cost was actually incurred than was budgeted. This would tend to lead to less profit. In theory, this is the responsibility of whoever controls overheads expenditure.

In practice, overheads tend to be a very slippery area, and one that is notoriously difficult to control. Of course, fixed overheads (and variable ones) are usually made up of more than one type of cost. Typically, they would include such things as rent, administrative costs, salaries of managerial staff, cleaning, electricity and so on. These could be individually budgeted and the actuals recorded. This would enable individual spending variances to be identified for each element of overheads, which in turn would enable managers to identify any problem areas.

Activity 13.10

Using the figures in Activity 13.4, what was the fixed overhead spending variance for June?

The fixed overhead spending variance for June was £700 (favourable) (that is, £20,000 – £19,300). It was favourable because less was spent on overheads than was budgeted, thereby having a favourable effect on profit.

We are now in a position to reconcile the original *May* budgeted operating profit with the actual operating profit, as follows:

	£	£
Budgeted operating profit		20,000
Add **Favourable variances**		
Sales price	2,000	
Direct materials price	100	
Direct labour efficiency	800	2,900
		22,900
Less **Adverse variances**		
Sales volume	4,000	
Direct materials usage	1,000	
Direct labour rate	300	
Fixed overhead spending	700	6,000
Actual operating profit		16,900

Activity (13.11)

Using the figures in Activity 13.4, try reconciling the original operating profit figure for June with the actual June figure.

	£	£
Budgeted operating profit		24,000
Add **Favourable variances**		
Sales volume	2,000	
Direct labour rate	480	
Fixed overhead spending	700	3,180
		27,180
Less **Adverse variances**		
Sales price	1,500	
Direct materials usage	300	
Direct labour efficiency	680	2,480
Actual operating profit		24,700

Activity (13.12)

The following are the budgeted and actual income statements for Baxter Ltd for the month of July:

	Budget	Actual
Output (production and sales)	1,000 units	1,050 units
	£	£
Sales revenue	100,000	104,300
Raw materials	(40,000) (40,000 metres)	(41,200) (40,500 metres)
Labour	(20,000) (2,500 hours)	(21,300) (2,600 hours)
Fixed overheads	(20,000)	(19,400)
Operating profit	20,000	22,400

Produce a reconciliation of the budgeted and actual operating profit, going into as much detail as possible with the variance analysis.

→

Activity 13.12 continued

The original budget, the flexed budget and the actual are as follows:

	Original budget	Flexed budget	Actual
Output (production and sales)	1,000 units	1,050 units	1,050 units
	£	£	£
Sales revenue	100,000	105,000	104,300
Raw materials	(40,000)	(42,000) (42,000m)	(41,200) (40,500m)
Labour	(20,000)	(21,000) (2,625 hr)	(21,300) (2,600 hr)
Fixed overheads	(20,000)	(20,000)	(19,400)
Operating profit	20,000	22,000	22,400

Reconciliation of the budgeted and actual operating profits for July

	£	£
Budgeted operating profit		20,000
Add **Favourable variances**		
Sales volume (22,000 − 20,000)	2,000	
Direct materials usage [(42,000 − 40,500) × £1]	1,500	
Direct labour efficiency [(2,625 − 2,600) × £8]	200	
Fixed overhead spending (20,000 − 19,400)	600	4,300
		24,300
Less **Adverse variances**		
Sales price (105,000 − 104,300)	700	
Direct materials price [(40,500 × £1) − 41,200]	700	
Direct labour rate [(2,600 × £8) − 21,300]	500	1,900
Actual operating profit		22,400

Real World 13.1 shows how two UK-based businesses, Next plc, the retailer, and British Airways, the airline operator, use **variance analysis** to exercise control over their operations. Many businesses explain in their annual reports how they operate systems of budgetary control.

Real World 13.1

Exercising control

What Next?

According to its annual report, Next has the following arrangements:

> The Board is responsible for approving semi-annual Group budgets. Performance against budget is reported to the Board monthly and any substantial variances are explained.

BA at the controls

BA makes it clear that it too uses budgets and variance analysis to help keep control over its activities. The annual report says:

A comprehensive management accounting system is in place providing financial and operational performance measurement indicators to management. Detailed management accounts are prepared monthly to cover each major area of the business. Variances from plan are analysed, explained and acted on in a timely manner.

The board of directors of these businesses will not seek explanations of variances arising at each branch/flight/department, but they will be looking at figures for the businesses as a whole or the results for major divisions of them.

Equally certainly, branch/department manager will receive a monthly (or perhaps more frequent) report of variances arising within their area of responsibility alone.

Sources: Next plc Annual Report 2006, p. 14; and British Airways plc Annual Report 2006, p. 8.

Real World 13.2 gives some indication of the importance of flexible budgeting in practice.

Real World 13.2

Flexing the budgets

A study of the UK food and drink industry by Abdel-Kader and Luther in 2004 provides some insight as to the importance attached by management accountants to flexible budgeting. The study asked those in charge of the management accounting function to rate the importance of flexible budgeting by selecting one of three possible categories: 'not important', 'moderately important' or 'important'. Figure 13.5 sets out the results, from the sample of 117 respondents.

Figure 13.5	Degree of importance attached to flexible budgeting

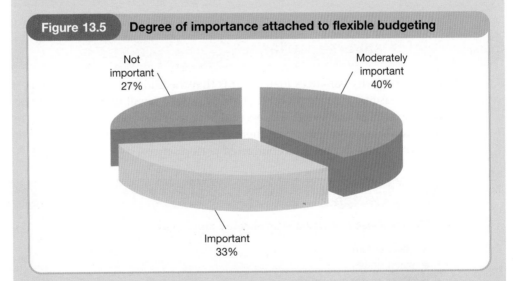

Respondents were also asked to state the frequency with which flexible budgeting was used within the business, using a five-point scale ranging from 1 (never) through to 5 (very often). Figure 13.6 sets out the results.

Real World 13.2 continued

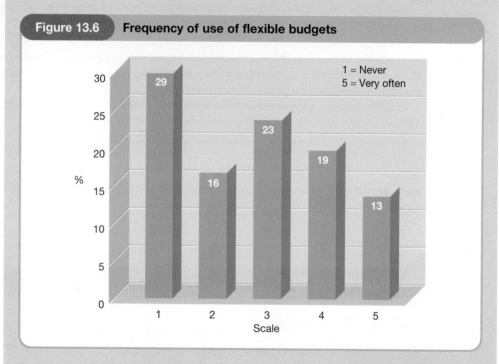

Figure 13.6   **Frequency of use of flexible budgets**

We can see that although flexible budgeting is regarded as important by a significant proportion of management accountants and is being used in practice, not all businesses use it.

Source: Based from information in Abdel-Kader and Luther (see reference 1 at the end of the chapter).

Reasons for adverse variances

One reason why variances may occur is that the budgets against which performance is being measured are unachievable. This is always a possibility that should be considered when examining variances. Unless budgets are achievable, they are not a useful means of exercising control. However, there are certainly other reasons that may lead to actual performance to deviate from budgeted performance.

Activity (13.13)

The variances that we have considered are:

- sales volume
- sales price
- direct materials usage
- direct materials price
- direct labour efficiency
- direct labour rate
- fixed overhead spending.

Assuming that the budget targets are reasonable, jot down some possible reasons for adverse variances for each of the above occurring.

The reasons that we thought of included the following:

Sales volume
- Poor performance by sales staff.
- Deterioration in market conditions between the time that the budget was set and the actual event.
- Lack of goods or services to sell as a result of some production problem.

Sales price
- Poor performance by sales staff.
- Deterioration in market conditions between the time of setting the budget and the actual event.

Direct materials usage
- Poor performance by production department staff, leading to high rates of scrap.
- Substandard materials, leading to high rates of scrap.
- Faulty machinery, causing high rates of scrap.

Direct materials price
- Poor performance by the buying department staff.
- Change in market conditions between the time that the budget was set and the actual event.

Labour efficiency
- Poor supervision.
- A low-skill grade of worker taking longer to do the work than was envisaged for the correct skill grade.
- Low-grade materials, leading to high levels of scrap and wasted labour time.
- Problems with a customer for whom a service is being rendered.
- Problems with machinery, leading to labour time being wasted.
- Dislocation of materials supply, leading to workers being unable to proceed with production.

Labour rate
- Poor performance by the personnel department.
- Using a higher grade of worker than was planned.
- Change in labour market conditions between the time of setting the budget and the actual event.

Fixed overheads
- Poor supervision of overheads.
- General increase in costs of overheads not taken into account in the budget.

Different variances may have the same underlying cause. For example, the purchase of low quality, cheaper materials may result in both an unfavourable direct materials usage variance and a favourable direct materials price variance.

Although we have tended to use the example of a manufacturing business to explain variance analysis, this should not be taken to imply that variance analysis is not equally applicable and useful in service sector businesses. It is simply that manufacturing businesses tend to have all of the variances found in practice. Service businesses, for example, may not have materials variances.

Non-operating-profit variances

There are many areas of business that have a budget but where a failure to meet the budget does not have a direct effect on profit. Frequently, however, it has an indirect effect on profit and, sometimes, a profound effect. For example, the cash budget sets out the planned receipts, payments and resultant cash balance for the period. If the person responsible for the cash budget gets things wrong, or is forced to make unplanned expenditures, this could lead to unplanned cash shortages and accompanying costs. These costs might be limited to lost interest on possible investments, which could otherwise have been made, or to the need to pay overdraft interest. If the cash shortage cannot be covered by some form of borrowing, the consequences could be more profound, such as the loss of profits on business that was not able to be undertaken because of the lack of funds.

→ It is clearly necessary that control be exercised over areas such as cash management as well as over those like production and sales in an attempt to avoid adverse **non-operating-profit variances**.

Investigating variances

It is unreasonable to expect budget targets to be met precisely each month and so variances will usually occur. Whatever the reason for a variance, finding out what went wrong will take staff time, and this is costly. Since small variances are almost inevitable, yet investigating variances can be expensive, management needs to establish a policy concerning which variances to investigate and which to accept. For example, for Baxter Ltd (Example 13.1 on page 473) the budgeted usage of materials during May was 40,000 metres at a cost of £1 a metre. Suppose that production had been the same as the budgeted quantity of output, but that 40,005 metres of material, costing £1 a metre, had actually been used. Would this adverse variance of £5 be investigated? Perhaps not, but what if the variance were £50 or £500 or £5,000?

Activity (13.14)

What broad approach do you feel should be taken as to whether to spend money investigating a particular variance?

The general approach to this policy must be concerned with cost and benefit. The benefit likely to be gained from knowing why a variance arose needs to be balanced against the cost of obtaining that knowledge. The issue of balancing the benefit of having information with the cost of having it was discussed in Chapter 1, on page 9.

Unfortunately, in practice, both the cost of investigation and the value of the benefit are difficult to assess in advance of the investigation.

Knowing the reason for a variance can have a value only when it might provide management with the means to bring things back under control, enabling future targets to be met. It should be borne in mind here that variances will normally be either zero, or very close to zero. This is to say that achieving targets, give or take small variances, should be normal.

Broadly, we suggest that the following approach seems sensible:

- Significant *adverse* variances should be investigated because the continuation of the fault that they represent could be very costly. Management must decide what 'significant' means. A certain amount of science, in the form of statistical models, can be used in making this decision. Ultimately, however, it must be a matter of managerial judgement as to what is significant. Perhaps a variance of 5 per cent from the budgeted figure would be deemed to be significant.

- Significant *favourable* variances should probably be investigated as well as those that are unfavourable. Though such variances would not cause such immediate management concern as adverse ones, they still represent things not going according to plan. If actual performance is significantly better than target, it may well mean that the target is unrealistically low.

- Insignificant variances, though not triggering immediate investigation, should be kept under review. For each aspect of operations, the cumulative sum of variances, over a series of control periods, should be zero, with small adverse variances in some periods being compensated for by small favourable ones in others. This should be the case with variances caused by chance factors, which will not necessarily recur.

Where a variance is caused by a more systematic factor, which will recur, the cumulative sum of the periodic variances will not be zero but an increasing figure. Even though the individual variances may be insignificant, this situation may well be worth investigating, particularly if the variances are adverse.

To illustrate this last point, let us consider Example 13.2.

Example 13.2

Indisurers Ltd finds that the variances for direct labour efficiency for processing motor insurance claims, since the beginning of the year, are as follows:

	£		£
January	25 (adverse)	July	20 (adverse)
February	15 (favourable)	August	15 (favourable)
March	5 (favourable)	September	23 (adverse)
April	20 (adverse)	October	15 (favourable)
May	22 (adverse)	November	5 (favourable)
June	8 (favourable)	December	26 (adverse)

The average total cost of labour performing this task is about £1,200 a month. Management believes that none of these variances, taken alone, is significant given the labour cost each month. The question is, are they significant when taken together? If we add them together, taking account of the signs, we find that we have a net adverse variance for the year of £73. Of itself, this too is probably not significant, but we should expect the cumulative total to be close to zero where the variances are random. We might feel that a pattern is developing and, given long enough, a net adverse variance of significant size might build up.

Investigating the labour efficiency might be worth doing. Finding the cause of the variance would put management in a position to correct something systematically going wrong, which could lead to future cost savings. (We should note that twelve periods are probably not enough to reach a statistically sound conclusion on whether the variances are random or not, but it provides an illustration of the point.)

Plotting the cumulative variances, from month to month, as in Figure 13.7, makes it clear what is happening as time proceeds.

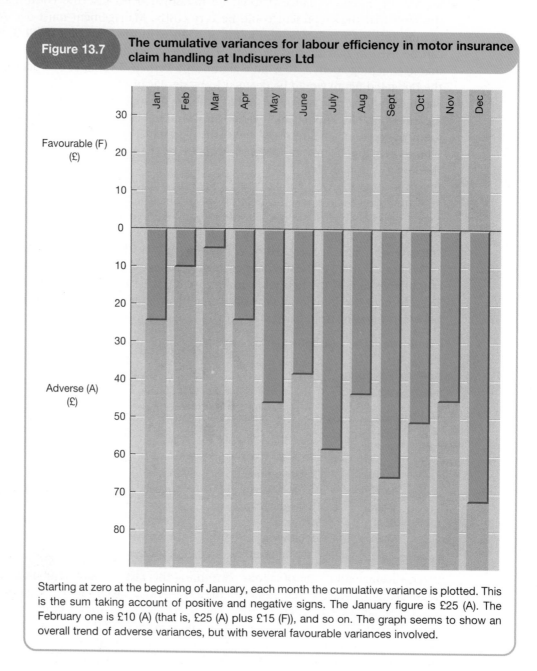

Figure 13.7 The cumulative variances for labour efficiency in motor insurance claim handling at Indisurers Ltd

Starting at zero at the beginning of January, each month the cumulative variance is plotted. This is the sum taking account of positive and negative signs. The January figure is £25 (A). The February one is £10 (A) (that is, £25 (A) plus £15 (F)), and so on. The graph seems to show an overall trend of adverse variances, but with several favourable variances involved.

Real World 13.3 provides some insight to how managers determine whether to investigate variances in practice.

Real World 13.3

Deciding whether to investigate

The table shows the methods used by respondents to decide whether to investigate a particular variance. It is based on a survey of UK manufacturing businesses by Drury *et al*.

	% 'Often' or 'Always'
Decisions based on managerial judgement	75
Variance exceeds a specific monetary amount	41
Variance exceeds a given percentage of the budgeted figure	36
Statistical models	3

Source: Reproduced from Drury *et al*. (see reference 2 at the end of the chapter), p. 39, table 5.7.

It is interesting to note the large extent, revealed by this survey, to which decisions on whether to investigate variances are made on the basis of some, presumably subjective, judgement. We might have expected businesses to adopt a more systematic approach. The survey is not very recent but it probably provides some helpful indication of current practice.

Compensating variances

There is superficial appeal in the idea of **compensating variances**. This involves trading off linked favourable and adverse variances against each other, without further consideration. For example, a sales manager may believe that she could sell more of a particular service if prices were lowered, and that this would feed through to increased operating profit. This would lead to a favourable sales volume variance, but also to an adverse sales price variance. On the face of it, provided that the former is greater than the latter, all would be well.

Activity 13.15

What possible reason is there why the sales manager mentioned above should not go ahead with the price reduction?

The change in policy will have ramifications for other areas of the business, including the following:

- The need for more provision of the service to be available to sell. Staff and other resources may not be available to supply this increase.
- Increased sales volumes would involve an increased need for finance to pay for increased activity, for example to pay additional staff costs.

Thus 'trading off' variances is not automatically acceptable, without a more far-reaching consultation and revision of plans.

Making budgetary control effective

It should be clear from what we have seen of **budgetary control** that a system, or a set of routines, must be put in place to enable the potential benefits to be gained. Most businesses that operate successful budgetary control systems tend to share some common features. These include the following:

- A serious attitude taken to the system by all levels of management, right from the very top. For example, senior managers need to make clear to junior managers that they take notice of the monthly variance reports and base some of their actions and decisions upon them.
- Clear demarcation between areas of managerial responsibility so that accountability can more easily be ascribed for any area that seems to be going out of control. It needs to be clear which manager is responsible for each business area.
- Budget targets that are challenging yet achievable. Setting unachievable targets is likely to have a demotivating effect. There may be a case for getting managers to participate in establishing their own targets to help create a sense of ownership. This, in turn, can increase the managers' commitment and motivation. We shall consider this in more detail shortly.
- Established data collection, analysis and reporting routines, which take the actual results and the budget figures, and calculate and report the variances. This should be part of the business's regular accounting information system, so that the required reports are automatically produced each month.
- Producing reports aimed at individual managers, rather than general-purpose documents. This avoids managers having to wade through reams of reports to find the part that is relevant to them.
- Fairly short reporting periods, typically a month, so that things cannot go too far wrong before they are picked up.
- Variance reports being produced and made available to managers shortly after the end of the relevant reporting period. If it is not until the end of June that a manager is informed that the performance in May was below the budgeted level, it is quite likely that the performance for June will be below target as well. Reports on the performance in May ideally need to emerge in early June.
- Action being taken to get operations back under control if they are shown to be out of control. The report will not change things by itself. Managers need to take action to try to ensure that the reporting of significant adverse variances leads to action to put things right for the future.

Behavioural issues

Budgets are prepared with the objective of affecting the attitudes and behaviour of managers. The point was made in Chapter 12 that budgets are intended to motivate managers, and research evidence generally shows that budgets can be effective in achieving this. More specifically, the research shows that:

- the existence of budgets generally tends to improve performance;
- demanding, yet achievable, budget targets tend to motivate better than less demanding targets. It seems that setting the most demanding targets that will be accepted by managers is a very effective way to motivate them;
- unrealistically demanding targets tend to have an adverse effect on managers' performance;

- the participation of managers in setting their targets tends to improve motivation and performance. This is probably because those managers feel a sense of commitment to the targets and a moral obligation to achieve them.

It has been suggested that allowing managers to set their own targets will lead to slack (that is, easily achievable targets) being introduced. This would make achievement of the target that much easier. On the other hand, in an effort to impress, a manager may select a target that is not really achievable. These points imply that care must be taken in the extent to which managers have unfettered choice of their own targets.

The impact of management style

There has been a great deal of discussion among experts on the way in which managers use information generated by the budgeting system and the impact of its use on the attitudes and behaviour of subordinates (that is, the staff). A pioneering study by Hopwood (see reference 3 at the end of the chapter) examined the way that managers, working within a manufacturing environment, used budget information to evaluate the performance of subordinates. He argued that three distinct styles of management could be observed. These are:

- *Budget-constrained style.* This management style focuses rigidly on the ability of subordinates to meet the budget. Other factors relating to the performance of subordinates are not given serious consideration even though they might include improving the long-term effectiveness of the area for which the subordinate has responsibility,
- *Profit-conscious style.* This management style uses budget information in a more flexible way and often in conjunction with other data. The main focus is on the ability of each subordinate to improve long-term effectiveness.
- *Non-accounting style.* In this case, budget information plays no significant role in the evaluation of a subordinate's performance.

Activity (13.16)

How might a manager respond to budget information that indicates a subordinate has not met the budget targets for the period, assuming the manager adopts:

(a) a budget-constrained style
(b) a profit-conscious style
(c) a non-accounting style?

(a) A manager adopting a budget-constrained style is likely to take the budget information very seriously. This may result in criticism of the subordinate and perhaps some form of sanction.
(b) A manager adopting a profit-conscious style is likely to take a broader view when examining the budget information and so will take other factors into consideration (for example, factors that could not have been anticipated at the time of preparing the budgets), before deciding whether criticism or punishment is justified.
(c) A manager adopting a non-accounting style will regard the failure to meet the budget as being relatively unimportant and so no action may be taken.

Hopwood found that subordinates working for a manager who adopts a budget-constrained style had unfortunate experiences. They suffered higher levels of job-related stress and had poorer working relationships, with both their colleagues and their manager, than those subordinates whose manager adopted one of the other two styles. Hopwood also found that the subordinates of a budget-constrained style of manager were more likely to manipulate the budget figures, or to take other undesirable actions, to ensure the budgets were met.

Reservations about the Hopwood study

Although Hopwood's findings are interesting, subsequent studies have cast doubt on their universal applicability. Later studies confirm that human attitudes and behaviour are complex and can vary according to the situation. For example, it has been found that the impact of different management styles on such factors as job-related stress and the manipulation of budget figures seems to vary. The impact is likely to depend on such factors as the level of independence enjoyed by the subordinates and the level of uncertainty associated with the tasks to be undertaken.

It seems that where there is a high level of interdependence between business divisions, subordinate managers are more likely to feel that they have less control over their performance, because the performance of staff in other divisions could be an important influence on the final outcome. In such a situation, rigid application of the budget could be viewed as being unfair and may lead to undesirable behaviour. However, where managers have a high degree of independence, the application of budgets as a measure of performance is likely to be more acceptable. In this case, the managers are likely to feel that the final outcome is much less dependent on the performance of others.

Later studies have also shown that where a subordinate is undertaking a task that has a high degree of uncertainty concerning the outcome (for example, developing a new product for the market), budget targets are unlikely to be an adequate measure of performance. In such a situation, other factors and measures should be taken into account in order to derive a more complete assessment of performance. However, where a task has a low degree of uncertainty concerning the outcome (for example, producing a standard product using standard equipment and an experienced workforce), budget measures may be regarded as more reliable indicators of performance. Thus, it appears that a budget-constrained style is more likely to work where subordinates enjoy a fair amount of independence and where the tasks set have a low level of uncertainty concerning their outcomes.

Failing to meet the budget

The existence of budgets gives senior managers a ready means to assess the performance of their subordinates (that is, junior managers). If a junior manager fails to meet a budget, failure must be dealt with carefully by his or her senior manager. A harsh, critical approach may demotivate the junior manager. Adverse variances may imply that the manager needs some help.

→ **Real World 13.4** gives some indication of the effects of the **behavioural aspects of budgetary control** in practice.

Real World 13.4

Behavioural issues explored

The survey by Drury *et al.* referred to earlier indicates that there is a large degree of participation in setting budgets by those who will be expected to perform to the budget (the budget holders). It also indicates that senior managers have greater influence in setting the targets than their junior manager budget holders.

Where there is a conflict between the cost estimates submitted by the budget holders and their senior managers, in 40 per cent of respondent businesses the senior manager's view would prevail without negotiation, but in nearly 60 per cent of cases there would be a reduction that would be negotiated between the budget holder and the senior manager. Regarding the ability of budget holders to influence the setting of their own budgets, the survey revealed that:

- 23 per cent of respondents believe that budget holders should not have too much influence since they will seek to obtain easy budgets (build in slack) if they do;
- 69 per cent of respondents take an opposite view.

The general view on how senior managers should judge their subordinates is:

- 46 per cent of respondent businesses think that senior managers should judge junior managers mainly on their ability to achieve the budget;
- 40 per cent think otherwise.

Although this research is not very recent (1993), in the absence of more recent evidence it provides some feel for budget setting in practice.

Source: Drury *et al.* (see reference 2 at the end of the chapter).

Self-assessment question 13.1

Toscanini Ltd makes a standard product, which is budgeted to sell at £4/unit, in a competitive market. It is made by taking a budgeted 0.4 kg of material, budgeted to cost £2.40/kg, and working on it by hand by an employee, paid a budgeted £8/hour, for a budgeted 6 minutes. Monthly fixed overheads are budgeted at £4,800. The output for May was budgeted at 4,000 units.

The actual results for May were as follows:

	£
Sales revenue (3,500 units)	13,820
Materials (1,425 kg)	(3,420)
Labour (345 hours)	(2,690)
Fixed overheads	(4,900)
Actual operating profit	2,810

No inventories of any description existed at the beginning and end of the month.

Required:

(a) Deduce the budgeted profit for May and reconcile it, through variances, with the actual profit in as much detail as the information provided will allow.

(b) State which manager should be held accountable, in the first instance, for each variance calculated.

Self-assessment question 13.1 continued

(c) Assuming that the standards were all well set in terms of labour times and rates and materials usage and price, suggest at least one feasible reason for each of the variances that you identified in (a), given what you know about the business's performance for May.

(d) If it were discovered that the actual total world market demand for the business's product was 10 per cent lower than estimated when the May budget was set, explain how and why the variances that you identified in (a) could be revised to provide information that would be potentially more useful.

The answer to this question can be found at the back of the book on pages 705–6.

Standard quantities and costs

We have already seen that a budget is a business plan for the short term – typically one year – that is expressed mainly in financial terms. A budget is often constructed from standards. **Standard quantities and costs** (or revenues) are those planned for an individual unit of input or output and provide the building blocks for budgets.

We can say about Baxter Ltd's operations (see Example 13.1 on page 473) that:

- the standard selling price is £100 for one unit of output;
- the standard raw materials cost is £40 for one unit of output;
- the standard raw materials usage is 40 metres for one unit of output;
- the standard raw materials price is £1 a metre (that is, for one unit of input);
- the standard labour cost is £20 for one unit of output;
- the standard labour time is 2.50 hours for one unit of output;
- the standard labour rate is £8 an hour (that is, for one unit of input).

Standards, like the budgets to which they are linked, represent targets against which actual performance is measured. To maintain their usefulness for evaluation and control purposes, they should be subject to frequent review and, where necessary, revision. Standards provide the basis for variance analysis. The material usage variance, for example, is the difference between the standard materials usage for the level of output and the actual usage, costed at the standard materials price.

Setting standards

When setting standards various points have to be considered. We shall now explore some of the more important of these.

What kinds of standards should be used?

The starting point for setting standards is to decide on the type of standards to be used. There are basically two types: **ideal standards** and **practical standards**. Ideal standards, as the name suggests, assume perfect operating conditions where there is no inefficiency due to lost production time, defects and so on. The objective of setting ideal standards, which are attainable in theory at least, is to encourage employees to strive towards excellence. Practical standards, also as the name suggests, do not assume ideal operating conditions. Although they demand a high level of efficiency, account is taken of possible lost production time, defects and so on. They are designed to be challenging yet achievable.

Practical standards seem to enjoy more widespread support than ideal standards. There are two major difficulties with using the ideal standards:

● They do not provide a useful basis for exercising control. Unless the standards set are realistic, any variances computed are extremely difficult to interpret.
● They may not achieve their intended purpose of motivating managers: indeed, the opposite may occur. We saw earlier that the evidence suggests that where managers regard a target as beyond their grasp, it is likely to have a de-motivating effect.

Real World 13.5 provides some evidence on the use of ideal standards in practice.

Real World 13.5

Setting the standard

The study of UK manufacturers by Drury *et al.* showed that only 5 per cent of respondents to the survey set standards at a level that could be achieved if everything went perfectly all of the time. Although, the study is a little dated now (1993), it represents the most recent survey and is worth noting.

Source: Drury *et al.* (see reference 2 at the end of the chapter).

Information gathering

Setting standards involves gathering information concerning how much material should be used, how much machine time should be required, how much direct labour time should be spent and so on. Two possible ways of collecting information for standard setting are available.

Activity 13.17

Can you think what these might be?

The first is to examine the particular processes and tasks involved in producing the product or service and to develop suitable estimates. Standards concerning materials usage, machine time and direct labour hours may be established by carrying out dummy production runs, time-and-motion studies and so on. This will require close collaboration between the management accountant and those involved in the production process.

The second approach is to collect information relating to past costs, times and usage for the same, or similar, products and to use this information as a basis for predicting the future. This information may have to be adjusted to reflect changes in price, changes in the production process and so on.

Where the product or service is entirely new or involves entirely new processes, the first approach will probably have to be used, even though it is usually more costly.

The learning-curve effect

Where an activity undertaken by direct workers has been unchanged for some time, and the workers are experienced at performing it, the standard labour time will normally stay unchanged. However, where a new activity is introduced, or new workers are involved with performing an existing activity, a **learning-curve** effect will normally occur. This is shown in Figure 13.8.

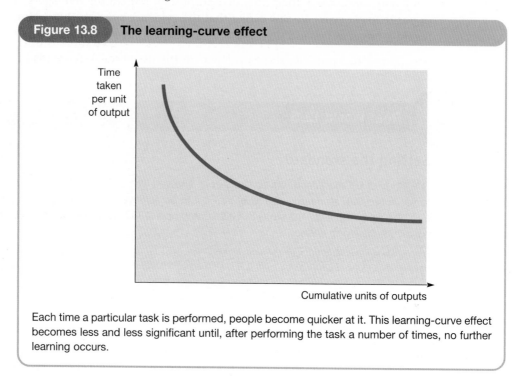

| Figure 13.8 | The learning-curve effect |

Each time a particular task is performed, people become quicker at it. This learning-curve effect becomes less and less significant until, after performing the task a number of times, no further learning occurs.

The first unit of output takes a long time to produce. As experience is gained, the worker takes less time to produce each unit of output. The rate of reduction in the time taken will, however, decrease as experience is gained. Thus, for example, the reduction in time taken between the first and second unit produced will be much bigger than the reduction between, say, the ninth and the tenth. Eventually, the rate of reduction in time taken will reduce to zero so that each unit will take as long as the preceding one. At this point, the point where the curve in Figure 13.8 becomes horizontal (the bottom right of the graph), the learning-curve effect will have been eliminated and a steady, long-term standard time for the activity will have been established.

The learning-curve effect seems to have little to do with whether workers are skilled or unskilled; if they are unfamiliar with the task, the learning-curve effect will arise. Practical experience shows that learning curves show remarkable regularity and, therefore, predictability from one activity to the next.

The learning-curve effect applies equally well to activities involved with providing a service (such as dealing with an insurance claim in an insurance business) as to manufacturing-type activities (like upholstering an armchair by hand in a furniture-making business).

Clearly, the learning-curve effect must be taken into account when setting standards, and when interpreting any adverse labour efficiency variances, where a new process and/or new personnel are involved.

Other uses for standard costing

We have seen that standards can play a valuable role in performance evaluation and control. However, standards, which are known to be broadly realistic, that relate to costs, usages, selling prices and so on, can be used for other purposes. In particular, they can be used to determine the cost of inventories and work in progress for income measurement purposes and the cost of items for use in pricing decisions.

Real World 13.6 provides some information on the use of standards in practice.

Real World 13.6

Standards in practice

The survey by Drury *et al.* showed that respondent businesses found standards to be useful for the following purposes:

	Percentage of respondents
Cost control and performance evaluation	72
Valuing inventory and work in progress	80
Deducing costs for decision-making purposes	62
To help in constructing budgets	69

Source: Drury *et al.* (see reference 2 at the end of the chapter).

Some problems . . .

Using standards and variances as a means of performance evaluation and control has obvious appeal. Nevertheless there are problems associated with this approach, which include the following:

- Large areas of business and commercial activity simply do not have the same direct relationship between inputs and outputs as is the case with, say, level of output and the number of direct labour hours worked. Many of the expenses of a modern business are in areas such as training and advertising, where the expense is discretionary and not linked to the level of output in a direct way.
- Standards can quickly become out of date as a result of both changes in the production process and price. This need not pose a major problem but it does require standards to be frequently monitored. We have already seen that standards that are unachievable are ineffective for control purposes. They may even have an adverse effect on performance. For example, a personnel manager who knows that it is

impossible to meet targets on rates of pay for labour, because of general labour cost rises, may have less incentive to minimise costs.

● Sometimes, factors beyond the control of the manager concerned may affect the variance for which that manager is held accountable. This problem may, however, go unrecognised when assessing the manager's performance. A more considered approach to the calculation of the variance, resulting in those factors controllable by the manager being separated from those that are not, is required to overcome this problem.

● In practice, creating clear lines of demarcation between the areas of responsibility of various managers may be difficult. Thus, one of the prerequisites of effective standard costing is lost.

The new business environment

The traditional standard costing approach was developed during an era when business operations were characterised by few product lines, long production runs and heavy reliance on direct labour. More recently, the increasingly competitive environment and the onward march of technology have changed the business landscape. Now, many business operations are characterised by a wide range of different products, shorter product life cycles (leading to shorter production runs) and automated production processes. The effect of these changes has resulted in:

● more frequent development of standards to deal with frequent changes to the product range;
● a change in the focus for control – where manufacturing systems are automated, for example, direct labour becomes less important than direct materials;
● a decline in the importance of monitoring from cost and usage variances – where manufacturing systems are automated, deviations from standards relating to costs and usage become less frequent and less significant.

Thus, where a business has highly automated production systems, traditional standard costing, with its emphasis on costs and usage, is likely to take on less importance. Other elements of the production process such as quality, production levels, product cycle times, delivery times and the need for continuous improvement become the focus of attention. This does not mean, however, that a standards-based approach is not useful for the new manufacturing environment. It can still provide valuable control information and there is no reason why standard costing systems cannot be redesigned to reflect a concern for some of the elements mentioned earlier. Nevertheless, other measures, including non-financial ones, may help to augment the information provided by the standard costing system. We considered this issue in Chapter 11.

Real World 13.7 reveals that, despite the problems mentioned above, standard costing is still alive and well.

Real World 13.7

Standard practice

A study was carried out involving interviews with senior financial managers. For 33 of the businesses studied, the use of standards might have been expected. It was found that 29 of the 33 (88 per cent) use standards. The popularity of each type of standard among these 29 businesses is set out in Figure 13.9.

Figure 13.9	The popularity of standards in practice

Standards for materials were used by all businesses in the survey. Although overhead variances were the least popular, they were still used by more than two-thirds of the businesses.

Source: Figure based on information in Dugdale *et al.* (see reference 4 at the end of the chapter)

Summary

The main points of this chapter may be summarised as follows:

Controlling through budgets
- Budgets act as a system of both feedback and feedforward control.
- To exercise control, budgets can be flexed to match actual volume of output.

Variance analysis
- Variances may be favourable or adverse according to whether they result in an increase to, or decrease from, the budgeted profit figure.
- Budgeted profit plus all favourable variances less all adverse variances equals actual profit.
- Commonly calculated variances:
  - Sales volume variance = difference between budgeted and actual volume (in units) multiplied by the standard contribution (for one unit).

- Sales price variance = difference between actual sales revenue and actual volume at the standard sales price.
- Total direct materials variance = difference between the actual direct materials cost and the direct materials cost according to the flexed budget.
- Direct materials usage variance = difference between actual usage and budgeted usage, for the actual volume of output, multiplied by the standard materials cost.
- Direct materials price variance = difference between the actual materials cost and the actual usage multiplied by the standard materials cost.
- Total direct labour variance = difference between the actual direct labour cost and the direct labour cost according to the flexed budget.
- Direct labour efficiency variance = difference between actual labour time and budgeted time, for the actual volume of output, multiplied by the standard labour rate.
- Direct labour rate variance = difference between the actual labour cost and the actual labour time multiplied by the standard labour rate.
- Fixed overhead spending variance = difference between the actual and budgeted spending on fixed overheads.

- Significant and/or persistent variances need to be investigated to establish their cause.

- Trading off favourable variances against linked adverse variances should not be automatically acceptable.

- Not all activities can usefully be controlled through traditional variance analysis.

Effective budgetary control

- Good budgetary control requires establishing systems and routines to ensure such things as a clear distinction between individual managers' areas of responsibility; prompt, frequent and relevant variance reporting; and senior management commitment.

- There are behavioural aspects of control relating to management style, participation in budget setting and the failure to meet budget targets that should be taken into account by senior managers.

Standard costing

- Standards = budgeted physical quantities and financial values for one unit of inputs and outputs.

- Two types of standards: ideal and practical.

- Information necessary for developing standards can be gathered by analysing the task or by using past data.

- There tends to be a learning-curve effect: routine tasks are performed more quickly with experience.

- Standards are useful in providing data for income measurement and pricing decisions.

- Standards have their limitations, particularly in modern manufacturing environments. However, they are still widely used.

MyAccountingLab *Now check your progress in your personal Study Plan*

Key terms

management by exception p. 471	non-operating-profit variances p. 486
feedback control p. 472	compensating variances p. 489
feedforward control p. 472	budgetary control p. 490
flexing the budget p. 474	behavioural aspects of budgetary
flexible budget p. 474	control p. 492
variance p. 475	standard quantities and costs p. 494
favourable variance p. 475	ideal standards p. 494
adverse variance p. 475	practical standards p. 494
variance analysis p. 482	learning curve p. 496

References

1 **An Empirical Investigation of the Evolution of Management Accounting Practices**, *Abdel-Kader M. and Luther R.*, Working paper no. 04/06, University of Essex, October 2004.

2 **A Survey of Managment Accounting Practices in UK Manufacturing Companies**, *Drury C., Braund S., Osborne P. and Tayles M.*, Chartered Association of Certified Accountants, 1993.

3 'An empirical study of the role of accounting data in performance evaluation', *Hopwood A.G.*, Empirical Research in Accounting, a supplement to the **Journal of Accounting Research**, 1972, pp. 156–82.

4 **Contemporary Management Accounting Practices in UK Manufacturing**, *Dugdale D., Jones C. and Green S.*, CIMA Research Publication, vol. 1, no. 13, 2005.

Further reading

If you would like to explore the topics covered in this chapter in more depth, we recommend the following books:

Cost Accounting: A managerial emphasis, *Horngren C., Datar S. and Foster G.*, 12th edn, Prentice Hall International, 2006, chapters 7 and 8.

Management Accounting, *Atkinson A., Kaplan R., Young S.M. and Matsumura*, E., 5th edn, Prentice Hall, 2007, chapter 12.

Management and Cost Accounting, *Drury C.*, 6th edn, Thomson Learning, 2004, chapters 16, 18 and 19.

Managerial Accounting, *Hilton R.*, 6th edn. McGraw-Hill/Irwin, 2005, chapter 10.

Review questions

Answers to these questions can be found at the back of the book on pages 783–4.

13.1 Explain what is meant by feedforward control and distinguish it from feedback control.

13.2 What is meant by a variance? What is the point in analysing variances?

13.3 What is the point in flexing the budget in the context of variance analysis? Does flexing imply that differences between budget and actual in the volume of output are ignored in variance analysis?

13.4 Should all variances be investigated to find their cause? Explain your answer.

Exercises

Exercises 13.4 to 13.8 are more advanced than 13.1 to 13.3. Those with coloured numbers have answers at the back of the book, starting on page 749.

If you wish to try more exercises, visit the students' side of the Companion Website.

13.1 You have recently overheard the following remarks:

(a) 'A favourable direct labour rate variance can only be caused by staff working more efficiently than budgeted.'
(b) 'Selling more units than budgeted, because the units were sold at less than standard price, automatically leads to a favourable sales volume variance.'
(c) 'Using below-standard materials will tend to lead to adverse materials usage variances but cannot affect labour variances.'
(d) 'Higher-than-budgeted sales could not possibly affect the labour rate variance.'
(e) 'An adverse sales price variance can only arise from selling a product at less than standard price.'

Required:
Critically assess these remarks, explaining any technical terms.

13.2 Pilot Ltd makes a standard product, which is budgeted to sell at £5.00 a unit. It is made by taking a budgeted 0.5 kg of material, budgeted to cost £3.00 a kilogram, and working on it by hand by an employee, paid a budgeted £5.00 an hour, for a budgeted 15 minutes. Monthly fixed overheads are budgeted at £6,000. The output for March was budgeted at 5,000 units.

The actual results for March were as follows:

	£
Sales revenue (5,400 units)	26,460
Materials (2,830 kg)	(8,770)
Labour (1,300 hours)	(6,885)
Fixed overheads	(6,350)
Actual operating profit	4,455

No inventories existed at the start or end of March.

Required:

(a) Deduce the budgeted profit for March and reconcile it with the actual profit in as much detail as the information provided will allow.

(b) State which manager should be held accountable, in the first instance, for each variance calculated.

13.3 Antonio plc makes product X, the standard costs of which are:

	£
Sales revenue	31
Direct labour (2 hours)	(11)
Direct materials (1 kg)	(10)
Fixed overheads	(3)
Standard profit	7

The budgeted output for March was 1,000 units of product X; the actual output was 1,100 units, which was sold for £34,950. There were no inventories at the start or end of March.

The actual production costs were:

	£
Direct labour (2,150 hours)	12,210
Direct materials (1,170 kg)	11,630
Fixed overheads	3,200

Required:

Calculate the variances for March as fully as you are able from the available information, and use them to reconcile the budgeted and actual profit figures.

13.4 You have recently overheard the following remarks:

(a) 'When calculating variances, we, in effect, ignore differences of volume of output, between original budget and actual, by flexing the budget. If there were a volume difference, it is water under the bridge by the time that the variances come to be calculated.'

(b) 'It is very valuable to calculate variances because they will tell you what went wrong.'

(c) 'Research evidence shows that the more demanding the target, the more motivated the manager.'

(d) 'Most businesses do not have feedforward controls of any type, just feedback controls through budgets.'

Required:

Critically assess these remarks, explaining any technical terms.

13.5 Bradley-Allen Ltd makes one standard product. Its budgeted operating statement for May is as follows:

		£	£
Sales (volume and revenue):	800 units		64,000
Direct materials:	Type A	12,000	
	Type B	16,000	
Direct labour:	Skilled	4,000	
	Unskilled	10,000	
Overheads:	(All fixed)	12,000	
			54,000
Budgeted operating profit			10,000

The standard costs were as follows:

Direct materials: Type A   £50/kg
                 Type B   £20/m
Direct labour: Skilled   £10/hour
                Unskilled   £8/hour

During May, the following occurred:

(i)   950 units were sold for a total of £73,000.
(ii) 310 kilos (costing £15,200) of type A material were used in production.
(iii) 920 metres (costing £18,900) of type B material were used in production.
(iv) Skilled workers were paid £4,628 for 445 hours.
(v) Unskilled workers were paid £11,275 for 1,375 hours.
(vi) Fixed overheads cost £11,960.

There was no inventory of finished production or of work in progress at either the beginning or end of May.

Required:

(a) Prepare a statement that reconciles the budgeted to the actual profit of the business for May, through variances. Your statement should analyse the difference between the two profit figures in as much detail as you are able.
(b) Explain how the statement in (a) might be helpful to managers.

13.6 Mowbray Ltd makes and sells one product, the standard costs of which are as follows:

	£
Direct materials (3 kg at £2.50/kg)	7.50
Direct labour (15 minutes at £9.00/hr)	2.25
Fixed overheads	3.60
	13.35
Selling price	20.00
Standard profit margin	6.65

The monthly production and sales are planned to be 1,200 units.
The actual results for May were as follows:

	£	
Sales revenue	18,000	
Less		
Direct materials	(7,400)	(2,800 kg)
Direct labour	(2,300)	(255 hr)
Fixed overheads	(4,100)	
Operating profit	4,200	

There were no inventories at the start or end of May. As a result of poor sales demand during May, the business reduced the price of all sales by 10 per cent.

Required:

Calculate the budgeted profit for May and reconcile it to the actual profit through variances, going into as much detail as is possible from the information available.

13.7 Varne Chemprocessors is a business that specialises in plastics. It uses a standard costing system to monitor and report its purchases and usage of materials. During the most recent month, accounting period six, the purchase and usage of chemical UK194 were as follows:

Purchases/usage   28,100 litres
Total price   £51,704

Because of fire risk and the danger to health, no inventories are held by the business. UK194 is used solely in the manufacture of a product called Varnelyne. The standard cost specification shows that, for the production of 5,000 litres of Varnelyne, 200 litres of UK194 is needed at a total standard cost of £392. During period six, 637,500 litres of Varnelyne were produced.

Required:
(a) Calculate the price and usage variances for UK194 for period six.
(b) The following comment was made by the production manager:
   'I knew at the beginning of period six that UK194 would be cheaper than the standard cost specification, so I used rather more of it than normal; this saved £4,900 on other chemicals.'
   What changes do you need to make in your analysis for (a) as a result of this comment?
(c) Calculate, for each material, the cumulative variances and comment briefly on the results.

Variances: periods one to six

Period	UK500 £		UK800 £	
1	301	F	298	F
2	251	A	203	F
3	102	F	52	A
4	202	A	98	A
5	153	F	150	A
6	103	A	201	A

where F = cost saving and A = cost overrun.

13.8 Brive plc has the following standards for its only product:

Selling price	£110/unit
Direct labour	2 hours at £5.25/hour
Direct materials	3 kg at £14.00/kg
Fixed overheads	£27.00, based on a budgeted output of 800 units/month

During May, there was an actual output of 850 units and the operating statement for the month was as follows:

	£
Sales revenue	92,930
Direct labour (1,780 hours)	(9,665)
Direct materials (2,410 kg)	(33,258)
Fixed overheads	(21,365)
Operating profit	28,642

There was no inventory of any description at the beginning and end of May.

Required:
Prepare the original budget and a budget flexed to the actual volume. Use these to compare the budgeted and actual profits of the business for the month, going into as much detail with your analysis as the information given will allow.

PART 3

Financial management

14 Making capital
   investment decisions

15 Financing the business

16 Managing working capital

Part 3 is concerned with the area of accounting and finance usually known as 'business finance' or 'financial management'. Broadly, we shall be looking at decisions concerning the raising and investment of finance. Businesses can be seen, from a purely economic perspective, as organisations that raise money from investors and others (for example, shareholders and lenders) and that use those funds to make investments (typically in plant and other assets) that will make the business and its owners wealthier. Clearly, these are important decision-making areas typically involving large amounts of money and relatively long-term commitments.

Chapter 14 considers how businesses make decisions about what represents a worthwhile investment. We shall be looking particularly at investments in such things as factories, offices and plant, which might enable businesses to provide some product or service for which a profitable market is seen. The decision-making techniques that we shall consider could equally well be applied to making investments in the shares of a business, or any other type of 'financial' investment, which individuals might make using their own money.

Chapter 15 deals with the other side of the investment: where the investment finance comes from. Here we shall be reviewing the various types of funding used by businesses of various sizes, including raising funds from

→ the owners of the business (the shareholders in the case of limited companies).

Chapter 16 looks at a particular area of fundraising and investment: the management of working capital. Working capital consists of the short-term assets and claims of the business: inventories, trade receivables, cash and trade payables. These items typically involve large amounts of finance and need to be managed carefully. The chapter considers how working capital can be managed effectively.

Making capital investment decisions

Introduction

In this chapter we shall look at how businesses can make decisions involving investments in new plant, machinery, buildings and similar long-term assets. In making these decisions, businesses should be trying to pursue their strategic objectives by trying to maximise value through investments that provide a suitable strategic fit.

Investment appraisal and management is a very important area for businesses; expensive and far-reaching consequences can flow from bad investment decisions.

We shall look at the research evidence relating to the use of the various appraisal techniques in practice. We shall also consider the problem of risk, a major aspect of all decision making. Lastly, we shall discuss the ways in which managers can oversee capital investment projects and how control may be exercised throughout the life of the project.

Learning outcomes

When you have completed this chapter, you should be able to:

● Explain the nature and importance of investment decision making.

● Identify, discuss and apply the four main investment appraisal methods found in practice.

● Discuss the strengths and weaknesses of various techniques for dealing with risk in investment appraisal.

● Explain the methods used to review and control capital expenditure projects.

 Remember to create your own personalised Study Plan

The nature of investment decisions

The essential feature of investment decisions is *time*. Investment involves making an outlay of something of economic value, usually cash, at one point in time, which is expected to yield economic benefits to the investor at some other point in time. Usually, the outlay precedes the benefits. Also, the outlay is typically one large amount and the benefits arrive as a series of smaller amounts over a fairly protracted period.

Investment decisions tend to be of profound importance to the business because:

- *Large amounts of resources are often involved.* Many investments made by businesses involve laying out a significant proportion of their total resources (see Real World 14.2). If mistakes are made with the decision, the effects on the businesses could be significant, if not catastrophic.
- *It is often difficult and/or expensive to bail out of an investment once it has been undertaken.* It is often the case that investments made by a business are specific to its needs. For example, a hotel business may invest in a new, custom-designed hotel complex. The specialist nature of this complex will probably lead to its having a rather limited second-hand value to another potential user with different needs. If the business found, after having made the investment, that room occupancy rates were not as buoyant as was planned, the only possible course of action might be to close down and sell the complex. This would probably mean that much less could be recouped from the investment than it had originally cost, particularly if the costs of design are included as part of the cost, as they logically should be.

Real World 14.1 gives an illustration of a major investment by a well-known business operating in the UK.

Real World 14.1

Brittany Ferries launches an investment

In the spring of 2004, Brittany Ferries, the cross-Channel ferry operator, launched a new ship. The ship had cost the business about £100m. Although Brittany Ferries is a substantial business, this level of expenditure is significant. Clearly, the business believes that acquisition of the new ship will be profitable for it, but how would it have reached this conclusion? Presumably the anticipated future cash flows from passengers and freight operators will have been major inputs to the decision. The ship was specifically designed for Brittany Ferries, so it would be difficult for the business to recoup a large proportion of its £100m should these projected cash flows not materialise.

Source: Publicity material published by Brittany Ferries.

The issues raised by Brittany Ferries' investment will be the main subject of this chapter.

Real World 14.2 indicates the level of annual investment for a number of randomly selected, well-known UK businesses. It can be seen that the scale of investment varies from one business to another. (It also tends to vary from one year to the next for a particular business.) In nearly all of these businesses the scale of investment is very significant.

Real World 14.2

The scale of investment by UK businesses

	Expenditure on additional non-current assets as a percentage of:	
	Annual sales revenue	*End-of-year non-current assets*
BT plc (telecommunications)	15.1	16.3
BAA plc (airports)	65.3	10.6
Tesco plc (supermarkets)	6.5	13.7
BA plc (airline)	3.4	3.4
Marks and Spencer plc (stores)	3.4	6.5
United Utilities plc (utilities)	52.5	8.5
J. Sainsbury plc (supermarkets)	3.4	6.2
First Group plc (passenger transport)	6.4	13.4

Source: Annual reports of the businesses concerned for the financial year ending in 2006.

Real World 14.2 is limited to considering the non-current asset investment, but most non-current asset investment also requires a level of current asset investment to support it (additional inventories, for example), meaning that the real scale of investment is even greater, typically considerably so, than indicated above.

Activity 14.1

When managers are making decisions involving capital investments, what should the decision seek to achieve?

Investment decisions must be consistent with the objectives of the particular business. For a private-sector business, increasing the wealth of the owners (shareholders) is usually assumed to be the key objective.

Investment appraisal methods

Given the importance of investment decisions, it is essential that there is proper screening of investment proposals. An important part of this screening process is to ensure that the business uses appropriate methods of evaluation.

Research shows that there are basically four methods used in practice by businesses throughout the world to evaluate investment opportunities. They are:

● accounting rate of return (ARR)
● payback period (PP)
● net present value (NPV)
● internal rate of return (IRR).

It is possible to find businesses that use variants of these four methods. It is also possible to find businesses, particularly smaller ones, which do not use any formal appraisal method but rely instead on the 'gut feeling' of their managers. Most businesses, however, seem to use one (or more) of these four methods.

We are going to assess the effectiveness of each of these methods and we shall see that only one of them (NPV) is a wholly logical approach. The other three all have flaws. We shall also see how popular these four methods seem to be in practice.

To help us to examine each of the methods, it might be useful to consider how each of them would cope with a particular investment opportunity. Let us consider the following example.

Example 14.1

Billingsgate Battery Company has carried out some research that shows that the business could provide a standard service that it has recently developed.

Provision of the service would require investment in a machine that would cost £100,000, payable immediately. Sales of the service would take place throughout the next five years. At the end of that time, it is estimated that the machine could be sold for £20,000.

Sales of the service would be expected to occur as follows:

	Number of units
Next year	5,000
Second year	10,000
Third year	15,000
Fourth year	15,000
Fifth year	5,000

It is estimated that the new service can be sold for £12 a unit, and that the relevant (variable) costs will total £8 a unit.

To simplify matters, we shall assume that the cash from sales and for the costs of providing the service are paid and received, respectively, at the end of each year. This is clearly unlikely to be true in real life. Money will have to be paid to employees (for salaries and wages) on a weekly or a monthly basis. Customers will pay within a month or two of buying the service. On the other hand, making the assumption probably does not lead to a serious distortion. It is a simplifying assumption that is often made in real life, and it will make things more straightforward for us now. We should be clear, however, that there is nothing about any of the four approaches that *demands* that this assumption is made.

Bearing in mind that each unit of the service sold will give rise to a net cash inflow of £4 (that is, £12 – £8), the total net cash flows (receipts less payments) for each year will be as follows:

Time		£000
Immediately	Cost of machine	(100)
1 year's time	Operating profit before depreciation (£4 × 5,000)	20
2 years' time	Operating profit before depreciation (£4 × 10,000)	40
3 years' time	Operating profit before depreciation (£4 × 15,000)	60
4 years' time	Operating profit before depreciation (£4 × 15,000)	60
5 years' time	Operating profit before depreciation (£4 × 5,000)	20
5 years' time	Disposal proceeds from the machine	20

Note that, broadly speaking, the operating profit before deducting depreciation (that is, before non-cash items) equals the net amount of cash flowing into the business. Apart from depreciation, all of this business's expenses cause cash to flow out of the business. Sales revenues lead to cash flowing in.

Having set up the example, we shall now go on to consider how each of the appraisal methods works.

Accounting rate of return (ARR)

→ The **accounting rate of return (ARR)** method takes the average accounting operating profit that the investment will generate and expresses it as a percentage of the average investment made over the life of the project. Thus:

$$\text{ARR} = \frac{\text{Average annual operating profit}}{\text{Average investment to earn that profit}} \times 100\%$$

We can see from the equation that, to calculate the ARR, we need to deduce two pieces of information about the particular project:

- the annual average operating profit; and
- the average investment.

In our example, the average annual operating profit *before depreciation* over the five years is £40,000 (that is, £(20 + 40 + 60 + 60 + 20)/5). Assuming 'straight-line' depreciation (that is, equal annual amounts), the annual depreciation charge will be £16,000 (that is, £(100,000 – 20,000)/5). Thus the average annual operating profit *after depreciation* is £24,000 (that is, £40,000 – £16,000).

The average investment over the five years can be calculated as follows:

$$\text{Average investment} = \frac{\text{Cost of machine} + \text{Disposal value}}{2}$$

$$= \frac{£100,000 + £20,000}{2}$$

$$= £60,000$$

Thus, the ARR of the investment is:

$$\text{ARR} = \frac{£24,000}{£60,000} \times 100\% = 40\%$$

Users of ARR should apply the following decision rules:

- For any project to be acceptable it must achieve a target ARR as a minimum.
- Where there are competing projects that all seem capable of exceeding this minimum rate (where the business must choose between more than one project), the one with the higher or highest ARR would normally be selected.

To decide whether the 40 per cent return is acceptable, we need to compare this percentage return with the minimum rate required by the business.

Activity 14.2

Chaotic Industries is considering an investment in a fleet of ten delivery vans to take its products to customers. The vans will cost £15,000 each to buy, payable immediately. The annual running costs are expected to total £20,000 for each van (including the driver's salary). The vans are expected to operate successfully for six years, at the end of which period they will all have to be sold, with disposal proceeds expected to be about £3,000 a van. At present, the business uses a commercial carrier for all of its deliveries. It is expected that this carrier will charge a total of £230,000 each year for the next six years to undertake the deliveries.

What is the ARR of buying the vans? (Note that cost savings are as relevant a benefit from an investment as are net cash inflows.)

The vans will save the business £30,000 a year (that is, £230,000 − (£20,000 × 10)), before depreciation, in total. Thus, the inflows and outflows will be:

Time		£000
Immediately	Cost of vans (10 × £15,000)	(150)
1 year's time	Net saving before depreciation	30
2 years' time	Net saving before depreciation	30
3 years' time	Net saving before depreciation	30
4 years' time	Net saving before depreciation	30
5 years' time	Net saving before depreciation	30
6 years' time	Net saving before depreciation	30
6 years' time	Disposal proceeds from the vans (10 × £3,000)	30

The total annual depreciation expense (assuming a straight-line approach) will be £20,000 (that is, (£150,000 − £30,000)/6). Thus, the average annual saving, after depreciation, is £10,000 (that is, £30,000 − £20,000).

The average investment will be

$$\text{Average investment} = \frac{£150,000 + £30,000}{2}$$

$$= £90,000$$

Thus, the ARR of the investment is

$$\text{ARR} = \frac{£10,000}{£90,000} \times 100\%$$

$$= 11.1\%$$

ARR and ROCE

We should note that ARR and the return on capital employed (ROCE) ratio, that we met in Chapter 7, take the same approach to performance measurement, in that they both relate accounting profit to the cost of the assets invested to generate that profit. ROCE is a popular means of assessing the performance of a business, as a whole, *after* it has performed. ARR is an approach that assesses the potential performance of a particular investment, taking the same approach as ROCE, but *before* it has performed.

As we have just seen, managers using ARR will require that any investment undertaken should achieve a target ARR as a minimum. Perhaps the minimum target would be based on the rate that previous investments had actually achieved (as measured by ROCE). Perhaps it would be the industry-average ROCE.

Since private sector businesses are normally seeking to increase the wealth of their owners, ARR may seem to be a sound method of appraising investment opportunities. Operating profit can be seen as a net increase in wealth over a period, and relating it to the size of investment made to achieve it seems a logical approach.

ARR is said to have a number of advantages as a method of investment appraisal. It was mentioned earlier that ROCE seems to be a widely used measure of business performance. Shareholders seem to use this ratio to evaluate management performance, and sometimes the financial objective of a business will be expressed in terms of a target ROCE. It therefore seems sensible to use a method of investment appraisal that is consistent with this overall approach to measuring business performance. It also gives the result expressed as a percentage. It seems that some managers feel comfortable using measures expressed in percentage terms.

Problems with ARR

Activity (14.3)

ARR suffers from a very major defect as a means of assessing investment opportunities. Can you reason out what this is? Consider the three competing projects whose cash flows are shown below. All three involve investment in a machine that is expected to have no residual value at the end of the five years. Note that all of the projects have the same total operating profits over the five years.

Time		Project A £000	Project B £000	Project C £000
Immediately	Cost of machine	(160)	(160)	(160)
1 year's time	Operating profit after depreciation	20	10	160
2 years' time	Operating profit after depreciation	40	10	10
3 years' time	Operating profit after depreciation	60	10	10
4 years' time	Operating profit after depreciation	60	10	10
5 years' time	Operating profit after depreciation	20	160	10

(*Hint*: The defect is not concerned with the ability of the decision maker to forecast future events, although this too can be a problem. Try to remember the essential feature of investment decisions, which we identified at the beginning of this chapter.)

Activity 14.3 continued

The problem with ARR is that it almost completely ignores the time factor. In this example, exactly the same ARR would have been computed for each of the three projects.

Since the same total operating profit over the five years (£200,000) arises in all three of these projects, and the average investment in each project is £80,000 (that is, £160,000/2), this means that each case will give rise to the same ARR of 50 per cent (that is, £40,000/£80,000).

Given a financial objective of increasing the wealth of the owners of the business, any rational decision maker faced with a choice between the three projects set out in Activity 14.3 would strongly prefer Project C. This is because most of the benefits from the investment arise within twelve months of investing the £160,000 to establish the project. Project A would rank second and Project B would come a poor third. Any appraisal technique that is not capable of distinguishing between these three situations is seriously flawed. We shall look at why timing is so important later in the chapter.

There are further problems associated with the use of ARR. One of these problems concerns the approach taken to derive the average investment in a project.

Example 14.2 illustrates the daft result that ARR can produce.

Example 14.2

George put forward an investment proposal to his boss. The business employs ARR to assess investment proposals using a minimum 'hurdle' rate of 27 per cent. Details of the proposal were as follows:

Cost of equipment	£200,000
Estimated residual value of equipment	£40,000
Average annual operating profit before depreciation	£48,000
Estimated life of project	10 years
Annual straight-line depreciation charge	£16,000 (that is, (200,000 − £40,000)/10)

The ARR of the project will be:

$$\text{ARR} = \frac{48,000 - 16,000}{(200,000 + 40,000)/2} \times 100\% = 26.7\%$$

The boss rejected George's proposal because it failed to achieve an ARR of at least 27 per cent. Although George was disappointed, he realised that there was still hope. In fact, all that the business had to do was to give away the piece of equipment at the end of its useful life rather than to sell it. The residual value of the equipment then became zero and the annual depreciation charge became ([£200,000 − £0]/10) = £20,000 a year. The revised ARR calculation was then as follows:

$$\text{ARR} = \frac{48,000 - 20,000}{(200,000 + 0)/2} \times 100\% = 28\%$$

ARR is based on the use of accounting profit. When measuring performance over the whole life of a project, however, it is cash flows rather than accounting profits that are important. Cash is the ultimate measure of the economic wealth generated by an investment. This is because it is cash that is used to acquire resources and for distribution to owners. Accounting profit, on the other hand is more appropriate for reporting achievement on a periodic basis. It is a useful measure of productive effort for a relatively short period, such as a year or half year. Thus, it is really a question of 'horses for courses'. Accounting profit is fine for measuring performance over short period but cash is the appropriate measure when considering the performance over the life of a project.

The ARR method can also create problems when considering competing investments of different size.

Activity (14.4)

Sinclair Wholesalers plc is currently considering opening a new sales outlet in Coventry. Two possible sites have been identified for the new outlet. Site A has an area of 30,000 sq m. It will require an average investment of £6m, and will produce an average operating profit of £600,000 a year. Site B has an area of 20,000 sq m. It will require an average investment of £4m, and will produce an average operating profit of £500,000 a year.

What is the ARR of each investment opportunity? Which site would you select, and why?

The ARR of Site A is £600,000/£6m = 10 per cent. The ARR of Site B is £500,000/£4m = 12.5 per cent. Thus, Site B has the higher ARR. However, in terms of the absolute operating profit generated, Site A is the more attractive. If the ultimate objective is to increase the wealth of the shareholders of Sinclair Wholesalers plc, it might be better to choose Site A even though the percentage return is lower. It is the absolute size of the return rather than the relative (percentage) size that is important. This is a general problem of using comparative measures, such as percentages, when the objective is measured in absolute ones, like an amount of money. If businesses were seeking through their investments to generate a percentage rate of return on investment, ARR would be more helpful. The problem is that most businesses seek to achieve increases in their absolute wealth (measured in pounds, euros, dollars and so on), through their investment decisions.

Real World 14.3 illustrates how using percentage measures can lead to confusion.

Real World 14.3

Increasing road capacity by sleight of hand

During the 1970s, the Mexican government wanted to increase the capacity of a major four-lane road. It came up with the idea of repainting the lane markings so that there were six narrower lanes occupying the same space as four wider ones had previously done. This increased the capacity of the road by 50 per cent (that is, $\frac{2}{4} \times 100$). A tragic outcome of the narrower lanes was an increase in deaths from road accidents. A year later the Mexican government had the six narrower lanes changed back to the original four wider

Real World 14.3 continued

ones. This reduced the capacity of the road by 33 per cent (that is, $^{2}/_{6} \times 100$). The Mexican government reported that, overall, it had increased the capacity of the road by 17 per cent (that is, 50% − 33%), despite the fact that its real capacity was identical to that which it had been originally. The confusion arose because each of the two percentages (50 per cent and 33 per cent) is based on different bases (four and six).

Source: Gigerenzer (see reference 1 at the end of the chapter).

Payback period (PP)

→ The **payback period (PP)** is the length of time it takes for an initial investment to be repaid out of the net cash inflows from a project. Since it takes time into account, the PP method seems to go some way to overcoming the timing problem of ARR – or at first glance it does.

It might be useful to consider PP in the context of the Billingsgate Battery example. We should recall that essentially the project's cash flows are:

Time		£000
Immediately	Cost of machine	(100)
1 year's time	Operating profit before depreciation	20
2 years' time	Operating profit before depreciation	40
3 years' time	Operating profit before depreciation	60
4 years' time	Operating profit before depreciation	60
5 years' time	Operating profit before depreciation	20
5 years' time	Disposal proceeds	20

Note that all of these figures are amounts of cash to be paid or received (we saw earlier that operating profit before depreciation is a rough measure of the cash flows from the project).

As the payback period is the length of time it takes for the initial investment to be repaid out of the net cash inflows, it will be three years before the £100,000 outlay is covered by the inflows. This is still assuming that the cash flows occur at year ends. The payback period can be derived by calculating the cumulative cash flows as follows:

Time		Net cash flows £000	Cumulative cash flows £000	
Immediately	Cost of machine	(100)	(100)	
1 year's time	Operating profit before depreciation	20	(80)	(−100 + 20)
2 years' time	Operating profit before depreciation	40	(40)	(−80 + 40)
3 years' time	Operating profit before depreciation	60	20	(−40 + 60)
4 years' time	Operating profit before depreciation	60	80	(20 + 60)
5 years' time	Operating profit before depreciation	20	100	(80 + 20)
5 years' time	Disposal proceeds	20	120	(100 + 20)

We can see that the cumulative cash flows become positive at the end of the third year. (Had we assumed that the cash flows arise evenly over the year, the precise payback period would be:

$$2 \text{ years} + (^{40}\!/_{60}) \text{ years} = 2^{2}/_{3} \text{ years}$$

where 40 represents the cash flow still required at the beginning of the third year to repay the initial outlay, and 60 is the projected cash flow during the third year.

We must now ask how to decide whether three years is an acceptable payback period. The decision rule for using PP is:

- For a project to be acceptable it would need to have a payback period shorter than a maximum payback period set by the business.
- If there were two or more competing projects whose payback periods were both shorter than the maximum payback period requirement, the decision maker should select the project with the shorter payback period.

If, for example, Billingsgate Battery had a maximum acceptable payback period of four years, the project would be undertaken. A project with a longer payback period than four years would not be acceptable.

Activity (14.5)

What is the payback period of the Chaotic Industries project from Activity 14.2?

The inflows and outflows are expected to be:

Time		Net cash flows £000	Cumulative net cash flows £000	
Immediately	Cost of vans	(150)	(150)	
1 year's time	Net saving before depreciation	30	(120)	(−150 + 30)
2 years' time	Net saving before depreciation	30	(90)	(−120 + 30)
3 years' time	Net saving before depreciation	30	(60)	(−90 + 30)
4 years' time	Net saving before depreciation	30	(30)	(−60 + 30)
5 years' time	Net saving before depreciation	30	0	(−30 + 30)
6 years' time	Net saving before depreciation	30	30	(0 + 30)
6 years' time	Disposal proceeds from the machine	30	60	(30 + 30)

The payback period here is five years; that is, it is not until the end of the fifth year that the vans will pay for themselves out of the savings that they are expected to generate.

The PP approach has certain advantages. It is quick and easy to calculate, and can be easily understood by managers. The logic of using PP is that projects that can recoup their cost quickly are economically more attractive than those with longer payback periods, that is, it emphasises liquidity. PP is probably an improvement on ARR in respect of the timing of the cash flows. PP is not, however, the whole answer to the problem.

Problems with PP

Activity (14.6)

In what respect is PP not the whole answer as a means of assessing investment opportunities? Consider the cash flows arising from three competing projects:

Time		Project 1 £000	Project 2 £000	Project 3 £000
Immediately	Cost of machine	(200)	(200)	(200)
1 year's time	Operating profit before depreciation	40	10	80
2 years' time	Operating profit before depreciation	80	20	100
3 years' time	Operating profit before depreciation	80	170	20
4 years' time	Operating profit before depreciation	60	20	200
5 years' time	Operating profit before depreciation	40	10	500
5 years' time	Disposal proceeds	40	10	20

(*Hint:* Again, the defect is not concerned with the ability of the manager to forecast future events. This is a problem, but it is a problem whatever approach we take.)

The PP for each project is three years and so the PP method would regard the projects as being equally acceptable. It cannot distinguish between those projects that pay back a significant amount early in the three-year payback period and those that do not.

In addition, this method ignores cash flows after the payback period. A decision maker concerned with increasing owners' wealth would prefer Project 3 because the cash flows come in earlier (most of the initial cost of making the investment has been repaid by the end of the second year) and they are greater in total.

The cumulative cash flows of each project in Activity 14.6 are set out in Figure 14.1.

Figure 14.1 The cumulative cash flows of each project in Activity 14.6

The payback method of investment appraisal would view Projects 1, 2 and 3 as being equally attractive. In doing so, the method completely ignores the fact that Project 3 provides the payback cash earlier in the three-year period and goes on to generate large benefits in later years.

We can see that the PP method is not concerned with the profitability of projects; it is concerned simply with their payback period. Thus cash flows arising beyond the payback period are ignored. While this neatly avoids the practical problems of forecasting cash flows over a long period, it means that relevant information may be ignored.

We may feel that, by favouring projects with a short payback period, the PP approach does at least provide a means of dealing with the problems of risk and uncertainty. However, this is a fairly crude approach to the problem. It looks only at the risk that the project will end earlier than expected. However, this is only one of many risk areas. What, for example, about the risk that the demand for the product may be less than expected? There are more systematic approaches to dealing with risk that can be used and we shall look at these later in the chapter.

PP takes some note of the timing of the costs and benefits from the project. Its key deficiency, however, is that it is not linked to promoting increases in the wealth of the business and its owners. PP will tend to recommend undertaking projects that pay for themselves quickly.

The PP method requires the managers of a business to select a maximum acceptable payback period. This maximum period, in practice, will vary from one business to the next. **Real World 14.4** provides some evidence of the length of payback period required by UK manufacturing businesses.

Real World 14.4

Payback time

A survey of 337 UK manufacturing businesses undertaken by the Confederation of British Industry in 2001 found that the average payback period required among those using the PP method was 3.6 years. Figure 14.2 shows the spread of required payback periods.

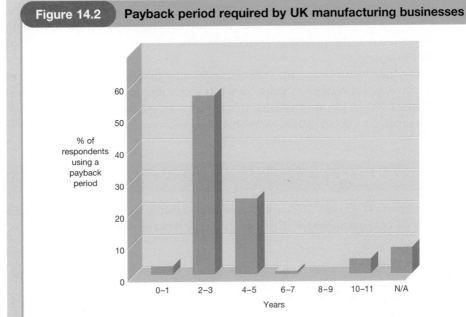

| Figure 14.2 | Payback period required by UK manufacturing businesses |

Over half (54 per cent) of businesses require a payback period of 2 to 3 years. The next most popular period is 4 to 5 years, which 24 per cent of businesses adopt.

Source: Figure adapted from a diagram in *Investment Appraisal in UK Manufacturing: Has it changed since the mid-1990s?*, D. Godden, www.cbi.org.uk.

Net present value (NPV)

From what we have seen so far, it seems that to make sensible investment decisions, we need a method of appraisal that both:

- considers *all* of the costs and benefits of each investment opportunity; and
- makes a logical allowance for the *timing* of those costs and benefits.

 The **net present value (NPV)** method provides us with this.

Consider the Billingsgate Battery example's cash flows, which we should recall can be summarised as follows:

Time		£000
Immediately	Cost of machine	(100)
1 year's time	Operating profit before depreciation	20
2 years' time	Operating profit before depreciation	40
3 years' time	Operating profit before depreciation	60
4 years' time	Operating profit before depreciation	60
5 years' time	Operating profit before depreciation	20
5 years' time	Disposal proceeds	20

Given that the principal financial objective of the business is to increase owners' wealth, it would be very easy to assess this investment if all of the cash inflows and outflows were to occur now (all at the same time). All that we should need to do would be to add up the cash inflows (total £220,000) and compare them with the cash outflows (£100,000). This would lead us to the conclusion that the project should go ahead because the business, and its owners, would be better off by £120,000. Of course, it is not as easy as this because time is involved. The cash outflow (payment) will occur immediately if the project is undertaken. The inflows (receipts) will arise at a range of later times.

The time factor is an important issue because people do not normally see £100 paid out now as equivalent in value to £100 receivable in a year's time. If we were to be offered £100 in 12 months' time in exchange for paying out £100 now, we should not be prepared to do so unless we wished to do someone a favour.

Activity (14.7)

Why would you see £100 to be received in a year's time as not equal in value to £100 to be paid immediately? (There are basically three reasons.)

The reasons are:

- interest lost
- risk
- effects of inflation.

We shall now take a closer look at these three reasons in turn.

Interest lost

If we are to be deprived of the opportunity to spend our money for a year, we could equally well be deprived of its use by placing it on deposit in a bank or building society. In this case, at the end of the year we could have our money back and have interest as well. Thus, by investing the funds in some other way, we shall be incurring an *opportunity cost*. As we saw in Chapter 8, an opportunity cost occurs where one course of action, for example making an investment, deprives us of the opportunity to derive some benefit from an alternative action, for example putting the money in the bank and earning interest.

From this we can see that any investment opportunity must, if it is to make us wealthier, do better than the returns that are available from the next best opportunity. Thus, if Billingsgate Battery Company sees putting the money in the bank on deposit as the alternative to investment in the machine, the return from investing in the machine must be better than that from investing in the bank. If the bank offered a better return, the business, and its owners, would become wealthier by putting the money on deposit.

Risk

Buying a machine to manufacture a product, or to provide a service, to be sold in the market, on the strength of various estimates made in advance of buying the machine, exposes the business to **risk**. Things may not turn out as expected.

Activity 14.8

Can you suggest some areas where things could go other than according to plan in the Billingsgate Battery Company example?

We have come up with the following:

● The machine might not work as well as expected; it might break down, leading to loss of the business's ability to provide the service.
● Sales of the service may not be as buoyant as expected.
● Labour costs may prove to be higher than expected.
● The sale proceeds of the machine could prove to be less than were estimated.

It is important to remember that the decision whether to invest in the machine must be taken *before* any of these things are known. It is only after the machine has been purchased that we could discover that the level of sales, which had been estimated before the event, is not going to be achieved. It is not possible to wait until we know for certain whether the market will behave as we expected before we buy the machine. We can study reports and analyses of the market. We can commission sophisticated market surveys, and these may give us more confidence in the likely outcome. We can advertise widely and try to promote sales. Ultimately, however, we have to decide whether to jump off into the dark and accept the risk if we want the opportunity to make profitable investments.

Normally, people expect to receive greater returns where they perceive risk to be a factor. Examples of this in real life are not difficult to find. One such example is that banks tend to charge higher rates of interest to borrowers whom the bank perceives as more risky. Those who can offer good security for a loan, and who can point to a regular source of income, tend to be charged lower rates of interest.

Going back to Billingsgate Battery Company's investment opportunity, it is not enough to say that we should not advise making the investment unless the returns from it are as high as those from investing in a bank deposit. Clearly we should want returns above the level of bank deposit interest rates, because the logical equivalent to investing in the machine is not putting the money on deposit but making an alternative investment that is risky.

In practice, we tend to expect a higher rate of return from investment projects where the risk is perceived as being higher. How risky a particular project is, and therefore how large this **risk premium** should be, are matters that are difficult to handle. It is usually necessary to make some judgement on these questions.

Inflation

If we are to be deprived of £100 for a year, when we come to spend that money it will not buy as many goods and services as it would have done a year earlier. Generally, we shall not be able to buy as many tins of baked beans or loaves of bread or bus tickets as we could have done a year earlier. This is because of the loss in the purchasing power of money, or **inflation**, which occurs over time. Clearly, the investor needs compensating for this loss of purchasing power if the investment is to be made. This compensation is on top of a return that takes account of what could have been gained from an alternative investment of similar risk.

In practice, interest rates observable in the market tend to take inflation into account. Rates that are offered to potential building society and bank depositors include an allowance for the rate of inflation that is expected in the future.

What will a logical investor do?

A logical investor who is seeking to increase his or her wealth will only be prepared to make investments that will compensate for the loss of interest and purchasing power of the money invested and for the fact that the returns expected may not materialise (risk). This is usually assessed by seeing whether the proposed investment will yield a return that is greater than the basic rate of interest (which would include an allowance for inflation) plus a risk premium.

These three factors (interest lost, risk and inflation) are set out in Figure 14.3.

Figure 14.3 The factors influencing the returns required by investors from a project

Three factors influence the required returns for inventory (opportunity cost of finance).

Naturally, investors need at least the minimum returns before they are prepared to invest. However, it is in terms of the effect on their wealth that they should logically assess an investment project. Usually it is the investment with the highest percentage return that will make the investor most wealthy, but we shall see later in this chapter that this is not always the case. For the time being, therefore, we shall concentrate on wealth.

Let us now return to the Billingsgate Battery Company example. We should recall that the cash flows expected from this investment are:

Time		£000
Immediately	Cost of machine	(100)
1 year's time	Operating profit before depreciation	20
2 years' time	Operating profit before depreciation	40
3 years' time	Operating profit before depreciation	60
4 years' time	Operating profit before depreciation	60
5 years' time	Operating profit before depreciation	20
5 years' time	Disposal proceeds	20

Let us assume that, instead of making this investment, the business could make an alternative investment with similar risk and obtain a return of 20 per cent a year.

We have already seen that it is not sufficient just to compare the basic cash inflows and outflows for the investment. It would be useful if we could express each of these cash flows in similar terms, so that we could make a direct comparison between the sum of the inflows over time and the immediate £100,000 investment. Fortunately, we can do this.

Activity (14.9)

We know that Billingsgate Battery Company could alternatively invest its money at a rate of 20 per cent a year. How much do you judge the present (immediate) value of the expected first year receipt of £20,000 to be? In other words, if instead of having to wait a year for the £20,000, and being deprived of the opportunity to invest it at 20 per cent, you could have some money now, what sum to be received now would you regard as exactly equivalent to getting £20,000 but having to wait a year for it?

We should obviously be happy to accept a lower amount if we could get it immediately than if we had to wait a year. This is because we could invest it at 20 per cent (in the alternative project). Logically, we should be prepared to accept the amount that, with a year's income, will grow to £20,000. If we call this amount PV (for present value) we can say:

$$PV + (PV \times 20\%) = £20,000$$

that is, the amount plus income from investing the amount for the year equals the £20,000.
If we rearrange this equation we find:

$$PV \times (1 + 0.2) = £20,000$$

(Note that 0.2 is the same as 20 per cent, but expressed as a decimal.) Further rearranging gives:

$$PV = £20,000/(1 + 0.2) = £16,667$$

Thus, rational investors who have the opportunity to invest at 20 per cent a year would not mind whether they have £16,667 now or £20,000 in a year's time. In this sense we can say that, given a 20 per cent alternative investment opportunity, the present value of £20,000 to be received in one year's time is £16,667.

If we could derive the present value (PV) of each of the cash flows associated with Billingsgate's machine investment, we could easily make the direct comparison between the cost of making the investment (£100,000) and the various benefits that will derive from it in years 1 to 5. Fortunately we can do this.

We can make a more general statement about the PV of a particular cash flow. It is:

> **PV of the cash flow of year n = Actual cash flow of year n divided by $(1 + r)^n$**

where n is the year of the cash flow (that is, how many years into the future) and r is the opportunity investing rate expressed as a decimal (instead of as a percentage).

We have already seen how this works for the £20,000 inflow for year 1. For year 2 the calculation would be:

$$\text{PV of year 2 cash flow (that is, £40,000)} = £40,000/(1 + 0.2)^2 = £40,000/(1.2)^2$$
$$= £40,000/1.44 = £27,778$$

Thus the present value of the £40,000 to be received in two years' time is £27,778.

Activity (14.10)

See if you can show that an investor would be indifferent to £27,778 receivable now, or £40,000 receivable in two years' time, assuming that there is a 20 per cent investment opportunity.

The reasoning goes like this:

	£
Amount available for immediate investment	27,778
Add Interest for year 1 (20% × 27,778)	5,556
	33,334
Add Interest for year 2 (20% × 33,334)	6,667
	40,001

(The extra £1 is only a rounding error.)

Thus, because the investor can turn £27,778 into £40,000 in two years, these amounts are equivalent. We can say that £27,778 is the present value of £40,000 receivable after two years (given a 20 per cent rate of return).

Now let us calculate the present values of all of the cash flows associated with the Billingsgate machine project and hence the *net present value (NPV)* of the project as a whole.

The relevant cash flows and calculations are as follows:

Time	Cash flow £000	Calculation of PV	PV £000
Immediately (time 0)	(100)	$(100)/(1 + 0.2)^0$	(100.00)
1 year's time	20	$20/(1 + 0.2)^1$	16.67
2 years' time	40	$40/(1 + 0.2)^2$	27.78
3 years' time	60	$60/(1 + 0.2)^3$	34.72
4 years' time	60	$60/(1 + 0.2)^4$	28.94
5 years' time	20	$20/(1 + 0.2)^5$	8.04
5 years' time	20	$20/(1 + 0.2)^5$	8.04
Net present value (NPV)			24.19

Note that $(1 + 0.2)^0 = 1$.

Once again, we must ask how we can decide whether the machine project is acceptable to the business. In fact, the decision rule is simple:

- If the NPV is positive the project should be accepted; if it is negative the project should be rejected.
- If there are two or more competing projects that have positive NPVs, the decision maker should select the project with the highest NPV.

In this case, the NPV is positive, so we should accept the project and buy the machine. The reasoning behind this decision rule is quite straightforward. Investing in the machine will make the business, and its owners, £24,190 better off than they would be by taking up the next best opportunity available to it. The gross benefits from investing in this machine are worth a total of £124,190 today, and since the business can 'buy' these benefits for just £100,000 today, the investment should be made. If, however, the present value of the gross benefits were below £100,000, it would be less than the cost of 'buying' those benefits.

Activity 14.11

What is the *maximum* the Billingsgate Battery Company would be prepared to pay for the machine, given the potential benefits of owning it?

The business would be prepared to pay up to £124,190 since the wealth of the owners of the business would be increased up to this price – although the business would prefer to pay as little as possible.

Using discount tables

Deducing the present values of the various cash flows is a little laborious using the approach that we have just taken. To deduce each PV we took the relevant cash flow and multiplied it by $1/(1 + r)^n$. There is a slightly different way to do this. Tables exist that show values of this **discount factor** for a range of values of r and n. Such a table appears in Appendix F at the end of this book. Take a look at it.

Look at the column for 20 per cent and the row for one year. We find that the factor is 0.833. This means that the PV of a cash flow of £1 receivable in one year is £0.833. So the present value of a cash flow of £20,000 receivable in one year's time is £16,660 (that is, 0.833 × £20,000), the same result as we found doing it in longhand.

Activity 14.12

What is the NPV of the Chaotic Industries project from Activity 14.2, assuming a 15 per cent opportunity cost of finance (discount rate)? You should use the discount table in Appendix F.

Activity 14.12 continued

Remember that the inflows and outflow are expected to be:

Time		£000
Immediately	Cost of vans	(150)
1 year's time	Net saving before depreciation	30
2 years' time	Net saving before depreciation	30
3 years' time	Net saving before depreciation	30
4 years' time	Net saving before depreciation	30
5 years' time	Net saving before depreciation	30
6 years' time	Net saving before depreciation	30
6 years' time	Disposal proceeds from the machine	30

The calculation of the NPV of the project is as follows:

Time	Cash flows £000	Discount factor (15% – from the table)	Present value £000
Immediately	(150)	1.000	(150.00)
1 year's time	30	0.870	26.10
2 years' time	30	0.756	22.68
3 years' time	30	0.658	19.74
4 years' time	30	0.572	17.16
5 years' time	30	0.497	14.91
6 years' time	30	0.432	12.96
6 years' time	30	0.432	12.96
		NPV	(23.49)

Activity 14.13

How would you interpret this result?

The fact that the project has a negative NPV means that the present values of the benefits from the investment are worth less than the cost of entering into it. Any cost up to £126,510 (the present value of the benefits) would be worth paying, but not £150,000.

The discount table reveals how the value of £1 diminishes as its receipt goes further into the future. Assuming an opportunity cost of finance of 20 per cent a year, £1 to be received immediately, obviously, has a present value of £1. However, as the time before it is to be received increases, the present value diminishes significantly, as is shown in Figure 14.4.

The discount rate and the cost of capital

We have seen that the appropriate discount rate to use in NPV assessments is the opportunity cost of finance. This is often known as the cost of capital.

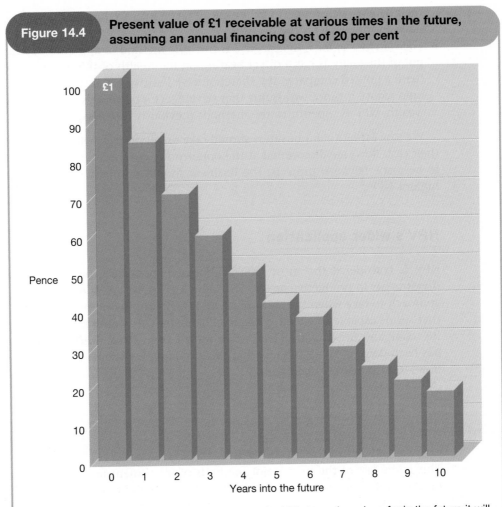

Figure 14.4   Present value of £1 receivable at various times in the future, assuming an annual financing cost of 20 per cent

The present value of a future receipt (or payment) of £1 depends on how far in the future it will occur. Those that will occur in the near future will have a larger present value than those whose occurrence is more distant in time.

Why NPV is better

From what we have seen, NPV seems to be a better method of appraising investment opportunities than either ARR or PP. This is because it fully takes account of each of the following:

● *The timing of the cash flows*. By discounting the various cash flows associated with each project according to when each one is expected to arise, NPV takes account of the time value of money. Associated with this is the fact that by discounting, using the opportunity cost of finance (that is, the return that the next best alternative opportunity would generate), the net benefit after financing costs have been met is identified (as the NPV of the project).

● *The whole of the relevant cash flows*. NPV includes all of the relevant cash flows irrespective of when they are expected to occur. It treats them differently according to their date of occurrence, but they are all taken into account in the NPV, and they all have an influence on the decision.

● *The objectives of the business.* NPV is the only method of appraisal in which the output of the analysis has a direct bearing on the wealth of the owners of the business (with a limited company, the shareholders). Positive NPVs enhance wealth; negative ones reduce it. Since we assume that private sector businesses seek to increase owners' wealth, NPV is superior to the methods previously discussed.

We saw earlier that a business should take on all projects with positive NPVs, when their cash flows are discounted at the opportunity cost of finance. Where a choice has to be made between projects, the business should normally select the one with the highest NPV.

NPV's wider application

NPV is considered the most logical approach to making business decisions about investments in productive assets. The same logic makes NPV equally valid as the best approach to take when trying to place a value on any economic asset, that is, an asset that seems capable of yielding financial benefits. This would include a share in a limited company and a loan. In fact, when we talk of *economic value*, we mean a value that has been derived by adding together the discounted (present) values of all future cash flows from the asset concerned.

Internal rate of return (IRR)

This is the last of the four major methods of investment appraisal that are found in practice. It is quite closely related to the NPV method in that, like NPV, it also involves discounting future cash flows. The **internal rate of return (IRR)** of a particular investment is the discount rate that, when applied to its future cash flows, will produce an NPV of precisely zero. In essence, it represents the yield from an investment opportunity.

Activity (14.14)

We should recall that, when we discounted the cash flows of the Billingsgate Battery Company machine investment opportunity at 20 per cent, we found that the NPV was a positive figure of £24,190 (see page 527). What does the NPV of the machine project tell us about the rate of return that the investment will yield for the business?

The fact that the NPV is positive when discounting at 20 per cent implies that the rate of return that the project generates is more than 20 per cent. The fact that the NPV is a pretty large figure implies that the actual rate of return is quite a lot above 20 per cent. We should expect increasing the size of the discount rate to reduce NPV, because a higher discount rate gives a lower discounted figure.

It is somewhat laborious to deduce the IRR by hand, since it cannot usually be calculated directly. Iteration (trial and error) is the approach that must usually be adopted. Fortunately, computer spreadsheet packages can deduce the IRR with ease. The package will also use a trial and error approach, but at high speed.

For the Billingsgate Battery Company, let us try a higher rate, say 30 per cent, and see what happens.

Time	Cash flow £000	Discount factor (30% – from the table)	PV £000
Immediately (time 0)	(100)	1.000	(100.00)
1 year's time	20	0.769	15.38
2 years' time	40	0.592	23.68
3 years' time	60	0.455	27.30
4 years' time	60	0.350	21.00
5 years' time	20	0.269	5.38
5 years' time	20	0.269	5.38
		NPV	(1.88)

In increasing the discount rate from 20 per cent to 30 per cent, we have reduced the NPV from £24,190 (positive) to £1,880 (negative). Since the IRR is the discount rate that will give us an NPV of exactly zero, we can conclude that the IRR of Billingsgate Battery Company's machine project is very slightly below 30 per cent. Further trials could lead us to the exact rate, but there is probably not much point, given the likely inaccuracy of the cash flow estimates. It is probably good enough, for practical purposes, to say that the IRR is about 30 per cent.

The relationship between the NPV method discussed earlier and the IRR is shown graphically in Figure 14.5 using the information relating to the Billingsgate Battery Company.

Figure 14.5   The relationship between the NPV and IRR methods

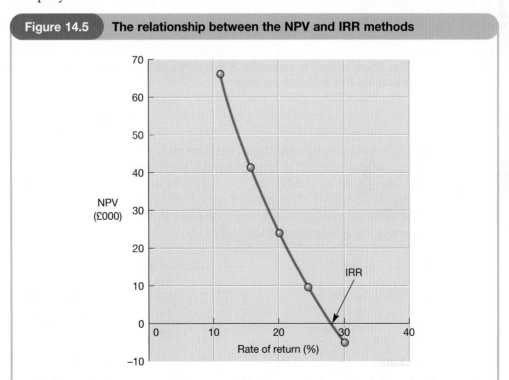

If the discount rate were zero, the NPV would be the sum of the net cash flows. In other words, no account would be taken of the time value of money. However, if we assume increasing discount rates, there is a corresponding decrease in the NPV of the project. When the NPV line crosses the horizontal axis there will be a zero NPV, and the point where it crosses is the IRR.

We can see that, where the discount rate is zero, the NPV will be the sum of the net cash flows. In other words, no account is taken of the time value of money. However, as the discount rate increases there is a corresponding decrease in the NPV of the project. When the NPV line crosses the horizontal axis there will be a zero NPV, and that represents the IRR.

Activity 14.15

What is the internal rate of return of the Chaotic Industries project from Activity 14.2? You should use the discount table in Appendix F. (*Hint*: Remember that you already know the NPV of this project at 15 per cent (from Activity 14.12).)

Since we know that, at a 15 per cent discount rate, the NPV is a relatively large negative figure, our next trial is using a lower discount rate, say 10 per cent:

Time	Cash flows £000	Discount factor (10% – from the table)	Present value £000
Immediately	(150)	1.000	(150.00)
1 year's time	30	0.909	27.27
2 years' time	30	0.826	24.78
3 years' time	30	0.751	22.53
4 years' time	30	0.683	20.49
5 years' time	30	0.621	18.63
6 years' time	30	0.565	16.95
6 years' time	30	0.565	16.95
		NPV	(2.40)

This figure is close to zero NPV. However, the NPV is still negative and so the precise IRR will be a little below 10 per cent.

We could undertake further trials in order to derive the precise IRR. In practice, most businesses have computer software packages that will do this quickly. If, however, we have to calculate the IRR manually, further iterations can be time consuming.

We can get an acceptable approximation to the answer fairly quickly by first calculating the change in NPV arising from a 1 per cent change in the discount rate. This can be done by taking the difference between the two trials (that is, 15 per cent and 10 per cent) that we have already carried out (in Activities 10.12 and 10.15):

Trial	Discount factor %	Present value £000
1	15	(23.49)
2	10	(2.40)
Difference	5	21.09

The change in NPV for every 1 per cent change in the discount rate will be:

$$(21.09/5) = 4.22$$

The reduction in the 10% discount rate required to achieve a zero NPV would therefore be:

$$(2.40)/4.22 = 0.57\%$$

The IRR is therefore:

$$(10.00 - 0.57) = 9.43\%$$

However to say that the IRR is about 9 per cent is near enough for most purposes.

Note that this approach assumes a straight-line relationship between the discount rate and NPV. We can see from Figure 14.5, however, that this assumption is not strictly correct. Over a relatively short range, however, this simplifying assumption is not usually a problem and so we can still arrive at a reasonable approximation.

Users of the IRR approach should apply the following decision rules:

- For any project to be acceptable, it must meet a minimum IRR requirement. This is often referred to as the *hurdle rate* and, logically, this should be the opportunity cost of finance.
- Where there are competing projects (the business can choose only one of two or more viable projects), the one with the highest IRR would be selected.

IRR has certain attributes in common with NPV. All cash flows are taken into account, and their timing is logically handled.

Real World 14.5 provides some idea of IRRs sought in practice.

Real World 14.5

Rates of return

IRR rates for investment projects can vary considerably. Here are a few examples of the expected returns from investment projects of large businesses.

- Associated British Ports, the UK's largest port operator, concentrates on projects that generate an IRR of at least 15 per cent.
- Brascan, a Canadian property and energy business, made a bid to acquire Canary Wharf, a property estate in London, and expected to generate an IRR of at least 20 per cent if the bid price was accepted.
- Hutchison Whampoa, a large telecommunications business, requires an IRR of at least 25 per cent from its telecom projects.
- Airbus expects an IRR of 13 per cent from the sale of its A380 superjumbo aircraft.

Sources: 'Brascan raises offer for Canary Wharf', FT.com, 13 February 2004; 'Spread of risks gives ABP confident outlook', FT.com, 13 February 2003; Hutchison Whampoa, FT.com, Lex column, 31 March 2004; and 'Airbus hikes A380 break-even target', FT.com, 20 October 2006.

Problems with IRR

The main disadvantage of IRR is the fact that it does not correctly address the question of wealth generation. It could therefore lead to the wrong decision being made. This is because IRR would, for example, always see an IRR of 25 per cent being preferable to a 20 per cent IRR, assuming an opportunity cost of finance of, say, 15 per cent. Although accepting the project with the higher percentage return will often generate more wealth, this may not always be the case. This is because IRR completely ignores the *scale of investment*.

With a 15 per cent cost of finance, £15 million invested at 20 per cent for one year, will make us wealthier by £0.75 million (that is, $15 \times (20 - 15)\% = 0.75$). With the same cost of finance, £5 million invested at 25 per cent for one year will make us only £0.5 million (that is, $5 \times (25 - 15)\% = 0.50$). IRR does not recognise this. It should be acknowledged that it is not usual for projects to be competing where there is such a large difference in scale. Even though the problem may be rare and so, typically, IRR will give the same signal as NPV, a method that is always reliable (NPV) must be better to use than IRR. This problem with percentages is another example illustrated by the Mexican road discussed in Real World 14.3.

A further problem with the IRR method is that it has difficulty handling projects with unconventional cash flows. In the examples studied so far, each project has a negative cash flow arising at the start of its life and then positive cash flows thereafter. However, in some cases, a project may have both positive and negative cash flows at future points in its life. Such a pattern of cash flows can result in there being more than one IRR, or even no IRR at all. This would make the IRR method impossible to use, although it should be said that this is quite rare in practice.

Some practical points

When undertaking an investment appraisal, there are several practical points that we should bear in mind:

- *Past costs*. As we saw in Chapter 7, with all decisions we should take account only of **relevant costs** in our analysis. This means that only costs that vary with the decision should be considered. Thus, all past costs should be ignored as they cannot vary with the decision. In some cases, a business may incur costs (such as development costs and market research costs) *before* the evaluation of an opportunity to launch a new product. As those costs have already been incurred, they should be disregarded, even though the amounts may be substantial. Costs that have already been committed but not yet paid should also be disregarded. Where a business has entered into a binding contract to incur a particular cost, it becomes in effect a past cost even though payment may not be due until some point in the future.

- *Common future costs*. It is not only past costs that do not vary with the decision; some future costs may also be the same. For example, the cost of raw materials may not vary with the decision whether to invest in a new piece of manufacturing plant or to continue to use existing plant.

- *Opportunity costs*. Opportunity costs arising from benefits forgone must be taken into account. Thus, for example, when considering a decision concerning whether or not to continue to use a machine already owned by the business, the realisable value of the machine might be an important **opportunity cost**.

- *Taxation*. Owners will be interested in the after-tax returns generated from the business, and so taxation will usually be an important consideration when making an investment decision. The profits from the project will be taxed, the capital investment may attract tax relief, and so on. Tax is levied on these at significant rates. This means that, in real life, unless tax is formally taken into account, the wrong decision could easily be made. The timing of the tax outflow should also be taken into account when preparing the cash flows for the project.

- *Cash flows not profit flows*. We have seen that for the NPV, IRR and PP methods, it is cash flows rather than profit flows that are relevant to the assessment of investment projects. In an investment appraisal requiring the application of any of these methods we may be given details of the profits for the investment period. These need to be adjusted in order to derive the cash flows. We should remember that the operating profit *before* non-cash items (such as depreciation) is an approximation to the cash flows for the period, and so we should work back to this figure.

When the data are expressed in profit rather than cash flow terms, an adjustment in respect of working capital may also be necessary. Some adjustment should be made to take account of changes in working capital. For example, launching a new product may give rise to an increase in the net cash investment made in trade receivables, inventories and trade payables, requiring an immediate outlay of cash. This outlay for additional working capital should be shown in the NPV calculations as part of the initial cost. However, at the end of the life of the project, the additional working capital will be released. This divestment, resulting in an inflow of cash at the end of the project should also be taken into account at the point at which it is received.

- *Year-end assumption.* In the examples and activities that we have considered so far in this chapter, we have assumed that cash flows arise at the end of the relevant year. This is a simplifying assumption that is used to make the calculations easier. (However, it is perfectly possible to deal more precisely with the cash flows.) The assumption is clearly unrealistic, as money will have to be paid to employees on a weekly or monthly basis and credit customers will pay within a month or two of buying the product or service. Nevertheless, it is probably not a serious distortion. We should be clear, however, that there is nothing about any of the appraisal methods that demands that this assumption be made.

- *Interest payments.* When using discounted cash flow techniques, interest payments should not be taken into account in deriving the cash flows for the period. The discount factor already takes account of the costs of financing, and so to take account of interest charges in deriving cash flows for the period would be double counting.

- *Other factors.* Investment decision making must not be viewed as simply a mechanical exercise. The results derived from a particular investment appraisal method will be only one input to the decision-making process. There may be broader issues connected to the decision that have to be taken into account but which may be difficult or impossible to quantify.

The reliability of the forecasts and the validity of the assumptions used in the evaluation will also have a bearing on the final decision.

Activity (14.16)

The directors of Manuff (Steel) Ltd are considering closing one of the business's factories. There has been a reduction in the demand for the products made at the factory in recent years, and the directors are not optimistic about the long-term prospects for these products. The factory is situated in the north of England, in an area where unemployment is high.

The factory is leased, and there are still four years of the lease remaining. The directors are uncertain whether the factory should be closed immediately or at the end of the period of the lease. Another business has offered to sublease the premises from Manuff at a rental of £40,000 a year for the remainder of the lease period.

The machinery and equipment at the factory cost £1,500,000, and have a balance sheet value of £400,000. In the event of immediate closure, the machinery and

Activity 14.16 continued

equipment could be sold for £220,000. The working capital at the factory is £420,000, and could be liquidated for that amount immediately, if required. Alternatively, the working capital can be liquidated in full at the end of the lease period. Immediate closure would result in redundancy payments to employees of £180,000.

If the factory continues in operation until the end of the lease period, the following operating profits (losses) are expected:

	Year 1 £000	Year 2 £000	Year 3 £000	Year 4 £000
Operating profit (loss)	160	(40)	30	20

The above figures include a charge of £90,000 a year for depreciation of machinery and equipment. The residual value of the machinery and equipment at the end of the lease period is estimated at £40,000.

Redundancy payments are expected to be £150,000 at the end of the lease period if the factory continues in operation. The business has an annual cost of capital of 12 per cent. Ignore taxation.

Required:
(a) Determine the relevant cash flows arising from a decision to continue operations until the end of the lease period rather than to close immediately.
(b) Calculate the net present value of continuing operations until the end of the lease period, rather than closing immediately.
(c) What other factors might the directors take into account before making a final decision on the timing of the factory closure?
(d) State, with reasons, whether or not the business should continue to operate the factory until the end of the lease period.

Your answer should be as follows:

(a) *Relevant cash flows*

	Years				
	0 £000	*1* £000	*2* £000	*3* £000	*4* £000
Operating cash flows (Note 1)		250	50	120	110
Sale of machinery (Note 2)	(220)				40
Redundancy costs (Note 3)	180				(150)
Sublease rentals (Note 4)		(40)	(40)	(40)	(40)
Working capital invested (Note 5)	(420)				420
	(460)	210	10	80	380

Notes:
1 Each year's operating cash flows are calculated by adding back the depreciation charge for the year to the operating profit for the year. In the case of the operating loss, the depreciation charge is deducted.
2 In the event of closure, machinery could be sold immediately. Thus an opportunity cost of £220,000 is incurred if operations continue.
3 By continuing operations, there will be a saving in immediate redundancy costs of £180,000. However, redundancy costs of £150,000 will be paid in four years' time.

4 By continuing operations, the opportunity to sublease the factory will be foregone.

5 Immediate closure would mean that working capital could be liquidated. By continuing operations this opportunity is foregone. However, working capital can be liquidated in four years' time.

(b)

Discount rate 12 per cent	1.000	0.893	0.797	0.712	0.636
Present value	(460)	187.5	8.0	57.0	241.7
Net present value	34.2				

(c) Other factors that may influence the decision include:

● *The overall strategy of the business.* The business may need to set the decision within a broader context. It may be necessary to manufacture the products at the factory because they are an integral part of the business's product range. The business may wish to avoid redundancies in an area of high unemployment for as long as possible.

● *Flexibility.* A decision to close the factory is probably irreversible. If the factory continues, however, there may be a chance that the prospects for the factory will brighten in the future.

● *Creditworthiness of sub-lessee.* The business should investigate the creditworthiness of the sub-lessee. Failure to receive the expected sublease payments would make the closure option far less attractive.

● *Accuracy of forecasts.* The forecasts made by the business should be examined carefully. Inaccuracies in the forecasts or any underlying assumptions may change the expected outcomes.

(d) The NPV of the decision to continue operations rather than close immediately is positive. Hence, shareholders would be better off if the directors took this course of action. The factory should therefore continue in operation rather than close down. This decision is likely to be welcomed by employees and would allow the business to maintain its flexibility.

Investment appraisal in practice

Many surveys have been conducted in the UK into the methods of investment appraisal used by businesses. They have shown the following features:

● Businesses tend to use more than one method to assess each investment decision, increasingly so over time.

● The discounting methods (NPV and IRR) have become increasingly popular over time, with these two becoming the most popular in recent years.

● The continued popularity of ARR and PP, despite their theoretical shortcomings and the rise in popularity of the discounting methods.

● A tendency for larger businesses to use the discounting methods and to use more than one method in respect of each decision.

Real World 14.6 shows the results of one of the most recent (1997) surveys conducted of UK businesses regarding their use of investment appraisal methods.

Real World 14.6

A survey of UK business practice

Method	Percentage of businesses using the method
Net present value	80
Internal rate of return	81
Payback period	70
Accounting rate of return	56
	287

Source: Arnold and Hatzopoulos (see reference 2 at the end of the chapter). Reproduced by kind permission of Blackwell Publishing Ltd.

A more recent survey of US businesses also shows considerable support for the NPV and IRR methods. There is less support, however, for the payback method and ARR. **Real World 14.7** sets out some of the main findings.

Real World 14.7

A survey of US practice

A survey of the chief financial officers (CFOs) of 392 US businesses examined the popularity of various methods of investment appraisal. Figure 14.6 shows the percentage of businesses surveyed that always, or almost always, used the four methods discussed in this chapter.

Figure 14.6 The use of investment appraisal methods among US businesses

Percentage of CFOs who always or almost always use a given technique

Both the IRR and NPV methods are widely used and are much more popular than PP and ARR. Nevertheless, PP is still used always, or almost always, by a majority of US businesses.

Source: Based on information in Graham and Harvey (see reference 3 at the end of the chapter).

Activity 14.17

Earlier in the chapter we discussed the theoretical limitations of the PP method. How do you explain the fact that it still seems to be a popular method of investment appraisal among businesses?

A number of possible reasons may explain this finding:

- PP is easy to understand and use.
- It can avoid the problems of forecasting far into the future.
- It gives emphasis to the early cash flows when there is greater certainty concerning the accuracy of their predicted value.
- It emphasises the importance of liquidity. Where a business has liquidity problems, a short payback period for a project is likely to appear attractive.

PP can provide a convenient, though rough and ready, assessment of the profitability of a project, in the way that it is used in **Real World 14.8**.

Real World 14.8

An investment lifts off

FT

SES Global is the world's largest commercial satellite operator. This means that it rents satellite capacity to broadcasters, governments, telecommunications groups and Internet service providers. It is a risky venture that few are prepared to undertake. As a result, a handful of businesses dominates the market.

Launching a satellite requires a huge initial outlay of capital, but relatively small cash outflows following the launch. Revenues only start to flow once the satellite is in orbit. A satellite launch costs around €250m. The main elements of this cost are the satellite (€120m), the launch vehicle (€80m), insurance (€40m) and ground equipment (€10m).

According to Romain Bausch, president and chief executive of SES Global, it takes three years to build and launch a satellite. However, the average lifetime of a satellite is fifteen years during which time it is generating revenues. The revenues generated are such that the payback period is around four to five years.

Source: 'Satellites need space to earn', Tim Burt, FT.com, 14 July 2003.

The popularity of PP may suggest a lack of sophistication by managers, concerning investment appraisal. This criticism is most often made against managers of smaller businesses. This point is borne out by both of the surveys discussed above which have found that smaller businesses are much less likely to use discounted cash flow methods (NPV and IRR) than are larger ones. Other surveys have tended to reach a similar conclusion.

The survey evidence suggests that many businesses use more than one method to appraise investments. The sum of percentage usage for each appraisal method in the UK survey, for example, is 287 per cent (see Real World 14.6). This survey also suggests that most businesses use one, or both, of the two discounted cash flow methods. Generally survey evidence has shown a strong increase in the rate of usage of both NPV and IRR, in the UK, over the years. Similar trends seem to prevail in most of the world.

IRR may be as popular as NPV, despite its shortcomings, because it expresses outcomes in percentage terms rather than in absolute terms. This form of expression appears to be more acceptable to managers, despite the problems of percentage measures that we discussed earler. This may be because managers are used to using percentage figures as targets (for example, return on capital employed).

Real World 14.9 shows extracts from the 2006 annual report of a well-known business: Rolls-Royce plc, the builder of engines for aircraft and other purposes.

Real World 14.9

The use of NPV at Rolls-Royce

In its 2006 annual report and accounts, Rolls-Royce plc stated that:

> The Group continues to subject all investments to rigorous examination of risks and future cash flows to ensure that they create shareholder value. All major investments require Board approval. The Group has a portfolio of projects at different stages of their life cycles. Discounted cash flow analysis of the remaining life of projects is performed on a regular basis.

Source: Rolls-Royce plc Annual Report and Accounts 2006.

Rolls-Royce makes clear that it uses NPV (the report refers to creating shareholder value and to discounted cash flow, which strongly imply NPV). It is interesting to note that Rolls-Royce not only assesses new projects but also reassesses existing ones. This must be a sensible commercial approach. Businesses should not continue with existing projects unless those projects have a positive NPV based on future cash flows. Just because a project seemed to have a positive NPV before it started does not mean that this will persist, in the light of changing circumstances. Activity 14.16 considered a decision to close down a project.

Self-assessment question 14.1

Beacon Chemicals plc is considering buying some equipment to produce a chemical named X14. The new equipment's capital cost is estimated at £100,000. If its purchase is approved now, the equipment can be bought and production can commence by the end of this year. £50,000 has already been spent on research and development work. Estimates of revenues and costs arising from the operation of the new equipment appear below:

	Year 1	Year 2	Year 3	Year 4	Year 5
Sales price (£/litre)	100	120	120	100	80
Sales volume (litres)	800	1,000	1,200	1,000	800
Variable costs (£/litre)	50	50	40	30	40
Fixed costs (£000)	30	30	30	30	30

If the equipment is bought, sales of some existing products will be lost, and this will result in a loss of contribution of £15,000 a year over its life.

The accountant has informed you that the fixed costs include depreciation of £20,000 a year on the new equipment. They also include an allocation of £10,000 for fixed overheads. A separate study has indicated that if the new equipment were bought, additional overheads, excluding depreciation, arising from producing the chemical would be £8,000 a year. Production would require additional working capital of £30,000.

For the purposes of your initial calculations ignore taxation.

Required:
(a) Deduce the relevant annual cash flows associated with buying the equipment.
(b) Deduce the payback period.
(c) Calculate the net present value using a discount rate of 8 per cent.

(*Hint*: You should deal with the investment in working capital by treating it as a cash outflow at the start of the project and an inflow at the end.)

The answer to this question can be found at the back of the book on page 706.

Dealing with risk

We have already encountered the fact that risk is an important aspect of financial decision making. Risk, in this context, is the extent and likelihood that what is projected to occur will not actually happen. It is a particularly important issue in the context of investment decisions, because of:

- the relatively long timescales involved – there is more time for things to go wrong between the decision being made and the end of the project;
- the size of the investment – if things go wrong, the impact can be both significant and lasting.

Various approaches to dealing with risk have been proposed. These fall into two categories: assessing the level of risk and reacting to the level of risk. We now consider formal methods of dealing with risk that fall within each category.

Assessing the level of risk

Sensitivity analysis

One popular way of attempting to assess the level of risk is to carry out a **sensitivity analysis** on the proposed project. This involves an examination of the key input values affecting the project to see how changes in each input might influence the viability of the project.

First, the investment is appraised, using the best estimates for each of the input factors (for example, labour cost, material cost, discount rate and so on). Assuming that the NPV is positive, each input value is then examined to see how far the estimated figure could be changed before the project becomes unviable for that reason alone.

Let us suppose that the NPV for an investment in a machine to provide a particular service is a positive value of £50,000. If we were to carry out a sensitivity analysis on this project, we should consider in turn each of the key input factors:

- cost of the machine
- sales volume and price
- relevant labour costs
- length of the project
- the discount rate.

We should seek to find the value that each of them could have before the NPV figure would become negative (that is, the value for the factor at which NPV would be zero). The difference between the value for that factor at which the NPV would equal zero and the estimated value represents the margin of safety for that particular input. The process is set out in Figure 14.7.

Figure 14.7 **Factors affecting the sensitivity of NPV calculations**

Sensitivity analysis involves identifying the key factors that affect the project. In the figure, six factors have been identified for the particular project. (In practice, the key factors are likely to vary between projects.) Once identified, each factor will be examined in turn to find the value it should have for the project to have a zero NPV.

A computer spreadsheet model of the project can be extremely valuable for this exercise because it then becomes a very simple matter to try various values for the input data and to see the effect of each. As a result of carrying out a sensitivity analysis, the decision maker is able to get a feel for the project, which otherwise might not be possible. Example 14.3, which illustrates a sensitivity analysis is, however, straightforward and can be undertaken without recourse to a spreadsheet.

Example 14.3

S. Saluja (Property Developers) Ltd intends to bid at an auction, to be held today, for a manor house that has fallen into disrepair. The auctioneer believes that the house will be sold for about £450,000. The business wishes to renovate the property and to divide it into flats, to be sold for £150,000 each. The renovation will be in two stages and will cover a two-year period. Stage 1 will cover the first year of the project. It will cost £500,000 and the six flats completed during this stage are expected to be sold for a total of £900,000 at the end of the first year. Stage 2 will cover the second year of the project. It will cost £300,000 and the three remaining flats are expected to be sold at the end of the second year for a total of £450,000. The cost of renovation is subject to an agreed figure with local builders; however, there is some uncertainty over the remaining input values. The business estimates its cost of capital at 12 per cent a year.

Required:
(a) What is the NPV of the proposed project?
(b) Assuming none of the other inputs deviates from the best estimates provided:
   (i) What auction price would have to be paid for the manor house to cause the project to have a zero NPV?
   (ii) What cost of capital would cause the project to have a zero NPV?
   (iii) What is the sale price of each of the flats that would cause the project to have a zero NPV? (Each flat will be sold for the same price: £150,000.)
(c) Is the level of risk associated with the project high or low? Discuss your findings.

Solution
(a) The NPV of the proposed project is as follows:

	Cash flows £	Discount factor 12%	Present value £
Year 1 (£900,000 – £500,000)	400,000	0.893	357,200
Year 2 (£450,000 – £300,000)	150,000	0.797	119,550
Less Initial outlay			(450,000)
NPV			26,750

(b) (i) To obtain a zero NPV, the auction price would have to be £26,750 higher than the current estimate, that is, a total price of £476,750. This is about 6 per cent above the current estimated price.
   (ii) As there is a positive NPV, the cost of capital that would cause the project to have a zero NPV must be higher than 12 per cent. Let us try 20 per cent.

	Cash flows £	Discount factor 20%	Present value £
Year 1 (£900,000 – £500,000)	400,000	0.833	333,200
Year 2 (£450,000 – £300,000)	150,000	0.694	104,100
Less Initial outlay			(450,000)
NPV			(12,700)

As the NPV, using a 20 per cent discount rate is negative, the 'break-even' cost of capital lies somewhere between 12 per cent and 20 per cent. A reasonable approximation is obtained as follows:

	Discount rate %	NPV £
	12	26,750
	20	(12,700)
Difference	8 Range	39,450

→ The change in NPV for every 1 per cent change in the discount rate will be:

$$39{,}450/8 = £4{,}931$$

The reduction in the 20 per cent discount rate required to achieve a zero NPV would therefore be:

$$12{,}700/4{,}931 = 2.6\%$$

The cost of capital (that is, the discount rate) would, therefore, have to be 17.4 per cent (that is, 20.0 – 2.6) for the project to have a zero NPV.

This calculation is, of course, the same as that used earlier in the chapter when calculating the IRR of the project. In other words, 17.4 per cent is the IRR of the project.

(iii) To obtain a zero NPV, the sale price of each flat must be reduced so that the NPV is reduced by £26,750. In year 1, six flats are sold (in year 2, three flats are sold). The discount factor at the 12 per cent rate for year 1 is 0.893, and for year 2 is 0.797. We can derive the fall in value per flat (Y) to give a zero NPV by using the equation:

$$(6Y \times 0.893) + (3Y \times 0.797) = £26{,}750$$

$$Y = £3{,}452$$

The sale price of each flat necessary to obtain a zero NPV is therefore:

$$£150{,}000 - £3{,}452 = £146{,}548$$

This represents a fall in the estimated price of 2.3 per cent.

(c) These calculations indicate that the auction price would have to be about 6 per cent above the estimated price before a zero NPV is obtained. The margin of safety is, therefore, not very high for this factor. The calculations also reveal that the price of the flats would only have to fall by 2.3 per cent from the estimated price before the NPV is reduced to zero. Hence, the margin of safety for this factor is even smaller. However, the cost of capital is less sensitive to changes and there would have to be an increase from 12 per cent to 17.4 per cent before the project produced a zero NPV. It seems from the calculations that the sale price of the flats is the most sensitive factor to consider. A careful re-examination of the market value of the flats seems appropriate before a final decision is made.

There are two major drawbacks with the use of sensitivity analysis:

- It does not give managers clear decision rules concerning acceptance or rejection of the project and so they must rely on their own judgement.
- It is a static form of analysis. Only one input is considered at a time, while the rest are held constant. In practice, however, it is likely that more than one input value will differ from the best estimates provided. Even so, it would be possible to deal with changes in various inputs simultaneously were the project data put on to a spreadsheet model. This approach, where more than one variable is altered at a time, is known as **scenario building**.

Real World 14.10 shows that it is not only the business that may carry out sensitivity analysis, or scenario building, in order to assess risk. A supplier or a lender may also use these tools to see whether the business is a credit risk.

No fear of flying

Ryanair is a low-cost airline that has enjoyed considerable success over recent years. As part of its expansion programme, the business ordered 153 Boeing 737–800 aircraft, with an option to purchase a further 125 aircraft, over a period up to 2009. It has been reported that these aircraft cost Ryanair around $32 million each. This represents a huge order for the Boeing Corporation and, of course, a huge risk if the aircraft were built for Ryanair and the business was then unable to pay for them. Around the time of the sale agreement, therefore, Boeing decided to evaluate the future profitability of Ryanair.

Boeing prepared a computer model to test whether changes in key variables such as a fall in passenger demand, changes in currency exchange rates and a rise in aviation fuel prices would damage the profitability of the low-cost airline. Ryanair passed the tests with flying colours: the worst scenario generated was that Ryanair would break even. According to Boeing's sales director for the UK and Ireland, the Ryanair model was probably the most robust that Boeing had encountered.

Source: 'How low can you go?', *Financial Times Magazine*, 21 June 2003; and 'Ryanair: feeding time at the zoo', 11 February 2003, Research report, Goodbody Stockbrokers.

Expected net present value

Another means of assessing risk is through the use of statistical probabilities. It may be possible to identify a range of feasible values for each of the items of input data and to assign a probability of occurrence to each of these values. Using this information, we can derive an **expected net present value (ENPV)**, which is, in effect, a weighted average of the possible outcomes where the probabilities are used as weights. To illustrate this method, let us consider Example 14.4.

Example 14.4

C. Piperis (Properties) Ltd has the opportunity to acquire a lease on a block of flats that has only two years remaining before it expires. The cost of the lease would be £100,000. The occupancy rate of the block of flats is currently around 70 per cent and the flats are let almost exclusively to naval personnel. There is a large naval base located nearby, and there is little other demand for the flats. The occupancy rate of the flats will change in the remaining two years of the lease, depending on the outcome of a defence review. The navy is currently considering three options for the naval base. These are:

● *Option 1*. Increase the size of the base by closing down a base in another region and transferring the personnel to the one located near the flats.

- *Option 2.* Close down the naval base near to the flats and leave only a skeleton staff there for maintenance purposes. The personnel would be moved to a base in another region.
- *Option 3.* Leave the base open but reduce staffing levels by 20 per cent.

The directors of Piperis have estimated the following net cash flows for each of the two years under each option and the probability of their occurrence:

	£	Probability
Option 1	80,000	0.6
Option 2	12,000	0.1
Option 3	40,000	0.3
		1.0

Note that the sum of the probabilities is 1.0 (in other words it is certain that one of the possible options will arise). The business has a cost of capital of 10 per cent.

Required:

Should the business purchase the lease on the block of flats?

Solution

To calculate the expected NPV of the proposed investment, we must first calculate the weighted average of the expected outcomes for each year where the probabilities are used as weights, by multiplying each cash flow by its probability of occurrence. Thus, the expected annual net cash flows will be:

	Cash flows (a) £	Probability (b)	Expected cash flows (a × b) £
Option 1	80,000	0.6	48,000
Option 2	12,000	0.1	1,200
Option 3	40,000	0.3	12,000
Expected cash flows in each year			61,200

Having derived the expected annual cash flows, we can now discount these using a rate of 10 per cent to reflect the cost of capital:

Year	Expected cash flows £	Discount rate 10%	Expected present value £
1	61,200	0.909	55,631
2	61,200	0.826	50,551
			106,182
Less Initial investment			100,000
Expected NPV			6,182

We can see that the expected NPV is positive. Hence, the wealth of shareholders is expected to increase by purchasing the lease.

The expected NPV approach has the advantage of producing a single numerical outcome and of having a clear decision rule to apply. If the expected NPV is positive, we should invest; if it is negative, we should not.

However, the approach produces an average figure that may not be capable of occurring. This point was illustrated in Example 14.4 where the expected NPV does not correspond to any of the stated options.

Perhaps more importantly, using an average figure can obscure the underlying risk associated with the project. Simply deriving the ENPV, as in Example 14.4, can be misleading. Without some idea of the individual possible outcomes and their probability of occurring, the decision maker is in the dark. In Example 14.4, were either of options 2 and 3 to occur, the investment would be adverse (wealth destroying). It is 40 per cent probable that one of these two options will occur, so this is a significant risk. Only should option 1 arise (60 per cent probable) would investing in the flats represent a good decision. Of course, in advance of making the investment, which option will actually occur is not known. None of this should be taken to mean that the investment in the flats should not be made, simply that the decision maker is better placed to make a judgement where information on the possible outcomes is available. Activity 14.18 further illustrates this point.

Activity (14.18)

Qingdao Manufacturing Ltd is considering two competing projects. Details are as follows:

- Project A has a 0.9 probability of producing a negative NPV of £200,000 and a 0.1 probability of producing a positive NPV of £3.8m.
- Project B has a 0.6 probability of producing a positive NPV of £100,000 and a 0.4 probability of producing a positive NPV of £350,000.

What is the expected net present value of each project?

The expected NPV of Project A is:

$$(0.1 \times £3.8m) - (0.9 \times £200,000) = £200,000$$

The expected NPV of Project B is:

$$(0.6 \times £100,000) + (0.4 \times £350,000) = £200,000$$

Although the expected NPV of each project in Activity 14.18 is identical, this does not mean that the business will be indifferent about which project to undertake. We can see from the information provided that Project A has a high probability of making a loss whereas Project B is not expected to make a loss under either possible outcome. If we assume that the shareholders dislike risk – which is usually the case – they will prefer the directors to take on Project B as this provides the same level of expected return as Project A but for a lower level of risk.

It can be argued that the problem identified above may not be significant where the business is engaged in several similar projects, as it will be lost in the averaging process. However, in practice, investment projects may be unique events and this argument will not then apply. Also, where the project is large in relation to other projects undertaken, the argument loses its force. There is also the problem that a factor that might cause one project to have an adverse outcome could also have adverse effects on other projects. For example, a large, unexpected increase in the price of oil may have a simultaneous adverse effect on all of the investment projects of a particular business.

Where the expected NPV approach is being used, it is probably a good idea to make known to managers the different possible outcomes and the probability attached to each outcome. By so doing, the managers will be able to gain an insight to the *downside risk* attached to the project. The information relating to each outcome can be presented in the form of a diagram if required. The construction of such a diagram is illustrated in Example 14.5.

Example 14.5

Zeta Computing Services Ltd has recently produced some software for a client organisation. The software has a life of two years and will then become obsolete. The cost of producing the software was £10,000. The client has agreed to pay a licence fee of £8,000 a year for the software if it is used in only one of its two divisions, and £12,000 a year if it is used in both of its divisions. The client may use the software for either one or two years in either division but will definitely use it in at least one division in each of the two years.

Zeta believes there is a 0.6 chance that the licence fee received in any one year will be £8,000 and a 0.4 chance that it will be £12,000. There are four possible outcomes attached to this project (where p denotes probability):

- *Outcome 1.* Year 1 cash flow £8,000 ($p = 0.6$) and year 2 cash flow £8,000 ($p = 0.6$). The probability of both years having cash flows of £8,000 will be:

$$0.6 \times 0.6 = 0.36$$

- *Outcome 2.* Year 1 cash flow £12,000 ($p = 0.4$) and year 2 cash flow £12,000 ($p = 0.4$). The probability of both years having cash flows of £12,000 will be:

$$0.4 \times 0.4 = 0.16$$

- *Outcome 3.* Year 1 cash flow £12,000 ($p = 0.4$) and year 2 cash flow £8,000 ($p = 0.6$). The probability of this sequence of cash flows occurring will be:

$$0.4 \times 0.6 = 0.24$$

- *Outcome 4.* Year 1 cash flow £8,000 ($p = 0.6$) and year 2 cash flow £12,000 ($p = 0.4$). The probability of this sequence of cash flows occurring will be:

$$0.6 \times 0.4 = 0.24$$

The information in Example 14.5 can be displayed in the form of a diagram (Figure 14.8).

The source of probabilities

As we might expect, assigning probabilities to possible outcomes can often be a problem. There may be many possible outcomes arising from a particular investment project, and to identify each outcome and then assign a probability to it may prove to be an impossible task. When assigning probabilities to possible outcomes, an objective or

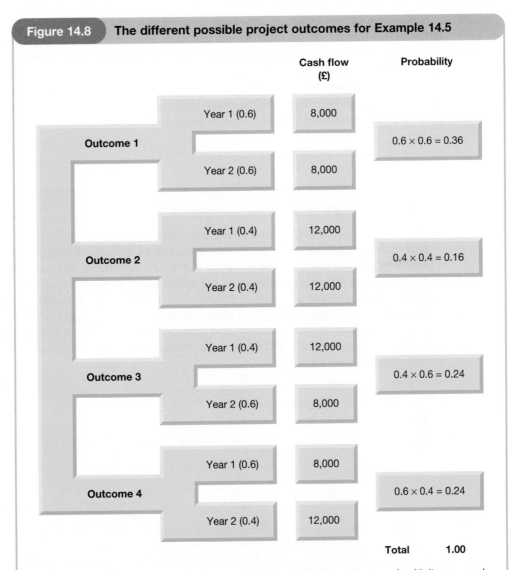

Figure 14.8 **The different possible project outcomes for Example 14.5**

There are four different possible outcomes associated with the project, each with its own probability of occurrence. The sum of the probabilities attached to each outcome must equal 1.00, in other words it is certain that one of the possible outcomes will occur. For example, outcome 1 would occur where only one division uses the software in each year.

a subjective approach may be used. **Objective probabilities** are based on information gathered from experience. Thus, for example, the transport manager of a business operating a fleet of motor vans may be able to provide information concerning the possible life of a new van purchased based on the record of similar vans acquired in the past. From the information available, probabilities may be developed for different possible lifespans. However, the past may not always be a reliable guide to the future, particularly during a period of rapid change. In the case of the motor vans, for example, changes in design and technology or changes in the purpose for which the vans are being used may undermine the validity of past data.

Subjective probabilities are based on opinion and will be used where past data are either inappropriate or unavailable. The opinions of independent experts may provide a useful basis for developing subjective probabilities, though even these may contain bias which will affect the reliability of the judgements made.

Despite these problems, we should not be dismissive of the use of probabilities. Assigning probabilities can help to make explicit some of the risks associated with a project and should help decision makers to appreciate the uncertainties that have to be faced.

Activity 14.19

Devonia (Laboratories) Ltd has recently carried out successful clinical trials on a new type of skin cream that has been developed to reduce the effects of ageing. Research and development costs incurred relating to the new product amount to £160,000. In order to gauge the market potential of the new product, independent market research consultants were hired at a cost of £15,000. The market research report submitted by the consultants indicates that the skin cream is likely to have a product life of four years and could be sold to retail chemists and large department stores at a price of £20 per 100 ml container. For each of the four years of the new product's life, sales demand has been estimated as follows:

Number of 100 ml containers sold	Probability of occurrence
11,000	0.3
14,000	0.6
16,000	0.1

If the business decides to launch the new product, it is possible for production to begin at once. The equipment necessary to produce the skin cream is already owned by the business and originally cost £150,000. At the end of the new product's life, it is estimated that the equipment could be sold for £35,000. If the business decides against launching the new product, the equipment will be sold immediately for £85,000, as it will be of no further use.

The new skin cream will require one hour's labour for each 100 ml container produced. The cost of labour for the new product is £8.00 an hour. Additional workers will have to be recruited to produce the new product. At the end of the product's life, the workers are unlikely to be offered further work with the business and redundancy costs of £10,000 are expected. The cost of the ingredients for each 100 ml container is £6.00. Additional overheads arising from production of the new product are expected to be £15,000 a year.

The new skin cream has attracted the interest of the business's competitors. If the business decides not to produce and sell the skin cream, it can sell the patent rights to a major competitor immediately for £125,000.

Devonia has a cost of capital of 12 per cent. Ignore taxation.

Required:
(a) Calculate the expected net present value (ENPV) of the new product.
(b) State, with reasons, whether or not Devonia should launch the new product.

Your answer should be as follows:

(a) Expected sales volume per year = $(11,000 \times 0.3) + (14,000 \times 0.6) + (16,000 \times 0.1)$

                                                   = 13,300 units

      Expected annual sales revenue = 13,300 × £20

                                                   = £266,000

      Annual labour   = 13,300 × £8

                                                   = £106,400

      Annual ingredient costs   = 13,300 × £6

                                                   = £79,800

Incremental cash flows:

	__0__	_1_	_2_	_3_	_4_
			Years		
	0	1	2	3	4
	£000	£000	£000	£000	£000
Sale of patent rights	(125.0)				
Sale of equipment	(85.0)				35.0
Sales revenue		266.0	266.0	266.0	266.0
Cost of ingredients		(79.8)	(79.8)	(79.8)	(79.8)
Labour costs		(106.4)	(106.4)	(106.4)	(106.4)
Redundancy					(10.0)
Additional overheads		(15.0)	(15.0)	(15.0)	(15.0)
	(210.0)	64.8	64.8	64.8	89.8
Discount factor (12%)	1.000	0.893	0.797	0.712	0.636
	(210.0)	57.9	51.6	46.1	57.1
ENPV	2.7				

(b) As the ENPV of the project is positive, accepting the project would increase the wealth of shareholders. However, the ENPV is very low in relation to the size of the project and careful checking of the key estimates and assumptions would be advisable. A relatively small downward revision of sales (volume and/or price) or upward revision of costs could make the project ENPV negative.

    It would be helpful to derive the NPV for each of the three possible outcomes regarding sales levels. This would enable the decision maker to have a clearer view of the risk involved with the investment.

Reacting to the level of risk

The logical reaction to a risky project is to demand a higher rate of return. Both theory and observable evidence show that there is a relationship between risk and the return required by investors. It was mentioned earlier, for example, that a bank would normally ask for a higher rate of interest on a loan where it perceives the lender to be less likely to be able to repay the amount borrowed.

When assessing investment projects, it is normal to increase the NPV discount rate in the face of increased risk – that is, to demand a risk premium: the higher the level of risk, the higher the risk premium that will be demanded. The risk premium is usually added to a 'risk-free' rate of return to derive the total return required. The risk-free rate is normally taken to be equivalent to the rate of return from government loan stock. In practice, a business may divide projects into low-, medium- and high-risk categories and then assign a risk premium to each category. The cash flows from a particular project will then be discounted using a rate based on the risk-free rate plus the appropriate risk premium. This relationship between risk and return is illustrated in Figure 14.9.

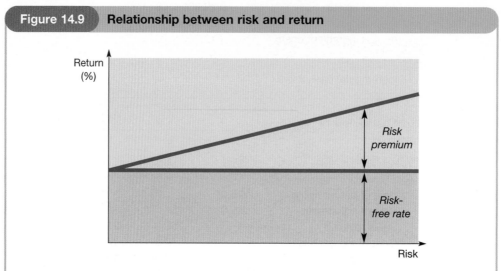

Figure 14.9 Relationship between risk and return

It is logical to take account of the riskiness of projects by changing the discount rate. A risk premium is added to the risk-free rate to derive the appropriate discount rate. A higher return will normally be expected from projects where the risks are higher; thus, the riskier the project, the higher the risk premium.

The use of a **risk-adjusted discount rate** provides managers with a single value that can be used when making a decision either to accept or to reject a project. Moreover, managers are likely to have an intuitive grasp of the relationship between risk and return and may well feel comfortable with this technique. However, there are practical difficulties with implementing this approach.

Activity 14.20

Can you think of any practical problems with the use of risk-adjusted discount rates?

Subjective judgement tends to be required when assigning an investment project to a particular risk category and then in assigning a risk premium to each category. The choices made will reflect the personal views of the managers responsible and this may differ from the views of the shareholders they are supposed to represent. The choices made can, nevertheless, make the difference between accepting and rejecting a particular project.

Managing investment projects

So far, we have been concerned with the process of carrying out the necessary calculations that enable managers to select among already identified investment opportunities. This topic is given a great deal of emphasis in the literature on investment appraisal.

Although the assessment of projects is undoubtedly important, we must bear in mind that it is only *part* of the process of investment decision making. There are other important aspects that managers must also consider.

It is possible to see the investment process as a sequence of five stages, each of which managers must consider. The five stages are set out in Figure 14.10 and described below.

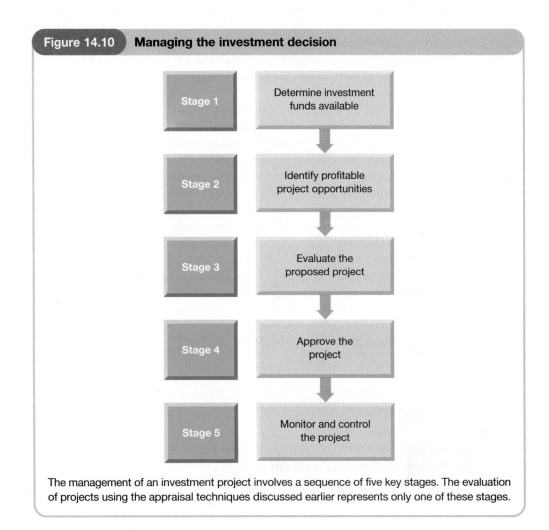

Figure 14.10   **Managing the investment decision**

Stage 1 — Determine investment funds available

Stage 2 — Identify profitable project opportunities

Stage 3 — Evaluate the proposed project

Stage 4 — Approve the project

Stage 5 — Monitor and control the project

The management of an investment project involves a sequence of five key stages. The evaluation of projects using the appraisal techniques discussed earlier represents only one of these stages.

Stage 1: Determine investment funds available

The amount of funds available for investment may be determined by the external market for funds or by internal management. In practice, it is often the latter that has the greater influence on the amount available. In either case, it may be that the funds will not be sufficient to finance the profitable investment opportunities available. This shortage of investment funds is known as **capital rationing**. When it arises, managers are faced with the task of deciding on the most profitable use of those funds available.

Stage 2: Identify profitable project opportunities

A vital part of the investment process is the search for profitable investment opportunities. The business should carry out methodical routines for identifying feasible projects. This may be done through a research and development department or by some other means. Failure to do so will inevitably lead to the business losing its competitive position with respect to product development, production methods or market penetration. To help identify investment opportunities, some businesses provide financial incentives to members of staff who come forward with good investment proposals. The search process will, however, usually involve looking outside the business to identify changes in technology, customer demand, market conditions and so on. Information will need to be gathered and this may take some time, particularly for unusual or non-routine investment opportunities.

It is important that the business's investments should fit in with its strategic plans, a point that we discussed in Chapter 1. The business should seek out investment projects that use its strengths (such as management expertise in a particular activity) to exploit opportunities (such as an expansion of the market). At the same time, investment projects selected should avoid exposing the business's weaknesses (such as a shortage of suitably skilled labour) to threats (such as other businesses poaching skilled staff). The business is likely to be able to generate greater amounts of wealth by investing in particular types of project, rather than in others. It is also possible that the business will be able to generate greater benefits from a particular project than could a different business with different strengths and weaknesses.

Where there is unlikely to be problems in raising investment funds, this stage may sometimes begin the process, followed by a search for suitable funding.

Stage 3: Evaluate the proposed project

If management is to agree to the investment of funds in a project, there must be a proper screening of each proposal. For larger projects, this will involve providing answers to a number of questions, including:

- What are the nature and purpose of the project?
- Does the project align with the overall objectives of the business?
- How much finance is required?
- What other resources (such as expertise, work space and so on) are required for successful completion of the project?
- How long will the project last and what are its key stages?
- What is the expected pattern of cash flows?
- What are the major problems associated with the project and how can they be overcome?
- What is the NPV of the project? How does this compare with other opportunities available?
- Have risk and inflation been taken into account in the appraisal process and, if so, what are the results?

The ability and commitment of those responsible for proposing and managing the project will be vital to its success. This means that, when evaluating a new project, one consideration will be the quality of those proposing it. In some cases, senior managers may decide not to support a project that appears profitable on paper if they lack confidence in the ability of key managers to see it through to completion.

Stage 4: Approve the project

Once the managers responsible for investment decision making are satisfied that the project should be undertaken, formal approval can be given. However, a decision on a project may be postponed if senior managers need more information from those proposing the project, or if revisions are required to the proposal. In some cases, the proposal may be rejected if the project is considered unprofitable or likely to fail. Before rejecting a proposal, however, the implications of not pursuing the project for such areas as market share, staff morale and existing business operations must be carefully considered.

Stage 5: Monitor and control the project

Making a decision to invest in, say, the plant needed to provide a new service does not automatically cause the investment to be made and provision of the service to go smoothly ahead. Managers will need to manage the project actively through to completion. This, in turn, will require further information gathering.

Management should receive progress reports at regular intervals concerning the project. These reports should provide information relating to the actual cash flows for each stage of the project, which can then be compared against the forecast figures provided when the proposal was submitted for approval. The reasons for significant variations should be ascertained and corrective action taken where possible. Any changes in the expected completion date of the project or any expected variations in future cash flows from budget should be reported immediately. In extreme cases, managers may even abandon the project if circumstances appear to have changed dramatically for the worse. We saw in Real World 14.9 that Rolls-Royce undertakes this kind of reassessment of existing projects. No doubt most other well-managed businesses do this too.

Project management techniques (for example, critical path analysis) should be employed wherever possible and their effectiveness reported to senior management.

 An important part of the control process is a **post-completion audit** of the project. This is, in essence, a review of the project performance to see if it lived up to expectations and whether any lessons can be learned from the way that the investment process was carried out. In addition to an evaluation of financial costs and benefits, non-financial measures of performance such as the ability to meet deadlines and levels of quality achieved should also be reported. We should recall that total life-cycle costing, which we discussed in Chapter 11, is based on similar principles.

The fact that a post-completion audit is an integral part of the management of the project should also encourage those who submit projects to use realistic estimates. Various studies have shown that there is a tendency for managers to use over-optimistic estimates when preparing investment proposals. (See reference 4 at the end of the chapter.) It seems that sometimes this is done deliberately in an attempt to secure project approval. Where over-optimistic estimates are used, the managers responsible may well find themselves accountable at the post-completion audit stage. Such audits, however, can be difficult and time consuming to carry out, and so the likely benefits must be weighed against the costs involved. Senior management may feel, therefore, that only projects above a certain size should be subject to a post-completion audit.

Real World 14.11 shows how Tesco uses post-completion audit approaches to evaluate past investment projects.

Real World 14.11

Reviewing investment decisions

In its 2006 annual report, Tesco plc, the supermarket chain, stated that:

> All major initiatives require business cases to be prepared, normally covering a minimum of five years. Post investment appraisals, carried out by management, determine the reasons for any significant variance from expected performance.

Source: Tesco plc Annual Report 2006.

As a footnote to our discussion of business investment decision making, **Real World 14.12** looks at one of the world's biggest investment project which has proved to be a commercial disaster, despite being a technological success.

Real World 14.12

Wealth lost in the chunnel

The tunnel, which runs for 31 miles between Folkestone in the UK and Sangatte in northern France was started in 1986 and opened for public use in 1994. From a technological and social perspective it has been a success, but from a financial point of view it has been a disaster. The tunnel was purely a private sector venture for which a new business, Eurotunnel plc, was created. Relatively little public money was involved. To be a commercial success the tunnel needed to cover all of its costs, including interest charges, and leave sufficient to enhance the shareholders' wealth. In fact, the providers of long-term finance (lenders and shareholders) have lost virtually all of their investment. Although the main losers were banks and institutional investors, many individuals, particularly in France, bought shares in Eurotunnel.

Key inputs to the pre-1986 assessment of the project were the cost of construction and creating the infrastructure, the length of time required to complete construction and the level of revenue that the tunnel would generate when it became operational.

In the event:

- construction cost was £10bn – it was originally planned to cost £5.6bn;
- construction time was seven years – it was planned to be six years;
- revenues from passengers and freight have been well below projected – for example, 21 million annual passenger journeys on Eurostar trains were projected; the numbers have consistently remained at around 7 million.

The failure to generate revenues at the projected levels has probably been the biggest contributor to the problem. When preparing the projection pre 1986, planners failed to take adequate account of two crucial factors:

- fierce competition from the ferry operators – at the time, many thought that the ferries would roll over and die; and
- the rise of no-frills, cheap air travel between the UK and the continent.

The commercial failure of the tunnel means that it will be very difficult in future for projects of this nature to be funded by private funds.

Sources: Annual reports of Eurotunnel plc; and 'How Eurotunnel went wrong', J. Randall, BBC news, www.newsvote.bbc.co.uk.

Summary

The main points of this chapter may be summarised as follows.

Accounting rate of return (ARR) is the average accounting profit from the project expressed as a percentage of the average investment.

- Decision rule: projects with an ARR above a defined minimum are acceptable; the greater the ARR, the more attractive the project becomes.
- Conclusions on ARR:
  - it does not relate directly to shareholders' wealth – can lead to illogical conclusions;
  - takes almost no account of the timing of cash flows;
  - ignores some relevant information and may take account of some irrelevant;
  - relatively simple to use;
  - much inferior to NPV.

Payback period (PP) is the length of time that it takes for the cash outflow for the initial investment to be repaid out of resulting cash inflows.

- Decision rule: projects with a PP up to defined maximum period are acceptable, the shorter the PP, the more desirable.
- Conclusions on PP:
  - does not relate to shareholders' wealth, ignores inflows after the payback date;
  - takes little account of the timing of cash flows;
  - ignores much relevant information;
  - does not always provide clear signals and can be impractical to use;
  - much inferior to NPV, but it is easy to understand and can offer a liquidity insight, which might be the reason for its widespread use.

Net present value (NPV) is the sum of the discounted values of the net cash flows from the investment.

- Money has a time value.
- Decision rule: all positive NPV investments enhance shareholders' wealth; the greater the NPV, the greater the enhancement and the more desirable.
- PV of a cashflow = cashflow $\times 1/(1 + r)^n$, assuming a constant discount rate.
- The act of discounting brings cash flows at different points in time to a common valuation basis (their present value), which enables them to be directly compared.
- Conclusions on NPV:
  - relates directly to shareholders' wealth objective;
  - takes account of the timing of cash flows;
  - takes all relevant information into account;
  - provides clear signals and practical to use.

Internal rate of return (IRR) is the discount rate that, when applied to the cash flows of a project, causes it to have a zero NPV.

- Represents the average percentage return on the investment, taking account of the fact that cash may be flowing in and out of the project at various points in its life.
- Decision rule: projects that have an IRR greater than the cost of capital are acceptable; the greater the IRR, the more attractive the project.

- Cannot normally be calculated directly; a trial and error approach is often necessary.
- Conclusions on IRR:
  - does not relate directly to shareholders' wealth. Usually gives the same signals as NPV but can mislead where there are competing projects of different size;
  - takes account of the timing of cash flows;
  - takes all relevant information into account;
  - problems of multiple IRRs when there are unconventional cash flows;
  - inferior to NPV.

Use of appraisal methods in practice

- All four methods identified are widely used.
- The discounting methods (NPV and IRR) show a steady increase in usage over time.
- Many businesses use more than one method.
- Larger businesses seem to be more sophisticated in their choice and use of appraisal methods than smaller ones.

Dealing with risk

- Sensitivity analysis (SA) is an assessment, taking each input factor in turn, of how much each one can vary from estimate before a project is not viable.
  - Provides useful insights to projects.
  - Does not give a clear decision rule, but provides an impression.
  - It can be rather static, but scenario building solves this problem.
- Expected net present value (ENPV) is the weighted average of the possible outcomes for a project, based on probabilities for each of the inputs:
  - Provides a single value and a clear decision rule.
  - The single ENPV figure can hide the real risk.
  - Useful for the ENPV figure to be supported by information on the range and dispersion of possible outcomes.
  - Probabilities may be subjective (based on opinion) or objective (based on evidence).
- Reacting to the level of risk:
  - Logically, high risk should lead to high returns.
  - Using a risk-adjusted discount rate, where a risk premium is added to the risk-free rate, is a logical response to risk.

Managing investment projects

- Determine investment funds available – dealing, if necessary, with capital rationing problems.
- Identify profitable project opportunities.
- Evaluate the proposed project.
- Approve the project.
- Monitor and control the project – using a post-completion audit approach.

MyAccountingLab **Now check your progress in your personal Study Plan**

Key terms

accounting rate of return (ARR) p. 513	opportunity cost p. 534
payback period (PP) p. 518	sensitivity analysis p. 541
net present value (NPV) p. 522	scenario building p. 544
risk p. 523	expected net present value (ENPV) p. 545
risk premium p. 524	objective probabilities p. 549
inflation p. 524	subjective probabilities p. 550
discount factor p. 527	risk-adjusted discount rate p. 552
internal rate of return (IRR) p. 530	capital rationing p. 553
relevant cost p. 534	post-completion audit p. 555

References

1 **Reckoning with Risk**, *Gigerenzer G.*, Penguin, 2002.

2 'The theory–practice gap in capital budgeting: evidence from the United Kingdom', *Arnold G.C. and Hatzopoulos P.D.*, **Journal of Business Finance and Accounting**, June/July 2000.

3 'How do CFOs make capital budgeting and capital structure decisions?', *Graham R. and Harvey C.*, **Journal of Applied Corporate Finance**, vol. 15, no. 1, 2002.

4 'Fifty years of research on accuracy of capital expenditure project estimates: a review of findings and their validity', *Linder S.*, Otto Beisham Graduate School of Management, April 2005.

Further reading

If you would like to explore the topics covered in this chapter in more depth, we recommend the following books:

Business Finance: Theory and practice, *McLaney E.*, 7th edn, Financial Times Prentice Hall, 2006, chapters 4, 5 and 6.

Corporate Finance and Investment, *Pike R. and Neale B.*, 5th edn, Prentice Hall, 2005, chapters 5, 6 and 7.

Corporate Financial Management, *Arnold G.*, 3rd edn, Financial Times Prentice Hall, 2005, chapters 2, 3 and 4.

Management and Cost Accounting, *Drury C.*, 6th edn, Thomson Learning, 2004, chapters 13 and 14.

Review questions

Answers to these questions can be found at the back of the book on pages 784–5.

14.1 Why is the net present value method of investment appraisal considered to be theoretically superior to other methods that are found in practice?

14.2 The payback method has been criticised for not taking the time value of money into account. Could this limitation be overcome? If so, would this method then be preferable to the NPV method?

14.3 Research indicates that the IRR method is a more popular method of investment appraisal than the NPV method. Why might this be?

14.4 Why are cash flows rather than profit flows used in the IRR, NPV and PP methods of investment appraisal?

Exercises

Exercises 14.3 to 14.8 are more advanced than 14.1 and 14.2. Those with coloured numbers have answers at the back of the book, starting on page 752.

If you wish to try more exercises, visit the students' side of the Companion Website.

14.1 The directors of Mylo Ltd are currently considering two mutually exclusive investment projects. Both projects are concerned with the purchase of new plant. The following data are available for each project:

	Project 1 £000	Project 2 £000
Cost (immediate outlay)	(100)	(60)
Expected annual operating profit (loss):		
Year 1	29	18
2	(1)	(2)
3	2	4
Estimated residual value of the plant	7	6

The business has an estimated cost of capital of 10 per cent, and uses the straight-line method of depreciation for all non-current (fixed) assets when calculating operating profit. Neither project would increase the working capital of the business. The business has sufficient funds to meet all capital expenditure requirements.

Required:

(a) Calculate for each project:
   (i)   The net present value.
   (ii) The approximate internal rate of return.
   (iii) The payback period.

(b) State which, if any, of the two investment projects the directors of Mylo Ltd should accept, and why.

(c) State, in general terms, which method of investment appraisal you consider to be most appropriate for evaluating investment projects, and why.

14.2 C. George (Controls) Ltd manufactures a thermostat that can be used in a range of kitchen appliances. The manufacturing process is, at present, semi-automated. The equipment used costs £540,000, and has a written-down (balance sheet) value of £300,000. Demand for the product has been fairly stable, and output has been maintained at 50,000 units a year in recent years.

The following data, based on the current level of output, have been prepared in respect of the product:

	Per unit	
	£	£
Selling price		12.40
Less		
Labour	3.30	
Materials	3.65	
Overheads: Variable	1.58	
Fixed	1.60	
		10.13
Operating profit		2.27

Although the existing equipment is expected to last for a further four years before it is sold for an estimated £40,000, the business has recently been considering purchasing new equipment that would completely automate much of the production process. The new equipment would cost £670,000 and would have an expected life of four years, at the end of which it would be sold for an estimated £70,000. If the new equipment is purchased, the old equipment could be sold for £150,000 immediately.

The assistant to the business's accountant has prepared a report to help assess the viability of the proposed change, which includes the following data:

	Per unit	
	£	£
Selling price		12.40
Less		
Labour	1.20	
Materials	3.20	
Overheads: Variable	1.40	
Fixed	3.30	
		9.10
Operating profit		3.30

Depreciation charges will increase by £85,000 a year as a result of purchasing the new machinery; however, other fixed costs are not expected to change.

In the report the assistant wrote:

> The figures shown above that relate to the proposed change are based on the current level of output and take account of a depreciation charge of £150,000 a year in respect of the new equipment. The effect of purchasing the new equipment will be to increase the operating profit to sales revenue ratio from 18.3% to 26.6%. In addition, the purchase of the new equipment will enable us to reduce our inventories level immediately by £130,000.
>
> In view of these facts, I recommend purchase of the new equipment.

The business has a cost of capital of 12 per cent. Ignore taxation.

Required:

(a) Prepare a statement of the incremental cash flows arising from the purchase of the new equipment.

(b) Calculate the net present value of the proposed purchase of new equipment.

(c) State, with reasons, whether the business should purchase the new equipment.

(d) Explain why cash flow forecasts are used rather than profit forecasts to assess the viability of proposed capital expenditure projects.

14.3 The accountant of your business has recently been taken ill through overwork. In his absence his assistant has prepared some calculations of the profitability of a project, which are to be discussed soon at the board meeting of your business. His workings, which are set out below, include some errors of principle. You can assume that the statement below includes no arithmetical errors.

	Year 1 £000	Year 2 £000	Year 3 £000	Year 4 £000	Year 5 £000	Year 6 £000
Sales revenue	—	450	470	470	470	470
Less Costs:						
Materials		126	132	132	132	132
Labour		90	94	94	94	94
Overheads		45	47	47	47	47
Depreciation		120	120	120	120	120
Working capital	180					
Interest on working capital		27	27	27	27	27
Write-off of development costs	—	30	30	30		
Total costs	180	438	450	450	420	420
Operating profit/(loss)	(180)	12	20	20	50	50

$$\frac{\text{Total profit (loss)}}{\text{Cost of equipment}} = \frac{(£28,000)}{£600,000} = \text{Return on investment (4.7\%)}$$

You ascertain the following additional information:

- The cost of equipment contains £100,000, being the carrying (balance sheet) value of an old machine. If it were not used for this project it would be scrapped with a zero net realisable value. New equipment costing £500,000 will be purchased on 31 December Year 0. You should assume that all other cash flows occur at the end of the year to which they relate.
- The development costs of £90,000 have already been spent.
- Overheads have been costed at 50 per cent of direct labour, which is the business's normal practice. An independent assessment has suggested that incremental overheads are likely to amount to £30,000 a year.
- The business's cost of capital is 12 per cent.

Ignore taxation in your answer.

Required:

(a) Prepare a corrected statement of the incremental cash flows arising from the project. Where you have altered the assistant's figures you should attach a brief note explaining your alterations.

(b) Calculate:
  (i) The project's payback period.
  (ii) The project's net present value as at 31 December Year 0.

(c) Write a memo to the board advising on the acceptance or rejection of the project.

14.4 Arkwright Mills plc is considering expanding its production of a new yarn, code name X15. The plant is expected to cost £1m and have a life of five years and a nil residual value. It will be bought, paid for and ready for operation on 31 December Year 0. £500,000 has already been spent on development costs of the product, and this has been charged in the income statement in the year it was incurred.

The following results are projected for the new yarn:

	Year 1 £m	Year 2 £m	Year 3 £m	Year 4 £m	Year 5 £m
Sales revenue	1.2	1.4	1.4	1.4	1.4
Costs, including depreciation	1.0	1.1	1.1	1.1	1.1
Profit before tax	0.2	0.3	0.3	0.3	0.3

Tax is charged at 50 per cent on annual profits (before tax and after depreciation) and paid one year in arrears. Depreciation of the plant has been calculated on a straight-line basis. Additional working capital of £0.6m will be required at the beginning of the project and released at the end of year 5. You should assume that all cash flows occur at the end of the year in which they arise.

Required:
(a) Prepare a statement showing the incremental cash flows of the project relevant to a decision concerning whether or not to proceed with the construction of the new plant.
(b) Compute the net present value of the project using a 10 per cent discount rate.
(c) Compute the payback period to the nearest year. Explain the meaning of this term.

14.5 Newton Electronics Ltd has incurred expenditure of £5m over the past three years researching and developing a miniature hearing aid. The hearing aid is now fully developed, and the directors are considering which of three mutually exclusive options should be taken to exploit the potential of the new product. The options are as follows:

1 The business could manufacture the hearing aid itself. This would be a new departure, since the business has so far concentrated on research and development projects. However, the business has manufacturing space available that it currently rents to another business for £100,000 a year. The business would have to purchase plant and equipment costing £9m and invest £3m in working capital immediately for production to begin.

A market research report, for which the business paid £50,000, indicates that the new product has an expected life of five years. Sales of the product during this period are predicted as follows:

	Predicted sales for the year ended 30 November				
	Year 1	Year 2	Year 3	Year 4	Year 5
Number of units ('000)	800	1,400	1,800	1,200	500

The selling price per unit will be £30 in the first year but will fall to £22 in the following three years. In the final year of the product's life, the selling price will fall to £20. Variable production costs are predicted to be £14 a unit, and fixed production costs (including depreciation) will be £2.4m a year. Marketing costs will be £2m a year.

The business intends to depreciate the plant and equipment using the straight-line method and based on an estimated residual value at the end of the five years of £1m. The business has a cost of capital of 10 per cent a year.

2 Newton Electronics Ltd could agree to another business manufacturing and marketing the product under licence. A multinational business, Faraday Electricals plc, has offered to undertake the manufacture and marketing of the product, and in return will make a royalty payment to Newton Electronics Ltd of £5 per unit. It has been estimated that the annual

number of sales of the hearing aid will be 10 per cent higher if the multinational business, rather than if Newton Electronics Ltd, manufactures and markets the product.

3 Newton Electronics Ltd could sell the patent rights to Faraday Electricals plc for £24m, payable in two equal instalments. The first instalment would be payable immediately and the second at the end of two years. This option would give Faraday Electricals the exclusive right to manufacture and market the new product.

Ignore taxation.

Required:

(a) Calculate the net present value of each of the options available to Newton Electronics Ltd.
(b) Identify and discuss any other factors that Newton Electronics Ltd should consider before arriving at a decision.
(c) State what you consider to be the most suitable option, and why.

14.6 Chesterfield Wanderers is a professional football club that has enjoyed considerable success in both national and European competitions in recent years. As a result, the club has accumulated £10m to spend on its further development. The board of directors is currently considering two mutually exclusive options for spending the funds available.

The first option is to acquire another player. The team manager has expressed a keen interest in acquiring Basil ('Bazza') Ramsey, a central defender, who currently plays for a rival club. The rival club has agreed to release the player immediately for £10m if required. A decision to acquire 'Bazza' Ramsey would mean that the existing central defender, Vinnie Smith, could be sold to another club. Chesterfield Wanderers has recently received an offer of £2.2m for this player. This offer is still open but will only be accepted if 'Bazza' Ramsey joins Chesterfield Wanderers. If this does not happen, Vinnie Smith will be expected to stay on with the club until the end of his playing career in five years' time. During this period, Vinnie will receive an annual salary of £400,000 and a loyalty bonus of £200,000 at the end of his five-year period with the club.

Assuming 'Bazza' Ramsey is acquired, the team manager estimates that gate receipts will increase by £2.5m in the first year and £1.3m in each of the four following years. There will also be an increase in advertising and sponsorship revenues of £1.2m for each of the next five years if the player is acquired. At the end of five years, the player can be sold to a club in a lower division and Chesterfield Wanderers will expect to receive £1m as a transfer fee. During his period at the club, 'Bazza' will receive an annual salary of £800,000 and a loyalty bonus of £400,000 after five years.

The second option is for the club to improve its ground facilities. The west stand could be extended and executive boxes could be built for businesses wishing to offer corporate hospitality to clients. These improvements would also cost £10m and would take one year to complete. During this period, the west stand would be closed, resulting in a reduction of gate receipts of £1.8m. However, gate receipts for each of the following four years would be £4.4m higher than current receipts. In five years' time, the club has plans to sell the existing grounds and to move to a new stadium nearby. Improving the ground facilities is not expected to affect the ground's value when it comes to be sold. Payment for the improvements will be made when the work has been completed at the end of the first year. Whichever option is chosen, the board of directors has decided to take on additional ground staff. The additional wages bill is expected to be £350,000 a year over the next five years.

The club has a cost of capital of 10 per cent. Ignore taxation.

Required:

(a) Calculate the incremental cash flows arising from each of the options available to the club.
(b) Calculate the net present value of each of the options.
(c) On the basis of the calculations made in (b) above, which of the two options would you choose and why?
(d) Discuss the validity of using the net present value method in making investment decisions for a professional football club.

14.7 Simtex Ltd has invested £120,000 to date in developing a new type of shaving foam. The shaving foam is now ready for production and it has been estimated that the new product will sell 160,000 cans a year over the next four years. At the end of four years, the product will be discontinued and replaced by a new product.

The shaving foam is expected to sell at £6 a can and variable costs are estimated at £4 a can. Fixed costs (excluding depreciation) are expected to be £300,000 a year. (This figure includes £130,000 in fixed costs incurred by the existing business that will be apportioned to this new product.)

To manufacture and package the new product, equipment costing £480,000 must be acquired immediately. The estimated value of this equipment in four years' time is £100,000. The business calculates depreciation using the straight-line method, and has an estimated cost of capital of 12 per cent.

Required:
(a) Deduce the net present value of the new product.
(b) Calculate by how much each of the following must change before the new product is no longer profitable.
  (i)   The discount rate.
  (ii) The initial outlay on new equipment.
  (iii) The net operating cash flows.
  (iv) The residual value of the equipment.
(c) Should the business produce the new product?

14.8 Kernow Cleaning Services Ltd provides street-cleaning services for local councils in the far south west of England. The work is currently labour intensive and few machines are employed. However, the business has recently been considering the purchase of a fleet of street-cleaning vehicles at a total cost of £540,000. The vehicles have a life of four years and are likely to result in a considerable saving of labour costs. Estimates of the likely labour savings and their probability of occurrence are set out below:

	Estimated savings £	Probability of occurrence
Year 1	80,000	0.3
	160,000	0.5
	200,000	0.2
Year 2	140,000	0.4
	220,000	0.4
	250,000	0.2
Year 3	140,000	0.4
	200,000	0.3
	230,000	0.3
Year 4	100,000	0.3
	170,000	0.6
	200,000	0.1

Estimates for each year are independent of other years. The business has a cost of capital of 10 per cent.

Required:
(a) Calculate the expected net present value (ENPV) of the street-cleaning machines.
(b) Calculate the net present value (NPV) of the worst possible outcome and the probability of its occurrence.

CHAPTER 15

Financing the business

Introduction

In this chapter we shall examine various aspects of financing the business. We begin by considering the main sources of finance available. Some of these sources have already been touched upon when we discussed the financing of limited companies in Chapters 4 and 7. In this chapter we shall look at these in more detail as well as discuss other sources of finance that have not yet been mentioned. The factors to be taken into account when choosing an appropriate source of finance are also considered.

Following our consideration of the main sources of finance, we shall go on to examine various aspects of the capital markets, including the role of the Stock Exchange, the financing of smaller businesses and the ways in which share capital may be issued.

Learning outcomes

When you have completed this chapter, you should be able to:

- Identify the main sources of finance available to a business and explain the advantages and disadvantages of each.

- Outline the ways in which share capital may be issued.

- Explain the role and nature of the Stock Exchange.

- Discuss the ways in which smaller businesses may seek to raise finance.

MyAccountingLab *Remember to create your own personalised Study Plan*

Sources of finance

When considering the various sources of finance available to a business, it is useful to distinguish between *internal* and *external* sources of finance. By internal sources we mean sources that do not require the agreement of anyone beyond the directors and managers of the business. Thus, retained profit is considered an internal source because the directors of the business have power to retain profits without the agreement of the shareholders, whose profits they are. Finance from an issue of new shares, on the other hand, is an external source because it requires the compliance of potential shareholders.

Within each of the two categories just described, we can further distinguish between *long-term* and *short-term* sources of finance. There is no agreed definition concerning each of these terms but, for the purpose of this chapter, long-term sources of finance are defined as sources of finance that are expected to provide finance for at least one year. Short-term sources typically provide finance for a shorter period. As we shall see, sources that are seen as short term when first used by the business often end up being used for quite long periods.

We shall begin the chapter by considering the various sources of internal finance available. We shall then go on to consider the various sources of external finance. This is probably an appropriate order to deal with these since, in practice, businesses tend to look first to internal sources before going outside for new funds.

Sources of internal finance

Internal sources of finance usually have the advantage that they are flexible. They may also be obtained quickly – particularly from working capital sources – and need not require the compliance of other parties. The main sources of internal funds are described below and are summarised in Figure 15.1.

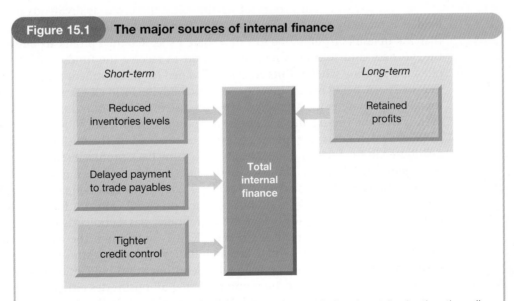

Figure 15.1   **The major sources of internal finance**

The major long-term source of internal finance is the profit that is retained rather than distributed to shareholders. The major short-term sources of internal finance involve reducing the level of trade receivables and inventories and increasing the level of trade payables.

Long-term sources of internal finance

Retained profits

Retained profit is the major source of finance for most businesses. By retaining profits within the business rather than distributing them to shareholders in the form of dividends, the funds of the business are increased.

Activity 15.1

Are retained profits a free source of finance to the business?

It is tempting to think that retained profits are a cost-free source of funds for a business. However, this is not the case. If profits are reinvested rather than distributed to shareholders in cash, those shareholders cannot invest this cash in other forms of investment. They will therefore expect a rate of return from the profits reinvested that is equivalent to what they would have received had the funds been invested in another opportunity with the same level of risk.

The reinvestment of profits rather than the issue of new shares can be a useful way of raising capital from ordinary share investors. There are no issue costs associated with retaining profits, and the amount raised is certain, once the profit has been made.

An obvious alternative way to increase equity investment, instead of retaining profit, is to issue new shares. When issuing new shares, however, the issue costs may be substantial and there may be uncertainty over the success of the issue. We shall look at these two problem areas later in the chapter.

Retaining profits will have no effect on the extent to which existing shareholders control the business, whereas when new shares are issued to outside investors there will be some dilution of control.

The decision to retain profits rather than pay them out as dividends to the shareholders is made by the directors. They may find it easier simply to retain profits rather than ask investors to subscribe to a new share issue. Retained profits are already held by the business, and so it does not have to wait to receive the funds. Moreover, there is often less scrutiny when profits are being retained for reinvestment purposes than when new shares are being issued. Investors and their advisers will closely examine the reasons for any new share issue. A problem with the use of profits as a source of finance, however, is that the timing and level of future profits cannot always be reliably estimated.

Some shareholders may prefer profits to be retained by the business, rather than be distributed in the form of dividends. By ploughing back profits, it may be expected that the business will expand, and that share values will increase as a result. Not all capital gains are liable for taxation. (For the tax year 2006/07, an individual with capital gains totalling less than £8,800 would not be taxed on those gains.) A further advantage of capital gains over dividends is that the shareholder has a choice as to when the shares are sold and the gain is realised. In the UK, it is only when the gain is realised that capital gains tax comes into play. Research indicates that investors may be attracted to particular businesses according to the dividend/retention policies that they adopt.

It would be wrong to get the impression that all businesses either retain all of their profit or pay it all out as a dividend. Where businesses pay dividends, and most of the larger ones do pay dividends, they typically pay no more than 50 per cent of the profit, retaining the remainder to fund expansion.

Retained profit is much the most important source of new finance for UK businesses, on average, in terms of value of funds raised.

Short-term sources of internal finance

Tighter credit control

By exerting tighter control over amounts owed by credit customers, it may be possible for a business to reduce the proportion of assets held in this form and so release funds for other purposes. Having funds tied up in trade receivables represents an opportunity cost in that those funds could be used for profit generating activities. It is important, however, to weigh the benefits of tighter credit control against the likely costs in the form of lost customer goodwill and lost sales. To remain competitive, a business must take account of the needs of its customers and the credit policies adopted by rival businesses within the industry. We shall consider this further in Chapter 16.

Activity 15.2

Rusli Ltd provides a car valet service for car-hire businesses when their cars are returned from hire. Details of the service costs are as follows:

	Per car	
	£	£
Car valet charge		20
Less Variable costs	14	
Fixed costs	4	18
Profit		2

Sales revenue is £10m a year and is all on credit. The average credit period taken by Rusli Ltd's customers is 45 days, although the terms of credit state that payment should be made within 30 days. Allowances for receivables (bad debts) are currently £100,000 a year. Trade receivables are financed by a bank overdraft costing 10 per cent a year.

Rusli Ltd's credit control department believes it can eliminate allowances for receivables (bad debts) and can reduce the average credit period to 30 days if new credit control procedures are implemented. These will cost £50,000 a year and are likely to result in a loss of business leading to a reduction in sales revenue of 5 per cent a year.

Should Rusli Ltd implement the new credit control procedures? (*Hint*: To answer this activity it is useful to compare the current cost of trade credit with the costs under the proposed approach.)

The current annual cost of trade credit is:

	£
Allowances for receivables (bad debts)	100,000
Overdraft interest [(£10m × 45/365) × 10%]	123,288
	223,288

The annual cost of trade credit under the new policy will be:

	£
Overdraft interest [(95% × (£10m) × (30/365)) × 10%]	78,082
Cost of control procedures	50,000
Net cost of lost sales [(£(10m/20) × 5%) × (20 − 14*)]	150,000
	278,082

* The loss will be the contribution per unit (that is, the difference between the selling price and the variable costs).

The above figures reveal that the business will be worse off if the new policies are adopted.

Reducing inventories levels

Reducing the level of inventories is an internal source of funds that may prove attractive to a business. If the business has a proportion of its assets in the form of inventories there is an opportunity cost, as the funds tied up cannot be used for other purposes. By reducing inventories, funds become available for those opportunities. However, a business must try to ensure that there are sufficient inventories available to meet likely future sales demand. Failure to do so will result in lost customer goodwill and lost sales revenue.

The nature and condition of the inventories held will determine whether it is possible to exploit this form of finance. A business may have too much inventories as a result of poor buying decisions. This may mean that a significant proportion of the inventories held are slow moving or obsolete and cannot, therefore, be reduced easily. These issues will be picked up again in Chapter 16.

Delaying payment to trade payables

By providing a period of credit, suppliers are in effect offering a business an interest-free loan. If the business delays payment, the period of the 'loan' is extended and funds can be retained within the business. This can be a cheap form of finance for a business, though this is not always the case. If a business fails to pay within the agreed credit period, there may be significant costs. For example, the business may find it difficult to buy on credit when it has a reputation as a slow payer.

These so-called short-term sources are short term to the extent that they can be reversed at short notice. For example, a reduction in the level of trade receivables can be reversed within a couple of weeks. Typically, however, once a business has established a reduced receivable collection period, a reduced inventory holding period and/or an expanded payables payment period, it will tend to maintain these new levels.

As we shall see in Chapter 16, for the typical business, the level of funds involved with the working capital items is vast. This means that highly significant amounts of funds can be raised through exercising tighter control of trade receivables and inventories and by exploiting opportunities to delay payment to trade payables.

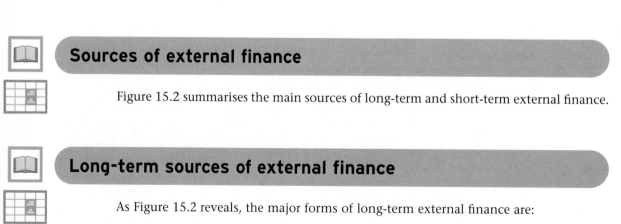

Sources of external finance

Figure 15.2 summarises the main sources of long-term and short-term external finance.

Long-term sources of external finance

As Figure 15.2 reveals, the major forms of long-term external finance are:

● ordinary shares
● preference shares
● borrowings

Figure 15.2   **The major sources of external finance**

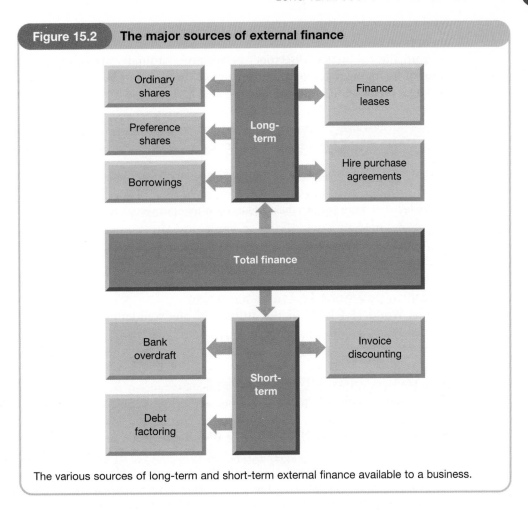

The various sources of long-term and short-term external finance available to a business.

- finance leases, including sale-and-leaseback arrangements
- hire purchase agreements.

We shall now discuss each of the sources identified.

Ordinary shares

As we saw in Chapter 4, ordinary shares form the backbone of the financial structure of a business. Ordinary share capital represents the business's risk capital. There is no fixed rate of dividend and ordinary shareholders can receive a dividend only if profits available for distribution still remain after other investors (preference shareholders and lenders) have received their dividend or interest payments. If the business is wound up, the ordinary shareholders will receive any proceeds from asset disposals only after any lenders, creditors and preference shareholders have received their entitlements. Because of the high risks associated with this form of investment, ordinary shareholders will normally require a comparatively high rate of return.

Although ordinary shareholders have a potential loss liability that is limited to the amount that they have invested or agreed to invest, the potential returns from their investment are unlimited. In other words, their downside risk is limited whereas their upside potential is not. Ordinary shareholders have control over the business, through their voting rights. This gives them the power both to elect the directors and to remove them from office.

From the business's (directors') perspective, ordinary shares can be an attractive form of financing, relative to borrowing. At times, it can be useful to be able to avoid paying a dividend. It is not usually possible to avoid paying interest on borrowings.

Activity (15.3)

Under what circumstances might a business find it useful to avoid paying a dividend?

We feel that there are two main situations where this would apply:

● An expanding business may prefer to retain funds to help fuel future growth.
● A business in difficulties may need the funds to meet its operating costs and so may find making a dividend payment a real burden.

Real World 15.1 looks at the attitude of one well-known businessman to paying dividends.

Real World 15.1

No frills, no dividends and no brains

Michael O'Leary, the colourfully-spoken chief executive of Ryanair Holdings plc, the 'no-frills' airline was very clear on his attitude to dividends. He said, 'We are never paying a dividend as long as I live and breathe and as long as I'm the largest shareholder. If you are stupid enough to invest in an airline for its dividend flow you should be put back in the loony bin where you came from.' Presumably Ryanair is expanding at a rate that eats up all available finances.

Source: 'Ryanair blunted by Buzz takeover', *A. Osborne, Daily Telegraph*, 6 August 2004.

Although a business financed by ordinary shares can avoid making cash payments to shareholders when it is not prudent to do so, the market value of the shares may go down. The cost to the business of financing through ordinary shares may become higher if shareholders feel uncertain about future dividends. On the other hand, for a business like Ryanair, which is clearly expanding its operations in a profitable way, share prices are likely to reflect this despite the lack of dividends.

It is also worth pointing out that the business does not obtain any tax relief on dividends paid to shareholders, whereas interest on borrowings is tax deductible. This makes it more expensive to the business to pay £1 of dividend than £1 of loan interest on borrowings.

Preference shares

Preference shares offer investors a lower level of risk than ordinary shares. Provided there are sufficient profits available, preference shares will normally be given a fixed rate of dividend each year, and preference shareholders will be paid the first slice of any dividend paid. Should the business be wound up, preference shareholders may be given priority over the claims of ordinary shareholders. (The business's own particular documents of incorporation will state the precise rights of preference shareholders in this respect.)

Activity 15.4

Would you expect the returns on preference shares to be higher or lower than those of ordinary shares?

We expect returns on preference shareholders to be lower than those on ordinary shares. This is because of the lower level of risk associated with this form of investment (preference shareholders have priority over ordinary shareholders regarding dividends).

Preference shares are no longer an important source of new finance. A major reason for this is that dividends paid to preference shareholders, like those paid to ordinary shareholders, are not allowable against taxable profits, whereas interest on loan capital is an allowable expense. From the business's point of view, preference shares and loans are quite similar, so the tax deductibility of loan interest is an important issue.

Activity 15.5

Would you expect the market price of ordinary shares or of preference shares to be the more volatile? Why?

The share price, which reflects the expected future returns from the share, will normally be less volatile for preference shares than for ordinary shares. The dividends of preference shares tend to be fairly stable over time, and there is usually an upper limit on the returns that can be received.

Both preference shares and ordinary shares are, in effect, *redeemable*. The business is allowed to buy back the shares from shareholders at any time.

Loans (borrowings)

Most businesses rely on loans or borrowings as well as share capital to finance operations. Lenders enter into a contract with the business in which the rate of interest, dates of interest payments, capital repayments and security for the loan are clearly stated. In the event that the interest payments or capital repayments are not made on the due dates, the lender will usually have the right, under the terms of the contract, to seize the assets on which the loan is secured and sell them in order to repay the amount outstanding. Security for a loan may take the form of a fixed charge on particular assets of the business (land and buildings are often favoured by lenders) or a floating charge on the whole of its assets. A floating charge will 'float' over the assets and will only fix on particular assets in the event that the business defaults on its loan obligations.

Activity (15.6)

What do you think is the advantage for the business of having a floating charge rather than a fixed charge on its assets?

A floating charge on assets allows the managers greater flexibility in their day-to-day operations than a fixed charge. Individual assets can be sold without reference to the lenders.

Term loans

One form of long-term loan is the **term loan**. This type of loan is offered by banks and other financial institutions, and is usually tailored to the needs of the client business. The amount of the loan, the time period, the repayment terms and the interest payable are all open to negotiation and agreement, which can be very useful. For example, where all of the funds to be borrowed are not required immediately, a business may agree with the lender that funds are drawn only as and when required. This means that interest will be paid only on amounts drawn and the business will not have to pay interest on amounts borrowed that are temporarily surplus to requirements. Term loans tend to be cheap to set up (from the borrower business's perspective) and can be quite flexible as to conditions.

Loan notes (or loan stock)

Another form of long-term loan finance is the **loan note** (or **loan stock**). Loan notes are frequently divided into units (rather like share capital), and investors are invited to purchase the number of units they require. The loan notes may be redeemable or irredeemable. Loan notes of public limited companies are often traded on the Stock Exchange, and their listed value will fluctuate according to the fortunes of the business, movements in interest rates and so on.

Loan notes are usually referred to as *bonds* in the US and, increasingly, in the UK.

Real World 15.2, describes how a world-famous football club has made secured borrowings.

Real World 15.2

Gunning for success

The Arsenal Football Club plc (Arsenal) has recently moved from its traditional home to a new 'state of the art' stadium at Ashburton Grove (the Emirates Stadium). It has been financing the stadium mainly with a £200m bond issue. The bonds are secured, not on the stadium itself, but on future cash receipts from ticket sales. This means that it is essential that Arsenal continues to be successful and generates a good level of attendances at matches. This type of security is quite common for UK and other European football clubs.

Source: Information taken from 'Gunners need on pitch success to pay off bond', *Accountancy Age*, 8 September 2005.

Eurobonds

Eurobonds are unsecured loan notes denominated in a currency other than the home currency of the business that issued them. Eurobonds are issued by businesses (and other large organisations) in various countries, and the finance is raised on an international basis. They are often denominated in US dollars, but many are issued in other major currencies. Interest is normally paid annually. Eurobonds are part of an ever-expanding international capital market, and they are not subject to regulations imposed by authorities in particular countries. Numerous financial institutions throughout the world have created a market for eurobonds, where holders of eurobonds are able to sell them to would-be holders. The business issuing the eurobonds usually makes them available to large banks and other financial institutions, which may either retain them as an investment or sell them to their clients.

The extent of borrowing, by UK businesses, in currencies other than sterling has expanded massively in recent years. Businesses are often attracted to issue eurobonds because of the size of the international capital market. Access to a large number of international investors is likely to increase the chances of a successful issue. In addition, the lack of regulation in the eurobond market means that national restrictions regarding loan issues may be overcome.

Real World 15.3 provides an example of a eurobond issue by a well-known UK business.

Real World 15.3

Taking off with eurobonds

FT

A growing number of companies are entering the euro bond market for the first time, encouraged by the opportunity to reach new investors with low financing costs. . . . This week BAA, the operator of Heathrow and six other airports in the UK, raised €750m ($913m) from its first euro-denominated bond. . . .

'This deal gave the company access to capital at a similar cost to what it could have done in sterling,' said Jean-Marc Mercier at HSBC's corporate syndicate desk, which managed the deal with BNP Paribas and Deutsche Bank.

'In addition, two-thirds of the investors in the deal were new to the company,' he added.

Diversifying the investor base is important for companies, as it increases their flexibility to raise capital when they need to.

Source: 'New appetite develops for Eurobonds', *Financial Times*, 18 September 2004, FT.com.

Activity 15.7

Would you expect the returns to loan capital to be higher or lower than those of preference shares?

Investors are usually prepared to accept a lower rate of return. This is because they will normally view loans as being less risky than preference shares. Lenders have priority over any claims from preference shareholders, and will usually have security for their loans.

The risk-return characteristics of loan, preference share and ordinary share finance are shown graphically in Figure 15.3.

Interest rates and deep discount bonds

Interest rates on loan finance may be either floating or fixed. A floating rate means that the rate of return required by lenders will rise and fall with market rates of interest.

Figure 15.3   The risk/return characteristics of long-term capital

The higher the level of risk associated with a particular form of long-term finance, the higher will be the returns expected by investors. Ordinary shares are the most risky and have the highest expected return, and, as a general rule, loan capital is the least risky and has the lowest expected return.

However, the market value of the lender's investment in the business is likely to remain fairly stable over time. The converse will normally be true for fixed-interest loans. The interest payments will remain unchanged with rises and falls in market rates of interest, but the value of the loan investment will fall when interest rates rise and will rise when interest rates fall.

A business may issue redeemable loan capital that offers a rate of interest below the market rate. In some cases, the loan capital even may have a zero rate of interest. Such loans are issued at a discount to their redeemable value and are referred to as **deep discount bonds**. Thus loan capital may be issued at, say, £80 for every £100 of nominal value. Although lenders will receive little or no interest during the period of the loan, they will receive a £20 gain when the loan is finally redeemed at the full £100. The redemption yield, as it is referred to, is often quite high and, when calculated on an annual basis, may compare favourably with returns from other forms of loan capital with the same level of risk. Deep discount bonds may have particular appeal to businesses with short-term cash flow problems. Such businesses receive an immediate injection of cash and there are no significant cash outflows associated with the loan until the maturity date. Deep discount bonds are likely to appeal to investors who do not have short-term cash flow needs, since they must wait for the loan to mature before receiving a cash return.

Convertible loan notes

Convertible loan notes (or convertible bonds) give investors the right, but not the obligation, to exchange the loan notes for ordinary shares in the business at a specified price (the 'exercise' price) on a given future specified date or within a range of specified dates. The exercise price is usually higher than the market price of those ordinary shares at the time of issue of the convertible loan notes. In effect the investor swaps the loan notes for a particular number of shares. The investor remains a lender to the business, and will receive interest on the amount of the loan, until such time as the conversion takes place. The investor is not obliged to convert to ordinary shares. This will be done only if the market price of the shares at the conversion date exceeds the specified conversion price.

An investor may find this form of investment a useful hedge against risk. This may be particularly useful when investment in a new business is being considered. Initially the investment is in the form of a loan, and regular interest payments will be made. If the business is successful, the investor can then decide to benefit from the success by converting the investment into ordinary shares.

The business may also find this form of financing useful. If the business is successful, the loan becomes self-liquidating (no cash payment is required), as investors will exercise their option to convert. The business may also be able to offer a lower rate of interest to investors because they expect future benefits to arise from conversion. There will be, however, some dilution of both control and earnings for existing shareholders if holders of convertible loans exercise their option to convert.

Real World 15.4 details one particular convertible loan issue.

Real World 15.4

Power conversion

In July 2006, International Power plc issued convertible bonds for a total of £140m. The business is a major generator of electricity throughout the world, including through six power stations in the UK. The business is listed on the London Stock Exchange.

It needed the cash to help finance a coal-fired electricity generation plant in Texas. The share price at which, in 2013, the bonds may be converted is £3.91 and, at the time of the issue, the market price of International Power's shares was £2.89. The offer was over-subscribed despite the annual interest rate attaching to the bonds being only 3.25 per cent (fixed). This implies a strong belief among investors that International Power's share price is set to rise.

Source: Information taken from 'Volatility prompts European issuance', Joanna Chung, *Financial Times*, 12 July 2006.

Warrants

→ Holders of **warrants** have the right, but not the obligation, to buy newly issued ordinary shares in a particular business, from that business, at a given price (the exercise price). As with convertible loan notes, the price at which shares may be bought is usually higher than the market price of those shares at the time of the issue of the warrants. The warrant will usually state the number of shares that the holder may buy and the time limit within which the option to buy them can be exercised. Occasionally, perpetual warrants are issued that have no set time limits. Warrants do not confer voting rights or entitle the holders to make any claims on the assets of the business. Warrants are themselves neither shares nor loan notes.

Share warrants are often sold to investors by the business concerned. In some cases, they are given away 'free' as a 'sweetener' to accompany an issue of loan notes, that is, as an incentive to potential lenders. The issue of warrants in this way may enable the business to offer lower rates of interest on the loan or to negotiate less restrictive loan conditions. Sometimes, businesses sell share warrants without there being a link to a loan notes issue. Warrants enable investors to benefit from any future increases in the business's ordinary share price without having to buy the shares themselves. On the other hand, if the share price remains below the exercise price, the warrant will not be used and the investor will lose out as a result.

Activity (15.8)

Under what circumstances will the holders of share warrants exercise their option to purchase?

Holders will exercise this option only if the market price of the shares exceeds the exercise price within the time limit specified. If the exercise price were higher than the market price, it would be cheaper for the investor to buy the shares in the market.

To the business issuing the warrants, warrants represent a source of funds (the proceeds of selling them). Alternatively, they represent an encouragement for the issue of another source of funds (a loan notes issue) to be successful.

Share warrants issued with a loan may be *detachable*, which means that they can be sold separately from the loan capital. The warrants of businesses whose shares are listed on the Stock Exchange are often themselves listed, providing a ready market for buying and selling the warrants.

It is probably worth mentioning the difference in status within a business between holders of convertible loan notes and holders of loan notes with share warrants attached, if both groups decide to exercise their right to convert. Convertible loan note holders become ordinary shareholders and are no longer lenders to the business. They will have used the value of the loan notes to 'buy' the shares. Warrant holders become ordinary shareholders by paying cash for the shares. If the warrant holders hold loan notes, this will be unaffected by their exercising their right to buy the shares bestowed by the warrant.

→ Both convertibles and warrants are examples of **financial derivatives**. These are any form of financial instrument, based on share or loan capital, that can be used by investors to increase their returns or reduce risk.

Mortgages

→ A **mortgage** is a form of loan that is secured on an asset, typically land. Financial institutions such as banks, insurance businesses and pension funds are often prepared to lend to businesses on this basis. The mortgage may be over a long period (twenty years or more).

Loan covenants

Lenders often impose certain obligations and restrictions on borrowers in an attempt to protect themselves. **Loan covenants** (as they are called) often form part of a loan agreement, and may deal with such matters as:

● *Financial statements*. The lender may require access to the financial statements of the borrowing business on a regular basis.
● *Other loans*. The lender may require the business to ask the lender's permission before taking on further loans from other sources.
● *Dividend payments*. The lender may require dividend payments to be limited during the period of the loan.
● *Liquidity*. The lender may require the business to maintain a certain level of liquidity during the period of the loan. This would typically be a requirement that the borrower business's current ratio is maintained at, or above, a specified level.

Any breach of these restrictive covenants can have serious consequences for the business. The lender may require immediate repayment of the loan in the event of a material breach.

Real World 15.5 shows how one well-known UK business was accused of breaching the covenants imposed by its lenders.

Real World 15.5

Capital problems

The stockbrokers Merrill Lynch (ML) claimed that GCap Media plc (Capital), the business that owns the London-based Capital Radio commercial station, breached its loan covenants. Capital's bankers required the business to maintain a net debt to annual earnings ratio of at most 3.0 and an interest cover ratio of at least 4.0. ML claims that both ratios were actually 3.3, meaning that Capital had broken the covenant on both counts. ML claimed that this had arisen as a result of falling advertising revenues for the radio station, particularly for its breakfast programme.

Capital denied breaching the covenants and referred to forecasts that it would do so as 'speculation'.

Source: Information taken from 'GCap attacks note on breaching covenants', *Financial Times*, 9 September 2006, FT.com.

Activity 15.9

Both preference shares and loan notes are forms of finance that require the business to provide a particular rate of return to investors. What are the factors that may be taken into account by a business when deciding between these two sources of finance?

The main factors are as follows:

● Preference shares tend to have a higher rate of return than loan notes. From the investor's point of view, preference shares are more risky. The amount invested cannot be secured, and the return is paid after the returns paid to lenders.

● A business has a legal obligation to pay interest and, typically, make capital repayments on loan stocks at the agreed dates. It will usually make every effort to meet its obligations because failure to do so can have serious consequences. (These consequences have been mentioned earlier.) Failure to pay a preference dividend, on the other hand, is less important. There is no legal obligation to pay if profits are not available for distribution. Failure to pay a preference dividend may prove an embarrassment for the business, however, because it may make it difficult to persuade investors to take up future preference share issues.

● It was mentioned above that the taxation system in the UK permits interest on loans to be allowable against profits for taxation, whereas preference dividends are not. As a result, the cost of servicing loan capital is, £ for £, usually much less for a business than the cost of servicing preference shares.

● The issue of loan notes may result in the management of a business having to accept some restrictions on its freedom of action. We saw earlier that loan agreements often contain covenants that can be onerous. However, preference shareholders can impose no such restrictions.

A further point is that preference shares issued form part of the permanent capital base of the business. If they are redeemed, the law requires that they be replaced, either by a new issue of shares or by a transfer from revenue reserves, so that the business's capital base stays intact. Loan capital, however, is not viewed in law as part of the business's permanent capital base, and therefore there is no legal requirement to replace any loan capital that has been redeemed.

Finance leases and sale-and-leaseback arrangements

When a business needs a particular asset (for example, an item of plant), instead of buying it direct from a supplier, the business may decide to arrange for another business (typically a bank) to buy it and then lease it to the first business. The business that owns the asset and leases it out is known as a 'lessor'. The one that uses it is known as the 'lessee'.

→ A **finance lease**, as such an arrangement is known, is, in essence, a form of lending. This is because, had the lessee borrowed the funds and then used them to buy the asset itself, the effect would be much the same. The lessee would have use of the asset, but have a financial obligation to the lender – much the same position as the leasing arrangement would lead to.

Although, with finance leasing, legal ownership of the asset rests with the financial institution (the lessor), a finance lease agreement transfers to the user (the lessee) virtually all the rewards and risks that are associated with the item being leased. The finance lease agreement covers a significant part of the life of the item being leased, and often cannot be cancelled.

Finance leasing is a very important source of finance for UK businesses. The Finance and Leasing Association estimates that 30 per cent of finance for non-current assets (excluding land and buildings) comes from finance leasing.

Finance leasing is by no means limited to smaller businesses. It is popular with many larger businesses. **Real World 15.6** gives an example of the use of finance leasing in a leading airline business.

Real World 15.6

Finance leasing at BA

Many airline businesses use finance leasing as a means of acquiring new aeroplanes. The financial statements for British Airways plc (BA) for the year ended 31 March 2006 show that approximately 27 per cent (totalling £1,792m) of the net book value of its fleet of aircraft had been acquired through this method.

Source: British Airways plc Annual Report and Accounts 2006.

→ A finance lease can be contrasted with an **operating lease**, where the rewards and risks of ownership stay with the owner and where the lease is short term. An example of an operating lease is where a builder hires some earthmoving equipment for a week to carry out a particular job.

In recent years, some important benefits associated with finance leasing have disappeared. Changes in UK tax law no longer make it such a tax-efficient form of financing, and changes in accounting disclosure requirements no longer make it possible to conceal this form of 'borrowing' from investors. Nevertheless, the popularity of finance leases has continued. Other reasons must therefore exist for businesses to adopt this form of financing. These reasons are said to include the following:

- *Ease of borrowing.* Leasing may be obtained more easily than other forms of long-term finance. Lenders normally require some form of security and a profitable track record before making advances to a business. However, a lessor may be prepared to lease assets to a new business without a track record, and to use the leased assets as security for the amounts owing.
- *Cost.* Leasing agreements may be offered at reasonable cost. As the asset leased is used as security, standard lease arrangements can be applied and detailed credit checking of lessees may be unnecessary. This can reduce administrative costs for the lessor and, thereby, help in providing competitive lease rentals.
- *Flexibility.* Leasing can help provide flexibility where there are rapid changes in technology. If an option to cancel can be incorporated into the lease, the business may be able to exercise this option and invest in new technology as it becomes available. This will help the business to avoid the risk of obsolescence.
- *Cash flows.* Leasing, rather than purchasing an asset outright, means that large cash outflows can be avoided. The leasing option allows cash outflows to be smoothed out over the asset's life. In some cases, it is possible to arrange for low lease payments to be made in the early years of the asset's life, when cash inflows may be low, and for these to increase over time as the asset generates positive cash flows.

Real World 15.7 provides some impression of the importance of finance leasing over recent years.

Real World 15.7

Finance leasing 1999 to 2005

There is an upward trend in the amount of asset finance provided through finance leasing by FLA members over the seven-year period.

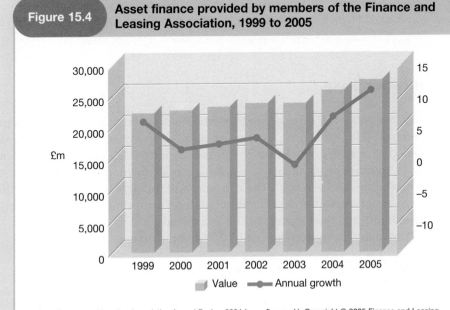

| Figure 15.4 | Asset finance provided by members of the Finance and Leasing Association, 1999 to 2005 |

Source: Finance and Leasing Association Annual Review 2004 (www.fla.org.uk). Copyright © 2005 Finance and Leasing Association.

→ A **sale-and-leaseback** arrangement involves a business raising finance by selling an asset to a financial institution. The sale is accompanied by an agreement to lease the asset back to the business to allow it to continue to use the asset. The lease payment is allowable against profits for taxation purposes. There are usually reviews at regular intervals throughout the period of the lease, and the amounts payable in future years may be difficult to predict. At the end of the lease agreement, the business must try either to renew the lease or to find an alternative asset. Although the sale of the asset will result in an immediate injection of cash for the business, the business will lose benefits from any future capital appreciation on the asset. Where a capital gain arises on the sale of the asset to the financial institution, a liability for taxation may also arise. Freehold property is often the asset that is the subject of such an arrangement. Many of the well-known UK high-street retailers (for example, Boots, Debenhams, Marks and Spencer, and Sainsbury) have recently sold off their store sites under sale-and-leaseback arrangements.

A sale-and-leaseback agreement can be used to help a business focus on its core areas of competence. In recent years, many hotel businesses have entered into sale-and-leaseback agreements to enable them to become purely hotel operators rather than a combination of hotel operators and owners.

Real World 15.8 provides an example of a sale-and-leaseback agreement undertaken by a well-known UK business.

Real World 15.8

Bingo

The Rank Group plc, the UK-based international gaming and leisure business, entered into an agreement for the sale and leaseback of 40 Mecca bingo clubs and four Grosvenor casinos. The deal, which was agreed on 14 July 2006, raised cash for Rank of £211m. The properties were sold to Solarus Estates Ltd and Earth Estates Ltd. Rank will now pay annual rents of £11.2m to lease back the properties, from Solarus and Earth, under 15-year leases.

Source: Information taken from 'Rank Group agrees sale and leaseback', 14 July 2006, FT.com.

Hire purchase

→ **Hire purchase** is a form of credit used to acquire an asset. Under the terms of a hire purchase (HP) agreement a customer pays for an asset by instalments over an agreed period. Normally, the customer will pay an initial deposit (downpayment) and then make instalment payments at regular intervals (perhaps monthly) until the balance outstanding has been paid. The customer will usually take possession of the asset after payment of the initial deposit, although legal ownership of the asset will not be transferred until the final instalment has been paid.

Hire purchase agreements will often involve three parties:

- the supplier
- the customer
- a financial institution.

Although the supplier will deliver the asset to the customer, the financial institution will buy the asset from the supplier and then enter into a hire purchase agreement with the customer. This intermediary role played by the financial institution enables the supplier to receive immediate payment for the asset but allows the customer a period of extended credit.

Real World 15.9 describes how one well-known holiday operator uses hire purchase to help finance its assets.

Real World 15.9

Paying by instalments

Holidaybreak plc has a camping division that includes well-known brands such as Eurocamp and Keycamp. The division provides mobile homes for holidaymakers, and the company's 2005 annual report revealed that the cost of mobile homes held was £75.9m against which £17.4m was owing under hire purchase agreements. The financing of the mobile homes involves hire purchase agreements with a number of financial institutions.

Source: Based on information in Holidaybreak plc Annual Report 2005.

HP agreements are similar to finance leases in so far that they allow a customer to obtain immediate possession of the asset without paying its full cost. Under the terms of an HP agreement, however, the customer will eventually become the legal owner of the asset, whereas under the terms of a finance lease, ownership will stay with the lessor.

Gearing and the long-term financing decision

In Chapter 7 we saw that financial gearing occurs when a business is financed, at least in part, by contributions from fixed-charge capital (preference shares and loans). We also saw that the level of gearing associated with a business is often an important factor in assessing the risk and returns to ordinary shareholders. In Example 15.1, we consider the implications of making a choice between a geared and an ungeared approach to raising long-term finance.

Example 15.1

The following are the summarised financial statements of Woodhall Engineers plc:

Woodhall Engineers plc
Income statement for the year ended 31 December

	Year 1	Year 2
	£m	£m
Revenue	47	50
Operating costs	(42)	(48)
Operating profit	5	2
Interest payable	(1)	(1)
Profit before tax	4	1
Taxation	–	–
Profit for the year	4	1

Balance sheet at 31 December

	Year 1 £m	Year 2 £m
Non-current assets (less depreciation)	21	20
Current assets		
Inventories	10	18
Receivables	16	17
Cash at bank	3	1
	29	36
Total assets	50	56
Equity		
Called-up share capital 25p ordinary shares	16	16
Retained earnings	4	4
	20	20
Non-current liabilities		
Borrowings – Long-term loans (secured)	15	15
Current liabilities		
Trade payables	10	10
Short-term borrowings	5	11
	15	21
	30	36
Total equity and liabilities	50	56

The business is making plans to expand its premises. New plant will cost £8m, and an expansion in output will increase working capital by £4m. Over the 15 years' life of the project, incremental profits arising from the expansion will be £2m a year before interest and tax. In addition, Year 3's profits before interest and tax from its existing activities are expected to return to Year 1 levels.

Two possible methods of financing the expansion have been discussed by Woodhall's directors. The first is the issue of £12m, 10 per cent loan notes repayable in Year 18. The second is a rights issue of 40m 25p ordinary shares, which will give the business 30p per share after expenses.

The business has substantial tax losses, which can be offset against future profits, so taxation can be ignored in the calculations. The Year 3 total dividend is expected to be £1.0m assuming that the expansion is financed by loan notes and £1.6m if the rights issue is made.

Prepare Woodhall's projected income statement (excluding revenue and operating costs) for the year ended 31 December Year 3, and of its capital and reserves, long-term loans and number of shares outstanding at that date, assuming that the business issues:

- loan notes
- ordinary shares.

The first part of the example requires the preparation of a projected income statement under each financing option. These will be as follows:

Projected income statement for the year ended 31 December Year 3

	Loan issue £m	Share issue £m
Operating profit (5.0 + 2.0)	7.0	7.0
Loan notes interest	(2.2)	(1.0)
Profit before tax	4.8	6.0
Taxation	–	–
Profit for the year	4.8	6.0

The capital structure of the business under each option as at the end of Year 3 will be as follows:

	Loan issue £m	Share issue £m
Equity		
Share capital 25p ordinary shares	16.0	26.0
Share premium account*	–	2.0
Retained profit†	7.8	8.4
	23.8	36.4
Number of shares in issue (25p shares)	64 million	104 million

* This represents the amount received from the issue of shares that is above the nominal value of the shares. The amount is calculated as follows:

$$40\text{m shares} \times (30\text{p} - 25\text{p}) = £2\text{m}$$

† This is the retained profit figure after deducting the dividend paid.

Activity (15.10)

Compute Woodhall's interest cover and earnings per share for the year ended 31 December Year 3 and its gearing on that date, assuming that the business issues:

(a) loan notes;
(b) ordinary shares.

Your answer should be as follows:

	(a) Loan notes issue	(b) Share issue
Interest cover ratio		
$\dfrac{\text{Profit before interest and tax}}{\text{Interest payable}}$	$= \dfrac{7.0}{2.2}$	$= \dfrac{7.0}{1.0}$
	= 3.2 times	= 7.0 times
Earning per share		
$\dfrac{\text{Earning available to ordinary shareholders}}{\text{Number of ordinary shares}}$	$= \dfrac{£4.8\text{m}}{64\text{m}}$	$= \dfrac{£6.0\text{m}}{104\text{m}}$
	= 7.5p	= 5.8p
Gearing ratio		
$\dfrac{\text{Non-current liabilities}}{\text{Share capital} + \text{Reserves} + \text{Non-current liabilities}}$	$= \dfrac{£27\text{m}}{£23.8\text{m} + £27\text{m}}$	$= \dfrac{£15\text{m}}{£36.4\text{m} + £15\text{m}}$
	= 53.1%	= 29.2%

Activity (15.11)

What would your views of the proposed schemes be in each of the following circumstances?

(a) If you were an investor who had been asked to take up some of the loan notes.
(b) If you were an ordinary shareholder in Woodhall and you were asked to subscribe to a rights issue.

(a) Investors may be unenthusiastic about lending money to the business. The gearing ratio of 53.1 per cent is rather high, and would leave the loan note holders in an exposed position. The existing loan is already secured on the business's assets, and it is not clear whether the business is in a position to offer an attractive form of security for the new loan. The interest cover ratio of 3.2 times is also rather low. If the business is unable to achieve the expected returns from the new project, or if it is unable to restore profits from the remainder of its operations to Year 1 levels, this ratio would be even lower.

(b) Ordinary share investors may need some convincing that it would be worthwhile to make further investments in the business. The return on ordinary shareholders' funds in Year 1 was 20 per cent (£4m/£20m). The incremental profit from the new project is £2m and the investment required is £12m, which represents a return of 16.7 per cent. Thus, the returns from the project are expected to be lower than for existing operations. In making their decision, investors should discover whether the new investment is of a similar level of risk to their existing investment and how the returns from the investment compare with those available from other opportunities with similar levels of risk.

Share issues

A business may issue shares in a number of ways. These may involve direct appeals to investors or the use of financial intermediaries. The most common methods of share issues for cash are:

● rights issues;
● offers for sale and public issues;
● private placings.

These are discussed below.

Rights issue

 As we saw in Chapter 4, **rights issues** are made when businesses that have been established for some time seek to raise additional share capital for expansion, or even to solve a liquidity problem (cash shortage) by issuing additional shares for cash. Company law gives existing shareholders the first right of refusal on these new shares, so the new shares would be offered to shareholders in proportion to their existing holding. Thus existing shareholders are each given the right to buy some new shares. Only where the existing shareholders agree to waive their right would the shares be offered to the investing public generally. Rights issues are now the most common form of share issue. The business (in effect, the existing shareholders) would typically prefer that existing shareholders buy the shares through a rights issue, irrespective of the legal position. This is for two reasons:

- The ownership (and, therefore, control) of the business remains in the same hands.
- The costs of making the issue (advertising, complying with various company law requirements) tend to be less if the shares are to be offered to existing shareholders.

To encourage existing shareholders to take up their 'rights' to buy some new shares, those shares are always offered at a price below the current market price of the existing ones.

Activity 15.12

In Chapter 4 (Example 4.2, page 132) the point was made that issuing new shares at below their current worth was to the advantage of the new shareholders at the expense of the old ones. In view of this, does it matter that rights issues are always made at below the current value of the shares?

The answer is that it does not matter *in these particular circumstances*, because, in a rights issue, the existing shareholders and the new shareholders are exactly the same people. Moreover, the shareholders will hold the new shares in the same proportion as they currently hold the existing shares. Thus, shareholders will gain on the new shares exactly as much as they lose on the existing ones: in the end, no one is better or worse off as a result of the rights issue being made at a discount.

Calculating the value of the rights offer received by shareholders is quite straightforward, as shown in Example 15.2.

Example 15.2

Shaw Holdings plc has 20 million ordinary shares of 50p in issue. These shares are currently valued on the Stock Exchange at £1.60 per share. The directors have decided to make a 1-for-4 issue (that is, one new share for every four shares held) at £1.30 per share.

The first step in the valuation process is to calculate the price of a share following the rights issue. This is known as the *ex-rights price*, and is simply a weighted average of the price of shares before the issue of rights and the price of the rights shares. In the above example, we have a 1-for-4 rights issue. The theoretical ex-rights price is therefore calculated as follows:

	£
Price of four shares before the rights issue (4 × £1.60)	6.40
Price of taking up one rights share	1.30
	7.70
Theoretical ex-rights price $= £\dfrac{7.70}{5}$	= £1.54

As the price of each share, in theory, should be £1.54 following the rights issue and the price of a rights share is £1.30, the value of the rights offer will be the difference between the two:

$$£1.54 - £1.30 = £0.24 \text{ per share}$$

Market forces will usually ensure that the actual and theoretical price of rights will be fairly close.

Activity 15.13

An investor with 2,000 shares in Shaw Holdings plc (see Example 15.2) has contacted you for investment advice. She is undecided whether to take up the rights issue, sell the rights or allow the rights offer to lapse.

Calculate the effect on the net wealth of the investor of each of the options being considered.

	£
Before the rights issue the investor had shares worth (2,000 × £1.60)	3,200

If she takes up the rights issue, she will be in the following position:

	£
Value of holding after rights issue [(2,000 + 500) × £1.54]	3,850
Less Cost of buying the rights shares (500 × £1.30)	650
	3,200

If the investor sells the rights, she will be in the following position:

	£
Value of holding after rights issue (2,000 × £1.54)	3,080
Sale of rights (500 × £0.24)	120
	3,200

If the investor lets the rights offer lapse, she will be in the following position:

	£
Value of holding after rights issue (2,000 × £1.54)	3,080

As we can see, the first two options should leave her in the same position concerning net wealth as she was before the rights issue. Before the rights issue she had 2,000 shares worth £1.60 each, or £3,200. However, she will be worse off if she allows the rights offer to lapse than under the other two options. In practice, however, the business may sell the rights, on behalf of the investor, and pass on the proceeds in order to ensure that she is not worse off as a result of the issue.

When considering a rights issue, the directors must first consider the amount of funds that needs to be raised. This will depend on the future plans and commitments of the business (rights issues are frequently made to raise cash for expansion). The directors must then decide on the issue price of the rights shares. Normally, this decision is not critical. In Example 15.2, the business made a 1-for-4 issue with the price of the rights shares set at £1.30. However, it could have raised the same amount by making a 1-for-2 issue and setting the rights price at £0.65, a 1-for-1 issue and setting the price at £0.325, and so on. The issue price that is finally decided upon will not affect the value of the underlying assets of the business or the proportion of the underlying assets and earnings to which each shareholder is entitled. The directors must ensure that the issue price is not above the current market price of the shares, however, or the issue will be unsuccessful.

Real World 15.10 describes how Premier Foods plc, the well-known UK food business, made a rights issue to fund the acquisition of another business.

Real World 15.10

The rights stuff puts Campbell in the Premiership

In August 2006, Premier Foods plc made a 1-for-1 rights issue that raised £450m. Shareholders took up 98 per cent of the issue. The remaining 2 per cent were placed with other investors.

Premier Foods makes a number of household-name products, including Branston Pickle, Hartley's Jam, Ambrosia Rice, and Crosse and Blackwell's soups. The new finance was raised to fund the acquisition of the UK and Irish division of the US Campbell Soup Company.

Source: www.premierfoods.co.uk.

Offer for sale and public issue

An **offer for sale** involves a business, that trades as a public limited company, selling a new issue of shares to a financial institution known as an *issuing house*. However, shares that are already in issue may also be sold to an issuing house. In this case, existing shareholders agree to sell all or some of their shares to the issuing house. The issuing house will, in turn, sell the shares, purchased from either the business or its shareholders, to the public. The issuing house will publish a prospectus that sets out details of the business and the type of shares to be sold and investors will be invited to apply for shares. The advantage of this type of issue, from the business's viewpoint, is that the sale proceeds of the shares are certain.

A **public issue** involves the business making a direct invitation to the public to purchase its shares. Typically, this is done through a newspaper advertisement. The shares may, once again, be a new issue or those already in issue. An offer for sale and a public issue will both result in a widening of share ownership in the business.

In practical terms, the net effect on the business is much the same whether there is an offer for sale or a public issue.

Issue by tender

When making an issue of shares, the business or the issuing house will usually set a price for the shares. Establishing this may not be an easy task, however, particularly where the market is volatile or where the business has unique characteristics. One way of dealing with this issue-price problem is to make a **tender issue** of shares. This involves the investors determining the price at which the shares are issued. Although the business (or issuing house) may publish a reserve price to help guide investors, it will be up to the individual investor to determine the number of shares to be purchased and the price the investor is prepared to pay. Once the offers from investors have all been received and recorded, a price at which all the shares can be sold will be established (known as the *striking price*). Investors who have made offers at, or above, the striking price will be issued shares at the striking price; offers received below the striking price will be rejected. Note that all of the shares will be issued at the same price irrespective of the prices actually offered by individual investors.

Although this form of issue is adopted occasionally, it is not popular with investors, and is therefore not in widespread use.

Private placing

 A **private placing** does not involve an invitation to the public to subscribe for shares. Instead the shares are 'placed' with selected investors, such as large financial institutions. This can be a quick and relatively cheap form of raising funds, because savings can be made in advertising and legal costs. However, it can result in the ownership of the business being concentrated in a few hands. Sometimes, unlisted businesses seeking relatively small amounts of cash will make this form of issue.

Real World 15.11 describes how Aviva plc, the insurance business, used a placing to raise finance.

Real World 15.11

Insuring a successful placing

Aviva plc is world's fifth largest insurance business and it strengthened its position still further by raising about £900m, in July 2006, through a placing of new ordinary shares. The shares were offered to clients of three leading merchant banks and were taken up by a variety of institutional and other investors. The funds raised led to an increase of about 5 per cent of Aviva plc's equity.

The cash raised by the placing provided most of the £1.6bn that Aviva plc is paying, in cash, to acquire AmerUs Group Company, a major US life insurance and annuity business.

Source: www.aviva.com.

Bonus issue

We should recall from Chapter 4 that a bonus issue is not a means of raising finance. It is simply converting one part of the equity (reserves) into another (ordinary shares). No cash changes hands; this benefits neither the business nor the shareholders.

The role of the Stock Exchange

Earlier we considered the various forms of long-term capital that are available to a business. In this section we examine the role that the **Stock Exchange** plays in the provision of finance for businesses. The Stock Exchange acts as both an important *primary* and *secondary* market in capital for businesses. As a primary market, its function is to enable businesses to raise new capital. As a secondary market, its function is to enable investors to sell their securities (including shares and loan notes) with ease. Thus, it provides a 'second-hand' market where shares and loan notes already in issue may be bought and sold.

To enable it to issue shares or loan notes through the Stock Exchange, a business must be 'listed'. This means that the business must meet fairly stringent requirements concerning size, profit history, information disclosure and so on. Some share issues by Stock Exchange listed businesses arise from the initial listing of the business, often known as an *initial public offering (IPO)*. Other share issues are undertaken by businesses that are already listed and that are seeking additional finance from investors.

Real World 15.12 describes how Air Lingus Group plc, the London Stock Exchange listed Irish airline, made a major IPO.

Real World 15.12

Air Lingus off to a flying start

Air Lingus Group plc was floated in September 2006 through an IPO, that raised £335m. The shares offered were oversubscribed 3.8 times (for every share available 3.8 shares were sought by investors).

The group planned to use much of the funds raised to expand operations mainly by investing in additional planes.

Source: Information taken from 'Air Lingus IPO has a smooth takeoff', Alistair Osborne and Stephen Seawright, *Daily Telegraph*, 28 September 2006.

Real World 15.13 explains how new issues are not always good investments for those who take up the shares concerned.

Real World 15.13

New issues but old problems

FT

It seems that we should be cautious when invited to subscribe to a new issue of shares arising from an initial listing on the Stock Exchange. The following extract from the *Financial Times* tells us why investing in new business flotations may be bad for our wealth.

> Back in 1940 Benjamin Graham and David Dodd, the fathers of security analysis, wrote: 'the odds are so strongly against the man who buys into these new flotations that he might as well throw three-quarters of the money out the window and keep the rest in the bank.'
>
> Now confirmation of the poor record of recent new issues comes from an Ernst and Young survey. The accountancy group looked at the records of 200 companies that floated on the UK market between 1998 and 2002. It found that only 39% of the sample had increased profits since flotation (although 82% had seen their sales grow).
>
> This should not come as too much of a surprise. Companies are most likely to float on the market when their recent trading record is impressive. But periods of rapid growth can be very dangerous for a company – costs and management ambitions can get out of hand. Furthermore, no business can grow rapidly forever, and there is a risk that the flotation occurs just at the moment when the decline is beginning.
>
> And, as Ernst and Young points out, the very act of flotation incurs significant costs and can divert management focus from the business. The money raised can also burn a hole in the management's pockets, leading to a flurry of spending that would disgrace a football manager.
>
> All this is slightly discouraging, given that the primary role of the stock market is to allow growing businesses to raise capital. But perhaps a certain amount of investor greed (and gullibility) is necessary if industry is to gain access to finance. New issue investors have been fooled before; they will be fooled again.

Source: Financial Times, 8 August 2003, p. 22.

Despite the problems with IPOs they have been quite popular, in terms of the value of funds raised over recent years, as is shown in **Real World 15.14**.

Real World 15.14

IPOs still popular

Figure 15.5 shows the number of IPOs, together with their average value, that have been made by businesses with a full London Stock Exchange listing during the ten years 1996 to 2005.

Figure 15.5 IPOs, 1996 to 2005

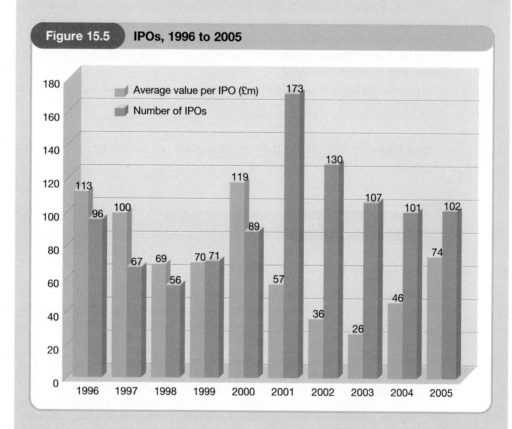

Although the number of issues has fluctuated quite widely, the average funds raised per IPO has tended to show an increase over time.

Source: Based on information contained on the KPMG Corporate Finance website www.kpmg.co.uk.

Advantages of a listing

The secondary market role of the Stock Exchange means that shares and other financial claims are easily transferable. Furthermore, their prices are constantly under scrutiny by investors and skilled analysts. This helps to promote the tendency for the price quoted for a particular business's share to reflect its true worth at that particular time. These factors can bring real benefits to a business.

Activity 15.14

What kinds of benefits might a business gain from its shares being listed?

If it is generally accepted that shares can easily be sold for prices that tend to reflect their true worth, investors will have more confidence to invest. The business may benefit from this greater investor confidence by finding it easier to raise long-term finance and by obtaining this finance at a lower cost, as investors will view their investment as being less risky.

It is worth pointing out that investors are not obliged to use the Stock Exchange as the means of transferring shares in a listed business. However, it is usually the most convenient way of buying or selling shares.

The Stock Exchange can be a useful vehicle for a successful entrepreneur wishing to realise the value of the business that has been built up. By floating (listing) the shares on the Stock Exchange, and thereby making the shares available to the public, the entrepreneur will usually benefit from a gain in the value of the shares held and will be able to realise that gain easily, if required, by selling some shares. **Real Worlds 15.15** and **15.16** give examples of businesses floating on the Stock Exchange and making their owners a lot of money.

Real World 15.15

Granny goes from Leicester market to Stock Market

Duelm Group plc floated on the London Stock Exchange and Jean Adderly realised £120m for her investment. The business was started, in 1979, by Jean (now a grandmother) and her husband Bill trading in curtains on a market stall in Leicester. The business has grown and expanded its range to include most types of household furnishings. It has also moved into more solid premises, with 82 retail outlets.

Source: Based on 'From the market to the market', Harry Wallop, *Daily Telegraph*, 22 September 2006.

Real World 15.16

Cashing in

Mark Mills, a 33-year-old entrepreneur, made himself a fortune in the form of the value of shares worth £4.6m, when his business (Cardpoint) was floated. The business owns 1,900 cash dispensing machines installed in garages and other locations. Everyone using the machines is charged £1.50 to withdraw cash. The business also owns 3,600 mobile phone top-up terminals.

Cardpoint was not Mark Mills' first business venture. He started young, selling bags of broken biscuits to his friends at age 6. At 18 he was in business as a party organiser. He then moved on to selling payphone systems to publicans, then to selling advertising to go on the outside of post boxes. These businesses had mixed success, but he really hit the jackpot with Cardpoint.

Source: Based on information in *Sunday Times*, Business Section, 11 January 2004, p. 11.

Disadvantages of a listing

A Stock Exchange listing can have certain disadvantages for a business. These include:

- Strict rules are imposed on listed businesses, including requiring additional levels of financial disclosure to those already imposed by International Financial Reporting Standards (for example, the listing rules require that half-yearly financial reports are published).
- Financial analysts, financial journalists and others tend to monitor closely the activities of listed businesses, particularly larger ones. Such scrutiny may not be welcome, particularly if the business is dealing with sensitive issues or is experiencing operational problems.
- It is often suggested that listed businesses are under pressure to perform well over the short term. This pressure may detract from undertaking projects that will yield benefits only in the longer term. If the market becomes disenchanted with the business, and the price of its shares falls, this may make it vulnerable to a takeover bid from another business.
- The costs of obtaining a listing are huge and this may be a real deterrent for some businesses.

To make an initial public offering, a business will rely on the help of various specialists such as lawyers, accountants and bankers. However, their services do not come cheap. **Real World 15.17** provides some information.

 Real World 15.17

Floating under heavy fees

According to the London Stock Exchange:

> While the total costs vary widely depending on individual circumstances, as a rule of thumb they tend to come to between four and eight percent of the total proceeds of the sale, although this proportion may be higher for relatively small share offers as some of the fees, for example for accountants and solicitors, are a fixed cost.

Source: Practical Guide to Listing, London Stock Exchange, p. 24.

Though there are over 1,000 UK businesses listed on the London Stock Exchange, in terms of equity market value, the market is dominated by just a few large ones, as is shown in **Real World 15.18**.

 Real World 15.18

Listing to one side

At 30 September 2006 there were 1,158 businesses that had a London Stock Exchange listing. Just 129 of them (11 per cent) accounted for 85 per cent of their total equity market value.

A total of 663 businesses (57 per cent of listed businesses) accounted for 98 per cent of total equity market value.

Source: Main Market Fact Sheet, London Stock Exchange, September 2006, table 8.

Real World 15.19 provides an analysis of the ownership of shares in UK listed businesses at the end of 2004.

Real World 15.19

Ownership of UK listed shares

At the end of 2004, the proportion of shares of UK listed businesses held by various groups was as shown in Figure 15.6.

Figure 15.6   **Ownership of UK listed shares**

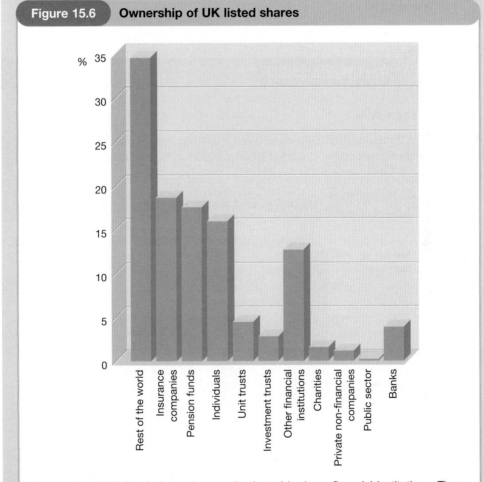

Ownership of UK listed shares is now dominated by large financial institutions. These figures do not fully portray the shareholdings of individuals, however, as individuals will also hold shares in unit trusts.

Source: Financial Statistics, Office for National Statistics, October 2005. Copyright © 2005 Crown Copyright. Crown copyright material is reproduced with the permission of the Controller of HMSO.

Going private

Such are the disadvantages of a stock market listing that many businesses have 'delisted'. This has obviously denied them the advantages of a listing, but it has avoided the disadvantages.

Alternative Investment Market

→ The **Alternative Investment Market (AIM)** was established in June 1995 by the London Stock Exchange for smaller, young and growing businesses. AIM is similar in style to the main London Stock Exchange but it is cheaper for the business to enter. Obtaining an AIM listing and raising funds, costs the typical business about £500,000. Many AIM-listed businesses are family-based ones. AIM has proved to be a very successful market where new equity finance can be raised and shares can be traded. Businesses listed on AIM tend to have market values in the range £1m to £250m, though a half of them fall within the £5m to £50m range, as is shown by **Real World 15.20**.

Real World 15.20

Take AIM

At 30 September 2006, there were 1,589 businesses that had an AIM listing. Their distribution according to market value is shown in Figure 15.7.

| Figure 15.7 | Distribution of AIM-listed businesses by equity market value |

It seems that few AIM-listed businesses have a market capitalisation greater than £250m. The most popular range is £10m–£25m.

Source: AIM Market Statistics, London Stock Exchange, September 2006.

The listing requirements of AIM are less stringent than those of a full listing. However AIM-listed businesses tend to be more risky than fully listed ones, which can make AIM-listed shares less attractive.

Currently there are just over 1,500 businesses listed on AIM. These include Monsoon plc, the high street fashion retailer, Heavitree Brewery plc, the Devon brewer and pub owner, and the football clubs Charlton Athletic and Preston North End. Also AIM listed is LiDCO Group plc, the heart monitoring equipment developer that we met in Real World 6.4 in the context of the cash flow statement.

Short-term sources of external finance

Short term, in this context, is usually taken to mean up to one year. Figure 15.2 revealed that the major sources of short-term external finance were:

- bank overdrafts
- debt factoring
- invoice discounting.

These are discussed below.

Bank overdraft

→ A **bank overdraft** enables a business to maintain a negative balance on its bank account. It represents a very flexible form of borrowing as the size of the overdraft can (subject to bank approval) be increased or decreased more or less instantaneously. An overdraft is relatively inexpensive to arrange, and interest rates are often very competitive, though often higher than those for a term loan. As with all loans, the rate of interest charged on an overdraft will vary according to how creditworthy the customer is perceived to be by the bank. An overdraft is fairly easy to arrange – sometimes it can be agreed by a telephone call to the bank. In view of these advantages, it is not surprising that an overdraft is an extremely popular form of short-term finance.

Banks prefer to grant overdrafts that are self-liquidating, that is, the funds applied will result in cash inflows that will extinguish the overdraft balance. The banks may ask for a cash budget (projected cash flow statement) from the business to see when the overdraft will be repaid and how much finance is required. The bank may also require some form of security on amounts advanced. One potential drawback with this form of finance is that the overdraft is repayable on demand. This may pose problems for a business that is illiquid. However, many businesses operate for many years using an overdraft, simply because the bank remains confident of their ability to repay and the arrangement suits the businesses. Thus the bank overdraft, though in theory regarded as short term, often becomes a long-term source of finance.

Debt factoring

→ **Debt factoring** is a service offered by a financial institution (known as a *factor*). Many of the large factors are subsidiaries of commercial banks. Debt factoring involves the factor taking over the business's debt collection. In addition to operating normal credit control procedures, a factor may offer to undertake credit investigations and to provide protection for approved credit sales. The factor is usually prepared to make an advance to the business of a maximum of 80 per cent of approved trade receivables. The charge made for the factoring service is based on total sales revenue, and is often 2 to 3 per cent of sales revenue. Any advances made to the business by the factor will attract a rate of interest similar to the rate charged on bank overdrafts.

Debt factoring is, in effect, outsourcing the trade receivables control to a specialist subcontractor. Many businesses find a factoring arrangement very convenient. It can result in savings in credit management and create more certainty with the cash flows. It can also release the time of key personnel for more profitable activities. This may be extremely important for smaller businesses that rely on the talent and skills of a few key individuals. However, there is a possibility that some will see a factoring arrangement as an indication that the business is experiencing financial difficulties. This may have an adverse effect on the confidence of customers, suppliers and staff. For this reason, some businesses try to conceal the factoring arrangement by collecting debts on behalf of the factor. When considering a factoring agreement, the costs and likely benefits arising must be identified and carefully weighed.

Figure 15.8 shows the factoring process diagrammatically.

Figure 15.8 **The factoring process**

There are three main parties to the factoring agreement. The client business will sell goods or services on credit and the factor will take responsibility for invoicing the customer and collecting the amount owing. The factor will then pay the client business the invoice amount, less fees and interest, in two stages. The first stage typically represents 80 per cent of the invoice value and will be paid immediately after the goods or service have been delivered to the customer. The second stage will represent the balance outstanding and will usually be paid when the customer has paid the factor the amount owing.

Invoice discounting

Invoice discounting involves a factor or other financial institution providing a loan based on a proportion of the face value of a business's credit sales outstanding. The amount advanced is usually 75 to 80 per cent of the value of the approved sales invoices outstanding. The business must agree to repay the advance within a relatively short period, perhaps 60 or 90 days. The responsibility for collecting the trade receivables outstanding remains with the business, and repayment of the advance is not dependent on the trade receivables being collected. Invoice discounting will not result in such a close relationship developing between the business and the financial institution as results with factoring. It may be a short-term arrangement, whereas debt factoring usually involves a longer-term relationship.

There are three main reasons for the relative popularity of invoice discounting:

● It is a confidential form of financing that the business's customers will know nothing about.
● The service charge for invoice discounting is generally only 0.2 to 0.3 per cent of sales revenue, compared with 2.0 to 3.0 per cent for factoring.
● Many businesses are unwilling to relinquish control of their customers' records. Customers are an important resource of the business, and many wish to retain control over all aspects of their relationship with their customers.

Real World 15.21 shows the relative importance of invoice discounting and factoring.

Real World 15.21

The popularity of invoice discounting and factoring

| Figure 15.9 | Client sales: domestic invoice discounting and factoring, 2000 to 2005 |

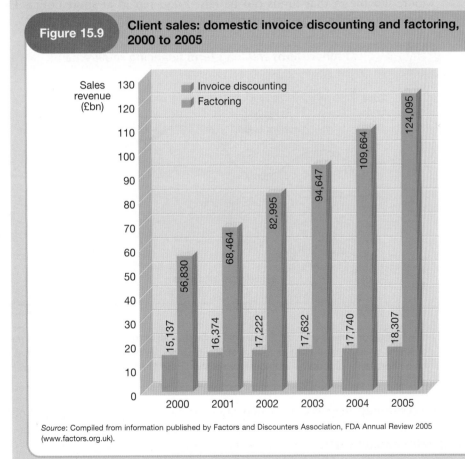

Source: Compiled from information published by Factors and Discounters Association, FDA Annual Review 2005 (www.factors.org.uk).

In recent years, client sales for invoice discounting has risen much more sharply than client sales from factoring. During 2005, for example, client sales for factoring grew by 3 per cent whereas invoice discounting grew by 13 per cent. Client sales for invoice discounting in 2005 were nearly seven times the client sales for factoring.

→ Factoring and invoice discounting are forms of **asset-based financing**, as the asset of trade receivables is in effect used as security for the cash advances received by the business.

Long-term versus short-term borrowing

Having decided that some form of borrowing is required to finance the business, managers must then decide whether it should be long term or short term in form. There are many issues that should be taken into account when making this decision. These include the following:

● *Matching.* The business may attempt to match the type of borrowing with the nature of the assets held. Thus, long-term borrowing might finance assets that form part of the permanent operating base of the business, including non-current assets and a certain level of current assets. This leaves assets held for a short period, such as current assets held to meet seasonal increases in demand (for example, inventories), to be financed by short-term borrowing, because short-term borrowing tends to be more flexible in that funds can be raised and repaid at short notice. Figure 15.10 shows this funding division graphically.

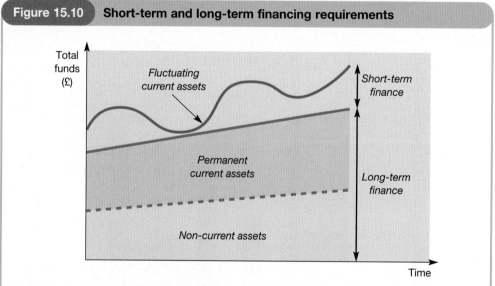

Figure 15.10 **Short-term and long-term financing requirements**

The broad consensus on financing seems to be that all of the permanent financial needs of the business should come from long-term sources. Only that part of current assets that fluctuates on a short-term, probably a seasonal, basis should be financed from short-term sources.

A business may wish to match the asset life exactly with the period of the related loan; however, this may not be possible because of the difficulty of predicting the life of many assets.

● *Flexibility.* Short-term borrowing may be a useful means of postponing a commitment to taking on a long-term loan. This may be seen as desirable if interest rates are high and it is forecast that they will fall in the future. Short-term borrowing does not usually incur penalties if there is early repayment of the amount outstanding, whereas some form of financial penalty may arise if long-term borrowing is repaid early.

- *Refunding risk.* Short-term borrowing has to be renewed more frequently than long-term borrowing. This may create problems for the business if it is already in financial difficulties or if there is a shortage of funds available for lending.
- *Interest rates.* Interest payable on long-term borrowing is often higher than for short-term borrowing, as lenders require a higher return where their funds are locked up for a long period. This fact may make short-term borrowing a more attractive source of finance for a business. However, there may be other costs associated with borrowing (arrangement fees, for example) to be taken into account. The more frequently borrowings must be renewed, the higher these costs will be.

Activity (15.15)

Some businesses may take up a less cautious financing position than that shown in Figure 15.10, and others may take up a more cautious one. How would the diagram differ under each of these options?

A less cautious position would mean relying on short-term finance to help fund part of the permanent capital base. A more cautious position would mean relying on long-term finance to help finance the fluctuating assets of the business.

Providing long-term finance for the small business

Although the Stock Exchange provides an important source of long-term finance for large businesses, it is not really suitable for small businesses. The aggregate market value of shares that are to be listed on the Stock Exchange must be at least £700,000 and, in practice, the amounts are much higher because of the high costs of listing. Thus, small businesses must look elsewhere for help in raising long-term finance. The more important sources of finance that are available to small businesses are **private equity** (venture capital and business angels) and government assistance. We shall now consider these.

Venture capital

Venture capital is long-term capital provided to small and medium-sized businesses wishing to grow but which do not have ready access to stock markets because of the prohibitively large costs of obtaining a listing. The businesses of interest to the venture capitalist will have higher levels of risk than would normally be acceptable to traditional providers of finance, such as the major clearing banks. The attraction for the venture capitalist of investing in higher-risk businesses is the prospect of higher returns.

Many small businesses are designed to provide the owners with a particular lifestyle and with job satisfaction. These kinds of businesses are not of interest to venture capitalists, as they are unlikely to provide the desired financial returns. Instead, venture capitalists look for businesses where the owners are seeking significant sales revenue and profit growth and need some outside help in order to achieve this.

The risks associated with the business can vary in practice. They are often due to the nature of the products or the fact that it is a new business that either lacks a trading record or has new management or both of these.

Venture capitalists provide long-term capital in the form of share and loan finance for different situations, including:

- *Start-up capital*. This is available to businesses that are not fully developed. They may need finance to help refine the business concept or to engage in product development or initial marketing. They have not yet reached the stage where they are trading.
- *Early-stage capital*. This is available for businesses that are ready to start trading.
- *Expansion capital*. This is aimed at providing additional funding for existing, growing businesses.
- *Buy-out or buy-in capital*. This is used to fund the acquisition of a business either by the existing management team ('buy-out') or by a new management team ('buy-in'). Management buy-outs (MBOs) and buy-ins (MBIs) often occur where a large business wishes to divest itself of one of its operating units or where a family business wishes to sell out because of succession problems.

The venture capitalist will often make a substantial investment in the business, and this will often take the form of ordinary shares. However, some of the funding may be in the form of preference shares or loan capital. To keep an eye on the sum invested, the venture capitalist will usually require a representative on the board of directors as a condition of the investment. The venture capitalist may not be looking for a quick return, and may well be prepared to invest in a business for five years or more. The return may take the form of a capital gain on the realisation of the investment (typically selling the shares).

Though venture capital is extremely important for some small businesses, the vast majority of small businesses obtain their finance from other sources. **Real World 15.22** shows the main sources of finance for small businesses in the UK.

Real World 15.22

Small business funding

Bank finance, such as overdrafts and loans, is the main source of external finance as the pie chart in Figure 15.11 shows.

Figure 15.11   **Financing small businesses, 2000 to 2002**

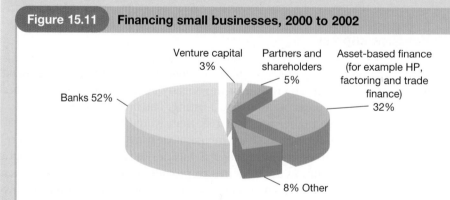

Venture capital, though very important to some small businesses, represents a very small part of the total finance raised. Bank finance remains the most important source of external finance, followed by asset-based finance, such as hire purchase, factoring and trade finance.

Source: Finance for Small Firms – An eleventh report, Bank of England, April 2004.

Business angels

→ **Business angels** are often wealthy individuals who have been successful in business. They are usually willing to invest, through a shareholding, between £10,000 and £100,000 in a start-up business or in a business that is at an early stage of development. They will often invest for a period of between three and five years, and sometimes even longer. They normally have a minority stake in the business, and although they do not usually become involved in its day-to-day management, they tend to take an interest in the way that the business is managed more generally. Business angels fill an important gap in the market as the size and the nature of the investment that they find appealing will not often appeal to venture capitalists.

Business angels may be attractive to small businesses for a number of reasons, including:

- They may be able to make investment decisions quickly, particularly if they are familiar with the industry in which the new business operates.
- They may also be able to offer a wealth of business experience to budding tycoons.
- Some business angels are prepared to accept lower financial returns than those required from venture capitalists in order to have the opportunity to become involved in a new and interesting project.

Business angels offer an informal source of share finance and it is not always easy for owners of small businesses to identify a suitable angel. However, numerous business angel networks have now developed to help owners of small businesses find their 'perfect partner'.

Government assistance

One of the most effective ways in which the UK government assists small businesses is through the Small Firms Loan Guarantee Scheme. This scheme aims to help small businesses that have viable business plans but lack the security to obtain a loan. The scheme guarantees loans made over a two- to ten-year period to small businesses from lending institutions for sums of £5,000 to £100,000 (increased to £250,000 for businesses that have been trading for at least two years). The government will guarantee up to 70 per cent (increased to 85 per cent for businesses that have been trading for at least two years) of the amount borrowed.

In addition to other forms of financial assistance, such as government grants and tax incentives for investors to buy shares in small businesses, the government also helps by providing information concerning the sources of finance available.

Self-assessment question 15.1

Helsim Ltd is a wholesaler and distributor of electrical components. The most recent draft financial statements of the business revealed the following:

Income statement for the year

	£m	£m
Sales revenue		14.2
Opening inventories	3.2	
Purchases	8.4	
	11.6	
Closing inventories	(3.8)	(7.8)
Gross profit		6.4
Administration expenses		(3.0)
Distribution expenses		(2.1)
Operating profit		1.3
Finance costs		(0.8)
Profit before taxation		0.5
Taxation		(0.2)
Profit for the period		0.3

Balance sheet as at the end of the year

	£m
Non-current assets	
Property, plant and equipment	
Land and buildings	3.8
Equipment	0.9
Motor vehicles	0.5
	5.2
Current assets	
Inventories	3.8
Trade receivables	3.6
Cash at bank	0.1
	7.5
Total assets	12.7
Equity	
Share capital	2.0
Retained earnings	1.8
	3.8
Non-current liabilities	
Loan notes (secured on freehold land)	3.5
Current liabilities	
Trade payables	1.8
Short-term borrowings	3.6
	5.4
Total equity and liabilities	12.7

Notes:

1 Land and buildings are shown at their current market value. Equipment and motor vehicles are shown at their written-down values (that is, cost less accumulated depreciation).

2 No dividends have been paid to ordinary shareholders for the past three years.

In recent months, trade payables have been pressing for payment. The managing director has therefore decided to reduce the level of trade payables to an average of 40 days outstanding. To achieve this, he has decided to approach the bank with a view to increasing the overdraft (the short-term borrowings comprise only a bank overdraft). The business is currently paying 10 per cent a year interest on the overdraft.

Required:

(a) Comment on the liquidity position of the business.

(b) Calculate the amount of finance required to reduce trade payables, from the level shown on the balance sheet, to an average of 40 days outstanding.

(c) State, with reasons, how you consider the bank would react to the proposal to grant an additional overdraft facility.

(d) Identify four sources of finance (internal or external, but excluding a bank overdraft) that may be suitable to finance the reduction in trade payables, and state, with reasons, which of these you consider the most appropriate.

The answer to this question can be found at the back of the book on pages 707–8.

Summary

The main points in this chapter may be summarised as follows.

Sources of finance

- Internal sources of finance do not require the agreement of anyone beyond the directors and managers of the business, whereas external sources of finance do require the compliance of 'outsiders'.

- Long-term sources of finance are not due for repayment within one year whereas short-term sources are due for repayment within one year.

- The higher the level of risk associated with investing in a particular form of finance, the higher the level of return that will be expected by investors.

Internal sources of finance

- The major internal source of long-term finance is retained profits.

- The main short-term sources of internal finance are tighter credit control of receivables, reducing inventories levels and delaying payments to trade payables.

External sources of finance

- The main external, *long-term* sources of finance are ordinary shares, preference shares, loans, leases and hire purchase agreements.

- Ordinary shares are normally considered to be the most risky form of investment and, therefore, provide the highest expected returns. Loan capital is normally the least risky and provides the lowest expected returns to investors.

- Leases and hire purchase agreements allow a business to obtain immediate possession of an asset without having to pay the cost of acquiring the asset.

- The level of gearing associated with a business is often an important factor in assessing the level of risk and returns to ordinary shareholders.

- The main sources of external *short-term* finance are bank overdrafts, debt factoring and invoice discounting.

- When considering the choice between long-term and short-term sources of borrowing, factors such as matching the type of borrowing with the nature of the assets held, the need for flexibility, refunding risk and interest rates should be taken into account.

Share issues

- Share issues that involve the payment of cash by investors can take the form of a rights issue, public issue, offer for sale or a private placing.

- A rights issue is made to existing shareholders. Most share issues are of this type as the law requires that shares that are to be issued for cash must first be offered to existing shareholders.

- A public issue involves a direct issue to the public and an offer for sale involves an indirect issue to the public.

- A private placing is an issue of shares to selected investors.

The Stock Exchange

- The Stock Exchange is an important primary and secondary market in capital for large businesses. However, obtaining a Stock Exchange listing can have certain drawbacks for a business.

The Alternative Investment Market (AIM)

- AIM is another important primary and secondary market managed by the London Stock Exchange for smaller, growing businesses. It tends to be a cheaper way for a business to become listed.

Small businesses

- Venture capital is long-term capital for small or medium-sized businesses that are not listed on the Stock Exchange. These businesses often have higher levels of risk but provide the venture capitalist with the prospect of higher levels of return.

- Business angels are wealthy individuals who are willing to invest in businesses at an early stage of development.

- The government assists small businesses through guaranteeing loans and by providing grants and tax incentives.

MyAccountingLab **Now check your progress in your personal Study Plan**

Key terms

term loan p. 574	**offer for sale** p. 589
loan notes p. 574	**public issue** p. 589
loan stock p. 574	**tender issue** p. 589
eurobond p. 574	**private placing** p. 590
deep discount bond p. 576	**Stock Exchange** p. 590
convertible loan notes p. 576	**Alternative Investment Market**
warrants p. 577	**(AIM)** p. 596
financial derivatives p. 578	**bank overdraft** p. 597
mortgage p. 578	**debt factoring** p. 597
loan covenant p. 578	**invoice discounting** p. 598
finance lease p. 580	**asset-based financing** p. 600
operating lease p. 580	**private equity** p. 601
sale and leaseback p. 582	**venture capital** p. 601
hire purchase p. 582	**business angel** p. 603
rights issue p. 586	

Further reading

If you would like to explore the topics covered in this chapter in more depth, we recommend the following books:

Business Finance: Theory and Practice, *McLaney E.,* 7th edn, Financial Times Prentice Hall, 2006, chapter 8.

Corporate Finance, *Brealey R., Myers S. and Allen F.,* 8th edn, McGraw-Hill, 2005, chapters 14, 25 and 26.

Corporate Finance and Investment, *Pike R. and Neale B.,* 5th edn, Prentice Hall International, 2005, chapters 15 and 16.

Corporate Financial Management, *Arnold G.,* 3rd edn, Financial Times Prentice Hall, 2005, chapters 9 to 12.

Review questions

Answers to these questions can be found at the back of the book on pages 785–6.

15.1 What are the benefits to a business of issuing share warrants?

15.2 Why might a business that has a Stock Exchange listing revert to being unlisted?

15.3 Distinguish between an offer for sale and a public issue of shares.

15.4 Distinguish between invoice discounting and factoring.

Exercises

Exercises 15.4 to 15.8 are more advanced than 15.1 to 15.3. Those with coloured numbers have answers at the back of the book, starting on page 758.

If you wish to try more exercises, visit the students' side of the Companion Website.

15.1 H. Brown (Portsmouth) Ltd produces a range of central heating systems for sale to builders' merchants. As a result of increasing demand for the business's products, the directors have decided to expand production. The cost of acquiring new plant and machinery and the increase in working capital requirements are planned to be financed by a mixture of long-term and short-term borrowing.

Required:
(a) Discuss the major factors that should be taken into account when deciding on the appropriate mix of long-term and short-term borrowing necessary to finance the expansion programme.
(b) Discuss the major factors that a lender should take into account when deciding whether to grant a long-term loan to the business.
(c) Identify three conditions that might be included in a long-term loan agreement, and state the purpose of each.

15.2 Devonian plc has the following equity as at 30 November Year 4:

	£m
Ordinary shares 25p fully paid	50.0
General reserve	22.5
Retained profit	25.5
	98.0

The business has no long-term borrowings.

In the year to 30 November Year 4, the operating profit (net profit before interest and taxation) was £40m and it is expected that this will increase by 25 per cent during the forthcoming year. The business is listed on the London Stock Exchange and the share price as at 30 November Year 4 was £2.10.

The business wishes to raise £72m in order to re-equip one of its factories and is considering two possible financing options. The first option is to make a 1-for-5 rights issue at a discount price of £1.80 per share. The second option is to take out a long-term loan at an interest rate of

10 per cent a year. If the first option is taken, it is expected that the price/earnings (P/E) ratio will remain the same for the forthcoming year. If the second option is taken, it is estimated that the P/E ratio will fall by 10 per cent by the end of the forthcoming year.

Assume a tax rate of 30 per cent.

Required:

(a) Assuming a rights issue of shares is made, calculate:
  (i) the theoretical ex-rights price of an ordinary share in Devonian plc; and
  (ii) the value of the rights for each original ordinary share.
(b) Calculate the price of an ordinary share in Devonian plc in one year's time assuming:
  (i) a rights issue is made; and
  (ii) a loan issue is made.
  Comment on your findings.
(c) Explain why rights issues are usually made at a discount.
(d) From the business's viewpoint, how critical is the pricing of a rights issue likely to be?

15.3 Brocmar plc has 10m ordinary £0.50 shares in issue. The market price of the shares is £1.80. The board of the business wishes to finance a major project at a cost of £2.88m. Forecasts suggest that the implementation of the project will add £0.4m to after-tax earnings available to ordinary shareholders in the coming year. After-tax earnings for the year just completed were £2m, but this figure is expected to decline to £1.8m in the coming year if the project proposed is not undertaken. A rights issue at a 20 per cent discount on the existing market price is proposed. Issue expenses can be ignored.

Required:

(a) To assist the board in coming to a final decision, you are required to present information in the following format:
  ● Project not undertaken
    (i) earnings per share for the coming year.
  ● Project undertaken and financed by a rights issue
    (ii) rights issue price per share
    (iii) number of shares to be issued
    (iv) earnings per share for the coming year
    (v) the theoretical ex-rights price per share.
  All workings should be shown separately.
(b) What information, other than that provided in the question, is needed before the board can make the investment decision?

15.4 Raphael Ltd is a small engineering business that has annual sales revenue of £2.4m, all of which is on credit. In recent years, the business has experienced credit control problems. The average collection period for trade receivables has risen to 50 days even though the stated policy of the business is for payment to be made within 30 days. In addition, 1.5 per cent of sales are written off as bad debts each year.

The business has recently been in talks with a factor, which is prepared to make an advance to the business equivalent to 80 per cent of trade receivables, based on the assumption that customers will, in future, adhere to a 30-day payment period. The interest rate for the advance will be 11 per cent a year. The trade receivables are currently financed through a bank overdraft, which has an interest rate of 12 per cent a year. The factor will take over the credit control procedures of the business and this will result in a saving to the business of £18,000 a year. However, the factor will make a charge of 2 per cent of sales revenue for this service. The use of the factoring service is expected to eliminate the bad debts incurred by the business.

Required:

Calculate the net cost of the factor agreement to the business and state whether the business should take advantage of the opportunity to factor its trade receivables. (*Hint*: To answer this question, compare the cost of existing trade credit policies (cost of investment in trade receivables and cost of bad debts) with the cost of using a factor (interest and other charges less the credit control savings.))

15.5 Russell Ltd installs and services heating and ventilation systems for commercial premises. The business's most recent balance sheet and income statement are as follows:

Balance sheet

	£000	£000
Non-current assets		
Property, plant and equipment		
Machinery and equipment at cost	883.6	
Less Accumulated depreciation	328.4	555.2
Motor vehicles at cost	268.8	
Less Accumulated depreciation	82.2	186.6
		741.8
Current assets		
Inventories at cost		293.2
Trade receivables		510.3
		803.5
Total assets		1,545.3
Equity		
£1 ordinary shares		400.0
General reserve		50.2
Retained profit		382.2
		832.4
Non-current liabilities		
Borrowings – 12% loan notes (repayable Year 10/11)		250.0
Current liabilities		
Trade payables		199.7
Taxation		128.0
Borrowings – Bank overdraft		135.2
		462.9
Total equity and liabilities		1,545.3

Income statement for the year

	£000
Sales revenue	5,207.8
Operating profit	542.0
Interest payable	(30.0)
Profit before taxation	512.0
Taxation (25%)	(128.0)
Profit for the year	384.0

Note:
Dividend paid during the year   153.6

The business wishes to invest in more machinery and equipment in order to cope with an upsurge in demand for its services. An additional operating profit of £120,000 a year is expected if an investment of £600,000 is made in plant and machinery.

The directors are considering an offer from venture capitalists to finance the expansion programme. The finance will be made available immediately through either:

(i)   an issue of £1 ordinary shares at a premium on par of £3 a share; or

(ii) an issue of £600,000 10 per cent loan notes at par.

The directors wish to maintain the same dividend payout ratio in future years as in past years whichever method of finance is chosen.

Required:

(a) For each of the financing schemes:
   (i)   prepare a projected income statement for next year;
   (ii) calculate the projected earnings per share for next year;
   (iii) calculate the projected level of gearing as at the end of next year.

(b) Briefly assess both of the financing schemes under consideration from the viewpoint of the existing shareholders.

15.6 Carpets Direct plc wishes to increase the number of its retail outlets in the south of England. The board of directors has decided to finance this expansion programme by raising the funds from existing shareholders through a 1-for-4 rights issue. The most recent income statement of the business is as follows:

Income statement for the year ended 30 April

	£m
Sales revenue	164.5
Operating profit	12.6
Interest	(6.2)
Profit before taxation	6.4
Taxation	(1.9)
Profit for the year	4.5

A £2m ordinary dividend had been paid in respect of the year.

The share capital consists of 120m ordinary shares with a par value of £0.50 a share. These are currently being traded on the Stock Exchange at a price/earnings ratio of 22 times and the board of directors has decided to issue the new shares at a discount of 20 per cent on the current market value.

Required:

(a) Calculate the theoretical ex-rights price of an ordinary share in Carpets Direct plc.

(b) Calculate the price at which the rights in Carpet Direct plc are likely to be traded.

(c) Identify and evaluate, at the time of the rights issue, each of the options arising from the rights issue to an investor who holds 4,000 ordinary shares before the rights announcement.

(*Hint*: To answer part (a), first calculate the earnings per share and then use this and the P/E ratio to calculate the marker value per share.)

15.7 Gainsborough Fashions Ltd operates a small chain of fashion shops in North Wales. In recent months the business has been under pressure from its suppliers to reduce the average credit period taken from three months to one month. As a result, the directors have approached the bank to ask for an increase in the existing overdraft for one year to be able to comply with the suppliers' demands. The most recent financial statements of the business are as follows:

Balance sheet as at 31 May

	£	£
Non-current assets		
Property, plant and equipment		
Fixtures and fittings at cost	90,000	
Less Accumulated depreciation	23,000	67,000
Motor vehicles at cost	34,000	
Less Accumulated depreciation	27,000	7,000
		74,000
Current assets		
Inventories at cost		198,000
Trade receivables		3,000
		201,000
Total assets		275,000
Equity		
£1 ordinary shares		20,000
General reserve		4,000
Retained profit		17,000
		41,000
Non-current liabilities		
Borrowings – Loan notes repayable in just over one year's time		40,000
Current liabilities		
Trade payables		162,000
Accrued expenses		10,000
Borrowings – Bank overdraft		17,000
Taxation		5,000
		194,000
Total equity and liabilities		275,000

Abbreviated income statement for the year ended 31 May

	£
Sales revenue	740,000
Operating profit	38,000
Interest charges	(5,000)
Profit before taxation	33,000
Taxation	(10,000)
Profit for the year	23,000

A dividend of £23,000 was paid for the year.

Notes:
1 The loan notes are secured by personal guarantees from the directors.
2 The current overdraft bears an interest rate of 12 per cent a year.

Required:
(a) Identify and discuss the major factors that a bank would take into account before deciding whether to grant an increase in the overdraft of a business.
(b) State whether, in your opinion, the bank should grant the required increase in the overdraft for Gainsborough Fashions Ltd. You should provide reasoned arguments and supporting calculations where necessary.

15.8 Telford Engineers plc, a medium-sized Midlands manufacturer of automobile components, has decided to modernise its factory by introducing a number of robots. These will cost £20m and will reduce operating costs by £6m a year for their estimated useful life of 10 years starting next year (Year 10). To finance this scheme, the business can raise £20m by issuing either:

1 20 million ordinary shares at 100p; or
2 loan notes at 7 per cent interest a year with capital repayments of £3m a year commencing at the end of Year 11.

Extracts from Telford Engineers' financial statements appear below:

Summary of balance sheet at 31 December

	Year 6 £m	Year 7 £m	Year 8 £m	Year 9 £m
Non-current assets	48	51	65	64
Current assets	55	67	57	55
	103	118	122	119
Equity	48	61	61	63
Non-current liabilities	30	30	30	30
Current liabilities				
Trade payables	20	27	25	18
Short-term borrowings	5	–	6	8
	25	27	31	26
	103	118	122	119
Number of issued 25p shares	80m	80m	80m	80m
Share price	150p	200p	100p	145p

Note that the short-term borrowings consisted entirely of bank overdrafts.

Summary of income statements for years ended 31 December

	Year 6 £m	Year 7 £m	Year 8 £m	Year 9 £m
Sales revenue	152	170	110	145
Operating profit	28	40	7	15
Interest payable	(4)	(3)	(4)	(5)
Profit before taxation	24	37	3	10
Taxation	(12)	(16)	(0)	(4)
Profit for the period	12	21	3	6
Dividends paid during each year	6	8	3	4

For your answer you should assume that the tax rate for Year 10 is 30 per cent, that sales revenue and operating profit will be unchanged except for the £6m cost saving arising from the introduction of the robots, and that Telford Engineers will pay the same dividend per share in Year 10 as in Year 9.

Required:

(a) Prepare, for each financing arrangement, Telford Engineers' projected income statement for the year ending 31 December Year 10 and a statement of its share capital, reserves and loans on that date.

(b) Calculate Telford's projected earnings per share for Year 10 for both schemes.

(c) Which scheme would you advise the business to adopt? You should give your reasons and state what additional information you would require.

Managing working capital

Introduction

In this chapter we shall consider the factors that must be taken into account when managing the working capital of a business. Each element of working capital will be identified and the major issues surrounding them will be discussed. Working capital represents a significant investment for many businesses and so its proper management and control can be vital. We saw in Chapter 14 that an investment in working capital is typically an important aspect of new investment proposals. Some useful tools in the management of working capital are financial ratios, which were considered in Chapter 7, and budgets, which we examined in Chapter 12.

Learning outcomes

When you have completed this chapter, you should be able to:

● Identify the main elements of working capital.

● Discuss the purpose of working capital and the nature of the working capital cycle.

● Explain the importance of establishing policies for the control of working capital.

● Explain the factors that have to be taken into account when managing each element of working capital.

MyAccountingLab *Remember to create your own personalised Study Plan*

The nature and purpose of working capital

→ **Working capital** is usually defined as current assets less current liabilities. The major elements of current assets are:

- inventories
- trade receivables
- cash (in hand and at bank).

The major elements of current liabilities are:

- trade payables
- bank overdrafts.

The size and composition of working capital can vary between industries. For some types of business, the investment in working capital can be substantial. For example, a manufacturing business will typically invest heavily in raw material, work in progress and finished goods, and will normally sell its goods on credit, giving rise to trade receivables. A retailer, on the other hand, will hold only one form of inventories (finished goods), and will usually sell goods for cash. Many service businesses hold no inventories. Most businesses buy goods and/or services on credit, giving rise to trade payables. Few, if any, businesses operate without a cash balance, though in some cases it is a negative one (a bank overdraft).

Working capital represents a net investment in short-term assets. These assets are continually flowing into and out of the business, and are essential for day-to-day operations. The various elements of working capital are interrelated, and can be seen as part of a short-term cycle. For a manufacturing business, the working capital cycle can be depicted as shown in Figure 16.1.

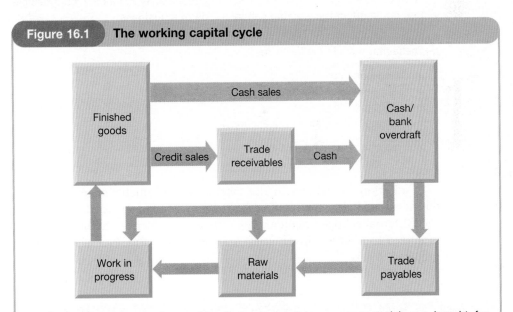

Figure 16.1   The working capital cycle

Cash is used to pay trade payables for raw materials, or raw materials are bought for immediate cash settlement. Cash is also spent on labour and other items that turn raw materials into work in progress and, finally, into finished goods. The finished goods are sold to customers either for cash or on credit. In the case of credit customers, there will be a delay before the cash is received from the sales. Receipt of cash completes the cycle.

For a retailer the situation would be as in Figure 16.1 except that there would be no work in progress and the raw materials and the finished inventories would be the same. For a purely service business, the working capital cycle would also be similar to that depicted in Figure 16.1 except that there would be no inventories of raw materials and finished goods. There may well be work in progress, however, since many services, for example a case handled by a firm of solicitors, will take some time to complete and costs will build up before the client is billed for them.

Managing working capital

The management of working capital is an essential part of the business's short-term planning process. It is necessary for management to decide how much of each element should be held. As we shall see later in this chapter, there are costs associated with holding either too much or too little of each element. Management must be aware of these costs, which include opportunity costs, in order to manage effectively. Hence, the potential benefits must be weighed against the likely costs in an attempt to achieve the optimum investment.

The working capital needs of a particular business are likely to change over time as a result of changes in the business environment. This means that working capital decisions are constantly being made. Managers must try to identify changes in an attempt to ensure that the level of investment in working capital is appropriate.

Activity 16.1

What kinds of changes in the commercial environment might lead to a decision to change the level of investment in working capital? Try to identify four possible changes that could affect the working capital needs of a business.

These may include the following:

● changes in interest rates
● changes in market demand
● changes in the seasons
● changes in the state of the economy.

You may have thought of others.

In addition to changes in the external environment, changes arising within the business could alter the required level of investment in working capital. Examples of such internal changes include using different production methods (resulting, perhaps, in a need to hold less inventories) and changes in the level of risk that managers are prepared to take.

The scale of working capital

We might imagine that, compared with the scale of investment in non-current assets by the typical business, the amounts involved with working capital are pretty trivial. This would be unrealistic – the scale of the working capital elements for most businesses is vast.

Real World 16.1 gives some impression of the working capital involvement for five UK businesses that are either very well known by name, or whose products are everyday commodities for most of us. These businesses were randomly selected, except that each one is high profile and from a different industry. For each business the major balance sheet items are expressed as a percentage of the total investment by the providers of long-term finance (equity and non-current liabilities).

Real World 16.1

A summary of the balance sheets of five UK businesses

Business:	Next plc	British Airways plc	Rolls-Royce plc	Tesco plc	Severn Trent plc
Balance sheet date:	28.1.06	31.3.06	31.12.05	25.2.06	31.3.06
Non-current (fixed) assets	78	97	62	124	114
Current assets					
Inventories	45	1	22	10	–
Trade receivables	72	8	34	6	5
Other receivables	–	5	8	–	–
Cash and near cash	10	28	29	9	–
	127	42	93	25	5
Total assets	205	139	155	149	119
Equity and non-current liabilities	100	100	100	100	100
Current liabilities					
Trade payables	79	32	45	34	–
Taxation	8	1	3	3	1
Other short-term liabilities	–	–	2	–	7
Overdrafts and short-term loans	18	6	5	12	11
	105	39	55	49	19
Total equity and liabilities	205	139	155	149	119

The non-current assets, current assets and current liabilities are expressed as a percentage of the total net long-term investment (equity plus non-current liabilities) of the business concerned. Next is a major retail and home shopping business. British Airways (BA) is a major airline. Rolls-Royce makes aero and other engines. Tesco is one of the major UK supermarkets. Severn Trent is a major supplier of water, sewerage services and waste management, mainly in the UK.

Source: Table constructed from information appearing in the annual reports of the five businesses concerned.

The totals for current assets are pretty large when compared with the total long-term investment. This is particularly true of Next and Rolls-Royce. The amounts vary considerably from one type of business to the next. When we look at the nature of working capital held we can see that Next, Rolls-Royce and Tesco, which produce and/or sell goods, are the only ones that hold significant amounts of inventories. The other two businesses are service providers and so inventories are not a significant item. We can see from the table that Tesco does not sell a lot on credit and very few of BA's and Severn Trent's sales are on credit as these businesses have little or nothing invested in trade receivables. It is interesting to note that Tesco's trade payables are much higher than its inventories. Since most of these payables will be suppliers of inventories, it means that the business is able, on average, to have the cash from a particular sale in the bank before it needs to pay for the goods concerned.

These types of variation in the amounts and types of working capital elements are typical of other businesses.

In the sections that follow, we shall consider each element of working capital separately and how they might be properly managed. It seems from the evidence presented in **Real World 16.2** that there is much scope for improvement in working capital management among UK businesses.

Real World 16.2

Capital not working hard enough!

According to a survey of 285 of the UK's largest businesses, conducted in 2005 by REL Consultancy Group, working capital is not as well managed as it could be. It is estimated that larger UK businesses have £62bn tied up in working capital that could be released with better management of the inventories, trade receivables, trade payables and cash. Were the businesses able to manage their working capital more efficiently, REL estimates that they would increase their return on capital employed by a staggering 12 per cent on average. This, however, represented an improvement on the results shown by a similar survey undertaken by REL in 2004.

It appears that businesses in other European countries tend to be even less efficient in their management of working capital than those in the UK.

Source: Information taken from 'Poor cash management hits profits', Jonathan Moules, *Financial Times*, 29 August 2005. The survey referred to is REL Consultancy Group's *2005 Annual Working Capital Survey Europe*.

Managing inventories

A business may hold inventories for various reasons, the most common of which is to meet the immediate day-to-day requirements of customers and production. However, a business may hold more than is necessary for this purpose if it is believed that future supplies may be interrupted or scarce. Similarly, if the business believes that the cost of inventories will rise in the future, it may decide to stockpile.

For some types of business the inventories held may represent a substantial proportion of the total assets held. For example, a car dealership that rents its premises may have nearly all of its total assets in the form of inventories. Inventories levels of manufacturers tend to be higher than in many other types of business as it is necessary to hold three kinds of inventories: raw materials, work in progress and finished goods. Each form of inventories represents a particular stage in the production cycle. For some types of business, the level of inventories held may vary substantially over the year owing to the seasonal nature of the industry. An example of such a business is a greetings card manufacturer. For other businesses, inventories levels may remain fairly stable throughout the year.

Where a business holds inventories simply to meet the day-to-day requirements of its customers and for production, it will normally seek to minimise the amount of inventories held. This is because there are significant costs associated with holding inventories. These include:

● storage and handling costs
● financing costs
● the costs of pilferage and obsolescence
● the cost of opportunities forgone in tying up funds in this form of asset.

However, a business must also recognise that, if the level of inventories held is too low, there will also be associated costs.

Activity 16.2

What costs might a business incur as a result of holding too low a level of inventories? Try to jot down at least three types of cost.

In answering this activity you may have thought of the following costs:

● loss of sales, from being unable to provide the goods required immediately;
● loss of customer goodwill, for being unable to satisfy customer demand;
● high transport costs incurred to ensure that inventories are replenished quickly;
● lost production due to shortage of raw materials;
● inefficient production scheduling due to shortages of raw materials;
● purchasing inventories at a higher price than might otherwise have been possible in order to replenish inventories quickly.

Before we go on to deal with the various approaches that can be taken to managing inventories, **Real World 16.3** provides an example of how badly things can go wrong if inventories are not adequately controlled.

Real World 16.3

Pallets lost at Brambles

Brambles Industries plc (BI) is an Anglo-Australian industrial services business, formed in 2001 when the industrial services subsidiary of GKN plc, the UK engineering business, was merged with the Australian business Brambles Ltd.

BI uses 'pallets' on which it delivers its products to customers. These are returnable by customers so BI holds a 'pool' of pallets. Each pallet costs the business about £10. Unfortunately, BI lost 14 million pallets during the year ended in June 2002 as a result of poor control and this led to a significant decline in the business's profits and share price.

At BI's annual general meeting in Sydney, Australia, one of the shareholders was quoted as saying: 'Running a pallet pool is not rocket science. I can teach one of my employees about pallets in 20 minutes.'

Source: Information taken from an article appearing in the *Financial Times*, 27 November 2002.

To try to ensure that the inventories are properly managed, a number of procedures and techniques may be used. These are reviewed below.

Budgeting future demand

One of the best ways to ensure that there will be inventories available to meet future production and sales requirements is to make appropriate plans. The budgets should deal with each product that the business makes and/or sells. It is important that every attempt is made to ensure that plans are realistic, as they will determine future ordering and production levels. The budgets may be derived in various ways. They may be developed using statistical techniques such as time series analysis, or they may be based on the judgement of the sales and marketing staff. We considered inventories budgets and their link to production and sales budgets in Chapter 12.

Financial ratios

One ratio that can be used to help monitor inventories levels is the average inventories turnover period, which we examined in Chapter 7. As we should recall, this ratio is calculated as follows:

$$\text{Average inventories turnover period} = \frac{\text{Average inventories held}}{\text{Cost of sales}} \times 365$$

This will provide a picture of the average period for which inventories are held, and can be useful as a basis for comparison. It is possible to calculate the average inventories turnover period for individual product lines as well as for inventories as a whole.

Recording and reordering systems

The management of inventories in a business of any size requires a sound system of recording inventories movements. There must be proper procedures for recording inventories purchases and usages. Periodic inventories checks may be required to ensure that the amount of physical inventories held is consistent with what is indicated by the inventories records.

There should also be clear procedures for the reordering of inventories. Authorisation for both the purchase and the issue of inventories should be confined to a few senior staff. This should avoid problems of duplication and lack of co-ordination. To determine the point at which inventories should be reordered, information will be required concerning the **lead time** (that is, the time between the placing of an order and the receipt of the goods) and the likely level of demand.

Activity 16.3

An electrical retailer stocks a particular type of light switch. The annual demand for the light switch is 10,400 units, and the lead time for orders is four weeks. Demand for the light switch is steady throughout the year. At what quantity of the light switch should the business reorder, assuming that it is confident of the information given above?

The average weekly demand for the switch is 10,400/52 = 200 units. During the time between ordering new switches and receiving them, the quantity sold will be 4 × 200 units = 800 units. So the business should reorder no later than when the level held reaches 800 units, in order to avoid running out of inventories.

In most businesses, there will be some uncertainty surrounding the above factors and so a buffer or safety inventories level may be maintained in case problems occur. The amount of the buffer to be held is really a matter of judgement. This judgement will depend on:

- the degree of uncertainty concerning the above factors;
- the likely costs of running out of the item concerned;
- the cost of holding the buffer inventories.

The effect of holding a buffer will be to raise the inventories level (the reorder point) at which an order for new inventories is placed.

Activity 16.4

Assume the same facts as in Activity 16.3. However, we are also told that the business maintains buffer inventories of 300 units. At what level should the business reorder?

Reorder point = expected level of demand during the lead time plus the level of buffer inventories

= 800 + 300

= 1,100 units

Carrying buffer inventories will increase the cost of holding inventories; however, this must be weighed against the cost of running out of inventories, in terms of lost sales, production problems and so on.

Real World 16.4 provides an example of how small businesses can use technology in inventories reordering to help compete against their larger rivals.

Real World 16.4

Taking on the big boys

The use of technology in inventories recording and reordering may be of vital importance to the survival of small businesses that are being threatened by larger rivals. One such example is that of small independent bookshops. Technology can come to their rescue in two ways. First, electronic point-of-sale (EPOS) systems can record books as they are sold and can constantly update records of inventories held. Thus, books that need to be reordered can be quickly and easily identified. Second, the reordering process can be improved by using web-based technology, which allows books to be ordered in real time. Many large book wholesalers provide free web-based software to their customers for this purpose and try to deliver books ordered during the next working day. This means that a small bookseller, with limited shelf space, may keep one copy only of a particular book but maintain a range of books that competes with that of a large bookseller.

Source: Information taken from 'Small stores keep up with the big boys', *Financial Times*, 5 February 2003, FT.com.

Levels of control

Senior managers must make a commitment to the management of inventories. However, the cost of controlling inventories must be weighed against the potential benefits. It may be possible to have different levels of control according to the nature of the inventories held. The **ABC system of inventories control** is based on the idea of selective levels of control.

A business may find that it is possible to divide its inventories into three broad categories: A, B and C. Each category will be based on the value of inventories held, as is illustrated in Example 16.1.

Example 16.1

Alascan Products plc makes door handles and door fittings. It makes them in brass, in steel and in plastic. The business finds that brass fittings account for 10 per cent of the physical volume of the finished inventories that it holds, but these represent 65 per cent of its total value. This is treated as Category A inventories. There are sophisticated recording procedures, tight control is exerted over inventories movements and there is a high level of security where the brass inventories are stored. This is economic because the inventories represent a relatively small proportion of the total volume.

The business finds that steel fittings account for 30 per cent of the total volume of finished inventories and represent 25 per cent of its total value. This is treated as Category B inventories, with a lower level of recording and management control being applied.

The remaining 60 per cent of the volume of inventories is plastic fittings, which represent the least valuable items that account for only 10 per cent of the total value of finished inventories held. This is treated as Category C inventories, so the level of recording and management control would be lower still. Applying to these inventories, the level of control that is applied to Category A or even Category B inventories would be uneconomic.

Categorising inventories in this way seeks to direct management effort to the most important areas, and tries to ensure that the costs of controlling inventories are appropriate to its importance.

Figure 16.2 shows the nature of the ABC approach to inventories control.

Inventories' management models

Economic order quantity

It is possible to use decision models to help manage inventories. The **economic order quantity (EOQ)** model is concerned with answering the question 'How much inventories should be ordered?' In its simplest form, the EOQ model assumes that demand is constant, so that inventories will be depleted evenly over time, and replenished just at the point that it runs out. These assumptions would lead to a 'saw-tooth' pattern to represent inventories' movements, as shown in Figure 16.3.

The EOQ model recognises that the key costs associated with inventories management are the cost of holding the inventories and the cost of ordering them. The model

Figure 16.2 ABC method of analysing and controlling inventories

Category A contains inventories that, though relatively few in quantity, account for a large proportion of the total value. Category B inventories consists of those items that are less valuable but more numerous. Category C comprises those inventories items that are very numerous but relatively low in value. Different inventories' control rules would be applied to each category. For example, only Category A inventories would attract the more expensive and sophisticated controls.

Figure 16.3 Patterns of inventories movements over time

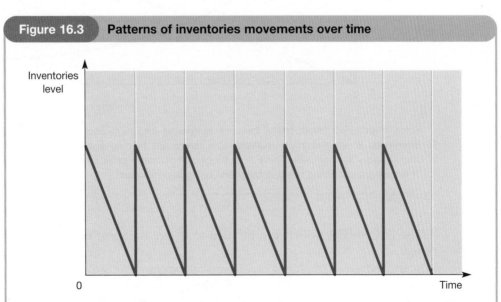

Here we assume that there is a constant rate of usage of the inventories item, and that inventories are reduced to zero just as new inventories arrive. At time 0 there is a full level of inventories. This is steadily used as time passes; and just as it falls to zero it is replaced. This pattern is then repeated.

can be used to calculate the optimum size of a purchase order by taking account of both of these cost elements. The cost of holding inventories can be substantial, and so management may try to minimise the average amount of inventories held. However, by reducing the level of inventories held, and therefore the holding costs, there will be a need to increase the number of orders during the period, and so ordering costs will rise.

Figure 16.4 shows how, as the level of inventories and the size of inventories orders increase, the annual costs of placing orders will decrease because fewer orders will be placed. However, the cost of holding inventories will increase, as there will be higher average inventories levels. The total costs curve, which is based on the sum of holding costs and ordering costs, will fall until the point E, which represents the minimum total cost. Thereafter, total costs begin to rise. The EOQ model seeks to identify point E at which total costs are minimised. This will represent half of the optimum amount that should be ordered on each occasion. Assuming, as we are doing, that inventories are used evenly over time and that they fall to zero before being replaced, the average inventories level equals half of the order size.

Figure 16.4 **Inventories holding and order costs**

Small inventories' levels imply frequent reordering and high annual ordering costs. Small inventories levels also imply relatively low inventories holding costs. High inventories levels imply exactly the opposite. There is, in theory, an optimum order size that will lead to the sum of ordering and holding costs (total costs) being at a minimum.

The EOQ model, which can be used to derive the most economic order quantity, is:

$$\mathrm{EOQ} = \sqrt{\frac{2DC}{H}}$$

where: D = the annual demand for the inventories item (expressed in units of the inventories item);
C = the cost of placing an order;
H = the cost of holding one unit of inventories for one year.

Activity (16.5)

HLA Ltd sells 2,000 bags of cement each year. It has been estimated that the cost of holding one bag of cement for a year is £4. The cost of placing an order for new inventories is estimated at £250.

Calculate the EOQ for bags of cement.

Your answer to this activity should be as follows:

$$EOQ = \sqrt{\frac{2 \times 2,000 \times 250}{4}} = 500 \text{ units}$$

This will mean that the business will have to order bags of cement four times each year (that is 2,000/500) so that sales demand can be met.

Note that the cost of the inventories concerned, which is the price paid to the supplier, does not directly impact on the EOQ model. The EOQ model is concerned only with the administrative costs of placing each order and the costs of looking after the inventories. Where the business operates an ABC system of inventories control, however, more expensive inventories items will have greater holding costs. For example, Category A inventories would tend to have a lower EOQ than Category B ones. So the cost of the inventories may have an indirect effect on the economic order size that the model recommends.

The basic EOQ model has a number of limiting assumptions. In particular, it assumes that:

● demand for the particular inventories item can be predicted with accuracy;
● demand is constant over the period and does not fluctuate through seasonality or for other reasons;
● no 'buffer' inventories are required;
● there are no discounts for bulk purchasing.

However, the model can be developed to overcome each of these limiting assumptions. Many businesses use this model (or a development of it) to help in the management of inventories.

Materials requirement planning systems

A **materials requirement planning (MRP) system** takes planned sales demand as its starting point. It then uses a computer package to help schedule the timing of deliveries of bought-in parts and materials to coincide with production requirements. It is a co-ordinated approach that links materials and parts deliveries to the scheduled time of their input to the production process. By ordering only those items that are necessary to ensure the flow of production, inventories levels are likely to be reduced. MRP is really a 'top-down' approach to inventories management, which recognises that inventories ordering decisions cannot be viewed as being independent of production decisions. In recent years, this approach has been extended to provide a fully integrated approach to production planning. The approach also takes account of other manufacturing resources such as labour and machine capacity.

Just-in-time inventories management

In recent years, many businesses have tried to eliminate the need to hold inventories by adopting **just-in-time (JIT) inventories management**. This approach was first used in the US defence industry during the Second World War, but was first used on a wide scale by Japanese manufacturing businesses. The essence of JIT is, as the name suggests, to have supplies delivered to the business just in time for them to be used in the production process or in a sale. By adopting this approach the inventories holding costs rest with suppliers rather than with the business itself. On the other hand, a failure by a particular supplier to deliver on time could cause enormous problems and costs to the business. Thus JIT can save cost, but it tends to increase risk.

For JIT to be successful, it is important that the business informs suppliers of its inventories requirements in advance, and that suppliers, in their turn, deliver materials of the right quality at the agreed times. Failure to do so could lead to a dislocation of production or supply to customers and could be very costly. Thus a close relationship is required between the business and its suppliers.

This close relationship enables suppliers to schedule their own production to that of their customers. This should mean that between supplier and customer there will be a net saving in the amount of inventories that need to be held, relative to that that would apply were JIT not in operation.

Although a business that applies JIT will not have to hold inventories, there may be other costs associated with this approach. As the suppliers may need to hold inventories for the customer, they may try to recoup this additional cost through increased prices. On the other hand, the close relationship between customer and supplier should enable the supplier to predict its customers' inventories needs. This means that suppliers can tailor their own production to that of the customer. The close relationship necessary between the business and its suppliers may also prevent the business from taking advantage of cheaper sources of supply if they become available.

Many people view JIT as more than simply an inventories control system. The philosophy underpinning this approach is concerned with eliminating waste and striving for excellence. There is an expectation that suppliers will always deliver inventories on time and that there will be no defects in the items supplied. There is also an expectation that, for manufacturers, the production process will operate at maximum efficiency. This means there will be no production breakdowns and the queuing and storage times of products manufactured will be eliminated, as only that time spent directly on processing the products is seen as adding value. While these expectations may be impossible to achieve, they do help to create a culture that is dedicated to the pursuit of excellence and quality.

Real Worlds 16.5 and **16.6** show how two very well-known businesses operating in the UK (one a retailer, the other a manufacturer) use JIT to advantage.

Real World 16.5

JIT at Boots

The Boots Company plc, the UK's largest healthcare retailer, has improved inventories management at its stores. The business is working towards a JIT system where delivery from its one central warehouse in Nottingham will be made every day to each retail branch, with nearly all of the inventories lines being placed directly on to the sales shelves, not into a branch stock room. The business says that this will bring significant savings of stores staff time and lead to significantly lower levels of inventories being held, without any lessening of the service offered to customers. The new system is expected to lead to major economic benefits for the business.

Source: Information taken from The Boots Company plc Annual Report and Accounts 2005.

Real World 16.6

JIT at Nissan

Nissan Motors UK Limited, the UK manufacturing arm of the world famous Japanese car business has a plant in Sunderland in the north east of England. Here it operates a well-developed JIT system. Sommer supplies carpets and soft interior trim from a factory close to the Nissan plant. It makes deliveries to Nissan once every 20 minutes on average, so as to arrive exactly as they are needed in production. This is fairly typical of all of the 200 suppliers of components and materials to the Nissan plant.

Source: Information taken from Partnership Sourcing Best Practice Case Study (www.pslcbi.com/studies/docnissan.htm).

Managing receivables

Selling goods or services on credit will result in costs being incurred by a business. These costs include credit administration costs, bad debts and opportunities forgone to use the funds for more profitable purposes. However, these costs must be weighed against the benefits of increased sales resulting from the opportunity for customers to delay payment.

Selling on credit is very widespread and is the norm outside the retail industry. When a business offers to sell its goods or services on credit, it must have clear policies concerning:

- which customers should receive credit;
- how much credit should be offered;
- what length of credit it is prepared to offer;
- whether discounts will be offered for prompt payment;
- what collection policies should be adopted;
- how the risk of non-payment can be reduced.

In this section, we shall consider each of these issues.

Which customers should receive credit and how much should they be offered?

A business offering credit runs the risk of not receiving payment for goods or services supplied. Thus, care must be taken over the type of customer to whom credit facilities are offered and how much credit is allowed. When considering a proposal from a customer for the supply of goods or services on credit, the business must take a number of factors into account. The following **five Cs of credit** provide a business with a useful checklist.

- *Capital.* The customer must appear to be financially sound before any credit is extended. Where the customer is a business, its financial statements should be examined. Particular regard should be given to the customer's likely future profitability and liquidity. In addition, any major financial commitments (for example, capital expenditure, contracts with suppliers) must be taken into account.

- *Capacity.* The customer must appear to have the capacity to pay amounts owing. Where possible, the payment record of the customer to date should be examined. If the customer is a business, the type of business operated and the physical resources of the business will be relevant. The value of goods that the customer wishes to buy on credit must be related to the customer's total financial resources.
- *Collateral.* On occasions, it may be necessary to ask for some kind of security for goods supplied on credit. When this occurs, the business must be convinced that the customer is able to offer a satisfactory form of security.
- *Conditions.* The state of the industry in which the customer operates, and the general economic conditions of the particular region or country, may have an important influence on the ability of a customer to pay the amounts outstanding on the due date.
- *Character.* It is important for a business to make some assessment of the customer's character. The willingness to pay will depend on the honesty and integrity of the individual with whom the business is dealing. Where the customer is a limited company this will mean assessing the characters of its directors. The business must feel satisfied that the customer will make every effort to pay any amounts owing.

It is clear from the above that the business will need to gather information concerning the ability and willingness of the customer to pay the amounts owing at the due dates.

Activity (16.6)

Assume that you are the credit manager of a business and that a limited company approaches you with a view to buying goods on credit. What sources of information might you decide to use to help assess the financial health of the potential customer?

There are various possibilities. You may have thought of some of the following:

- *Trade references.* Some businesses ask potential customers to supply them with references from other suppliers who have made sales on credit to them. This may be extremely useful provided that the references supplied are truly representative of the opinions of a customer's suppliers. There is a danger that a potential customer will be selective when giving details of other suppliers, in order to create a more favourable impression than is deserved.
- *Bank references.* It is possible to ask the potential customer for a bank reference. Although banks are usually prepared to supply references, the contents of such references are not always very informative. If customers are in financial difficulties, the bank may be unwilling to add to their problems by supplying poor references. It is worth remembering that the bank's loyalty is likely to be with the customer rather than the enquirer. The bank will usually charge a fee for providing a reference.
- *Published financial statements.* A limited company is obliged by law to file a copy of its annual financial statements with the Registrar of Companies. These financial statements are available for public inspection and provide a useful source of information. Apart from the information contained in the financial statements, company law requires public limited companies to state in the directors' report the average time taken to pay suppliers. The annual reports of many companies are available on their own websites or on computer-based information systems (for example, FAME).
- *The customer.* Interviews with the directors of the customer business and visits to its premises may be carried out to gain an impression of the way that the customer conducts its business. Where a significant amount of credit is required, the business may

ask the customer for access to internal budgets and other unpublished financial information to help assess the level of risk involved.

- *Credit agencies.* Specialist agencies exist to provide information that can be used to assess the creditworthiness of a potential customer. The information that a credit agency supplies may be gleaned from various sources, including the financial statements of the customer and news items relating to the customer from both published and unpublished sources. The credit agencies may also provide a credit rating for the business.
- *Register of County Court Judgments.* Any money judgments given against the business or an individual in a county court will be maintained on the register for six years. This register is available for inspection by any member of the public for a small fee.
- *Other suppliers.* Similar business will often be prepared to exchange information concerning slow payers or defaulting customers through an industry credit circle. This can be a reliable and relatively cheap way of obtaining information.

Length of credit period

A business must determine what credit terms it is prepared to offer its customers. The length of credit offered to customers can vary significantly between businesses, and may be influenced by such factors as:

- the typical credit terms operating within the industry;
- the degree of competition within the industry;
- the bargaining power of particular customers;
- the risk of non-payment;
- the capacity of the business to offer credit;
- the marketing strategy of the business.

The last point identified may require some explanation. If, for example, a business wishes to increase its market share, it may decide to be more generous in its credit policy in an attempt to stimulate sales. Potential customers may be attracted by the offer of a longer credit period. However, any such change in policy must take account of the likely costs and benefits arising.

To illustrate this point, consider Example 16.2.

Example 16.2

Torrance Ltd produces a new type of golf putter. The business sells the putter to wholesalers and retailers and has an annual turnover of £600,000. The following data relate to each putter produced.

	£	£
Selling price		40
Variable costs	20	
Fixed cost apportionment	6	26
Profit		14

The business's cost of capital is estimated at 10 per cent a year.

→ Torrance Ltd wishes to expand the sales volume of the new putter. It believes that offering a longer credit period can achieve this. The business's average receivables collection period is currently 30 days. It is considering three options in an attempt to increase sales revenue. These are as follows:

	Option		
	1	*2*	*3*
Increase in average collection period (days)	10	20	30
Increase in sales revenue (£)	30,000	45,000	50,000

To enable the business to decide on the best option to adopt, it must weigh the benefits of the options against their respective costs. The benefits arising will be represented by the increase in profit from the sale of additional putters. From the cost data supplied we can see that the contribution (that is, selling price (£40) less variable costs (£20)) is £20 a putter, that is, 50 per cent of the selling price. So, whatever increase there may be in sales revenue, the additional contributions will be half of that figure. The fixed costs can be ignored in our calculations, as they will remain the same whichever option is chosen.

The increase in contribution under each option will therefore be:

	Option		
	1	*2*	*3*
50% of the increase in sales revenue (£)	15,000	22,500	25,000

The increase in trade receivables under each option will be as follows:

	Option		
	1	*2*	*3*
	£	£	£
Projected level of trade receivables			
40 × £630,000/365 (Note 1)	69,041		
50 × £645,000/365		88,356	
60 × £650,000/365			106,849
Current level of trade receivables			
30 × £600,000/365	(49,315)	(49,315)	(49,315)
Increase in trade receivables	19,726	39,041	57,534

The increase in receivables that results from each option will mean an additional finance cost to the business.

The net increase in the business's profit arising from the projected change is:

	Option		
	1	*2*	*3*
	£	£	£
Increase in contribution (see above)	15,000	22,500	25,000
Increase in finance cost (Note 2)	(1,973)	(3,904)	(5,753)
Net increase in profits	13,027	18,596	19,247

The calculations show that Option 3 will be the most profitable one.

Notes:

1 If the annual sales revenue total £630,000 and 40 days' credit are allowed (both of which will apply under Option 1), the average amount that will be owed to the business by its customers, at any point during the year, will be the daily sales revenue (that is, £630,000/365) multiplied by the number of days that the customers take to pay (that is 40).

   Exactly the same logic applies to Options 2 and 3 and to the current level of trade receivables.

2 The increase in the finance cost for Option 1 will be the increase in trade receivables (£19,726) × 10 per cent. The equivalent figures for the other options are derived in a similar way.

Example 16.2 illustrates the way in which a business should assess changes in credit terms. However, if there is a risk that, by extending the length of credit, there will be an increase in bad debts, this should also be taken into account in the calculations, as should any additional trade receivable collection costs that will be incurred.

Real World 16.7 provides some insight into the typical length of credit taken by UK businesses.

Real World 16.7

Credit where it's due

The average collection period for trade receivables in the UK is around 60 days, according to survey evidence from Experian, the information services business.

Where the credit customers are large UK businesses, the average time that the supplier has to wait for the cash is about 78 days.

Source: Information taken from 'Legislation fails to curb late payment problems', Jonathon Moules, *Financial Times*, 28 July 2004, FT.com.

An alternative approach to evaluating the credit decision

It is possible to view the credit decision as a capital investment decision. Granting trade credit involves an outlay of resources in the form of cash (which has been temporarily forgone) in the expectation that future cash flows will be increased (through higher sales) as a result. A business will usually have choices concerning the level of investment to be made in credit sales and the period over which credit is granted. These choices will result in different returns and different levels of risk. There is no reason in principle why the NPV investment appraisal method, which we considered in Chapter 14, should not be used to evaluate these choices. We have seen that the NPV method takes into account both the time value of money and the level of risk involved.

Cash discounts

A business may decide to offer a **cash discount** in an attempt to encourage prompt payment from its credit customers. The size of any discount will be an important influence on whether a customer decides to pay promptly.

From the business's viewpoint, the cost of offering discounts must be weighed against the likely benefits in the form of a reduction both in the cost of financing receivables and in the amount of bad debts.

In practice, there is always the danger that a customer may be slow to pay and yet may still take the discount offered. Where the customer is important to the business it may be difficult to insist on full payment. An alternative to allowing the customer to take discounts by reducing payment is to agree in advance to provide discounts for prompt payment through quarterly credit notes. As credit notes will be given only for those debts paid on time, the customer will often make an effort to qualify for the discount.

Self-assessment question (16.1)

Williams Wholesalers Ltd at present requires payment from its customers by the end of the month after the month of delivery. On average, customers take 70 days to pay. Sales revenue amounts to £4m a year and bad debts to £20,000 a year.

It is planned to offer customers a cash discount of 2 per cent for payment within 30 days. Williams estimates that 50 per cent of customers will accept this facility but that the remaining customers, who tend to be slow payers, will not pay until 80 days after the sale. At present the business has an overdraft facility at an interest rate of 13 per cent a year. If the plan goes ahead, bad debts will be reduced to £10,000 a year and there will be savings in credit administration expenses of £6,000 a year.

Required:
Should Williams Wholesalers Ltd offer the new credit terms to customers? You should support your answer with any calculations and explanations that you consider necessary.

The answer to this question can be found at the back of the book on page 708.

Debt factoring and invoice discounting

We saw in Chapter 15 (pages 597–8) that trade payables can, in effect, be turned into cash by either factoring them or having sales invoices discounted. These both seem to be fairly popular approaches to managing trade receivables.

Collection policies and reducing the risk of non-payment

A business offering credit must ensure that amounts owing are collected as quickly as possible so that the risk of non-payment is minimised. Various steps can be taken to achieve this, including the following.

Develop customer relationships

For major customers it is often useful to cultivate a relationship with the key staff responsible for paying sales invoices. By so doing, the chances of prompt payment may be increased. For less important customers, the business should at least identify key staff responsible for paying invoices, who can be contacted in the event of a payment problem.

Publicise credit terms

The credit terms of the business should be made clear in all relevant correspondence, such as order acknowledgements, invoices and statements. In early negotiations with the prospective customer, credit terms should be openly discussed and an agreement reached.

Issue invoices promptly

An efficient collection policy requires an efficient accounting system. Invoices (bills) must be sent out promptly to customers, as must monthly statements. Reminders must also be despatched promptly to customers who are late in paying. If a customer fails to respond to a reminder, the accounting system should alert managers so that a stop can be placed on further deliveries.

Monitor outstanding debts

Management can monitor the effectiveness of collection policies in a number of ways. One method is to calculate the **average settlement period for trade receivables** ratio, which we met in Chapter 7. This ratio, we should recall, is calculated as follows:

$$\text{Average settlement period for trade receivables} = \frac{\text{Trade receivables}}{\text{Credit sales}} \times 365$$

Although this ratio can be useful, it is important to remember that it produces an *average* figure for the number of days for which debts are outstanding. This average may be badly distorted by a few large customers who are very slow or very fast payers.

Produce an ageing schedule of trade receivables

A more detailed and informative approach to monitoring receivables may be to produce an **ageing schedule of trade receivables**. Debts are divided into categories according to the length of time the debt has been outstanding. An ageing schedule can be produced, on a regular basis, to help managers see the pattern of outstanding debts. An example of an ageing schedule is set out in Example 16.3.

Example 16.3

Ageing schedule of trade receivables at 31 December

Customer	Days outstanding				Total
	1 to 30 days	31 to 60 days	61 to 90 days	More than 90 days	
	£	£	£	£	£
A Ltd	20,000	10,000	–	–	30,000
B Ltd	–	24,000	–	–	24,000
C Ltd	12,000	13,000	14,000	18,000	57,000
Total	32,000	47,000	14,000	18,000	111,000

This shows a business's trade receivables figure at 31 December, which totals £111,000. Each customer's balance is analysed according to how long the debt has been outstanding. (This business has just three credit customers.)

Thus we can see from the schedule that A Ltd has £20,000 outstanding for 30 days or less (that is, arising from sales during December) and £10,000 outstanding for between 31 and 60 days (arising from November sales). This information can be very useful for credit control purposes.

Many accounting software packages now include this ageing schedule as one of the routine reports available to managers. Such packages often have the facility to put customers 'on hold' when they reach their credit limits. Putting a customer on hold means that no further credit sales will be made to that customer until debts arising from past sales have been settled.

Answer queries quickly

It is important for relevant staff to deal with customer queries on goods and services supplied quickly and efficiently. Payment is unlikely to be made by customers until their queries have been dealt with.

Deal with slow payers

It is almost inevitably the case that a business making significant sales on credit will be faced with customers who do not pay. When this occurs, there should be agreed procedures for dealing with the situation. However, the cost of any action to be taken against delinquent credit customers must be weighed against the likely returns. For example, there is little point in taking legal action against a customer, incurring large legal expenses, if there is evidence that the customer does not have the necessary resources to pay. Where possible, an estimate of the cost of bad debts should be taken into account when setting prices for products or services.

Real World 16.8 shows that businesses are not always as efficient as they might be with their management of trade receivables.

Real World 16.8

Would you credit it?

According to a 2004 survey of 6,500 UK businesses, 44 per cent of businesses leave it a fortnight, or longer, after the due date for payment before sending reminders to their credit cutomers, while 13 per cent leave it for a month or more. In other words, many businesses are very slow to react to their customers failing to pay on time.

Intrim Justia UK, who conducted the survey, said: 'A clear credit policy, consistent checks on overdue payments and robust credit management systems are just some of the critical measures that businesses need to adopt.'

Source: Information taken from 'Late reminders lead to late payments', Jonathon Moules, *Financial Times*, 12 July 2004.

As a footnote to our consideration of managing receivables, **Real World 16.9** outlines some of the excuses that long-suffering credit managers must listen to when chasing payment for outstanding debt.

Real World 16.9

It's in the post

Accountants' noses should be growing, if we're to believe a new survey listing the bizarre excuses given by businesses that fail to pay their debts.

'The director's been shot' and 'I'll pay you when God tells me to' are just two of the most outrageous excuses listed in a survey published by the Credit Services Association, the debt collection industry body.

The commercial sector tends to blame financial problems, and excuses such as 'you'll get paid when we do' and 'the finance director is off sick' are common. However, those in the consumer sector apparently feel no shame in citing personal relationship problems as the reason for not paying the bill.

Source: Accountancy, April 2000, p. 18.

Managing cash

Why hold cash?

Most businesses hold a certain amount of cash. The amount of cash held tends to vary considerably between businesses.

Activity 16.7

Why do you think a business may decide to hold at least some of its assets in the form of cash? (*Hint*: There are broadly three reasons.)

The three reasons are:

1 To meet day-to-day commitments, a business requires a certain amount of cash. Payments for wages, overhead expenses, goods purchased and so on must be made at the due dates. Cash has been described as the lifeblood of a business. Unless it circulates through the business and is available for the payment of maturing obligations, the survival of the business will be at risk. Profitability is not enough; a business must have sufficient cash to pay its debts when they fall due.

2 If future cash flows are uncertain for any reason, it would be prudent to hold a balance of cash. For example, a major customer that owes a large sum to the business may be in financial difficulties. Given this situation, the business can retain its capacity to meet its obligations by holding a cash balance. Similarly, if there is some uncertainty concerning future outlays, a cash balance will be required.

3 A business may decide to hold cash to put itself in a position to exploit profitable opportunities as and when they arise. For example, by holding cash, a business may be able to acquire a competitor's business that suddenly becomes available at an attractive price.

How much cash should be held?

Although cash can be held for each of the reasons identified, doing so may not always be necessary. If a business is able to borrow quickly, the amount of cash it needs to hold can be reduced. Similarly, if the business holds assets that can easily be converted to cash (for example, marketable securities such as shares in Stock Exchange listed businesses or government bonds), the amount of cash held can be reduced.

The decision as to how much cash a particular business should hold is a difficult one. Different businesses will have different views on the subject.

Activity 16.8

What do you think are the major factors that influence how much cash a business will hold? See if you can think of five possible factors.

You may have thought of the following:

- *The nature of the business*. Some businesses, such as utilities (for example, water, electricity and gas suppliers), may have cash flows that are both predictable and reasonably certain. This will enable them to hold lower cash balances. For some businesses, cash balances may vary greatly according to the time of year. A seasonal business may accumulate cash during the high season to enable it to meet commitments during the low season.
- *The opportunity cost of holding cash*. Where there are profitable opportunities it may not be wise to hold a large cash balance.
- *The level of inflation*. Holding cash during a period of rising prices will lead to a loss of purchasing power. The higher the level of inflation, the greater will be this loss.
- *The availability of near-liquid assets*. If a business has marketable securities or inventories that may easily be liquidated, high cash balances may not be necessary.
- *The availability of borrowing*. If a business can borrow easily (and quickly) there is less need to hold cash.
- *The cost of borrowing*. When interest rates are high, the option of borrowing becomes less attractive.
- *Economic conditions*. When the economy is in recession, businesses may prefer to hold cash so that they can be well placed to invest when the economy improves. In addition, during a recession, businesses may experience difficulties in collecting trade receivables. They may therefore hold higher cash balances than usual in order to meet commitments.
- *Relationships with suppliers*. Too little cash may hinder the ability of the business to pay suppliers promptly. This can lead to a loss of goodwill. It may also lead to discounts being forgone.

Controlling the cash balance

Several models have been developed to help control the cash balance of the business. One such model proposes the use of upper and lower control limits for cash balances and the use of a target cash balance. The model assumes that the business will invest in marketable investments that can easily be liquidated. These investments will be purchased or sold, as necessary, in order to keep the cash balance within the control limits.

The model proposes two upper and two lower control limits (see Figure 16.5). If the business exceeds an *outer* limit, the managers must decide whether the cash balance is likely to return to a point within the *inner* control limits set, over the next few days. If this seems likely, then no action is required. If, on the other hand, it does not seem likely, management must change the cash position of the business by either lending or borrowing (or possibly by buying or selling marketable securities).

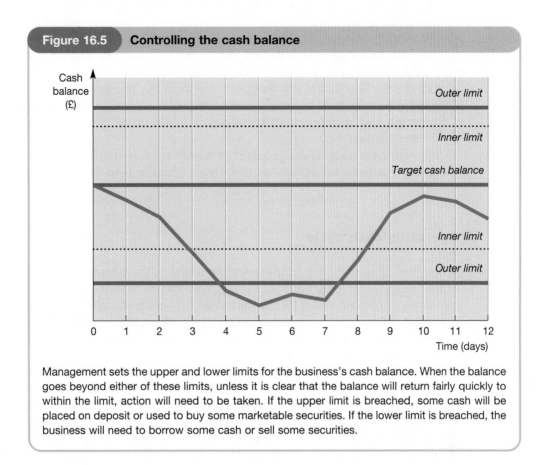

Figure 16.5 Controlling the cash balance

Management sets the upper and lower limits for the business's cash balance. When the balance goes beyond either of these limits, unless it is clear that the balance will return fairly quickly to within the limit, action will need to be taken. If the upper limit is breached, some cash will be placed on deposit or used to buy some marketable securities. If the lower limit is breached, the business will need to borrow some cash or sell some securities.

In Figure 16.5 we can see that the lower outer control limit has been breached for four days. If a four-day period is unacceptable, managers must sell marketable securities to replenish the cash balance.

The model relies heavily on management judgement to determine where the control limits are set and the period within which breaches of the control limits are acceptable. Past experience may be useful in helping managers decide on these issues. There are other models, however, that do not rely on management judgement. Instead, these use quantitative techniques to determine an optimal cash policy. One model proposed, for example, is the cash equivalent of the inventories economic order quantity model, discussed earlier in the chapter.

Cash budgets and managing cash

To manage cash effectively, it is useful for a business to prepare a cash budget. This is a very important tool for both planning and control purposes. Cash budgets were considered in Chapter 12, and so we shall not consider them again in detail. However, it is worth repeating that these statements enable managers to see how planned events are expected to affect the cash balance. The cash budget will identify periods when cash surpluses and cash deficits are expected.

When a cash surplus is expected to arise, managers must decide on the best use of the surplus funds. When a cash deficit is expected, managers must make adequate provision by borrowing, liquidating assets or rescheduling cash payments or receipts to deal with this. Projected cash flow statements are useful in helping to control the cash held. The actual cash flows can be compared with the planned cash flows for the period. If there is a significant divergence between the budgeted and the actual cash flows, explanations must be sought and corrective action taken where necessary.

To refresh your memory on cash budgets, it would probably be worth looking back at Chapter 12, page 447.

Although cash budgets are prepared primarily for internal management purposes, prospective lenders sometimes require them when a loan to a business is being considered.

Operating cash cycle

 When managing cash, it is important to be aware of the **operating cash cycle (OCC)** of the business. For a retailer, for example, this may be defined as the period between the outlay of cash necessary for the purchase of inventories and the ultimate receipt of cash from the sale of the goods. In the case of a business that purchases goods on credit for subsequent resale on credit (for example, a wholesaler), the OCC is as shown in Figure 16.6.

Figure 16.6 shows that payment for inventories acquired on credit occurs some time after those inventories have been purchased and, therefore, no immediate cash outflow arises from the purchase. Similarly, cash receipts from credit customers will occur some time after the sale is made, and so there will be no immediate cash inflow as a result of the sale. The OCC is the period between the payment made to the supplier for goods concerned and the cash received from the credit customer. Although Figure 16.6 depicts the position for a wholesaling business, the precise definition of the OCC can easily be adapted for other types of business.

The OCC is important because it has a significant influence on the financing requirements of the business. Broadly, the longer the cycle, the greater the financing requirements of the business and the greater the financial risks. For this reason, the business is likely to want to reduce the OCC to the minimum possible period.

For the type of business mentioned above, which buys and sells on credit, the OCC can be calculated from the financial statements by the use of certain ratios. It is calculated as shown in Figure 16.7.

Figure 16.6 The operating cash cycle

The OCC is the time lapse between paying for goods and receiving the cash from the sale of those goods. The length of the OCC has a significant impact on the amount of funds that the business needs to apply to working capital.

Figure 16.7 Calculating the operating cash cycle

For businesses that buy and sell on credit, three ratios are required to calculate the OCC.

Activity (16.9)

The financial statements of Freezeqwik Ltd, a distributor of frozen foods, are set out below for the year ended 31 December last year.

Income statement for the year ended 31 December last year

	£000	£000
Sales revenue		820
Cost of sales		
Opening inventories	142	
Purchases	568	
	710	
Closing inventories	166	544
Gross profit		276
Administration expenses		(120)
Distribution expenses		(95)
Operating profit		61
Financial expenses		(32)
Profit before taxation		29
Taxation		(7)
Profit for the period		22

Balance sheet as at 31 December last year

	£000
Non-current assets	
Property, plant and equipment	
Freehold premises at valuation	180
Fixtures and fittings at cost less depreciation	82
Motor vans at cost less depreciation	102
	364
Current assets	
Inventories	166
Trade receivables	264
Cash	24
	454
Total assets	818
Equity	
Ordinary share capital	300
Share premium account	200
Retained earnings	152
	652
Current liabilities	
Trade payables	159
Taxation	7
	166
	818

All purchases and sales are on credit. There has been no change in the level of trade receivables or payables over the period.

Calculate the length of the OCC for the business and go on to suggest how the business may seek to reduce this period.

The OCC may be calculated as follows:

Number of days

Average inventories holding period:

$$\frac{\text{(Opening inventories + Closing inventories)/2}}{\text{Cost of sales}} \times 365 = \frac{(142 + 166)/2}{544} \times 365 \qquad 103$$

Average settlement period for trade receivables:

$$\frac{\text{Trade receivables}}{\text{Credit sales}} \times 365 = \frac{264}{820} \times 365 \qquad \underline{118}$$

$$221$$

Less Average settlement period for trade payables:

$$\frac{\text{Trade payables}}{\text{Credit purchases}} \times 365 = \frac{159}{568} \times 365 \qquad \underline{102}$$

OCC $$\underline{119}$$

The business can reduce the length of the OCC in a number of ways. The average inventories holding period seems quite long. At present, average inventories held represent more than three months' sales requirements. Lowering the level of inventories held will reduce this. Similarly, the average settlement period for trade receivables seems long, at nearly four months' sales. Imposing tighter credit control, offering discounts, charging interest on overdue accounts and so on may reduce this. However, any policy decisions concerning inventories and trade receivables must take account of current trading conditions.

Extending the period of credit taken to pay suppliers could also reduce the OCC. However, for reasons that will be explained later, this option must be given careful consideration.

Cash transmission

A business will normally wish to benefit from receipts from customers at the earliest opportunity. The benefit is immediate where payment is made in cash. However, when payment is made by cheque, there is normally a delay of three to four working days before the cheque can be cleared through the banking system. The business must therefore wait for this period before it can benefit from the amount paid in. In the case of a business that receives large amounts in the form of cheques, the opportunity cost of this delay can be significant.

To avoid this delay, a business could require payments to be made in cash. This is not usually very practical, mainly because of the risk of theft and/or the expense of conveying cash securely. Another option is to ask for payment to be made by standing order or by direct debit from the customer's bank account. This should ensure that the amount owing is always transferred from the bank account of the customer to the bank account of the business on the day that has been agreed.

It is also possible for funds to be transferred directly to a business's bank account. As a result of developments in computer technology, customers can pay for items by using debit cards, which results in the appropriate account being instantly debited and seller's bank account being instantly credited with the required amount. This method of payment is widely used by large retail businesses, and may well extend to other types of business.

Bank overdrafts

Bank overdrafts are simply bank current accounts that have a negative balance. They are a type of bank loan. We looked at these in Chapter 15 in the context of short-term bank borrowing (page 597). They can be a useful tool in managing the business's cash flow requirements.

Managing trade payables

Trade credit arises from the fact that most businesses buy their goods and service requirements on credit. In effect, suppliers are lending the business money, interest free, on a short-term basis. Trade payables are the other side of the coin from trade receivables. One business's trade payable is another one's trade receivable, in respect of a particular transaction. Trade payables are an important source of finance for most businesses. They have been described as a 'spontaneous' source, as they tend to increase in line with the increase in the level of activity achieved by a business. Trade credit is widely regarded as a 'free' source of finance and, therefore, a good thing for a business to use. There may be real costs, however, associated with taking trade credit.

First, customers who take credit may not be as well treated as those who pay immediately. For example, when goods are in short supply, credit customers may receive lower priority when allocating the goods available. In addition, credit customers may be less favoured in terms of delivery dates or the provision of technical support services. Sometimes, the goods or services provided may be more costly if credit is required. However, in most industries, trade credit is the norm. As a result, the above costs will not apply except, perhaps, to customers that abuse the credit facilities. A business that purchases supplies on credit will normally have to incur additional administration and accounting costs in dealing with the scrutiny and payment of invoices, maintaining and updating payables' accounts and so on.

In some cases, delaying payment to payables can be a sign of financial distress. One such example is given in **Real World 16.10**.

Real World 16.10

Can't pay, won't pay

Kmart, a large US retailer, suffered a cash crisis during 2001. The crisis was largely as a result of one manager ordering $850m worth of inventories, which was later described in an internal report as 'excessive'. To conserve cash, the business implemented Project Slow It Down. This involved systematically delaying or reducing payments to trade payables. The project also involved denying suppliers access to records of the amounts owed by Kmart and giving false reasons as to why they had not been paid on time.

Source: Information taken from 'Kmart's fall is tale of poor governance', *Financial Times*, 29 January 2003.

The above points are not meant to imply that taking credit is a burden to a business. There are, of course, real benefits that can accrue. Provided that trade credit is not abused, it can represent a form of interest-free loan. It can be a much more convenient method of paying for goods and services than paying by cash, and, during a period of inflation there will be an economic gain by paying later rather than sooner for goods and services purchased. For most businesses, these benefits will exceed the costs involved.

Taking advantage of cash discounts

Where a supplier offers a discount for prompt payment, the business should give careful consideration to the possibility of paying within the discount period. An example may be useful to illustrate the cost of forgoing possible discounts.

Example 16.4

Hassan Ltd takes 70 days to pay for goods from its supplier. To encourage prompt payment, the supplier has offered the business a 2 per cent discount if payment for goods is made within 30 days.

Hassan Ltd is not sure whether it is worth taking the discount offered.

If the discount is taken, payment could be made on the last day of the discount period (that is, the 30th day). However, if the discount is not taken, payment will be made after 70 days. This means that, by not taking the discount, the business will receive an extra 40 days' (that is, 70 – 30) credit. The cost of this extra credit to the business will be the 2 per cent discount forgone. If we annualise the cost of this discount forgone, we have:

$$365/40 \times 2\% = 18.3\%*$$

We can see that the annual cost of forgoing the discount is very high, and so it may be profitable for the business to pay the supplier within the discount period, even if it means that it will have to borrow to enable it to do so.

* This is an approximate annual rate. For the more mathematically minded, the precise rate is:

$$\{[(1 + 2/98)^{9.125}] - 1\} \times 100\% = 20.2\%$$

Controlling trade payables

To help monitor the level of trade credit taken, management can calculate the **average settlement period for trade payables**. As we saw in Chapter 7, this ratio is:

$$\text{Average settlement period for trade payables} = \frac{\text{Trade payables}}{\text{Credit purchases}} \times 365$$

Once again, this provides an average figure, which could be misleading. A more informative approach would be to produce an ageing schedule for payables. This would look much the same as the ageing schedule for receivables described earlier.

Since, as was pointed out earlier in this section, one business's trade payable is another one's trade receivable, the information contained in Real World 16.7 (page 631) provides some indication of typical lengths of trade credit taken by UK businesses.

Working capital problems of the small business

We saw earlier (Real World 16.1, page 617) that the amounts invested by businesses in working capital are often high in proportion to the total assets employed. It is, therefore, important that these amounts are properly managed. Although this point applies to businesses of all sizes, it may be of particular importance to small businesses. It is often claimed that many small businesses suffer from a lack of capital and, where this is the case, tight control over working capital investment becomes critical. There is evidence, however, that small businesses are not very good at managing their working capital and this has been cited as a major cause of their high failure rate compared with that of large businesses. In this section, we consider the working capital management problems associated with small businesses.

Managing inventories

A lack of financial management skills within a small business often creates problems in managing inventories in an efficient and effective way. The owners of small businesses are not always aware that there are costs involved in holding too much inventories and that there are also costs involved in holding too little. These costs, which were discussed earlier, may be very high in certain industries such as manufacturing and wholesaling, where inventories account for a significant proportion of the total assets held.

It was mentioned earlier in the chapter that the starting point for an effective inventories management system is good planning and budgeting systems. In particular, there should be reliable sales forecasts, or budgets, available for inventories ordering purposes. However, it seems that not all small businesses prepare these forecasts or budgets. A survey by Chittenden *et al.* (see reference 1 at the end of the chapter) of small and medium-sized businesses indicated that only 78 per cent of those replying prepare a sales budget. Inventories management can also benefit from good reporting systems and the application of quantitative techniques (for example, the economic order quantity model) to try to optimise inventories levels. However, the same survey found that more than one-third of small businesses rely on manual methods of inventories control, and the majority do not use inventories optimisation techniques. Although the Chittenden survey is now rather old (1998) it represents the most recent reliable evidence available. There is no reason to believe that practices of small businesses have changed much since this evidence was gathered.

Credit management

Small businesses often lack the resources to manage their trade receivables effectively. It is not unusual for a small business to operate without a separate credit control department. This tends to mean that neither the expertise nor the information required to make sound judgements concerning terms of sale and so on is available. A small business may also lack proper debt collection procedures, such as prompt invoicing and sending out regular statements. This will increase the risks of late payment and defaulting credit customers.

These risks probably increase where there is an excessive concern for growth. In an attempt to increase sales, small businesses may be too willing to extend credit to customers that are poor credit risks. While this kind of problem can occur in businesses of all sizes, small businesses seem particularly susceptible.

Another problem faced by small businesses is their lack of market power. They will often find themselves in a weak position when negotiating credit terms with larger businesses. Moreover, when a large customer exceeds the terms of credit, the small supplier may feel unwilling to press the customer for payment in case future sales are lost.

In the UK, the government has intervened to help deal with this problem and the law now permits small businesses to charge interest on overdue accounts. In addition, large companies are now required to disclose in their published financial statements the payment policy adopted towards suppliers in the hope that this requirement will improve the behaviour of those that delay payments. However, it is unlikely that legislation alone will make a significant improvement. Although small businesses may be able to charge interest on overdue accounts, they will often avoid doing so because they fear that large customers would view this as a provocative act. What is really needed to help small businesses is a change in the payment culture.

We saw in Chapter 15 that one way of dealing with the credit management problem is to factor the outstanding trade receivables. Under this kind of arrangement, the factor will take over the sales records of the business and will take responsibility for the prompt collection of trade receivables. However, some businesses are too small to take advantage of this facility. The set-up costs of a factoring arrangement often make businesses with a small turnover (say, £100,000 a year or less) an uneconomic proposition for the factor.

Managing cash

The management of cash raises similar issues to those relating to the management of inventories. There are costs involved both in holding too much and too little cash. Thus, there is a need for careful planning and monitoring of cash flows over time. The Chittenden survey (see reference 1 at the end of the chapter) found, however, that only 63 per cent of those replying prepared a cash budget. It was also found that cash balances are generally proportionately higher for smaller businesses than for larger ones. More than half of those in the survey held surplus cash balances on a regular basis. Although this may reflect a more conservative approach to liquidity among the owners of smaller businesses, it may suggest a failure to recognise the opportunity costs of cash balances.

Managing credit suppliers

In practice, small businesses often try to cope with the late payment of credit customers by delaying payments to their credit suppliers. We saw earlier in the chapter, however, that this can be an expensive option. Where discounts are forgone, the annual cost of this financing option compares unfavourably with most other forms of short-term financing. Nevertheless, the vast majority of small and medium-sized businesses are unaware of the very high cost of delaying payment, according to the Chittenden survey (see reference 1 at the end of the chapter).

Summary

The main points of this chapter may be summarised as follows.

Working capital

- Working capital is the difference between current assets and current liabilities.
- That is, working capital = inventories + receivables + cash – payables – bank overdrafts.
- An investment in working capital cannot be avoided in practice – typically large amounts are involved.

Inventories

- There are costs of holding inventories, which include:
  - lost interest
  - storage cost
  - insurance cost
  - obsolescence.
- There are also costs of not holding sufficient inventories, which include:
  - loss of sales and customer goodwill
  - production dislocation
  - loss of flexibility – cannot take advantage of opportunities
  - reorder costs – low inventories imply more frequent ordering.
- Practical points on inventories management include:
  - identify optimum order size – models can help with this
  - set inventories reorder levels
  - use budgets
  - keep reliable inventories records
  - use accounting ratios (for example, inventories turnover period ratio)
  - establish systems for security of inventories and authorisation
  - consider just-in-time (JIT) inventories management.

Trade receivables

- When assessing which customers should receive credit, the five Cs of credit can be used:
  - capital
  - capacity
  - collateral
  - condition
  - character.
- The costs of allowing credit include:
  - lost interest
  - lost purchasing power
  - costs of assessing customer creditworthiness
  - administration cost
  - bad debts
  - cash discounts (for prompt payment).
- The costs of denying credit include:
  - loss of customer goodwill.
- Practical points on receivables management:
  - establish a policy
  - assess and monitor customer creditworthiness
  - establish effective administration of receivables
  - establish a policy on bad debts
  - consider cash discounts

    – use financial ratios (for example, average settlement period for trade receivables ratio)
    – use ageing summaries.

Cash

- The costs of holding cash include:
  - lost interest
  - lost purchasing power.

- The costs of holding insufficient cash include:
  - loss of supplier goodwill if unable to meet commitments on time
  - loss of opportunities
  - inability to claim cash discounts
  - costs of borrowing (should an obligation need to be met at short notice).

- Practical points on cash management:
  - establish a policy
  - plan cash flows
  - make judicious use of bank overdraft finance – it can be cheap and flexible
  - use short-term cash surpluses profitably
  - bank frequently
  - operating cash cycle (for a wholesaler) = length of time from buying inventories to receiving cash from receivables less payables' payment period (in days)
  - transmit cash promptly;

- An objective of working capital management is to limit the length of the operating cash cycle (OCC), subject to any risks that this may cause.

Trade payables

- The costs of taking credit include:
  - higher price than purchases for immediate cash settlement
  - administrative costs
  - restrictions imposed by seller.

- The costs of not taking credit include:
  - lost interest-free borrowing
  - lost purchasing power
  - inconvenience – paying at the time of purchase can be inconvenient.

- Practical points on payables management:
  - establish a policy
  - exploit free credit as far as possible
  - use accounting ratios (for example, average settlement period for trade payables ratio).

Working capital and the small business

- Small businesses often lack the skills and resources to manage working capital effectively.
- Small businesses often suffer from large businesses delaying payments for goods and services supplied.
- Changes in the law designed to help small businesses have had limited success.

 Now check your progress in your personal Study Plan

Key terms

working capital   p. 615
lead time   p. 620
ABC system of inventories control
   p. 622
economic order quantity (EOQ)
   p. 622
materials requirement planning (MRP)
   system   p. 625
just-in-time (JIT) inventories
   management   p. 625

five Cs of credit   p. 627
cash discount   p. 631
average settlement period for trade
   receivables   p. 633
ageing schedule of trade receivables
   p. 633
operating cash cycle (OCC)   p. 638
average settlement period for trade
   payables   p. 643

Reference

Financial Management and Working Capital Practices in UK SMEs, *Chittenden F., Poutziouris P. and Michaelis N.*, Manchester Business School, 1998.

Further reading

If you would like to explore the topics covered in this chapter in more depth, we recommend the following books:

Business Finance: Theory and practice, *McLaney E.*, 7th edn, Financial Times Prentice Hall, 2006, chapter 13.

Corporate Finance, *Brealey B., Myers S. and Allen F.*, 8th edn, McGraw-Hill, 2005, chapters 30 and 31.

Corporate Finance and Investment, *Pike R. and Neale B.*, 5th edn, Prentice Hall, 2005, chapters 13 and 14.

Corporate Financial Management, *Arnold G.*, 3rd edn, Financial Times Prentice Hall, 2005, chapter 13.

Review questions

Answers to these questions can be found at the back of the book on page 786.

16.1 Tariq is the credit manager of Heltex plc. He is concerned that the pattern of monthly cash receipts from credit sales shows that credit collection is poor compared with budget. Heltex's sales director believes that Tariq is to blame for this situation, but Tariq insists that he is not. Why might Tariq not be to blame for the deterioration in the credit collection period?

16.2 How might each of the following affect the level of inventories held by a business?

(a) An increase in the number of production bottlenecks experienced by the business.
(b) A rise in the level of interest rates.
(c) A decision to offer customers a narrower range of products in the future.
(d) A switch of suppliers from an overseas business to a local business.
(e) A deterioration in the quality and reliability of bought-in components.

16.3 What are the reasons for holding inventories? Are these reasons different from the reasons for holding cash?

16.4 Identify the costs of holding:

(a) too little cash;
(b) too much cash.

Exercises

Exercises 16.4 to 16.8 are more advanced than 16.1 to 16.3. Those with coloured numbers have an answer at the back of the book starting on page 762.

If you wish to try more exercises, visit the students' side of the Companion Website.

16.1 Hercules Wholesalers Ltd has been particularly concerned with its liquidity position in recent months. The most recent income statement and balance sheet of the business are as follows:

Income statement for the year ended 31 December last year

	£000	£000
Sales revenue		452
Cost of sales		
Opening inventories	125	
Purchases	341	
	466	
Closing inventories	(143)	323
Gross profit		129
Expenses		(132)
Loss for the period		(3)

Balance sheet as at 31 December last year

	£000
Non-current assets	
Property, plant and equipment	
Freehold premises at valuation	280
Fixtures and fittings at cost less depreciation	25
Motor vehicles at cost less depreciation	52
	357
Current assets	
Inventories	143
Trade receivables	163
	306
Total assets	663
Equity	
Ordinary share capital	100
Retained earnings	158
	258
Non current liabilities	
Borrowings – Loans	120
Current liabilities	
Trade payables	145
Borrowings – Bank overdraft	140
	285
Total equity and liabilities	663

The trade receivables and payables were maintained at a constant level throughout the year.

Required:
(a) Explain why Hercules Wholesalers Ltd is concerned about its liquidity position.
(b) Calculate the operating cash cycle for Hercules Wholesalers Ltd based on the information above. (Assume a 360-day year.)
(c) State what steps may be taken to improve the operating cash cycle of the business.

16.2 International Electric plc at present offers its customers 30 days' credit. Half the customers, by value, pay on time. The other half takes an average of 70 days to pay. The business is considering offering a cash discount of 2 per cent to its customers for payment within 30 days.

The credit controller anticipates that half of the customers who now take an average of 70 days to pay (that is, a quarter of all customers) will pay in 30 days. The other half (the final quarter) will still take an average of 70 days to pay. The scheme will also reduce bad debts by £300,000 a year.

Annual sales revenue of £365m is made evenly throughout the year. At present the business has a large overdraft (£60m) with its bank at an interest cost of 12 per cent a year.

Required:
(a) Calculate the approximate equivalent annual percentage cost of a discount of 2 per cent, which reduces the time taken by credit customers to pay from 70 days to 30 days. (*Hint:* This part can be answered without reference to the narrative above.)
(b) Calculate the value of trade receivables outstanding under both the old and new schemes.
(c) How much will the scheme cost the business in discounts?
(d) Should the business go ahead with the scheme? State what other factors, if any, should be taken into account.
(e) Outline the controls and procedures that a business should adopt to manage the level of its trade receivables.

16.3 The managing director of Sparkrite Ltd, a trading business, has just received summary sets of financial statements for last year and this year:

Sparkrite Ltd
Income statements for years ended 30 September last year and this year

	Last year £000	Last year £000	This year £000	This year £000
Sales revenue		1,800		1,920
Cost of sales				
Opening inventories	160		200	
Purchases	1,120		1,175	
	1,280		1,375	
Closing inventories	(200)		(250)	
		1,080		1,125
Gross profit		720		795
Expenses		(680)		(750)
Profit for the period		40		45

Balance sheets as at 30 September last year and this year

	Last year £000	This year £000
Non-current assets	950	930
Current assets		
Inventories	200	250
Trade receivables	375	480
Bank	4	2
	579	732
Total assets	1,529	1,662
Equity		
Fully paid £1 ordinary shares	825	883
Retained earnings	509	554
	1,334	1,437
Current liabilities	195	225
Total equity and liabilities	1,529	1,662

The finance director has expressed concern at the increase in inventories and trade receivables levels.

Required:
(a) Show, by using the data given, how you would calculate ratios that could be used to measure inventories and trade receivables levels during last year and this year.
(b) Discuss the ways in which the management of Sparkrite Ltd could exercise control over:
  (i) inventories levels;
  (ii) trade receivables levels.

16.4 Your superior, the general manager of Plastics Manufacturers Limited, has recently been talking to the chief buyer of Plastic Toys Limited, which manufactures a wide range of toys for young children. At present, Plastic Toys is considering changing its supplier of plastic granules and has offered to buy its entire requirement of 2,000 kg a month from you at the going market rate, provided that you will grant it three months' credit on its purchases. The following information is available:

1 Plastic granules sell for £10 a kilogram, variable costs are £7 a kilogram, and fixed costs £2 a kilogram.

2 Your own business is financially strong, and has sales revenue of £15m a year. For the foreseeable future it will have surplus capacity, and it is actively looking for new outlets.

3 Extracts from Plastic Toys' financial statements:

	Year 1 £000	Year 2 £000	Year 3 £000
Sales revenue	800	980	640
Profit before interest and tax	100	110	(150)
Capital employed	600	650	575
Current assets			
Inventories	200	220	320
Trade receivables	140	160	160
	340	380	480
Current liabilities			
Trade payables	180	190	220
Short-term borrowings (overdraft)	100	150	310
	280	340	530

Required:

(a) Write some short notes suggesting sources of information that you would use to assess the creditworthiness of potential customers who are unknown to you. You should critically evaluate each source of information.

(b) Describe the accounting controls that you would use to monitor the level of your business's trade receivables.

(c) Advise your general manager on the acceptability of the proposal. You should give your reasons and do any calculations you consider necessary. (*Hint*: To answer this question you must weigh the costs of administration and cash discounts against the savings in bad debts and interest charges.)

16.5 Mayo Computers Ltd has an annual sales turnover of £20m. Bad debts amount to £0.1m a year. All sales made by the business are on credit, and, at present, credit terms are negotiable by the customer. On average, the settlement period for trade receivables is 60 days. Trade receivables are financed by an overdraft bearing a 14 per cent rate of interest per year. The business is currently reviewing its credit policies to see whether more efficient and profitable methods could be employed. Only one proposal has so far been put forward concerning the management of trade credit.

The credit control department has proposed that customers should be given a $2\frac{1}{2}$ per cent discount if they pay within 30 days. For those who do not pay within this period, a maximum of 50 days' credit should be given. The credit department believes that 60 per cent of customers will take advantage of the discount by paying at the end of the discount period, and the remainder will pay at the end of 50 days. The credit department believes that bad debts can be effectively eliminated by adopting the above policies and by employing stricter credit investigation procedures, which will cost an additional £20,000 a year. The credit department is confident that these new policies will not result in any reduction in sales revenue.

Required:

Calculate the net annual cost (savings) to the business of abandoning its existing credit policies and adopting the proposals of the credit control department. (*Hint*: To answer this question you must weigh the costs of administration and cash discounts against the savings in bad debts and interest charges.)

16.6 Boswell Enterprises Ltd is reviewing its trade credit policy. The business, which sells all of its goods on credit, has estimated that sales revenue for the forthcoming year will be £3m under the existing policy. Credit customers representing 30 per cent of trade receivables are expected to pay one month after being invoiced and 70 per cent are expected to pay two months after being invoiced. These estimates are in line with previous years' figures.

At present, no cash discounts are offered to customers. However, to encourage prompt payment, the business is considering giving a $2^1/_2$ per cent cash discount to credit customers who pay in one month or less. Given this incentive, the business expects that credit customers accounting for 60 per cent of trade receivables to pay one month after being invoiced and those accounting for 40 per cent of trade receivables to pay two months after being invoiced. The business believes that the introduction of a cash discount policy will prove attractive to some customers and will lead to a 5 per cent increase in total sales revenue.

Irrespective of the trade credit policy adopted, the gross profit margin of the business will be 20 per cent for the forthcoming year and three months' inventories will be held. Fixed monthly expenses of £15,000 and variable expenses (excluding discounts), equivalent to 10 per cent of sales revenue, will be incurred and will be paid one month in arrears. Trade payables will be paid in arrears and will be equal to two months' cost of sales. The business will hold a fixed cash balance of £140,000 throughout the year, whichever trade credit policy is adopted. Ignore taxation.

Required:

(a) Calculate the investment in working capital at the end of the forthcoming year under:
   (i) the existing policy;
   (ii) the proposed policy.
(b) Calculate the expected net profit for the forthcoming year under:
   (i) the existing policy;
   (ii) the proposed policy.
(c) Advise the business as to whether it should implement the proposed policy.

(*Hint*: The investment in working capital will be made up of inventories, trade receivables and cash, *less* trade payables and any unpaid expenses at the year end.)

16.7 Delphi plc has recently decided to enter the expanding market for MP3 players. The business will manufacture the players and sell them to small TV and hi-fi specialists, medium-sized music stores and large retail chain stores. The new product will be launched next February and predicted sales revenue for the product from each customer group for February and the expected rate of growth for subsequent months are as follows:

Customer type	February sales revenue (£000)	Monthly compound sales revenue growth (%)	Credit sales (months)
TV and hi-fi specialists	20	4	1
Music stores	30	6	2
Retail chain stores	40	8	3

The business is concerned about the financing implications of launching the new product, as it is already experiencing liquidity problems. In addition, it is concerned that the credit control department will find it difficult to cope. This is a new market for the business and there are likely to be many new customers who will have to be investigated for creditworthiness.

Workings should be in £000 and calculations made to one decimal place only.

Required:

(a) Prepare an ageing schedule of the monthly receivables' balance relating to the new product for each of the first four months of the new product's life, and comment on the results. The schedule should analyse the trade receivables outstanding according to customer type. It should also indicate, for each customer type, the relevant percentage outstanding in relation to the total amount outstanding for each month.

(b) Identify and discuss the factors that should be taken into account when evaluating the creditworthiness of the new business customers.

16.8 Goliath plc is a retail business operating in Ireland. The most recent financial statements of the business are as follows:

Income statement for the year to 31 May

	£000	£000
Sales revenue		2,400.0
Cost of sales		
Opening inventories	550.0	
Purchases	1,450.0	
	2,000.0	
Closing inventories	560.0	(1,440.0)
Gross profit		960.0
Administration expenses		(300.0)
Selling expenses		(436.0)
Operating profit		224.0
Interest payable		(40.0)
Profit before taxation		184.0
Taxation (25%)		(46.0)
Profit for the period		138.0

Balance sheet as at 31 May

	£000	£000
Non-current assets		
Property, plant and equipment		
Machinery and equipment at cost	424.4	
Accumulated depreciation	(140.8)	283.6
Motor vehicles at cost	308.4	
Accumulated depreciation	(135.6)	172.8
		456.4
Current assets		
Inventories at cost		560.0
Trade receivables		565.0
Cash at bank		36.4
		1,161.4
Total assets		1,617.8

	£000
Equity	
£1 ordinary shares	200.0
Retained earnings	520.8
	720.8
Non-current liabilities	
Borrowings – Loan notes	400.0
Current liabilities	
Trade payables	451.0
Taxation	46.0
	497.0
Total equity and liabilities	1,617.8

All sales and purchases are made on credit.

The business is considering whether to grant extended credit facilities to its customers. It has been estimated that increasing the settlement period for trade receivables by a further 20 days will increase the turnover of the business by 10 per cent. However, inventories will have to be increased by 15 per cent to cope with the increased demand. It is estimated that purchases will have to rise to £1,668,000 during the next year as a result of these changes. To finance the increase in inventories and trade receivables, the business will increase the settlement period taken for suppliers by 15 days and use a loan facility bearing a 10 per cent rate of interest for the remaining balance.

If the policy is implemented, bad debts are likely to increase by £120,000 a year and administration costs will rise by 15 per cent.

Required:
(a) Calculate the increase or decrease to each of the following that will occur in the forth-coming year if the proposed policy is implemented:
   (i)   operating cash cycle (based on year-end figures);
   (ii) net investment in inventories, trade receivables and trade payables;
   (iii) net profit after taxation.
(b) Should the business implement the proposed policy? Give reasons for your conclusion.

PART 4

Supplementary information

Appendix A
Recording financial
transactions

Appendix B
Glossary of key terms

Appendix C
Solutions to self-assessment
questions

Appendix D
Solutions to review questions

Appendix E
Solutions to selected
exercises

Appendix F
Present value table

Part 4 provides information that is supplementary to the main text of the book.

Appendix A takes the format of a normal textual chapter and describes the way in which financial transactions are recorded in books of account. Generally, this is by means of the 'double entry' system, described in basic terms in the appendix.

Appendix B gives definitions of the key terms highlighted throughout the main text and listed at the end of each chapter. The aim of the appendix is to provide a single location to check on the meanings of the major accounting terms used in this book and in the world of finance.

Appendices C, D and E give answers to some of the questions set in the course of the main text. Appendix C gives answers to the self-assessment questions, Appendix D gives the answers to the review questions and Appendix E gives answers to those of the exercises that are marked as having their answers provided in the book.

Appendix F is a table of present value factors that can be used to discount future cash flows.

Recording financial transactions

Introduction

In Chapters 2 and 3, we saw how the financial transactions of a business may be recorded by making a series of entries on the balance sheet and/or the income statement. Each of these entries had its corresponding 'double', meaning that both sides of the transaction were recorded. However, adjusting the financial statements, by hand, for each transaction can be very messy and confusing. With a reasonably large number of transactions it is pretty certain to result in mistakes.

For businesses whose accounting systems are on a computer, this problem is overcome because suitable software can deal with a series of 'plus' and 'minus' entries very reliably. Where the accounting system is not computerised, however, it would be helpful to have some more practical way of keeping accounting records. Such a system not only exists but, before the advent of the computer, was the routine way of keeping accounts. It is this system that is explained in this appendix. We should be clear that the system we are going to consider follows exactly the same rules as those that we have already met. Its distinguishing feature is its ability to provide those keeping accounting records by hand with a methodical approach that allows each transaction to be clearly identified and errors to be minimised.

Learning outcomes

When you have completed this appendix, you should be able to:

- Explain the basic principles of double-entry bookkeeping.

- Write up a series of business transactions and balance the accounts.

- Extract a trial balance and explain its purpose.

- Prepare a set of financial statements from the underlying double-entry accounts.

The basics of double-entry bookkeeping

→ When we record accounting transactions by hand, we use a recording system known as **double-entry bookkeeping**. This system does not use plus and minus entries on the face of a balance sheet and income statement to record a particular transaction, in the way described in Chapters 2 and 3. Instead, these are recorded in accounts.

→ An **account** is simply a record of one or more transactions relating to a particular item, such as cash, fixtures and fittings, borrowings, sales revenue, rent payable and capital. A business may keep few or many accounts, depending on the size and complexity of its operations. Broadly, businesses tend to keep a separate account for each item that appears in either the income statement or the balance sheet.

An example of an account, in this case the cash account, is as follows:

Cash

£ | £

We can see that an account has three main features:

- A title indicating the item to which it relates
→ - A left-hand side, known as the **debit** side
→ - A right-hand side, known as the **credit** side.

One side of an account will record increases in the particular item and the other will record decreases. This, of course, is slightly different from the approach we used when adjusting the financial statements. When adjusting the balance sheet, for example, we put a reduction in an asset or claim in the same column as any increases, but with a minus sign against it. However, when accounts are used, a reduction is shown on the opposite side of the account.

The side on which an increase or decrease is shown will depend on the nature of the item to which the account relates. For example, an account for an asset, such as cash, will show increases on the left-hand (debit) side of the account and decreases on the right-hand (credit) side. However, for claims (that is, capital and liabilities) it is the other way around. An increase in the account for capital or for a liability will be shown on the right-hand (credit) side and a decrease will be shown on the left-hand (debit) side.

To understand why this difference exists, we should recall from Chapter 2 that the balance sheet equation is:

Assets = Capital + Liabilities

We can see that assets appear on one side of the equation and capital and liabilities appear on the other. Recording transactions in accounts simply expresses this difference in the recording process. Increases in assets are shown on the left-hand side of an account and increases in capital and liabilities are shown on the right-hand side of the account. We should recall the point made in Chapter 2 that each transaction has two aspects. Thus, when we record a particular transaction, two separate accounts will be affected. Recording transactions in this way is known as double-entry bookkeeping.

It is worth going through a simple example to see how transactions affecting balance sheet items would be recorded under the double-entry bookkeeping system. Suppose a new business started on 1 January with the owner putting £5,000 into a newly opened business bank account, as initial capital. This entry would appear in the cash account as follows:

Cash

	£			£
1 January Capital	5,000			

The corresponding entry would be made in the capital account as follows:

Capital

	£			£
		1 January Cash		5,000

It is usual to show, in each account by way of note, where the other side of the entry will be found. Thus, someone looking at the capital account will know that the £5,000 arose from a receipt of cash. This provides potentially useful information, partly because it establishes a 'trail' that can be followed when checking for errors. Including the date of the transaction provides additional information to the reader of the accounts.

Now suppose that, on 2 January, £600 of the cash is used to buy some inventories. This would affect the cash account as follows:

Cash

	£			£
1 January Capital	5,000	2 January Inventories		600

This cash account, in effect, shows 'positive' cash of £5,000 and 'negative' cash of £600, a net amount of £4,400.

Activity A.1

As you know, we must somehow record the other side of the transaction involving the acquisition of the inventories for £600. See if you can work out what to do in respect of the inventories.

We must open an account for inventories. Since inventories are assets, an increase in it will appear on the left-hand side of the account, as follows:

Inventories

	£			£
2 January Cash	600			

What we have seen so far highlights the key rule of double-entry bookkeeping: each left-hand entry must have a right-hand entry of equal size. Using the jargon, we can say that *every debit must have a credit*.

It might be helpful at this point to make clear that the words 'debit' and 'credit' are no more than accounting jargon for left and right, respectively. Generally, in English, (that is, when not referring to accounting), people tend to use credit to imply something good and debit something undesirable. Debit and credit have no such implication in accounting. Each transaction requires both a debit entry and a credit one. This is equally true whether the transaction is a 'good' one, like being paid by a credit customer, or a 'bad' one, like having to treat a credit customer's balance as worthless because that customer has gone bankrupt.

Recording trading transactions

The rules of double entry also extend to 'trading' transactions, that is, making revenue (sales and so on) and incurring expenses. To understand how these transactions are recorded, we should recall that in Chapter 3 the extended balance sheet equation was set out as follows:

$$\text{Assets} = \text{Capital} + (\text{Revenues} - \text{Expenses}) + \text{Liabilities}$$

This equation can be rearranged so that:

$$\text{Assets} + \text{Expenses} = \text{Capital} + \text{Revenues} + \text{Liabilities}$$

We can see that increases in expenses are shown on the same side as assets and this means that they will be dealt with in the same way for recording purposes. Thus, an increase in an expense, such as wages, will be shown on the left-hand (debit) side of the wages account and a decrease will be shown on the right-hand (credit) side. Increases in revenues are shown on the same side as capital and liabilities and so will be dealt with in the same way. Thus, an increase in revenue, such as sales, will be shown on the right-hand (credit) side and a decrease will be shown on the left hand (debit) side.

To summarise, therefore, we can say that:

- **Debits (left-hand entries) represent increases in assets and expenses and decreases in claims and revenues.**
- **Credits (right-hand entries) represent increases in claims and revenues and decreases in assets and expenses.**

Let us continue with our example by assuming that, on 3 January, the business paid £900 to rent business premises for the three months to 31 March. To record this transaction, we should normally open a 'rent account' and make entries in this account and in the cash account as follows:

Rent

		£			£
3 January	Cash	900			

Cash

		£			£
1 January	Capital	5,000	2 January	Inventories	600
			3 January	Rent	900

The fact that assets and expenses are dealt with in the same way should not be altogether surprising since assets and expenses are closely linked. Assets actually transform into expenses as they are 'used up'. Rent, which, as here, is usually paid in advance, is an asset when it is first paid. It represents the value to the business of being entitled to occupy the premises for the forthcoming period (until 31 March in this case). As the three months progress, this asset becomes an expense; it is 'used up'. We need to remember that the debit entry in the rent account does not necessarily represent either an asset or an expense; it could be a mixture of the two. Strictly, by the end of the day on which it was paid (3 January), £30 would have represented an expense for the three days; the remaining £870 would have been an asset. As each day passes, an additional £10 (that is, £900/90 (there are 90 days in January, February and March altogether)) will transform from an asset into an expense. As we have already seen, it is not necessary for us to make any adjustment to the rent account as the days pass.

Assume, now, that on 5 January the business sold inventories costing £200 for £300 on credit. As usual, when we are able to identify the cost of the inventories sold at the time of sale, we need to deal with the sale and the cost of sales as two separate issues, each having its own set of debits and credits.

First, let us deal with the sale. We now need to open accounts for both 'sales revenue' and 'trade receivables' – which do not, as yet, exist. The sale gives rise to an increase in revenue and so there is a credit entry in the sales revenue account. The sale also creates an asset of trade receivables and so there is debit entry in trade receivables:

Sales revenue

	£		£
		5 January Trade receivables	300

Trade receivables

	£		£
5 January Sales revenue	300		

Let us now deal with the inventories sold. Since the inventories sold have become the expense 'cost of sales', we need to reduce the figure on the inventories account by making a credit entry and to make the corresponding debit in a 'cost of sales' account, opened for the purpose:

Inventories

	£		£
2 January Cash	600	5 January Cost of sales	200

Cost of sales

	£		£
5 January Inventories	200		

We shall now look at the other transactions for our hypothetical business for the remainder of January. These can be taken to be as follows:

8 January	Bought some inventories on credit costing £800
11 January	Bought some office furniture for £600 cash
15 January	Sold inventories costing £600 for £900, on credit
18 January	Received £800 from trade receivables
21 January	Paid trade payables £500
24 January	Paid wages for the month £400
27 January	Bought inventories on credit for £800
31 January	Borrowed £2,000 from the Commercial Finance Company

Naturally, we shall have to open several additional accounts to enable us to record all of these transactions in any meaningful way. By the end of January, the set of accounts would appear as follows:

Cash

		£			£
1 January	Capital	5,000	2 January	Inventories	600
18 January	Trade receivables	800	3 January	Rent	900
31 January	Comm. Fin. Co.	2,000	11 January	Office furniture	600
			21 January	Trade payables	500
			24 January	Wages	400

Capital

		£			£
			1 January	Cash	5,000

Inventories

		£			£
2 January	Cash	600	5 January	Cost of sales	200
8 January	Trade payables	800	15 January	Cost of sales	600
27 January	Trade payables	800			

Rent

		£		£
3 January	Cash	900		

Sales revenue

		£			£
			5 January	Trade receivables	300
			15 January	Trade receivables	900

Trade receivables

		£			£
5 January	Sales revenue	300	18 January	Cash	800
15 January	Sales revenue	900			

Cost of sales

		£		£
5 January	Inventories	200		
15 January	Inventories	600		

Trade payables

		£			£
21 January	Cash	500	8 January	Inventories	800
			27 January	Inventories	800

Office furniture

	£		£
11 January Cash	600		

Wages

	£		£
24 January Cash	400		

Borrowings – Commercial Finance Company

	£		£
		31 January Cash	2,000

All of the transactions from 8 January onwards are quite similar in nature to those up to that date, which we discussed in detail, and so we should be able to follow them using the date references as a guide.

Balancing accounts and the trial balance

Businesses keeping their accounts in the way shown would find it helpful to summarise their individual accounts periodically – perhaps weekly or monthly – for two reasons:

- To be able to see at a glance how much is in each account (for example, to see how much cash the business has left).
- To help to check the accuracy of the bookkeeping so far.

Let us look at the cash account again:

Cash

		£			£
1 January	Capital	5,000	2 January	Inventories	600
18 January	Trade receivables	800	3 January	Rent	900
31 January	Comm. Fin. Co.	2,000	11 January	Office furniture	600
			21 January	Trade payables	500
			24 January	Wages	400

Does this account tell us how much cash the business has at 31 January? The answer is partly yes and partly no.

We do not have a single figure showing the cash **balance** but we can fairly easily deduce this by adding up the debit (receipts) column and deducting the sum of the credit (payments) column. However, it would be better if a cash balance were provided for us.

To summarise or balance this account, we add up the column with the largest amount (in this case, the debit side) and put this total on *both* sides of the account. We then put in, on the credit side, the figure that will make that side add up to the total that appears in the account. We cannot put in this balancing figure only once, as the double-entry rule would be broken. Thus, to preserve the double entry, we also put it in on the other side of the same account below the totals, as follows:

Cash

		£			£
1 January	Capital	5,000	2 January	Inventories	600
18 January	Trade receivables	800	3 January	Rent	900
31 January	Borrowings	2,000	11 January	Office furniture	600
			21 January	Trade payables	500
			24 January	Wages	400
			31 January	Balance carried down	4,800
		7,800			7,800
1 February	Balance brought down	4,800			

Note that the balance carried down (usually abbreviated to 'c/d') at the end of one period becomes the balance brought down ('b/d') at the beginning of the next. Now we can see at a glance what the present cash position is, without having to do any mental arithmetic.

Activity (A.2)

Try balancing the inventories account and then say what we know about the inventories position at the end of January.

The inventories account will be balanced as follows:

Inventories

		£			£
2 January	Cash	600	5 January	Cost of sales	200
8 January	Trade payables	800	15 January	Cost of sales	600
27 January	Trade payables	800	31 January	Balance c/d	1,400
		2,200			2,200
1 February	Balance b/d	1,400			

We can see at a glance that the business held inventories that had cost £1,400 at the end of January. We can also see quite easily how this situation arose.

We can balance all of the other accounts in a similar fashion. However, there is no point in formally balancing accounts that have only one entry at the moment (for example, the capital account) because we cannot summarise one figure; it is already in as summarised a form as it can be. After balancing, the remaining accounts will be as follows:

Capital

	£			£
		1 January	Cash	5,000

Rent

	£		£
3 January Cash	900		

Sales revenue

	£			£
31 January Balance c/d	1,200	5 January	Trade receivables	300
		15 January	Trade receivables	900
	1,200			1,200
		1 February	Balance b/d	1,200

Trade receivables

		£			£
5 January	Sales revenue	300	18 January	Cash	800
15 January	Sales revenue	900	31 January	Balance c/d	400
		1,200			1,200
1 February	Balance b/d	400			

Cost of sales

		£			£
5 January	Inventories	200	31 January	Balance c/d	800
15 January	Inventories	600			
		800			800
1 February	Balance b/d	800			

Trade payables

		£			£
21 January	Cash	500	8 January	Inventories	800
31 January	Balance c/d	1,100	27 January	Inventories	800
		1,600			1,600
			1 February	Balance b/d	1,100

Office furniture

	£		£
11 January Cash	600		

Wages

	£		£
24 January Cash	400		

Borrowings – Commercial Finance Company

	£		£
		31 January Cash	2,000

Activity (A.3)

If we now separately total the debit balances and the credit balances, what should we expect to find?

We should expect to find that these two totals are equal. This must, in theory be true since every debit entry was matched by an equally sized credit entry.

Let us see if our expectation in Activity A.3 works in our example, by listing the debit and credit balances as follows:

	Debits £	Credits £
Cash	4,800	
Inventories	1,400	
Capital		5,000
Rent	900	
Sales revenue		1,200
Trade receivables	400	
Cost of sales	800	
Trade payables		1,100
Office furniture	600	
Wages	400	
Borrowings		2,000
	9,300	9,300

This statement is known as a **trial balance**. The fact that it agrees gives us *some* indication that we have not made bookkeeping errors.

This situation, does not, however, give us total confidence that no error could have occurred. Consider the transaction that took place on 3 January (paid rent for the month of £900). In each of the following cases, all of which would be wrong, the trial balance would still have agreed:

- The transaction was completely omitted from the accounts, that is, no entries were made at all.
- The amount was misread as £9,000 but then (correctly) debited to the rent account and credited to cash.
- The correct amount was (incorrectly) debited to cash and credited to rent.

Nevertheless, a trial balance that agrees does give some confidence that accounts have been correctly written up.

Activity (A.4)

Why do you think the words 'debtor' and 'creditor' are used to describe those who owe money or are owed money by a business?

The answer simply is that debtors have a debit balance (that is, a balance brought down on the debit side) in the books of the business, whereas creditors have a credit balance.

Preparing the financial statements (final accounts)

If the trial balance agrees and we are confident that there are no errors in recording, the next stage is to prepare the income statement and balance sheet. Preparing the income statement is simply a matter of going through the individual accounts, identifying those amounts that represent revenue and expenses of the period, and transferring them to the income statement, which is itself part of the double-entry system.

We shall now do this for the example we have been using. The situation is complicated slightly for three reasons:

- As we know, the £900 rent paid during January relates to the three months January, February and March.
- The business's owner estimates that the electricity used during January is about £110. There is no bill yet from the electricity supply business because it normally bills customers only at the end of each three-month period.
- The business's owner believes that the office furniture should be depreciated by 20 per cent each year (straight-line).

These three factors need to be taken into account. As we shall see, however, the end-of-period adjustments of these types are very easily handled in double-entry accounts. Let us deal with these three areas first.

The rent account will appear as follow, after we have completed the transfer to the income statement:

Rent

		£			£
3 January	Cash	900	31 January	Income statement	300
				Balance c/d	600
		900			900
1 February	Balance b/d	600			

At 31 January, because two months' rent is still an asset, this is carried down as a debit balance. The remainder (representing January's rent) is credited to the rent account and debited to a newly opened income statement. As we shall see shortly, the £600 debit balance remaining will appear in the 31 January balance sheet.

Now let us deal with the electricity. The electricity account will be as follows after the transfer to the income statement:

Electricity

	£			£
		31 January	Income statement	110

Because there has been no cash payment or other transaction recorded so far for electricity, we do not already have an account for it. It is necessary to open one. We need to debit the income statement with the £110 of electricity used during January and credit the electricity account with the same amount. At 31 January, this credit balance reflects the amount owed by this business to the electricity supplier. Once again, we shall see shortly that this balance will appear on the balance sheet.

Next we shall consider what is necessary regarding the office furniture. The depreciation for the month will be $20\% \times £600 \times \frac{1}{12}$, that is £10. Normal accounting practice is to charge (debit) this to the income statement, with the corresponding credit going to a 'provision for depreciation of office furniture' account. The latter entry will appear as follows:

Provision for depreciation of office furniture account

	£			£
		31 January	Income statement	10

This £10 balance will be reflected in the balance sheet at 31 January by being deducted from the office furniture itself, as we shall see.

The balances on the following accounts represent straightforward revenue and expenses for the month of January:

- Sales revenue
- Cost of sales
- Wages.

The balances on these accounts will simply be transferred to the income statement.

To transfer balances to the income statement, we simply debit or credit the account concerned, such that any balance amount is eliminated, and make the corresponding credit or debit in the income statement. Take sales revenue, for example. This has a credit balance (because the balance represents a revenue). We must debit the sales revenue account with £1,200 and credit the income statement with the same amount. So a credit balance on the sales revenue account becomes a credit entry in the income statement. For the three accounts, then, we have the following:

Sales revenue

		£			£
31 January	Balance c/d	1,200	5 January	Trade receivables	300
			15 January	Trade receivables	900
		1,200			1,200
31 January	Income statement	1,200	1 February	Balance b/d	1,200

Cost of sales

		£			£
5 January	Inventories	200	31 January	Balance c/d	800
15 January	Inventories	600			
		800			800
1 February	Balance b/d	800	31 January	Income statement	800

Wages

		£			£
24 January	Cash	400	31 January	Income statement	400

The income statement will now look as follows:

Income statement

		£			£
31 January	Cost of sales	800	31 January	Sales revenue	1,200
31 January	Rent	300			
31 January	Wages	400			
31 January	Electricity	110			
31 January	Depreciation	10			

We must now transfer the balance on the income statement (a debit balance of £420).

Activity A.5

What does the balance on the income statement represent, and to where should it be transferred?

The balance is either the profit or the loss for the period. In this case it is a loss as the total expenses exceed the total revenue. This loss must be borne by the owner, and it must therefore be transferred to the capital account.

The two accounts would now appear as follows:

Income statement

		£			£
31 January	Cost of sales	800	31 January	Sales revenue	1,200
31 January	Rent	300			
31 January	Wages	400			
31 January	Electricity	110			
31 January	Depreciation	10	31 January	Capital (loss)	420
		1,620			1,620

Capital

		£			£
31 January	Income statement (loss)	420	1 January	Cash	5,000
31 January	Balance c/d	4,580			
		5,000			5,000
			1 February	Balance b/d	4,580

The last thing done was to balance the capital account.

Now all of the balances remaining on accounts represent either assets or claims as at 31 January. These balances can now be used to produce a balance sheet, as follows:

Balance sheet as at 31 January

	£
Non-current assets	
Property, plant and equipment	
Office furniture: cost	600
depreciation	(10)
	590
Current assets	
Inventories	1,400
Prepaid expense	600
Trade receivables	400
Cash	4,800
	7,200
Total assets	7,790
Capital (owners' equity)	4,580
Non-current liability	
Borrowings	2,000
Current liabilities	
Accrued expense	110
Trade payables	1,100
	1,210
Total equity and liabilities	7,790

The income statement could be written in a more stylish manner, for reporting to users, as follows:

Income statement for the month ended 31 January

	£
Sales revenue	1,200
Cost of sales	(800)
Gross profit	400
Rent	(300)
Wages	(400)
Electricity	(110)
Depreciation	(10)
Loss for the month	(420)

The ledger and its division

→ The book in which the accounts are traditionally kept is known as the **ledger**, and 'accounts' are sometimes referred to as 'ledger accounts', even where they are computerised.

In a handwritten accounting system, the ledger is often divided into various sections. This tends to be for two main reasons:

- Having all of the accounts in one book means that it is only possible for one person at a time to use the accounts, either to make entries or to extract useful information.
- Dividing the ledger along logical grounds can allow specialisation, so that various individual members of the accounts staff can look after their own part of the system. This can lead to more efficient record keeping. It can also lead to greater security, that is, less risk of error and fraud by limiting an individual's access to only part of the entire set of accounts.

There are no clear, universal rules on the division of the ledger, but the following division is fairly common:

- *The cash book.* This tends to be all of the accounts relating to cash either loose or in the bank.
- *The sales (or trade receivables) ledger.* This contains the accounts of all of the business's individual trade receivables.
- *The purchases (or trade payables) ledger.* This consists of the accounts of all of the business's individual trade payables.
- *The nominal ledger.* These accounts tend to be those of expenses and revenue, for example, sales revenue, wages, rent, and so on.
- *The general ledger.* This contains the remainder of the business's accounts, mainly those to do with non-current assets and long-term finance.

Summary

The main points in this appendix may be summarised as follows.

Double-entry bookkeeping = a system for keeping accounting records by hand, such that a relatively large volume of transactions can be handled effectively and accurately.

- There is a separate account for each asset, claim, expense and liability that needs to be separately identified.
- Each account looks like a letter T.
- Left-hand (debit) side of the account records increases in assets and expenses and decreases in revenues and claims.
- Right-hand (credit) side records increases in revenues and claims and decreases in assets and expenses.
- There is an equal credit entry in one account for a debit entry in another.
- Double-entry bookkeeping can be used to record day-to-day transactions.
- It can also follow through to generate the income statement.
- The balance sheet is a list of the net figure (the 'balance') on each of the accounts after appropriate transfers have been made to the income statement.
- The accounts are traditionally kept in a 'ledger', a term that persists even with computerised accounting.
- The ledger is traditionally broken down into several sections, each containing particular types of account.

 Key terms

double-entry bookkeeping p. 660	**balance** p. 665
account p. 660	**trial balance** p. 668
debit p. 660	**ledger** p. 672
credit p. 660	

Further reading

If you would like to explore the topics covered in this appendix in more depth, we recommend the following books:

An Introduction to Financial Accounting, *Thomas A.*, 5th edn, McGraw-Hill, 2005, chapters 3 to 8.

Financial Accounting, *Bebbington J., Gray R. and Laughlin R.*, 3rd edn, Thomson Learning, 2001, chapters 2 to 7.

Foundations of Business Accounting, *Dodge R.*, 2nd edn, Thomson Business Press, 1997, chapter 3.

Practical Accounting, *Benedict A. and Elliott B.*, Financial Times Prentice Hall, 2007, chapters 2 to 5.

Exercises

The answers to all three of these exercises are at the back of the book, starting on page 766.
If you wish to try more exercises, visit the students' side of the Companion Website.

A.1   In respect of each of the following transactions, state in which two accounts must an entry be made and whether the entry is a debit or a credit. (For example, if the transaction were buying inventories for cash, the answer would be debit the inventories account and credit the cash account.)

(a) Bought inventories on credit.
(b) Owner made cash drawings.
(c) Paid interest on business borrowings.
(d) Bought inventories for cash.
(e) Received cash from a credit customer.
(f) Paid wages to employees.
(g) The owner received some cash from a credit customer, which was taken as drawings rather than being paid into the business's bank account.
(h) Paid a credit supplier.
(i) Paid electricity bill.
(j) Made cash sales.

A.2   (a) Record the following transactions in a set of double-entry accounts:

1 February	Lee (the owner) put £6,000 into a newly-opened business bank account to start a new business
3 February	Bought inventories for £2,600 for cash
5 February	Bought some equipment (non-current asset) for cash for £800
6 February	Bought inventories costing £3,000 on credit
9 February	Paid rent for the month of £250
10 February	Paid fuel and electricity for the month of £240
11 February	Paid general expenses of £200
15 February	Sold inventories for £4,000 in cash; the inventories had cost £2,400
19 February	Sold inventories for £3,800 on credit; the inventories had cost £2,300
21 February	Lee withdrew £1,000 in cash for personal use
25 February	Paid £2,000 to trade payables
28 February	Received £2,500 from trade receivables

(b) Balance the relevant accounts and prepare a trial balance (making sure that it agrees).
(c) Prepare an income statement for the month and a balance sheet at the month end. Assume that there are no prepaid or accrued expenses at the end of the month and ignore any possible depreciation.

A.3   The following is the balance sheet of David's business at 1 January of last year.

Non-current assets		£	Capital (owners' equity)	£ 25,050
Property, plant and equipment				
Buildings		25,000	Non-current liability	
Fittings: cost	10,000		Borrowings	12,000
dep'n	(2,000)	8,000		
Current assets			Current liabilities	
Inventories of stationery		140	Trade payables	1,690
Trading inventories		1,350	Accrued electricity	270
Prepaid rent		500		
Trade receivables		1,840		
Cash		2,180		
Total assests		39,010	Total equity and liabilities	39,010

The following is a summary of the transactions that took place during the year:

1 Inventories were bought on credit for £17,220.
2 Inventories were bought for £3,760 cash.
3 Credit sales revenue amounted to £33,100 (cost £15,220).
4 Cash sales revenue amounted to £10,360 (cost £4,900).
5 Wages of £3,770 were paid.
6 Rent of £3,000 was paid. The annual rental amounts to £3,000.
7 Electricity of £1,070 was paid.
8 General expenses of £580 were paid.
9 Additional fittings were purchased on 1 January for £2,000. The cash for this was raised from additional borrowings of this amount. The interest rate is 10 per cent a year, the same as for the existing borrowings.
10 £1,000 of the borrowing was repaid on 30 June.
11 Cash received from trade receivables amounted to £32,810.
12 Cash paid to trade payables amounted to £18,150.
13 The owner withdrew £10,400 cash and £560 inventories for private use.

At the end of the year it was found that:

● The electricity bill for the last quarter of the year for £290 had not been paid.
● Trade receivables amounting to £260 were unlikely to be received.
● The value of stationery remaining was estimated at £150. Stationery is included in general expenses.
● The borrowings carried interest of 10 per cent a year and was unpaid at the year end.
● Depreciation to be taken at 20 per cent on the cost of the fittings owned at the year end. Buildings are not depreciated.

Required:
(a) Open ledger accounts and bring down all of the balances in the opening balance sheet.
(b) Make entries to record the transactions 1 to 13 (above), opening any additional accounts as necessary.
(c) Open an income statement (part of the double entry, remember). Make the necessary entries for the bulleted list above and the appropriate transfers to the income statement.
(d) List the remaining balances in the same form as the opening balance sheet (above).

ABC system of inventories control   A method of applying different levels of inventories control, based on the value of each category of inventories. *p. 622*

Absorption costing   A method at costing in which a 'fair share' of all manufacturing overhead costs is included when calculating the cost of a particular product or service. *p. 337*

Account   A section of a double-entry bookkeeping system that deals with one particular asset, claim, expense or revenue. *p. 660*

Accounting   The process of identifying, measuring and communicating information to permit informed judgements and decisions by users of the information. *p. 2*

Accounting conventions   Accounting rules that have evolved over time in order to deal with practical problems rather than to reflect some theoretical ideal. *p. 55*

Accounting information system   The system used within a business to identify, record, analyse and report accounting information. *p. 11*

Accounting period   The time span for which a business prepares its financial statements. *p. 73*

Accounting rate of return (ARR)   The average profit from an investment, expressed as a percentage of the average investment made. *p. 513*

Accruals accounting   The system of accounting that follows the accruals convention. This is the system followed in drawing up the balance sheet and income statement. *p. 86*

Accruals convention   The convention of accounting that asserts that profit is the excess of revenue over expenses, not the excess of cash receipts over cash payments. *p. 86*

Accrued expense   An expense that is outstanding at the end of an accounting period. *p. 83*

Acid test ratio   A liquidity ratio that relates the current assets (less inventories) to the current liabilities. *p. 241*

Activity-based budgeting (ABB)   A system of budgeting based on the philosophy of activity-based costing (ABC). *p. 454*

Activity-based costing (ABC)   A technique for more accurately relating overheads to specific production or provision of a service. It is based on acceptance of the fact that overheads do not just occur but are caused by activities, such as holding products in stores, which 'drive' the costs. *p. 376*

Adverse variance A difference between planned and actual performance, usually where the difference will cause the actual profit to be lower than the budgeted one. *p. 475*

Ageing schedule of trade receivables A report dividing trade receivables into categories, depending on the length of time outstanding. *p. 633*

Allotted share capital *See* Issued share capital.

Allowance for trade receivables An amount set aside out of profit to provide for anticipated losses arising from debts (trade receivables) that may prove irrecoverable. *p. 102*

Alternative Investment Market A stock market for the shares of smaller, young and growing businesses. AIM is similar in style to the main London Stock Exchange, but is cheaper for a business to enter and has a lighter regulatury regime. *p. 596*

Assets Resources held by a business, that have certain characteristics. *p. 42*

Asset-based financing A form of financing where assets are used as security for cash advances to the business. Factoring and invoice discounting, where the security is trade receivables, are examples of asset-based financing. *p. 600*

Auditors Professionals whose main duty is to make a report as to whether, in their opinion, the financial statements of a company do what they are supposed to do, namely show a true and fair view and comply with statutory, and financial reporting standard, requirements. *p. 170*

Average inventories turnover period ratio An efficiency ratio that measures the average period for which inventories are held by a business. *p. 233*

Average settlement period for trade payables ratio The average time taken for a business to pay its trade payables. *pp. 235, 643*

Average settlement period for trade receivables ratio The average time taken for trade receivables to pay the amounts owing. *pp. 234, 633*

Bad debt An amount owed to the business that is considered to be irrecoverable. *p. 102*

Balance The net of the debit and credit totals in an account in a double-entry bookkeeping system. *p. 665*

Balance sheet A statement of financial position that shows the assets of a business and the claims on those assets. *p. 38*

Balanced Scorecard A framework for translating the aims and objectives of a business into a series of key performance measures and targets. *p. 394*

Bank overdraft A flexible form of borrowing that allows an individual or business to have a negative current account balance. *p. 597*

Batch costing A technique for identifying full cost, where the production of many types of goods and services – particularly goods – involves producing in a batch of identical or nearly identical units of output, but where each batch is distinctly different from other batches. *p. 358*

Behavioural aspects of budgetary control The effect on people's attitudes and behaviour of using budgets as the basis for planning and controlling a business. *p. 492*

Benchmarking Identifying a successful business, or part of a business, and measuring the effectiveness of one's own business by comparison with this standard. *p. 392*

Bonus issue *See* Bonus shares.

Bonus shares Reserves that are converted into shares and given 'free' to shareholders. *p. 134*

Break-even analysis The activity of deducing the break-even point of some activity through analysing costs and revenue. *p. 302*

Break-even chart A graphical representation of the costs and revenue of some activity, at various levels of output, that enables the break-even point to be identified. *p. 303*

Break-even point (BEP) The level of activity at which total revenue will equal total cost, so that there is neither profit nor loss. *p. 303*

Budget A financial plan for the short term, typically one year or less. *p. 431*

Budget committee A group of managers formed to supervise and take responsibility for the budget-setting process. *p. 440*

Budget holder An individual responsible for a particular budget. *p. 446*

Budget officer An individual, often an accountant, appointed to carry out the technical tasks of the budget committee. *p. 440*

Budgetary control Using the budget as a yardstick against which the effectiveness of actual performance may be assessed. *p. 490*

Business angel An individual who supplies finance (usually equity finance) and advice to a small business. Usually the amount of finance supplied falls between £10,000 and £100,000. *p. 603*

Business entity convention The convention that holds that, for accounting purposes, the business and its owner(s) are treated as quite separate and distinct. *p. 55*

Called-up share capital That part of a company's share capital for which the shareholders have been asked to pay the agreed amount. It is part of the claim of the owners against the business. *p. 136*

Capital The owner's claim on the assets of the business. *p. 44*

Capital rationing A situation where a business has insufficient funds to undertake all of the investments that it judges to be beneficial. *p. 553*

Capital reserves Reserves that arise from an unrealised 'capital' profits or gains rather than from normal realised trading activities. *p. 131*

Carrying amount The difference between the cost (or fair value) of a non-current asset and the accumulated depreciation relating to the asset. The carrying value is also referred to as the written-down value (WDV) and the net book value (NBV). *p. 90*

Cash discount A reduction in the amount due for goods or services sold on credit in return for prompt payment. *p. 631*

Cash flow statement A statement that shows the sources and uses of cash for a period. *p. 38*

Cash generated from operations per ordinary shares ratio An investment ratio that relates the cash generated from operations and available to ordinary shareholders to the number of ordinary shares. *p. 250*

Cash generated from operations to maturing obligations ratio A liquidity ratio that compares the cash generated from operations to the current liabilities of the business. *p. 241*

Claims Obligations on the part of a business to provide cash or some other benefit to outside parties. *p. 42*

Combined Code A code of practice for companies listed on the London Stock Exchange that deals with corporate governance matters. *p. 124*

Committed cost A cost that has been incurred but not yet paid, but which must, under some contract or obligation, be paid. *p. 286*

Common costs Another name for indirect costs or overheads. These are costs that do not relate directly to, and are not measurable in respect of, particular units of output, but relate to all output. *p. 336*

Comparability The requirement that items, which are basically the same, should be treated in the same manner for measurement and reporting purposes. Lack of comparability will limit the usefulness of accounting information. *p. 8*

Compensating variances The situation that exists when two variances, one adverse the other favourable, are of equal size and therefore cancel each other out. *p. 489*

Consistency convention The accounting convention that holds that, when a particular method of accounting is selected to deal with a transaction, this method should be applied consistently over time. *p. 101*

Consolidated financial statements *See* Group financial statements.

Continual budget A budgeting system that continually updates budgets so that there is always a budget for a full planning period. (Also known as a rolling budget.) *p. 434*

Contribution per unit Sales revenue per unit less variable costs per unit. *p. 307*

Control Compelling events to conform to a plan. *pp. 432, 492*

Convertible loan notes Long-term borrowings that can be converted into equity share capital at the option of the holders. *p. 576*

Corporate governance Matters concerned with directing and controlling a company. *p. 123*

Corporation tax Taxation that a limited company is liable to pay on its profits. *p. 122*

Cost The amount of resources, usually measured in monetary terms, sacrificed to achieve a particular objective. *p. 280*

Cost allocation Assigning costs to cost centres according to the amount of cost that has been incurred in each centre. *p. 351*

Cost apportionment Dividing costs between cost centres on a basis that is considered to reflect fairly the costs incurred in each centre. *p. 351*

Cost behaviour The manner in which costs alter with changes in the level of activity. *p. 339*

Cost centre Some area, object, person or activity for which costs are separately collected. *p. 349*

Cost driver An activity that causes costs. *p. 376*

Cost of sales   The cost of the goods sold during a period. Cost of sales can be derived by adding the opening inventories held to the inventories purchases for the period and then deducting the closing inventories held. *p. 76*

Cost-plus pricing   An approach to pricing output that is based on full cost, plus a percentage profit loading. *p. 360*

Cost pool   The sum of the overhead costs that are seen as being caused by the same cost driver. *p. 376*

Cost unit   The objective for which the cost is being deduced, usually a product or service. *p. 340*

Creative accounting   Adopting accounting policies to achieve a particular view of performance and position that preparers would like users to see rather than what is a true and fair view. *p. 180*

Credit   An entry made in the right-hand side of an account in double-entry book-keeping. *p. 660*

Current assets   Assets that are held for the short term. They include cash itself and other assets that are held for sale or consumption in the normal course of a business's operating cycle. *p. 50*

Current liabilities   Claims against the business which are expect to be settled within the normal course of the business's operating cycle or within 12 months of the balance sheet date, or which are held primarily for trading purposes, or for which the business does not have the right to defer settlement beyond 12 months of the balance sheet date. *p. 52*

Current ratio   A liquidity ratio that relates the current assets of the business to the current liabilities. *p. 240*

Debit   An entry made in the left-hand side of an account in double-entry bookkeeping. *p. 660*

Debt factoring   A service offered by a financial institution (a factor) that involves the factor taking over the management of the trade receivables of the business. The factor is often prepared to make an advance to the business, based on the amount of trade receivables outstanding. *p. 597*

Deep discount bonds   Redeemable loan notes (bonds) offering a rate of interest below the market rate and issued at a discount to their redeemable value. *p. 576*

Depreciation   A measure of that portion of the cost (or fair value) of a non-current asset that has been consumed during an accounting period. *p. 87*

Direct costs   Costs that can be identified with specific cost units, to the extent that the effect of the cost can be measured in respect of each particular unit of output. *p. 336*

Direct method   An approach to deducing the cash flows from operating activities, in a cash flow statement, by analysing the business's cash records. *p. 201*

Director   An individual who is appointed (normally by being elected) to act as the most senior level of management of a company. *p. 123*

Directors' report   A report containing information of a financial and non-financial nature that the directors must produce as part of the annual financial report to shareholders. *p. 171*

Discount factor   The rate applied to future cash flows to derive the present value of those cash flows. *p. 527*

Discretionary budget   A budget based on a sum allocated at the discretion of senior management. *p. 446*

Discriminate function   A boundary line, produced by multiple discriminate analysis, which can be used to identify those businesses that are likely to suffer financial distress and those that are not. *p. 262*

Dividend   The transfer of assets (usually cash) made by a company to its shareholders. *p. 129*

Dividend cover ratio   An investment ratio that relates the earnings available for dividends to the dividend announced, to indicate how many times the former covers the latter. *p. 248*

Dividend payout ratio   An investment ratio that relates the dividends announced for the period to the earnings available for dividends that were generated in that period. *p. 248*

Dividend per share   An investment ratio that relates the dividends announced for a period to the number of shares in issue. *p. 249*

Dividend yield ratio   An investment ratio that relates the cash return from a share to its current market value. *p. 249*

Double-entry bookkeeping   A system for recording financial transactions where each transaction is recorded twice, once as a debit and once as a credit. *p. 660*

Dual aspect convention   The accounting convention that holds that each transaction has two aspects and that each aspect must be recorded in the financial statements. *p. 57*

Earnings per share   An investment ratio that relates the earnings generated by the business during a period, and available to shareholders, to the number of shares in issue. *p. 250*

Economic order quantity (EOQ)   The quantity of inventories that should be bought in each order so as to minimise total inventories' costs. *p. 622*

Economic value added (EVA®)   A measure of business performance that concentrates on wealth generation. It is based on economic profit rather than accounting profit and takes full account of the costs of financing. *p. 403*

Economies of scale   Cost savings per unit that result from undertaking a large volume of activities; they are due to factors such as division and specialisation of labour and discounts from bulk buying. *p. 313*

Elasticity of demand   The extent to which the level of demand alters with changes in price. *p. 409*

Equity   Ordinary shares and reserves of a company. *p. 128*

Eurobond   A form of long-term borrowing where the finance is raised on an international basis. Eurobonds are issued in a currency that is not that of the country in which the bonds are issued. *p. 574*

Expected net present value (ENPV)   A weighted average of the possible present value outcomes, where the probabilities associated with each outcome are used as weights. *p. 545*

Expense A measure of the outflow of assets (or increase in liabilities) incurred as a result of generating revenue. *p. 72*

Fair values The values ascribed to assets as an alternative to historic cost. They are usually the current market value (that is, the exchange values in an arm's-length transaction). *p. 61*

Favourable variance A difference between planned and actual performance, where the difference will cause the actual profit to be higher than the budgeted one. *p. 475*

Feedback control A control device where actual performance is compared with planned and where action is taken to try to avoid future divergences between these. *p. 472*

Feedforward control A control device where forecast future performance is compared with planned performance and where action is taken to deal with divergences between these. *p. 472*

Final accounts The income statement, cash flow statement and balance sheet taken together. *p. 41*

Finance The study of how businesses raise funds and select appropriate investments. *p. 2*

Finance lease A financial arrangement where the asset title remains with the owner (the lessor) but the lease agreement transfers virtually all the rewards and risks to the business (the lessee). *p. 580*

Financial accounting The measuring and reporting of accounting information for external users (those users other than the managers of the business). *p. 13*

Financial derivative Any form of financial instrument, based on share capital or borrowings, which can be used by investors either to increase their returns or to decrease their exposure to risk. *p. 578*

Financial gearing The existence of fixed payment-bearing sources of finance (for example, borrowings) in the capital structure of a business. *p. 242*

Financial management A subject area concerned with the financing and investing decisions of businesses. *p. 2*

First in, first out (FIFO) A method of inventories costing which assumes that the earliest acquired inventories are used (in production or sales) first. *p. 97*

Five Cs of credit A checklist of factors to be taken into account when assessing the creditworthiness of a customer. *p. 627*

Fixed cost A cost that stays the same when changes occur to the volume of activity. *p. 298*

Flexible budget A budget that is adjusted to reflect the actual level of output achieved. *p. 474*

Flexing the budget Revising the budget to what it would have been had the planned level of output been different. *p. 474*

Forecast A prediction of future outcomes, or of the future state of the environment. *p. 434*

Framework of principles The main principles that underpin accounting, which can help in identifying best practice and in developing accounting rules. *p. 169*

Full cost The total amount of resources, usually measured in monetary terms, sacrificed to achieve a particular objective. *p. 334*

Full cost (cost-plus) pricing Pricing output on the basis of its full cost, normally with a loading for profit. *p. 417*

Full costing Deducting the total direct and indirect (overhead) costs of pursuing some activity or objective. *p. 334*

Fully paid shares Shares on which the shareholders have paid the full issue price. *p. 136*

Gearing ratio A ratio that relates the contribution of finance that required a fixed return (such as borrowings) to the total long-term finance of the business. *p. 244*

Going concern convention The accounting convention that holds that it is assumed that the business will continue operations for the foreseeable future, unless there is reason to believe otherwise. In other words, there is no intention, or need, to liquidate the business. *p. 57*

Gross profit The amount remaining (if positive) after trading expenses (for example, cost of sales) have been deducted from trading revenue. *p. 74*

Gross profit margin ratio A profitability ratio relating the gross profit to the sales revenue for a period. *p. 231*

Group financial statements Sets of financial accounting statements that combine the performance and position of a group of companies under common control. *p. 146*

Hire purchase A method of acquiring an asset by paying the purchase price by instalments over a period. Normally, control of the asset will pass as soon as the hire purchase contract is signed and the first instalment is paid, whereas ownership will pass on payment of the final instalment. *p. 582*

Historic cost What was paid for an asset when it was originally acquired. *p. 280*

Historic cost convention The accounting convention that holds that assets should be recorded at their historic (acquisition) cost. *p. 56*

Holding company *See* Parent company.

Ideal standards Standards that assume perfect operating conditions, where there is no inefficiency due to lost production time, defects and so on. The objective of setting ideal standards is to encourage employees to strive towards excellence. *p. 494*

Income statement A financial statement (also known as profit and loss account) that measures and reports the profit (or loss) the business has generated during a period. It is derived by deducting from total revenue for a period, the total expenses associated with that revenue. *pp. 38, 72*

Incremental budgeting Constructing budgets on the basis of what happened in the previous period, with some adjustment for expected changes in the forthcoming budget period. *p. 446*

Indirect costs (or overheads) All of those costs that cannot be directly measured in respect of each particular unit of output, that is all costs except direct costs. *p. 336*

Indirect method An approach to deducing the cash flows from operating activities, in a cash flow statement, by analysing the business's financial statements. *p. 201*

Inflation An increase in the general prices of goods and services resulting in a corresponding decline in the purchasing power of money. *p. 524*

Intangible assets Assets that do not have a physical substance (for example, patents, goodwill and trade receivables). *p. 44*

Interest cover ratio A gearing ratio that divides the operating profit (that is, profit before interest and taxation) by the interest payable for a period. *p. 245*

Internal rate of return (IRR) The discount rate for an investment that will have the effect of producing a zero NPV. *p. 530*

International Accounting Standards *See* International Financial Reporting Standards.

International Financial Reporting Standards Transnational accounting rules that have been adopted, or developed, by the International Accounting Standards Board and which should be followed in preparing the published financial statements of listed limited companies. *p. 161*

Invoice discounting A loan provided by a financial institution based on a proportion of the face value of credit sales outstanding. *p. 598*

Irrelevant cost A cost that is not relevant to a particular decision. *p. 281*

Issued share capital That part of the share capital that has been issued to shareholders. Also known as allotted share capital. *p. 136*

Job costing A technique for identifying the full cost per unit of output, where that output is not similar to other units of output. *p. 337*

Just-in-time (JIT) inventories management A system of inventories management that aims to have supplies delivered, to production or sales, just in time for their required use. *p. 625*

***Kaizen* costing** An approach to cost control where an attempt is made to control costs by trying continually to make cost savings, often only small ones, from one time period to the next during the production stage of the product life cycle. *p. 390*

Last in, first out (LIFO) A method of inventories costing which assumes that the most recently acquired inventories are used (in production or sales) first. *p. 97*

Lead time The time lag between placing an order for goods or services and their delivery to the required location. *p. 620*

Learning curve A graph that represents the tendency for people to carry out tasks more quickly as they become more experienced in doing them. *p. 496*

Ledger The book in which accounts are traditionally kept. *p. 672*

Liabilities Claims of individuals and organisations, apart from the owner, that have arisen from past transactions or events such as supplying goods or lending money to the business. *p. 45*

Limited company An artificial legal person that has an identity separate from that of those who own and manage it. *pp. 20, 116*

Limited liability The restriction of the legal obligation of shareholders to meet all of the company's debts. *p. 118*

Limiting factor Some aspect of the business (for example, lack of sales demand) that will prevent it achieving its objectives to the maximum extent. *p. 434*

Loan notes Long-term borrowings usually made by limited companies. *pp. 137, 574*

Loan covenant A condition contained within a loan agreement that is designed to help protect the lenders. *p. 578*

Loan stock *See* Loan note.

Management accounting The measuring and reporting of accounting information for the managers of a business. *p. 13*

Management by exception A system of control, based on a comparison of planned and actual performance, that allows managers to focus on areas of poor performance rather than dealing with areas where performance is satisfactory. *pp. 438, 471*

Marginal analysis The activity of decision making through analysing variable costs and revenues, ignoring fixed costs. *p. 318*

Marginal cost The additional cost of producing one more unit. This is often the same as the variable cost. *p. 318*

Marginal cost pricing Pricing output on the basis of its marginal cost, normally with a loading for profit. *p. 420*

Master budget A summary of the individual budgets, usually consisting of a budgeted income statement, a budgeted balance sheet and a budgeted cash flow statement. *p. 435*

Matching convention The accounting convention that holds that, in measuring income, expenses should be matched to revenue, which they helped generate in the same accounting period as that revenue was realised. *p. 82*

Materiality The requirement that material information should be disclosed to users in financial statements. *p. 8*

Materiality convention The accounting convention that states that, where the amounts involved are immaterial, only what is expedient should be considered. *p. 86*

Materials requirement planning (MRP) system A computer-based system of inventories control that schedules the timing of deliveries of bought-in parts and materials to coincide with production requirements to meet demand. *p. 625*

Mission statement A brief statement setting out the aims of the business. *pp. 26, 431*

Mortgage A loan secured on property. *p. 578*

Multiple discriminate analysis A statistical technique that can be used to predict financial distress; it involves using an index based on a combination of financial ratios. *p. 262*

Net book value *See* Carrying amount.

Net present value (NPV) A method of investment appraisal based on the present value of all relevant cash flows associated with an investment. *p. 522*

Nominal value The face value of a share in a company. (Also called par value.) *p. 129*

Non-current assets Assets held that do not meet the criteria of current assets. They are held for the long-term operations of the business rather than continuously circulating within the business. Non-current assets can be seen as the tools of the business. (Also known as fixed asset.) *p. 50*

Non-current liabilities Those amounts due to other parties that are not current liabilities. *p. 52*

Non-operating-profit variances Differences between budgeted and actual performance that do not lead directly to differences between budgeted and actual operating profit. *p. 486*

Objective probabilities Probabilities based on information gathered from past experience. *p. 549*

Offer for sale An issue of shares that involves a public limited company (or its shareholders) selling the shares to a financial institution that will, in turn, sell the shares to the public. *p. 589*

Operating and financial review (OFR) A narrative report that helps users to understand the operating and financial results of a business for a period. *p. 176*

Operating cash cycle (OCC) The period between the outlay of cash to buy supplies and the ultimate receipt of cash from the sale of goods. *p. 638*

Operating gearing The relationship between the total fixed and the total variable costs for some activity. *p. 311*

Operating lease An arrangement where a business hires an asset, usually for a short time. Hiring an asset under an operating lease tends to be seen as an operating, rather than a financing, decision. *p. 580*

Operating profit The profit achieved during a period after all operating expenses have been deducted from revenues from operations. Financing expenses are deducted after the calculation of operating profit. *p. 75*

Operating profit margin ratio A profitability ratio relating the operating profit to the sales revenue for the period. *p. 230*

Operational gearing *See* Operating gearing.

Opportunity cost The cost incurred when one course of action prevents an opportunity to derive some benefit from another course of action. *pp. 280, 534*

Ordinary shares Shares of a company owned by those who are due the benefits of the company's activities after all other stakeholders have been satisfied. *p. 130*

Outlay cost A cost that involves the spending of money or some other transfer of assets. *p. 282*

Outsourcing Subcontracting activities to (sourcing goods or services from) outside organisations. *p. 322*

Overhead (or indirect cost) Any cost except a direct cost; a cost which cannot be directly measured in respect of each particular cost objective. *p. 336*

Overhead absorption (recovery) rate The rate at which overheads are charged to cost units (jobs), usually in a job costing system. *p. 341*

Overtrading The situation arising when a business is operating at a level of activity which cannot be supported by the amount of finance that has been committed. *p. 256*

Paid-up share capital That part of the share capital of a company that has been called and paid. *p. 136*

Par value *See* Nominal value.

Parent company A company that has a controlling interest in another company. *p. 145*

Partnership A form of business unit where there are at least two individuals, but usually no more than twenty, carrying on a business with the intention of making a profit. *p. 20*

Past cost A cost that has been incurred in the past. *p. 282*

Payback period (PP) The time taken for the initial outlay for an investment to be repaid from its future net cash inflows. *p. 518*

Penetration pricing   Setting prices at a level low enough to encourage wide market acceptance of a product or service. *p. 422*

Periodic budget   A budget developed on a one-off basis to cover a particular planning period. *p. 434*

Post-completion audit   A review of the performance of an investment project to see whether actual performance matched planned performance and whether any lessons can be drawn from the way in which the investment was appraised and carried out. *p. 555*

Practical standards   Standards that do not assume perfect operating conditions. Although they demand a high level of efficiency, account is taken of possible lost production time, defects and so on. They are designed to be challenging, yet achievable. *p. 494*

Preference shares   Shares of a company owned by those who are entitled to the first part of any dividend that the company may pay. *p. 130*

Prepaid expenses   Expenses that have been paid in advance at the end of the accounting period. *p. 85*

Price/earnings ratio   An investment ratio that relates the market value of a share to the earnings per share. *p. 251*

Price skimming   Setting prices at a high level to make the maximum profit from the product or service before the price is lowered to attract the next segment of the market. *p. 423*

Private company   A limited company for which the directors can restrict the ownership of its shares. *p. 119*

Private equity   Equity finance primarily for small and medium-sized businesses provided by venture capitalists and/or business angels. *p. 601*

Private placing   An issue of shares that involves a limited company arranging for the shares to be sold to the clients of particular issuing houses or stockbrokers, rather than to the general investing public. *p. 590*

Process costing   A technique for deriving the full cost per unit of output, where the units of output are the same or it is reasonable to treat them as being so. *p. 335*

Product cost centre   Some area, object, person or activity for which costs are separately collected, in which cost units have costs added. *p. 350*

Profit   The increase in wealth attributable to the owners of a business that arises through business operations. *p. 72*

Profit and loss account   *See* Income statement.

Profit before taxation   The result when all of the appropriately matched expenses of running a business have been deducted from the revenue for the year, but before the taxation charge is deducted. *p. 144*

Profit for the year   The result when all of the appropriately matched expenses of running a business have been deducted from the revenue for the year and then, in the case of a limited company the taxation charge deducted. *pp. 75, 144*

Profit–volume (PV) chart   A graphical representation of the contributions (revenue less variable costs) of some activity, at various levels, which enables the break-even point and the profit at various activity levels to be identified. *p. 313*

Property, plant and equipment Those non-current assets that have a physical substance (for example, plant and machinery, motor vehicles). *p. 61*

Prudence convention The accounting convention that holds that financial statements should err on the side of caution. *p. 56*

Public company A limited company for which the directors cannot restrict the ownership of its shares. *p. 119*

Public issue An issue of shares that involves a public limited company (plc) making a direct invitation to the public to buy shares in the company. *p. 589*

Quality costs The cost of establishing procedures that promote the quality of output, either by preventing quality problems in the first place or by dealing with them when they occur. *p. 389*

Reducing-balance method A method of calculating depreciation that applies a fixed percentage rate of depreciation to the carrying amount of an asset in each period. *p. 90*

Relevance The ability of accounting information to influence decisions; regarded as a key characteristic of useful accounting information. *p. 7*

Relevant cost A cost that is relevant to a particular decision. *pp. 281, 534*

Relevant range The range of output within which a particular business is expected to operate. *p. 315*

Reliability The requirement that accounting information should be free from significant errors or bias and should represent what it purports to represent. Reliability is regarded as a key characteristic of useful accounting information. *p. 7*

Reserves Part of the owners' claim (equity) of a limited company that has arisen from profits and gains, to the extent that these have not been distributed to the shareholders or reduced by losses. *p. 128*

Residual value The amount for which a non-current asset is sold when the business has no further use for it. *p. 89*

Return on capital employed ratio (ROCE) A profitability ratio expressing the relationship between the operating profit (that is, profit before interest and taxation) and the long-term funds (equity and borrowings) invested in the business. *p. 229*

Return on ordinary shareholders' funds ratio (ROSF) A profitability ratio that compares the amount of profit for the period available to the ordinary shareholders with their stake in the business. *p. 228*

Revenue A measure of the inflow of assets (for example, cash or amounts owed to a business by credit customers), or a reduction in liabilities, arising as a result of trading operations. *p. 72*

Revenue reserve Part of the owners' claim (equity) of a company that arises from realised profits and gains, including after-tax trading profits and gains from disposals of non-current assets. *p. 129*

Rights issue An issue of shares for cash to existing shareholders on the basis of the number of shares already held. *p. 586*

Risk The extent and likelihood that what is projected to occur will not actually occur. *p. 523*

Risk-adjusted discount rate A discount rate applied to investment projects that is increased (decreased) in the face of increased (decreased) risk. *p. 552*

Risk premium The additional return required from an investment, owing to a perceived level of risk: the greater the perceived risk, the larger the required risk premium. *p. 524*

Rolling budget *See* Continual budget.

Sale and leaseback An agreement to sell an asset (usually property) to another party and simultaneously to lease the asset back in order to continue using the asset. *p. 582*

Sales revenue per employee ratio An efficiency ratio that relates the sales revenue generated during a period to the average number of employees of the business. *p. 237*

Sales revenue to capital employed ratio An efficiency ratio that relates the sales revenue generated during a period to the capital employed. *p. 236*

Scenario building Creating a model of a business decision, usually on a computer spreadsheet, enabling the decision maker to look at the effect of different assumptions on the decision outcome. *p. 544*

Segmental financial report A report that breaks down the operating results of a business according to its business or geographical segments. *p. 173*

Semi-fixed (semi-variable) cost A cost that has an element of both fixed and variable cost. *p. 301*

Sensitivity analysis An examination of the key variables affecting a decision (for example an investment project), to see how changes in each input might influence the outcome. *p. 541*

Service cost centre Some area, object, person or activity for which costs are collected separately, in which cost units do not have cost added, because service cost centres only render services to product cost services and to other service cost centres. *p. 350*

Shares Portions of the ownership, or equity, of a company. *pp. 6, 116*

Share premium account A capital reserve reflecting any amount, above the nominal value of shares, that is paid for those shares when issued by a company. *p. 132*

Sole proprietorship An individual in business on his or her own account. *p. 19*

Standard quantities and costs Planned quantities and costs (or revenue) for individual units of input or output. Standards are the building blocks used to produce the budget. *p. 494*

Statement of changes in equity A financial statement, required by IAS 1, which shows the effect of gains/losses and capital injections/withdrawals on the equity base of a company. *p. 166*

Stepped fixed cost A fixed cost that does not remain fixed over all levels of output but which changes in steps as a threshold level of output is reached. *p. 300*

Stock exchange A market where 'second-hand' shares may be bought and sold and new capital raised. *p. 590*

Straight-line method A method of accounting for depreciation that allocates the amount to be depreciated evenly over the useful life of the asset. *p. 89*

Strategic management The process of setting a course to achieve the business's objectives, taking account of the commercial and economic environment in which the business operates. *p. 24*

Subjective probabilities Probabilities that are based on opinion rather than past data. *p. 550*

Summary financial statements A summarised version of the complete annual financial statements, which shareholders may receive as an alternative to the complete statements. *p. 180*

Sunk cost A cost that has been incurred in the past; the same as a past cost. *p. 286*

Takeover The acquisition of control of one company by another, usually as a result of acquiring a majority of the ordinary shares of the former. *p. 146*

Tangible assets Those assets that have a physical substance (for example, plant and machinery, motor vehicles). *p. 44*

Target costing An approach to deriving product costs where the business starts with the projected selling price and from it deduces the target cost per unit that must be met to enable the business to meet its profit objectives. *p. 388*

Tender issue A public issue of shares or loan notes (by a public limited company) where potential investors are invited to place bids for the securities concerned, rather than the company setting the price itself. *p. 589*

Term loan Finance provided by financial institutions, like banks and insurance companies, under a contract with the borrowing business that indicates the interest rate and dates of payments of interest and repayment of the loan. The loan is not normally transferable from one lender to another. *p. 574*

Total cost The sum of the variable and fixed costs of pursuing some activity. *p. 340*

Total life-cycle costing Paying attention to all of the costs that will be incurred during the entire life of a product or service. *p. 386*

Transfer price The price at which goods or services are sold, or transferred, between divisions of the same business. *p. 174*

Trial balance A totalled list of the balances on each of the accounts in a double-entry bookkeeping system. *p. 668*

Understandability The requirement that accounting information should be understood by those for whom the information is primarily compiled. Lack of understandability will limit the usefulness of accounting information. *p. 8*

Univariate analysis A method that can be used to help predict financial distress, which involves the use of a single ratio as a predictor. *p. 262*

Value chain analysis Analysing each activity undertaken by a business to identify any that do not add value to the output of goods or services. *p. 390*

Value driver A factor that creates wealth, such as employee satisfaction, customer loyalty and level of product innovation. *p. 393*

Variable cost A cost that varies according to the volume of activity. *p. 298*

Variable costing An approach to costing in which only those costs that vary with the level of output are included in the product cost. *p. 362*

Variance The financial effect, usually on the budgeted profit, of the particular factor under consideration being more, or less, than budgeted. *p. 475*

Variance analysis Carrying out calculations to find the area of the business's operations that has caused the budgets not to have been met. *p. 482*

Venture capital Long-term finance provided by certain institutions to small and medium-sized businesses to exploit relatively high-risk opportunities. *p. 601*

Warrant A document giving the holder the right, but not the obligation, to acquire ordinary shares in a company at an agreed price. *p. 577*

Weighted average cost (AVCO) A method of inventories costing, which assumes that inventories entering the business lose their separate identity and any issues of inventories reflect the weighted average cost of the inventories held. *p. 97*

Working capital Current assets less current liabilities. *p. 615*

Written-down value (WDV) *See* Carrying amount.

Zero-base budgeting (ZBB) An approach to budgeting, based on the philosophy that all spending needs to be justified annually and that each budget should start as a clean sheet. *p. 446*

Solutions to self-assessment questions

Chapter 2

2.1 **Simonson Engineering**

The balance sheet you prepare should be set out as follows:

Simonson Engineering
Balance sheet as at 30 September 2006

	£
Non-current assets	
Property, plant and equipment	
Property	72,000
Plant and machinery	25,000
Motor vehicles	15,000
Fixtures and fittings	9,000
	121,000
Current assets	
Inventories	45,000
Trade receivables	48,000
Cash in hand	1,500
	94,500
Total assets	215,500
Capital (owners' equity)	
Opening balance	117,500
Profit	18,000
	135,500
Drawings	(15,000)
	120,500
Non-current liabilities	
Long-term borrowings	51,000
Current liabilities	
Trade payables	18,000
Short-term borrowings	26,000
	44,000
Total equity and liabilities	215,500

Chapter 3

3.1 **TT and Co.**

Balance sheet as at 31 December 2006

Assets	£	Claims	£
Delivery van		Capital	
(12,000 − 2,500)	9,500	(50,000 + 26,900)	76,900
Inventories (143,000 +		Trade payables	
12,000 − 74,000 − 16,000)	65,000	(143,000 − 121,000)	22,000
Trade receivables		Accrued expenses	
(152,000 − 132,000 − 400)	19,600	(630 + 620)	1,250
Cash at bank (50,000 − 25,000			
− 500 − 1,200 − 12,000 −			
33,500 − 1,650 − 12,000			
+ 35,000 + 132,000			
− 121,000 − 9,400)	750		
Prepaid expenses			
(5,000 + 300)	5,300		
Total assets	100,150	**Total equity and liabilities**	100,150

Income statement for the year ended 31 December 2006

	£
Sales revenue (152,000 + 35,000)	187,000
Cost of goods sold (74,000 + 16,000)	(90,000)
Gross profit	97,000
Rent	(20,000)
Rates (500 + 900)	(1,400)
Wages (33,500 + 630)	(34,130)
Electricity (1,650 + 620)	(2,270)
Bad debts	(400)
Van depreciation [(12,000 − 2,000)/4]	(2,500)
Van expenses	(9,400)
Profit for the year	26,900

The balance sheet could now be rewritten in a more stylish form as follows:

Balance sheet as at 31 December 2006

	£
Non-current assets	
Property, plant and equipment	
Delivery van at cost	12,000
Accumulated depreciation	(2,500)
	9,500
Current assets	
Inventories	65,000
Trade receivables	19,600
Prepaid expenses	5,300
Cash	750
	90,650
Total assets	100,150
Capital (owners' equity)	
Original	50,000
Retained profit	26,900
	76,900
Current liabilities	
Trade payables	22,000
Accrued expenses	1,250
	23,250
Total equity and liabilities	100,150

Chapter 4

4.1 Dev Ltd

(a) The summarised balance sheet of Dev Ltd, immediately following the rights and bonus issue, is as follows:

Balance sheet as at 31 December 2006

	£
Net assets [235 + 40 (cash from the rights issue)]	275,000
Equity	
Share capital: 180,000 shares @ £1 [(100 + 20) + 60]	180,000
Share premium account (30 + 20 − 50)	–
Revaluation reserve (37 − 10)	27,000
Retained earnings	68,000
Total equity	275,000

Note that the bonus issue of £60,000 is taken from capital reserves (reserves unavailable for dividends) as follows:

	£
Share premium account	50,000
Revaluation reserve	10,000
	60,000

More could have been taken from the revaluation reserve and less from the share premium account without making any difference to dividend payment possibilities.

(b) There may be pressure from a potential lender for the business to limit its ability to pay dividends. This would place lenders in a more secure position because the maximum buffer or safety margin between the value of the assets and the amount owed by the business is maintained. It is not unusual for potential lenders to insist on some measure to lock up shareholders' funds in this way as a condition of granting the loan.

(c) The summarised balance sheet of Dev Ltd, immediately following the rights and bonus issue, assuming a minimum dividend potential objective, is as follows:

Balance sheet as at 31 December 2006

	£
Net assets [235 + 40 (cash from the rights issue)]	275,000
Equity	
Share capital: 180,000 shares @ £1 [(100 + 20) + 60]	180,000
Share premium account (30 + 20)	50,000
Revaluation reserve	37,000
Retained earnings (68 – 60)	8,000
Total equity	275,000

(d) Before the bonus issue, the maximum dividend was £68,000. Now it is £8,000. Thus the bonus issue has had the effect of locking up an additional £60,000 of the business's assets in terms of the business's ability to pay dividends.

(e) Before the issues, Lee had 100 shares worth £2.35 (that is, £235,000/100,000) each or £235 in total. Lee would be offered 20 shares in the rights issue at £2 each or £40 in total. After the rights issue, Lee would have 120 shares worth £2.2917 (that is, £275,000/120,000) each or £275 in total.

The bonus issue would give Lee 60 additional shares. After the bonus issue, Lee would have 180 shares worth £1.5278 (that is, £275,000/180,000) each or £275 in total.

None of this affects Lee's wealth. Before the issues, Lee had £235 worth of shares and £40 more in cash. After the issues, Lee has the same total wealth but all £275 is in the value of the shares.

(f) The things that we know about the company are as follows:

(i) It is a private (as opposed to a public) limited company, for it has 'Ltd' (limited) as part of its name, rather than plc (public limited company).

(ii) It has made an issue of shares at a premium, almost certainly after it had traded successfully for a period. (There is a share premium account. It is very unlikely that the original shares, issued when the company was first formed, would have been issued at a premium.)

(iii) Certain of the assets in the balance sheet have been upwardly revalued by at least £37,000. (There is a revaluation reserve of £37,000. This may just be what is left after a previous bonus issue had taken part of the balance.)

(iv) The company has traded at an aggregate profit (though there could have been losses in some years), net of tax and any dividends paid. (There is a positive balance on retained earnings.)

Chapter 5

5.1 J Baxter plc

We can see from the table below that the Italian segment generates the highest revenue, but also generates the lowest profit. We shall be considering financial ratios in detail in Chapter 7; however, it is helpful to compare the profit generated with the sales revenue for each geographical segment. We can see from the table below that the French segment generates the most profit in relation to sales revenue. 15 per cent, or £0.15 in every £1, of profit is derived from the sales revenue generated. However, for the Italian segment, only 2.1%, or £0.02 in every £1, of profit is derived from the sales revenue generated.

We can also compare the profit generated with the net assets employed (that is, total assets – total liabilities) for each segment. We can see from the table below that the UK segment produces the best return on net assets employed: £0.36 for every £1 invested. Once again, the Italian segment produces the worst results.

The reasons for the relatively poor results from the Italian segment need further investigation. There may be valid reasons; for example, this segment may have deliberately engaged in low pricing during the period in an attempt to increase market share. However, it may suggest that the business needs to re-evaluate its presence in this geographical region.

It is interesting to note that the Italian segment benefited most from capital expenditure during the period. The reason for such a large investment in such a poorly performing segment needs to be justified. It is possible that the business will reap rewards for the investment in the future; however, we do not have enough information to understand the reasons for the investment decision.

The reasons why the depreciation charges in the Italian segment are significantly lower than in the other geographical segments should also be investigated. The depreciation charge as a percentage of total assets is much lower. It is possible that the mix of assets is different in the Italian segment from that in the other two segments. If, however, this is not the case and a higher depreciation charge is really warranted, the profitability of this segment would be even worse.

Table of key results

	UK	France	Italy
Total revenue	270	200	390
Segment result	34	30	8
Net assets (assets – liabilities)	94	122	94
Segment result as a percentage of sales revenue	12.6%	15.0%	2.1%
Segment result as a percentage of net assets employed	36.2%	24.6%	8.5%
Capital expenditure	£20m	£15m	£35m
Depreciation as a percentage of total assets	21.7%	23.3%	9.5%

Chapter 6

6.1 Touchstone plc

Touchstone plc
Cash flow statement for the year ended 31 December 2007

	£m	£m
Cash flows from operating activities		
Profit before taxation (after interest) (see Note 1 below)	60	
Adjustments for:		
Depreciation	16	
Interest expense (Note 2)	4	
	80	
Increase in trade receivables (26 – 16)	(10)	
Decrease in trade payables (38 – 37)	(1)	
Decrease in inventories (25 – 24)	1	
Cash generated from operations	70	
Interest paid	(4)	
Taxation paid (Note 3)	(12)	
Dividend paid	(18)	
Net cash from operating activities		36
Cash flows from investing activities		
Payments to acquire tangible non-current assets (Note 4)	(41)	
Net cash used in investing activities		(41)
Cash flows from financing activities		
Issue of loan notes (40 – 20)	20	
Net cash used in financing activities		20
Net increase in cash and cash equivalents		15
Cash and cash equivalents at 1 January 2007		
Cash		4
Cash and cash equivalents at 31 December 2007		
Cash		4
Treasury bills		15
		19

To see how this relates to the cash of the business at the beginning and end of the year it can be useful to provide a reconciliation as follows:

Analysis of cash and cash equivalents during the year ended 31 December 2007

	£m
Cash and cash equivalents at 1 January 2007	4
Net cash inflow	15
Cash and cash equivalents at 31 December 2007	19

Notes:

1 This is simply taken from the income statement for the year.
2 Interest payable expense must be taken out, by adding it back to the profit before taxation figure. We subsequently deduct the cash paid for interest payable during the year. In this case the two figures are identical.
3 Companies pay 50% of their tax during their accounting year and the other 50% in the following year. Thus the 2007 payment would have been half the tax on the 2006 profit (that is, the figure that would

have appeared in the current liabilities at the end of 2006), plus half of the 2007 tax charge (that is, 4 + ($\frac{1}{2} \times 16$) = 12).

4   Since there were no disposals, the depreciation charges must be the difference between the start and end of the year's non-current asset values, adjusted by the cost of any additions:

	£m
Carrying amount at 1 January 2007	147
Add Additions (balancing figure)	41
	188
Less Depreciation (6 + 10)	16
Carrying amount at 31 December 2007	172

Chapter 7

7.1   Financial ratios

In order to answer this question you may have used the following ratios:

	Ali plc	Bhaskar plc
Current ratio	$\dfrac{853.0}{422.4} = 2.0$	$\dfrac{816.5}{293.1} = 2.8$
Acid test ratio	$\dfrac{(853.0 - 592.0)}{422.4} = 0.6$	$\dfrac{(816.5 - 403.0)}{293.1} = 1.4$
Gearing ratio	$\dfrac{190}{(687.6 + 190)} \times 100 = 21.6\%$	$\dfrac{250}{(874.6 + 250)} \times 100 = 22.2\%$
Interest cover ratio	$\dfrac{151.3}{19.4} = 7.8$ times	$\dfrac{166.9}{27.5} = 6.1$ times
Dividend payout ratio	$\dfrac{135.0}{99.9} \times 100 = 135\%$	$\dfrac{95.0}{104.6} \times 100 = 91\%$
Price/earnings ratio	$\dfrac{£6.50}{31.2p} = 20.8$ times	$\dfrac{£8.20}{41.8p} = 19.6$ times

Ali plc has a much lower current ratio and acid test ratio than Bhaskar plc. The reasons for this may be partly due to the fact that Ali plc has a lower average settlement period for receivables. The acid test ratio of Ali plc is substantially below 1.0: this may suggest a liquidity problem.

The gearing ratio of each business is quite similar. Neither business seems to have excessive borrowing. The interest cover ratio for each business is also similar. The ratios indicate that both businesses have good profit coverage for their interest charges.

The dividend payout ratio for each business seems very high. In the case of Ali plc, the dividends announced for the year are considerably higher than the profit for the year that is available for dividend. As a result, part of the dividend was paid out of retained profits from previous years. This is an unusual occurrence; although it is quite legitimate, such action may nevertheless suggest a lack of prudence on the part of the directors.

The P/E ratios for both businesses seem high, which indicates market confidence in their future prospects.

Chapter 8

8.1 JB Limited

(a)

	£	
Material M1		The original cost is irrelevant since any
(1,200 @ £5.50)	6,600	inventories used will need to be replaced
Material P2		The best alternative use of this material is
(800 @ £2.00 (that is,		as a substitute for P4 – an effective
£3.60 – £1.60))	1,600	opportunity cost of £2.00/kg
Part no. 678 (400 @ £50)	20,000	
Labour		
Skilled (2,000 @ £12)	24,000	The effective cost is £12/hour
Unskilled (2,000 @ £10)	20,000	
Overheads	3,200	It is only the additional cost that is
		relevant; the method of apportioning
		total overheads is not relevant
Total relevant cost	75,400	
Potential revenue		
(400 @ £200)	80,000	

Clearly, on the basis of the information available it would be beneficial for the business to undertake the contract.

(b) There is an almost infinite number of possible answers to this part of the question, including:

- If material P2 had not already been held, it may be that it would not be possible to buy it in and still leave the contract as a beneficial one. In this case the business may be unhappy about accepting a price under the particular conditions that apply, which could not be accepted under other conditions.
- Will the replacement for the skilled worker be able to do the normal work of that person to the necessary standard?
- Is JB Limited confident that the additional unskilled employee can be made redundant at the end of this contract without cost to itself?

Chapter 9

9.1 Khan Ltd

(a) The break-even point if only the Alpha service were rendered would be:

$$\frac{\text{Fixed costs}}{\text{Sales revenue per unit} - \text{Variable cost per unit}} = \frac{£40,000}{£30 - £(15 + 6)} = 4,445 \text{ units (a year)}$$

(Strictly it is 4,444.44 but 4,445 is the smallest number of units of the service that must be rendered to avoid a loss.)

(b)

	Alpha £/unit	Beta £/unit	Gamma £/unit
Selling price	30	39	20
Variable materials	(15)	(18)	(10)
Variable production costs	(6)	(10)	(5)
Contribution	9	11	5
Staff time (hr/unit)	2	3	1
Contribution/staff hour	£4.50	£3.67	£5.00
Order of priority	2nd	3rd	1st

(c)

	Hours		Contribution £
Render:			
5,000 Gamma using	5,000	generating (that is, 5,000 × £5 =)	25,000
2,500 Alpha using	5,000	generating (that is, 2,500 × £9 =)	22,500
	10,000		47,500
		Less Fixed costs	40,000
		Operating profit	7,500

This leaves a demand for 500 units of Alpha and 2,000 units of Beta unsatisfied.

Chapter 10

10.1 Hector and Co. Ltd

Job-costing basis:

			£
Materials:	Metal wire	1,000 × 2 × £2.20*	4,400
	Fabric	1,000 × 0.5 × £1.00*	500
Labour:	Skilled	1,000 × (10/60) × £12.00	2,000
	Unskilled	1,000 × (5/60) × £7.50	625
Overheads		1,000 × (15/60) × (50,000/12,500)	1,000
Total cost			8,525
Add Profit loading		12.5% thereof	1,066
Total tender price			9,591

* In the traditional approach to full costing, historic costs of materials tend to be used. It would not necessarily have been incorrect to have used the 'relevant' (opportunity) costs here.

Minimum contract price (relevant cost basis):

			£
Materials:	Metal wire	1,000 × 2 × £2.50 (replacement cost)	5,000
	Fabric	1,000 × 0.5 × £0.40 (scrap value)	200
Labour:	Skilled	(there is no effective cost of skilled staff)	–
	Unskilled	1,000 × (5/60) × £7.50	625
Minimum tender price			5,825

The difference between the two prices is partly that the relevant costing approach tends to look to the future, partly that it considers opportunity costs, and partly that the job-costing basis total has a profit loading.

Chapter 11

11.1 **Psilis Ltd**

(a) *Full cost (present basis)*

	Basic		Super	
	£		£	
Direct labour (all £10/hour)	40.00	(4 hours)	60.00	(6 hours)
Direct material	15.00		20.00	
Overheads	18.20	(£4.55* × 4)	27.30	(£4.55* × 6)
	73.20		107.30	

* Total direct labour hours worked = (40,000 × 4) + (10,000 × 6) = 220,000 hours. Overhead recovery rate = £1,000,000/220,000 = £4.55 per direct labour hour.

Thus the selling prices are currently:

Basic: £73.20 + 25% = £91.50
Super: £107.30 + 25% = £134.13

(b) *Full cost (activity cost basis)*
Here, the cost of each cost-driving activity is apportioned between total production of the two products.

Activity	Cost £000	Basis of apportionment	Basic £000		Super £000	
Machine set-ups	280	Number of set-ups	56	(20/100)	224	(80/100)
Quality inspection	220	Number of inspections	55	(500/2,000)	165	(1,500/2,000)
Sales order processing	240	Number of orders processed	72	(1,500/5,000)	168	(3,500/5,000)
General production	260	Machine hours	182	(350/500)	78	(150/500)
Total	1,000		365		635	

The overheads per unit are:

$$\text{Basic:} \quad \frac{£365,000}{40,000} = £9.13$$

$$\text{Super:} \quad \frac{£635,000}{10,000} = £63.50$$

Thus, on an activity basis, the full costs are as follows:

	Basic	Super
	£	£
Direct labour (all £10/hour)	40.00 (4 hours)	60.00 (6 hours)
Direct material	15.00	20.00
Overheads	9.13	63.50
Full cost	64.13	143.50
Current selling price	£91.50	£134.13

(c) It seems that the Supers are being sold for less than they cost to produce. If the price cannot be increased, there is a very strong case for abandoning this product. At the same time, the Basics are very profitable to the extent that it may be worth considering lowering the price to attract more sales revenue.

The fact that the overhead costs can be related to activities and, more specifically, to products does not mean that abandoning Super production would lead to immediate overhead cost savings. For example, it may not be possible or desirable to dismiss machine-setting staff overnight. It would certainly rarely be possible to release factory space occupied by machine setters and make immediate cost savings. Nevertheless, in the medium term, these costs can be avoided and it may be sensible to do so.

Chapter 12

12.1 Antonio Ltd

(a) (i) The raw materials inventories budget for the six months ending 31 December (physical quantities) is as follows:

	July Units	Aug Units	Sept Units	Oct Units	Nov Units	Dec Units
Opening inventories (Current month's production)	500	600	600	700	750	750
Purchases (Balance figure)	600	600	700	750	750	750
	1,100	1,200	1,300	1,450	1,500	1,500
Less Issues to production (From question)	500	600	600	700	750	750
Closing inventories (Next month's production)	600	600	700	750	750	750

The raw materials' inventories budget for the six months ending 31 December (in financial terms), that is, the physical quantities × £8 is:

	July £	Aug £	Sept £	Oct £	Nov £	Dec £
Opening inventories	4,000	4,800	4,800	5,600	6,000	6,000
Purchases	4,800	4,800	5,600	6,000	6,000	6,000
	8,800	9,600	10,400	11,600	12,000	12,000
Less Issues to prod'n	4,000	4,800	4,800	5,600	6,000	6,000
Closing inventories	4,800	4,800	5,600	6,000	6,000	6,000

(ii) The trade payables budget for the six months ending 31 December is:

	July £	Aug £	Sept £	Oct £	Nov £	Dec £
Opening balance (Current month's payment)	4,000	4,800	4,800	5,600	6,000	6,000
Purchases (From raw materials inventories budget)	4,800	4,800	5,600	6,000	6,000	6,000
	8,800	9,600	10,400	11,600	12,000	12,000
Less Payments	4,000	4,800	4,800	5,600	6,000	6,000
Closing balance (Next month's payment)	4,800	4,800	5,600	6,000	6,000	6,000

(iii) The cash budget for the six months ending 31 December is:

	July £	Aug £	Sept £	Oct £	Nov £	Dec £
Inflows						
Receipts:						
Trade receivables (40% of sales revenue of two months previous)	2,800	3,200	3,200	4,000	4,800	5,200
Cash sales revenue (60% of current month's revenue)	4,800	6,000	7,200	7,800	8,400	9,600
Total inflows	7,600	9,200	10,400	11,800	13,200	14,800
Outflows						
Trade payables (from trade payables budget)	(4,000)	(4,800)	(4,800)	(5,600)	(6,000)	(6,000)
Direct costs	(3,000)	(3,600)	(3,600)	(4,200)	(4,500)	(4,500)
Advertising	(1,000)	–	–	(1,500)	–	–
Overheads: 80%	(1,280)	(1,280)	(1,280)	(1,280)	(1,600)	(1,600)
20%	(280)	(320)	(320)	(320)	(320)	(400)
New plant			(2,200)	(2,200)	(2,200)	
Total outflows	(9,560)	(10,000)	(12,200)	(15,100)	(14,620)	(12,500)
Net inflows (outflows)	(1,960)	(800)	(1,800)	(3,300)	(1,420)	2,300
Balance c/f	5,540	4,740	2,940	(360)	(1,780)	520

The balances carried forward are deduced by deducting the deficit (net outflows) for the month from (or adding the surplus for the month to) the previous month's balance.

Note how budgets are linked; in this case the inventories budget to the trade payables budget and the trade payables budget to the cash budget.

(b) The following are possible means of relieving the cash shortages revealed by the budget:

- Make a higher proportion of sales on a cash basis.
- Collect the money from trade receivables more promptly, for example during the month following the sale.
- Hold lower inventories, both of raw materials and of finished goods.
- Increase the trade payables payment period.
- Delay the payments for advertising.
- Obtain more credit for the overhead costs; at present only 20% are on credit.
- Delay the payments for the new plant.

Chapter 13

13.1 Toscanini Ltd

(a) and (b)

	Budget		Actual
	Original	Flexed	
Output (prod'n and sales) (units)	4,000	3,500	3,500
	£	£	£
Sales revenue	16,000	14,000	13,820
Raw materials	(3,840)	(3,360) (1,400 kg)	(3,420) (1,425 kg)
Labour	(3,200)	(2,800) (350 hr)	(2,690) (345 hr)
Fixed overheads	(4,800)	(4,800)	(4,900)
Operating profit	4,160	3,040	2,810

	£		Manager accountable
Sales volume variance (4,160 – 3,040)	(1,120)	(A)	Sales
Sales price variance (14,000 – 13,820)	(180)	(A)	Sales
Materials price variance (1,425 × 2.40) – 3,420	0	–	–
Materials usage variance [(3,500 × 0.4) – 1,425] × £2.40	(60)	(A)	Production
Labour rate variance (345 × £8) – 2,690	70	(F)	Personnel
Labour efficiency variance [(3,500 × 0.10) – 345] × £8	40	(F)	Production
Fixed overhead spending (4,800 – 4,900)	(100)	(A)	Various depending on the nature of the overheads
Total net variances	(1,350)	(A)	
Budgeted operating profit	4,160		
Less Total net variance	(1,350)		
Actual operating profit	2,810		

(c) Feasible explanations include the following:

- Sales volume – unanticipated fall in world demand would account for 400 × £2.24 = £896 of this variance (£2.24 is the budgeted contribution per unit). The remainder is probably caused by ineffective marketing, though a lack of availability of inventories to sell may be a reason.
- Sales price – ineffective selling seems the only logical reason.
- Materials usage – inefficient usage of materials, perhaps because of poor performance by labour or substandard materials.
- Labour rate – less overtime worked or lower production bonuses paid as a result of lower volume of activity.
- Labour efficiency – more effective working.
- Overheads – ineffective control of overheads.

(d) Clearly, not all of the sales volume variance can be attributed to poor marketing, given a 10% reduction in demand.

It will probably be useful to distinguish between that part of the variance that arose from the shortfall in general demand (a planning variance) and a volume variance, which is more fairly attributable to the manager concerned. Thus accountability will be more fairly imposed.

	£
Planning variance (10% × 4,000) × £2.24	896
'New' sales volume variance	
[4,000 − (10% × 4,000) − 3,500] × £2.24	224
Original sales volume variance	1,120

Chapter 14

14.1 Beacon Chemicals plc

(a) Relevant cash flows are as follows:

	Year 0 £000	Year 1 £000	Year 2 £000	Year 3 £000	Year 4 £000	Year 5 £000
Sales revenue	–	80	120	144	100	64
Loss of contribution		(15)	(15)	(15)	(15)	(15)
Variable costs		(40)	(50)	(48)	(30)	(32)
Fixed costs (Note 1)		(8)	(8)	(8)	(8)	(8)
Operating cash flows		17	47	73	47	9
Working capital	(30)					30
Capital cost	(100)					
Net relevant cash flows	(130)	17	47	73	47	39

Notes:

1. Only the fixed costs that are incremental to the project (existing only because of the project) are relevant. Depreciation is irrelevant because it is not a cash flow.
2. The research and development cost is irrelevant since it has been spent irrespective of the decision on X14 production.

(b) The payback period is as follows:

	Year 0 £000	Year 1 £000	Year 2 £000	Year 3 £000
Cumulative cash flows	(130)	(113)	(66)	7

Thus the equipment will have repaid the initial investment by the end of the third year of operations.

(c) The net present value is as follows:

	Year 0 £000	Year 1 £000	Year 2 £000	Year 3 £000	Year 4 £000	Year 5 £000
Discount factor	1.00	0.926	0.857	0.794	0.735	0.681
Present value	(130)	15.74	40.28	57.96	34.55	26.56
NPV	45.09	(that is, the sum of the present values for years 0 to 5)				

Chapter 15

15.1   **Helsim Ltd**

(a) The liquidity position may be assessed by using the liquidity ratios discussed in Chapter 7:

$$\text{Current ratio} = \frac{\text{Current assets}}{\text{Current liabilities}}$$

$$= \frac{£7.5\text{m}}{£5.4\text{m}}$$

$$= 1.4$$

$$\text{Acid test ratio} = \frac{\text{Current assets (excluding inventories)}}{\text{Current liabilities}}$$

$$= \frac{£3.7\text{m}}{£5.4\text{m}}$$

$$= 0.7$$

These ratios reveal a fairly weak liquidity position. The current ratio seems quite low and the acid test ratio very low. This latter ratio suggests that the business does not have sufficient liquid assets to meet its maturing obligations. It would, however, be useful to have details of the liquidity ratios of similar businesses in the same industry in order to make a more informed judgement. The bank overdraft represents 67% of the current liabilities and 40% of the total liabilities of the business. The continuing support of the bank is therefore important to the ability of the business to meet its commitments.

(b) The finance required to reduce trade payables to an average of 40 days outstanding is calculated as follows:

	£m
Trade payables at balance sheet date	1.80
Trade payables outstanding based on 40 days' credit	
40/365 × £8.4m (that is, credit purchases)	(0.92)
Finance required	0.88 (say £0.9m)

(c) The bank may not wish to provide further finance to the business. The increase in overdraft will reduce the level of trade payables but will increase the risk exposure of the bank. The additional finance invested by the bank will not generate further funds and will not therefore be self-liquidating. The question does not make it clear whether the business has sufficient security to offer the bank for the increase in overdraft facility. The profits of the business will be reduced and the interest cover ratio, based on the profits generated last year, would reduce to about 1.6* times if the additional overdraft were granted (based on interest charged at 10% each year). This is very low and means that only a small decline in profits would leave interest charges uncovered.

* Existing bank overdraft (3.6) + extension of overdraft to cover reduction in trade payables (0.9) + loan notes (3.5) = £8.0m. Assuming a 10% interest rate means a yearly interest payment of £0.8m. The operating profit was £1.3m (that is, 6.4 – 3.0 – 2.1). Interest cover would be 1.63 (that is, 1.3/0.8).

(d) A number of possible sources of finance might be considered. Four possible sources are as follows:

- *Issue equity shares.* This option may be unattractive to investors. The return on equity is fairly low at 7.9% (that is, profit for the year (0.3)/equity (3.8)) and there is no evidence that the profitability of the business will improve. If profits remain at their current level the effect of issuing more equity will be to reduce further the returns to equity.

- *Make other borrowings.* This option may also prove unattractive to investors. The effect of making further borowings will have a similar effect to that of increasing the overdraft. The profits of the business will be reduced and the interest cover ratio will decrease to a low level. The gearing ratio of the business is already quite high at 48% (that is, loan notes (3.5)/(loan notes + equity (3.5 + 3.8)) and it is not clear what security would be available for the loan. The gearing ratio would be much higher if the overdraft were to be included.

- *Chase trade receivables.* It may be possible to improve cash flows by reducing the level of credit outstanding from customers. At present, the average settlement period is 93 days (that is, (trade receivables (3.6)/sales revenue (14.2)) × 365), which seems quite high. A reduction in the average settlement period by approximately one-quarter would generate the funds required. However, it is not clear what effect this would have on sales.

- *Reduce inventories.* This appears to be the most attractive of the four options. At present, the average inventories holding period is 178 days (that is, (closing inventories (3.8)/cost of sales (7.8)) × 365), which seems very high. A reduction in this period by less than one-quarter would generate the funds required. However, if the business holds a large amount of slow-moving and obsolete items, it may be difficult to reduce inventories levels.

Chapter 16

16.1 Williams Wholesalers Ltd

	£	£
Existing level of trade receivables (£4m × 70/365)		767,123
New level of trade receivables: £2m × 80/365	438,356	
£2m × 30/365	164,384	602,740
Reduction in trade receivables		164,383
Costs and benefits of policy		
Cost of discount (£2m × 2%)		40,000
Less Savings		
Interest payable (£164,384* × 13%)	21,370	
Administration costs	6,000	
Bad debts (20,000 − 10,000)	10,000	37,370
Net cost of policy		2,630

* It could be argued that the interest should be based on the amount expected to be received, that is the value of the trade receivables *after* taking account of the discount.

The above calculations reveal that the business will be worse off by offering the discounts.

Solutions to review questions

Chapter 1

1.1 The objective of providing accounting information is to enable users to make more informed decisions and judgements about the organisation concerned. Accounting has no other valid purpose or justification.

1.2

Students	Whether to enrol on a course of study. This would probably involve an assessment of the university's ability to continue to operate and to fulfil students' needs.
Other universities and colleges	How best to compete against the university. This might involve using the university's performance in various aspects as a 'benchmark' when evaluating their own performance.
Employees	Whether to take up or to continue in employment with the university. Employees might assess this by considering the ability of the university to continue to provide employment and to reward employees adequately for their labour.
Government/ funding authority	How efficient the university is in undertaking its various activities.
Local community representatives	Whether to allow/encourage the university to expand its premises. To assess this, the university's ability to continue to provide employment for the community, to use community resources and to help fund environmental improvements might be considered.
Suppliers	Whether to continue to supply the university at all; also whether to supply on credit. This would involve an assessment of the university's ability to pay for any goods and services supplied.
Lenders	Whether to lend money to the university and/or whether to require repayment of any existing loans. To assess this, the university's ability to meet its obligations to pay interest and to repay the principal would be considered.
Board of governors and other managers (Faculty deans and so on)	Whether the performance of the university requires improvement. Here performance to date would be compared with earlier plans or some other 'benchmark' to decide whether action needs to be taken. Whether there should be a change in the university's future direction. In making such decisions, management will need to look at the university's ability to perform and at the opportunities available to it.

1.3   Most businesses are far too large and complex for managers to be able to see and assess everything that is going on in their own areas of responsibility merely by personal observation. Managers need information on all aspects within their control. Management accounting reports can provide them with this information, to a greater or lesser extent. These reports can be seen, therefore, as acting as the eyes and ears of the managers, providing insights not necessarily obvious without them.

1.4   Since we can never be sure what is going to happen in the future, the best that we can do is to make judgements on the basis of past experience. Thus information concerning flows of cash and of wealth in the recent past is likely to be a useful source on which to base judgements about possible future outcomes.

Chapter 2

2.1   The confusion arises because the owner seems unaware of the business entity convention in accounting. This convention requires a separation of the business from the owner(s) of the business for accounting purposes. The business is regarded as a separate entity and the balance sheet is prepared from the perspective of the business rather than that of the owner. As a result, funds invested in the business by the owner will be regarded as a claim that the owner has on the business. In the balance sheet, this claim will be shown alongside other claims on the business from outsiders.

2.2   A balance sheet does not show what a business is worth, for two major reasons:

- Only those items which can be measured reliably in monetary terms are shown on the balance sheet. Thus, things of value such as the reputation for product quality, skills of employees and so on will not normally appear in the balance sheet.
- The historic cost convention results in assets being recorded at their outlay cost rather than their current value. In the case of certain assets, the difference between historic cost and current value may be significant.

2.3   The balance sheet equation is simply the relationship between a business's assets, liabilities and capital. In the horizontal layout it is

Assets (current and non-current) = Capital + Liabilities (current and non-current)

In the vertical layout, the equation is the same but it is set out in columnar form. Assets are shown first and capital and liabilities are shown underneath.

2.4   Some object to the idea of humans being treated as assets for inclusion on the balance sheet. It can be seen as demeaning for humans to be listed alongside inventories, plant and machinery and other assets. However, others argue that humans are often the most valuable resource of a business and by placing a value on this resource will help bring to the attention of managers the importance of nurturing and developing this 'asset'. There is a saying in management that 'the things that count are the things that get counted'. As the value of the 'human assets' is not stated in the financial statements, there is a danger that managers will treat these 'assets' less favourably than other assets that are on the balance sheet.

Humans are likely to meet the first criterion of an asset listed in the chapter, that is, a probable future benefit exists. There would be little point in employing people if this were not the case. The second criterion concerning exclusive right of control is more problematic. Clearly a business cannot control humans in the same way as most other assets. However, a business can have the exclusive right to the employment services that a person provides. This distinction between control over the services provided, rather than control over the person, makes it possible to argue that the second criterion can be met.

Humans sign a contract of employment with the business normally and so the third criterion is normally met. The difficulty, however, is with the fourth criterion, that is, whether the value of humans (or their services) can be measured with any degree of reliability. To date, none of the measurement methods proposed enjoy widespread acceptance.

Chapter 3

3.1 At the time of preparing the income statement, it is not always possible to determine accurately the expenses that need to be matched to the sales revenue figure for the period. It will only be at some later point in time that the true position becomes clear. However, it is still necessary to try to include all relevant expenses in the income statement and so estimates of the future will have to be made. Examples of estimates that may have to be made include:

- Expenses accrued at the end of the period such as the amount of telephone expenses incurred since the last quarter's bill.
- The amount of depreciation based on estimates of the life of the non-current asset and future residual value.
- The amount of bad and doubtful debts incurred.

3.2 Depreciation attempts to allocate the cost, or fair value, (less any residual value) of the asset over its useful life. Depreciation does not attempt to measure the fall in value of the asset during the period. Thus, the carrying amount of the asset appearing on the balance sheet normally represents the unexpired cost of the asset rather than its current market value.

3.3 The convention of consistency is designed to provide a degree of uniformity concerning the application of accounting policies. We have seen, that in certain areas, there may be more than one method of accounting for an item, for example inventories. The convention of consistency states that, having decided on a particular accounting policy, a business should continue to apply the policy in successive periods. While this policy helps to ensure that users can make valid comparisons concerning business performance *over time*, it does not ensure that valid comparisons can be made *between businesses*. This is because different businesses may consistently apply different accounting policies.

3.4 An expense is that element of the cost incurred that is used up during the accounting period. An asset is that element of cost which is carried forward on the balance sheet and which will normally be used up in future periods. Thus, both assets and expenses arise from costs being incurred. The major difference between the two is the period over which the benefits (resulting from the costs incurred) accrue.

Chapter 4

4.1 It does not differ. In both cases they are required to meet their debts to the full extent that there are assets available. To this extent they both have a liability that is limited to the extent of their assets. This is a particularly important fact for the shareholders of a limited company because they know that those owed money by the company cannot demand that the shareholders contribute additional funds to help meet debts. Thus the liability of the shareholders is limited to the amount that they have paid for their shares, or have agreed to pay in the case of partially unpaid shares. This contrasts with the position of the owner or part owner of an unincorporated (non-company) business. Here all of the individual's assets could be required to meet the unsatisfied liabilities of the business.

4.2 A private limited company may place restrictions on the transfer of its shares, that is, the directors can veto an attempt by a shareholder to sell his or her shares to another person to whom the directors object. Thus, in effect, the majority can avoid having as a shareholder someone that they would prefer not to have. A public company cannot do this.

A public limited company must have authorised share capital of at least £50,000. There is no minimum for a private limited company.

The main advantage of being a public limited company is that the company may offer its shares and debentures to the general public; a private company cannot make such an offer.

4.3 A reserve is that part of the equity (owners' claim) of a company that is not share capital. Reserves represent gains or surpluses that enhance the claim of the shareholders above the nominal value of their shares. For example, the share premium account is a reserve that represents the excess over the nominal value of shares that is paid for them on a share issue. The retained profit balance is a reserve that arises from ploughed-back profits earned by the company.

4.4 A preference share represents part of the ownership of a company. Preference shares entitle their owners to the first part of any dividend paid by the company, up to a maximum amount. The maximum is usually expressed as a percentage of the nominal or par value of the preference shares.

(a) They differ from ordinary shares to the extent that they only entitle their holders to dividends to a predetermined maximum value. Dividends to ordinary shareholders have no predetermined maximum. Usually preference shares attract a maximum payout equal to their nominal value on liquidation, the ordinary shareholders receive the residue after all other claimants, including the preference shareholders.

(b) They differ from loan notes in that these represent borrowings for the company, where normally holders have a contract with the company that specifies the rate of interest, interest payment dates and redemption date. They are often secured on the company's assets. Preference shareholders have no such contract.

Chapter 5

5.1 Accounting is an evolving subject. It is not static and so the principles that are laid down at any particular point in time may become obsolete as a result of changes in our understanding of the nature of accounting information and its impact on users and changes in the economic environment within which accounting is employed. We must accept, therefore, that accounting principles will continue to evolve and that existing principles must be regularly reviewed.

5.2 Apart from increases in accounting regulation, financial reports have increased because of:

- increasing demands by influential user groups, such as shareholders and financial analysts, for financial information relating to the company;
- the increasing sophistication of influential user groups, such as financial analysts, to deal with financial information;
- the increasing complexity of business operations requiring greater explanation;

- increasing recognition of the need for greater accountability towards certain user groups (such as employees and community groups) requiring the need for additional reports, such as environmental reports and social reports.

5.3 There are various problems associated with the measurement of business segments. These include:

- the definition of a segment;
- the treatment of inter-segmental transactions, such as sales;
- the treatment of common costs.

There is no single correct method of dealing with these problems and variations will arise in practice. This, in turn, will hinder comparisons between businesses.

5.4 Preparing an OFR may present a problem for accountants. For information to be credible to all interested parties, accountants should be as neutral as possible in measuring and reporting the financial performance and position of the business. The OFR requires some interpretation of results and there is a danger that the directors will wish to portray the business activities in as favourable a light as possible. This will affect what items are reported and how they are reported. The OFR is not normally independently audited and so the risks of bias in reporting are therefore increased. The board of directors should therefore accept full responsibility for preparing the OFR and this should be made clear to users.

Chapter 6

6.1 People and organisations will not normally accept other than cash in settlement of their claims against the business. If a business wants to employ people it must pay them in cash. If it wants to buy a new non-current asset to exploit a business opportunity, the supplier will normally insist on being paid in cash, normally after a short period of credit. When businesses fail, it is their inability to find the cash to pay claimants that actually drives them under. These factors lead to cash being the pre-eminent business asset and, therefore, the one that analysts and others watch carefully in trying to assess the ability of the business to survive and/or to take advantage of commercial opportunities as they arise.

6.2 With the direct method, the business's cash records are analysed for the period concerned. The analysis reveals the amounts of cash, in total, which have been paid and received in respect of each category of the cash flow statement. This is not difficult in principle, or in practice if it is done by computer as a matter of routine.

The indirect method takes the approach that, while the profit (loss) for the year is not equal to the net inflow (outflow) of cash from operations, they are fairly closely linked to the extent that appropriate adjustment of the profit (loss) for the year figure will produce the correct cash flow one. The adjustment is concerned with depreciation charge for, and movements in relevant working capital items over, the period.

6.3 (a) *Cash flows from operating activities.* This would normally be positive, even for a business with small profits or even losses. The fact that depreciation is not a cash flow tends to lead to positive cash flows in this area in most cases.

(b) *Cash flows from investing activities.* Normally this would be negative in cash flow terms since assets become worn out and need to be replaced in the normal course of business. This means that, typically, old items of property, plant and equipment are generating less cash on their disposal than is having to be paid out to replace them.

(c) *Cash flows from financing activities.* There is a tendency for businesses either to expand or to fail. In either case, this is likely to mean that, over the years, more finance will be raised than will be redeemed or retired.

6.4 There are several reasons for this, including the following:

- Changes in inventories, trade receivables and trade payables. For example, an increase in trade receivables during an accounting period would mean that the cash received from credit sales would be less than the credit sales revenue for the same period.
- Cash may have been spent on new non-current assets or received from disposals of old ones; these would not directly affect profit.
- Cash may have been spent to redeem or repay a financial claim or received as a result of the creation or the increase of a claim. These would not directly affect profit.
- The taxation charged in the income statement would not be the same tax that is paid during the same accounting period.

Chapter 7

7.1 The fact that a business operates on a low operating profit margin indicates that only a small operating profit is being produced for each £1 of sales revenue generated. However, this does not necessarily mean that the ROCE will be low. If the business is able to generate a large amount of sales revenue during a period, the operating profit may be very high even though the operating profit per £1 of sales revenue is low. If the overall operating profit is high, this can lead, in turn, to a high ROCE, since it is the total operating profit that is used as the numerator (top part of the fraction) in this ratio. Many businesses (including supermarkets) pursue a strategy of 'low margin, high turnover'.

7.2 The balance sheet is drawn up at a single point in time – the end of the financial period. As a result, the figures shown on the balance sheet represent the position at that single point in time and may not be representative of the position during the period. Wherever possible, average figures (perhaps based on monthly figures) should be used. However, an external user may only have access to the opening and closing balance sheets for the year and so a simple average based on these figures may be all that it is possible to calculate. Where a business is seasonal in nature or is subject to cyclical changes, this simple averaging may not be sufficient.

7.3 Three possible reasons for a long inventories turnover period are:

- poor inventories controls, leading to excessive investment in inventories;
- inventories hoarding in anticipation of price rises or shortages;
- inventories building in anticipation of increased future sales.

A short inventories turnover period may be due to:

- tight inventories controls, thereby reducing excessive investment in inventories and/or the amount of obsolete and slow-moving inventories;
- an inability to finance the required amount of inventories to meet sales demand;
- a difference in the mix of inventories carried by similar businesses (for example, greater investment in perishable goods which are held for a short period only).

7.4 The P/E ratio may vary between businesses within the same industry for the following reasons:

- *Accounting conventions*. Differences in the methods used to compute profit (for example, inventories valuation and depreciation) can lead to different profit figures and, therefore, different P/E ratios.
- *Different prospects*. One business may be regarded as having a much brighter future owing to factors such as the quality of management, the quality of products, location. This will

affect the market price that investors are prepared to pay for the share and, hence, it will also affect the P/E ratio.

- *Different asset structure*. One business's underlying asset base may be much higher than the other's and this may affect the market price of its shares.

Chapter 8

8.1 The two attributes are:

- They must relate to the objective(s) that the decision is intended to work towards. In most businesses this is taken to be wealth enhancement. This means that any information relating to the decision that does not impact on wealth enhancement is irrelevant, where wealth enhancement is the sole objective. In practice a business may have more than one objective.
- The costs must differ between the options under consideration. Where a cost will be the same irrespective of the outcome of the decision that is to be taken, that cost is irrelevant. It is only on the basis of things that differ from one outcome to another that decisions can be made.

8.2 A sunk cost is a past and, therefore, an irrelevant cost in the context of any decision about the future. Thus, for example, the cost of an item of inventories already bought is a sunk cost. It is irrelevant, in any decision involving the use of the inventories, because this cost will be the same irrespective of the decision made.

An opportunity cost is the cost of being deprived of the next best option to the one under consideration. For example, where using an hour of a worker's time on activity A deprives the business of the opportunity to use that time in a profitable activity B, the benefit lost from activity B is an opportunity cost of pursuing activity A.

8.3 Cost may be defined as the amount of resources, usually measured in monetary terms, sacrificed to achieve a particular objective.

8.4 A committed cost is like a past cost in that an irrevocable decision has been made to incur the cost. This might be because the business has entered into a binding contract, for example to rent some premises for the next two years. Thus it is effectively a past cost though the payment (for rent, in our example) has yet to be made. Since the business cannot avoid a committed cost, committed costs cannot be relevant costs.

Chapter 9

9.1 A fixed cost is one that is the same irrespective of the level of activity or output. Typical examples of costs that are fixed, irrespective of the level of production or provision of a service, include rent of business premises, salaries of supervisory staff, and electricity charges for heating and lighting.

A variable cost is one that varies with the level of activity or output. Examples include raw materials and labour, where labour is rewarded in proportion to the level of output.

Note particularly that it is relative to the level of activity that costs are fixed or variable. Fixed costs will be affected by inflation and they will be greater for a longer period than for a shorter one.

For a particular product or service, knowing which costs are fixed and which variable enables managers to predict the total cost for any particular level of activity. It also enables them to concentrate only on the variable costs in circumstances where a decision will not alter the fixed costs.

9.2   The break-even point (BEP) is the level of activity, measured either in physical units or in value of sales revenue, at which the sales revenues exactly cover all of the costs, both fixed and variable.

BEP is calculated as:

$$\text{Fixed costs}/(\text{Sales revenue per unit} - \text{Variable costs per unit})$$

which may alternatively be expressed as:

$$\text{Fixed costs}/(\text{contribution per unit})$$

Thus break even will occur when the contributions for the period are sufficient to cover the fixed costs for the period.

The BEP tends to be useful as a comparison with planned level of activity in an attempt to assess the riskiness of the activity.

9.3   Operating (or operational) gearing refers to the extent of fixed costs relative to variable costs in the total costs of some activity. Where the fixed costs form a relatively high proportion of the total, we say that the activity has high operational gearing.

Typically, high operating gearing is present in environments where there is a relatively high level of mechanisation (that is, capital intensive). This is because such environments tend simultaneously to involve relatively high fixed costs of depreciation, maintenance and so on and relatively low variable costs.

High operating gearing tends to mean that the effects of increases or decreases in the level of activity have an accentuated effect on operating profit. For example, a 20% decrease in output of a particular service will lead to a greater than 20% decrease in operating profit, assuming no cost or price changes.

9.4   In the face of a restricting scarce resource, profit will be maximised by using the scarce resource on output where the contribution per unit of the scarce resource is maximised.

This means that the contribution per unit of the scarce resource (for example, hour of scarce labour, unit of scarce raw material and so on) for each competing product or service needs to be identified. It is then a question of allocating the scarce resource to the product or service that provides the highest contribution per unit of the particular scarce resource.

The logic of this approach is that the scarce resource is allocated to the activity that uses it most effectively in terms of contribution and, therefore, profit.

Chapter 10

10.1   In process costing, the total production costs for a period are divided by the number of completed units of output for the period to deduce the full cost. Where there is work in progress at the beginning and/or the end of the period complications arise.

The problem is that some of the completed output incurred costs in the preceding period. Similarly, some of the costs incurred in the current period lead to completed production in the subsequent period. Account needs to be taken of these facts if reliable full cost information is to be obtained.

10.2   The only reason for distinguishing between direct and indirect costs is to help to deduce the full cost of a unit of output in a job-costing environment. In an environment where all units of output are identical, or can reasonably be regarded as being so, a process-costing approach will be taken. This avoids the need for identifying direct and indirect costs separately.

Direct costs form that part of the total costs of pursuing some activity that can, unequivocally, be associated with that particular activity. Examples of direct costs in the typical job-costing environment include direct labour and direct materials.

Indirect costs are the remainder of the costs of pursuing some activity. Identifying direct costs reduces the extent to which costs must be related to individual jobs on a, more or less, arbitrary basis. In practice, knowledge of the direct costs tends to provide the basis used to charge overheads to jobs.

The distinction between direct and indirect costs is irrelevant for any other purpose.

Directness and indirectness is dictated as much by the nature of what is being costed as by the nature of the cost.

10.3 The notion of direct and indirect costs is concerned only with the extent to which particular costs can unequivocally be related to and measured in respect of a particular cost unit, usually a product or service. The distinction between direct and indirect costs is made exclusively for the purpose of deducing the full cost of some cost unit, in an environment where each cost unit is not identical, or close enough to being identical for it to be treated as such. Thus, it is typically in the context of job costing, or some variant of it, that the distinction between direct and indirect costs is usefully made.

The notion of variable and fixed costs is concerned entirely with how costs behave in the face of changes in the volume of output. The value of being able to distinguish between fixed and variable costs is that predictions can be made of what total costs will be at particular levels of volume and/or what reduction or addition to costs will occur if the volume of output is reduced or increased.

Thus the notion of direct and indirect costs, on the one hand, and that of variable and fixed costs, on the other, are not connected with one another. Although it is true that, in most contexts, some direct costs are variable, some direct costs are fixed. Similarly, indirect costs might be fixed or variable.

10.4 The full cost includes all of the costs of pursuing the cost objective, including a 'fair' share of the overheads. Generally the full cost represents an average cost of the various elements, rather than a cost that arises because the business finds itself in a particular situation.

The fact that the full cost reflects all aspects of cost should mean that, were the business to sell its output at a price exactly equal to the full cost, the sales revenue for the period would exactly cover all of the costs and the business would break even, that is, make neither profit nor loss.

Chapter 11

11.1 ABC is a means of dealing with charging overheads to units of output to derive full costs in a multi-product (job- or batch-costing) environment.

The traditional approach tends to accept that once identifiable direct costs, normally labour and materials, have been taken out, all of the other costs (overheads) must be treated as common costs and applied to jobs using the same formula, typically on the basis of direct labour hours.

ABC takes a much more enquiring approach to overheads. It follows the philosophy that overheads do not occur for no reason, but they must be driven by activities. For example, a particular type of product may take up a disproportionately large part of supervisors' time. If that product were not made, in the long run, supervision costs could be cut (fewer supervisors would be needed). Whereas the traditional approach would just accept that supervisory salaries are an overhead which needs to be apportioned along with other overheads, ABC would seek to charge that part of the supervisors' salaries which is driven by the particular type of product, to that product.

11.2 One criticism is on the issue of the cost–benefit balance. It is claimed that the work necessary to analyse overheads and identify the cost drivers tends to be more expensive than is justified by the increased quality of the full costs that emerge.

Linked to this is the belief of many that full cost information is of rather dubious value for most purposes, irrespective of how the full costs are deduced. Many argue that full cost information is flawed by the fact that it takes no account of opportunity costs.

ABC enthusiasts would probably argue that deducing better quality full costs is not the only benefit which is available, if the overhead cost drivers can be identified. Knowing what drives costs can enable management to exercise more control over them. This benefit needs to be taken into account when assessing the cost–benefit of using ABC.

11.3 Generally, a rise in price of a commodity causes a fall in demand. A commodity is said to have a relatively elastic demand where demand reacts relatively dramatically (stretches more). Elastic demand tends to be associated with commodities that are not essential, perhaps because there is a ready substitute.

It can be very helpful for those involved with pricing decisions to have some feel for the elasticity of demand of the commodity that will be the subject of a decision. The sensitivity of the demand to the decision is obviously much greater (and the pricing decision more crucial) with commodities whose demand is elastic than with commodities whose demand is relatively inelastic.

11.4 A business will make the most profit from one of its products or services at the point where marginal sales revenue equals marginal cost of production. In other words, the point where the increase in total sales revenue that will result from selling one more unit equals the increase in total costs which will result from selling that unit.

Chapter 12

12.1 A budget can be defined as a financial plan for a future period of time. Thus it sets out the intentions which management has for the period concerned. Achieving the budget plans should help to achieve the long-term plans of the business. Achievement of the long-term plans should mean that the business is successfully working towards its objectives.

A budget differs from a forecast in that a forecast is a statement of what is expected to happen without the intervention of management, perhaps because managers cannot intervene (as with a weather forecast). A plan is an intention to achieve.

Normally, management would take account of reliable forecasts when making its plans.

12.2 The five uses of budgets are:

- They tend to promote forward thinking and the possible identification of short-term problems. Managers must plan and the budgeting process tends to force them to do so. In doing so, they are likely to encounter potential problems. If the potential problems can be identified early enough, solutions might be easily found.
- They can be used to help co-ordination between various sections of the business. It is important that the plans of one area of the business fit in with those of other areas; a lack of co-ordination could have disastrous consequences. Having formal statements of plans for each aspect of the business enables a check to be made that plans are complementary.

- They can motivate managers to better performance. It is believed that people are motivated by having a target to aim for. Provided that the inherent goals are achievable, budgets can provide an effective motivational device.
- They can provide a basis for a system of control. Having a plan against which actual performance can be measured, provides a potentially useful tool of control.
- They can provide a system of authorisation. Many managers have 'spending' budgets for research and development, staff training and so on. For these people, the size of their budget defines their authority to spend.

12.3 Control can be defined as 'compelling things to occur as planned'. This implies that control can be achieved only if a plan exists. Budgets are financial plans. This means that, if actual performance can be compared with the budget (plan) for each aspect of the business, divergences from plan can be spotted. Steps can then be taken to bring matters back under control where they are going out of control.

12.4 A budget committee is a group of senior staff that is responsible for the budget preparation process within an organisation. The existence of the committee places the budget responsibility clearly with an identifiable group of people. This group can focus on the tasks involved.

Chapter 13

13.1 Feedforward controls are devices to try to identify what is likely to happen in the future and to assist in action being taken to make the actual outcome match the desired outcome. It contrasts with feedback controls that simply compare actual to budget after the event. Thus the use of feedforward controls reflects a more proactive management style.

13.2 A variance is the effect on budgeted operating profit of the particular aspect of the business that is being considered. Thus it is the difference between the budgeted operating profit and what the actual operating profit would have been had all other matters, except the one under consideration, gone according to budget. From this it must be the case that: budgeted operating profit plus favourable variances less unfavourable variances equals actual operating profit.

The objective of analysing and assessing variances is to identify whether, and if so where, things are not going according to plan. If this can be done, it may be possible to find out the actual cause of things going out of control. If this can be discovered, it may be possible to put things right for the future.

13.3 Where the budgeted and actual volumes of output do not coincide, it is impossible to make a valid comparison of 'allowed' and actual expenses and revenues. Flexing the original budget to reflect the actual output level enables a more informative comparison to be made.

Flexing certainly does not mean that output volume differences do not matter. Flexing will show (as the difference between flexed and original budget operating profits) the effect on operating profit of output volume differences.

13.4 The attitude taken to investigating variances is at management's discretion and a matter of its judgement. It is probably true to say, however, that management should set a threshold of significance, for example 5% of the budgeted figure for that revenue or expense or a percentage of budgeted operating profit. All variances above this threshold should automatically be investigated.

Even where variances are below the threshold, any sign of a systematic variance shown, for example, by an increasing cumulative total for the factor, should trigger an investigation.

Knowledge of the cause of a particular variance may well put management in a position to take actions that will be beneficial to the business in the future. Investigating variances, however, is likely to be relatively expensive in staff time and so on. A judgement needs to be made on whether the value or benefit of knowing the cause of the variance will justify the cost of this knowledge. As with most investigation of this type, it is difficult to judge the value of the knowledge until after the variance has been investigated.

Chapter 14

14.1 NPV is usually considered the best method of assessing investment opportunities because it takes account of:

- *The timing of the cash flows.* By *discounting* the various cash flows associated with each project according to when they are expected to arise, the NPV method recognises the fact that cash flows do not all occur simultaneously. Associated with this is the fact that, by discounting, using the opportunity cost of finance (that is, the return that the next best alternative opportunity would generate), the net benefit after financing costs have been met is identified (as the NPV).
- *The whole of the relevant cash flows.* NPV includes all of the relevant cash flows irrespective of when they are expected to occur. It treats them differently according to their date of occurrence, but they are all taken account of in the NPV and they all have, or can have, an influence on the decision.
- *The objectives of the business.* NPV is the only method of appraisal where the output of the analysis has a direct bearing on the wealth of the owners of the business. (Positive NPVs enhance wealth; negative ones reduce it.) Since most private-sector businesses seek to increase their owners' wealth, NPV clearly is the best approach to use.

NPV provides clear decision rules concerning acceptance/rejection of projects and the ranking of projects. It is fairly simple to use, particularly with the availability of modern computer software that takes away the need for routine calculations to be done manually.

14.2 The payback method, in its original form, does not take account of the time value of money. However, it would be possible to modify the payback method to accommodate this requirement. Cash flows arising from a project could be discounted, using the cost of finance as the appropriate discount rate, in the same way as the NPV and IRR methods. The discounted payback approach is used by some businesses and represents an improvement on the original approach described in the chapter. However, it retains the other flaws of the original payback approach that were discussed. For example, it ignores relevant data after the payback period. Thus, even in its modified form, the PP method cannot be regarded as superior to NPV.

14.3 The IRR method does appear to be preferred to the NPV method among practising managers. The main reasons for this appear to be as follows:

- A preference for a percentage return ratio rather than an absolute figure as a means of expressing the outcome of a project. This preference for a ratio may reflect the fact that other financial goals of the business are often set in terms of ratios, for example return on capital employed.
- A preference for ranking projects in terms of their percentage return. Managers feel it is easier to rank projects on the basis of percentage returns (though NPV outcomes should be just as easy for them). We saw in the chapter that the IRR method could provide misleading advice on the ranking of projects and the NPV method was preferable for this purpose.

14.4 Cash flows are preferred to profit flows because cash is the ultimate measure of economic wealth. Cash is used to acquire resources and for distribution to shareholders. When cash is invested in an investment project, an opportunity cost is incurred, as the cash cannot be used in other investment projects. Similarly, when positive cash flows are generated by the project, the cash can be used to reinvest in other investment projects.

Profit, on the other hand, is relevant to reporting the productive effort for a period. This measure of effort may have only a tenuous relationship to cash flows for a period. The conventions of accounting may lead to the recognition of gains and losses in one period and the relevant cash inflows and outflows occurring in another period.

Chapter 15

15.1 Share warrants may be particularly useful for young expanding businesses that wish to attract new investors. They can help provide a 'sweetener' for the issue of loan notes. By attaching warrants it may be possible to agree a lower rate of interest or less restrictive loan covenants. If the business is successful, the warrants will provide a further source of finance. Investors will exercise their option to acquire shares if the market price of the shares exceeds the exercise price of the warrant. However, this will have the effect of diluting the control of existing shareholders.

15.2 A listed business may wish to revert to unlisted status for a number of possible reasons. These include:

- *Cost.* A Stock Exchange listing can be costly, as the business must adhere to certain administrative regulations and financial disclosures.
- *Scrutiny.* Listed companies are subject to close scrutiny by analysts and this may not be welcome if the business is engaged in sensitive negotiations or controversial business activities.
- *Takeover risk.* The shares of the business may be purchased by an unwelcome bidder and this may result in a takeover.
- *Investor profile.* If the business is dominated by a few investors who wish to retain their interest in the business and do not wish to raise further capital by public issues, the benefits of a listing are few.

15.3 An offer for sale involves an issuing house buying the shares in the business and then, in turn, selling the shares to the public. The issue will be advertised by the publication of a prospectus, which will set out details of the business and the issue price of the shares (or reserve price if a tender issue is being made). The shares issued by the issuing house may be either new shares or shares which have been purchased from existing shareholders. A public issue is where the business undertakes direct responsibility for issuing shares to the public. If an issuing house is employed it will usually be in the role of adviser and administrator of the issue. However, the issuing house may also underwrite the issue. A public issue runs the risk that the shares will not be taken up and is a less popular form of issue for businesses.

15.4 Invoice discounting is a service offered to businesses by a financial institution whereby the institution is prepared to advance a sum equivalent to 75% to 80% of outstanding trade receivables. The amount advanced is usually payable within 60 to 90 days. The business will retain responsibility for collecting the amounts owing from credit customers and the advance must be repaid irrespective of whether the trade receivables have been collected. Factoring is a service that is also offered to businesses by financial institutions. In this case, the factor will take over the business's sales and trade receivables records and will undertake to collect trade receivables on behalf of the client business. The factor will also be prepared to make an advance of 80% to 85% of approved trade receivables that is repayable from the amounts received from customers. The service charge for invoice discounting is up to 0.5% of turnover, whereas the service charge for factoring is up to 3% of turnover. This difference explains, in part, why businesses have shown a preference for invoice discounting rather than factoring in recent years. However, the factor provides additional services, as explained.

Chapter 16

16.1 Although the credit manager is responsible for ensuring that trade receivables pay on time, Tariq may be right in denying blame. Various factors may be responsible for the situation described which are beyond the control of the credit manager. These include:

- a downturn in the economy leading to financial difficulties among trade receivables;
- a decision made by other managers to liberalise credit policy in order to stimulate sales;
- an increase in competition among suppliers offering credit that is being exploited by customers;
- disputes with customers over the quality of goods or services supplied; and
- problems in the delivery of goods leading to delays.

You may have thought of others.

16.2 Inventories levels could be affected in the following ways:

(a) An increase in production bottlenecks is likely to result in an increase in raw materials and work in progress being processed within the plant. Therefore, inventories levels should rise.

(b) A rise in interest rates will make the cost of holding inventories more expensive (if they are financed by debt). This may, in turn, lead to a decision to reduce inventories levels.

(c) The decision to reduce the range of products should result in fewer inventories being held. It would no longer be necessary to hold certain items in order to meet customer demand.

(d) Switching to a local supplier may reduce the lead time between ordering an item and receiving it. This should, in turn, reduce the need to carry such high levels of the item.

(e) A deterioration in the quality of bought-in items may result in the purchase of higher quantities of inventories in order to take account of the defective element in inventories acquired and, perhaps, an increase in the inspection time for items received. This would lead to a rise in inventories levels.

16.3 Inventories are held to meet customer demand, to avoid the problems of running out of supplies and to take advantage of profitable opportunities (for example, buying items that are expected to rise steeply in price in the future). These reasons are similar to the transactionary, precautionary and speculative motives that were used to explain why cash is held by a business.

16.4 (a) The costs of holding too little cash are:

- failure to meet obligations when they fall due which can damage the reputation of the business and may, in the extreme, lead to the business collapsing;
- having to borrow and thereby incur interest charges; and
- an inability to take advantage of profitable opportunities.

(b) The costs of holding too much cash are:

- failure to use the funds available for more profitable purposes; and
- loss of value during a period of inflation.

APPENDIX E

Solutions to selected exercises

Chapter 2

2.1 Paul

Cash flow statement for Thursday

	£
Opening balance (from Wednesday)	59
Cash from sale of wrapping paper	47
	106
Cash paid to purchase wrapping paper	(53)
Closing balance	53

Income statement for Thursday

	£
Sales revenue	47
Cost of goods sold	(33)
Profit	14

Balance sheet as at Thursday evening

	£
Cash	53
Inventories of goods for resale (23 + 53 − 33)	43
Total business wealth	96

2.2 Paul (continued)

	£
Cash introduced by Paul on Monday	40
Profit for Monday	15
Profit for Tuesday	18
Profit for Wednesday	9
Profit for Thursday	14
	96

Thus the wealth of the business, all of which belongs to Paul as sole owner, consists of the cash he put in to start the business plus the profit earned each day.

2.3 **Helen**

Income statement for day 1

	£
Sales revenue (70 × £0.80)	56
Cost of sales (70 × £0.50)	(35)
Profit	21

Cash flow statement for day 1

	£
Opening balance	40
Cash from sales	56
	96
Cash for purchases (80 × £0.50)	(40)
Closing balance	56

Balance sheet as at end of day 1

	£
Cash balance	56
Inventory of unsold goods (10 × £0.50)	5
Helen's business wealth	61

Income statement for day 2

	£
Sales revenue (65 × £0.80)	52.0
Cost of sales (65 × £0.50)	(32.5)
Profit	19.5

Cash flow statement for day 2

	£
Opening balance	56.0
Cash from sales	52.0
	108.0
Cash for purchases (60 × £0.50)	(30.0)
Closing balance	78.0

Balance sheet as at end of day 2

	£
Cash balance	78.0
Inventory of unsold goods (5 × £0.50)	2.5
Helen's business wealth	80.5

Income statement for day 3

	£
Sales revenue (20 × £0.80) + (45 × £0.40)	34.0
Cost of sales (65 × £0.50)	(32.5)
Profit	1.5

Cash flow statement for day 3

	£
Opening balance	78.0
Cash from sales	34.0
	112.0
Cash for purchases (60 × £0.50)	(30.0)
Closing balance	82.0

Balance sheet as at end of day 3

	£
Cash balance	82.0
Inventory of unsold goods	–
Helen's business wealth	82.0

2.5 Crafty Engineering Ltd

(a)
Crafty Engineering Ltd
Balance sheet as at 30 June last year

	£000
Non-current assets	
Property, plant and equipment	
Property	320
Equipment and tools	207
Motor vehicles	38
	565
Current assets	
Inventories	153
Trade receivables	185
	338
Total assets	903
Capital (Owners' equity, which is the missing figure)	441
Non-current liabilities	
Long-term borrowings (Loan Industrial Finance Co.)	260
Current liabilities	
Trade payables	86
Short-term borrowings	116
	202
Total equity and liabilities	903

(b) The balance sheet reveals a high level of investment in non-current assets. In percentage terms, we can say that more than 60% of the total investment in assets (565/903) has been in non-current assets. The nature of the business may require a heavy investment in non-current assets. The investment in current assets exceeds the current liabilities by a large amount (approximately 1.7 times). As a result, there is no obvious sign of a liquidity problem. However, the balance sheet reveals that the business has no cash balance and is therefore dependent on the continuing support of short-term borrowing in order to meet obligations when they fall due. When considering the long-term financing of the business, we can see that about 37% (that is, 260/(260 + 441)) of the total long-term finance for the business has been supplied by borrowings and about 63% (that is, 441/(260 + 441)) by the owners. This level of long-term borrowing seems quite high but not excessive. However, we would need to know more about the ability of the business to service the borrowing (that is, make interest payments and repayments of the amount borrowed) before a full assessment could be made.

2.8

(a) The income statement shows the increase in wealth, as a result of trading, generated during the period (revenue), the decrease in wealth caused by the generation of that revenue (expenses) and the resulting net increase (profit) or decrease (loss) in wealth for the period. Though most businesses hold some of their wealth in cash, wealth is held in many other forms: non-current assets, receivables and so on.

(b) Assets, to be included in a balance sheet, must be judged as likely to produce future economic benefits. The economic benefit may come from selling the asset in the short term, in which case the statement is broadly true for those assets that it is the intention of the business to liquidate (turn into cash) in the short term. Many assets have an economic benefit that is not related to liquidation value but to use – for example, in production. For these types of asset, the statement is certainly not true.

There are other conditions that must be met in order for an item to be included in the balance sheet. These are:

- the business must have an exclusive right to control the asset;
- the benefit must arise from some past transaction or event; and
- the asset must be measurable in monetary terms.

(c) The balance sheet equation is:

$$\text{Assets} = \text{Capital} + \text{Liabilities}$$

(d) Non-current assets are assets that do not meet the criteria for current assets. They are normally held for the long-term operations of the business. Some non-current assets may be immovable (for example, property) but others are not (for example, delivery vans).

(e) Goodwill may or may not have an infinite life – it will depend on the nature of the goodwill. There are no hard and fast rules that can be applied. Where this asset has a finite life, it should be amortised. Where it is considered to have an infinite life, it should not be amortised but should be tested annually for impairment.

Chapter 3

3.1 (a) Capital does increase as a result of the owners introducing more cash into the business, but it will also increase as a result of introducing other assets (for example, a motor car) and by the business generating revenue by trading. Similarly, capital decreases not only as a result of withdrawals of cash by owners but also by withdrawals of other assets (for example, inventory for the owners' personal use) and through trading expenses being incurred. For the typical business in a typical accounting period, capital will alter much more as a result of trading activities than for any other reason.

(b) An accrued expense is not one that relates to next year. It is one that needs to be matched with the revenue of the accounting period under review, but that has yet to be met in terms of cash payment. As such, it will appear on the balance sheet as a current liability.

(c) The purpose of depreciation is not to provide for asset replacement. Rather, it is an attempt to allocate the cost, or fair value, of the asset (less any residual value) over its useful life. Depreciation is an attempt to provide a measure of the amount of the non-current asset that has been consumed during the period. This amount will then be charged as an expense for the period in deriving the profit figure. Depreciation is a book entry (the outlay of cash occurs when the asset is purchased) and does not normally entail setting aside a separate amount of cash for asset replacement. Even if this were done, there would be no guarantee that sufficient funds would be available at the end of the asset's life for its replacement. Factors such as inflation and technological change may mean that the replacement cost is higher than the original cost of the asset.

(d) In the short term, it is possible for the current value of a non-current asset to exceed its original cost. However, nearly all non-current assets will wear out over time as a result of being used to generate wealth for the business. This will be the case for freehold buildings. As a result, some measure of depreciation should be calculated to take account of the fact that the asset is being consumed. Some businesses revalue their freehold buildings where the current value is significantly different from the original cost. Where this occurs, the depreciation charged should be based on the revalued amount (fair value). This will normally result in higher depreciation charges than if the asset remained at its historic cost.

3.3 The existence of profit and downward movement in cash may be for various reasons, which include the following:

- The purchase of assets for cash during the period (for example, motor cars and inventories), which were not all consumed during the period and are therefore not having as great an effect on expenses as they are on cash.
- The payment of an outstanding liability (for example, borrowings), which will have an effect on cash but not on expenses in the income statement.
- The withdrawal of cash by the owners from the capital invested, which will not have an effect on the expenses in the income statement.
- The generation of revenue on credit where the cash has yet to be received. This will increase the sales revenue for the period but will not have a beneficial effect on the cash balance until a later period.

3.5
(a)	Rent payable – expense for period	£9,000
(b)	Rates and insurance – expense for period	£6,000
(c)	General expenses – paid in period	£7,000
(d)	Interest (on borrowings) payable – prepaid	£500
(e)	Salaries – paid in period	£6,000
(f)	Rent receivable – received during period	£3,000

3.7 **WW Associates**

WW Associates
Balance sheet as at 31 December 2006

Assets	£	Claims	£
Machinery		Capital (owners' equity)	
(+25,300 + 6,000 + 9,000		(+48,900 – 23,000 + 26,480)	52,380
– 13,000 + 3,900 – 9,360)	21,840*		
Inventory			
(+12,200 + 143,000 + 12,000			
– 127,000 – 25,000)	15,200		
		Trade payables	
		(+16,900 + 143,000 – 156,000)	3,900
Trade receivables		Accrued expenses	
(+21,300 + 211,000 – 198,000)	34,300	(+1,700 – 1,700 + 860)	860
Cash at bank (overdraft)			
(+8,300 – 23,000 – 25,000 –			
2,000 – 6,000 – 23,800 – 2,700			
– 12,000 + 42,000 + 198,000 –			
156,000 – 17,500)	–19,700		
Prepaid expenses			
(+400 – 400 + 500 + 5,000)	5,500		
Total assets	**57,140**	**Total equity and liabilities**	**57,140**

*	£
Cost less accumulated depreciation at 31 December 2005	25,300
Less Carrying amount of machine disposed of (£13,000 – £3,900)	(9,100)
	16,200
Add Cost of new machine	15,000
	31,200
Depreciation for 2006 (£31,200 × 30%)	(9,360)
Carrying amount (written-down value) of machine at 31 December 2006	21,840

Income statement for the year ended 31 December 2006

	£
Sales revenue (+211,000 + 42,000)	253,000
Cost of goods sold (+127,000 + 25,000)	(152,000)
Gross profit	101,000
Rent (+20,000)	(20,000)
Rates (+400 + 1,500)	(1,900)
Wages (−1,700 + 23,800 + 860)	(22,960)
Electricity (+2,700)	(2,700)
Machinery depreciation (+9,360)	(9,360)
Loss on disposal of the old machinery (+13,000 − 3,900 − 9,000)	(100)
Van expenses (+17,500)	(17,500)
Profit for the year	26,480

The loss on disposal of the old machinery is the carrying amount (cost less depreciation) less the disposal proceeds. Since the machinery had only been owned for one year, with a depreciation rate of 30%, the depreciation on it so far is £3,900 (that is, £13,000 × 30%). The effective disposal proceeds were £9,000 because, as a result of trading it in, the business saved £9,000 on the new asset.

The depreciation expense for 2006 is based on the cost less accumulated depreciation of the assets owned at the end of 2006. Accumulated depreciation must be taken into account because the business uses the reducing-balance method.

The balance sheet could now be rewritten in a more stylish form as follows:

WW Associates
Balance sheet as at 31 December 2006

	£
Non-current assets	
Property, plant and equipment	
Machinery at cost less depreciation	21,840
Current assets	
Inventory	15,200
Trade receivables	34,300
Prepaid expenses	5,500
	55,000
Total assets	76,840
Capital (owners' equity)	
Original	48,900
Profit	26,480
	75,380
Drawings	(23,000)
	52,380
Current liabilities	
Trade payables	3,900
Accrued expenses	860
Borrowings – Bank overdraft	19,700
	24,460
Total equity and liabilities	76,840

3.8 Nikov and Co.

An examination of the income statements for the two years reveals a number of interesting points, which include:

- An increase in sales value and gross profit of 9.9% in 2006.
- The gross profit expressed as a percentage of sales revenue remaining at 70%.
- An increase in salaries of 7.2%.
- An increase in selling and distribution costs of 31.2%.
- An increase in bad debts of 392.5%.
- A decline in profit for the year of 39.3%.
- A decline in the profit for the year as a percentage of sales revenue from 13.3% to 7.4%.

Thus, the business has enjoyed an increase in sales revenue and gross profits, but this has failed to translate to an increase in profit for the year because of the significant rise in overheads. The increase in selling costs during 2006 suggests that the increase in sales revenue was achieved by greater marketing effort, and the huge increase in bad debts suggests that the increase in sales revenue may be attributable to selling to less creditworthy customers or to a weak debt-collection policy. There appears to have been a change of policy in 2006 towards sales, and this has not been successful overall as the profit for the year has shown a dramatic decline.

Chapter 4

4.1 Limited companies can no more set a limit on the amount of debts they will meet than can human beings. They must meet their debts up to the limit of their assets, just as we as individuals must. In the context of owners' claim, 'reserves' mean part of the owners' claim against the assets of the company. These assets may or may not include cash. The legal ability of the company to pay dividends is not related to the amount of cash that it has.

Preference shares do not carry a guaranteed dividend. They simply guarantee that the preference shareholders have a right to the first slice of any dividend that is paid. Shares of many companies can, in effect, be bought by one investor from another through the Stock Exchange. Such a transaction has no direct effect on the company, however. These are not new shares being offered by the company, but existing shares that are being sold 'second-hand'.

4.2 (a) The first part of the quote is incorrect. Bonus shares should not, of themselves, increase the value of the shareholders' wealth. This is because reserves, belonging to the shareholders, are used to create bonus shares. Thus, each shareholder's stake in the company has not increased.

(b) This statement is incorrect. Shares can be issued at any price, provided that it is not below the nominal value of the shares. Once the company has been trading profitably for a period, the shares will not be worth the same as they were (the nominal value) when the company was first formed. In such circumstances, issuing shares at above their nominal value would not only be legal, but essential to preserve the wealth of the existing shareholders relative to any new ones.

(c) This statement is incorrect. From a legal perspective, the company is limited to a maximum dividend of the current extent of its revenue reserves. This amounts to any after-tax profits or gains realised that have not been eroded through, for example, payments of previous dividends. Legally, cash is not an issue; it would be perfectly legal for a company to borrow the funds to pay a dividend – although whether such an action would be commercially prudent is another question.

(d) This statement is partly incorrect. Companies do indeed have to pay tax on their profits. Depending on their circumstances, shareholders might also have to pay tax on their dividends.

4.4   Iqbal Ltd

Year	Maximum dividend £	
2002	0	No profit exists out of which to pay a dividend.
2003	0	There remains a cumulative loss of £7,000. Since the revaluation represents a gain that has not been realised, it cannot be used to justify a dividend.
2004	13,000	The cumulative net realised gains are derived as (−£15,000 + £8,000 + £15,000 + £5,000).
2005	14,000	The realised profits and gains for the year.
2006	22,000	The realised profits and gains for the year.

4.6   Pear Limited

Balance sheet as at 30 September 2006

	£000
Non-current assets	
Property, plant and equipment	
Cost (1,570 + 30)	1,600
Depreciation (690 + 12)	(702)
	898
Current assets	
Inventories	207
Receivables (182 + 18 − 4)	196
Cash at bank	21
	424
Total assets	1,322
Equity	
Share capital	300
Share premium account	300
Retained earnings (104 + 41 − 25)	120
	720
Non-current liabilities	
Borrowings – 10% loan (repayable 2009)	300
Current liabilities	
Trade payables	88
Other payables (20 + 30 + 15 + 2)	67
Taxation	17
Dividend approved	25
Borrowings – Bank overdraft	105
	302
Total equity and liabilities	1,322

Income statement for the year ended 30 September 2006

	£000
Revenue (1,456 + 18)	1,474
Cost of sales	(768)
Gross profit	706
Salaries	(220)
Depreciation (249 + 12)	(261)
Other operating costs [131 + (2% × 200) + 2]	(137)
Operating profit	88
Interest payable (15 + 15)	(30)
Profit before taxation	58
Taxation (58 × 30%)	(17)
Profit for the year	41

4.7 Chips Limited

Balance sheet as at 30 June 2006

	Cost £000	Depreciation £000	£000
Non-current assets			
Property, plant and equipment			
Buildings	800	(112)	688
Plant and equipment	650	(367)	283
Motor vehicles (102 − 8); (53 − 5 + 19)	94	(67)	27
	1,544	(546)	998
Current assets			
Inventories			950
Trade receivables (420 − 16)			404
Cash at bank (16 + 2)			18
			1,372
Total assets			2,370
Equity			
Ordinary shares of £1, fully paid			800
Reserves at 1 July 2005			248
Retained profit for year			60
			1,108
Non-current liabilities			
Borrowings − secured 10% loan			700
Current liabilities			
Trade payables (361 + 23)			384
Other payables (117 + 35)			152
Taxation			26
			562
Total equity and liabilities			2,370

Income statement for the year ended 30 June 2006

	£000
Revenue (1,850 − 16)	1,834
Cost of sales (1,040 + 23)	(1,063)
Gross profit	771
Depreciation [220 − 2 − 5 + 8 + (94 × 20%)]	(240)
Other operating costs	(375)
Operating profit	156
Interest payable (35 + 35)	(70)
Profit before taxation	86
Taxation (86 × 30%)	(26)
Profit for the year	60

Chapter 5

5.1 Some believe that the annual reports of companies are becoming too long and contain too much information. A few examples of the length of the 2006 accounts of large companies are as follows:

Marks and Spencer plc	108 pages
Tesco plc	116 pages
BT Group plc	150 pages
3i Group plc	100 pages

There is a danger that users will suffer from information overload if they are confronted with an excessive amount of information and that they will be unable to cope with it. This may, in turn, lead them to:

- fail to distinguish between important and less important information;
- fail to approach the analysis of information in a logical and systematic manner;
- feel a sense of confusion and avoid the task of analysing the information.

Lengthy annual reports are likely to be a problem for the less sophisticated user. This problem has been recognised and many companies publish summarised accounts for private investors, which include only the key points. However, for sophisticated users the problem may be that the annual reports are still not long enough. They often wish to glean as much information as possible from the company in order to make investment decisions.

5.3 **I. Ching (Booksellers) plc**

I. Ching (Booksellers) plc
Income statement for the year ended 31 December 2006

	£000
Revenue	943
Cost of sales	(460)
Gross profit	483
Distribution costs	(110)
Administrative expenses	(212)
Other expenses	(25)
Operating profit	136
Finance costs	(40)
Profit before tax	96
Taxation	(24)
Profit for the period	72

5.4 **Manet plc**

Manet plc
Statement of changes in equity for the year ended 30 June 2007

	Share capital £m	Share premium £m	Revaluation reserve £m	Translation reserve £m	Retained earnings £m	Total £m
Balance as at 30 June 2006	250	50	120	15	380	815
Changes in equity for the year ended 30 June 2007						
Gain on revaluation of properties			30			30
Exchange differences on translation of foreign operations	—	—	—	(5)	—	(5)
Net income recognised directly to equity			30	(5)		25
Profit for the period	—	—	—	—	160	160
Total recognised income and expense for the period			30	(5)	160	185
Dividends					(80)	(80)
Balance at 30 June 2007	250	50	150	10	460	920

5.5 Here are some points that might be made concerning accounting regulation and accounting measurement:

For

- It seems reasonable that companies, particularly given their limited liability, should be required to account to their members and to the general public and that rules should prescribe how this should be done – including how particular items should be measured. It also seems sensible that these rules should try to establish some uniformity of practice. Investors could be misled if the same item appeared in the financial statements of two separate companies but had been measured in different ways.
- Companies would find it difficult to attract finance, credit and possibly employees without publishing credible information about themselves. An important measure of performance is profit, and investors often need to make judgements concerning relative performance within an industry sector. Without clear benchmarks by which to judge performance, investors may not invest in a company.

Against

- It could be argued that it is up to the companies to decide whether or not they can survive and prosper without publishing information about themselves. If they can, then so much the better for them as they will have saved large amounts of money by not doing so. If it is necessary for a company to provide financial information in order to be able to attract investment finance and other necessary factors, then the company can make the necessary judgement of how much information is necessary and what forms of measurement are required.
- Not all company managements view matters in the same way. Allowing companies to select their own approaches to financial reporting enables them to reflect their personalities. Thus, a conservative management will adopt conservative accounting policies, such as writing off research and development expenditure quickly, whereas more adventurous management may adopt less conservative accounting policies, such as writing off research and development expenditure over several years. The impact of these different views will have an effect on profit and will give the reader an insight to the approach adopted by the management team.

5.8   Carpetright plc

Table of key results
This table extracts some of the information from the segmental report and calculates a few ratios to help gain an insight to financial health. (Ratios will be explored in detail in Chapter 7.)

	2006		2005	
	UK and RoI £m	Rest of Europe £m	UK and RoI £m	Rest of Europe £m
Segment revenue	397.7	53.7	409.2	53.3
Gross profit	241.2	29.7	245.2	27.8
Operating profit	55.1	3.6	60.4	3.0
Total assets	162.7	74.8	147.9	64.2
Net assets (total assets – total liabilities)	52.7	60.2	47.0	52.4
Capital expenditure	30.8	4.3	23.6	9.5
Key ratios				
Gross profit as % revenue	60.6%	55.3%	59.9%	52.2%
Operating profit as % revenue	13.9%	6.7%	14.8%	5.6%
Operating profit as % of net assets	104.6%	6.0%	128.5%	5.7%
Capital expenditure as % of total assets	18.9%	5.7%	16.0%	14.8%

Comparing 2006 with the 2005 segment results

UK and RoI segment

- For the UK and RoI segment, revenue, gross profit and operating profit fell slightly in 2006 compared with the previous year.
- Operating profit as a percentage of revenue slipped slightly in 2006.
- Net assets increased during 2006.
- Given the decline in the operating profits and the increase in net assets, it was inevitable that the operating profits as a percentage of net assets would decline.
- Overall, some deterioration in financial results has occurred during 2006.

Rest of Europe segment

- Revenue increased slightly in 2006 compared with the previous year.
- Gross profit and operating profits increased by a greater amount than the increase in revenue compared with the previous year.
- Net assets increased by nearly 15% in 2006 compared with the previous year.
- The increase in net assets was greater than the increase in operating profits.
- The operating profit as a percentage of net assets did not increase significantly.
- Overall, some improvement in financial results has occurred for the Rest of Europe during 2006.

Comparing the two segments

- There is a significant difference in the size of the two segments – the UK and RoI segment dwarfs the Rest of Europe segment.
- For 2006, sales revenue for the UK and RoI is more than seven times higher and operating profits are more than 15 times than for the rest of Europe.
- The UK and RoI segment is the more profitable segment in both years and across all measures.
- Capital expenditure, as a percentage of total assets, is much higher for the UK and RoI than for the Rest of Europe in both years.
- The Rest of Europe requires a much higher investment of assets to generate each £1 of sales revenue and each £1 of profit.

The reasons for the differences in profitability between the two segments are not clear from the information available. Possible reasons may include:

- a more difficult economic environment in the Rest of Europe segment;
- the Rest of Europe segment is not yet fully established in its markets;
- problems in applying, or adapting, the UK and RoI business model to the Rest of Europe.

Chapter 6

6.1 (a) An increase in the level of inventories would, ultimately, have an adverse effect on cash.

(b) A rights issue of ordinary shares will give rise to a positive cash flow, which will be included in the 'financing' section of the cash flow statement.

(c) A bonus issue of ordinary shares has no cash flow effect.

(d) Writing off some of the value of the inventories has no cash flow effect.

(e) A disposal for cash of a large number of shares by a major shareholder has no cash flow effect as far as the business is concerned.

(f) Depreciation does not involve cash at all. Using the indirect method of deducing cash flows from operating activities involves the depreciation expense in the calculation, but this is simply because we are trying to find out from the profit before taxation (after depreciation) figure what the profit before taxation *and* depreciation must have been.

6.3 Torrent plc

Torrent plc
Cash flow statement for the year ended 31 December 2007

	£m	£m
Cash flows from operating activities		
Profit before taxation (after interest) (see Note 1 below)	170	
Adjustments for:		
Depreciation (Note 2)	78	
Interest expense (Note 3)	26	
	274	
Decrease in inventories (41 – 35)	6	
Increase in trade receivables (145 – 139)	(6)	
Decrease in trade payables (54 – 41)	(13)	
Cash generated from operations	261	
Interest paid	(26)	
Taxation paid (Note 4)	(41)	
Dividend paid	(60)	
Net cash from operating activities		134
Cash flows from investing activities		
Payments to acquire plant and machinery	(67)	
Net cash used in investing activities		(67)
Cash flows from financing activities		
Redemption of loan notes (250 – 150) (Note 5)	(100)	
Net cash used in financing activities		(100)
Net decrease in cash and cash equivalents		(33)
Cash and cash equivalents at 1 January 2007		
Bank overdraft		(56)
Cash and cash equivalents at 31 December 2007		
Bank overdraft		(89)

To see how this relates to the cash of the business at the beginning and end of the year it can be useful to provide a reconciliation as follows:

Analysis of cash and cash equivalents during the year ended 31 December 2007

	£m
Cash and cash equivalents at 1 January 2007	(56)
Net cash outflow	(33)
Cash and cash equivalents at 31 December 2007	(89)

Notes:
1 This is simply taken from the income statement for the year.
2 Since there were no disposals, the depreciation charges must be the difference between the start and end of the year's plant and machinery values, adjusted by the cost of any additions.

	£m
Carrying amount at 1 January 2007	325
Add Additions	67
	392
Less Depreciation (balancing figure)	78
Carrying amount at 31 December 2007	314

3 Interest payable expense must be taken out, by adding it back to the profit before taxation figure. We subsequently deduct the cash paid for interest payable during the year. In this case the two figures are identical.
4 Companies pay 50% of their tax during their accounting year and 50% in the following year. Thus the 2007 payment would have been half the tax on the 2006 profit (that is, the figure that would

have appeared in the current liabilities at the end of 2006), plus half of the 2007 tax charge (that is, $23 + (\frac{1}{2} \times 36) = 41$).

5 It is assumed that the cash payment to redeem the debentures was simply the difference between the two balance sheet figures.

It seems that there was a bonus issue of ordinary shares during the year. These increased by £100m. At the same time, the share premium account balance reduced by £40m (to zero) and the revaluation reserve balance fell by £60m.

6.6 Blackstone plc

Blackstone plc
Cash flow statement for the year ended 31 March 2007

	£m	£m
Cash flows from operating activities		
Profit before taxation (after interest)		
(see Note 1 below)	1,853	
Adjustments for:		
Depreciation (Note 2)	1,289	
Interest expense (Note 3)	456	
	3,598	
Increase in inventories (2,410 − 1,209)	(1,201)	
Increase in trade receivables (1,173 − 641)	(532)	
Increase in trade payables (1,507 − 931)	576	
Cash generated from operations	2,441	
Interest paid	(456)	
Taxation paid (Note 4)	(300)	
Dividend paid	(400)	
Net cash from operating activities		1,285
Cash flows from investing activities		
Proceeds of disposals	54	
Payment to acquire intangible non-current asset	(700)	
Payments to acquire property, plant and equipment	(4,578)	
Net cash used in investing activities		(5,224)
Cash flows from financing activities		
Bank borrowings	2,000	
Net cash from financing activities		2,000
Net decrease in cash and cash equivalents		(1,939)
Cash and cash equivalents at 1 April 2006		
Cash at bank		123
Cash and cash equivalents at 31 March 2007		
Bank overdraft		(1,816)

To see how this relates to the cash of the business at the beginning and end of the year it can be useful to provide a reconciliation as follows:

Analysis of cash and cash equivalents during the year ended 31 March 2007

	£m
Cash and cash equivalents at 1 April 2006	123
Net cash outflow	(1,939)
Cash and cash equivalents at 31 March 2007	1,816

Notes:

1 This is simply taken from the income statement for the year.

2 The full depreciation charge was that stated in Note 2 to the question (£1,251m), plus the deficit on disposal of the non-current assets. According to Note 2, these non-current assets had originally cost £581m and had been depreciated by £489m, that is a net carrying amount of £92m. They were

sold for £54m, leading to a deficit on disposal of £38m. Thus the full depreciation expense for the year was £1,289m (that is, £1,251m + £38m).

3 Interest payable expense must be taken out, by adding it back to the profit before taxation figure. We subsequently deduct the cash paid for interest payable during the year. In this case the two figures are identical.

4 Companies pay tax at 50% during their accounting year and the other 50% in the following year. Thus the 2007 payment would have been half the tax on the 2006 profit (that is, the figure that would have appeared in the current liabilities at 31 March 2006), plus half of the 2007 tax charge (that is, $105 + (^1/_2 \times 390) = 300$).

6.7 York plc

York plc
Cash flow statement for the year ended 30 September 2007

	£m	£m
Cash flows from operating activities		
Profit before taxation (after interest)		
(see Note 1 below)	10.0	
Adjustments for:		
Depreciation (Note 2)	9.8	
Interest expense (Note 3)	3.0	
	22.8	
Increase in inventories and trade receivables		
(122.1 – 119.8)	(2.3)	
Increase in trade payables (82.5 – 80.0)	2.5	
Cash generated from operations	23.0	
Interest paid	(3.0)	
Taxation paid (Note 4)	(2.3)	
Dividend paid	(3.5)	
Net cash from operating activities		14.2
Cash flows from investing activities		
Proceeds of disposals (Note 2)	5.2	
Payments to acquire non-current assets	(20.0)	
Net cash used in investing activities		(14.8)
Cash flows from financing activities		
Increase in long-term borrowings	3.0	
Share issue (Note 5)	5.0	
Net cash from financing activities		8.0
Net increase in cash and cash equivalents		7.4
Cash and cash equivalents at 1 October 2006		
Cash at bank		9.2
Cash and cash equivalents at 30 September 2007		
Cash at bank		16.6

To see how this relates to the cash of the business at the beginning and end of the year it can be useful to provide a reconciliation as follows:

Analysis of cash and cash equivalents
during the year ended 30 September 2007

	£m
Cash and cash equivalents at 1 October 2006	9.2
Net cash inflow	7.4
Cash and cash equivalents at 30 September 2007	16.6

Notes:

1 This is simply taken from the income statement for the year.

2 The full depreciation charge was the £13.0m, less the surplus on disposal (£3.2m), both stated in Note 1 to the question. (According to the table in Note 4 to the question, the non-current assets disposed of had a net carrying value of £2.0m. To produce a surplus of £3.2m, they must have been sold for £5.2m.)

3 Interest payable expense must be taken out, by adding it back to the profit before taxation figure. We subsequently deduct the cash paid for interest payable during the year. In this case the two figures are identical.

4 Companies pay 50% of their tax during their accounting year and the other 50% in the following year. Thus the 2007 payment would have been half the tax on the 2006 profit (that is, the figure that would have appeared in the current liabilities at 30 September 2006), plus half of the 2007 tax charge (that is, $1.0 + (\frac{1}{2} \times 2.6) = 2.3$).

5 This issue must have been for cash since it could not have been a bonus issue – the share premium is untouched and 'Reserves' had altered over the year only by the amount of the 2007 retained profit (profit for the year, less the dividend). The shares seem to have been issued at par (that is, at their nominal value). This is a little surprising since the business has assets that seem to be above that value. On the other hand, were this a rights issue, the low issue price would not have disadvantaged the existing shareholders since they were also the beneficiaries of the advantage of the low issue price.

6.8 Axis plc

Axis plc
Cash flow statement for the year ended 31 December 2007

	£m	£m
Cash flows from operating activities		
Profit before taxation (after interest) (see Note 1 below)	34	
Adjustments for:		
Depreciation (Note 2)	19	
Interest expense (Note 3)	2	
	55	
Decrease in inventories (25 – 24)	1	
Increase in trade receivables (26 – 16)	(10)	
Increase in trade payables (36 – 31)	5	
Cash generated from operations	51	
Interest paid	(2)	
Taxation paid (Note 4)	(15)	
Dividend paid	(14)	
Net cash from operating activities		20
Cash flows from investing activities		
Proceeds of disposals (Note 2)	4	
Payments to acquire non-current assets	(25)	
Net cash used in investing activities		(21)
Cash flows from financing activities		
Issue of loan notes	20	
Net cash from financing activities		20
Net increase in cash and cash equivalents		19
Cash and cash equivalents at 1 January 2007		
Cash at bank		nil
Short-term investments		nil
		nil
Cash and cash equivalents at 31 December 2007		
Cash at bank		7
Short-term investments		12
		19

To see how this relates to the cash of the business at the beginning and end of the year it can be useful to provide a reconciliation as follows:

Analysis of cash and cash equivalents during the year ended 31 December 2007

	£m
Cash and cash equivalents at 1 January 2007	nil
Net cash inflow	19
Cash and cash equivalents at 31 December 2007	19

Notes:

1 This is simply taken from the income statement for the year.

2 The full depreciation charge for the year is the sum of two figures labelled 'depreciation' and the deficit on disposal of non-current assets (that is, £2m + £16m + £1m = £19m). These were detailed in the income statement.

   According to the note in the question, the non-current assets disposed of had a net carrying amount of £5.0m (that is, £15m − £10m). To produce a deficit of £1m, they must have been sold for £4m.

3 Interest payable expense must be taken out, by adding it back to the profit before taxation figure. We subsequently deduct the cash paid for interest payable during the year. In this case the two figures are identical.

4 Companies pay 50% of their tax during their accounting year and the other 50% in the following year. Thus the 2007 payment would have been half the tax on the 2006 profit (that is, the figure that would have appeared in the current liabilities at 31 December 2006), plus half of the 2007 tax charge (that is, $7 + (\frac{1}{2} \times 16) = 15$).

Chapter 7

7.1 I. Jiang (Western) Ltd

The effect of each of the changes on ROCE is not always easy to predict.

1 On the face of it, an increase in the gross profit margin would tend to lead to an increase in ROCE. An increase in the gross profit margin may, however, lead to a decrease in ROCE in particular circumstances. If the increase in the margin resulted from an increase in sales prices, which in turn led to a decrease in sales revenue, a fall in ROCE can occur. A fall in sales revenue can reduce the operating profit (the numerator (top part of the fraction) in ROCE) if the overheads of the business did not decrease correspondingly.

2 A reduction in sales revenue can reduce ROCE for the reasons mentioned above.

3 An increase in overhead expenses will reduce the operating profit and this in turn will result in a reduction in ROCE.

4 An increase in inventories held would increase the amount of capital employed by the business (the denominator [bottom part of the fraction] in ROCE) where long-term funds are employed to finance the inventories. This will, in turn, reduce ROCE.

5 Repayment of the borrowings at the year end will reduce the capital employed and this will increase the ROCE, assuming that the year-end capital employed figure has been used in the calculation. Since the operating profit was earned during a period in which the borrowings existed, there is a strong argument for basing the capital employed figure on what was the position during the year, rather than at the end of it.

6 An increase in the time taken for credit customers to pay will result in an increase in capital employed if long-term funds are employed to finance the trade receivables. This increase in long-term funds will, in turn, reduce ROCE.

7.2   Amsterdam Ltd and Berlin Ltd

The ratios for Amsterdam Ltd and Berlin Ltd reveal that the trade receivables turnover ratio for Amsterdam Ltd is three times that for Berlin Ltd. Berlin Ltd is therefore much quicker in collecting amounts outstanding from customers. On the other hand, there is not much difference between the two businesses in the time taken to pay trade payables.

It is interesting to compare the difference in the trade receivables and payables collection periods for each business. As Amsterdam Ltd allows an average of 63 days' credit to its customers, yet pays suppliers within 50 days, it will require greater investment in working capital than Berlin Ltd, which allows an average of only 21 days to its customers but takes 45 days to pay its suppliers.

Amsterdam Ltd has a much higher gross profit margin than Berlin Ltd. However, the operating profit margin for the two businesses is identical. This suggests that Amsterdam Ltd has much higher overheads (as a percentage of sales revenue) than Berlin Ltd. The inventories turnover period for Amsterdam Ltd is more than twice that of Berlin Ltd. This may be due to the fact that Amsterdam Ltd maintains a wider range of inventories in an attempt to meet customer requirements. The evidence therefore suggests that Amsterdam Ltd is the one that prides itself on personal service. The higher average settlement period for trade receivables is consistent with a more relaxed attitude to credit collection (thereby maintaining customer goodwill) and the high overheads are consistent with incurring the additional costs of satisfying customers' requirements. Amsterdam Ltd's high inventories levels are consistent with maintaining a wide range of inventories, with the aim of satisfying a range of customer needs.

Berlin Ltd has the characteristics of a more price-competitive business. Its gross profit margin is much lower than that of Amsterdam Ltd, that is, a much lower gross profit for each £1 of sales revenue. However, overheads have been kept low, the effect being that the operating percentage is the same as Amsterdam Ltd's. The low inventories turnover period and average collection period for trade receivables are consistent with a business that wishes to minimise investment in current assets, thereby reducing costs.

7.6   Bradbury Ltd

(a)

	2006	2007
1 Operating profit margin	$\frac{914}{9,482} \times 100\% = 9.6\%$	$\frac{1,042}{11,365} \times 100\% = 9.2\%$
2 ROCE	$\frac{914}{11,033} \times 100 = 8.3\%$	$\frac{1,042}{13,943} \times 100\% = 7.5\%$
3 Current ratio	$\frac{4,926}{1,508} = 3.3{:}1$	$\frac{7,700}{5,174} = 1.5{:}1$
4 Gearing ratio	$\frac{1,220}{11,033} \times 100\% = 11.1\%$	$\frac{3,675}{13,943} \times 100\% = 26.4\%$
5 Days trade receivables	$\left(\frac{2,540}{9,482}\right) \times 365 = 98$ days	$\left(\frac{4,280}{11,365}\right) \times 365 = 137$ days
6 Sales revenue to capital employed	$\frac{9,482}{(9,813 + 1,220)} = 0.9$ times	$\frac{11,365}{(10,268 + 3,675)} = 0.8$ times

(b) The operating profit margin was slightly lower in 2007 than in 2006. Although there was an increase in sales revenue in 2007, this could not prevent a slight fall in ROCE in that year. The lower operating margin and increases in sales revenue may well be due to the new contract. The capital employed by the company increased in 2007 by a larger percentage than the increase in revenue. Hence, the sales revenue to capital employed ratio decreased over the period. The increase in capital during 2007 is largely due to an increase in borrowing. However, the gearing ratio is probably still low in comparison with other businesses. Comparison of the premises and borrowings figures indicates possible unused borrowing (debt) capacity.

The major cause for concern has been the dramatic decline in liquidity during 2007. The current ratio has more than halved during the period. There has also been a similar decrease in the acid test ratio, from 1.7:1 in 2006 to 0.8:1 in 2007. The balance sheet shows that the business now has a large overdraft and the trade payables outstanding have nearly doubled in 2007.

The trade receivables outstanding and inventories have increased much more than appears to be warranted by the increase in sales revenue. This may be due to the terms of the contract that has been negotiated and may be difficult to influence. If this is the case, the business should consider whether it is overtrading. If the conclusion is that it is, increasing its long-term funding may be a sensible policy.

7.7 **Harridges Ltd**

(a)

	2006	2007
ROCE	$\dfrac{310}{1,600} = 19.4\%$	$\dfrac{350}{1,700} = 20.6\%$
ROSF	$\dfrac{155}{1,100} = 14.1\%$	$\dfrac{175}{1,200} = 14.6\%$
Gross profit margin	$\dfrac{1,040}{2,600} = 40\%$	$\dfrac{1,150}{3,500} = 32.9\%$
Operating profit margin	$\dfrac{310}{2,600} = 11.9\%$	$\dfrac{350}{3,500} = 10\%$
Current ratio	$\dfrac{735}{400} = 1.8$	$\dfrac{660}{485} = 1.4$
Acid test ratio	$\dfrac{485}{400} = 1.2$	$\dfrac{260}{485} = 0.5$
Days trade receivables	$\dfrac{105}{2,600} \times 365 = 15$ days	$\dfrac{145}{3,500} \times 365 = 15$ days
Days trade payables	$\dfrac{300}{1,560} \times 365 = 70$ days	$\dfrac{375}{2,350^*} \times 365 = 58$ days
Inventories turnover period	$\dfrac{250}{1,560} \times 365 = 58$ days	$\dfrac{400}{2,350} \times 365 = 62$ days
Gearing ratio	$\dfrac{500}{1,600} = 31.3\%$	$\dfrac{500}{1,700} = 29.4\%$
EPS	$\dfrac{155}{490} = 31.6\text{p}$	$\dfrac{175}{490} = 35.7\text{p}$

* Used because the credit purchases figure is not available.

(b) There has been a considerable decline in the gross profit margin during 2007. This fact, combined with the increase in sales revenue by more than one-third, suggests that a price-cutting policy has been adopted in an attempt to stimulate sales. The resulting increase in sales revenue, however, has led to only a small improvement in ROCE and ROSF. Similarly, there has only been a small improvement in EPS.

Despite a large cut in the gross profit margin, the operating profit margin has fallen by less than 2%. This suggests that overheads have been tightly controlled during 2007. Certainly, overheads have not risen in proportion to sales revenue.

The current ratio has fallen and the acid test ratio has fallen by more than half. Even though liquidity ratios are lower in retailing than in manufacturing, the liquidity of the business should now be a cause for concern. However, this may be a passing problem. The business is investing heavily in non-current assets and is relying on internal funds to finance this growth. When this investment ends, the liquidity position may improve quickly.

The trade receivables period has remained unchanged over the two years, and there has been no significant change in the inventories turnover period in 2007. The gearing ratio seems quite low and provides no cause for concern given the profitability of the business.

Overall, the business appears to be financially sound. Although there has been rapid growth during 2007, there is no real cause for alarm provided that the liquidity of the business can be improved in the near future. In the absence of information concerning share price, it is not possible to say whether an investment should be made.

7.8 Genesis Ltd

(a) and (b) These parts have been answered in the text of the chapter and you are referred to it for a discussion on overtrading and its consequences.

(c)

$$\text{Current ratio} = \frac{232}{550} = 0.42$$

$$\text{Acid test ratio} = \frac{104}{550} = 0.19$$

$$\text{Inventories turnover period} = \frac{128}{1,248} \times 365 = 37 \text{ days}$$

$$\text{Average settlement period for trade receivables} = \frac{104}{1,640} \times 365 = 23 \text{ days}$$

$$\text{Average settlement period for trade payables} = \frac{184}{1,260} \times 365 = 53 \text{ days}$$

(d) Overtrading must be dealt with either by increasing the level of funding to match the level of activity or by reducing the level of activity to match the funds available. The latter option may result in a reduction in operating profit in the short term but may be necessary to ensure long-term survival.

Chapter 8

8.1 Lombard Ltd

Relevant costs of undertaking the contract are:

	£
Equipment costs	200,000
Component X (20,000 × 4 × £5)	400,000
Component Y (20,000 × 3 × £8)	480,000
Additional costs (20,000 × £8)	160,000
	1,240,000
Revenue from the contract (20,000 × £80)	1,600,000

Thus, from a purely financial point of view the project is acceptable. (Note that there is no relevant labour cost since the staff concerned will be paid irrespective of whether the contract is undertaken.)

8.2 The local authority

(a) *Net benefit of accepting the touring company proposal*

	£
Net reduction in ticket revenues (see workings below)	(20,000)
Savings on: Costumes	5,600
Scenery	3,300
Casual staff	3,520
Net deficit	7,580

Since there is a net deficit, on financial grounds the touring company's proposal should be rejected.

Note that all of the following are irrelevant, because they will occur irrespective of the decision:

- non-performing staff salaries
- artistes' salaries
- heating and lighting
- administration costs
- refreshment revenues and costs
- programme advertising.

Workings		£	£
Normal ticket sales revenue:	200 @ £24 =	4,800	
	500 @ £16 =	8,000	
	300 @ £12 =	3,600	
		16,400	
Ticket revenue at 50 per cent capacity for 20 performances:			
(£16,400 × 50% × 20)			164,000

Touring company ticket sales:
Total revenue for each performance for a full house:

		£	
	200 @ £22 =	4,400	
	500 @ £14 =	7,000	
	300 @ £10 =	3,000	
		14,400	
Ticket revenues	(£14,400 × 10 × 50%)		72,000
	(£14,400 × 15 × ⅔ × 50%)		72,000
			144,000
Net loss of revenue	(£164,000 − £144,000)		20,000

(b) Other possible factors to consider include:

- The reliability of the estimations, including the assumption that the level of occupancy will not alter programme and refreshment sales revenue.
- A desire to offer theatregoers the opportunity to see another group of players.
- Dangers of loss of morale of staff not employed, or employed to do other than their usual work.

8.3 Andrews and Co. Ltd

Minimum contract price:

			£
Materials	Steel core:	10,000 × £2.10	21,000
	Plastic:	10,000 × 0.10 × £0.10	100
Labour	Skilled:		–
	Unskilled:	10,000 × 5/60 × £7.50	6,250
Minimum tender price			27,350

8.6 The local education authority

(a) *One-off financial net benefits of closing:*

	D only	A and B	A and C
Capacity reduction	800	700	800
	£m	£m	£m
Property developer (A)	–	14.0	14.0
Shopping complex (B)	–	8.0	–
Property developer (D)	9.0	–	–
Safety (C)	–	–	3.0
Adapt facilities	(1.8)	–	–
Total	7.2	22.0	17.0
Ranking based on total one-off benefits	3	1	2

(Note that all past costs of buying and improving the schools are irrelevant.)

Recurrent financial net benefits of closing:

	D only £m	A and B £m	A and C £m
Rent (C)	–	–	0.3
Administrators	0.2	0.4	0.4
Total	0.2	0.4	0.7
Ranking based on total of recurrent benefits	3	2	1

On the basis of the financial figures alone, closure of either A and B or A and C looks best. It is not possible to add the one-off and the recurring costs directly, but the large one-off cost saving associated with closing Schools A and B makes this option look attractive. (In Chapter 14 we shall see that it is possible to add one-off and recurring costs in a way that should lead to sensible conclusions.)

(b) The costs of acquiring and improving the schools in the past are past costs or sunk costs and, therefore, irrelevant. The costs of employing the chief education officer is a future cost, but irrelevant because it is not dependent on outcomes, it is a common cost.

(c) There are many other factors, some of a non-quantifiable nature. These include:
- accuracy of projections of capacity requirements;
- locality of existing schools relative to where potential pupils live;
- political acceptability of selling schools to property developers;
- importance of purely financial issues in making the final decision;
- the quality of the replacement sporting facilities compared with those at School D;
- political acceptability of staff redundancies;
- possible savings/costs of employing fewer teachers, which might be relevant if economies of scale are available by having fewer schools;
- staff morale.

8.7 Rob Otics Ltd

(a) The minimum price for the proposed contract would be:

	£
Materials	
Component X (2 × 8 × £180)	2,880
Component Y	0
Component Z [(75 + 32) × £20] − (75 × £25)	265
Other miscellaneous items	250
Labour	
Assembly (25 + 24 + 23 + 22 + 21 + 20 + 19 + 18) × £48*	8,256
Inspection (8 × 6 × £18)	864
Total	12,515

* £60 − £12 = £48.

The assembly labour cost is irrelevant here because it will be incurred irrespective of which work the members of staff do. The historic cost of the inventories of Component X and the fact that it is not yet paid for are both irrelevant. The historic cost and the £1,500 relating to component Y are also irrelevant. Thus the minimum price is £12,515.

(b) Other factors include:
- competitive state of the market;
- the fact that the above figure is unique to the particular circumstances at the time – for example, having component Y in available but having no use for it. Any subsequent order might have to take account of an outlay cost;
- breaking even (that is, just covering the costs) on a contract will not fulfil the business's objective;
- charging a low price may cause marketing problems. Other customers may resent the low price for this contract. The current enquirer may expect a similar price in future.

Chapter 9

9.4 Motormusic Ltd

(a) Break-even point = fixed costs/contribution per unit

$$= (80{,}000 + 60{,}000)/[60 − (20 + 14 + 12 + 3)] = 12{,}727 \text{ radios}$$

These would have a sales value of £763,620 (that is, 12,727 × £60).

(b) The margin of safety is 7,273 radios (that is, 20,000 − 12,727). This margin would have a sales value of £436,380 (that is, 7,273 × £60).

9.5 **Products A, B and C**

(a) Total time required on cutting machines is:

$$(2,500 \times 1.0) + (3,400 \times 1.0) + (5,100 \times 0.5) = 8,450 \text{ hours}$$

Total time available on cutting machines is 5,000 hours. Therefore, this is a limiting factor. Total time required on assembling machines is:

$$(2,500 \times 0.5) + (3,400 \times 1.0) + (5,100 \times 0.5) = 7,200 \text{ hours}$$

Total time available on assembling machines is 8,000 hours. Therefore, this is not a limiting factor.

	A (per unit) £	B (per unit) £	C (per unit) £
Selling price	25	30	18
Variable materials	(12)	(13)	(10)
Variable production costs	(7)	(4)	(3)
Contribution	6	13	5
Time on cutting machines	1.0 hour	1.0 hour	0.5 hour
Contribution per hour on cutting machines	£6	£13	£10
Order of priority	3rd	1st	2nd

Therefore, produce:

3,400 product B using	3,400 hours
3,200 product C using	1,600 hours
	5,000 hours

(b) Assuming that the business would make no saving in variable production costs by sub-contracting, it would be worth paying up to the contribution per unit (£5) for product C, which would therefore be £5 × (5,100 − 3,200) = £9,500 in total.

Similarly it would be worth paying up to £6 per unit for product A, that is, £6 × 2,500 = £15,000 in total.

9.6 **Darmor Ltd**

(a) Contribution per hour of skilled labour of product X is:

$$\frac{£(30 - 6 - 2 - 12 - 3)}{(6/12)} = £14$$

Given the scarcity of skilled labour, if the management is to be indifferent between the products, the contribution per skilled-labour-hour must be the same. Thus for product Y the selling price must be:

$$£[14 \times (9/12)] + 9 + 4 + 25 + 7 = £55.50$$

(that is, the contribution plus the variable costs), and for product Z the selling price must be:

$$£[14 \times (3/12)] + 3 + 10 + 14 + 7 = £37.50$$

(b) The business could pay up to £26 an hour (£12 + £14) for additional hours of skilled labour. This is the potential contribution per hour, before taking account of the labour rate of £12 an hour.

9.7 Intermediate Products Ltd

(a)

	A £	B £	C £	D £
Total costs per unit	(65)	(41)	(36)	(46)
Less Fixed costs	20	8	8	12
Variable cost per unit	(45)	(33)	(28)	(34)
Buying/selling price per unit	70	45	40	55
Contribution per unit	25	12	12	21
Hours on special machine	0.5	0.4	0.5	0.3
Contribution per hour	50	30	24	70
Order of preference	2nd	3rd	4th	1st

Optimum use of hours on special machine	Balance of hours
D 3,000 × 0.3 = 900	5,100 (that is, 6,000 − 900)
A 5,000 × 0.5 = 2,500	2,600 (that is, 5,100 − 2,500)
B 6,000 × 0.4 = 2,400	200 (that is, 2,600 − 2,400)
C 400 × 0.5 = 200	–
6,000	

Therefore, make all of the demand for Ds, As and Bs plus 400 (of 4,000) Cs.

(b) The contribution per hour from Cs is £24, and so this is the maximum amount per hour that it would be worth paying to rent the machine, for a maximum of 1,800 hours (that is, 3,600 × 0.5, the time necessary to make the remaining demand for Cs).

(c) Other possible actions to overcome the shortage of machine time include:
- Alter the design of the products to avoid the use of the special machine.
- Increase the selling price of the product so that the demand will fall, making the available machine time sufficient but making production more profitable.

9.8 Gandhi Ltd

(a) Given that the spare capacity could not be used by other services, the standard service should continue to be offered. This is because it renders a positive contribution.

(b) The standard service renders a contribution per unit of £15 (that is, £80 − £65), or £30 during the time it would take to render one unit of the nova service. The nova service would provide a contribution of only £25 (that is, £75 − £50). The nova service should, therefore, not replace the standard service.

(c) Under the original plans, the following contributions would be rendered by the basic and standard services:

		£
Basic	11,000 × (£50 − £25) =	275,000
Standard	6,000 × (£80 − £65) =	90,000
		365,000

If the basic were to take the standard's place, 17,000 units (that is, 11,000 + 6,000) of them could be produced in total. To generate the same total contribution, each unit of the standard service would need to provide £21.47 (that is, £365,000/17,000) of contribution. Given the basic's variable cost of £25, this would mean a selling price of £46.47 each (that is £21.47 + £25.00).

Chapter 10

10.4 Promptprint Ltd

(a) The budget may be summarised as:

	£	
Sales revenue	196,000	
Direct materials	(38,000)	
Direct labour	(32,000)	
Total overheads	(77,000)	(2,400 + 3,000 + 27,600 + 36,000 + 8,000)
Operating profit	49,000	

The job may be priced on the basis that both overheads and operating profit should be apportioned to it on the basis of direct labour cost, as follows:

	£	
Direct materials	4,000	
Direct labour	3,600	
Overheads	8,663	(£77,000 × 3,600/32,000)
Operating profit	5,513	(£49,000 × 3,600/32,000)
	21,776	

This answer assumes that variable overheads vary in proportion to direct labour cost.

Various other bases of charging overheads and profit loading the job could have been adopted. For example, materials cost could have been included (with direct labour) as the basis for profit loading, or even apportioning overheads.

(b) This part of the question is, in effect, asking for comments on the validity of 'full cost-plus' pricing. This approach can be useful as an indicator of the average long-run cost of doing the job. On the other hand, it fails to take account of relevant opportunity costs as well as the state of the market and other external factors. For example, it ignores the price that a competitor printing business may quote.

(c) Revised estimates of direct material costs for the job:

	£	
Paper grade 1	1,500	(£1,200 × 125%; this item of inventories needs to be replaced)
Paper grade 2	0	(it has no opportunity cost value)
Card	510	(£640 – £130: using the card on another job would save £640, but cost £130 to achieve that saving)
Inks etc.	300	(this item of inventories needs to be replaced)
	2,310	

10.5 Bookdon plc

(a) To answer this question, we need first to allocate and apportion the overheads to product cost centres, as follows:

Cost	Basis of apportionment	Total	Machine shop	Fitting section	Canteen	Machine main'ce section
		£	£	£	£	£
Allocated items:	Specific	90,380	27,660	19,470	16,600	26,650
Rent, rates, heat, light	Floor area	17,000	9,000	3,500	2,500	2,000
			(3,600/ 6,800)	(1,400/ 6,800)	(1,000/ 6,800)	(800/ 6,800)
Dep'n and insurance	Carrying value	25,000	12,500	6,250	2,500	3,750
			(150/300)	(75/300)	(30/300)	(45/300)
		132,380	49,160	29,220	21,600	32,400
Canteen	Number of employees	–	10,800	8,400	(21,600)	2,400
			(18/36)	(14/36)		(4/36)
		132,380	59,960	37,620	–	34,800
Machine main'ce section	Specified %	–	24,360	10,440	–	(34,800)
			(70%)	(30%)		
		132,380	84,320	48,060	–	–

Note that the canteen overheads were reapportioned to the other cost centres first because the canteen renders a service to the machine maintenance section but does not receive a service from it.

Calculation of the overhead absorption (recovery) rates can now proceed:

(i) Total budgeted machine hours are:

	Hours
Product X (4,200 × 6)	25,200
Product Y (6,900 × 3)	20,700
Product Z (1,700 × 4)	6,800
	52,700

Overhead absorption rate for the machine shop is:

$$\frac{£84,320}{52,700} = £1.60/\text{machine-hour}$$

(ii) Total budgeted direct labour cost for the fitting section is:

	£
Product X (4,200 × £12)	50,400
Product Y (6,900 × £3)	20,700
Product Z (1,700 × £21)	35,700
	106,800

Overhead absorption rate for the fitting section is:

$$\frac{£48,060}{£106,800} \times 100\% = 45\% \quad \text{or £0.45 per £ of direct labour cost}$$

(b) The cost of one unit of product X is calculated as follows:

	£
Direct materials	11.00
Direct labour:	
Machine shop	6.00
Fitting section	12.00
Overheads:	
Machine shop (6 × £1.60)	9.60
Fitting section (£12 × 45%)	5.40
	44.00

Therefore, the cost of one unit of Product X is £44.00.

10.6 Products A, B and C

Allocation and apportionment of overheads to product cost centres

	Basis of apportionment	Cutting £	Machining £	Pressing £	Engineering £	Personnel £
Total		154,482	64,316	58,452	56,000	34,000
Personnel	Specified	18,700 (55%)	3,400 (10%)	6,800 (20%)	5,100 (15%)	(34,000)
		173,182	67,716	65,252	61,100	–
Engineering	Specified	12,220 (20%)	27,495 (45%)	21,385 (35%)	(61,100)	
		185,402	95,211	86,637	–	–

Note that the personnel overheads were reapportioned to the other cost centres first because the canteen renders a service to the engineering department section, but does not receive a service from it.

Calculation of the overhead absorption (recovery) rates
In both the cutting and pressing departments no machines seem to be used, and so a direct labour hour basis of overhead absorption seems reasonable.

In the machining department, machine hours are far in excess of labour hours and the overheads are probably machine related. In this department, machine hours seem a fair basis for cost units to absorb overheads.

Total planned direct labour hours for the cutting department are thus:

	£
Product A [4,000 × (3 + 6)]	36,000
Product B [3,000 × (5 + 1)]	18,000
Product C [6,000 × (2 + 3)]	30,000
	84,000

The overhead absorption rate for the cutting department = £185,402/84,000 = £2.21 per direct labour hour.

Total planned machine hours for the machining department are thus:

	£
Product A (4,000 × 2.0)	8,000
Product B (3,000 × 1.5)	4,500
Product C (6,000 × 2.5)	15,000
	27,500

The overhead absorption rate for the machining department = £95,211/27,500 = £3.46 per machine hour.

Total planned direct labour hours for the pressing department are:

	£
Product A (4,000 × 2)	8,000
Product B (3,000 × 3)	9,000
Product C (6,000 × 4)	24,000
	41,000

The overhead absorption rate for the cutting department = £86,637/41,000 = £2.11 per direct labour hour.

(a) Cost of one completed unit of Product A

		£
Direct materials		7.00
Direct labour:		
Cutting department: Skilled	(3 × £16)	48.00
Unskilled	(6 × £10)	60.00
Machining department	(0.5 × £12)	6.00
Pressing department	(2 × £12)	24.00
Overheads:		
Cutting department	(9 × £2.21)	19.89
Machining department	(2 × £3.46)	6.92
Pressing department	(2 × £2.11)	4.22
		176.03

(b) Cost of one uncompleted unit of Product B

		£
Direct materials		4.00*
Direct labour:		
Cutting department: Skilled	(5 × £16)	80.00
Unskilled	(1 × £10)	10.00
Machining department	(0.25 × £12)	3.00
Overheads:		
Cutting department	(6 × £2.21)	13.26
Machining department	(1.5 × £3.46)	5.19
		115.45

* This assumes that all of the materials are added in the cutting or machining departments.

10.7

Offending phrase	Explanation
'Necessary to divide up the business into departments'	This can be done but it will not always be of much benefit. Only in quite restricted circumstances will it give significantly different job costs.
'Fixed costs (or overheads)'	This implies that fixed costs and overheads are the same thing. They are not really connected with one another. 'Fixed' is to do with how costs behave as the level of output is raised or lowered; 'overheads' are to do with the extent to which costs can be directly measured in respect of a particular unit of output. Although it is true that many overheads are fixed, not all are. Also, direct labour is usually a fixed cost. All of the other references to fixed and variable costs are wrong. The person should have referred to indirect and direct costs.
'Usually this is done on the basis of area'	Where overheads are apportioned to departments, they will be apportioned on some logical basis. For certain costs – for example, rent – the floor area may be the most logical; for others, such as machine maintenance costs, the floor area would be totally inappropriate.
'When the total fixed costs for each department have been identified, this will be divided by the number of hours that were worked'	Where overheads are dealt with on a departmental basis, they may be divided by the number of direct labour hours to deduce a recovery rate. However, this is only one basis of applying overheads to jobs. For example, machine hours or some other basis may be more appropriate to the particular circumstances involved.
'It is essential that this approach is taken in order to deduce a selling price'	It is relatively unusual for the 'job cost' to be able to dictate the price at which the manufacturer can price its output. For many businesses, the market dictates the price.

10.8 (a) Charging overheads to jobs on a departmental basis means that overheads are collected 'product' cost centre (department) by 'product' cost centre. This involves picking up the overheads that are direct to each department and adding to them a share of overheads that are general to the business as a whole. The overheads of 'service' cost centres must then be apportioned to the product cost centres. At this point, all of the overheads for the whole business are divided between the 'product' cost centres, such that the sum of the 'product' cost centre overheads equals those for the whole business.

Dealing with overheads departmentally is believed to provide more fair and useful information to decision makers, because different departments may have rather different overheads, and applying overheads departmentally can take account of that and reflect it in job costs.

In theory, dealing with overheads on a departmental basis is more costly than on a business-wide basis. In practice, it possibly does not make too much difference to the cost of collecting the information. This is because, normally, businesses are divided into departments, and the costs are collected departmentally, as part of the normal routine for exercising control over the business.

(b) In order to make any difference to the job cost that will emerge as a result of dealing with overheads departmentally, as compared with a business-wide basis, the following *both* need to be the case:

- The overheads per unit of the basis of charging (for example direct labour hours) need to be different from one department to the next; and
- The proportion (but not the actual amounts) of total overheads that are charged to jobs must differ from one job to the next.

Assume, for the sake of argument, that direct labour hours are used as the basis of charging overheads in all departments. Also assume that there are three departments, A, B and C.

There will be no difference in the overheads charged to a job if the rate of overheads per direct labour hour is the same for all departments. Obviously, if the charging rate is the same in all departments, that same rate must also apply to the business taken as a whole.

Also, even where overheads per direct labour hour differ significantly from one department to another – if all jobs spend, say, about 20% of their time in Department A, 50% in Department B and 30% in Department C – it will not make any difference whether overheads are charged departmentally or overall.

These conclusions are not in any way dependent on the basis of charging overheads or even that overheads are charged on the same basis in each department.

The statements above combine to mean that, probably in many cases in practice, departmentalising overheads is not providing information that is significantly different from that which would be provided by charging overheads to jobs on a business-wide basis.

Chapter 11

11.1 Woodner Ltd

A	B	C	D	E	F	G	H
Output	Sales price per unit	Total sales revenue (A × B)	Marginal unit sales revenue	Total variable cost (A × £20)	Total cost (variable cost + £2,500)	Marginal cost per unit	Profit/(loss)
Units	£	£	£	£	£	£	£
0	0	0	0	0	2,500	–	(2,500)
10	95	950*	95†	200	2,700	20	(1,750)
20	90	1,800	85	400	2,900	20	(1,100)
30	85	2,550	75	600	3,100	20	(550)
40	80	3,200	65	800	3,300	20	(100)
50	75	3,750	55	1,000	3,500	20	250
60	70	4,200	45	1,200	3,700	20	500
70	65	4,550	35	1,400	3,900	20	650
80	60	4,800	25	1,600	4,100	20	700
90	55	4,950	15	1,800	4,300	20	650
100	50	5,000	5	2,000	4,500	20	500

* (10 × £95)
† (950 – 0)/(10 – 0)

An output of 80 units each week will maximise profit at £700 a week. This is the nearest, given the nature of the input data, to the level of output where marginal cost per unit equals marginal revenue per unit. (For the mathematically minded, calculus could have been used to find the point at which the slopes of the total sales revenue and total cost curves were equal.)

11.2 Cost-plus pricing means that prices are based on calculations/assessments of how much it costs to produce the good or service, and includes a margin for profit. 'Cost' in this context might mean relevant cost, variable cost, direct cost or full cost. Usually, cost-plus prices are based on full costs.

If a business charges the full cost of its output as a selling price, it will in theory break even. This is because the sales revenue will exactly cover all of the costs. Charging something above full cost will yield a profit. Thus, in theory, cost-plus pricing is logical.

If a cost-plus approach to pricing is to be taken, the issue that must be addressed is the level of profit required from each unit sold. This must logically be based on the total profit that is required for the period. Normally, businesses seek to enhance their wealth through trading. The extent to which they expect to do this is normally related to the amount of wealth that is invested to promote wealth enhancement. Businesses tend to seek to produce a particular percentage increase in wealth. In other words, they seek to generate a particular return on capital employed. It seems logical, therefore, that the profit loading on full cost should reflect the business's target profit and that the target should itself be based on a target return on capital employed.

An obvious problem with cost-plus pricing is that the market may not agree with the price. Put another way, cost-plus pricing takes no account of the market demand function (the relationship between price and quantity demanded). A business may fairly deduce the full cost of some product and then add what might be regarded as a reasonable level of profit, only to find that a rival producer is offering a similar product for a much lower price, or that the market simply will not buy at the cost-plus price.

Most suppliers are not strong enough in the market to dictate pricing: most are 'price takers', not 'price makers'. They must accept the price offered by the market or they do not sell any of their wares. Cost-plus pricing may be appropriate for price makers, but it has less relevance for price takers.

The cost-plus price is not entirely useless to price takers. When contemplating entering a market, knowing the cost-plus price will tell the price taker whether it can profitably enter the market. As has been said above, the full cost can be seen as a long-run break-even selling price. If entering a market means that this break-even price, plus an acceptable profit, cannot be achieved, then the business should probably stay out. Having a breakdown of the full cost may put the business in a position to examine where costs might be capable of being cut in order to bring the full cost-plus profit to within a figure acceptable to the market.

Being a price maker does not always imply that the business dominates a particular market. Many small businesses are, to some extent, price makers. This tends to be where buyers find it difficult to make clear distinctions between the prices offered by various suppliers. An example of this might be a car repair. Though it may be possible to obtain a series of binding estimates for the work from various garages, most people would not normally do so. As a result, garages normally charge cost-plus prices for car repairs.

11.3 **Kaplan plc**

(a) At present, the business makes each model of suitcase in a batch. The direct materials and labour costs will be recorded in respect of each batch. To these costs will be added a share of the overheads of the business for the period in which production of the batch takes place. The basis of the batch absorbing overheads is a matter of managerial judgement. Direct labour hours spent working on the batch, relative to total direct labour hours worked during the period, is a popular method. This is not the 'correct' way, however. There is no correct way. If the activity is capital intensive, some machine hour basis of dealing with overheads might be more appropriate, though still not 'correct'. Overheads might be collected, department by department, and charged to the batch as it passes through each department. Alternatively, all of the overheads for the entire production facility might be totalled and the overheads dealt with more globally. It is only in restricted circumstances that overheads charged to batches will be affected by a decision to deal with them departmentally rather than globally.

Once the 'full cost' (direct costs plus a share of indirect costs) has been ascertained for the batch, the cost per suitcase can be established by dividing the batch cost by the number in the batch.

(b) The uses to which full cost information can be put have been identified as:
- *Pricing*. Usually the customer will want to know the price in advance of placing the order. Thus, it is not possible to wait until all of the costs have been incurred, and are known, before the price can be deduced. Even where a job is not for an identified customer, the business still needs to have some idea of whether it can produce the good or service at a price that the market will bear. In practice, a luggage manufacturer would be unlikely to be able to base prices on full cost. It would have to compete with others and would likely be a 'price taker'.
- *Exercising control*. Where the cost of doing something is planned (budgeted), the actual cost of doing it can be compared with the plan and steps taken to get things back on track if there are divergences between plans and actual. Using full costs in this way can lead to managers being held accountable for costs, particularly overheads, over which they have no control. This could weaken the control process.
- *Assessing relative efficiency*. Full costs can also be used to help assess operational efficiency. Comparing costs for the forthcoming period with those of previous periods, or with similar businesses, can provide some insight to relative efficiency. This can give misleading information where costs are being derived on different bases; for example overheads might be absorbed on a business-wide basis in one business and on a departmental one in the other.
- *Assessing performance*. Valuing work in progress is an important purpose for which full costs are required. If managers are to benefit fully from accounting information, the costs (including overheads) of generating revenues for a period must be identified. The relatively arbitrary nature of overhead absorption by cost units can weaken the value of the financial reports.

(c) Whereas the traditional approach to dealing with overheads is just to accept that they exist and deal with them in a fairly broad manner, ABC takes a much more enquiring approach. ABC takes the view that overheads do not just 'occur', but that they are caused or 'driven' by 'activities'. It is a matter of finding out which activities are driving the costs and how much cost they are driving.

For example, a significant part of the costs of making suitcases of different sizes might be resetting machinery to cope with a batch of a different size from its predecessor batch. Where a particular model is made in very small batches, because it has only a small market, ABC would advocate that this model is charged directly with its machine-setting costs. The traditional approach would be to treat machine setting as a general overhead that the individual suitcases (irrespective of the model) might bear equally. ABC, it is claimed, leads to more accurate costing and thus to more accurate assessment of profitability.

(d) The other advantage of pursuing an ABC philosophy and identifying cost drivers is that, once the drivers have been identified, costs are likely to become much more susceptible to being controlled. Thus the ability of management to assess the benefit of certain activities against their cost becomes more feasible.

11.6 **GB Company**

(a) The minimum acceptable price of 120,000 motors to be supplied over the next four months is:

	£000	
Direct materials	600	(120,000 × £5.00)
Direct labour	720	(120,000 × £6.00)
Variable manufacturing overheads	360	(120,000 × £3.00 (that is, £3.00 for half an hour))
Fixed manufacturing overheads	60	(4 × £15,000)
Total	1,740	

The offer price is:

$$120,000 \times £19.00 = £2,280,000$$

On this basis, the price of £19 per machine could be accepted, subject to a number of factors identified in (b) below.

(b) The assumptions on which the above analysis and decision in (a) are based include the following:

- That the contract can be accommodated within the 30% spare capacity of GB. If this is not so, then there will be an opportunity cost relating to lost 'normal' production, which must be taken account of in the decision.
- That sales commission and freight costs will not be affected by the contract.
- It is unlikely that work more remunerative to GB than the contract will be available during the period of the contract.

There are also some strategic issues involved in the decision, including:

- The possibility that the contract could lead to other and better-remunerated work from II.
- A problem of selling similar products in the same market at different prices. Other customers, knowing that GB is selling at marginal prices, may make it difficult for the business to resist demand from other customers for similarly priced output.

11.7 **Sillycon Ltd**

(a) *Overhead analysis*

	Electronics £000	Testing £000	Service £000
Variable overheads	1,200	600	700
Apportionment of service dept (800:600)	400	300	(700)
	1,600	900	–
Direct labour hours ('000)	800	600	
Variable overheads per direct labour hour	£2.00	£1.50	

	Electronics £000	Testing £000	Service £000
Fixed overheads	2,000	500	800
Apportionment of service dept (equally)	400	400	(800)
	2,400	900	–
Direct labour hours	800	600	
Fixed overheads per direct labour hour	£3.00	£1.50	

Product cost (per unit)

		£	
Direct materials		7.00	
Direct labour:	electronics	40.00	(4 × £10.00)
	testing	18.00	(3 × £6.00)
Variable overheads:	electronics	8.00	(4 × £2.00)
	testing	4.50	(3 × £1.50)
Total variable cost		77.50	(assuming direct labour to be variable)
Fixed overheads:	electronics	12.00	(4 × £3.00)
	testing	4.50	(3 × £1.50)
Total 'full' cost		94.00	
Add Mark-up, say 30%		28.20	
		122.20	

On the basis of the above, the business could hope to compete in the market at a price that reflects normal pricing practice.

(b) At this price, and only taking account of incremental fixed overheads, the break-even point (BEP) would be given by:

$$\text{BEP} = \frac{\text{Fixed costs}}{\text{Contribution per unit}} = \frac{£150,000^*}{£122.20 - £77.50} = 3,356 \text{ units}$$

* (£13,000 + £100,000 + £37,000) namely the costs specifically incurred.

As the potential market for the business is around 5,000 to 6,000 units a year, the new product looks viable.

Chapter 12

12.3 Nursing Home

(a) The rates per patient for the variable overheads, on the basis of experience during months 1 to 6, are as follows:

Expense	Amount for 2,700 patients	Amount per patient
	£	£
Staffing	59,400	22
Power	27,000	10
Supplies	54,000	20
Other	8,100	3
	148,500	55

Since the expected level of activity for the full year is 6,000, 3,300 (that is, 6,000 − 2,700) is the expected level of activity for the second six months.

Thus the budget for the second six months will be:

	£	
Variable element:		
Staffing	72,600	(3,300 × £22)
Power	33,000	(3,300 × £10)
Supplies	66,000	(3,300 × £20)
Other	9,900	(3,300 × £3)
	181,500	(3,300 × £55)

Fixed element:

Supervision	60,000 ⎫	
Depreciation/finance	93,600 ⎬	6/12 of the values given in the question
Other	32,400 ⎭	
	186,000	(per patient = £56.36 (= £186,000/3,300))
Total (second six months)	367,500	(per patient = £111.36 (= £56.36 + 55.00))

(b) For the second six months the actual activity was 3,800 patients. For a valid comparison with the actual outcome, the budget will need to be revised to reflect this activity.

	Actual costs	Budget (3,800 patients)	Difference
	£	£	£
Variable element	203,300	209,000 (3,800 × £55)	5,700 (saving)
Fixed element	190,000	186,000	4,000 (overspend)
Total	393,300	395,000	1,700 (saving)

(c) Relative to the budget, there was a saving of nearly 3% on the variable element and an overspend of about 2% on fixed costs. Without further information, it is impossible to deduce much more than this.

   The differences between the budget and the actual may be caused by some assumptions made in framing the budget for 3,800 patients in the second part of the year. There may be some element of economies of scale in the variable costs, that is, the costs may not be strictly linear. If this were the case, basing a relatively large activity budget on the experience of a relatively small activity period would tend to overstate the large activity budget. The fixed-cost budget was deduced by dividing the budget for twelve months by two. In fact, there could be seasonal factors or inflationary pressures at work that might make such a crude division of the fixed-cost element unfair.

12.4 Linpet Ltd

(a) Cash budgets are extremely useful for decision-making purposes. They allow managers to see the likely effect on the cash balance of the plans that they have set in place. Cash is an important asset and it is necessary to ensure that it is properly managed. Failure to do so can have disastrous consequences for the business. Where the cash budget indicates a surplus balance, managers must decide whether this balance should be reinvested in the business or distributed to the owners. Where the cash budget indicates a deficit balance, managers must decide how this deficit should be financed or how it might be avoided.

(b) The cash budget to 30 November is:

	June £	July £	Aug £	Sept £	Oct £	Nov £
Receipts						
Cash sales revenue						
(Note 1)	4,000	5,500	7,000	8,500	11,000	11,000
Credit sales revenue						
(Note 2)	–	–	4,000	5,500	7,000	8,500
	4,000	5,500	11,000	14,000	18,000	19,500
Payments						
Purchases						
(Note 3)	–	29,000	9,250	11,500	13,750	17,500
Overheads	500	500	500	500	650	650
Wages	900	900	900	900	900	900
Commission						
(Note 4)	–	320	440	560	680	880
Equipment	10,000					7,000
Motor vehicle	6,000					
Leasehold	40,000					
	57,400	30,720	11,090	13,460	15,980	26,930
Cash flow	(53,400)	(25,220)	(90)	540	2,020	(7,430)
Opening balance	60,000	6,600	(18,620)	(18,710)	(18,170)	(16,150)
Closing balance	6,600	(18,620)	(18,710)	(18,170)	(16,150)	(23,580)

Notes:

1 50% of the current month's sales revenue.
2 50% of sales revenue of two months previous.
3 To have sufficient inventories to meet each month's sales will require purchases of 75% of the month's sales revenue figures (25% is profit). In addition, each month the business will buy £1,000 more inventories than it will sell. In June, the business will also buy its initial inventories of £22,000. This will be paid for in the following month. For example, June's purchases will be (75% × £8,000) + £1,000 + £22,000 = £29,000, paid for in July.
4 This is 5% of 80% of the month's sales revenue, paid in the following month. For example, June's commission will be 5% × 80% × £8,000 = £320, payable in July.

12.5 Lewisham Ltd

(a) The finished goods inventories budget for the three months ending 30 September (in units of production) is:

	July '000 units	Aug '000 units	Sept '000 units
Opening inventories (Note 1)	40	48	40
Production (Note 2)	188	232	196
	228	280	236
Less Sales (Note 3)	180	240	200
Closing inventories	48	40	36

(b) The raw materials inventories budget for the two months ending 31 August is:

	July '000 kg	Aug '000 kg
Opening inventories (Note 1)	40	58
Purchases (Note 2)	112	107
	152	165
Less Production (Note 4)	94	116
Closing inventories	58	49

(c) The cash budget for the two months ending 30 September is:

	Aug £	Sept £
Inflows		
Trade receivables: Current month (Note 5)	493,920	411,600
Preceding month (Note 6)	151,200	201,600
Total inflows	645,120	613,200
Outflows		
Payments to trade payables (Note 7)	168,000	160,500
Labour and overheads (Note 4)	185,600	156,800
Fixed overheads	22,000	22,000
Total outflows	375,600	339,300
Net inflows/(outflows)	269,520	273,900
Balance c/f	289,520	563,420

Notes:

1 The opening balance is the same as the closing balance from the previous month.
2 This is a balancing figure.
3 This figure is given in the question.
4 This figure derives from the finished inventories budget.
5 This is 98% of 70% of the current month's sales revenue.
6 This is 28% of the previous month's sales revenue.
7 This figure derives from the raw materials inventories budget.

12.6 Newtake records

(a) The cash budget for the period to 30 November is:

	June £000	July £000	Aug £000	Sept £000	Oct £000	Nov £000
Cash receipts						
Sales (Note 1)	227	315	246	138	118	108
Cash payments						
Administration (Note 2)	(40)	(41)	(38)	(33)	(31)	(30)
Goods purchased	(135)	(180)	(142)	(94)	(75)	(66)
Borrowings repayments	(5)	(5)	(5)	(5)	(5)	(5)
Selling expenses	(22)	(24)	(28)	(26)	(21)	(19)
Taxation paid			(22)			
Shop refurbishment		(14)	(18)	(6)		
	(202)	(264)	(253)	(164)	(132)	(120)
Cash surplus (deficit)	25	51	(7)	(26)	(14)	(12)
Opening balance	(35)	(10)	41	34	8	(6)
Closing balance	(10)	41	34	8	(6)	(18)

Notes:

1 (50% of the current month's sales revenue) + (97% × 50% of that sales revenue). For example, the June cash receipts = (50% × £230,000) + (97% × 50% × £230,000) = £226,550.

2 The administration expenses figure for the month, *less* £15,000 for depreciation (a non-cash expense).

(b) The inventories budget for the six months to 30 November is:

	June £000	July £000	Aug £000	Sept £000	Oct £000	Nov £000
Opening balance	112	154	104	48	39	33
Inventories purchased	180	142	94	75	66	57
	292	296	198	123	105	90
Cost of inventories sold (60% sales revenue)	(138)	(192)	(150)	(84)	(72)	(66)
Closing balance	154	104	48	39	33	24

(c) The budgeted income statement for the six months ending 30 November is:

	£000
Sales revenue	1,170
Cost of goods sold	(702)
Gross profit	468
Selling expenses	(136)
Admin. expenses	(303)
Credit card charges	(18)
Operating profit	11
Interest payable	(6)
Profit for the period	5

(d) We are told that the business is required to eliminate the bank overdraft by the end of November. However, the cash budget reveals that this will not be achieved. There is a decline in the overdraft of nearly 50% over the period, but this is not enough and ways must be found to comply with the bank's requirements. It may be possible to delay the refurbishment programme that is included in the forecasts or to obtain an injection of funds from the owners or other investors. It may also be possible to stimulate sales in some way. However, there has been a decline in the sales revenue since the end of July and the November sales revenue is approximately one-third of the July figure. The reasons for this decline should be sought.

The inventories levels will fall below the preferred minimum level for each of the last three months. However, to rectify this situation it will be necessary to purchase more inventories, which will, in turn, exacerbate the cash flow problems of the business.

The budgeted income statement reveals a very low profit for the period. For every £1 of sales revenue, the business is managing to generate only 0.4p in profit. The business should look carefully at its pricing policies and its overhead expenses. The administration expenses, for example, absorb more than one-quarter of the total sales revenue. Any reduction in overhead expenses will have a beneficial effect on cash flows.

12.7 Prolog Ltd

(a) The cash budget for the six months to 30 June is:

	Jan £000	Feb £000	Mar £000	Apr £000	May £000	June £000
Receipts						
Credit sales revenue (Note 1)	100	100	140	180	220	260
Payments						
Trade payables (Note 2)	112	144	176	208	240	272
Operating expenses	4	6	8	10	10	10
Shelving				12		
Taxation			25			
	116	150	209	230	250	282
Cash flow	(16)	(50)	(69)	(50)	(30)	(22)
Opening balance	(68)	(84)	(134)	(203)	(253)	(283)
Closing balance	(84)	(134)	(203)	(253)	(283)	(305)

Notes:

1 Sales receipts will equal the month's sales revenue, but be received two months later. For example, the January sales revenue = £2,000 × (50 + 20) = £140,000, to be received in March.

2 Trade payables payments will equal the next month's sales requirements, payable the next month. For example, January purchases = £1,600 × (50 + 40) = £144,000, payable in February.

(b) A banker may require various pieces of information before granting additional overdraft facilities. These may include:
- Security available for the loan.
- Details of past profit performance.
- Profit projections for the next 12 months.
- Cash projections beyond the next six months to help assess the prospects of repayment.
- Details of the assumptions underlying projected figures supplied.
- Details of the contractual commitment between Prolog Ltd and its supplier.
- Details of management expertise. Can they manage the expansion programme?
- Details of new machine and its performance in relation to competing models.
- Details of funds available from owners to finance the expansion.

Chapter 13

13.1 (a) A favourable direct labour rate variance can only be caused by something that leads to the rate per hour paid being less than standard. Normally, this would not be linked to efficient working. Where, however, the standard envisaged some overtime working, at premium rates, the actual labour rate may be below standard if efficiency has removed the need for the overtime.

 (b) The statement is true. The action will lead to an adverse sales price variance and may well lead to problems elsewhere, but the sales volume variance must be favourable.

 (c) It is true that below-standard material could lead to adverse materials usage variances because there may be more than a standard amount of scrap. This could also cause adverse labour efficiency variances because working on materials that would not form part of the output would waste labour time.

 (d) Higher-than-budgeted sales volumes could well lead to an adverse labour rate variance because producing the additional work may require overtime working at premium rates.

 (e) The statement is true. Nothing else could cause such a variance.

13.2 **Pilot Ltd**

(a) and (b)

	Budget			Actual	
	Original	Flexed			
Output (production and sales) (units)	5,000	5,400		5,400	
	£	£		£	
Sales revenue	25,000	27,000		26,460	
Raw materials	(7,500)	(8,100)	(2,700 kg)	(8,770)	(2,830 kg)
Labour	(6,250)	(6,750)	(1,350 hr)	(6,885)	(1,300 hr)
Fixed overheads	(6,000)	(6,000)		(6,350)	
Operating profit	5,250	6,150		4,455	

	£		Manager accountable
Sales volume variance (5,250 – 6,150)	900	(F)	Sales
Sales price variance (27,000 – 26,460)	(540)	(A)	Sales
Materials price variance (2,830 × 3) – 8,770	(280)	(A)	Buyer
Materials usage variance [(5,400 × 0.5) – 2,830] × £3	(390)	(A)	Production
Labour rate variance (1,300 × £5) – 6,885	(385)	(A)	Personnel
Labour efficiency variance [(5,400 × 0.25) – 1,300] × £5	250	(F)	Production
Fixed overhead spending (6,000 – 6,350)	(350)	(A)	Various – depends on the nature of the overheads
Total net variances	(795)	(A)	

	£
Budgeted operating profit	5,250
Less Total net variance	(795)
Actual operating profit	4,455

13.4 (a) Flexing the budget identifies what the operating profit would have been had the only difference between the original budget and the actual figures been concerned with the difference in volume of output. Comparing this operating profit figure with that in the original budget reveals the operating profit difference (variance) arising solely from the volume difference (sales volume variance). Thus, flexing the budget does not mean at all that volume differences do not matter. Flexing the budget is the means of discovering the effect on operating profit of the volume difference.

In one sense, all variances are 'water under the bridge', to the extent that the past cannot be undone, and so it is impossible to go back to the last control period and put in a better performance. Identifying variances can, however, be useful in identifying where things went wrong, which should enable management to take steps to ensure that the same things do not to go wrong in the future.

(b) Variances will not tell you what went wrong. They should, however, be a great help in identifying the manager within whose sphere of responsibility things went wrong. That manager should know why it went wrong. In this sense, variances identify relevant questions, but not answers.

(c) Research evidence does not show this. It seems to show that managers tend to be most motivated by having as a target the most difficult goals that they find acceptable.

(d) Budgets normally provide the basis of feedforward and feedback control. During a budget preparation period, potential problems (for example, a potential inventories shortage) might be revealed. Steps can then be taken to revise the plans in order to avoid the potential problem. This is an example of a feedforward control: potential problems are anticipated and eliminated before they can occur.

Budgetary control is a very good example of feedback control, where a signal that something is going wrong triggers steps to take corrective action for the future.

13.5 **Bradley-Allen Ltd**

(a)

	Budget			Actual	
	Original	Flexed			
Output (production and sales) (units)	800	950		950	
	£	£		£	
Sales revenue	64,000	76,000		73,000	
Raw materials – A	(12,000)	(14,250)	(285 kg)	(15,200)	(310 kg)
– B	(16,000)	(19,000)	(950m)	(18,900)	(920m)
Labour – skilled	(4,000)	(4,750)	(475 hr)	(4,628)	(445 hr)
– unskilled	(10,000)	(11,875)	(1,484.375 hr)	(11,275)	(1,375 hr)
Fixed overheads	(12,000)	(12,000)		(11,960)	
Operating profit	10,000	14,125		11,037	

Sales variances

Volume:	$10,000 - 14,125 = £4,125$	(F)
Price:	$76,000 - 73,000 = £3,000$	(A)

Direct materials A variances

Usage:	$[(950 \times 0.3) - 310] \times £50 = £1,250$	(A)
Price:	$(310 \times £50) - £15,200 = £300$	(F)

Direct materials B variances

Usage:	$[(950 \times 1) - 920] \times £20 = £600$	(F)
Price:	$(920 \times £20) - £18,900 = £500$	(A)

Skilled direct labour variances

Efficiency:	$[(950 \times 0.5) - 445] \times £10 = £300$	(F)
Rate:	$(445 \times £10) - £4,628 = £178$	(A)

Unskilled direct labour variances

Efficiency:	$[(950 \times 1.5625) - 1,375] \times £8 = £875$	(F)
Rate:	$(1,375 \times £8) - £11,275 = £275$	(A)

Fixed overhead variances

Spending:	$(12,000 - 11,960) = £40$	(F)

		£		£
Budgeted operating profit				10,000
Sales:	Volume	4,125	(F)	
	Price	(3,000)	(A)	1,125
Direct material A:	Usage	(1,250)	(A)	
	Price	300	(F)	(950)
Direct material B:	Usage	600	(F)	
	Price	(500)	(A)	100
Skilled labour:	Efficiency	300	(F)	
	Rate	(178)	(A)	122
Unskilled labour:	Efficiency	875	(F)	
	Rate	(275)	(A)	600
Fixed overheads:	Expenditure			40
Actual operating profit				£11,037

(b) The statement in (a) is useful to management because it enables them not only to see where there have been failures to meet the original budget but also to quantify the extent of such failures. This means that junior managers can be held accountable for the performance of their particular area of responsibility.

13.7 Varne Chemprocessors

(a) The standard usage rate of UK194 (per litre of Varnelyne) is $200/5,000 = 0.04$.

The standard price $= £392/200 = £1.96$ per litre of UK194.

Materials usage variance (UK194) is

$$[(637,500 \times 0.04) - 28,100] \times £1.96 = £5,096 \text{ (A)}$$

Materials price variance is

$$(28,100 \times £1.96) - £51,704 = £3,372 \text{ (F)}$$

(b) The net variance on UK194 was, from the calculations in (a), £1,724 (A) (that is £5,096 - 3,372). This seems to have led directly to savings elsewhere of £4,900, giving a net cost saving of over £3,000 for the month.

Unfortunately things may not be quite as simple as the numbers suggest. Will the non-standard mix to make the Varnelyne lead to a substandard product, which could have very wide-ranging ramifications in terms of potential loss of market goodwill?

There is also the possibility that the material for which the UK194 was used as a substitute was already held in inventories. If this were the case, is there any danger that this material may deteriorate and, ultimately, prove to be unusable?

Other possible adverse outcomes of the non-standard mix could also arise.

The question is raised by the analysis in part (a) (and by the production manager's comment) of why the cost standard for UK194 had not been revised to take account of the lower price prevailing in the market.

(c) The variances, period by period and cumulatively, for each of the two materials are given as follows:

Period	UK500		UK800	
	Period £	Cumulative £	Period £	Cumulative £
1	301 (F)	301 (F)	298 (F)	298 (F)
2	(251) (A)	50 (F)	203 (F)	501 (F)
3	102 (F)	152 (F)	(52) (A)	449 (F)
4	(202) (A)	(50) (A)	(98) (A)	351 (F)
5	153 (F)	103 (F)	(150) (A)	201 (F)
6	(103) (A)	zero	(201) (A)	zero

Without knowing the scale of these variances relative to the actual costs involved, it is not possible to be too dogmatic about how to interpret the above information.

UK500 appears to show a fairly random set of data, with the period variances fluctuating from positive to negative and giving a net variance of zero. This is what would be expected from a situation that is basically in control.

UK800 also shows a zero cumulative figure over the six periods, *but* there seems to be a more systematic train of events, particularly the four consecutive adverse variances from period 3 onwards. This looks as if it may be out of control and worthy of investigation.

Chapter 14

14.1 Mylo Ltd

(a) The annual depreciation of the two projects is:

$$\text{Project 1:} \quad \frac{(£100,000 - £7,000)}{3} = £31,000$$

$$\text{Project 2:} \quad \frac{(£60,000 - £6,000)}{3} = £18,000$$

Project 1

(i)

	Year 0 £000	Year 1 £000	Year 2 £000	Year 3 £000
Operating profit/(loss)		29	(1)	2
Depreciation		31	31	31
Capital cost	(100)			
Residual value				7
Net cash flows	(100)	60	30	40
10% discount factor	1.000	0.909	0.826	0.751
Present value	(100.00)	54.54	24.78	30.04
NPV	9.36			

(ii)   Clearly the IRR lies above 10%. Try 15%:

15% discount factor	1.000	0.870	0.756	0.658
Present value	(100.00)	52.20	22.68	26.32
NPV	1.20			

Thus the IRR lies a little above 15%, perhaps around 16%.

(iii)   To find the payback period, the cumulative cash flows are calculated:

Cumulative cash flows	(100)	(40)	(10)	30

Thus the payback will occur within 3 years.

Project 2

(i)

	Year 0 £000	Year 1 £000	Year 2 £000	Year 3 £000
Operating profit/(loss)		18	(2)	4
Depreciation		18	18	18
Capital cost	(60)			
Residual value				6
Net cash flows	(60)	36	16	28
10% discount factor	1.000	0.909	0.826	0.751
Present value	(60.00)	32.72	13.22	21.03
NPV	6.97			

(ii)   Clearly the IRR lies above 10%. Try 15%:

15% discount factor	1.000	0.870	0.756	0.658
Present value	(60.00)	31.32	12.10	18.42
NPV	1.84			

Thus the IRR lies a little above 15%, perhaps around 17%.

    (iii) The cumulative cash flows are:

Cumulative cash flows	(60)	(24)	(8)	20

    Thus, the payback will occur within three years.

(b) Assuming that Mylo Ltd is pursuing a wealth-enhancement objective, Project 1 is preferable since it has the higher NPV. The difference between the two NPVs is not significant, however.

(c) NPV is the preferred method of assessing investment opportunities because it fully addresses each of the following:

- *The timing of the cash flows.* Discounting the various cash flows associated with each project, according to when they are expected to arise, takes account of the fact that cash flows do not all occur simultaneously. Associated with this is the fact that by discounting, using the opportunity cost of finance (namely the return that the next-best alternative opportunity would generate), the net benefit, after financing costs have been met, is identified (as the NPV).

- *The whole of the relevant cash flows.* NPV includes all of the relevant cash flows irrespective of when they are expected to occur. It treats them differently according to their date of occurrence, but they are all taken into account in the calculation of the NPV and they all have, or can have, an influence on the decision.

- *The objectives of the business.* NPV is the only method of appraisal where the output of the analysis has a direct bearing on the wealth of the owners of the business. (Positive NPVs enhance wealth; negative NPVs reduce it.) Since most private sector businesses seek to increase their owners' wealth, NPV clearly is the best approach to use.

14.5 Newton Electronics Ltd

(a) **Option 1**

	Year 0 £m	Year 1 £m	Year 2 £m	Year 3 £m	Year 4 £m	Year 5 £m
Plant and equipment	(9.0)					1.0
Sales revenue		24.0	30.8	39.6	26.4	10.0
Variable costs		(11.2)	(19.6)	(25.2)	(16.8)	(7.0)
Fixed costs (ex. dep'n)		(0.8)	(0.8)	(0.8)	(0.8)	(0.8)
Working capital	(3.0)					3.0
Marketing costs		(2.0)	(2.0)	(2.0)	(2.0)	(2.0)
Opportunity costs		(0.1)	(0.1)	(0.1)	(0.1)	(0.1)
	(12.0)	9.9	8.3	11.5	6.7	4.1
Discount factor 10%	1.000	0.909	0.826	0.751	0.683	0.621
Present value	(12.0)	9.0	6.9	8.6	4.6	2.5
NPV	19.6					

Option 2

	Year 0 £m	Year 1 £m	Year 2 £m	Year 3 £m	Year 4 £m	Year 5 £m
Royalties	–	4.4	7.7	9.9	6.6	2.8
Discount factor 10%	1.000	0.909	0.826	0.751	0.683	0.621
Present value	–	4.0	6.4	7.4	4.5	1.7
NPV	24.0					

Option 3

	Year 0	Year 2
Instalments	12.0	12.0
Discount factor 10%	1.000	0.826
Present value	12.0	9.9
NPV	21.9	

(b) Before making a final decision, the board should consider the following factors:
  - The long-term competitiveness of the business may be affected by the sale of the patents.
  - At present, the business is not involved in manufacturing and marketing products. Would a change in direction be desirable?
  - The business will probably have to buy in the skills necessary to produce the product itself. This will involve costs, and problems will be incurred. Has this been taken into account?
  - How accurate are the forecasts made and how valid are the assumptions on which they are based?

(c) Option 2 has the highest NPV and is therefore the most attractive to shareholders. However, the accuracy of the forecasts should be checked before a final decision is made.

14.6 Chesterfield Wanderers

(a) and (b)

Player option

	Year 0 £000	Year 1 £000	Year 2 £000	Year 3 £000	Year 4 £000	Year 5 £000
Sale of player	2,200					1,000
Purchase of Bazza	(10,000)					
Sponsorship and so on		1,200	1,200	1,200	1,200	1,200
Gate receipts		2,500	1,300	1,300	1,300	1,300
Salaries paid		(800)	(800)	(800)	(800)	(1,200)
Salaries saved		400	400	400	400	600
Net cash received (paid)	(7,800)	3,300	2,100	2,100	2,100	2,900
Discount factor 10%	1.000	0.909	0.826	0.751	0.683	0.621
Present values	(7,800)	3,000	1,735	1,577	1,434	1,801
NPV	1,747					

Ground improvement option

	Year 1 £000	Year 2 £000	Year 3 £000	Year 4 £000	Year 5 £000
Ground improvements	(10,000)				
Increased gate receipts	(1,800)	4,400	4,400	4,400	4,400
	(11,800)	4,400	4,400	4,400	4,400
Discount factor 10%	0.909	0.826	0.751	0.683	0.621
Present values	(10,726)	3,634	3,304	3,005	2,732
NPV	1,949				

(c) The ground improvement option provides the higher NPV and is therefore the preferable option, based on the objective of shareholder wealth maximisation.

(d) A professional football club may not wish to pursue an objective of shareholder wealth enhancement. It may prefer to invest in quality players in an attempt to enjoy future sporting success. If this is the case, the NPV approach will be less appropriate because the club is not pursuing a strict wealth-related objective.

14.7 Simtex Ltd

(a) Net operating cash flows each year will be:

	£000	£000
Sales revenue (160 × £6)		960
Less Variable costs (160 × £4)	640	
Relevant fixed costs	170	810
		150

The estimated NPV of the new product can then be calculated:

	£000
Annual cash flows (150 × 3.038*)	456
Residual value of equipment (100 × 0.636)	64
	520
Less Initial outlay	480
Net present value	40

* This is the sum of the discount rates over four years. Where the cash flows are constant, it is a quicker procedure than working out the present value of cash flows for each year and then adding them together.

(b) (i) Assume the discount rate is 18%. The net present value of the project would be:

	£000
Annual cash flows (150 × 2.690)	404
Residual value of equipment (100 × 0.516)	52
	456
Less Initial outlay	480
NPV	(24)

Thus an increase of 6%, from 12% to 18%, in the discount rate causes a fall from +40 to –24 in the NPV: a fall of 64, or 10.67 (that is, 64/6) for each 1% rise in the discount rate. So a zero NPV will occur with a discount rate approximately equal to 12 + (40/11.67) = 15.4%. (This is, of course, the IRR.)

This higher discount rate represents an increase of about 28% on the existing cost of capital figure.

(ii) The initial outlay on equipment is already expressed in present-value terms and so, to make the project no longer viable, the outlay will have to increase by an amount equal to the NPV of the project (that is, £40,000) – an increase of 8.3% on the stated initial outlay.

(iii) The change necessary in the annual net cash flows to make the project no longer profitable can be calculated as follows.

Let Y = change in the annual operating cash flows. Then (Y × cumulative discount rates for a four-year period) – NPV = 0. This can be rearranged as:

$$Y \times \text{cumulative discount rates for a four-year period} = \text{NPV}$$

That is:

$$Y \times 3.038 = £40{,}000$$
$$Y = £40{,}000/3.038$$
$$= £13{,}167$$

In percentage terms, this is a decrease of 8.8% on the estimated cash flows.

(iv) The change in the residual value required to make the new product no longer profitable can be calculated as follows.

Let V = change in the residual value. Then (V × discount factor at end of four years) – NPV of product = 0. This can be rearranged as:

$$V \times \text{discount factor at end of four years} = \text{NPV of product}$$

That is:

$$V \times 0.636 = £40{,}000$$
$$V = £40{,}000/0.636$$
$$= £62{,}893$$

This is a decrease of 63.9% in the residual value of the equipment.

(c) The NPV of the product is positive and so it will increase shareholder wealth. Thus, it should be produced. The sensitivity analysis suggests the initial outlay and the annual cash flows are the most sensitive variables for managers to consider.

14.8 Kernow Cleaning Services Ltd

(a) The first step is to calculate the expected annual cash flows:

Year 1	£	Year 2	£
£80,000 × 0.3	24,000	£140,000 × 0.4	56,000
£160,000 × 0.5	80,000	£220,000 × 0.4	88,000
£200,000 × 0.2	40,000	£250,000 × 0.2	50,000
	144,000		194,000
Year 3		Year 4	
£140,000 × 0.4	56,000	£100,000 × 0.3	30,000
£200,000 × 0.3	60,000	£170,000 × 0.6	102,000
£230,000 × 0.3	69,000	£200,000 × 0.1	20,000
	185,000		152,000

The expected net present value (ENPV) can now be calculated as follows:

Period	Expected cash flow £	Discount rate 10%	Expected PV £
0	(540,000)	1.000	(540,000)
1	144,000	0.909	130,896
2	194,000	0.826	160,244
3	185,000	0.751	138,935
4	152,000	0.683	103,816
ENPV			(6,109)

(b) The *worst possible outcome* can be calculated by taking the lowest values of savings each year, as follows:

Period	Cash flow £	Discount rate 10%	PV £
0	(540,000)	1.000	(540,000)
1	80,000	0.909	72,720
2	140,000	0.826	115,640
3	140,000	0.751	105,140
4	100,000	0.683	68,300
NPV			(178,200)

The probability of occurrence can be obtained by multiplying together the probability of *each* of the worst outcomes above, that is $0.3 \times 0.4 \times 0.4 \times 0.3 = 0.014$.

Thus, the probability of occurrence is 1.4%, which is very low.

Chapter 15

15.1 H. Brown (Portsmouth) Ltd

(a) The main factors to take into account are:

- *Risk.* If a business borrows, there is a risk that at the maturity date of the loan the business will not have the funds to repay the amount owing and will be unable to find a suitable form of replacement borrowing. With short-term borrowingss, the maturity dates will arrive more quickly and the type of risk outlined will occur at more frequent intervals.

- *Matching.* A business may wish to match the life of an asset with the maturity date of the borrowing. In other words, long-term assets will be purchased with long-term borrowed funds. A certain level of current assets, which form part of the long-term asset base of the business, may also be funded by long-term borrowing. Those current assets that fluctuate owing to seasonality and so on will be funded by short-term borrowing. This approach to funding assets will help reduce risks for the business.

- *Cost.* Interest rates for long-term borrowings may be higher than for short-term ones as investors may seek extra compensation for having their funds locked up for a long period. However, issue costs may be higher for short-term borrowings as there will be a need to refund at more frequent intervals.

- *Flexibility.* Short-term borrowings may be more flexible. It may be difficult to repay long-term ones before the maturity period.

(b) When deciding to grant a loan, a lender should consider the following factors:
- security
- purpose of the loan
- ability of the borrower to repay
- loan period
- availability of funds
- character and integrity of the senior managers.

(c) Loan conditions may include:
- the need to obtain permission before issuing further loans
- the need to maintain a certain level of liquidity during the loan period
- a restriction on the level of dividends and directors' pay.

15.2 **Devonian plc**

(a) (i) *Ex-rights price*

	£
5 original shares @ £2.10 per share	10.50
1 rights share @ £1.80	1.80
	12.30
Theoretical ex-rights price (£12.30/6)	£2.05

(ii) *Value of rights*

	£
Value of a share after the rights issue	2.05
Cost of a rights share	1.80
Value of rights	0.25
Value of rights attached to each original share = £0.25/5 =	£0.05

(b) (i) *Share price in one year's time*
Rights issue
We must first calculate the existing P/E ratio in order to determine the share price in one year's time. This can be done as follows:

	£m
Operating profit (Year 4)	40.0
Taxation (30%)	(12.0)
Profit for the year (available to shareholders)	28.0
Earnings per share (EPS) (£28.0m/200m)	= £0.14
P/E ratio	$= \dfrac{\text{Share price}}{\text{EPS}}$
	= £2.10/£0.14
	= 15 times

	£m
Operating profit (Year 5)	50.0
Taxation (30%)	(15.0)
Profit for the year (available to ordinary shareholders)	35.0
Earnings per share (£35m/240m)	= £0.146
Share price (Year 5)	= EPS × P/E ratio
	= £0.146 × 15
	= £2.19

(ii) *Borrowing*

	£m
Operating profit (Year 5)	50.0
Interest payable (£72m @ 10%)	(7.2)
	42.8
Taxation (30%)	(12.8)
Profit for the year (available to ordinary shareholders)	30.0
Earnings per share (£30m/200m)	= £0.15
Share price (Year 5)	= EPS × P/E ratio
	= £0.15 × 13.5
	= £2.03

These calculations reveal that in one year's time the share price is expected to rise by more than 4% above the current share price if a rights issue is made, whereas the share price will fall by more than 3% if the business borrows the money. Given the additional financial risks attached to borrowing, it seems that a rights issue offers the better option – at least in the short term.

(c) By issuing shares at a discount in a rights issue, pressure is put on the shareholders either to take up the shares or to sell the right to someone that will. Failure to do one of these will lead to a loss of wealth for the shareholder.

(d) The price at which rights issues are made is not critical. It needs to be sufficiently low to put pressure on shareholders to take them up or sell the rights. It also needs to be low enough to make it unlikely that, between setting the issue price and the date of the issue, the current market price of the existing share will not have fallen below the rights issue price. Since the discount does not represent a real bonus to the shareholders, it can be quite large.

15.3 Brocmar plc

(a) (i) EPS = £1.8m/10m   = £0.180

    (ii) Rights price = £1.80 – (20% × £1.80)   = £1.44

    (iii) Number of shares issued = £2.88m/£1.44   = 2m

    (iv) EPS for next year = (£1.8m + £0.4m)/(10m + 2m) = £0.183

    (v) Ex-rights price: 5 shares @ £1.80   = £9.00

                        1 share @ £1.44   = £1.44

                        6   £10.44

        Theoretical ex-rights price per share = £10.44/6   = £1.74

(b) Additional information should include:
- future cash flows from the project
- the degree of risk associated with the project
- the cost of capital required to undertake the project
- the NPV of the project
- the extent to which the project fits with the strategy of the business.

15.4 Raphael Ltd

The existing credit policies have the following costs:

	£
Cost of investment in trade receivables [(50/365) × £2.4m × 12%]	39,452
Cost of bad debts (1.5% × £2.4m)	36,000
Total cost	75,452

Employing a factor will result in the following costs and savings:

	£
Charges of the factor (2% × £2.4m)	48,000
Interest charges on advance [(30/365) × (80% × £2.4m) × 11%]	17,359
Interest charges on overdraft [(30/365) × (20% × £2.4m) × 12%]	4,734
Total cost	70,093
Less Credit control savings	(18,000)
Net cost	52,093

We can see the net cost of factoring is lower than the existing costs, and so there would be a benefit gained from entering into an agreement with the factor.

15.6 Carpets Direct plc

(a) The earnings per share (EPS) is:

$$\frac{\text{Profit after taxation}}{\text{Number of ordinary shares}} = \frac{£4.5m}{120m} = £0.0375$$

The current market value per share is:

$$\text{Earnings per share} \times \text{P/E} = £0.0375 \times 22 = £0.825$$

The rights issue price will be £0.825, less 20% discount = £0.66.
The theoretical ex-rights price is:

	£
Original shares (4 @ £0.825)	3.30
Rights share (1 @ £0.66)	0.66
Value of five shares following rights issue	3.96

Therefore, the value of one share following the rights issue is:

$$\frac{£3.96}{5} = 79.2\text{p}$$

(b)

Value of one share after rights issue	79.2p
Cost of a rights share	(66.0p)
Value of rights to shareholder	13.2p

(c) (i) *Taking up rights issue*

	£
Shareholding following rights issue [(4,000 + 1,000) × 79.2p]	3,960
Less Cost of rights shares (1,000 × 66p)	(660)
Shareholder wealth	3,300

(ii) *Selling the rights*

Shareholding following rights issue (4,000 × 79.2p)	3,168
Add Proceeds from sale of rights (1,000 × 13.2p)	132
Shareholder wealth	3,300

(iii) *Doing nothing*

As the rights are neither purchased nor sold, the shareholder wealth following the rights issue will be:

Shareholding (4,000 × 79.2p)	3,168

We can see that the investor will have the same wealth under the first two options. However, by the investor doing nothing, the rights offer will lapse and so the investor will lose the value of the rights and will be worse off.

Chapter 16

16.1 Hercules Wholesalers Ltd

(a) The liquidity ratios of the business seem low. The current ratio is only 1:1.1 (that is, 306/285) and its acid test ratio is 1:0.6 (that is, 163/285). This latter ratio suggests that the business has insufficient liquid assets to pay its short-term obligations. A cash flow projection for the next period would provide a better insight to the liquidity position of the business. The bank overdraft seems high and it would be useful to know whether the bank is pressing for a reduction and what overdraft limit has been established for the business.

(b) The operating cash cycle can be calculated as follows:

Number of days

Average inventories holding period:

$$\frac{[(\text{Opening inventories} + \text{Closing inventories})/2] \times 360}{\text{Cost of sales}} = \frac{[(125 + 143)/2] \times 360}{323}$$

149

Add Average settlement period for trade receivables:

$$\frac{\text{Trade receivables} \times 360}{\text{Credit sales revenue}} = \frac{163}{452} \times 360$$

130
279

Less Average settlement period for trade payables:

$$\frac{\text{Trade payables} \times 360}{\text{Credit purchases}} = \frac{145}{341} \times 360$$

153
126

(c) The business can reduce the operating cash cycle in a number of ways. The average inventories holding period seems quite long. At present, average inventories held represent almost five months' sales needs. This period can be shortened by reducing the level of inventories held. Similarly, the average settlement period for trade receivables seems long at more than four months' sales revenue. This may be shortened by imposing tighter credit control, offering discounts, charging interest on overdue accounts and so on. However, any policy decisions concerning inventories and trade receivables must take account of current trading conditions.

The operating cash cycle would also be reduced by extending the period of credit taken to pay suppliers. However, for the reasons mentioned in the chapter, this option must be given careful consideration.

16.5

Mayo Computers Ltd
New proposals from credit control department

	£000	£000
Current level of investment in trade receivables		
[£20m × (60/365)]		3,288
Proposed level of investment in trade receivables		
[(£20m × 60%) × (30/365)]	(986)	
[(£20m × 40%) × (50/365)]	(1,096)	(2,082)
Reduction in level of investment		1,206

The reduction in overdraft interest as a result of the reduction in the level of investment will be £1,206,000 × 14% = £169,000.

	£000	£000
Cost of cash discounts offered (£20m × 60% × 2½%)		300
Additional cost of credit administration		20
		320
Bad debt savings	(100)	
Interest charge savings (see above)	(169)	(269)
Net cost of policy each year		51

These calculations show that the business would incur additional annual costs if it implemented this proposal. It would therefore be cheaper to stay with the existing credit policy.

16.6 **Boswell Enterprises Ltd**

(a) The investment in working capital will be:

	Current policy		New policy	
	£000	£000	£000	£000
Trade receivables				
[(£3m × $\frac{1}{12}$ × 30%) + (£3m × $\frac{2}{12}$ × 70%)]		425.0		
[(£3.15m × $\frac{1}{12}$ × 60%) + (£3.15m × $\frac{2}{12}$ × 40%)]				367.5
Inventories				
[£3m − (£3m × 20%)] × $\frac{3}{12}$]		600.0		
{[£3.15m − (£3.15m × 20%)] × $\frac{3}{12}$}				630.0
Cash (fixed)		140.0		140.0
		1,165.0		1,137.5
Trade payables				
[[£3m − (£3m × 20%)] × $\frac{2}{12}$]	(400.0)			
{[£3.15m − (£3.15m × 20%)] × $\frac{2}{12}$}			(420.0)	
Accrued variable expenses				
[£3m × $\frac{1}{12}$ × 10%]	(25.0)			
[£3.15m × $\frac{1}{12}$ × 10%]			(26.3)	
Accrued fixed expenses	(15.0)	(440.0)	(15.0)	(461.3)
Investment in working capital		725.0		676.2

(b) The forecast planned profit for the year will be:

	Current policy		New policy	
	£000	£000	£000	£000
Sales revenue		3,000.0		3,150.0
Cost of goods sold		(2,400.0)		(2,520.0)
Gross profit (20%)		600.0		630.0
Variable expenses (10%)	(300.0)		(315.0)	
Fixed expenses	(180.0)		(180.0)	
Discounts	–	(480.0)	(47.3)	(542.3)
Operating profit		120.0		87.7

(c) Under the proposed policy we can see that the investment in working capital will be slightly lower than under the current policy. However, profit will be substantially lower as a result of offering discounts. The increase in sales revenue resulting from the discounts will not be sufficient to offset the additional costs of making the discounts to customers. It seems that the business should, therefore, stick with its current policy.

16.7 **Delphi plc**

(a) The trade receivables ageing schedule is:

	1 month or less £000	%	1 to 2 months £000	%	2 to 3 months £000	%	Total receivables £000	%
February								
TV and hi-fi	20.0	(22.2)					20.0	(22.2)
Music	30.0	(33.3)					30.0	(33.3)
Retail	40.0	(44.5)					40.0	(44.5)
	90.0	(100.0)					90.0	(100.0)
March								
TV and hi-fi	20.8	(12.5)					20.8	(12.5)
Music	31.8	(19.2)	30.0	(18.1)			61.8	(37.3)
Retail	43.2	(26.1)	40.0	(24.1)			83.2	(50.2)
	95.8	(57.8)	70.0	(42.2)			165.8	(100.0)
April								
TV and hi-fi	21.6	(10.0)					21.6	(10.0)
Music	33.7	(15.6)	31.8	(14.7)			65.5	(30.3)
Retail	46.7	(21.4)	43.2	(19.9)	40.0	(18.4)	129.9	(59.7)
	102.0	(47.0)	75.0	(34.6)	40.0	(18.4)	217.0	(100.0)
May								
TV and hi-fi	22.5	(9.6)					22.5	(9.6)
Music	35.7	(15.4)	33.7	(14.6)			69.6	(30.0)
Retail	50.4	(21.7)	46.7	(20.1)	43.2	(18.6)	140.2	(60.4)
	108.6	(46.7)	80.4	(34.7)	43.2	(18.6)	232.3	(100.0)

Number of months outstanding

We can see that the trade receivables figure will increase substantially in the first four months. The retail chains will account for about 60% of the total trade receivables outstanding by May as this group has the fastest rate of growth. There is also a significant decline in the proportion of total amounts outstanding from TV and hi-fi shops over this period.

(b) In answering this part of the question, you should refer to the 'five Cs of credit' that were discussed in detail in the chapter.

16.8 **Goliath plc**

(a) (i) The existing operating cash cycle can be calculated as follows:

Number of days

$$\text{Inventories holding period} = \frac{\text{Inventories at year end}}{\text{Cost of sales}} \times 365$$

$$= \frac{560}{1,440} \times 365 \qquad\qquad 142$$

Add Trade receivables settlement period

$$= \frac{\text{Trade receivables at year end}}{\text{Sales revenue}} \times 365$$

$$= \frac{565}{2,400} \times 365 \qquad\qquad \underline{86}$$

$$228$$

Less Trade payables settlement period

$$= \frac{\text{Trade payables at year end}}{\text{Purchases}} \times 365$$

$$= \frac{451}{1,450} \times 365 \qquad\qquad \underline{(114)}$$

Operating cash cycle $\underline{114}$

The new operating cash cycle is:

Number of days

$$\text{Inventories holding period} = \frac{(560 \times 1.15)}{(2,400 \times 1.10) \times 0.60} \times 365 \qquad 148$$

Trade receivables settlement period = 86 + 20 $\underline{106}$

$$254$$

Less Trade payables settlement period = 114 + 15 $\underline{(129)}$

$$\underline{125}$$

New operating cash cycle   125

Existing operating cash cycle   (114)

Increase in operating cash cycle (days) $\underline{11}$

(ii)

	£000
Increase (decrease) in inventories held [(560 × 1.15) − 560]	84.0
Increase (decrease) in trade receivables {[(2,400 × 1.1) × (106/365)] − 565}	201.7
	285.7
(Increase) decrease in trade payables [1,668 × (129/365) − 451]	(138.5)
Increase (decrease) in net investment	147.2

(iii)

	£000	£000
Gross profit increase [(2,400 × 0.1) × 0.40]		96.0
Adjust for:		
Administration expenses increase (15%)	(45.0)	
Bad debts increase	(120.0)	
Interest (10%) on borrowing for increased net investment in working capital (147.2)	(14.7)	(179.7)
Increase (decrease) in profit before taxation		(83.7)
Decrease in taxation charge for the period (25% × 83.7)		20.9
Increase (decrease) in profit for the year		(62.8)

(b) There would be an increase in the operating cash cycle and this will have an adverse effect on liquidity. The existing trade payables and inventories holding periods already appear to be quite high. Any increase in either of these must be justified. The planned increase in the trade payables period must also be justified because it may risk the loss of goodwill from suppliers. Although there is an expected increase in sales revenue of £240,000 from adopting the new policy, the profit for the year will decrease by £62,800. This represents a substantial decrease when compared with the previous year. (The increase in bad debts is a major reason why the profit is adversely affected.) There is also a substantial increase in the net investment in inventories, trade receivables and trade payables, which seem high in relation to the expected increase in sales revenue. The new policy requires a significant increase in investment and is expected to generate lower profit than is currently being enjoyed. It should, therefore, be rejected.

Appendix A

A.1

Account to be debited	*Account to be credited*
(a) Inventories	Trade payables
(b) Capital (or a separate drawings account)	Cash
(c) Interest on borrowings	Cash
(d) Inventories	Cash
(e) Cash	Trade receivables
(f) Wages	Cash
(g) Capital (or a separate drawings account)	Trade receivables
(h) Trade payables	Cash
(i) Electricity (or heat and light)	Cash
(j) Cash	Sales revenue

Note that the precise name given to an account is not crucial so long as it is clear to those who are using the information what each account deals with.

A.2 (a) and (b)

Cash

		£			£
1 Feb	Capital	6,000	3 Feb	Inventories	2,600
15 Feb	Sales revenue	4,000	5 Feb	Equipment	800
28 Feb	Trade receivables	2,500	9 Feb	Rent	250
			10 Feb	Fuel and electricity	240
			11 Feb	General expenses	200
			21 Feb	Capital	1,000
			25 Feb	Trade payables	2,000
			28 Feb	Balance c/d	5,410
		12,500			12,500
1 Mar	Balance b/d	5,410			

Capital

		£			£
21 Feb	Cash	1,000	1 Feb	Cash	6,000
28 Feb	Balance c/d	5,000			
		6,000			6,000
			28 Feb	Balance b/d	5,000
28 Feb	Balance c/d	7,410	28 Feb	Income statement	2,410
		7,410			7,410
			1 Mar	Balance b/d	7,410

Inventories

		£			£
3 Feb	Cash	2,600	15 Feb	Cost of sales	2,400
6 Feb	Trade payables	3,000	19 Feb	Cost of sales	2,300
			28 Feb	Balance c/d	900
		5,600			5,600
1 Mar	Balance b/d	900			

Equipment

		£			£
5 Feb	Cash	800			

Trade payables

		£			£
25 Feb	Cash	2,000	6 Feb	Inventories	3,000
28 Feb	Balance c/d	1,000			
		3,000			3,000
			1 Mar	Balance b/d	1,000

Rent

		£			£
9 Feb	Cash	250	28 Feb	Income statement	250

Fuel and electricity

		£			£
10 Feb	Cash	240	28 Feb	Income statement	240

General expenses

		£			£
11 Feb	Cash	200	28 Feb	Income statement	200

Sales revenue

		£			£
28 Feb	Balance c/d	7,800	15 Feb	Cash	4,000
			19 Feb	Trade receivables	3,800
		7,800			7,800
28 Feb	Income statement	7,800	28 Feb	Balance b/d	7,800

Cost of sales

		£			£
15 Feb	Inventories	2,400	28 Feb	Balance c/d	4,700
19 Feb	Inventories	2,300			
		4,700			4,700
28 Feb	Balance b/d	4,700	28 Feb	Income statement	4,700

Trade receivables

		£			£
19 Feb	Sales revenue	3,800	28 Feb	Cash	2,500
			28 Feb	Balance c/d	1,300
		3,800			3,800
1 Mar	Balance b/d	1,300			

Trial balance as at 28 February

	Debits	Credits
	£	£
Cash	5,410	
Capital		5,000
Inventories	900	
Equipment	800	
Trade payables		1,000
Rent	250	
Fuel and electricity	240	
General expenses	200	
Sales revenue		7,800
Cost of sales	4,700	
Trade receivables	1,300	
	13,800	13,800

(c)

Income statement

			£			£
28 Feb	Cost of sales		4,700	28 February Sales revenue		7,800
28 Feb	Rent		250			
28 Feb	Fuel and electricity		240			
28 Feb	General expenses		200			
28 Feb	Capital (profit)		2,410			
			7,800			7,800

Balance sheet as at 28 February

	£
Non-current assets	
Equipment	800
Current assets	
Inventories	900
Trade receivables	1,300
Cash	5,410
	7,610
Total assets	8,410
Capital (owners' equity)	7,410
Current liabilities	
Trade payables	1,000
Total equity and liabilities	8,410

Income statement for the month ended 28 February

	£
Sales revenue	7,800
Cost of sales	(4,700)
Gross profit	3,100
Rent	(250)
Fuel and electricity	(240)
General expenses	(200)
Profit for the month	2,410

A.3

Buildings

		£			£
1 Jan	Balance brought down	25,000			

Fittings – cost

		£				£
1 Jan	Balance brought down	10,000	31 Dec	Balance carried down		12,000
	Cash	2,000				
		12,000				12,000
1 Jan	Balance brought down	12,000				

Fittings – depreciation

		£			£
31 Dec	Balance carried down	4,400	1 Jan	Balance brought down	2,000
			31 Dec	Income statement	
				(£12,000 × 20%)	2,400
		4,400			4,400
			1 Jan	Balance brought down	4,400

General expenses

		£			£
1 Jan	Balance brought down	140	31 Dec	Income statement	570
	Cash	580		Balance carried down	150
		720			720
1 Jan	Balance brought down	150			

Inventories

		£			£
1 Jan	Balance brought down	1,350	31 Dec	Cost of sales	15,220
31 Dec	Trade payables	17,220		Cost of sales	4,900
	Cash	3,760		Capital	560
				Balance carried down	1,650
		22,330			22,330
1 Jan	Balance brought down	1,650			

Cost of sales

		£			£
31 Dec	Inventories	15,220	31 Dec	Income statement	20,120
	Inventories	4,900			
		20,120			20,120

Rent

		£			£
1 Jan	Balance brought down	500	31 Dec	Income statement	3,000
31 Dec	Cash	3,000		Balance carried down	500
		3,500			3,500
1 Jan	Balance brought down	500			

Trade receivables

		£			£
1 Jan	Balance brought down	1,840	31 Dec	Cash	32,810
31 Dec	Sales revenue	33,100		Income statement (bad debt)	260
				Balance carried down	1,870
		34,940			34,940
1 Jan	Balance brought down	1,870			

Cash

		£			£
1 Jan	Balance brought down	2,180	31 Dec	Inventories	3,760
31 Dec	Sales revenue	10,360		Wages	3,770
	Borrowings	2,000		Rent	3,000
	Trade receivables	32,810		Electricity	1,070
				General expenses	580
				Fittings	2,000
				Borrowings	1,000
				Trade payables	18,150
				Capital	10,400
				Balance carried down	3,620
		47,350			47,350
1 Jan	Balance brought down	3,620			

Capital

		£			£
31 Dec	Inventories	560	1 Jan	Balance brought down	25,050
	Cash	10,400		Income statement (profit)	10,900
	Balance carried down	24,990			
		35,950			35,950
			1 Jan	Balance brought down	24,990

Borrowings

		£			£
30 June	Cash	1,000	1 Jan	Balance brought down	12,000
31 Dec	Balance carried down	13,000		Cash	2,000
		14,000			14,000
			1 Jan	Balance brought down	13,000

Trade payables

		£			£
31 Dec	Cash	18,150	1 Jan	Balance brought down	1,690
	Balance carried down	760	31 Dec	Inventories	17,220
		18,910			18,910
			1 Jan	Balance brought down	760

Electricity

		£			£
31 Dec	Cash	1,070	1 Jan	Balance brought down	270
31 Dec	Balance carried down	290	31 Dec	Income statement	1,090
		1,360			1,360
			1 Jan	Balance brought down	290

Sales revenue

		£			£
31 Dec	Income statement	43,460	31 Dec	Trade receivables	33,100
				Cash	10,360
		43,460			43,460

Wages

		£			£
31 Dec	Cash	3,770	31 Dec	Income statement	3,770

Interest on borrowings

	£			£
		31 Dec	Income statement	
			[(6/12 × 14,000) +	
			(6/12 × 13,000)] × 10%	1,350

Income statement for the year to 31 December

		£			£
31 Dec	Cost of sales	20,120	31 Dec	Sales revenue	43,460
	Depreciation	2,400			
	General expenses	570			
	Rent	3,000			
	Bad debts (Trade receivables)	260			
	Electricity	1,090			
	Wages	3,770			
	Interest on borrowings	1,350			
	Profit (Capital)	10,900			
		43,460			43,460

Balance sheet as at 31 December last year

		£		£
Non-current assets			**Capital (owners' equity)**	24,990
Property, plant and equipment				
Buildings		25,000		
Fittings: cost	12,000		**Non-current liabilities**	
depreciation	(4,400)	7,600	Borrowings	13,000
Current assets			**Current liabilities**	
Inventories of stationery		150	Trade payables	760
Inventories		1,650	Accrued electricity	290
Prepaid rent		500	Accrued interest on borrowings	1,350
Trade receivables		1,870		
Cash		3,620		
Total Assets		40,390	**Total equity and liabilities**	40,390

Present value table

Present value of £1, that is, $1/(1 + r)^n$

where r = discount rate

n = number of periods until payment

Periods (n)	Discount rates (r)										
	1%	2%	3%	4%	5%	6%	7%	8%	9%	10%	
1	0.990	0.980	0.971	0.962	0.952	0.943	0.935	0.926	0.917	0.909	1
2	0.980	0.961	0.943	0.925	0.907	0.890	0.873	0.857	0.842	0.826	2
3	0.971	0.942	0.915	0.889	0.864	0.840	0.816	0.794	0.772	0.751	3
4	0.961	0.924	0.888	0.855	0.823	0.792	0.763	0.735	0.708	0.683	4
5	0.951	0.906	0.863	0.822	0.784	0.747	0.713	0.681	0.650	0.621	5
6	0.942	0.888	0.837	0.790	0.746	0.705	0.666	0.630	0.596	0.564	6
7	0.933	0.871	0.813	0.760	0.711	0.665	0.623	0.583	0.547	0.513	7
8	0.923	0.853	0.789	0.731	0.677	0.627	0.582	0.540	0.502	0.467	8
9	0.914	0.837	0.766	0.703	0.645	0.592	0.544	0.500	0.460	0.424	9
10	0.905	0.820	0.744	0.676	0.614	0.558	0.508	0.463	0.422	0.386	10
11	0.896	0.804	0.722	0.650	0.585	0.527	0.475	0.429	0.388	0.350	11
12	0.887	0.788	0.701	0.625	0.557	0.497	0.444	0.397	0.356	0.319	12
13	0.879	0.773	0.681	0.601	0.530	0.469	0.415	0.368	0.326	0.290	13
14	0.870	0.758	0.661	0.577	0.505	0.442	0.388	0.340	0.299	0.263	14
15	0.861	0.743	0.642	0.555	0.481	0.417	0.362	0.315	0.275	0.239	15

(continued over)

					Discount rates (r)						
Periods (n)	11%	12%	13%	14%	15%	16%	17%	18%	19%	20%	
1	0.901	0.893	0.885	0.877	0.870	0.862	0.855	0.847	0.840	0.833	1
2	0.812	0.797	0.783	0.769	0.756	0.743	0.731	0.718	0.706	0.694	2
3	0.731	0.712	0.693	0.675	0.658	0.641	0.624	0.609	0.593	0.579	3
4	0.659	0.636	0.613	0.592	0.572	0.552	0.534	0.516	0.499	0.482	4
5	0.593	0.567	0.543	0.519	0.497	0.476	0.456	0.437	0.419	0.402	5
6	0.535	0.507	0.480	0.456	0.432	0.410	0.390	0.370	0.352	0.335	6
7	0.482	0.452	0.425	0.400	0.376	0.354	0.333	0.314	0.296	0.279	7
8	0.434	0.404	0.376	0.351	0.327	0.305	0.285	0.266	0.249	0.233	8
9	0.391	0.361	0.333	0.308	0.284	0.263	0.243	0.225	0.209	0.194	9
10	0.352	0.322	0.295	0.270	0.247	0.227	0.208	0.191	0.176	0.162	10
11	0.317	0.287	0.261	0.237	0.215	0.195	0.178	0.162	0.148	0.135	11
12	0.286	0.257	0.231	0.208	0.187	0.168	0.152	0.137	0.124	0.112	12
13	0.258	0.229	0.204	0.182	0.163	0.145	0.130	0.116	0.104	0.093	13
14	0.232	0.205	0.181	0.160	0.141	0.125	0.111	0.099	0.088	0.078	14
15	0.209	0.183	0.160	0.140	0.123	0.108	0.095	0.084	0.074	0.065	15

Index

Page numbers in **bold** refer to definitions in Glossary.

ABC system (stock control) 622, 623, **677**
absorption costing 337, **677**
accepting/rejecting contracts 318–19
account 660, **677**
accountability (of directors) 123–4
accounting 6–7, 16–17
  for business 18
  conventions 55–8, 169, **677**
  definitions 2, **677**
  framework of principles 169–70
  regulation 13
  role (in management control) 470–99
  scandals 15
accounting information 3–7, 9–11, 16–17
  characteristics 7–8, 11–12
  system 11–12, **677**
accounting period 73, 78, **677**
accounting rate of return 512, 513–18, 529, 537–40, **677**
accounting rules
  need for 160–1
  sources 161–3
accounting standards *see* financial reporting standards; International Accounting Standards; International Accounting Standards Board (ASB) 176
accruals accounting 86–7, **677**
accruals convention 86, **677**
accrued expenses (accruals) 83–5, **677**
acid test ratio 241, **677**
activity (efficiency) ratios 223, 233–8
activity, volume of 298–325
activity-based budgeting 454, 457, **677**
activity-based costing 374–85, 454, **677**
  criticisms 381–2
adverse variances 475, 484–5, **678**
ageing schedule of trade receivables 633–4, **678**
allotted share capital 136, **678**

allowances for trade receivables 102–5, **678**
Alternative Investment Market (AIM) 596–7, **678**
Altman, E. I. 263
amortisation *see* depreciation
annual accounts 119, 160
appraisal costs 389
arm's-length transaction 59
articles and memorandum of association 130
asset-based finance 600, **678**
assets 87–8, **678**
  characteristics 42–4
  classification 49–51
  liabilities and 45–7
  valuation 64–5
  see also current assets; non-current assets
audit 21, 124, 144
  post-completion 555, **688**
auditors 170–1, **678**
authorised share capital 136
average inventories turnover period 233–4, 620, **678**
average settlement period for trade payables 234–5, 643, **677**
average settlement period for trade receivables 234–5, 633, **678**

bad and doubtful debts 102–5, **678**
balance sheet 38, 42–7, 166, **678**
  accounting conventions 55–8
  assets 42–4, 66
  claims 45–7, 52
  effect of trading operations 47–9
  equation 45, 49
  examples 39, 40, 41
  income statement and 197
  interpretation 66
  layouts 52–4
  limited companies 144
  income statement and 73–4, 166, 197

balance sheet (*cont'd*)
  purpose 42
  ratios 265–6
  reporting interval 47
balance/balancing accounts 665–8, **678**
Balanced Scorecard 394–400, 457, **678**
bank overdraft 597, 642, **678**
bank references 628
batch costing 358, 374–5, **678**
Beaver, W. H. 262
behaviour 455–6, 490–1, **678**
benchmarking 223, 392–3, **678**
beyond conventional budgeting 457–60
board of directors 22, 123
bonds 574, 575–6
bonus issue 135, **679**
bonus shares 134–6, 141, 590, **679**
bottom line 107
bottom-up approach 442
brand image 59
brands 59–60
break-even analysis 303, 304–7, 315–17,
    413, **679**
break-even chart 303–4, 309, 313–15, **679**
break-even point 303–4, 305, 413, 414,
    679
  failure to reach 315
break-even price 359
budget-constrained style 491
budget holder 446, 454, **679**
budgetary control **679**
  process 471–2
  standard quantities and costs 494
  types 472–3
  variance analysis 475–7
budgets/budgeting
  activity-based 454, 457, **677**
  annual 434
  behavioural aspects 490–1, **678**
  beyond conventional 457–60
  cash 447–51, 638
  committee 440, **679**
  communication 440–1, 443
  comparisons 442
  continual 434–5, **680**
  definitions 434, 431, **679**
  discretionary 446–7, **682**
  failing to meet 492
  finished stock inventories 436–7, 452
  flexible 483–4, **683**
  flexing 474, 476–7, 483–4, **683**
  forecasts and 434, 457
  future demand 629

incremental 446–7, 457, **684**
interrelationships 435–7
link with strategic plans and objectives
    431–2
limiting factor 434, 441, **685**
management behaviour and 455–6,
    491–3
master 435, 442–3, **686**
non-financial measures 455
officer 440, **679**
periodic 434–5, **688**
preparation 441–2, 451–4
problems and limitations 456–7
production 435–7, 438
raw materials inventories 435–7, 452
review and co-ordination 442
rolling 435
sales 435–7
setting process 440–3, 444
in small and medium-sized businesses
    445
standard costing 494
style/format 448
time horizon 432–4
trade payables 435–7, 451–2, 453
trade receivables 435–7, 451, 453
uses 437–40, 443–5, 460
variances 473, 484–9
zero-base 446–7, **692**
business
  accounting for 18
  purpose of 18–19
business angels 603, **679**
business entity convention 55, **679**
business environment 498
business management 24–5
business objectives 25–7, 282, 394–400,
    431–2, 456–7, 530
business organisation 22–4
business ownership 19–22
business review 179
buy-out/buy-in capital 602

called-up share capital 136, **679**
capital 44–5, 128, 374, **679**
  restriction of drawings 130
capital investment *see* investment
capital rationing (investments) 553, **679**
capital reserves 131–3, 139, 141, **679**
carrying amount 61, **679**
cash 50, 82, 86–7
  amount required 636
  borrowing requirements 638

cash (cont'd)
  definition 195–6
  discounts 631–2, 643, **679**
  expenses more than 83–5
  generated from operations per ordinary
    share 250–1, **679**
  holding (motives) 635
  importance of 194–5
  management 635–42, 644–5
  net increase 199
  operating cash cycle 638–9, **687**
  surplus funds (use) 638
  transmission 641
cash account, balancing 665–8
cash balance 227, 636–7
cash budget 447–51, 638
cash equivalents, definition 195–6
  net increase 199
cash flow 581
  financing activities 198
  investing activities 198
  investment decision and 529
  maturing obligations ratio 241–4, **680**
  normal direction 199–201
  operating activities 197–8, 201–7
  relevant 529–30, 534
cash flow statement 38, 168, 193–4, 196,
  679, **688**
  diagrammatical representation 199
  examples 38, 40
  form of 197–9
  layout 197, 198
  main features 195–201
  net cash flows 201–4
  preparation 201–7
  relationships 197
  returns from investing activities 198
  taxation 199
  uses 208–9
channel stuffing 181
chief executive officer (CEO) 22
claims 42, 44–7, 52, **680**
  see also current liabilities; long-term
    liabilities
closing/continuation decisions 323–5
Combined Code 124–8, **680**
command and control structure 456
committed cost 286–7, **680**
common costs 336, **680**
comparability (accounting information) 8,
  11, **680**
compensating variances 489, **680**
computerised accounting system 659

consistency convention 101, **680**
consolidated financial statements 145–9, **684**
consolidating shares 133, **680**
construction contracts 80–1
continual budgets 434–5, **680**
contracts
  special 318–19
  long-term 80–1
contribution per unit 307–8, 320, **680**
control 438, 490, 555–6, 622
  definitions 432, **680**
  feedback/feedforward 472–3, **683**
  and planning process 432, 433
  see also budgetary control
controllable cost 373
convertible loan notes (convertible bonds)
  576–7, **680**
corporate governance 123–8, **680**
corporation tax 122, 144, 197, **680**
cost (definition) 281, **680**
cost allocation 351, **680**
cost apportionment 351–2, **680**
cost behaviour 338–40, **680**
cost centres 349–51, 378, **680**
cost drivers 376, 378, **680**
cost management 385–400
cost of sales (cost of goods-sold) 72, 76–7,
  681
cost pools 376–7, **681**
cost units 340, **681**
costing 373–4
  absorption 337–8
  activity-based 374–85, 454, **677**
  kaisen 390, **685**
  process 335, 359, **688**
  standards 497
  target 388, **691**
  total life-cycle 385–7, 388, **691**
  see also full costing; job costing
costing inventories 97–101
cost-plus pricing 360, **684**
cost-plus pricing 417–20, **681**
costs
  appraisal 389
  of assets 87–8
  break-even *see* break-even analysis
  committed 286–7, **680**
  controllable 373
  definitions 280–1, **680**
  direct 336–7, 373, 374, **681**
  external failure 389
  fixed 298–300, 301, 308–9, 338–40, **683**
  indirect 336–7, **684**

costs (cont'd)
  inflation and 299
  internal failure 389
  irrelevant 281, 286, 382, **685**
  marginal analysis 317–18, 338, **686**
  outlay 282–5, 286, **687**
  output and 411–12, 413–14
  prevention 389
  relevant 279–89, 335, 382, 534, **689**
  replacement 56, 335
  semi-fixed 301–2, **690**
  sunk 286–7, **691**
  variable 298, 300–1, 308, 314–15, 339, **691**
  see also historic cost; opportunity cost;
     past cost
cost-volume-profit analysis 297–325
covenants, loan 578–80, **685**
creative accounting 180–5, 264, **681**
credit 101, **681**
  agencies 629
  control 569
  management 627–35, 644–5
credit sales receipts 633–4
credit terms, publicity 633
creditors see trade payables
current assets 50, 615
  definitions 50, **681**
current liabilities 52, 615, **681**
current ratio 240, 257, 258, 260–4, **681**
current value accounting 56
customer relationships 632
customers 395, 396, 627–9
  loyalty 393
  satisfaction 455

debentures 137
  see also loans
debit 660, **681**
debt
  bad and doubtful 102–5, **678**
  capacity 227
debt factoring 597–8, **681**
debtors see trade receivables
deep discount bonds 575–6, **681**
demand 409–10, 629
departmental structure 23–4
depreciation **681**
  calculation of 87–97
  judgement and 95–7
  methods 89–93
  non-current assets 61, 63–4, 87–95
  overdepreciation 97
  underdepreciation 97

direct costs 336–7, 373, 374, **681**
direct labour 340–1, 345, 348–9, 359, 373,
     479–80, 484–5
direct material variances 478–9, 484–5
direct method 336–7, 373, 374, **681**
directors 22, 123–8, 171, **681**
directors' report 171, **681**
disclosure 123
  segment 173–4
discount factor 527, **682**
discount rate 528–9
  risk-adjusted 552
discount tables 527–9
discretionary budgets 446–7, **682**
discriminate function 262, **682**
diseconomies of scale 315
dividend cover ratio 248, **682**
dividend payout ratio 248–9, **682**
dividend per share **682**
dividend yield ratio 249, 253–4, **682**
dividends 130, 145, 578, **682**
  cash flow statement 197
  from revenue reserves 142
divisional structure 23–4
documents of incorporation 21
double-entry bookkeeping 660–5, 673, **682**
downside risk 548
dual aspect convention 57–8, **682**
duty to account 160

early stage capital 602
earnings per share 250, 585, **682**
economic order quantity 622–5, **682**
economic value added (EVA) 403–8, **682**
economies of scale 313–15, **682**
efficiency ratios 223, 233–8
elasticity of demand 409, **682**
employees 237–8, 393
equity 128, **682**
  withdrawing 139–41
equity finance 137
Eurobonds 574–5, **682**
expansion capital 602
expected net present value 545–8, **682**
expenses **683**
  accrued (accruals) 83–5, **677**
  classification of 77–8
  prepaid 85, **688**
  recognition 82–7
expertise 323
explanatory notes (financial statements)
     168
external failure costs 389

factor/factoring (debt) 597–8
failure costs, internal and external 389
fair representation 164
fair value 61, **683**
favourable variances 475, **683**
feedback control 472–3, **683**
feedforward control 472–3, **683**
final accounts 41, 669–72, **683**
   see also balance sheet; cash flow
      statement; income statement
finance, definition 2–3, **683**
finance leases 138, 580–2, **683**
finance sources (external) 570
   gearing and 583–6
   long-term 570–83, 601–3
   matching 600
   share issue 134–6, 137, 591, 586–90
   short-term 567, 597–600
   Stock Exchange role 590–5
   venture capital 601–2, **691**
   see also bank overdraft; debentures; debt
      factoring; finance leases; invoice
      discounting; loans; ordinary shares;
      preference shares; sale and leaseback
finance sources (internal) 567
   credit control 569
   delayed payments to trade payables 570
   reduced inventories levels 570
   retained profits 131, 137, 567
financial accounting 13–14, **683**
financial derivatives 578, **683**
financial failure (prediction) 260–4
financial gearing 242–8, **683**
   long-term financing decision 583–6
financial management 2–3, 15, **683**
financial performance (reporting) 71–107
financial period 73, 78
financial plan, budget as 432–4
financial ratios 620
   calculation 222, 225–6
   classification 223
   comparisons 223–5, 265
   description 222
   limitations of analysis 264–6
   overtrading 256–7
   predicting financial failure 260–4
   trend analysis 258–60
   uses 222
   see also efficiency ratios; gearing ratios;
      investment ratios; liquidity ratios;
      profitability ratios
financial reports, segmental 171–5
Financial Services Authority (FSA) 162

financial statements, analysis *see* financial
   ratios
   see also balance sheet; cash flow
      statement; income statement
financial transactions, recording
   balancing accounts 665–8
   computerised accounting system 659
   double-entry bookkeeping 660–5, 673
   final accounts 669–72
   trial balance 668
finished stock budget 436–7
first in, first out (FIFO) 97–8, 99–101, **683**
five Cs of credit 627–8, **683**
fixed assets *see* non-current assets
fixed costs 298–300, 301, 308–9, 338–9,
   683
   stepped 300, 316, **690**
fixed overhead spending variance 480
fixed overhead variance 480–4, 484–5
fixtures and fittings 44
flexibility (long-term) 537, 581, 600
flexible budgets 483–4, **683**
flexing the budget 474, 476–7, 483–4, **683**
forecasts 456, 537, **683**
framework 176–9
   business performance 177
   business, nature of 176–7
   financial position 178–9
   resources, risk and relationships 178
framework of principles 169–70, **683**
full cost 334, **683**
full cost (cost-plus) pricing **684**
full costing 382, 409
   alternative approach 375
   criticisms 362
   definition 334, **684**
   forward-looking nature 359
   impact of competitive environment 374
   multi-product operations 335–40
   need for knowledge 333–4
   overheads 340–60
   process costing 335
   single-product operations 334–5
   uses 360–2
   vs variable costing 362–4
fully paid shares 136, **684**

gearing ratios 223, 244–5, 586, **684**
   calculation 243
   interest cover ratio 245–8
general reserves 144
going concern 57, **684**
goodwill 59, 146, 148, 405

government assistance 603
gross profit 74, **684**
gross profit margin ratio 231–3, **684**
group financial statements 145–9, **684**
growth 395, 396

hire purchase 582–3, **684**
historic cost 56, 97, 280, 284, 335, **684**
historic cost convention 56, **684**
holding company 145, **684**
hollow swaps 181
Hopwood, A. G. 492
human resources 60
hurdle rate 533

ideal standards 494–5, **684**
in-and-out trading 181
income statement 38, 72–3, 164–6
    balance sheet and 73–4, 166, 197
    cash flow statement and 197
    classification of expenses 77–8
    cost of sales 72, 76–7, **681**
    definition **684**
    depreciation charge 95
    example 39, 40, 41
    interpretation 107
    layout 74–5
    limited companies 144
    preparation 669–72
    revenue recognition 79–82
incremental budgeting 446–7, 457, **684**
indirect costs 336–7, **684**
    see also overheads
indirect method 336–7, **684**
inflation 224, 264–5, 299, 524, **684**
information gathering 495–6
initial public offering (IPO) 590–2
intangible assets 44, 63, 93–4, 403, **684**
interest cover ratio 245–8, 586, **685**
interest lost (NPV method) 523
interest payments 535
interest rate 137, 575–6, 601
interim financial statement 78
internal business process 395, 396
internal failure costs 389
internal rate of return 512, 530–4, 537,
    539, **685**
International Accounting Standards (IASs)
    161, **685**
    IAS 1 (presentation of financial
        statements) 164–6
    IAS 7 194, 195, 198, 199
    IAS 14 172

International Accounting Standards Board
    (IASB) 161–2, 169–70
    framework of principles 169–70
International Financial Reporting Board
    161
international financial reporting standards
    93, **685**
inventories 50
    costing 97–101
    finished 436–7, 452
    movement over time (pattern) 623
    order costs 624
    raw materials 435–7, 452
    turnover period 233–4, 620
    valuation 64–5
inventories management 618–27
    models 622–7
investigating variances 486–9
investment 198, 551–2
    decisions 509–58
    marketable 405
    shareholder value analysis 402–3
investment appraisal 511–13
    accuracy of forecasts 537
    cash flows 534–5
    expected NPV 545–8
    inflation and 524
    interest payments 535
    non-quantifiable factors 535
    opportunity costs 534
    relevant costs 534
    risk-adjusted discount rate 552,
        689
    risk level 523–4, 541–52
    taxation 534
investment appraisal methods *see*
    accounting rate of return; internal
    rate of return; net present value;
    payback period
investment ratios 223, 253–5
    cash generated from operations per
        ordinary share 250–1, **679**
    comparison (industrial sectors) 253–5
    dividend cover ratio 248
    dividend payout ratio 248–9, **682**
    dividend per share **682**
    dividend yield ratio 249, 253–4, **682**
    earnings per share 250, 585, **682**
    price/earnings ratio 251–6
invoice discounting 598–600, **685**
invoices, issuing 633
issued (allotted) share capital 136, **685**
issuing house 589

job costing 359, 374–5, **685**
    multi-product operations 335–40
just-in-time system 625–7, **685**

kaizen costing 390, **685**
Kaplan, R. 394–400
key performance indicators (KPIs) 177

labour
    cost 339, 341, 494
    direct 341–4, 348–9, 359, 373
    variances 479–80, 484–5
last in, first out (LIFO) 97, 98, 99–101, **685**
lead time 620, **685**
learning (Balanced Scorecard) 395–400
learning-curve effect 496–7, **685**
leases 138, 580–2
ledger 672–3
liabilities 45–7, **685**
    long-term 52
    see also current liabilities
limited company 20–2, **685**
    accounting standards *see* accounting
        standards
    annual accounts 119, 160, 434
    audit/auditors 21, 124, 170–1
    balance sheet *see* balance sheet
    directors' duty to account 160
    documents of incorporation 21
    financial statements 142–4
    financing 128–33
    groups of companies 145–9
    legal nature 116
    legal safeguards 119
    management 123–8
    operating and financial review (OFR)
        176–9, **687**
    ownership 116
    partnership and 118
    perpetual life 116–17
    production of accounts 119
    profit and loss account *see* income
        statement
    public/private (comparison) 119–21
    regulation *see* regulation
    segmental financial reporting 171–5
    sole proprietorship and 118
    taxation 121–2, 144
    withdrawing equity 139–42
limited liability 21, 116, 117–19, **685**
limiting factor 434, 441, **685**
liquidity 86, 257, 578
liquidity ratios 223

acid test ratio 241, **677**
current ratio 240, 257, 258, 260–4, **681**
operating cash flows to maturing
        obligations 241–4, **680**
loan notes (loan stock) 137, 574, **685**
    convertible 576–7, **680**
loans (borrowings) 573–80
    conditions/restrictions 578–80
    convertible 576–7, **680**
    covenants 578–80
    debentures 137
    deep discount bonds 575–6, **681**
    Eurobonds 574–5, **682**
    interest rate 575–6, 601
    long-term 137–9, 574
    mortgages 578, **686**
    notes 574
    secured 138, 141, 573
    term 574
    unsecured 138
    warrants 577–8, **691**
London Stock Exchange 124, 125, 162, 592,
        594
long-term contracts 80–1
long-term liabilities 52
long-term loans 137–9, 198, 574
long-term sources of finance (external)
    business angels 603
    debentures 137
    gearing and 583–6
    government assistance 603
    leases 138, 580–2
    loans 137–9, 198, 574
    ordinary shares 250, 571–2, **687**
    preference shares 130, 572–3, **688**
    sale and leaseback 582, **690**
    share issues 134–6, 137, 586–90
    short-term and 600–1
    Stock Exchange role 590–5
    venture capital 601–2, **691**
long-term sources of finance (internal) 131,
        137–8, 567, 568, 601–3
loss on sale of non-current asset 97

machine hours 344, 345
make-or-buy decisions 322–3
management
    behaviour, budgets and 455–6
    business 24–5
    of companies 123–8
    control (role of accounting) 470–99
    of investment project 552–6
    motivation of 438

management (*cont'd*)
  style 491–3
  of working capital 614–45
  see also directors
management accounting 13–14, **685**
management buy-ins (MBIs) 602
management buy-outs (MBOs) 602
management-by-exception 438, 471, **686**
managers (authorisation system) 438
margin of safety 308–10, 542, **686**
  for lenders and suppliers 141
marginal analysis 317–25, 338, **686**
marginal cost **686**
marginal cost pricing 420–1, **686**
marginal sales revenue 414, 415
master budget 435, 442–3, **686**
matching convention 82, **686**
materiality 8–9, 11, **686**
materiality convention 86, **686**
materials requirements planning system
  625, **686**
materials variances 478–9, 485
minority interests 146, 148
mission statement 431, **686**
monetary stability 60–1
money measurement 58–61
mortgages 578, **686**
multi-product operations 316, 335–40
multiple discriminate analysis 262, **686**

narrative reporting 175–9
net book value 61, 90, **686**
net cash flow from operating activities
  197–8
net cash inflows, deducing 201–7
net current assets *see* working capital
net present value 512, 522–30, 537–40,
  686
  expected 545–8, **682**
net profit margin 230
nominal value 130, 131–2, **686**
non-accounting style 491
non-business assets 118
non-current (fixed) assets 227, **686**
  definitions 50–1, **686**
  depreciation 63–4, 89, 93–4
  examples 51
  impairment 63–4
  intangible 44, 63, 93–4, **684**
  profit/loss on sale 97
  tangible 44, 61–3, **691**
  valuation 61–5
non-current liabilities 52, **686**

non-financial measures of performance
  393–400
non-operating profit variances 486, **686**
Norton, D. 394–400
not-for-profit organisations 28–9

objective probabilities 549, **686**
offer for sale 589, **687**
operating activities 197–8, 201–4
operating and financial review (OFR)
  176–9, **687**
operating cash cycle 638–9, **687**
operating cash flows to maturing
  obligations ratio 241–4, **680**
operating gearing 311–12, **687**
operating lease 580, **687**
operating profit 75, **687**
operating profit margin 238–9, **687**
opportunity cost 280, 282–5, 382, 523, 528,
  534, **687**
ordinary shares 130, 571–2, **687**
  cash generated from operations per
    250–1, **679**
outlay cost 282–5, **687**
output 411–12, 413–14
  volume of activity 298–325
outsider interests 146
outsourcing 322, **687**
overdraft 597, 642, **678**
overhead absorption (recovery) rate 340,
  344, 347, **687**
overheads 374, **687**
  basis for charging 344–6
  departmentalisation 348–58
  fixed overhead variance 480–4
  indirect costs 336–7
  job costing 337–8, 340–1
  segmenting 347
  as service renderers 340–60
  see also activity-based costing
overtrading 256–7, **687**
owners' claim 128
owner's equity 44
ownership of limited company 116

paid-up share capital 136, **687**
par value *see* nominal value
parent company 145, **687**
partnerships 20, 118, **687**
past cost 282, 382, **687**
  see also committed cost; sunk cost
patents 44
payback period 512, 518–21, 529, **687**

penetration pricing 422, **688**
performance 224–5, 393–400
periodic budgets 434–5, **688**
perpetual life 116–17
placing (shares) 590, **688**
planning and control process 432
plant and equipment 44, **689**
position statement *see* balance sheet
post-completion audit 555, **688**
post-production phase 385, 387
practical standards 494–5, **688**
pre-dispatching 181
preference shares 130, 572–3, **688**
prepaid expenses 85, **688**
pre-production phase 385, 386
present value 525–6
prevention costs 389
price makers 360, 418
price skimming 423, **688**
price takers 360, 418–19
price/earnings ratio 251–6, **688**
pricing
    in competitive environment 409–23
    cost-plus 360
    demand and 409–10
    economic theory 409–23
    full (cost-plus) cost 417–20, **681**, **684**
    penetration 422, **688**
    profit maximisation 411, 414–15
    relevant/marginal cost 420–2
    strategies 422–3
    total (whole) life-cycle costing 385–7,
        691
private company 119–21, **688**
private equity 601, **688**
private placing (shares) 590, **688**
probabilities 548–51
process costing 335, **688**
product brands 59
product cost centres 350–1, **688**
product innovation 393
product life-cycle 386, 385
production budget 436–7, 438
production phase 385, 387, 389
profit 97, 227, 475, 534–5, **688**
    in balance sheet 49
    cost-volume-profit analysis 297–325
    gross 74, **684**
    maximisation 27, 411, 414–15
    retained 49, 131, 137, 567, 568
    see also reserves
profit and loss account *see* income
    statement

profit before taxation 144, **688**
profit for the year 75, **688**
profit measurement 72–3
    calculation of depreciation 87–97
    costing inventories 97–101
    expenses recognition 82–7
    revenue recognition 79–81
profit on sale of non-current asset 97
profitability 238–9, 554
profitability ratios 223, 228–33, 238–9
profit-conscious style 491
profit-volume charts 313, **688**
projected financial statements 42
property 44, 582, **689**
prudence convention 56–7, **689**
public issue (shares) 589, **689**
public limited company 119–21, 589, **689**
published accounts 628

qualitative factors of decisions 287–8
quality control 389
quality costs 289, **689**

raw materials 436–7, 452
realisable value 56, 100
receivables, trade
    ageing schedule of 633–4, **678**
    average settlement period 234–5, 633,
        678
    management of 627–35
recording/reordering system 620–1
redeemable preference shares 573
redemption yield 576
reducing-balance method 90–2, **689**
Registrar of Companies 21, 116, 119, 130,
        170, 628
regulation 13
relevance (accounting information) 7,
        689
relevant cost 279–89, 335, 534, **689**
relevant range 315, **689**
relevant/marginal cost pricing 420–2
reliability (accounting information) 7–8,
        689
rent 299–300
replacement costs 56, 94–5, 335
reporting interval 13, 47
reporting period 73, 78
research and development 385, 405
reserves 128, 144, **689**
    see also revenue reserves
residual value 89, 94, **689**
resources 319–21, 510

restructuring costs 405
retained profits 49, 131, 137, 567, 568
   see also reserves
return, balancing risk and 28
return on capital employed 229–30, 238–9,
   262, 265, 417, 515, **689**
return on investment 552
return on ordinary shareholders' funds
   228–9, **689**
revenue
   definition 72, **689**
   recognition of 79–81
   total 72–3
revenue reserves 131–3, 139, 141–2, **689**
rights issues 586–9, **689**
risk 130, **689**
   adjusted discount rate 552, **689**
   downside 548
   finance sources 572, 601
   investment appraisal 523–4, 541–52
   of non-payment 632–5
   and return, balancing 28
risk premium 524, **690**
rolling budgets 435, **690**
round tripping 181
RS 1 179–80

sale and leaseback 582, **690**
sales
   budget 436–7
   to capital employed 236–7, 238, **690**
   cost of 72, 76–7, **681**
   price variance 477, 485
   revenue 412–16
   revenue per employee 237–8, **690**
   volume 474–7, 485
scandals, accounting 15
scenario building 544, **690**
segmental disclosure 173–4
segmental financial reports 171–5, **690**
segmental reporting rules 172–3
semi-fixed (semi-variable) costs 301–2,
   690
sensitivity analysis 541–5, **690**
service cost centres 350–1, **690**
service industries 348–52
   ABC and 377–81
services, provision of 81–2
share capital 134, 139
   authorised 136
   called-up 136, **679**
   issued (allotted) 136, **685**
   nominal value 130, 131–2, **686**

   paid-up 136
   raising 136–7
share issues 137, 586–90
   bonus 134–6, 141, 590, **679**
   offer for sale 589, **687**
   placing 590, **688**
   public issue 589, **689**
   rights 586–9, **689**
share premium account 132, **690**
share warrants 577–8
shareholder value 401–7
   creation 401–2
   measurement 402–3
shareholders 116–22, 124, 125–6
   auditors and directors and 170–1
   election of directors 123, 170–1
   rights 130
shares 6–7, 116, **690**
   capital 116
   consolidating 133, **680**
   fully paid 136, **684**
   nominal value 130, 131–2, **686**
   ownership (transferring) 122
   splitting 133–4
   see also ordinary shares; preference
     shares; share issues
short-term finance (external) 567
   bank overdrafts 597, 642, **678**
   debt factoring 597–8, **681**
   invoice discounting 598–600, **685**
short-term finance (internal)
   credit control 569
   delayed payment to trade payables 570
   reduced inventories levels 570
single-product operations 334–5
small and medium-sized enterprises (SMEs)
   445
small companies, working capital problems
   644–5
sole proprietorship 19–20, 118, 128, **690**
standard costing 497
standard quantities/costs 494, **690**
standards 494–7
   problems 497–8
start-up capital 602
statement of changes in equity 166–8,
   690
statement of financial position *see* balance
   sheet
statistical probabilities 545–51
stepped fixed costs 300, 316, **690**
stock *see* inventories
stock account, balancing 666

Stock Exchange 137, 590–5, **690**
    see also London Stock Exchange
straight-line method 89, 92–3, **690**
strategic management 24–5, **690**
strategic plans and objectives, link with
        budgets 431–2
striking price 589
subcontracting 322–3
subjective probabilities 550, **690**
subsidiary budgets 437
subsidiary companies 145–9
summary financial statements **691**
sunk cost 286–7, **691**

Taffler, R. 264–5
takeover 146, 148, 264, **691**
tangible assets 44, 61–3, **691**
target costing 388, **691**
taxation 534
    cash flow statement 199
    corporation tax 122, 144, 197, **680**
    investment appraisal 534
    limited company 121–2, 144
tender issue 589, **691**
term loans 574, **691**
time factor 13, 432–4, 510, 529
top-down approach 442
total costs 340, **691**
total direct labour variance 479
total direct material variance 478
total life-cycle costing 385–7, **691**
trade payables (trade creditors) 46, 117, 668
    average settlement period 235–6, 643
    budget 435–7, 451–2, 453
    delaying payments to 570
    discount for prompt payment 631–2
    management of 642–3, 645
    margin of safety 141
trade receivables (trade debtors) 50, 668
    allowances for 102–5
    budget 435–7, 451, 453
    problems 101–7
trade references 628
trademarks 44, 59
trading operations 47–9
    double-entry bookkeeping 662–5
transfer price 174, **691**
treasury policy 179
trend analysis 258–60
trial balance 668, **691**

true and fair view 180
turnover analysis 233–4

understandability (accounting information)
        8, **691**
univariate analysis 262, **691**
user groups 3, 5

valuation 64–5, 97–101
value chain analysis 390–1, **691**
value drivers 393, **691**
variable costing 362–4, **691**
variable costs 298, 300–1, 308, 313, 338–9,
        691
variances/variance analysis 482, **691**
    adverse variance 475–7, 485–6, **678**
    compensating variance 489, **680**
    definitions 475, **691**
    favourable variance 475–7, **683**
    fixed overhead 480–4, 485
    fixed overhead spending 480
    investigating variance 486–9
    labour variances 479–80, 484–5
    material variances 478–9, 484–5
    non-operating profit 486, **686**
    problems 497–8
    sales price variance 477, 484–5
    sales volume variance 474–7, 484–5
venture capital 601–2, **691**

warrants 577–8, **691**
wealth 25, 72, 73
wealth creation 25–7
weighted average cost 97, 98–100, **692**
work in progress 335
working capital 208, 227
    cash management 635–42
    cycle 615–16
    receivables 627–35
    definition 615, **692**
    inventory management 618–27
    nature/purpose 615–16
    scale of 616–18
    trade credit 642–3
written-down value (WDV) 61, 90, 92, **692**
written-off debt 102–3, 105

Z score model 263–4
zero-base budgeting 446–7, 457, **692**
Zmijewski, M. E. 262